Friendship is one of life's most essential and rewarding forms of interaction. It is a feature of every culture and most persons interact with their friends on a daily basis. Thus far, most research on the subject of friendship has concentrated on peer acceptance, dyadic properties, and the contribution that friendship makes to development and adjustment. There has been little exploration of friendship's role in a child's social and emotional growth. *The Company They Keep* pioneers this area.

This book provides a forum in which internationally recognized scholars active in the study of friendship present the major conceptual issues, themes, and findings from their research. The authors describe the theoretical and empirical context and the goals of their own research programs. They discuss current research and the methodological strategies adopted for the purpose of studying friendship relations. A variety of topics is explored, including cultural variations in children's and adolescents' friendships, the association between friendship and cognitive and personality development, the effect of friendship on adjustment, and the links between experience within the family and relationships with friends. The authors also express their views on future directions for such research.

## Cambridge Studies in Social and Emotional Development

*General Editor: Martin L. Hoffman, New York University*

*Advisory Board: Robert N. Emde, Willard W. Hartup, Robert A. Hinde, Lois W. Hoffman, Carroll E. Izard, Nicholas Blurton Jones, Jerome Kagan, Franz J. Mönks, Paul Mussen, Ross D. Parke, and Michael Rutter.*

**The company they keep: Friendship in childhood and adolescence**

# The company they keep

## Friendship in childhood and adolescence

*Edited by*

WILLIAM M. BUKOWSKI
*Concordia University*

ANDREW F. NEWCOMB
*University of Richmond*

WILLARD W. HARTUP
*University of Minnesota*

CAMBRIDGE
UNIVERSITY PRESS

Published by the Press Syndicate of the University of Cambridge
The Pitt Building, Trumpington Street, Cambridge CB2 1RP
40 West 20th Street, New York, NY 10011–4211, USA
10 Stamford Road, Oakleigh, Melbourne 3166, Australia

First published 1996

Printed in the United States of America

*Library of Congress Cataloging-in-Publication Data*
The company they keep : friendship in childhood and adolescence /
edited by William M. Bukowski, Andrew F. Newcomb, Willard W. Hartup.
p.    cm. – (Cambridge studies in social and emotional
development)
ISBN 0-521-45198-1
1. Friendship in children.   2. Friendship in adolescence.
3. Interpersonal relations in children.   4. Interpersonal relations
in adolescence.   I. Bukowski, William M.   II. Newcomb, Andrew F.
III. Hartup, Willard W.   IV. Series.
BF723.F68C66   1996
302.3'4 – dc20                                              95–16855
                                                                CIP

A catalog record for this book is available from the British Library.

ISBN 0-521-45198-1 Hardback

# Contents

# Contributors

Frances E. Aboud
Department of Psychology
McGill University

Steven R. Asher
Bureau of Educational Research
University of Illinois

Catherine L. Bagwell
Department of Psychology
Duke University

Thomas J. Berndt
Department of Psychological
  Sciences
Purdue University

Duane Buhrmester
School of Human Development
University of Texas at Dallas

William M. Bukowski
Department of Psychology and
  Centre for Research in Human
  Development
Concordia University

Anna Beth Doyle
Department of Psychology and
  Centre for Research in Human
  Development
Concordia University

Wyndol Furman
Department of Psychology
University of Denver

Willard W. Hartup
Institute of Child Development
University of Minnesota

Carollee Howes
Graduate School of Education
University of California, Los Angeles

Kathryn A. Kerns
Department of Psychology
Kent State University

Becky J. Kochenderfer
Department of Educational
  Psychology
University of Illinois

Lothar Krappmann
Max Planck Institute for Human
  Development

Gary W. Ladd
Department of Educational
  Psychology and Children's
  Research Center
University of Illinois

vii

Brett Laursen
Department of Psychology
Florida Atlantic University

Dorothy Markiewicz
Departments of Applied Social
    Science and Psychology
Concordia University

Morton J. Mendelson
Department of Psychology
McGill University

Andrew F. Newcomb
Department of Psychology
University of Richmond

Jeffrey G. Parker
Department of Psychology
University of Michigan

Joseph M. Price
Department of Psychology
San Diego State University

Lorrie K. Sippola
Henry Murray Research Center
Radcliffe College
Harvard University

Diane L. Walker
Department of Educational
    Psychology
University of Illinois

# Preface

The chapters in this book are based on presentations made at an SRCD study group on friendship and development held at Concordia University in Montréal during November 1992. The purpose of this study group was to provide a forum for persons actively involved in the study of friendship to present and discuss their ideas and current research activities on this aspect of children's and adolescents' experiences with peers. At this meeting, the participants discussed the theoretical and empirical context of their own research programs, the goals of their research, and the methodological strategies they have adopted for the purpose of studying friendship relations.

The point of departure for much of the recent research on friendship is the hypothesis that friendship relations are uniquely implicated in children's social and emotional growth. Indeed, friendship relations appear to influence children's adaptation to school, adjustment following major life transitions, and the acquisition of social skills and values. Considering the pervasive nature of friendship and its effects, it is not surprising that this topic is of interest to persons from a wide variety of disciplines, including child psychology, clinical and social psychology, sociology, communications, anthropology, education, and sociolinguistics. This topic also interests persons who study normal development and those who are concerned with atypical development or special populations.

In spite of the cold, gray, and damp weather in Montréal on that November weekend, the discussions held indoors during this meeting were warm, bright, and very lively. In addition to the support from SRCD, the conference was supported by grants from the W. T. Grant Foundation, the University of Richmond, Concordia University, and the Williams Professorship at the University of Minnesota awarded to W. W. Hartup. The editors cheerfully acknowledge their gratitude to Larry Steinberg of the SRCD Panel on Study Groups and Summer Institutes, Lonnie Sherrod of the W. T. Grant Foundation, David Leary of the University of Richmond, and Charles Betrand and Larry Tansey of Concordia University for facilitating this support. We are grateful also to Lorrie

Sippola, Lynn Kratzer, Sepi Zargarpour, Paul James, and Carole Dubois for their help before, during, and after the conference, and to Anna Beth Doyle and Stan Shapiro for opening the doors of their home to the conference participants for a dinner during the meetings.

# 1 Friendship and its significance in childhood and adolescence: Introduction and comment

*William M. Bukowski, Andrew F. Newcomb, and Willard W. Hartup*

The social relations of children and adolescents are centered on their friends as well as their families. The word *friend* appears in most children's vocabularies by the fourth year and "best friends" are ubiquitous in social experience during middle childhood and adolescence. Mutually regulated "friendships" can be identified among infants and toddlers, too, although the cognitive and linguistic concomitants of these relationships are not always obvious. Once observable, however, these concomitants (e.g., attributions, expectations) change continuously through childhood and adolescence and on into adulthood.

Friendship is closely tied to "liking," that is, being attracted to someone who is attracted in return and taking pleasure in that person's company. Preschool-aged children understand this:

Interviewer: Why is Caleb your friend?
Tony: Because I like him.
Interviewer: And why do you like him?
Tony: Because he's my friend. (Rubin, 1980)

These attractions differ from the feelings that children have about other companions. Friendships are specific attachments carrying expectations that "best friends" spend more time with one another than "ordinary friends" or acquaintances, that cost-benefit balances in one's social exchanges with a friend are favorable; and, among older children and adolescents, that friends are loyal, trusting, and intimate with one another.

One must remember, though, that friendships are voluntary rather than obligatory relationships. Common ground and affirmation are necessities in both friendship formation and maintenance (Gottman, 1983); their cessation virtually guarantees termination. Such uncertainties, however, do not lessen the affective intensity that marks these relationships and one should not discount their significance in child and adolescent development simply because social sanctions do not guarantee their permanence.

1

Social scientists have been examining friendships among children and adolescents for a century or more. Until recently, research dealing with these relationships was sporadic. Other socialization issues commanded more attention (Hartup, 1983; Parker, Rubin, Price, & DeRosier, in press), including: (a) normative continuities in social understanding and social interaction; (b) social acceptance and rejection – that is, the extent to which children are liked or disliked collectively by classmates or associates; (c) group relations and social organization; and (d) differences among individuals and the implication of these differences for "risk."

Gradually, however, investigators are discovering that child attributes (e.g., cooperativeness or aggressiveness) and sociometric status (e.g., being popular, average, or rejected) do not account for developmental outcomes as completely as we would like. Mounting evidence suggests that developmental outcome derives from complex transactions among child attributes, close relationships, and the broader social context (Hartup & Van Lieshout, 1995). Realizing that child attributes alone are not sufficient for identifying major pathways in personality and social development, investigators are moving rapidly to include relationship variables in their developmental models – friendship measures being among them.

Current research is moving in two directions, which are only loosely connected to one another: (a) normative and descriptive studies establishing what children's friendships are, their behavioral and cognitive manifestations, and how these change with age; and (b) studies dealing with having friends, who one's friends are, as well as the quality of one's friendships and their significance for the individual child or adolescent. These studies increasingly reflect the conviction that these relationships must be treated as complex and multifaceted. Until recently, investigators seemed not to be aware that friendships should be regarded multidimensionally – that there is more to friendship than having friends; that all friendships are not alike; that friendships involve social interactions that are sometimes affirming but sometimes contentious; that different benefits and liabilities may derive from having friends than from who one's friends are; and that friendships can be described in numerous ways other than the time that children spend together or the intimacy of their social exchanges. Recent research efforts toward a multidimensional understanding of friendships in childhood and adolescence are described in this book along with a consensus among the contributors that these multidimensional efforts must continue.

## Friendships: Their nature

A major issue confronted by investigators concerns the friendship construct and its meaning. One can use natural language to specify these relationships but, inevitably, such specifications consist almost entirely of metaphors (e.g., "friendships are affectionate attachments between two individuals"). Using this strategy, an abstraction (the friendship construct) is instantiated with *fastening* or *adherence*, the concrete conditions that connote what *being attached* amounts to. These instantiations, however, contain much ambiguity and are not very useful in selecting the observables needed for scientific inquiry. Moreover, natural language does not differentiate between the "friendships" of infants and toddlers, on the one hand, and the "friendships" of adolescents and adults, on the other. Can a single construct be used to describe close peer relationships at any age? Or, are close relationships fundamentally different at different ages, requiring more differentiated language than everyday discourse provides?

Seeking to better specify the friendship construct, investigators now rely on three kinds of information: (a) What children and adolescents themselves tell us about these relationships; (b) what parents and teachers report; and (c) what trained observers identify in terms of behavioral manifestations in social interaction. This book makes clear that investigators frequently have strong biases as to which source(s) of information are most valid. One can argue, however, that most studies require information from all three: the children themselves who give us first-hand, insiders' views; observers who know the children well but whose views are less colored by the affective and cognitive biases of the participants themselves; and other observers who can specify these relationships in terms of the social exchanges that comprise them. Children may be the final authorities concerning who their friends are and what these relationships are like; nevertheless, their views can be idiosyncratic and their capacities for describing these relationships limited.

Utilizing child interviews, parent and teacher questionnaires, and direct observations, investigators generally agree that the conditions marking the friendships of children and adolescents are as follows: (a) *reciprocities*, that is, mutual regard, behavioral mutualities (including cooperation and effective conflict management), and equivalencies in the "benefits" that derive from the social exchanges occurring between the individuals; (b) *liking*, that is, the desire to spend time with one another in greater proportion to time spent with others; and (c) *affection* and *having fun*. Children articulate these conditions differently at different ages and behavioral manifestations become more distinct as children grow older (Bigelow, 1977; Berndt & Perry, 1986). But the general description of friendship relations with which this chapter opened is empirically grounded in both interview and observational studies; it is not impressionistic. A generally accepted common language now exists for identifying these relationships through reference to the number, nature, and patterns among the exchanges that constitute their substance.

Until recently, investigators have not felt sufficiently secure with these criteria to attempt further classification or categorization of child and adolescent friendships. Qualitative differentiation, however, has been the key to progress in studying other relationships. For example, the discovery that attachment security is a better predictor of developmental outcome than attachment occurrence (Ainsworth, Blehar, Waters, & Wall, 1978) was a major theoretical and empirical advance. Similar differentiation is needed in friendship relations. To begin with, one must distinguish between *having friends* (which seems to be a precursor of self-esteem and being successful in subsequent relationships, including romantic ones (see Neeman, Hubbard, & Kojetin, 1991), *the identity of one's friends* (which is related to both one's antisocial as well as prosocial tendencies; Dishion, 1990), and *friendship quality* (Bukowski & Hoza, 1989; Bukowski, Hoza, & Boivin, 1993; Parker & Asher, 1993).

Several contributors to this volume describe efforts to classify child and adolescent friendships in terms of their qualitative features. Readers will discover, first, that differentiating between "positive" and "negative" friendships forecasts school adaptation according to whether the "cost-benefit" balance rests on support and intimacy or coercion and emotional distance (Berndt, this volume). Second, differentiations among friendships in terms of warmth, conflict, status/power, and comparison features (e.g., their exclusivity) capture considerable relationship-to-relationship variation (see Furman, this volume; Buhrmester, this volume). Third, reliable differentiation can be achieved by referring to companionship and recreation, validation and caring, help and guidance, intimacy, and conflict and conflict resolution (Asher, Parker, & Walker, this volume; Bukowski, Hoza, & Boivin, 1993). Fourth, still other classifications can be based on the extent to which relationships are "close" or "not close" (Repinski, 1993; Laursen, this volume), "interdependent" or "disengaged" (Shulman, 1993). Sorting through these assessments and assimilating them to the general dimensions with which relationships can be classified (content, diversity, time spent together, intimacy, commitment, affective quality, personal attributions and perceptions; Hinde, 1979) is a formidable task.

### Normative issues

Normative studies are concentrated on several basic questions: (a) How many friends do children have at different ages and what expectations do children have about these relationships? (b) What is the size and character of the friendship network? (c) Are friends more similar to one another than nonfriends? Does similarity undergird attraction? Do friends become similar to one another over time? (d) Are friends more cooperative and less antagonistic toward one another than nonfriends are? (e) Does having friends buffer the child against stress and does not having them constitute a risk factor? Note that these questions imply that friendships are all pretty much alike and, furthermore, that having friends is generally a "good thing" in the child's experience.

Comparing social interaction between friends and between acquaintances (nonfriends) suggests that, indeed, these relationships generally seem to promote development and adaptation: (a) Social engagement, cooperation and conflict management, expressed emotions, and task orientation are greater among friends than they are among nonfriends (Newcomb & Bagwell, this volume); (b) self-awareness and self-esteem as well as knowledge about others and knowledge about the world are enhanced (Ladd and Kochenderfer, this volume); (c) friendships serve as both emotional and cognitive resources (Hartup, this volume; Kerns, this volume); and (d) these relationships are likely to be forerunners of subsequent ones (Kramer & Gottman, 1992; Neeman et al., 1991).

Between-group differences, however, are better documented in these studies than within-group variation, yet some friendships are clearly not benign. Known subtypes include "positive" and "negative" friendships (Berndt, this volume), interdependent and disengaged friendships (Shulman, 1993), and positive/coordinated versus negative/asynchronous friendships (Youngblade, Park, & Belsky, 1993). These attempts at differentiation are estimable, but our general lack of understanding concerning friendship heterogeneities is a significant shortcoming.

Normative studies in this field of inquiry are generally cross-sectional or short-term longitudinal investigations. One wishes for more extensive longitudinal studies, especially those extending beyond a single year. Univariate comparisons are more common than multivariate ones; differentiation or changes in factorial structure are rarely studied but should be (Berndt & Perry, 1986). Furthermore, relatively little is known about friendship beginnings, middles, and ends, especially as these relationship "developments" interact with chronological age. Generally, however, normative studies are accelerating and our understanding of friendships and their distinguishing characteristics in childhood and adolescence is increasing rapidly.

## Differential issues

Correlational studies show that children who have friends are more socially competent than children who do not. Children who have friends evidence many desirable characteristics, including friendliness, cooperativeness, altruism, good perspective-taking, and self-esteem (Newcomb & Bagwell, this volume). No one has ever reported that having friends is correlated with undesirable social attributes.

These correlations, however, are difficult to interpret for several reasons: First, having a friend usually amounts to having a *good, supportive* friend in these studies, so one does not know whether the sheer existence of a friendship or its quality accounts for the results. Second, direction of causation is impossible to establish; having friends may contribute to self-esteem but self-confidence may also enhance success in forming and maintaining these relationships. Furthermore, significant correlations between having friends and social competence may derive from some other, common source, for example, good social relationships in early childhood. Third, having friends seldom accounts for more than one-third of the variance in social outcome, suggesting moderating conditions and/or measurement limitations. Certainly, alternative possibilities must be considered: Having friends, for example, may have different effects according to stability in the home (this is not known). Friendship effects may vary according to whether these relationships are close and supportive or whether they are contentious and conflict-ridden (Berndt, this volume). Clearly, the developmental significance of friendships in childhood and adolescence cannot be established without conducting studies that: (a) utilize other friendship measures besides their sheer existence (e.g., qualitative features); (b) consider child characteristics and other social relationships together in multivariate studies with friendship experience; and (c) explore these effects over time.

Experimental analysis has been underutilized in establishing the developmental significance of child and adolescent friendships (Berndt, this volume). Investigators are too often content to establish (for example) that friends are more talkative than nonfriends, more frequently propose alternatives, offer explanations, criticize one another, and smile more during task performance than nonfriends do (Hartup, this volume). Only rarely, however, are results offered showing that these distinctive interactions affect the behavior of each individual separately at a later time. One exception: Azmitia and Montgomery (1993) showed that individual problem solving improved more following collaboration with a friend than with an acquaintance, and that performance was correlated with good conflict resolution during their collaboration. To be sure, these effects are short-term rather than long-term but their implications are considerable.

More extensive longitudinal studies are required in order to establish the long-term consequences of friendship experience. Current efforts must be expanded; most are narrowly focused on school adaptation (Ladd, this volume). Child characteristics, including temperament and personality, must be included in the study design as well as assessments of other relationships and the broader social context. ''Main effect'' friendship outcomes are not likely to turn up, only combinations with other measures cycling through relatively large blocks of time are apt to occur. Although it would be comforting to be able to say that friends make a direct contribution to self-awareness or self-esteem, for example, main effects showing developmental significance are likely to be few and far between.

Once again, these investigations must include multidimensional assessments of friendship relations. We know that aggressive and nonaggressive children have different friends and that aggressive children's friendships are more contentious and less stable than the friendships of nonaggressive children (Cairns, Cairns, Neckerman, Gest, & Gariéppy, 1988; Dishion, Andrews, & Crosby, in press). At the very least, then, longitudinal studies must focus on several constructs, including having friends, who the child's friends are, and the quality of these relationships. Such studies are discussed in this book as well as the many problems and issues connected with carrying out future ones.

## Organization of this volume

Our goal is to provide a forum for a group of internationally recognized scholars, who are active in the study of friendship, to present the major conceptual issues and themes of their areas of inquiry. The need for this type of book on friendship is acute. The last multiauthored volume on friendship and development dates back to the early 1980s (Asher & Gottman, 1981), and there have been dramatic advances in the field since that time. A principal point of departure for this new work has been the hypothesis that friendship relations are uniquely implicated in children's social and emotional growth. The pervasive nature of friendship and its effects have made this a topic of considerable interest to individuals in a variety of disciplines including child psychology, clinical and social psychology, sociology, communications, anthropology, education, and sociolinguistics.

Our charge to the volume's contributors was to describe the theoretical and empirical context of their own research programs and to present the goals and methodological strategies they have adopted for studying friendship relations. The reader should not anticipate either literature reviews or journal-style reports. Rather, the authors have written issue-based chapters in which they highlight their own work and research programs and discuss their views on future directions. Although the contributors share a common commitment to research in friendship relations, they are relatively heterogeneous in representing different theoretical views, methodological persuasions, and research foci. As such, this volume has a broad audience, specifically those individuals who want to understand better the complex and multifaceted nature and influence of child and adolescent friendships. Among this group are academics and graduate students, clinicians and health-care providers, and teachers and parents.

Over time, our thoughts on how to organize the chapters have changed as we have observed the richness of coverage offered by each contributor. For example, although the themes outlined in this introduction provide an excellent guide to the friendship literature, these themes do not afford an organizational template that can be superimposed on the chapters contributed by our diverse authors. As a result, we offer the reader a fairly simple heuristic for approaching the chapters in this book. In this organization plan, we have clustered the chapters into four groupings that might assist the reader in locating broader topics of interest. At the same time, we caution the reader about the considerable overlap of topical coverage across the various chapters and invite the reader to explore the interdependencies amongst the wealth of ideas in each chapter.

### The nature of friendship, its measurement, and development

A defining characteristic of all the chapters in this volume is that each contributor challenges others interested in child and adolescent friendships to move beyond the simple description of these relations. We begin this task with Krappmann's exploration of the universality of friendship and the relationship between friendship and culture. The study of the quality of children's friendships is another area that is representative of this new empirical approach. Furman provides a starting point for this journey with his consideration of conceptual and methodological issues in the measurement of children's friendship perceptions. As a companion to this critical evaluation of different approaches to the measure of friendship quality, Howes explores the challenge of examining the characteristics and quality of friendships among toddlers and young preschool children. Interestingly, her thesis provides a bridge between the study of the constructs of companionship, affection, and intimacy in early friendships and these same constructs in later friendships. In contrast, Aboud and Mendelson examine child characteristics that influence the development of close friendships. Their premise is that some children are more likely than others to be selected as friends and to participate in friendships of high quality, and they explore similarity and personal attributes as determinants of these outcomes.

### Interdependence of relationship systems

Friendship relations are not in a world of their own; instead, these relations are linked to, or even embedded in, other relationship systems. First among these interdependencies are the connections between family relationships and friendship. Interest in this issue speaks both to its importance and to the relative neglect previously afforded this topic. Doyle and Markiewicz explore the influence of family relationships on children's friendships and the mechanisms through which family relations affect children's friendships. In contrast, Kerns examines individual differences in the quality of children's friendships and considers the moderating influence of child–mother attachment on friendship quality. The other two chapters extend the issue of interdependence amongst relationship systems to other domains. Buhrmester focuses on need fulfillment and interpersonal competence across interpersonal contexts including children's networks of personal relationships. Laursen concludes this section with his examination of the interdependencies among friends and romantic partners during the critical developmental period of adolescence.

## *Friendship and its associations with other aspects of development*

The next set of chapters explores one issue related to the developmental significance of children's friendships: the type of contexts that friendships provide to promote development in other domains of functioning. A characteristic of the contributions to this section is that our relative knowledge in each area is limited. As a result, each contributor explores the overlapping boundaries and interfaces between children's friendships and different areas of development. Hartup begins this examination with his consideration of children's friendships as contexts for cognitive development. The result is an integration of the constructs of co-operation, close relationships, and cognitive development. The interrelationship of friendship and morality is explored by Bukowski and Sippola in their examination of friendship as an important context for the development of morality. Price considers the importance of friendship as a provider of developmental contexts from a unique perspective. In particular, he considers how the friendships of maltreated children and adolescents can reshape early relationship histories.

## *Friendship and adaptation*

What are the benefits of having friends and the implications of not having friends? Newcomb and Bagwell build upon the prior chapters' considerations of the contexts afforded by friendship through their quantitative review of friendship's contribution to developmental outcome and their exploration of differences between children who have and who do not have friends. The importance of friendship relations is further examined by Ladd and Kochenderfer through their work on the role friendship relations play in determining young children's adjustment to school. Berndt also explores friendship relations and adjustment to school, but his focus is on the adolescent years. He examines friendship quality as a predictor of self-esteem and behavior and exposes the merits and drawbacks of different experimental approaches. Finally, the distinction between friendship and acceptance provides fertile ground for Asher, Parker, and Walker's consideration of interventions to promote friendship relations. Especially interesting to the reader are the hypotheses these authors propose as to the interpersonal tasks and skills that underpin the formation and maintenance of friendship.

**Assumptions about friendship: Is friendship always positive?**

The chapters that comprise this volume cover a wide array of topics and issues and the age span covered extends from early childhood through adolescence. No single theory or perspective dominates this volume as several conceptual vantage points serve as the points of departure for the authors represented here. Nevertheless, in spite of this theoretical pluralism, some particular views are implicit in nearly every chapter.

*Is friendship always positive?*

Perhaps the most pervasive theme implicit in these works is the argument that friendship exerts a positive force on development. This view can be seen clearly in nearly every chapter of this book. There are, of course, several theoretical bases for this perspective (e.g., Sullivan, 1953), and there is a well-known empirical justification for it also. Indeed, several reports indicate that children without friends are more likely than children with friends to show signs of maladaptation (Parker, Rubin, DeRosier, & Price, in press). Nevertheless, there are reasons also to expect that the effects of friendship may not be always positive. One reason is related to the theme developed earlier in this essay, namely, that not all friendships are the same. Certain types of friendships, such as those that are imbalanced or asynchronous, may not provide the sorts of experiences that are likely to promote development and well-being, even if they are based on mutual liking. To the contrary, such friendships may be remarkably restrictive in the forms of interaction they facilitate and in the sorts of affective experiences they engender. Accordingly, in spite of a child's participation in a best-friendship relation, due to the particular qualities and features of the relationship the child's well-being may be stymied.

A second reason derives from the notion of mutual influence. Although empirical evidence of mutual influence between friends is currently slim, it is believed that friends influence one another. In this volume, the salience of this process is implicit in descriptions of the ways that friends collaborate to facilitate each other's performance in a writing task (see Hartup, this volume) or to develop a sense of mutual understanding and concern (see Bukowski & Sippola, this volume). It is unlikely, however, that this process is always beneficial. Theoretical support for the view that friends influence each other can be taken from several perspectives, with each theory adopting a different position on the expected outcome of this form of influence. Certainly, theory from a Piagetian perspective (Piaget, 1932) and from social learning (Bandura, 1977) imply that friends influence each other, although these theories propose that this influence happens through very different means. If it is the case that children imitate their friends (c.f., Newcomb & Brady, 1982), then how a child's friend behaves is of critical importance. Recent research by Dishion, Andrews, and Crosby (in press) suggests that the patterns of mutual influence between antisocial boys and their friends may not always produce positive outcomes.

## Some future directions

In spite of the breadth and the diversity among the chapters, one can think of topics and questions pertinent to friendship that are not represented, or are represented only marginally, in these works. What fundamental topics are either absent or only marginally represented in this volume? We would like to identify seven topics that receive only indirect or marginal treatment in this book, or have been given no attention at all.

Perhaps the most important "missing" topic is motivation. To be sure, discussions of motivation are implicit in the chapters written by Doyle and Markiewicz and by Buhrmester, but in each case this concept does not form the core of their chapters. Currently, there is no broad model for explaining why some children are more desirous of friendship than are other children. It is conceivable that such a model would have to be multifaceted, including factors such as the desire for associations with peers as well as what form this association would take. One would also have to consider children's appraisals of the likelihood that they would be successful at forming a friendship relation. And one would have to include the factors already identified by Buhrmester and Doyle and Markiewicz, namely, needs that derive from either one's relationship history or from particular developmental processes. The construction of such a model may result in a complex equation, but its importance to the understanding of the features and effects of friendship for individual children cannot be underestimated.

Another issue that is relatively absent from these pages is the notion of the social network. Friendships do not exist in isolation but are instead embedded in the constellation of relationships that exist among other members of the peer group. A concern with this network of relationships is not new – it was the basis of much of Moreno's (1934) original thoughts about sociometry. Considering the embeddedness of friendship within a broader network, it is likely that the structure and properties of this network are apt to have an impact on the formation and continuity of particular friendship relations. Eder and Hallinan (1978) have shown already that one can begin to understand something about the stability of friendship dyads by considering the structure of the triadic relations they are linked to. Considering the current interest in group structure (e.g., Kindermann, 1993) as a context for development, it is surprising that we know so little about how social contexts will facilitate or inhibit the development and stability of friendship.

Little is known also about the association between friendship and another network of relationships, namely, sibling relations. With the exception of Kramer and Gottman's (1992) study of friendship as an antecedent to sibling interaction, research on the link between friendship and "sibship" is generally lacking. Do children with many siblings have lower "needs" for friends than "sibless" children do? Are patterns of interaction with siblings transferred to friendship relations? These questions point to fundamental issues regarding the nature of personal needs and their satisfaction and the continuity and discontinuity of developmental experiences. When persons study the family and the peer system, the feature of the family that is emphasized is the parent–child relationship. Compared with the parent–child relationship, the sibling relation is much more like a child's relationship with friends. Accordingly, the sibling relationship may be a fruitful domain for identifying developmental antecedents of friendship.

A further issue in which there is a surprising lack of research is that of friendship stability. There is some evidence that stability is linked to structural properties of the friendship dyad (Bukowski & Newcomb, 1984) and it is also linked to properties of the individual (Parker & Seal, 1993). Overall, however, little is known about why some friendships last whereas others dissolve quickly. Consistent with the arguments of Hinde (1979), it is likely that the answer to this question will be found by looking at properties of individuals and the particular interactive match between them. This latter point, of course, is a recurrent theme in the peer literature, specifically, how features of the individual, aspects of individuals, and properties of relationships facilitate and influence each other. There is already an interest in the link between friendship and popularity (Bukowski & Newcomb, 1984; Bukowski, Hoza, & Newcomb, 1994; Parker and Asher, 1993). It is time to expand this interest to include a wider range of constructs and the study of friendship stability may be an ideal domain for the integration of these factors.

A fifth issue that receives little attention in the friendship literature is that of culture. Considering that there is a chapter on friendship and culture in this book, this comment may strike some readers as surprising. But as Krappmann points out in his chapter, there is hardly any information, of any sort, on cultural differences in friendship during childhood. There are some exceptions to this (DeRosier & Kupersmidt, 1991) but for the most part nothing is known about how the features and effects of friendship vary across culture. Research that would address this question is likely to be difficult insofar as many of the meanings of friendship may be, as Krappmann notes, linguistically determined. A further complication would be the necessity of recognizing how other aspects of the social world of children (e.g., the family) are organized and how they function. But well-done research on this topic is likely to be remarkably fruitful and exciting. And one would not need to go to the far-off corners of the world to conduct studies on friendship and culture. There may be sufficient cultural diversity in many metropolitan areas to provide a sufficient context for this sort of research.

A sixth topic that does not receive the attention that it deserves in this book is that of age differences. Identifying age differences in children's conceptions of friendship was a major concern of friendship researchers 20 years ago, but now age rarely seems to enter into most friendship research. It is true that most of the authors represented here place friendship within a particular developmental context, but, for the most part, age receives little attention. This is surprising for several reasons. First, we know already that the features of friendship vary with age. Second, the most prominent theories regarding friendship (e.g., Sullivan, 1953) are explicitly developmental in their approach. Third, the contexts in which friendships "happen" – the school environment, the social network – change with age. Moreover, children's capacity to engage effectively in relationships, independent of the family, change with age also. Again, researchers would be wise to return to a concern with age differences in the properties and the effects of friendship.

Research may be wise also to attend to the differences between same- and other-sex friendships. Much has been written about children's preference for same-sex peers (see Leaper, 1994). Although it is clear that children have more same-sex than other-sex friends, it is clear also that other-sex friendships occur frequently. Attempts at determining which children are most likely to have other-sex friendships have produced only modest results (Bukowski, Gauze, Hoza, & Newcomb, 1993) and even less is known about the features and effects of these relationships. As pointed out earlier, not all friendships are the same. Exploring the differences between same- and other-sex friendships will add to the understanding of the diversity of the friendship relation and the contributions it makes to development.

One final note regarding theory is in order: The chapters in this book are largely organized around theories familiar to child psychologists, specifically social learning theory, Sullivan's interpersonal model, attachment theory, and the constructivist ideas taken from Vygotsky. Ideas from other conceptual domains are relatively sparse, although they can be found (e.g., in the chapters by Laursen, Krappmann, and Bukowski and Sippola). Considering that interest in friendship is hardly restricted to child psychology, this conceptual insularity is surprising. In our view, the study of friendship by developmental psychologists would evolve more profitably if researchers were more willing to look beyond what is already our common currency.

## Summary

This book covers current theory and research on friendship during childhood and adolescence. The chapters show that research on friendship is alive and well, and moving in many directions. Ten years ago, the study of peers was concentrated on the popularity system. Now, a concern with the features, antecedents, and consequences of friendship occupies a significant place in the literature on peer relations. Clearly, the company that children keep is an aspect of the developmental niche that has consequences for children's long-term development and adaptation.

## References

Ainsworth, M. D. S., Blehar, M. C., Waters, E., & Wall, S. (1978). *Patterns of attachment*. Hillsdale, NJ: Erlbaum.

Asher, S. R., & Gottman, J. M. (1981). *The development of children's friendships*. New York: Cambridge University Press.

Azmitia, M., & Montgomery, R. (1993). Friendship, transactive dialogues, and the development of scientific reasoning. *Social Development, 2*, 202–221.

Bandura, A. (1977). *Social learning theory*. Englewood Cliffs, NJ: Prentice Hall.

Berndt, T. J., & Perry, T. B. (1986). Children's perceptions of friendship as supportive relationships. *Developmental Psychology, 22*, 640–648.

Bigelow, B. J. (1977). Children's friendship expectations: A cognitive developmental study. *Child Development, 48*, 246–253.

Bukowski, W. M., Gauze, C., Hoza, B., & Newcomb, A. F. (1993). Differences and consistency in relations with same-sex and other-sex peers during early adolescence. *Developmental Psychology, 29*, 255–263.

Bukowski, W. M., & Hoza, B. (1989). Popularity and friendship: Issues in theory, measurement, and outcomes. In T. Berndt & G. Ladd (Eds.), *Peer relations in child development* (pp. 15–45). New York: John Wiley.

Bukowski, W. M., Hoza, B., & Boivin, M. (1993). Popularity, friendship, and emotional adjustment during early adolescence. In B. Laursen (Ed.), *Close friendships in adolescence*. San Francisco: Jossey-Bass.

Bukowski, W. M., Hoza, B., & Newcomb, A. F. (1994). Using rating scale and nomination techniques to measure friendship and popularity. *Journal of Social and Personal Relationships, 11*, 485–488.

Bukowski, W. M., & Newcomb, A. F. (1984). The stability and determinants of sociometric status and friendship choice: A longitudinal perspective. *Developmental Psychology, 20*, 941–952.

Cairns, R. B., Cairns, B. D., Neckerman, H. J., Gest, S., & Gariéppy, J.-L (1988). Peer networks and aggressive behavior:Peer support or peer rejection? *Developmental Psychology, 24*, 815–823.

DeRosier, M., & Kupersmidt, J. B. (1991). Costa Rican children's perceptions of their social network. *Developmental Psychology, 29,* 656–662.

Dishion, T. J. (1990). The peer context of troublesome child and adolescent behavior. In P. Leone (Ed.), *Understanding troubled and troublesome youth.* Newbury Park, CA: Sage.

Dishion, T. J., Andrews, D. W., & Crosby, L. (in press). Anti-social boys and their friends in early adolescence: Relationship characteristics, quality, and interactional process. *Child Development.*

Eder, D., & Hallinan, M. T. (1978). Sex differences in children's friendships. *American Sociological Review, 43,* 237–250.

Gottman, J. M. (1983). How children become friends. *Monographs of the Society for Research in Child Development, 48* (3, Serial No. 201).

Hartup, W. W. (1983). Peer relations. In P. H. Mussen, Series Ed., E. M. Hetherington, Vol. Ed., *Handbook of child psychology, Vol. 4: Socialization, personality, and social development.* New York: John Wiley.

Hartup, W. W., & Van Lieshout, C. F. M. (1995). Personality development in social context. *Annual Review of Psychology, 46,* 655–687.

Hinde, R. A. (1979). *Towards understanding relationships.* New York: Academic Press.

Kindermann, T. (1993). Natural peer groups as contexts for individual development. *Developmental Psychology, 29,* 970–977.

Kramer, L., & Gottman, J. M. (1992). Becoming a sibling: "With a little help from my friends." *Developmental Psychology, 28,* 685–699.

Leaper, C. (1994). Childhood gender segregation: Causes and consequences. *New Directions For Child Development* (Number 65). San Francisco: Jossey-Bass.

Moreno, J. L. (1934). *Who shall survive?* New York: Beacon House.

Neeman, J. D., Hubbard, J., & Kojetin, B. A. (April, 1991). *Continuity in quality of friendships and romantic relationships from childhood to adolescence.* Poster presented at the biennial meetings of the Society for Research in Child Development, Seattle.

Newcomb, A. F., & Brady, J. (1982). Mutuality in boys' friendship relations. *Child Development, 53,* 392–395.

Parker, J. G., & Asher, S. R. (1993). Friendship and friendship quality in middle childhood: Links with peer group acceptance and feelings of loneliness and social dissatisfaction. *Developmental Psychology, 29,* 611–621.

Parker, J. G., Rubin, K. H., Price, J., & DeRosier, M. E. (in press). Peer relationships, child development, and adjustment: A developmental psychopathology perspective. In D. Cicchetti & D. Cohen (Eds.), *Developmental psychopathology, Vol. 2: Risk, disorder, and adaptation.* New York: John Wiley.

Parker, J. G., & Seal, J. (March, 1993). *Temporal patterning and behavioral and affective correlates of boys' and girls' friendship involvement in middle childhood.* Presented at the biennial meetings of the Society for Research in Child Development, New Orleans, Louisiana.

Piaget. J. (1932). *Moral judgement of the child.* New York: Harcourt Brace.

Repinski, D. J. (1993). *Adolescents' close relationships with parents and friends.* Unpublished doctoral dissertation, University of Minnesota.

Rubin, Z. (1980). *Children's friendships.* Cambridge, MA: Harvard University Press.

Shulman, S. (1993). Close friendships in early and middle adolescence: Typology and friendship reasoning. In B. Laursen (Ed.), *Close friendships in adolescence.* San Francisco: Jossey-Bass.

Sullivan, H. S. (1953). *The interpersonal theory of psychiatry.* New York: Norton.

Youngblade, L. M., Park, K. A., & Belsky, J. (1993). Measurement of young children's close friendship: A comparison of two independent assessment systems and their associations with attachment security. *International Journal of Behavioral Development, 16,* 563–587.

*Part I*

**The nature of friendship, its measurement, and development**

# 2 Amicitia, drujba, shin-yu, philia, freundschaft, friendship: On the cultural diversity of a human relationship

*Lothar Krappmann*

## Introduction

The aim of this chapter is to demonstrate that friendship is found across all, or at least most, societies but that it is manifested in a rich variety of ways depending on the cultural system. In the following pages the relationship between friendship and culture will be considered from several perspectives. First, we will see how friendship has been treated by sociologists and anthropologists as a unique form of human relationship. The central focus of this discussion will be on the features that make friendship distinct from other relationships such as those among family members. Second, we will consider cultural variations in the meaning of the word *friend* and study how the idea of friendship is constructed in different societies. Following this discussion, we will examine cultural differences in children's conceptions of friendship. The goal will be to determine whether variations in culture are reflected in children's constructions of friendship. The final sections are directed at questions regarding the associations between patterns of friendship and culture. There is a lack of well-focused research on these issues that is immediately pertinent to childhood. Nevertheless, the child-oriented evidence that does exist and the literature regarding adult friendships provide a sufficient basis for an understanding of how and why friendship patterns vary across societies.

## Features of friendship

A prominent aspect of the relationship called friendship is that it is a voluntary relationship. This voluntariness is seen in the processes of initiating, maintaining, and terminating a friendship, as well as in the expectations that friends have for each other. Under some circumstances this voluntariness may be more fiction

19

than reality, because the group of persons available for friendship may be either very small or the social constraints governing friendship patterns may be very rigid. The cost of breaking up a friendship may be extremely high with regard to social status or psychological well-being. Or friendship may even be defined in some cultures as indissoluble blood brotherhood, thus restricting a person's capacity to terminate friendships.

This aspect of voluntariness is also reflected in the behaviors that are judged to be appropriate among friends. Mutual obligations may be narrowly defined in certain communities, whereas in others it is debated whether the idea of rights is compatible with friendship at all (Meyer, 1992). In any case, it is widely accepted that friends should be committed to each other, give priority to the other's requests, and mutually assist the other when support is needed. Thus, reciprocity is a second important feature of friendships. Because it appears to be so obvious that friendship is a matter of consent from both partners and that it is a relationship maintained for the purpose of mutual support, this quality in itself has not received much attention in the literature.

Although in our society there are almost no formal descriptions exclusively related to friends, in other societies obligations and prohibitions are precisely determined. Almost no behavior can be excluded as an act of friendship. For example, in the name of friendship, help can be given or it can be denied, such as in a case when help would create an asymmetry that would be detrimental to the relationship. Friends may behave in very friendly manners or they may curse each other and call each other names in mock anger or battle "taking liberties that were reserved for and tolerated in close friends alone" (Liebow, 1967, p. 168). Friends mutually allow themselves "idiosyncrasy credits" (Hollander, 1958). For example, they may continue a dispute on controversial issues longer than would individuals who are not friends. They may tolerate in each other forms of behavior that nonfriends might see as deviant. Friends may give their life for the other, but also, in extreme and very rare situations, friends may take upon themselves the responsibility of ending a friend's life as a last service to the friend who is in a desperate situation.

These observations attest that friendship is a relationship oriented to the other's benefit, but also that it is futile to compile a list specifying the mutual obligations that underlie friendship. This does not mean that no attempts are made to specify what a friend has to do for his or her friend. Cohen's (1966) examination of 65 non-Western societies clearly demonstrates that the functions that friends perform for each other differ across these societies. Some societies give priority to material exchange, some demand support in love affairs and marriage arrangements, whereas in other societies friends adopt each others' children. Cohen also concludes, however, that neither personal traits and early socializing experiences nor social norms defined in the respective societies can finally explain the ways in which friends share, are generous, or trust each other.

Sociologists also have difficulty dealing with friendship (Allan, 1989). Friendships seem to be outside the usual sociological blueprint of a society in the sense that they emerge outside well-defined kinship systems and other institutions that are guardians of social norms and are likely to require conformity to rigid roles. In comparison, the superior function of friendships may be to make up for the deficits and dissatisfactions that these social systems and institutions create. Nevertheless, Suttles (1970), in an often quoted article, declared that friendship was a "social institution." However, his interpretation of this institution emphasizes that friendship is a social institution of its own kind: "Friendship fills in where the more mechanical and exclusionary institutions fail to define interpersonal affiliations" (Suttles, 1970, p. 96). He argues that, in contrast to other socially established associations, friendships can be formed across all relevant subdivisions of a society, such as across social classes, institutions, and organizations. Although Suttles acknowledges societal differences, he also emphasizes that friendships are essentially characterized by voluntariness and that what occurs within friendships is a matter of personal negotiation.

Thus, friendship may actually transcend kinship systems and institutions, but not for arbitrary reasons. Rather, friendship can counteract problems that result from social disorientation and dissatisfaction by the social organization and social institutions. To put it in a more positive light: Friends try to realize the values, aims, and desires that individuals in a given society are striving for. These efforts are sometimes made against societal obstacles and constraints. Therefore, friends do more for each other than one would do for a nonfriend; and when making decisions about their interactions, they consider the particular concerns, needs, and desires of their friend. In this way, they co-construct an individual agreement about the relevance, means, and even the goals of their friendship.

Suttles (1970) speaks of the "contrastive structures" generated by friends, which, on the one hand, are private cultures opposing usual conventions, but, on the other hand, are intrinsically shaped by the overarching meanings, ideals, expressive symbols, and the language that together constitute culture. Thus, if friendships solve, contrast, and transcend prescribed solutions and institutional regulations, they do it only from "within" a particular societal or cultural frame. That is, friendships may be unique but they are nevertheless embedded within a larger cultural context. Culture also defines the leeway that friends have as they balance social demands and concerns with individual desires.

Friendship is manifested in many ways by reflecting the weaknesses and strengths of the surrounding context. Such cultural differences may be seen between societies, such as those one might find in different parts of the world, as well as within societies. Therefore, it is important to examine patterns of friendship that are found in different sections of Western societies. The behaviors of the members of a society are influenced more by social class and ethnic traditions, religious affiliations, occupational and leisure subcultures, and standards based on age and gender than they are by the proclaimed common values and norms of a society. A goal of this chapter is to describe some of these cultural variations in friendship.

Unfortunately, the cultural differences that shape the understanding and the practice of friendships are not well investigated. Therefore, I am able to approach this subject only from different perspectives and cannot deliver an integrated outline of a cultural theory of friendship. It is also impossible to restrict this discussion to studies of friendship in childhood and adolescence, the general subject of this volume. I therefore include many studies of adult friendship patterns. This material is sufficient to demonstrate the diversity of culturally shaped friendships. The available studies differ with regard to their methodological orientation. Most work done by cultural anthropologists and sociologists uses ethnographic methods of data collection and interpretive procedures of data analysis. Only a small part of the research is comparative in a narrower sense. This lack of comparative studies limits the conclusions we can reach but the studies that do exist stimulate a future-oriented reconsideration of the issues regarding friendship. The main objective of this chapter is to encourage future researchers to consider the richness of meanings and manifestations of friendship, especially when they are conducting research from within the framework of a single society.

### The word *friend* and its connotations in different cultures

A term for friendship seems to be available in every language of the world. When we translate the original words directly into our mother tongue, we sometimes overlook the cultural particularities that are crystallized within the original word. One way of revealing cultural differences of friendship would be to examine the philological roots of the various verbal equivalents. Then, one would trace the implications that belonging to particular word families would have for particular words, such as the words *friend, amicus, philos*, or *tomodachi*. The history of a particular word and its relation to other words of the same language that are derived from the same source suggest the underlying or covered meanings of the word that are often unknown even to native speakers. One may assume that these networks of meanings that are linked with the respective words for friend may also affect the behaviors of the members of the distinct cultures.

## German and English

The modern English word *friend*, as well as the German word *freund*, are derived from the Germanic word *frijond* meaning "friend." The word frijond, however, also means "kinsman," namely, a relative from a widespread kinship network and, therefore, not just one of the very few persons whom we recognize today as our relatives. Frijond is based on the verb *frij-o*, which means "to treat somebody friendly" and "to court, to seek eagerly." This Germanic word can be traced to the old-Indian word *priyayate*, which means "to favor somebody," "to assist," and "to take care (for)." It is interesting that the Germanic word *fri*, which still means "free" (or "frei" in modern German) was also developed from this root. Thus, the aspect of voluntariness connected with friendship relations is actually embedded within the word *friend*. The German word *Frieden* was also developed from the root *pri-*. Frieden means to be close to one another and to mutually treat the other in the way members of the same kin do (Kluge, 1989).

## Latin and Greek

The Latin word *amicus* is derived from the verb *amo* (I love), which is based on *ama*. Ama is the same word as *mama* or *mamie*, phonemes from the child's first attempts to express affection for the mother. Thus, this word friend implies a kind of basic affection (Walde & Hoffmann, 1938). The Greek word *philos* means friend, but also means "belonging to" and "one's own." Therefore, the *phili* are an individual's own family, relatives, and friends (Fisk, 1970). Unlike in German, however, the word for voluntariness in Greek and Latin is unrelated to the word for friendship.

## Russian

The Russian word *drujba* stems from a word that expresses closeness, comradeship, and company. Here again we find the connection to kin. An older predecessor of the word means not only "dear," but also just "the other." The interesting ramifications of the word include meanings that are close to family issues as well as to war comradeship, perhaps related by the common reference to circumstances that engender serious mutual interdependence in one way or another (Kon, 1979).

## Japanese

The Japanese word for friend is *tomo*, represented by a Ghanji sign interpreted as two hands holding each other. Thus, the dominant component of the basic meaning of this word is the active mutual assistance offered in friendships. The connotations of the word tomo include meanings like mutuality, togetherness, and affiliation. The word *tomodachi* refers not only to individual friendships but also to relationships among the members of a group of friends. However, the individual aspect is present in the meaning because friendships are seen as based on personal respect and liking and, therefore, are distinguished from relationships with colleagues for which another word is available. When one wishes to refer to the high quality of a personal relationship, a special word (*shin-yu*) may be used (Takahashi, personal communication). The comparison of the cultural meaning embodied in Japanese friendships to the meaning of friendship in European societies is especially interesting because Japan often is regarded as a collective-oriented culture that emphasizes aspects of cohesion in friendship more than are emphasized in Western culture. However, in modern Japanese society, different meaning traditions seem to coexist, permitting a broad range of interpretations of friendship (Takahashi, 1993).

*Summary*

Philologists do not use a psychological perspective to examine the history of a word. As a consequence, philology cannot provide precise answers to questions regarding the psychological derivation of terms. Nevertheless, descriptive information about the origins of words can be very revealing. In regard to friendship, across all cultures and languages there is a word for a close relationship established outside the narrow family context. These words may have their roots in words referring to kinship relations but they have been gradually differentiated from these kin-relation words. We find indications that some languages, during some periods of their development, gave more emphasis to an objective or material reality, such as the importance of mutual help, in close relationships, whereas other languages stressed the affective union of friendship, referring to a subjective reality. These "subjective" voluntary relationships between independent individuals must be affirmed by means other than a blood relationship. The scope of the connotations related to the words used for friendship seems to reflect the sociohistorical circumstances under which friendship was important. The horizon of these meanings includes family issues, ritual functions, mutual assistance, kindness, war comradeship, conflict solution, intimacy, and affection. It should be noted that the history of the Germanic word friend can be read like the modern research agenda regarding children's conceptualizations of friendship. This striking parallel clearly demonstrates the value of a philological analysis of social and personal constructs such as friendship.

## The conception of friendship cross-culturally

The initial studies of children's conceptualizations of friendship were primarily conducted in English-speaking countries that border the North Atlantic. These studies approached conceptions of friendship from different vantage points focusing on either children's expectations about a friend's behavior (Bigelow, 1977; Bigelow & LaGaipa, 1975), or on operations children apply to confirm or terminate friendships (Youniss & Volpe, 1978), or on children's reasoning about different functions and aspects of friendships (Damon, 1977; Selman, 1976). Whether informed by a stage model of conceptual development or by other conceptualizations of development, these studies agree almost completely on the basic developmental process. In their thinking about friendship, children begin with a rather unilateral and momentary orientation that is based on joint play, physical proximity, and attractive toys. They then proceed to an understanding of friendship according to mutual and reciprocal processes. This level of understanding is more sophisticated than the initial conceptualization of friendship, but this level of understanding still leaves friendship vulnerable to problems that arise when friends are confronted with the need to coordinate plans of action. Later, preadolescents develop an understanding of friendship that is characterized by internal psychological processes such as intimacy, and trust, which allows them to overcome occasional conflicts (Shantz, 1983).

These results generally support the idea that children regard friendship as a form of relationship that is grounded in personal commitment. Studies outside the United States have examined the scope of this assumption. These studies include Bigelow's and LaGaipa's research in Canada and Scotland, and research using Selman's interview procedure with samples of Icelandic children (Keller & Edelstein, 1990; Keller & Wood, 1989), German children (Oswald & Krappmann, 1991; Valtin, 1991), and Chinese boys and girls (Keller, Schuster, & Edelstein, 1993). The study by Youniss and Volpe was replicated in Germany by Hofer, Becker, Schmidt, and Noack (1990). All these studies attest to the line of conceptual development that was first found in Anglo-Saxon countries.

The study that Keller, Schuster, and Edelstein (1993) conducted with Chinese children generally supports Selman's developmental model. However, these researchers met with some difficulties when assigning children's answers to some of the categories that had served to classify the answers given by Western children. In particular, young Chinese children appear to use prosocial reasons in decisions about action with friends earlier than Western children do. Perhaps the culture provides words and sentences that are interpreted as indicators of a higher level of understanding when European manuals are used, whereas these phrases may represent conventional expressions in China. It is also possible that the Chinese educational system, aiming at a strong collectivist orientation, may accelerate prosocial reasoning among young children. The authors claim that these differences concern the content of reasoning and do not call the developmental logic of friendship reasoning into question. Similarly, a study comparing Costa Rican and American children's perceptions of relationships shows that the quality dimensions describing relationships are applied by children of both cultures, but that the relative appraisal of peer and family relationships is influenced by the basic value system of the culture (DeRosier & Kupersmidt, 1991).

Overall, results obtained in research on the development of the friendship concept do not contradict the assumption that children and adolescents growing up in different cultures construct a similar concept of a mutual and trustful relationship called friendship. On the other hand, Keller and Wood's (1989) study demonstrates that even within the same culture children's increasing understanding of the distinct aspects of friendship does not develop uniformly. It may depend on the cultural definitions of goals and competencies that motivate interpersonal behaviors and which qualities of close relationships are given primacy at various points of development. Thus, the basic idea of an intimate, mutually supportive relationship apparently is widely spread across cultures, but the developmental progress and the actual realization of close relationships seem to be under the influence of interactions shaped by the respective culture.

### Friendships in different cultures

Studies of cultural anthropologists and ethnologists demonstrate the vast variety of behaviors regarded as proper performances of friendship. These studies impel us to recognize that the actual realizations of friendships in Western cultures vary as a function of value orientations and societal constraints. Unfortunately, societal and cultural variations have been included only rarely in these investigations. It is unfortunate also that in the well-known cross-cultural studies of Edwards, Whiting, Whiting, and their collaborators, which focused on children's social behavior in natural settings, the topic of children's friendships is not found in the indexes of two books comprehensively describing children's social activities (Whiting & Edwards, 1988; Whiting & Whiting, 1975).[1] This is all the more surprising as same-age peer interaction is an important domain of children's social lives and, according to the authors' interpretation, is similarly characterized by the dimensions of ''sociability'' and ''aggressiveness'' in each of the six communities studied (Whiting & Whiting, 1975). Perhaps the authors neglected to undertake a thorough analysis of children's friendships because they did not expect that children's friendships would play a role in the transmission of culture to the next generation.

Although we can assume that the children of these six farming villages actually form friendships, Konner (1981) reports that groups of same-age children do not exist in hunting and gathering societies. Under dangerous life circumstances, the multiaged juvenile group is apparently a more appropriate means of integrating a child into the community and transferring culturally and ecologically important information to the next generation. Solitary farm settlements can also limit children from finding playmates other than siblings or close relatives who live nearby (Iceland: Edelstein, 1983; Norway: Hollos, 1974).

In some of these societies friendships are established only later in life, often in connection with initiation ceremonies that accentuate the transition to young adulthood. Cohen (1966) studied 65 societies for which ethnographic reports were available. He found that in most of them friendship is an important relationship that offers an individual support from persons outside the kin network. Because of the indispensable social and ritual functions that friends in many societies have to fulfill for each other, friendships are often converted into ceremonial kin relationships (e.g., blood brotherhood) that carry the same obligations as consanguinal relationships and cannot be terminated. Cohen calls this type of a friendship *inalienable friendship* and underscores the ''institutionalization'' of this type of friendship.

The criterion of voluntariness, which is regarded as especially essential for friendship from our cultural point of view, seems to be contradicted by the ritual establishment and institutionalization of these relationships. However, Eisenstadt's (1956) analysis of ritualized relationships confirms that these relationships also contain the elements that are typical of friendship, namely that it is a personal relationship between individuals who are not interchangeable. Often, the partners can select the person with whom they initiate a ritualized friendship and individuals may also prefer one or some of their ritual friends with whom they develop a sense of intimacy.

In ritualized friendships, the role of supernatural forces may be used to explain why voluntariness in friendship may be limited. Indeed, indissoluble ritually established ties may help to avert the disorder that might result from free personal decisions about the continuation of important relationships. Also, the expansive prescriptions that regulate many rights and obligations among friends can conflict with the modern Western perspective emphasizing individual responsibility. Accordingly, instrumental functions in ritualized friendships seem to overshadow the affective qualities of these relationships. Of course, such a perspective fails to recognize that in a ritualistic system exchanged goods as well as performed functions have high symbolic value and, therefore, can elicit deep emotional responses. Besides, the instrumental aspects of close relationships in a ''modern'' society should not be underestimated.

In the 65 societies that he studied, Cohen (1966) identified three other forms of adult friendships in addition to the inalienable (i.e., the ritual-based institutionalized type). *Close friendship* is based on emotional propinquity, established without ceremonies, and may be broken. In close friendships, friends' duties are culturally prescribed, but their performance cannot be enforced legally or religiously. *Casual friendship* is not ritualized and not culturally recognized as a regulated relationship and hence can be dissolved easily. Casual friends are aware of each other, but little is shared among them. *Expedient friendship* is a relationship that gives both parties, often super- and subordinates, advantages that must not be literal equivalents (e.g., economic benefits vs. loyalty). The relationship lasts as long as mutual advantage is provided since no emotional ties bind the partners to each other.

Cohen finds that in most of the societies that he studied, one type of friendship dominates and that the prevailing type of friendship is related to the social structure of the community. Inalienable friendships are characteristic of territorially integrated communities with a joint economy in which the kin system is most influential (i.e., a "maximally solidary community"). Close friendships tend to prevail in communities in which the individual is strongly oriented to the clan, but also in which alliances with nonkinsmen are possible. This introduces the dimension of being either close to or distant from others in the social life of the community (i.e., a "solidary-fissile community"). Casual friendship exists in loose associations of isolated family groups, mostly belonging to nomadic groups that can hardly be termed a society. Temporary cooperation among these families does not overcome the distance between them (i.e., a "nonnucleated society"). Expedient friendship is found in societies in which kinship bonds are weak and the family unit is not internally integrated as persons compete with each other for individual profit and success (i.e., "individuated social structure").

Another attempt to differentiate friendships was proposed by Wolf (1966), who maintained that two types of friendship exist within communities: *expressive* or *emotional* friendship and *instrumental* friendship. He related the manifestation of distinct friendships to different social conditions. According to Wolf's model, emotional friendship has a special role in communities in which each individual has a fixed place in the social system and in which resources are distributed in accordance with this system. Individuals "escape" into emotionally supportive relationships so as to avoid the envy and suspicion that can exist in these societies. Wolf argued that instrumental friendships are most likely to be seen in cultures in which the distribution of resources is less dependent on social systems. In these societies, individuals who wish to expand their access to resources often need the help of others, and therefore they develop instrumental friendships. Wolf is careful to point out that emotional friendships may serve instrumental purposes and that instrumental friendships do not function without some emotional commitment.

Although the perspectives offered by Cohen, Eisenstadt, and Wolf help us appreciate the diversity of friendship relations, there is reason to be skeptical about the parallels they draw between friendship and specific community structures. All four of Cohen's (1966) types of friendship can be found in Western societies. Indeed, somehow the diversity and strangeness of at least some of the friendship phenomena vanish when we juxtapose them with the friendship categories that we use to conceive of and organize friendship relations within our own culture. Inalienable friendships may be rare, but they can be discovered in some exclusive secret associations (e.g., freemason lodges and fraternal organizations). Close friendship is hard to distinguish from voluntarily maintained intimate friendships. Casual friendship is similar to acquaintanceships, and expedient friendship resembles profit-oriented partnerships or patron–client relationships in the political and economic life of our society (Paine, 1970). It should be recognized also that Wolf's (1966) differentiation of emotional and instrumental friendships may be too vague, and too obvious, for disclosing deeper insight into the manifoldness of friendships. Paine (1969), though subscribing to a structural approach, extends his doubts to the distinction of friendship relationships as opposed to kin relationships, since many researchers have reported that subjects from many societies use kin terms in order to designate intense friendships. Paine concludes that some behaviors among particular kinsmen may be friendship behaviors and that, in some cultures, friendship values may have the values of certain kin relationships.

Paine (1969) recommends another way to understand the cultural diversity of friendship. He proposes that we start off with concepts that are useful in our society, specifically the qualities "personal," "private," and "affective." In Western middle-class societies, these qualities are important for the development of friendships that are characterized by autonomy, unpredictability, and terminality. According to Paine, we should then examine whether other societies or cultures construct alternative realizations of friendships with regard to the dimensions that are emphasized by our culture. Personal in our case means that friendship is relatively independent of kinship and institutions. Nevertheless, we learn from the anthropological literature that institutionalized friendships and friendships that are not clearly separated from the kin system coexist. Private means in our context that friendship is protected against the social control of others. But, again, anthropology shows that the behaviors of friends may be narrowly prescribed and their performance severely sanctioned. Affective means that friendship is not predominantly instrumental to achieve material advantage, but oriented to the other's well being. And yet in many societies, friends exchange goods, benefits, or even children, and fulfill social and ceremonial functions, but still these friendships are emotionally satisfying.

At the same time, we discover by these comparisons that friendships in our culture are not just personal, private, and affective. Individuals can realize their friendships as personal, private, and affective to varying degrees only. And in our culture, friends are not completely outside the control of others in the sense that we orient our behavior with friends according to an ethic of friendship. In Western societies friendships are also not completely independent of family and institutional affiliations. This is especially true with regard to children. It has been shown that until adolescence children's relationships with peers prosper when family and school cooperate to provide beneficial opportunities for socializing with agemates (Cooper & Cooper, 1992). It should be remembered also that competing influences of family and peer groups and the potentially negative impact of "bad company" on children's development are frequently an issue of discussion (Berndt, 1989).

Paine's (1969) observation that within Western societies one can find all of the different types of friendship that were regarded as closely linked to distinct cultural contexts makes us aware of the broad range of options that "modern" societies afford for choosing one's individual way of life. Already in childhood, parents begin to respect children's own responsibility for peer activities. Preadolescents know that many issues of friendships can be settled only by the friends themselves (Youniss, 1980). When considered from the perspective of sociologists like Eisenstadt (1956) or Riesman (1950), it is clear that the relative independence of children's social world contributes to adaptation to new conditions requiring coordinated interaction in societies that are challenged by increasing social differentiation, rapid change, and strengthened respect of multicultural orientations. The network of peer relationships and friendships offers ample opportunities for negotiating with others about plans, dissensions, objectives, and ways to achieve agreement, so that competencies are stimulated or expanded that society needs. Thus, the social world of childhood is instrumental not by conveying cultural patterns but by contributing to the formation of new patterns of living together. Without a doubt, the delicate balance of cultural traditions to be conserved and individual co-construction of shared cultural patterns is placed neither on the individual level nor on the societal level.

**Alternative features of friendship within a complex society**

A wide variety of forms of friendships can be found in Western society, largely due to the variability in cultural values that derive from a multicultural climate. This is especially so in North America, but can also be observed in other countries that have heterogeneous cultural traditions. Sociologists, especially those of the Chicago school, have intensely studied social settings of different cultural groups in the United States. For example, Gans (1962) has studied the relationship system among Italian (-American) urban villagers, and Whyte (1943) has studied the "street corner societies" formed by a generation of Italian-American adolescents and young adults who are still attached to their families but who nevertheless form independent social networks. Liebow (1967) has conducted similar studies of the "effortless sociability" of a group of young black men who gathered on the sidewalk in front of a take-out restaurant. (For an overview of other studies in this vein of research, see Lopata, 1990.)[2]

The persons described in these studies all lived under marginal, disadvantaged social conditions. These circumstances lead to the desire for reliable support from "true" friends while at the same time severely restrict objective, as well as subjective, capacities of overcoming crises in relationships. In spite of these similarities, however, these three groups represent different cultures and we see that friendship varies across these groups. For Gans's (1962) Italian-American urban villagers, friendships are subordinated to the peer group, which is formed of same-age, same-sex persons who have known each other from childhood on and, because of low mobility, stay together throughout their lives, sharing the tasks and problems of the respective life cycle. The peer group of these young adults is family- and kin-centered because peers and friends often are also cousins or in-laws. If you make a new friend in adulthood and the peer group accepts the person, you will try to make that person a godparent of a child in order to adequately integrate him or her into the network of peer and family relationships.

What does friendship mean in this context? Almost every member of the peer group is somehow a friend, at least a potential friend. Also a newly introduced friend becomes a "friend of the family." From childhood, friendship formation is mainly determined by occasions of prolonged contact provided by school, neighborhood, clique, church, or periods of extended help. However, the process of becoming more acquainted is strictly under the supervision of the group, which allows only relatively compatible persons to have access to the common social life. The reason is that "West-enders cannot cope effectively with disagreement" (Gans, 1962, p. 76). Thus, friendship is not a private matter in the sense that friends do not know much more about their friends than they know about any other members of the group. Moreover, friendship is not likely to be terminated. Yet within the group, there is much competition for respect and influence, manifested in joking, bragging, teasing, and denigrating "as long as this does not become too extreme" (p. 88). Although close friends may play a particular role in these activities, Gans refers to the contribution of group processes only, which, according to his analysis, do not equip the member with a "self" capable of tolerating personal differences. We may speculate that an emphasis on individual friendships may be dangerous to these groups because of the threat they might pose to the undifferentiated structure of the group.

Friendships are also a major part in the group life described in Whyte's (1943) discussions of the street corner societies formed by young adults. Whereas the family-centered peer group, which Gans depicts, strives for equality, street corner gangs, such as the group Whyte calls the Nortons, are hierarchically organized groups held together by a leader and strong mutual loyalties among members. The reason for this difference between the "Nortons" and the "West Enders" may be that the Nortons are not as embedded in kin networks that help to coordinate activities. However, since young adults like the Nortons have difficulties adjusting to unforseen changes, group leadership and the relative group status of the members serve to regulate the intragroup interactions so that everybody keeps to the usual routines. Order within the group builds coherence, and the group can defend its niche and protect its members.

In the street corner society, friendships apparently function only within the group context because the dyads and triads within the group are inactive and unable to make decisions without consultation with the group leader. Within that framework, friends give each other much support that remains unnoticed until the relationship is in crisis, for instance, when a member becomes involved with a woman outside the group. In that case, a neglected friend will complain about a lack of reciprocity from this person, considering that in the past he always did everything for the benefit of his friend. In this regard, friendships are hidden under the more manifest group processes. They seem to be "private," but not in a sense that they are a "resort" where you recover from strain in the public sphere. Instead, friendships offer mutual assistance to overcome everyday insufficiencies that could hamper group activities ("no money"). Friendships are instrumental for participation in group life, so that the group continues to be one's main source of satisfaction.

Friends are also extremely important for the young blacks studied by Liebow (1987) at "Tally's corner." These men do not form a structured group, but instead have personal relationships that differ in quality, have their ups and downs, and offer the opportunity for all kinds of vital and trivial activities ranging from badly needed help to time-wasting jokes. One has to question, however, whether these are actual friendships or if they are a fiction only, though a life-preserving one.

At Tally's corner, we observe that close relationships, perhaps because of the fragility of friendships, are often not declared to be friendships, but are transformed into kin relationships: Good friends are "going for brothers" and others treat them as if they were brothers. Even a man and a woman may "go for cousins," so that others know that they are friends and not lovers. At the same time, friendships are idealized: Friends claim that they will share every misfortune, give everything to the other, and will protect the friend against every danger. In fact, however, relationships are easily broken when unfavorable circumstances occur or selfish interests arise. Now it becomes apparent that these men do not know anything really personal about each other. What they know about each other, whether or not they are friends, is what is known to everybody strolling around Tally's corner. There is no substance in the relationships to which friends can appeal when they are in conflicts. They begin to blame each other for behaviors that are the product of their desperate life conditions more than the result of personal intentions. As every conflict between friends has consequences for all the others, the social situation among these men is very unstable, contrary to the claimed myth.[3]

From a middle-class perspective, the relationship praised as close friendships by these men would at best be regarded as casual friendships. These men try to stabilize them by applying kin terms, idealizing them, and ascribing long histories to them. Although these aspects are discredited by the evident reality, these men's claims represent an effort to create some stability in a social world marked by permanent transitions and shifts. Their efforts do not achieve what is desired, but repeatedly contribute to the realization of life periods characterized by more security and satisfaction. Thus, these fictitious friendships also serve a hardly dispensable function in these men's lives.

Although Liebow attempted to describe nothing more than life at Tally's corner, his analysis makes us understand that miserable living conditions as experienced by these men can produce a situation, which, on the one hand, elicits hopes about close relationships, but on the other hand, cannot be realized under just these conditions. The social rationale of this pattern seems to be effective not only at Tally's corner. "As-if" friendships or, using a more cautious formulation, friendships that are of another quality than is claimed, may be a relevant aspect in the actual social life of many individuals because contradictions between one's personal desire and socially offered opportunities are ubiquitous.

Whyte and Gans, likewise, are not only describing the social world of Italian-American first-, second-, or third-generation immigrants who inhabit a few blocks of Cornerville or West End. A similar network of interwoven kin and friendship relationships has also been described by Wilmott and Young in East London (Young & Wilmott, 1957; Wilmott & Young, 1960).[4] These particular social worlds emerge when individuals of common origin and shared traditions living in close contact experience their separateness from others. Such persons often feel language or educational deficits that prevent career and mobility on the one side and as a consequence produce a need for reliable support systems. Members of these groups avoid the risk of exposing themselves to contradictory life orientations and prefer to seek a "similar other" in their friendships. The interaction of these conditions is clearly demonstrated in Cornerville, West End, as well as in East London. To a lesser degree, this social pattern is widespread and forces persons to anchor themselves in socially meaningful places. Although friendships have the potential to transcend social barriers (Suttles, 1970), friendships under these living conditions primarily serve this purpose in conjunction with kin relationships.

When persons are better educated, career-oriented, and mobile, other qualities are seen in friendship (Seeley, Sim, & Loosley, 1967). Under these conditions we find friendships that emphasize voluntariness, unpredictability, affectivity (more than instrumentality), and terminality, which Paine (1969) relates to the "middle-class" culture. These friendships will flourish in a society, as Paine believes, where "an efficient and dispassionate bureaucracy [exists], so that an individual may enjoy private and uncompetitive relations without prejudice to those other relations that belong to the competitive public sector" (p. 521). This is the social sphere in which friendships are developed as predominantly personal constructions. This is not to say that friendships are less important in traditional "working-class" contexts, but in this cultural milieu friendships tend to be (a) more situation specific, (b) limited in the range of activities, and (c) more influenced by structural constraints (Allan, 1977). It should be recognized, however, that traditional working-class neighborhoods are dissolving, perhaps in some cases due to the influx of immigrants (see Williams, 1983). Little is known about the consequences of these processes for friendship formation (Allan, 1989).

## The cultural character of children's friendships

Children are almost completely absent in the reports on the cultural diversity of friendships, although some of the studies mention that the adult patterns of interwoven kin and friend relationships were already evolving in childhood. Remarkably, children's friendships were not an issue that cultural anthropologists chose to study. This may be the result of the researcher's unawareness of the potential contribution that friendships can make to socialization. Nevertheless, we are not informed in which way the next generation is introduced into these patterns.

Some "ethnographic" studies on childhood conducted mainly by sociologists have shown that children's friendship is a rich and manifold cultural phenomenon. This research indicates that children's friendships are responsive to the culture of their natural setting (Corsaro, 1985; Fine, 1987). Some of these studies were made outside of the North American context, but in related cultures. Unfortunately, though, most of these studies do not explicitly address the question of cultural differences and their impact on children's peer activities and friendships. Even when children from different cultural contexts are included, the effects of differing cultures as distinct meaning-generating contexts are not examined. Nevertheless, from this literature, we can develop ideas about the continuity of friendship across cultures. For example, we learn that children in an

American nursery school and an Italian *schola materna* use the same strategies to protect fragile interactions and, thereby, in the same way transform their practices and ideas of friendship without telling us why these culturally diverse contexts are of no relevance (Corsaro, 1985). Another study of friends debating future transformations of their friendships reveals that children often refer to the context, but this study does not pay attention to possible peculiarities influencing *discussione* among Italian preschoolers (Corsaro & Rizzo, 1988).

Other ethnographic studies report that some aspects of friendship are differentially meaningful in distinct contexts. Unfortunately these studies do not elaborate on the comparative cultural embeddedness of children's friendship. Fine (1981) shows the significance of friendship groups as a context for the acquisition of cultural roles. Sluckin (1981) emphasizes that friendship is an effective tool forcing the other to conform to the "friend's" expectation. And Davies (1982) observes in her study of Australian preschoolers that the initiation and frequent termination of friendships serve to maintain order in children's interactions. She remarks that this pragmatic aspect of friendship is typically not understood from an adult perspective, but is an important regulative element of children's own culture. Krappmann and Oswald (1991) found that children's acts of helping are not so much influenced by the context of instruction, but instead by behavioral standards of the peer culture. These standards are interpreted by helping friends either with special vigor or with peculiar indulgence due to the maintained relationship.[5] We can conclude from these studies that friendship is a social form provided with all the constituents of a cultural phenomenon that is also in the social world of children. However, more research explicitly focusing on this issue is needed.

## Conclusions and outlook

The scope of the cultural diversity of friendships could easily be further extended by including historical studies as well as studies conducted in various sections of social life such as in different professions or institutions. In addition, these studies would confirm that individuals almost universally, but not always successfully, are searching for others with whom they can establish a particular relationship, that is, a friendship. Friendships serve an important social role that differs from kin relationships and institutional roles.

The content and performance of these friendships, however, are much more determined by sociocultural factors than is typically recognized within the usual narrow focus of psychological research. Research from other disciplines provides evidence that friendships differ with respect to societies and their cultures as demonstrated by anthropological studies. Friendships also differ with respect to the social location of groups within one society and its culture as shown by ethnographic studies in lower-class milieus. Prosperous social groups whose survival is guaranteed can most easily afford to have voluntary, individually shaped, private friendships among its members. Groups that live under unfavorable conditions may limit the range of voluntariness, privacy, and individual negotiation.

The essential elements of friendship are sometimes hard to observe, because kin systems, societal institutions, and sociocultural traditions often try to restrict the achievements that friendship offers its members. They fear the relative independence of a relationship that may compete with kin relationships and institutional roles. Whether the maintenance of friendships is estimated as a contribution to the better functioning of the entire society or condemned as an attack against the integration of social life, it is strongly influenced by the basic structural conditions of societies. In the latter case, ritualization and institutionalization as well as rigid cultural definitions of rights and obligations function to decrease the danger of social dissolution. Sensitized by these observations, we discover tendencies of bringing friendships back to the joint social life in our middle-class culture. Some studies examined the strategies of "greedy" institutions or communal societies undertaken to prevent exclusive friendships among their members (Coser, 1974; Kanter, 1972). Also, children sometimes accuse peers of "dyadic withdrawal" (Slater, 1963).

The etymological findings demonstrate that research procedures must be appropriate to grasp the differences of meaning connected with the phenomena of friendships. Interviews and questionnaires that take for granted that every child asked about friendships will respond on the basis of a shared meaning of the word will not be useful as long as children come from different cultural worlds. Furthermore, we have to assume that within one world of childhood, children maintain friendships of different qualities that, at least when children grow older, comprise playmates, school friendships, sports buddies, hobby partnerships, and intimate friendships (Krappmann, 1992). These relationships have their own concerns, customs, and ethics.

Survey studies that provide data about the number of friends, expressed liking, and given or expected help, risk producing an idealized picture of friendships. In these studies it is difficult to realize many of the ambivalences, conditions, and counterarguments that can occur within these relationships. This idealization obscures the true impact of friendship, which is exerted not only by harmonic friendships, but also, or even more, by friends who fight their way through all the complications and contradictions that characterize different kinds of friendships in real peer life. For this reason, observations of children in natural settings should complement data collection because the meanings that allow children to understand intentions and to coordinate actions, as well as the rules that they apply, often can be inferred only from their behaviors (Rizzo, Corsaro, & Bates, 1992).

Using these procedures, researchers will discover and explore friendship as perhaps the most human of relationships, because friends try to construct their relationship in relative independence of, but not necessarily against, the most respectable institutions of their society. For that purpose they use a culturally based shared meaning system because it enables them to negotiate their relationship in a way that offers the best balance of personal desires and others' demands in a given context. Relative to the respective context, no relationship is less standardized than friendship. Because of the diversity of cultural contexts, no relationship can be realized in richer variations than friendship can be.

## Notes

1. The index of the *Handbook of cross-cultural human development* (Munroe, Munroe, & Whiting, 1981) contains "friendship," but refers the reader to go to "male solidarity" where one finds "male solidarity and drinking."
2. These are "classic" studies that are still frequently cited and are in no way replaced by recent network research that does not yield comparable results.
3. Liebow maintains that this is also true for family and kin relationships in the surrounding slum area, which differs from the organized and integrated patterns of life observed by Whyte (1943) in his study conducted in the 40s.
4. This same pattern of findings could be seen in the community where I grew up. This community was predominantly Protestant but it had a small Catholic subcommunity that was my actual cultural milieu. In this subcommunity there were refugees from the eastern part of Germany and unemployed sailors from the former German navy, which was located at the Baltic Sea. Starting in primary school, I knew four or five girls, who were either my friends' sisters or friends of those sisters, one of whom I probably would have married about 15 years later. For many years, sometimes still today, I sadly remember the warmth, the rivalries, and conflicts, as well as the pleasures of our peer and family worlds that I lost after I left the social place defined for me when I pursued my higher education in another city.
5. This does not mean that school has no impact on children's peer activities and friendships. One focus of culturally oriented research on childhood should be the interaction of peer and school cultures.

## References

Allan, G. (1977). Class variations in friendship patterns. *British Journal of Sociology, 28,* 389–393.

Allan, G. (1989). *Friendship.* New York: Harvester Wheatsheaf.

Berndt, T. J. (1989). Friendships in childhood and adolescence. In W. Damon (Ed.), *Child development – today and tomorrow* (pp. 323–348). San Francisco: Jossey-Bass.

Bigelow, B. J. (1977). Children's friendship expectations. *Child Development, 48,* 246–253.

Bigelow, B. J., & LaGaipa, J. J. (1975). Children's written descriptions of friendship. *Developmental Psychology, 11,* 857–858.

Cohen, Y. A. (1966). Patterns of friendship. In Y. A. Cohen (Ed.), *Social structure and personality* (pp. 351–386). New York: Holt, Rinehart, & Winston.

Cooper, C. R., & Cooper, R. G. J. (1992). Links between adolescents' relationships with their parents and peers: Models, evidence, and mechanisms. In R. D. Parke & G. W. Ladd (Eds.), *Parent–peer linkage* (pp. 135–158). Hillsdale, NJ: Erlbaum.

Corsaro, W. A. (1985). *Friendship and peer culture in the early years.* Norwood, NJ: Ablex.

Corsaro, W. A., & Rizzo, T. A. (1988). "Discussione" and friendship: Socialization processes in the peer culture of Italian nursery school children. *American Sociological Review, 53,* 879–894.

Coser, L. A. (1974). *Greedy institutions: Patterns of undivided commitment.* New York: Free Press.

Damon, W. (1977). *The social world of the child.* San Francisco: Jossey-Bass.

Davies, B. (1982). *Life in the classroom and playground.* London: Routledge & Kegan Paul.

DeRosier, M. E., & Kupersmidt, J. B. (1991). Costa Rican children's perceptions of their social networks. *Developmental Psychology, 27,* 656–662.

Edelstein, W. (1983). Cultural constraints on development and the vicissitudes of progress. In F. S. Kessel & A. W. Siegel (Eds.), *The child and other cultural inventions* (pp. 48–81). New York: Praeger.

Eisenstadt, S. N. (1956). From generation to generation – Age groups and social structure. Glencoe, IL: Free Press.

Fine, G. A. (1981). Friends, impression management, and preadolescent behavior. In S. R. Asher & J. M. Gottman (Eds.), *The development of children's friendships* (pp. 29–52). Cambridge: Cambridge University Press.

Fine, G. A. (1987). *With the boys: Little League baseball and preadolescent culture.* Chicago: University of Chicago Press.

Fisk, H. (1970). *Griechisches etymologisches Woerterbuch* [Greek etymological dictionary]. Vol. 2. Heidelberg: Winter.

Gans, H. J. (1962). *The urban villagers: Group and class in the life of Italian Americans.* New York: Free Press [exp. ed. 1982].

Hofer, M., Becker, U., Schmidt, B., & Noack, P. (1990). Die Altersabhaengigkeit von Vorstellungen ueber Freundschaft bei 6-bis 14jaehrigen [Friendship conceptions of six-to fourteen-year-olds as related to age]. In M. Knopf & W. Schneider (Eds.), *Entwicklung* [Development] (pp. 65–82). Goettingen: Hogrefe.

Hollander, E. (1958). Conformity, status, and idiosyncrasy credit. *Psychological Review, 65,* 117–127.

Hollos, M. (1974). *Growing up in Flathill. Social environment and cognitive development.* Oslo: Universitaetsforlaget.

Kanter, R. M. (1972). *Commitment and community: Communes and utopia in sociological perspective.* Cambridge, MA: Harvard University Press.

Keller, M., & Edelstein, W. (1990). The emergence of morality in personal relationships. In T. Wren (Ed.), *The moral domain* (pp. 255–282). Cambridge, MA: MIT Press.

Keller, M., Schuster, P., & Edelstein, W. (1993). Universelle und differentielle Aspekte in der Entwicklung sozio-moralischen Denkens. Ergebnisse einer Untersuchung mit isldndischen und chinesischen Kindern [Universal and differential aspects of the development of socio-moral reasoning. Results from a study of Islandic and Chinese children]. *Zeitschrift fuer Sozialisationsforschung und Erziehungssoziologie, 13,* 149–160.

Keller, M., & Wood, P. (1989). Development of friendship reasoning: A study of interindividual differences in intraindividual change. *Developmental Psychology, 25,* 820–826.

Kluge, F. (1989). *Etymologisches Woerterbuch der deutschen Sprache* [Etymological dictionary of the German language]. Berlin: deGruyter (22nd ed.).

Kon, I. S. (1979). *Freundschaft* [Friendship]. Reinbek: Rowohlt.

Konner, M. J. (1981). Evolution of human behavior development. In R. H. Munroe, R. L. Munroe, & B. B. Whiting (Eds.), *Handbook of cross-cultural human development* (pp. 3–51). New York: Garland STPM Press.

Krappmann, L. (1992). Die Entwicklung vielfaeltiger sozialer Beziehungen unter Kindern [The development of manifold social relationships among children]. In A. E. Auhagen & M. von Salisch (Eds.), *Zwischenmenschliche Beziehungen* [Interpersonal relationships] (pp. 37–58). Goettingen: Hogrefe.

Krappmann, L., & Oswald, H. (1991). Problems of helping among ten-year-old children: Results of a qualitative study in natural settings. In L. Montada & H. W. Bierhoff (Eds.), *Altruism in social systems* (pp. 142–158). Toronto: Hogrefe.

Liebow, E. (1967). *Tally's corner*. Boston: Little, Brown.

Lopata, H. Z. (1990). Friendship: Historical and theoretical introduction. In H. Z. Lopata & D. Maines (Eds.), *Friendship in context* (pp. 1–19). Greenwich, CT: JAI Press.

Meyer, M. J. (1992). Rights between friends. *Journal of Philosophy, 89,* 467–483.

Munroe, R. H., Munroe, R. L., & Whiting, B. B., Eds. (1981). *Handbook of cross-cultural human development*. New York: Garland STPM Press.

Oswald, H., & Krappmann, L. (1991). Der Beitrag der Gleichaltrigen zur sozialen Entwicklung von Kindern in der Grundschule [Peers' contribution to the social development of children in primary school]. In R. Pekrun & H. Fend (Eds.), *Schule und Persoenlichkeitsentwicklung* [School and personality development] (pp. 201–216). Stuttgart: Enke.

Paine, R. (1969). In search of friendship: An exploratory analysis in ''middle-class'' culture. *Man, 4,* 505–524.

Paine, R. (1970). Anthropological approaches to friendship. *Humanitas, 6,* 139–159.

Riesman, D. (1950). *The lonely crowd*. New Haven: Yale University Press.

Rizzo, T. A., Corsaro, W. A., & Bates, J. E. (1992). Ethnographic methods and interpretive analysis: Expanding the methodological options of psychologists. *Developmental Review, 12,* 101–123.

Seeley, J. R., Sim, A. R., & Loosley, E. W. (1967). *Crestwood heights*. New York: Science Editions.

Selman, R. L. (1976). Toward a structural analysis of developing interpersonal relations concepts. In A. D. Pick (Ed.), *Minnesota Symposia on Child Psychology*, Vol. 10 (pp. 156–200). Minneapolis: University of Minnesota Press.

Shantz, C. U. (1983). Social cognition. In J. H. Flavell & E. M. Markman (Eds.), *Handbook of child psychology*, Vol. 3: *Cognitive development* (pp. 495–555). New York: John Wiley.

Slater, P. E. (1963). On social regression. *American Sociological Review, 28,* 339–364.

Sluckin, A. M. (1981). *Growing up in the playground*. London: Routledge & Kegan Paul.

Suttles, G. D. (1970). Friendship as a social institution. In G. McCall, M. M. McCall, N. K. Denzin, G. D. Suttles, & S. B. Kurth (Eds.), *Social relationships* (pp. 95–135). Chicago: Aldine.

Takahashi, K. (1993). Life-span development of social relationships. *Newsletter of the International Society of Behavioural Development*, serial no. 24, 3–4.

Valtin, R. (1991). *Mit den Augen der Kinder* [With the eyes of the children]. Reinbek: Rowohlt.

Walde, A., & Hoffmann, J. B. (1938). *Lateinisches etymologisches Woerterbuch* [Latin etymological dictionary]. Heidelberg: Winter.

Whiting, B. B., & Edwards, C. P. (1988). *Children of different worlds*. Cambridge, MA: Harvard University Press.

Whiting, B. B., & Whiting, J. W. M. (1975). *Children of six cultures: A psycho-cultural analysis*. Cambridge, MA: Harvard University Press.

Whyte, W. F. (1943). *Street corner society*. Chicago: University of Chicago Press.

Williams, R. G. A. (1983). Kinship and migration strategies among settled Londoners. *British Journal of Sociology, 34,* 386–415.

Wilmott, P., & Young, M. (1960). *Family and class in a London suburb*. London: Routledge & Kegan Paul.

Wolf, E. R. (1966). Kinship, friendship, and patron–client relations in complex societies. In M. Banton (Ed.), *The social anthropology of complex societies* (pp. 1–22). London: Tavistock.

Young, M., & Wilmott, P. (1957). *Family and kinship in East London.* New York: The Free Press of Macmillan.

Youniss, J. (1980). *Parents and peers in social development.* Chicago: University of Chicago Press.

Youniss, J., & Volpe, J. (1978). A relational analysis of children's friendships. In W. Damon (Ed.), *New directions for child development*, Vol. 1: *Social cognition*, (pp. 1–22). San Francisco: Jossey-Bass.

# 3 The measurement of friendship perceptions: Conceptual and methodological issues

*Wyndol Furman*

The quality of children's friendships, as well as their popularity or status in the peer group, may be important determinants of social development and adjustment (Furman & Robbins, 1985; Hartup, 1992b). Although sociometric status has been studied extensively for a number of decades, research on children's friendships is more limited. Happily, the situation has recently changed, and today many investigators are examining children's friendships. A range of methodological approaches have been developed to study the quality of children's friendships. Observational systems exist for coding patterns of interaction, and both questionnaires and interviews are available for obtaining children's perspectives on their relationships. Although reservations are often expressed about questionnaires, interviews, or other types of self-report measures, they seem central to the study of interpersonal relationships. After all, friendships are affective bonds by definition. Children's perceptions of their partners and their relationships with them are fundamental determinants of the kind of the relationships that exist. In fact, symbolic theorists argue that perceptions of a relationship are the most valid indices of the quality of the relationship (Burr, Leigh, Day, & Constantine, 1979). In any event, children's perceptions are likely to shape the course of the relationship, both by affecting their own behavior and by affecting their interpretations of their partners' behavior.

This chapter provides a review of the measurement of friendship perceptions. In the first section, the existing measures of friendship perceptions are described. The conceptual background, psychometric properties, and validational evidence for each instrument are presented. In the second section, the general conceptual and methodological issues involved in the measurement of friendship perceptions are discussed.

Appreciation is expressed to Jeff Parker and Bill Bukowski for providing their data for the factor analyses described here. Preparation of this manuscript was supported by a grant from National Institute of Mental Health (BNS 5R01-MH-45830). The research described here was supported by a W. T. Grant Faculty Scholar Award and a grant from the National Institute of Child Health and Human Development (BNS 1R01HD16142).

41

The instruments that are described meet several criteria. First, the instruments assess specific friendships or could be adapted to do so. In effect, this eliminates several measures of peer social support. It is not clear if those measures actually assess support from friends in particular or peers in general; in either case, they are not measures of specific relationships. Second, the measures that are included provide relatively comprehensive, multidimensional evaluations of the features of friendships. This consideration excludes a number of the instruments that focus on only one or a limited number of characteristics, such as intimacy or social support (e.g., Hunter & Youniss, 1982; Mannarino, 1976; Sharabany, Gershoni, & Hofman, 1981; Wolchik, Sandler, & Braver, in press). Finally, the measures assess school-aged children or adolescents' friendships. Certainly, younger children have friendships, but different assessment approaches are required because questionnaires, interviews, and sociometric measures cannot be readily used (see Howes, 1987, this volume).

## Questionnaire measures of friendship features

### Berndt's assessment of friendship features

*Background.* In a series of investigations, Berndt and his colleagues have examined positive and negative features in friendships (Berndt & Hawkins, 1992; Berndt, Hawkins, & Hoyle, 1986; Berndt & Keefe, 1992; Berndt & Miller, 1992; Berndt & Perry, 1986). In the most recent version of their measure, a positive features scale focuses on characteristics, such as self-disclosure, prosocial behavior, and self-esteem support. A negative one assesses features such as conflict and rivalry. These positive and negative features were selected because they have been emphasized in past research on friendship conceptions and social support. Finally, the measure includes an assessment of the frequency of interactions.

*Description and psychometric properties.* Children are asked to rate the frequency of a particular type of interaction, using a 5-point Likert scale (1 = "never" to 5 = "very often" or "every day"). The measure can be used to assess either a single relationship or multiple relationships. Twelve positive and eight negative items are rated for each relationship; thus, 60 items are used in most instances. Scores can either be averaged across multiple relationships or derived separately for different relationships. In either case, the Cronbach alphas are excellent for the positive and negative scales (alphas ≥ .80). Factor analyses have repeatedly found the expected two factors. Written versions of Berndt's different measures have been used with preadolescents and adolescents (Grade

5 through college), and earlier versions, which were administered orally, have been used with children as young as second graders (Berndt & Perry, 1986).

*Validational evidence.* Studies show that students describe their closest friendships in more positive and less negative terms than they describe their second or third closest friendships (Berndt & Keefe, 1992) or their acquaintanceships (Berndt & Perry, 1986). Girls give higher ratings of positive features than boys do, but no gender differences are found in negative features (Berndt & Keefe, 1992; Berndt & Miller, 1992). Ratings based on average levels of positive and negative features in three friendships are very stable ($r$'s $> .50$) over the course of a school year, even when the ratings are not necessarily based on the same friendships (Berndt & Keefe, 1992). Stability of relationships was associated with the qualitative ratings in one study (Berndt, et al., 1986), but not a second one (Berndt & Keefe, 1992). Higher ratings of positive features and lower ratings of negative features are moderately related to school adjustment and perceived competence (Berndt & Miller, 1992; Berndt & Keefe, 1992); these links are more apparent when the mean scores of three friendships are used than when only the best friendship scores are (Berndt & Miller, 1992).

### Friendship qualities scale

*Background.* Bukowski, Boivin, and Hoza's (1994) Friendship Qualities Scale examines five features: (a) companionship, (b) help (encompassing both aid and protection from victimization), (c) security (encompassing trust and the idea that the relationship will transcend specific problems), (d) closeness (encompassing both the child's feelings toward the partner and his or her perceptions of the partner's feelings), and (e) conflict. Currently, a balance scale is being developed. The investigators selected these features by reviewing the literature and identifying the variables thought to be central components by both theorists and children themselves.

*Description and psychometric properties.* Children rate how true a sentence description is of one of their friendships, using a 5-point Likert scale (1 = "not true" to 5 = "really true"). Each of the five dimensions is assessed by four or five items (total number = 23). Cronbach alphas of scales are acceptable though slightly low (range = .71 to .80), perhaps reflecting the relatively small number of items per scale. The scale is said to be appropriate for school-age children and early adolescents, although no specific age range is provided.

Confirmatory factor analyses have been conducted separately for each scale. In preparing this chapter, the present author conducted principal component analyses of the investigators' data and found two plausible solutions. Consistent with their conceptualization, a five-factor solution accounted for 54% of the variance; the five factors corresponded closely to their five scales previously listed. At the same time, 35% of the variance was accounted for by a two-factor solution where the positive items loaded on the first factor and the conflict items on the second. The additional three factors met the normal Eigenvalue criterion, but each accounted for less than 10% of the variance. The implications of these findings are discussed in a subsequent section.

*Validational evidence.* Reciprocated friendships are described in more positive terms than unreciprocated ones (Bukowski et al., 1994). Similarly, stable friendships of 6 months' duration are described in more positive terms than unstable friendships on all but the conflict scale. Finally, friendship ratings are related to self-esteem and perceived competence (Bukowski, Hoza, & Boivin, 1993).

*Friendship quality questionnaire*

*Background.* Recently, Parker and Asher (1993) developed a Friendship Quality Questionnaire that was partially based on an early version of Bukowski et al.'s (1994) instrument. Six features are assessed: (a) companionship and recreation, (b) help and guidance, (c) validation and caring, (d) intimate exchange, (e) conflict and betrayal, and (f) conflict resolution. The authors assert that there is general consistency across studies that these features are the important aspects of friendship to examine.

*Description and psychometric properties.* Children rate how true a description is of a particular friendship, using a 5-point Likert scale (0 = "not at all true" to 4 = "really true"). The questionnaire consists of 40 questions with 3 to 10 items on each scale. The Cronbach alphas of scales are satisfactory ($M = .83$). Although the positively valenced scales are relatively highly intercorrelated (mean $r = .62$), a principal components analysis yields six oblique factors that closely resemble their six scales (58% of the variance accounted for); a reanalysis of these data by the present author revealed that 45% of the variance was accounted for by two oblique factors, which consisted of the positive items and the conflict items. Stability of scores over a two-week period is high ($M\ r = .75$). The measure has been administered to third- through sixth-grade children, but it is not known if the measure can be used with older or younger children.

*Validational evidence.* Friendship satisfaction is significantly related to all six features (Parker & Asher, 1993). Perceptions of friendships are moderately to highly related to partners' perceptions of the relationship. Additionally, children who are accepted by their peers describe their friendships more positively than do those who are not well accepted. Girls also describe their relationships more positively than boys. Finally, the qualitative features are significantly related to self-perceptions of loneliness, even after peer group acceptance is controlled for.

## Friendship Questionnaire

Furman and Adler's (1982) Friendship Questionnaire (FQ) assesses 16 features that fall under four factors: (a) Warmth/Closeness (which includes intimacy, affection, prosocial behavior, companionship, similarity, admiration, and affection scales [and in an earlier version acceptance and loyalty]), (b) Conflict (which includes quarreling, antagonism, and competition scales), (c) Exclusivity (two scales assessing desire by self and desire by friend for the relationship to be special or exclusive), and (d) Relative Status/Power (three scales assessing relative evaluations of oneself and one's friend in terms of academics, sports, and popularity). Based on work in other types of relationships, a fifth domain of Affective Mismatch was added recently (relative amount of affection and relative amount of negative interactions by the two participants toward each other). Most of the features were selected from culling the literature on children's friendships, particularly the research on their conceptions of friendships. The relative power/status, exclusivity, and mismatch domains were included because of work suggesting that they were important dimensions underlying other personal relationships (see Adler & Furman, 1988). Additionally, the FQ was designed to be comparable to other measures assessing sibling relationship qualities (Furman & Buhrmester, 1985) and parent–child relationship qualities (Furman & Adler, 1983). Specifically, the format is the same and many items and scales are identical, permitting comparisons among relationships.

*Description and psychometric properties.* For the warmth/closeness, conflict, and exclusivity scales, children rate how characteristic a description is of a particular friendship, using a 5-point Likert scale (1 = "hardly at all" to 5 = "Extremely much"). Each of the 16 scales includes three items (total $N = 48$). The Cronbach alphas of scales are satisfactory ($M = .77$). Although the assessment at the scale level is appropriate for some questions, the five factors are more commonly used ($M$ alpha of the original four factors $= .87$). The measure has been used with third- through seventh-grade children.

*Validational evidence.* Girls report less conflict in their relationships than boys do. Ratings of warmth/closeness are moderately related to the time the two children have known each other and the time they have been friends ($r = .40$, $r = .33$, respectively.). In one study of fourth to seventh graders, the subjects' and their friends' perceptions of all factors were moderately correlated with each other ($r$'s = .28 to .31), but in a second study of third and fourth graders, only perceptions of warmth were significantly correlated. Finally, ratings of friendships are related to the children's personality characteristics (Lanthier & Furman, 1992); specifically, ratings of warmth are associated with ratings of agreeableness and conscientiousness, whereas conflict ratings are negatively related to these two characteristics and positively related with openness to experience.

### Network of relationships inventory

Another measure that explicitly provides for comparisons across relationships is the Network of Relationships Inventory (NRI) (Furman & Buhrmester, 1985). In this measure children are asked about 12 features of their relationships with their parents, siblings, boy/girlfriends, and teachers (or other adults) as well as their close friends. The list of 12 includes 7 social provisions: (a) reliable alliance – a lasting dependable bond, (b) enhancement of worth, (c) instrumental help, (d) affection, (e) companionship, (f) intimacy, and (g) nurturance of the other. This list was derived from Weiss (1974) who hypothesized that individuals seek these specific social provisions in their relationships with others. Additionally, prior research indicates that relationships vary not only on a warmth or social provisions dimension, but also in terms of negative interactions and power (see Adler & Furman, 1988; Wiggens, 1979). Accordingly, five other features are assessed: (a) conflict, (b) punishment, (c) annoyance, (d) relative power/status, and (e) satisfaction with the relationship.

*Description and psychometric properties.* Participants rate how much each feature occurs in each relationship. Ratings are done using 5-point Likert scales. Anchors are the same on all scales except relative power (1 = "little or none" to 5 = "the MOST"); the relative power anchors refer to who has the most power (1 = "they almost always do" to 5 = "I almost always do"). Each of the 12 features is assessed by three items. Cronbach alphas of scales are satisfactory (typical mean alphas = .80) (Furman & Buhrmester, 1985; Furman & Buhrmester, 1992). Principal components analyses have revealed three factors: (a) Support Provisions, which is comprised of the seven provisions and the satisfaction ratings, (b) Negative Interactions, which contains the conflict, punishment, and annoyance scales, and (c) Relative Power, which contains the relative power scale and, secondarily, the nurturance-of-other scale. The third factor does not always emerge in analyses of friendships, though it does in assessments of other relationships (Furman, 1989). Support and negative interaction factor scores are quite reliable (alpha's > .90) (Connolly & Konarski, 1992; Gavin & Furman, 1992). Factor scores are stable over a 1-month period

($r$'s from .66 to .70) (Connolly & Konarski, 1992). The NRI has been used with second grade through college-aged students (Buhrmester & Furman, 1987; Furman & Buhrmester 1992).

*Validational evidence.* Adolescent friends' descriptions of their relationships are moderately to highly related to one another (support $r = .34$, negative interactions $r = .63$, power $r = .51$). Recently, we compared the interactions among female adolescent friends in relationships identified as satisfying (i.e., high in support and low in conflict) and unsatisfying (the reverse) (Gavin & Furman, 1992). In satisfying friendships, both adolescent girls and their friends display more positive affect, share power more equally, and are less jealous; additionally, their friends are more attuned, more socially skilled, and not as self-centered as friends in unsatisfying relationships. In another investigation, satisfying friendships were related to adolescents' perceptions of global worth and positive emotionality (Furman, 1987). Similarly, the amount of support in friendships is associated with perceptions of peer acceptance, particularly perceptions of being able to make and keep close friends (Connolly & Konarski, 1992). Rejected-aggressive children report more conflict with friends, whereas neglected children report less companionship (Patterson, Kupersmidt, & Griesler, 1990). Composite ratings of intimacy, companionship, and satisfaction are moderately related to interpersonal skills and adjustment in adolescence, but less consistently related in preadolescence (Buhrmester, 1990). In a similar vein, perceptions of support, particularly intimacy, are greater in early adolescence than preadolescence (Buhrmester & Furman, 1987; Furman & Buhrmester, 1992). Girls also generally give higher ratings than boys on the various support provisions, although specific differences vary slightly as a function of age (Buhrmester & Furman, 1987; Furman & Buhrmester, 1985, 1992). Finally, differences have been found in cross-cultural comparisons of friendships in Costa Rica and the United States (DeRosier & Kupersmidt, 1991).

*Behavioral systems questionnaire*

Recently, a behavioral systems conceptualization of romantic relationships, friendships, and parent–child relationships was proposed (Furman & Wehner, 1994). Drawing heavily on traditional attachment theory, adult romantic attachment theory, and neo-Sullivanian ideas, we hypothesized that romantic partners become major figures in the functioning of the affiliative, attachment, caregiving, and sexual/reproductive behavioral systems. Friends are expected to be major figures in the affiliative systems and in some instances in the attachment and caregiving systems.

A key concept in the theory is that of views, which refer to conscious perceptions and unconscious working models of a particular relationship, the self in that relationship, and the partner in that relationship. Views are seen as views of all behavioral systems and not just of the attachment system. Attachment theory's concepts of secure, dismissing, and preoccupied styles or models were, however, thought to be a promising way of describing such individual differences.

Views of a particular relationship are influenced by the nature of the experiences and interactions in that relationship, by past experiences in similar relationships, and finally by past experiences in other relationships. The existing data suggest that views are not highly concordant across particular relationships (see Furman & Wehner, 1994), but people may have general views of particular types of relationships (e.g., friendships) as well as specific views of each relationship (views of each of their friendships).

We developed a Behavioral Systems Questionnaire (BSQ) to assess conscious generalized views of four different types of relationships (friendships, romantic relationships, mother–child, and father–child relationships). Table 3.1 presents the different domains that are examined, and the stylistic scales within each domain. These domains were selected because they were thought to reflect stylistic differences in functioning, and because they are central aspects of these relationships.

*Description and psychometric properties.* Students are asked to rate on a 5-point scale how much they agree or disagree with each of a series of 92 statements about their friendships (1 = "strongly disagree" to 5 = "strongly agree"). Each of the 19 variables listed in Table 3.1 is assessed with four or five items. Secure, preoccupied, and dismissing scores are derived by standardizing and averaging the appropriate scales for the attachment, caretaking provided, and affiliation systems. Cronbach alphas of scales are satisfactory (mean alpha = .80); the composite style scores are particularly reliable (mean alpha = .88). Principal components analyses of each of the different domains yields the structure depicted in Table 3.1. Scores were moderately stable across an 8-month period ($r$'s = .51 to .80). Stylistic scores are only minimally related to Paulus's impression management index of social desirability. Parallel versions of the measure are available for assessing views of relationships with mothers, fathers, and romantic partners. The original BSQ referred to best or close friendships in general (past or present), but a comparable version has been developed to assess particular friendships. The psychometric properties of this measure are similar to the general version. The BSQ has been used with high school and college students, but the investigators believe that the measure could also be used with junior high or middle school students.

Table 3.1. *List of behavioral system questionnaire factors*

---

*Attachment*
1. Secure base (secure vs. dismissing)
2. Availability (preoccupied)

*Caretaking provided*
1. Secure care (secure)
2. Dislikes providing care (dismissing)
3. Provides excessive care (preoccupied)

*Affiliation*
1. Harmony (secure)
2. Low similarity (dismissing)
3. Less invested in relationship (dismissing)
4. More invested in relationship (preoccupied)

*Intimacy*
1. Self-discloses (secure vs. dismissing)
2. Dissatisfied with intimacy (preoccupied)

*Conflict*
1. Addresses and resolves difficulties (secure)
2. Denies conflict (dismissing)
3. Holds a grudge (preoccupied)

*Emotional expression*
1. Expresses emotions (secure)
2. Rational/unemotional (dismissing)
3. Emotionally confused (preoccupied)
4. Emotionally uncontrolled (preoccupied)

---

*Validational evidence.* Most work with the BSQ has focused on romantic views and their correlates. BSQ romantic style scores are significantly related to Collins and Read's (1990) and Hazan and Shavers' (1987) measures of attachment style. Adolescents who are secure in their relationships date more frequently and are more satisfied with dating life. Those who are more dismissing or preoccupied date less frequently. Consistent with the theory, secure views of romantic relationships are positively related to the frequency of engaging in mild forms of sexual behavior (hugging, kissing, necking, light petting), whereas dismissing views are negatively related. Preoccupied views are associated with earlier initiation of sexual behavior in a relationship.

In terms of friendship, ratings of secure styles for friendships are positively related to ratings of support in particular friendships, whereas dismissing and preoccupation ratings are negatively related. Secure ratings are also associated with a greater number of friendships and greater satisfaction with the number of friendships one has. Additionally, secure friendship styles are related to self-report ratings of social skills, particularly skillfullness in providing emotional support. Preoccupied style scores are negatively related to social skills ratings, especially conflict management and self-disclosure. Finally, general views of friendships, romantic relationships, and parent–child relationships are only mild to moderately related to one another, suggesting that views may be specific to different types of relationships.

## Interview measures of friendship characteristics

### Children's Friendship Interview

*Background.* Whereas the preceding measures are all questionnaires, Stocker developed two interview measures for assessing children's friendships (Stocker, 1988; Stocker & Dunn, 1990). An interview for children assesses closeness and hostility, whereas an interview for mothers assesses positive and negative features. The interviews include questions about association, prosocial behavior, intimacy, loyalty, similarity, co-operation, self-disclosure, reciprocity, and conflict. Stocker selected these features by reviewing the research on conceptions of friendships and children's behavior with friends.

*Description and psychometric properties.* The child and maternal interviews include 31 and 27 open-ended questions, respectively. Raters code the entire child interview for closeness and hostility using 5-point Likert scales. Interrater agreement for the child interview is satisfactory ($rs$ = .77 to .80). Because a global rating was used for the child interview, item properties were not determined. For the maternal interview, the frequency of behaviors is coded separately for each item using 5-point Likert scales (1 = "almost never" to 5 = "all the time"). If the rating is apparent from the mother's comments, it is coded; if not, the interviewer prompts the mother by referring to specific anchors. The internal consistency of the items in the maternal interview is low (positive alpha = .56; negative alpha = .62). These interviews have been used with a sample of first-grade children, but may be appropriate for children of other ages.

*Validational evidence.* Gender differences were not found on either measure. Child reports of hostility were moderately correlated with maternal reports of negativity ($r$ = .29). The other correlations between child and maternal reports were not significant. Neither report was strongly related to other measures of peer relationships, but a few links were found with sibling relationships and temperament.

*Other interviews*

Stocker's protocols are currently the only existing interview measures of friendship quality. In our own work (Wehner & Furman,1992), we have modified George, Kaplan, and Main's (1985) Adult Attachment Interview to assess working models of friendships, but this work is still in progress. Much of the early research on friendship conceptions was also based on interviews or open-ended essays (e.g., Bigelow & LaGaipa, 1975; Furman & Bierman, 1984), although individual differences in conceptions were not examined in that work. Thus, the potential richness of interview approaches has not been exploited sufficiently.

*Current status of the measurement of friendships*

This review of the various friendship measures gives rise to a number of observations. In the sections that follow I first discuss issues of measurement and then subsequently turn to general issues.

*Identifying friendships*

In order to use any of the preceding measures, one must first determine which relationships should be rated; that is, which relationships should be considered friendships? Two general approaches have been used. First, some investigators, particularly those studying adolescents, have simply asked the participants to pick the relationships they will rate. Alternatively, other investigators select the relationships to be rated on the basis of sociometric data. In particular, for a relationship to qualify as a friendship, both children must nominate each other as one of their best three friends. A variant of this approach is one in which one child must name the other as a best friend, and both must rate each other highly on a roster and rating sociometric scale (Berndt, 1984).

The first strategy (relying solely on the subject's nomination) is certainly easier, especially with adolescent samples where it is difficult to obtain sociometric data and less clear how to define the peer group (see Furman, 1993). The two strategies, however, are conceptually different. The former requires that both children name the other as a friend, whereas the latter requires only that the focal child designate the other as a friend.

The requirement of mutual nominations has several appealing features. First, friendships are commonly defined as mutual relationships. Second, almost all children will name others as friends when asked, but a significant proportion of such nominations are not reciprocated (Parker & Asher, 1993). For example, children will often name popular children as friends, because they would like to be friends with them (Ball, 1981; Leinhardt, 1972).

Although the requirement of mutual nominations has much appeal (and may, in fact, be the best solution), a number of psychometric problems arise in the typical methodology. In particular, nominations provide relatively insensitive indices of friendship because they are dichotomous ratings (i.e., friend/not a friend) (Berndt, 1984). The fixed number of nominations, typically three, can also lead to some misidentification of friendships. Those children who have only one or two friends may name other peers as their third friends. Conversely, by restricting the number of nominations a child may have, some friendships may be omitted or incorrectly classified as not being friendships. This selective omission of "secondary" friendships reduces the amount of variation among friendships and may present an overly positive picture of friendships. Moreover, if we take the idea seriously that there are multiple distinct perspectives on relationships (see the subsequent section), one could argue that some unilateral relationships are friendships – at least from the point of view of the child doing the nominating. That is, the child may see the peer as a friend and interact with that person as if she or he were a friend. Of course, other unilateral friendships may really be imaginary or desired relationships that do not resemble other friendships. Empirically, interactions in unilateral friendships differ from those of mutual friends, but they also differ from those of neutral associates, suggesting that we may have to treat unilateral friendships as a distinct category and not place them in one of the other groups (Hartup, Laursen, Stewart, & Eastenson, 1988).

In some instances, we may study friendships because we are interested in the child's "best" peer relationship. Unfortunately, the standard approach eliminates many children because they do not have reciprocally nominated friendships. Once again, we may be reducing the amount of variance and, in fact, missing a subgroup of particular interest clinically. For example, one estimate is that approximately half of low-accepted or rejected children are excluded (Parker & Asher, 1993). Empirical studies of the correlates of friendship characteristics have often yielded relatively small effect sizes. Perhaps this is an unintended consequence of the standard selection criteria.

If we are interested in the best relationships of those children who have a "good enough" relationship, then the current accepted approach makes sense, but one wonders if that is what we really are interested in. An alternative procedure is not being advocated as preferable here; instead, the point is that the issues deserve more careful consideration.

### Conceptual bases of measurement

With the exception of the Network of Relationships Inventory and the Behavioral Systems Questionnaire, the different measures have not been derived from theories per se, but instead have been based on reviews of past literature. Such a descriptive approach has much merit as it insures that the frameworks are relatively comprehensive ones that capture many of the phenomena in friendships. At the same time, this approach may make it difficult for us to make theoretical advances (Furman, 1993). In particular, the descriptive information that we obtain may not be readily amenable to theoretical analyses. If they have not been determined by theoretical considerations, our descriptive categories may put together behaviors that are different according to some theory; conversely, our categories may distinguish between behaviors that are theoretically equivalent. Moreover, we may simply fail to examine phenomena that are important to a particular theory.

The significance of theory is nicely illustrated by considering the historical changes in the literature on parent–infant interactions. Observational studies in the 1960's and 1970's yielded a number of classes of behavior that were hard to integrate; typically, behavioral frequencies were unreliable, unstable, or inconsistent from situation to situation (Masters & Wellman, 1974). When the behaviors were conceptualized in terms of attachment processes, however, the organization of behavior became more evident, and evidence for reliability and stability was obtained (Waters, 1978).

Although the primary point here is to emphasize the value of theory in designing our measures, theories serve other valuable purposes as well. Theories organize the findings of a field. By specifying underlying processes, they provide explanations of different empirical phenomena. They identify significant questions to be addressed and guide future research.

Unfortunately, relatively few theories of friendship have been proposed to date. Certainly, we have Sullivan's classic theory of socioemotional development to turn to (see Buhrmester & Furman, 1986; Sullivan, 1953), but since that time relatively few theories have emerged. Youniss and his colleagues have proposed an interesting integration of Sullivanian and Piagetian ideas (Youniss, 1980; Youniss & Smollar, 1985), but their work so far has primarily focused on comparing the contributions of parent–child and peer relations, and has not really examined individual variations in friendship. Attachment theorists have examined the links between parent–child and peer relations, but only a few efforts have been made to apply attachment theory to the study of friendships per se (Furman & Wehner, 1994; Shulman, 1993). Theoretical approaches and theoretically derived measures are needed to help guide our empirical work in more systematic directions.

## The features of friendships and their structure

As the preceding review indicates, only a moderate amount of agreement exists concerning which features should be examined in the assessment of friendships.

Some features, such as companionship, are included in all measures, but many others are specific to particular instruments. After all, the number of features assessed in the multidimensional measures ranges from 5 to 16. How do we determine which features should be examined? Certainly, theory is an important guide for selecting features. We should also insure that the children actually differentiate among the different features which are included. Ideally, categories should correspond with those that have emerged in observational studies so that the results from different methods can be integrated. Finally, empirical studies will also help us determine which features are centrally related to other phenomena, and which seem secondary in importance.

It is also worth noting that the vast majority of the features that have been included are positively valenced ones, which seem to reflect warmth, support, or positive interchanges. Although one would not want to dismiss the positive nature of friendships and their potential benefits, it is important to remember that friendships are also an arena for conflict and competition (Hartup, 1992a). As our measures develop further, we need to incorporate these other features of friendship.

Another important question is how the different features are related to one another. Elsewhere we proposed that four primary elements underlie the various features of friendship or other personal relationships. The four are: (a) Warmth, (b) Conflict, (c) Relative Power/Status, and (d) Comparisons of the relationship with other relationships (Adler & Furman, 1988). The meanings of the first three are self evident; the last refers to feelings, desires, or behaviors that implicitly or explicitly involve some comparison of the relationship to other relationships. For example, rivalry in sibling relationships involves comparisons of two siblings' relationships with their parents. Similarly, exclusivity in friendships refers to wishes for the relationship to be different from other ones.

A review of existing measures provides clear evidence for both a warmth and a conflict dimension. For example, analyses of Berndt's measures have yielded Positive and Negative factors, as have the reanalyses of Parker and Asher's and Bukowski et al.'s Friendship Quality scales. Most measures have not included items that assess power or compare different relationships. When such items are included, the factors emerge. For example, factor analyses of our Friendship Quality scale yield Relative Power and Exclusivity factors as well as Warmth and Conflict factors. It is interesting that a Relative Power factor does not consistently emerge in the analyses of friendship ratings on the Network of Relations Inventory. This measure assesses more overt differences in power than the Friendship Questionnaire does, suggesting that children perceive their friendships to be relatively egalitarian, but subtle differences in power may occur. In summary, each of the four elements appears to be present in friendships, although more attention should be given to the power and comparison of relationship elements in the subsequent development of measures.

Although the four may be the primary elements, further differentiations can be made. For example, the reanalyses of the Parker and Asher measure and the Bukowski et al. measure suggest that one can look both at a global Warmth factor and at the specific features that are parts of this factor. Similarly, analyses of the Network of Relationships Inventory yield both first-order factors for the specific support provisions and a second-order general support factor (Buhrmester, personal communication, October, 1992; Connolly & Konarski, 1993).

The appropriate level of analysis depends upon the nature of the questions being asked. Generally speaking, the issues are analogous to those that arise in choosing between molecular and molar coding strategies in observational research (see Grotevant & Carlson, 1989; Hartup, 1979; Patterson & Reid, 1984). Most theoretical constructs are at a molar level, but such an approach may not provide the level of detail that is required. It is possible that molecular categories can even provide more objective and reliable indices of molar constructs, but it is also possible that they will not capture the level of organization of behavior or the stable characteristics of the relationship (Cairns & Green, 1979).

In any event, it is important to remember that most measures simultaneously reflect both molecular and molar constructs. Thus, a molecular measure of self-disclosure is also a measure of general warmth or support, albeit an incomplete one. Conversely, variation in a global warmth measure may actually reflect variation in particular molecular constructs, such as self-disclosure. Because of the multileveled meaning of our measures, we must be careful in our interpretations of what we find. Observed effects of specific variables may actually be effects of the broader constructs. For example, Parker and Asher (1993) report significant differences in the friendships of low-, medium-, and high-accepted children. As the differences were significant or near significant on all of their scales, it appears that they actually found a difference in general support, rather than in any specific friendship feature. Conversely, seeming differences on broad dimensions may actually be limited to more specific features that are part of that dimension. For example, we found that a significant age difference in the supportiveness of preadolescents and adolescents' friendships actually reflected age differences in affection and intimacy and not the other provisions of support (Furman & Buhrmester, 1992).

## The validation of measures

Most of the measures described in this review have promising psychometric features. Investigators have been successful in developing internally consistent scales that are related to one another in meaningful ways. At the same time, the validational evidence for any of the measures is relatively limited. Few investigators have examined the stability of their measures, although it is unclear how stable a measure of a relationship should ideally be. To the best of our knowledge, normative data are not available for any of the instruments, making it difficult to compare samples across studies or use the measures for clinical purposes. Finally, the classic problems of response bias and social desirability have not been addressed very often. To avoid problems of rating a stereotypic friendship (vs. a specific one), Parker and Asher (1993) insert a particular friend's name into the phrasing of each item, a technique that other authors should consider.

Comparisons among the different instruments are badly needed. Not only would such comparisons provide convergent validity for the measures (it is hoped!), but also they would determine what is uniquely assessed by particular instruments. Such information would help determine what the underlying structure of friendships is. If broad dimensions, such as warmth and conflict, underlie most measures, the different instruments should be highly related. If particular scales are not highly related to other measures, they may either have some measurement problems or they may be tapping some distinct features of friendships.

The process of construct validation for the different measures has also just begun. Existing research provides encouraging evidence of links between friendship experiences and peer status, loneliness, self-esteem, and adjustment, but further work is obviously required. Particularly important would be work examining the links between perceptions of friendships and patterns of interaction. Observational systems have been developed that provide broad assessments of friendship characteristics (Stocker and Mantz-Simmons, 1992) or the characteristics of individuals in their interactions with friends (Gavin & Furman, 1992). A number of other observational tasks and coding schemes are available for examining specific facets of relationships, particularly intimacy, prosocial behavior, conflict, and competition. As yet, however, we know little about how perceptions are related to these different types of interactions.

Finally, one measurement issue that has not received much attention is the question of whether a dimensional or typological approach is a more promising way of describing individual differences in friendships. All of the existing measures rely on a dimensional approach. Shulman (1993), however, has recently developed a typology of adolescent friendships. Using Reiss's (1981) family system theory as a basis, he proposed three types of friendships: (a) interdependent, in which cooperation and autonomy are balanced, (b) disengaged, where the individuals act independently of each other, and (c) consensus-sensitive or enmeshed, where full agreement and cohesion are of utmost importance. Such a typological approach has the appeal of being able to identify potential patterns among variables. On the other hand, the dimensional approach has more appealing psychometric properties. For example, in our own work on friendships and romantic relationships, the relations among variables are stronger when a dimensional measure, such as the Behavioral Systems Questionnaire, is applied than when a typological one, such as Hazan and Shaver's attachment measure, is used. It is interesting to note that when our Behavioral System Questionnaire attachment items for each kind of relationship are subjected to cluster analyses, four types generally emerge: (a) a secure type, (b) a dismissing type, (c) a preoccupied type, and (d) an average type. These findings suggest that some relationships can be characterized as types, but other ones cannot be so readily classified. Nevertheless, the relative merits of the two approaches warrant further consideration.

*Perceptions of friendships*

Typically, friends' perceptions of their relationship are only moderately related to their partners' perceptions (Furman & Adler, 1982; Parker & Asher, 1993). This finding may mean that the measures are not valid, but not necessarily. It is incorrect to think of friendships or other personal relationships as unitary phenomena (see Furman, Jones, Buhrmester, & Adler, 1988). That is, there is no such beast as *the* friendship. Each of the children has a friendship, and thus, each can provide a distinct perspective on their relationship. Moreover, outside observers, such as social scientists, or "participant observers," such as parents or other peers, may also provide valuable insights into the nature of the relationship.

Perspectives differ because of different experiences in or exposures to the relationship. The context and reference points for interpreting behaviors also differ, and of course attitudes, feelings, ego involvement, competence, and motivation influence an individual's views as well (see Furman et al., 1988). Accordingly, the data we gather tell us what a person's or an observer's perspective on the relationship is like rather than what "the relationship" is like.

The concept of multiple perspectives complicates the process of validation. The correspondence among different perspectives may only be moderate even when the measure is valid. Yet, we need to insure that children's answers to our questions provide a veridical representation of their perceptions. That is, we need to insure that they are not describing the relationship in a more positive light than they perceive it, or otherwise distorting their perceptions of the relationship in their answers to our questions.

Incidentally, if the participants' perceptions are only moderately related to one another, one would expect that these perceptions would be only moderately related to patterns of interaction. Greater convergence, however, could be obtained by using composite perceptions or by using both participants' perceptions to predict interactions. The latter solution of having two sets of predictor variables in a regression equation requires a meaningful basis for determining who should be designated as the first and second participants. Perhaps this could be done on the basis of a characteristic of the two children (e.g., relative age) or on the basis of the relative positivity of the children's perceptions. It would be interesting to know whether the pattern of interaction is more related to the more positive than to the more negative view of the relationship.

Finally, one should also recognize that perspectives on relationships are not fully captured by conscious perceptions. The distinction between overt self-report and their unconscious or automated working model has been articulated most clearly by attachment theorists (Cassidy & Kobak, 1988; Main, Kaplan, & Cassidy, 1985). For example, individuals who experience early rejection from their parents may deny such events and instead describe their childhoods in a very favorable light. Their recollections, however, may be diffuse, nonspecific, and contradictory, whereas those who are securely attached present a more balanced perspective, substantiated by specific incidents. Should models of friendships work in the same manner, then simple self-reports may not distinguish between two very different types of relationships. At the same time, conscious styles may involve more than defensive strategies; if so, these perceptions would not correspond with automated models even if one adjusted for defensive responding (Furman & Wehner, 1994). Certainly, these comments are not intended to denigrate the significance of conscious styles; the point is simply that neither they nor automated models alone provide a complete picture of a person's perspective on a relationship.

### Developmental considerations

Several developmental issues need greater consideration in measuring friendship perceptions. First, the investigator must insure that the items are appropriate indices for the ages of the subjects. Within narrow age ranges, this task is not too difficult. For example, in the process of item development one may use interviews or observations to document that the behaviors being assessed commonly occur at a given age and that children understand what they are being asked about. When a wide age range is being examined, however, the task is more difficult because the manifestations of a construct may vary across the range. For example, intimacy among elementary school-aged children involves self-disclosure, but among adolescents, it includes genuineness, trust, and emotional support as well (Bigelow & LaGaipa, 1980; Furman & Bierman, 1984; Sharabany, Gershoni, & Hoffman, 1981). Even if these features are reflected in young children's behavior, it seems unlikely that the young children themselves would comprehend these abstract concepts. In our own measures, we chose to write items that refer to simple concrete behaviors (Furman & Buhrmester, 1985; Buhrmester & Furman, 1987). Although this approach insures that the items are appropriate across all ages, it can underestimate the magnitude of developmental changes that occur as a result of changes in the manifestation of the construct of interest.

In a related vein, one also should insure that the underlying structure of the measure is invariant over development. Coan (1960) described three forms of changes in structure; these were the emergence of new factors, the disintegration of factors, and the metamorphosis of a factor in which the underlying construct remains the same, but the manifestations change (see also Connell & Furman, 1984). Should such changes occur in the structure of friendships, then the interpretation of any age differences would be problematic. In effect, what is being measured at different ages would not be comparable or have the same meaning. Should, for example, a warmth factor in preadolescence divide into companionship and intimacy factors in adolescence, it would be difficult to describe any developmental changes in the mean levels of these variables as the variables are not the same. One solution has been to divide the constructs into the smallest consistent units. Thus, in the present hypothetical example, one would describe the changes in companionship and intimacy separately, even though the two are part of the same construct at the younger age. Although this solution understates the nature of the developmental change, it has much appeal. One drawback, however, is that the consistent units may not be representative of the larger constructs from which they were drawn. For example, our companionship and intimacy factors may not provide a complete or a representative picture of the warmth construct at the earlier age. As yet, few investigators have considered the possibility of changes in the underlying structure of friendships. In our work with the Network of Relations Inventory, we have found little evidence of such changes, but the question requires further consideration.

Interpretations of differences among children may also be complicated by developmental changes in friendships. For example, adolescents typically describe their relationships as being more intimate than those of preadolescents (e.g., Buhrmester & Furman, 1987; Furman & Buhrmester, 1992). Moreover, children or adolescents of any particular age vary in how intimate their friendships are. For example, some early adolescents describe their relationships as being less intimate than other early adolescents do. Should we interpret the low intimacy of some early adolescents' friendships as characteristic of the kind of relationships they are likely to have or is it because they are not as far along developmentally as their peers are in terms of the nature of their relationships? That is, in a year or two, they may "catch up" and have intimate relationships similar to those of other adolescents. In other words, are these adolescents with nonintimate friendships on a different developmental trajectory or are they displaying a developmental lag? Most interpretations imply that the differences are long lasting ones and do not simply reflect delays, yet this may not be the case. Longitudinal assessments are required to distinguish between these two interpretations, but unfortunately the existing studies are all cross-sectional ones. Until longitudinal data exist, we need to consider both the developmental lag and the different developmental trajectory interpretations as the two have very different conceptual and applied implications.

The preceding issues also apply to research on cultural and sex differences. For example, one of the most consistent findings in the literature is that girls self-disclose more than boys do (e.g., Buhrmester & Furman, 1987; Furman & Buhrmester, 1985; Hunter & Youniss, 1982; Sharabany et al., 1981). What is more controversial, however, is the assertion that girls' relationships are more intimate in the broadest sense of the word (e.g., closeness or Sullivan's concept of consensual validation). An alternative explanation is that intimacy is manifested differently by girls and boys. For example, girls may seek intimacy through self-disclosure and talk, whereas boys may seek it through shared activities, particularly frightening or dangerous ones. Regardless of what proves to be the case in this specific instance, we need to insure that our measures have comparable meaning for boys and girls or for children from different cultural backgrounds, just as we need to insure that our measures are comparable for children of different ages.

*Temporal changes within relationships.* Not only is our work complicated by age changes in the nature of friendships, but it is also complicated by changes over time in friendships themselves. Theoretically, one would expect friendships to become more supportive or closer as they develop. In fact, as noted previously, length of knowing someone and length of friendship are correlated with warmth/closeness ratings. Because of these temporal changes in friendships, it is difficult to compare different children's friendships that vary in length. Observed differences could reflect something about the children, but they could reflect differences in the length of their friendships. One solution is to covary out the length of relationships before examining the relations of friendship characteristics with other variables. Unfortunately, this solution presents its own set of problems. First, it assumes that the changes over the course of a relationship are linear – a dubious proposition. A more problematic issue is that it assumes that variations in the length of relationship are purely random or nonsystematic, yet children vary in how stable their friendships are. For example, adolescents with more stable friendships have better school adjustment (Berndt & Hawkins, 1992). By controlling for the length of relationship, we eliminate part of the meaningful variance. Moreover, the comparisons can be confounded (Meehl, 1970). When we match or covary, we are comparing the less stable relationships of children with stable friendships with the more stable relationships of children with unstable friendships. It is not clear what this comparison means. In fact, our matching on one variable (length) may result in mismatching on another variable (relative ranking of friendship). That is, because best friendships are likely to be longer lasting than other relationships, our matching or covariance techniques may result in comparisons of the best friendships of children with unstable relationships with the less significant friendships of children with stable relationships. Given the limitations of the alternatives, we should consider both controlling and not controlling for variation in length or other factors. That is, we should conduct both sets of analyses, hoping that the results are the same.

## Friendship characteristics, friendships, and individual differences

Often we are interested in how friendship experiences may be related to other facets of development or adjustment. When examining such questions, we need to look at more than just the qualitative features of friendships. Not only would we want to include other kinds of features, such as the length or stability of a relationship, but we would also want to consider the characteristics of the friend, and, in fact, the similarity between the child and friend. That is, some effects may occur because of the nature of the relationship, but others may result from whom one selects as a friend. For example, school adjustment is related to the characteristics of the friends and similarity with one's friends, as well as the characteristics of the relationships themselves (Berndt & Keefe, 1992). Separating individual and relationship characteristics presents some thorny conceptual and methodological issues, but this is essential if we are to understand the influence friendships have on development and adjustment (see Furman, 1984, 1993; Hartup, 1993, for further discussion).

Assessment problems are further complicated by the fact that children do not have one and only one friendship. On the one hand, as noted previously, some children do not have friendships, a fact likely to be significant itself. On the other hand, most children have more than one friendship. Which relationships should we examine? The characteristics of best friendships may be important predictors, but it is possible that the characteristics of other friendships are just as important. In fact, stronger effects are found when a composite of friendships is examined than when just best friendships are (Berndt & Miller, 1992). Admittedly, comparisons of multiple friendships present difficult methodological choices. For example, which relationships do you compare when one child has three close friends and six other friends, whereas another has two close ones and ten others? Should one average across various relationships? If so, which ones, when the size of the networks vary? Simple counts of numbers of friend-ships and even indices of quality do not seem to capture the variation in friend-ship networks fully. A different level of analysis seems necessary. These problems are compounded by the fact that one ultimately needs to examine other peer relationships or other close relationships to understand the contributions specific to friendship relations. Despite these headaches, studies of multiple friendships seem essential if we are to understand the contribution of children's friendships to adjustment and development.

## Concluding comments

During the last decade, many new measures of friendship perceptions have ap-peared. These measures have promising psychometric properties and the initial validational evidence is encouraging. At the same time, a number of measure-ment and conceptual questions must be addressed. In particular, we must re-consider which relationships qualify as friendships and which do not. The theoretical foundations of our measures require further articulation. Important questions exist concerning the underlying structure of our measures, typological versus dimensional approaches, and conscious and unconscious perceptions. De-velopmental factors and temporal changes also have significant implications for our measurement of friendships and the interpretation of results. Finally, it is important to remember that examining the qualitative features of friendships is just one part of understanding the role friendships play in development. Atten-tion to these conceptual issues should foster further advances in our measure-ment of friendships.

## References

Adler, T., & Furman, W. (1988). A model for close relationships and relationship dysfunctions. In S. W. Duck (Ed.), *Handbook of personal relationships: Theory, research, and interventions.* London: Wiley.

Ball, S. J. (1981). *Beachside comprehensive.* Cambridge: Cambridge University Press.

Berndt, T. J. (1984). Sociometric, social-cognitive, and behavioral measures for the study of friend-ship and popularity. In T. Field, M. Siegal, & J. L. Roopnarine (Eds.), *Friendships of normal and handicapped children.* NY: Ablex.

Berndt, T. J., & Hawkins, J. A. (1992). *Effects of friendship on adolescents' adjustment to junior high school.* Manuscript under review.

Berndt, T. J., Hawkins, J. A., & Hoyle, S. G. (1986). Changes in friendship during a school year: Effects on children's and adolescents' impressions of friendship and sharing with friends. *Child Development, 57,* 1284–1297.

Berndt, T. J., & Keefe, K. (1992). *Influences of friends' characteristics and friendship features on adolescents' behavior and adjustment.* Manuscript submitted for publication.

Berndt, T. J., & Miller, K. E. (1992). *Relations of adolescents' self-esteem and school adjustment to their friends' characteristics.* Manuscript submitted for publication.

Berndt, T. J., & Perry, T. B. (1986). Children's perceptions of friendships as supportive relationships. *Developmental Psychology, 22,* 640–648.

Bigelow, B. J., & LaGaipa, J. J. (1975). Children's friendship expectations: A cognitive developmental study. *Child Development, 48,* 246–253.

Bigelow, B. J., & LaGaipa, J. J. (1980). The development of friendship values and choice. In H. C. Foot, A. J. Chapman, & J. R. Smith (Eds.), *Friendships and social relationships in children.* New York: Springer.

Buhrmester, D. (1990). Intimacy of friendship, interpersonal competence, and adjustment in pre-adolescence and adolescence. *Child Development, 61,* 1101–1111.

Buhrmester, D., & Furman, W. (1986). The changing functions of friends in childhood: A neo-Sullivanian perspective. In V. G. Derlega & B. A. Winstead (Eds.), *Friendship and social interaction.* New York: Springer-Verlag.

Buhrmester, D., & Furman, W. (1987). The development of companionship and intimacy, *Child Development, 58,* 1101–1113.

Bukowski, W. M., Boivin, M., & Hoza, B. (1994). Measuring friendship quality during pre-and early adolescence: The development and psychometric properties of the Friendship Qualities Scale. *Journal of Social and Personal Relationships, II,* 471–484.

Bukowski, W. M., Hoza, B., & Boivin, M. (1993). The role of affect in the differential links between qualities of friendship and dimensions of "self" during early adolescence. In B. Laursen (Ed.), *New directions for child development: Close friendships in adolescence.* San Francisco: Jossey-Bass.

Burr, W. R., Leigh, G. K., Day, R. D., & Constantine, J. (1979). Symbolic interaction and the family. In W. R. Burr, R. Hill, & I. L. Reiss (Eds.), *Contemporary theories about the family* (Vol 2). New York: Free Press.

Cairns, R. B., & Green, J. A. (1979). Appendix A: How to assess personality and social patterns. In R. B. Cairns (Ed.), *The analysis of social interactions: Methods, issues and illustrations.* Hillsdale, NJ: Erlbaum.

Cassidy, J., & Kobak, R. (1988). Avoidance and its relation to other defensive processes. In J. Belsky & T. Neworski (Ed.), *Clinical implications of attachment.* Hillsdale, NJ: Erlbaum.

Coan, R. W. (1960). Child personality and developmental psychology. In R. B. Cattell (Ed.), *Handbook of multivariate experimental psychology.* Chicago: Rand McNally.

Collins, N. L., & Read, S. J. (1990). Adult attachment, working models, and relationship quality in dating couples. *Journal of Personality and Social Psychology, 58,* 644–663.

Connell, J. C., & Furman, W. (1984). Conceptual and methodological issues in the study of transitions. In R. Harmon & R. Emde (Eds.), *Continuity and discontinuity in development.* New York: Plenum.

Connolly, J., & Konarski, R. (1992). *The peer self-concept in adolescence: Components and interpersonal correlates.* Manuscript under review.

Connolly, J., & Konarski, R. (1993). *A structural analysis of adolescents' perceptions of social support.* Paper presented at the meetings of the American Psychological Association, Toronto, Canada.

DeRosier, M. E., & Kupersmidt, J. B. (1991). Costa Rican children's perceptions of their social networks. *Developmental Psychology, 27,* 656–662.

Furman, W. (1984). Issues in the assessment of social skills of normal and handicapped children. In T. Field, M. Siegal, & J. L. Roopnarine (Eds.), *Friendships of normal and handicapped children.* New York: Ablex.

Furman, W. (1987). *Social support, stress, and adjustment in adolescence.* Paper presented at the biennial meetings of the Society for Research in Child Development, Baltimore, MD.

Furman, W. (1989). Developmental changes in children's social networks. In D. Belle (Ed.), *Children's social networks and social supports*. New York: John Wiley & Son.

Furman, W. (1993). New directions and needed directions in the study of adolescent friendships. In B. Laursen (Ed.), *New directions for child development: Close friendships in adolescence*. San Francisco: Jossey-Bass.

Furman, W., & Adler, T. (1982). *The Friendship Questionnaire*. Unpublished manuscript, University of Denver.

Furman, W., & Adler, T. (1983). *The Parent–Child Relationship Questionnaire*. Unpublished manuscript, University of Denver.

Furman, W., & Bierman, K. L. (1984). Children's conceptions of friendship: A multimethod study of developmental changes. *Developmental Psychology, 20*, 925–933.

Furman, W., & Buhrmester, D. (1985). Children's perceptions of the personal relationships in their social networks. *Developmental Psychology, 21*, 1016–1022.

Furman, W., & Buhrmester, D. (1992). Age and sex differences in perceptions of networks of personal relationships. *Child Development, 63*, 103–115.

Furman, W., Jones, L., Buhrmester, D., & Adler, T. (1988). Children's, parents', and observers' perspective on sibling relationships. In P. G. Zukow (Ed.), *Sibling interaction across culture*. New York: Springer-Verlag.

Furman, W., & Robbins, P. (1985). What's the point? Issues in the selection of treatment objectives. In B. Schneider, K. Rubin, & J. Leddingham (Eds.), *Children's relations: Issues in assessment and intervention*. New York: Springer-Verlag.

Furman, W., & Wehner, E. A. (1994). Romantic views: Toward a theory of adolescent romantic relationships. In R. Montemayor (Ed.), *Advances in adolescent development, Vol. 6: Relationships in adolescence*. Newbury Park, CA: Sage.

Gavin, L. G., & Furman, W. (1992). *Adolescent girls' relationships with mothers and best friends*. Unpublished manuscript, University of Denver.

George, C., Kaplan, N., & Main, M. (1985). *An adult attachment interview*. Unpublished Manuscript, University of California, Berkeley.

Grotevant, H. D., & Carlson, C. I. (1989). *Family assessment: A guide to methods and measures*. New York: Guilford.

Hartup, W. W. (1979). Levels of analysis in the study of social interaction: An historical perspective. In M. E. Lamb, S. J. Suomi, & G. R. Stephenson (Eds.), *Social interaction analysis: Methodological issues*. Madison: University of Wisconsin Press.

Hartup, W. W. (1992a). Conflict and friendship relations. In C. U. Shantz & W. W. Hartup (Eds.), *Conflict in child and adolescent development*. Cambridge: Cambridge University Press.

Hartup, W. W. (1992b). Friendships and their developmental significance. In H. McGurk (Ed.), *Childhood social development*. Hove, England: Erlbaum.

Hartup, W. W. (1993). Adolescents and their friends. In B. Laursen (Ed.), *Close friendships in adolescence: New Directions for Child Development*, (pp. 3–22). San Francisco: Jossey-Bass.

Hartup, W. W., Laursen, B., Stewart, M. I., & Eastenson, A. (1988). Conflict and the friendship relations of young children. *Child Development, 59*, 1590–1600.

Hazan, C., & Shaver, P. (1987). Conceptualizing romantic love as an attachment process. *Journal of Personality and Social Psychology, 52*, 511–524.

Howes, C. (1987). Peer interactions of young children. *Society for Research in Child Development, 5*(1, Serial No. 217).

Hunter, F. T., & Youniss, J. (1982). Changes in functions of three relations during adolescence. *Developmental Psychology, 18*, 806–811.

Lanthier, R., & Furman, W. (1992). *Links between personality and children's peer and sibling relationships*. Paper presented at meetings of the American Psychological Association, Washington, D.C.

Leinhardt, S. (1972). Developmental changes in the sentiment structure of children's groups. *American Sociological Review, 37*, 202–212.

Main, M., Kaplan, N., & Cassidy, J. (1985). Security in infancy, childhood and adulthood: A move to the level of representation. In I. Bretherton & E. Waters (Eds.), *Monographs of the Society for Research in Child Development, 50*(1–2, Serial No. 209), 66–106.

Mannarino, A. P. (1976). Friendship patterns and altruistic behavior in preadolescent males. *Developmental Psychology, 12*, 555–556.

Masters, J. C., & Wellman, H. (1974). The study of human infant attachment: A procedural critique. *Psychological Bulletin, 81*, 218–237.

Meehl, P. E. (1970). Nuisance variables and the ex post facto design. In M. Radner & S. Winokur (Eds.), *Minnesota studies in the philosophy of science: Vol IV. Analyses of theories and methods of physics and psychology*. Minneapolis: University of Minnesota Press.

Parker, J. G., & Asher, S. R. (1993). Friendship and friendship quality in middle childhood: Links with peer group acceptance and feelings of loneliness and social dissatisfaction. *Developmental Psychology, 29*, 611–621.

Patterson, C. J., Kupersmidt, J. B., & Griesler, P. C. (1990). Children's perceptions of self and of relationships with others as a function of sociometric status. *Child Development, 61*, 1335–1349.

Patterson, G. R., & Reid, J. B. (1984). Social interaction processes within the family: The study of the moment-by-moment family transactions in which human social development is imbedded. *Journal of Applied Developmental Psychology, 5*, 237–262.

Reiss, D. (1981). *The family's construction of reality*. Cambridge, MA: Harvard University Press.

Sharabany, R., Gershoni, R., & Hofman, J. E. (1981). Girlfriend, boyfriend: Age and sex differences in intimate friendship. *Developmental Psychology, 17*, 691–703.

Shulman, S. (1993). Early and middle adolescence close friendship: Typology and friendship reasoning. In B. Laursen (Ed.), *New directions for child development: Close friendships in adolescence*. San Francisco: Jossey-Bass.

Stocker, C. (1988). *Interview about children's friendships*. Unpublished manuscript, Pennsylvania State University.

Stocker, C., & Dunn, J. (1990). Sibling relationships in childhood: Links with friendships and peer relationships. *British Journal of Developmental Psychology, 8*, 227–244.

Stocker, C., & Mantz-Simmons, L. A. (1992). *Children's friendships and peer status: Links with sibling relationships, temperament, and social skills*. Manuscript under review.

Sullivan, H. S. (1953). *The interpersonal theory of psychiatry*. New York: Norton.

Waters, E. (1978). The reliability and stability of individual differences in infant–mother attachment. *Child Development, 49*, 483–494.

Wehner, E. A., & Furman, W. (1992). *An interview for assessing working models of friendships*. Unpublished manuscript, University of Denver.

Weiss, R. S. (1974). The provisions of social relationships. In Z. Rubin (Ed.), *Doing unto others*. Englewood Cliffs, NJ: Prentice Hall.

Wiggens, J. S. (1979). A psychological taxonomy of trait-descriptive terms: The interpersonal domain. *Journal of Personality and Social Psychology, 37*, 395–412.

Wolchik, S. A., Sandler, I. N., & Braver, S. L. (in press). Social support: Its assessment and relation to children's adjustment. In N. Eisenberg (Ed.), *Contemporary issues in developmental psychology*. New York: Wiley.

Youniss, J. (1980). *Parents and peers in social development: A Sullivanian perspective*. Chicago: University of Chicago Press.

Youniss, J., & Smollar, J. (1985). *Adolescent relationships with mothers, fathers, and friends*. Chicago: University of Chicago Press.

# 4    The earliest friendships

*Carollee Howes*

Anna and Suzanne are not yet 2 years old. Their mothers became acquainted during their pregnancies and from their earliest weeks of life the little girls have visited each other's houses. When the girls were 6 months old they were enrolled in the same child care center. They now are frequent play partners, and sometimes insist that their naptime cots be placed side by side. Their greetings and play are often marked by shared smiles. Anna and Suzanne's parents and teachers identify them as friends.

The behavior of these children presents a dilemma for developmental psychologists. As toddlers these children cannot select each other as friends during a sociometric interview, describe the quality of their relationship in terms of affection or companionship on a questionnaire, or discuss friendships generally. Yet the children's behavior leads observers to conclude that they are friends.

In this chapter, earliest friendships are explored, that is, friendships between toddlers and young preschool-aged children. These relationships are difficult to examine because, unlike older children's friendships, self-reports cannot be used to understand them. We must, instead, rely on parental and teacher reports and inferences from the children's behavior to understand their meaning. When inferences are made from children's behavior, however, we risk confusing social skills with relationships (Hinde, 1979).

I argue that very young children form internal representations of peer and friendship relations in much the same way that they form internal representations of adult caregivers and attachments. Assuming that children construct these representations, we can make inferences about the nature of their relationships by observing their behaviors with one another. When these behaviors meet specified criteria, the existence of a ''friendship'' can be inferred. With young children, the researcher is concerned with the ''fit'' between the behavior indicative of the child's internal representation and the researcher's own definition of friendship relations. In contrast, with older children, the children themselves define

Leslie Phillipsen provided helpful comments on the chapter. Thank you.

the relationship, and the researcher merely asks the child whether another child is a friend or what type of friend the other child is.

In the following sections, the usefulness of certain propositions drawn from attachment theory for understanding friendships and friendship formation is first examined. Definitions and components of friendship used by researchers who study older children (who can define friendship for themselves) will then be discussed. In the final sections of the chapter the fit between the characteristics of older children's friendships and the manner in which young children behave with their friends will be examined.

## Relationships and friendships: Definitional issues

### Characteristics of relationships and their internal representations

A basic assumption of attachment theory is that, through multiple and recursive interactive experiences in being cared for, the child forms a mental representation of the self and the other (Bowlby, 1969). Recursive interactions are well-scripted social exchanges (Bretherton, 1985), for example, the child and caregiver's interactions around diaper changing and bedtime. These social exchanges are nearly identical from time to time and are repeated many times. From them, the child forms a set of internal representations of the other as one who will care for him or her – in either a sensitive or intrusive manner (Bowlby, 1969). The nature of the child's representation can be inferred from the child's behavior, particularly in times of stress when the attachment system is activated (Bowlby, 1969).

Attachment relationships are unique in that the biological survival of the child is intrinsically tied to them. In most cases, friendships are not implicated in survival functions (see Freud & Dann, 1951, for an exception). However, Emde (1989) argues that from a very early age, the child's interactions with adult caregivers lead to mental representations of several different aspects of that relationship, for example, play and teaching as well as caregiving. Toddlers also form relationships with noncaregiving adults and older siblings, based on play rather than caregiving interactions (Dunn, 1983; Schaffer & Emerson, 1964). Although these are not attachment relationships, they are still significant relationships in the child's social network. Children thus form relationships, including internal representations of those relationships, with familiar people other than caregiving adults, provided that they have opportunities for multiple recursive interactions.

Many young children, especially those enrolled in child care centers or family day homes, have opportunities for recursive interactions with other children. For example, day after day some children are expected to play in a constricted area with a fixed set of toys, to have snacks and lunches together, and to take naps side by side. Other children who are not enrolled in child care are known to have regular playdates in one another's homes once or twice a week (Ladd & Golter, 1988; Unger, 1991). These playdates also contain opportunities for recursive interactions. One example: the experience, recounted by parents, in which two children play together weekly and have a fight weekly over who gets to wear the firefighter hat before they settle into a routinized game of putting out the fire.

Assuming that children have the opportunity to form relationships with other children, we must then ask three further questions: (1) Are relations with peers specific relationships? That is, do the children differentiate among the children with whom they interact, forming relationships that differ in intensity and quality? (2) Are toddler social exchanges with peers sufficiently regular and consistent to lead to internal representation? (3) Can we infer the nature of these relationships from the children's behavior? That is, can we tap into children's internal representations of relationships when the children themselves are unable to identify and describe their friendship relationships verbally?

Many researchers working with young friendships conclude that, by the end of the first year, children form differential relationships with their peers. That is, they seem to be capable of selecting one particular child from among their playmates, initiating and responding more often to this child than to others in the group (Howes, 1983), and engaging in interactions with this child that are distinct from interaction patterns with other peers (Ross & Lollis, 1989).

Consistent with these notions, observational research on social interaction patterns suggests that toddler-age children discriminate among peer partners and form preferences within their peer groups (Howes, 1983; Lee, 1977; Ross & Lollis, 1989). Children by 12 to 18 months of age direct different frequencies of social bids to different members of their peer groups (Lee, 1977). Children have different patterns of interactions with different partners even when they have had equal opportunities for interaction with them (Howes, 1983; Ross & Lollis, 1989). Based on these observations, it appears that toddlers differentiate among their peers, selecting some children as targets of their social exchanges and changing their patterns of social interactions on the basis of who their partners are. Because relationships develop from particular interactions with particular partners we can assume, then, that toddlers develop specific relationships with some of their companions but not with others.

Even if a toddler has opportunities for recursive interactions with a small group of peers, and if there are specific relationships within the peer group, we still must ask if the social interaction between two children contains sufficient scripted regularities for the children to extract internal representations of these relationships. The literature on this question is mixed. Research suggests that by 12 months children have sufficient symbolic, memory, and cognitive capacities to mentally represent the adult–child relationship (Bretherton, 1985). Furthermore, this mental representation is consistent with observations of social interactions between the adult and the child (Ainsworth, Blehar, Waters, & Wall, 1978). Hay (1985) reviewed literature on the development of interaction sequences between adults and children as well as between peers and concluded that these sequences emerge within a similar developmental time frame, implying that adult–child interaction is not a prerequisite for child–child interaction. However, in adult–child interaction, the adult initially is responsible for producing regularities in social interaction (Bruner, 1983) whereas this is not the case in peer interactions. Extrapolation from studies of adult–child relationships to peer relationships is therefore difficult.

Studies of *unacquainted* infant and toddler peers reveal that extended social coordinations are not common in peer interaction until the end of the second year (Brownell, 1986; Eckerman, Davis, & Didow, 1989). Among well-acquainted peers, however, scripted regularities in social interaction sometimes emerge earlier. Dunn (1993), for example, found that 18-month-olds engaged in complex and scripted play sequences with their preschool siblings; the younger children in these sibling games were active in constructing the play script indicating that they understood the regularized scripted nature of the play. Some well-acquainted toddler peers also engage in complementary and reciprocal games by 13 to 15 months of age as well as scripted cooperative fantasy play before their second birthdays (Howes & Matheson, 1992; Howes, Unger, & Seidner, 1989).

Taken together, these results suggest that at least two conditions must be satisfied before we can conclude that specific relationships exist among very young children: First, there must be opportunities in the child's daily life for regular constricted play interactions. That is, there must be situational regularities in the child's experiences with peers. Second, the peers must be sufficiently well acquainted to have the opportunity to construct regular scripted interactions with one another. It is difficult to estimate the proportion of toddlers who experience these conditions. However, increasing numbers of toddlers are enrolled in child care settings containing stable peer groups. Other toddlers have peer interaction during regular playdates, and their interaction is known to be similar to the peer interaction of children enrolled in center child care (Rubenstein & Howes, 1976).

*Characteristics of friendship relationships*

To address the question of whether relationships among young children can ever be considered friendships, we must move away from an attachment perspective.

Friendship researchers studying older children or adults (Berndt, 1989; Furman & Buhrmester, 1985; Gottman & Parker, 1986; Sullivan, 1953; Weiss, 1974) suggest that friendships can be defined as relationships that satisfy a number of specified social needs, for example, companionship, intimacy, and affection. Although the specific list of social needs or functions served by children's friendships varies somewhat from theorist to theorist, these three features are considered here as necessary for friendship definition and as criteria for determining whether a relationship is a friendship.

These three criteria – companionship, intimacy, and affection – originated in a theory of adult friendships (Weiss, 1974). Research based on this theory, using children whose cognitive capacities are sufficiently advanced to enable them to articulate their friendship perceptions, shows that friends are indeed expected to provide companionship, intimacy, and affection to one another (Bigelow, 1977; Bigelow & LaGaipa, 1975; Furman & Buhrmester, 1985). Children also distinguish among various kinds of relationships, including friendships, in terms of these "provisions" (Furman & Buhrmester, 1985). By middle childhood, children describe their satisfaction with their friendships along these same dimensions (Buhrmester, 1990).

When children describe their friendship relations via interviews or questionnaires, they appear to draw upon mental representations of these relationships. But to determine whether relationships among younger children are based on these same representations (companionship, intimacy, and affection), we must examine behavioral rather than verbal data. That is, we must examine the social interactions within toddler and preschool dyads for evidence of differential companionship, intimacy, and affectional activity. Our working assumption is that the same goals undergird friendships at all ages, but that investigators must take different routes to access these goals among children of different ages. The remainder of this chapter evaluates existing research, suggesting that early friendships are based on these goals.

### Companionship

When researchers suggest that friendships provide children with opportunities for companionship, *companionship* is defined as spending time together and as having fun together (Berndt, 1989). Companionship is operationalized most frequently as spending time together, that is, as social preference or proximity. There is a long research tradition of using preference or proximity as the definitive criterion for defining friendships (Hartup, 1983, 1989). That is, when children prefer particular partners either by seeking them out for interaction or by maintaining proximity, the children are judged to be friends.

Companionship may also be defined as having fun or playing together. This definition is more complex than proximity, that is, what the children are doing together must be assessed. Once we consider companionship as having content – having fun or playing together – we also must consider the issue of social skills. Children who have more competent social skills may appear as friends if a criterion for friendship is playing together. This lack of independence between friendships and social skills is particularly true during early development because children are not very socially skilled (Howes, 1987).

In the following sections we first examine research in which companionship was operationalized as proximity. Then literature in which companionship was defined as having fun or playing together will be reviewed. By contrasting these literatures, we can determine whether proximity is a sufficient criterion for defining a friendship.

*Companionship defined as proximity*

One of the earliest examinations of infant and toddler peer relationships (Lee, 1973), conducted in a laboratory school setting, was a case study of a very small group of children. By coding proximity and social initiations, the investigator observed that the infants sought each other's company differently. The majority of later work on early friendships continues to be based in naturally occurring peer groups. Researchers then identify patterns of association or proximity among group members as a means of examining friendships or "strong associations" (Hinde, Titmus, Easton, & Tamplin, 1985).

Proximity has been defined in various ways. For example, in my own work on early friendships three different variations on a behavioral definition of friendship, each tied to the construct of companionship and each operationalized as proximity or preference, have been used. For example, companionship as mutual preference has been defined as: (a) social initiations between children of which at least 50% result in an interaction (Howes, 1983); (b) being within 3 feet of each other during at least 30% of the combined observations of the two children (Howes, 1988); or (c) being within 3 feet of each other during 30% of the "friendship scans" occurring within a specified data collection period (Howes & Phillipsen, 1992).[1] These proximity and preference measures are consistent with the practice of several other researchers who have examined friendships in very young children (George & Krantz, 1981; Hinde et al., 1985; Moller, 1991; Vandell & Mueller, 1980).

A second strand of research on infant and toddler friendships involves asking parents about the social networks of their children. By relying on parents as informants we can gather information on multiple social contexts rather than only one (e.g., in a child care classroom). Companionship is usually operation-alized in these studies by the frequency of contacts the children have over a week.

Ladd thus developed an interview for parents of preschool children that asks about the child's contacts with peers on a weekly or daily basis (Ladd & Golter, 1988; Ladd, Hart, Wadsworth, & Golter, 1988). Unger (1991) adapted this in-terview for use with 2-year-old children. She found that most of the children had two to three playdates per week with unrelated peers. The playdates were usually arranged by the mothers and occurred in the child's or the companion's home. The mothers reported that their children had clear preferences for partic-ular peers and would request playdates with them. Hinde (Hinde et al.,1985) identified preschool friends via observed proximity and then asked the parents to name their children's best friends. A significant overlap was evident between maternal responses and the friends identified according to a proximity criterion. In our most recent work, we interviewed parents to ask them to name the chil-dren from child care who their children talked about and wanted to invite to their homes. Substantial overlap (91%) occurred between the friends identified, in part by proximity, and the friends identified by the children's parents.

*Validating proximity measures*

Two tests of the proposition that friendships can be defined by measuring social preferences or differential proximity can be made: (a) We can determine whether these social preferences are determined by the children themselves or by parental management; and (b) we can determine whether children's preferences are stable over time rather than momentary attractions or interests in the others' activities.

*Sources of differential peer preferences.* Peer proximity can be determined by several conditions that have nothing to do with friendship. For example, two children might be near one another repeatedly because both are dependent on the teacher. In this case, the children's proximity to one another is probably more indicative of a competitive relationship than a mutual attraction. Another example: In child care settings, children are sometimes placed together when they are similar in physical ability. Teachers may place two crawlers in a section of the room protected from the children who prefer to walk and run. Although similarity underlies many friendships (Hartup, 1983), this teacher-initiated prox-imity based on similarity between the children does not indicate voluntary social choice.

In addition, interviews suggest that mothers sometimes select peer com-panions without taking the child's own preferences into account. Mothers often arrange peer contacts if they believe that the children get along and if they believe the child comes from a "nice" family with a likable mother (Rubin & Sloman, 1984; Unger, 1991). In other words, some mothers must feel comfortable with the peer's family before a relationship has a chance to develop. Thus, for children too young to initiate their own contacts, their range of potential friends may be limited to those children whom their own mothers want them to have as companions.

Our interviews with the mothers of children whose friendships were identified in child care classrooms suggest that some mothers determine children's friendship choices in a more indirect way. Some mothers, for example, reported that they did not know each other until after a friendship was identified by the children or the teachers. When the parents became aware of the friendship between their children they then initiated home visits – but only when the parents were also compatible.

Parental decisions concerning child care may be based in part on parent beliefs, for example, that children need companions and that acceptable ones can be found in a certain child care facility. Most of the mothers in the Unger (1991) sample used in-home housekeepers for child care yet enrolled their children for part of each day in activity classes so that they could meet other children in advance of attending nursery school. The mothers in our child care interview sample (Howes & Phillipsen, 1992) selected one of the few full-day child care centers in the geographic area that enroll both tuition-paying and subsidized children, and that are thus racially and economically diverse. Many of these parents wanted their children to be companions and friends with children who were different from themselves. Consistent with this belief system, more cross-race friendships were observed in the child care sample than in the 2-year-old home-based sample. Using only proximity as a criterion for friendship may thus identify pairs determined by parent management or other exogenous influences rather than by the children themselves.

*Stability of preferences.* Research identifying preferred companions from observations and from maternal reports suggests that early peer preferences or friendships tend to be stable. Within child care settings, friendships established among toddlers are maintained for several years (Howes, 1983, 1988; Howes & Phillipsen, 1992). For example, in one longitudinal sample 80% of the friendships that were not disrupted by one of the social partners leaving the child care group were maintained for 3 years (Howes & Phillipsen, 1992). Mothers of the 2-year-olds in the Unger (1991) study reported that 75% of their children's relationships lasted more than 13 months, or over half of these children's lives.

These findings are consistent with studies that examine the stability of preschool-aged children's friendships. Dunn (1993) reports that the average length of time the 4-year-old children in her study had been friends was 2 years. Most of these children had formed their friendships in the toddler period. Similar findings for preschool children are reported by Park, Lay, and Ramsay (1990). And, within the preschool period itself (3–5 years of age) children's friendships remain stable between 6 months (Gershman & Hayes, 1983) and a year (Howes, 1988).

Research on companionship among very young children thus suggests that children differentially seek the company of particular peers and that these preferences are fairly stable. When adult caregivers – teachers and mothers – talk about these relationships, they label them as friendships, in part owing to this stability. As mentioned earlier, teacher and parent nominations of friendship pairs are consistent with behaviorally identified friends (Howes, 1983, 1988; Howes & Phillipsen, 1992).

### Is preference enough to define a friendship?

In a short-term longitudinal study of early friendships, three criteria were used to identify friendships from patterns of interaction and mutual preference was found to be the most inclusive (Howes, 1983). In other words, if friendships were identified only by using the mutual preference criterion, these relationships would be overidentified, that is, too many would have been identified if more than one criterion was used. Adding skillful interaction and mutual enjoyment to the friendship criteria more closely ties the relationships identified to the construct of companionship (defined as having fun or playing together); the overidentification of friendships is consequently lessened (Howes, 1983).

### Companionship as having fun or playing together

When companionship is defined as having fun or playing together, a new problem arises. Toddler-age children are in a developmental period in which they are rapidly constructing the social skills that permit complex games and interactional sequences (Howes & Matheson, 1992). In studying friendships it is important not to consider only the more skillful children as potential friendship partners. Alternatively, a certain level of play complexity may be the best indication that the researcher can infer that the children are aware of the others as social partners. In this discussion, we must be mindful of Hinde's (1979) warning not to confuse social skills with relationships.

### Skillful interaction as a necessary component of friendship

Infant- and toddler-age children are beginners not only at developing friendships; they are also in the first stages of developing skillful, reciprocal, peer interaction (Howes, 1988; Howes & Matheson, 1992). Recent studies describing the development of social play with peers suggest that, during the second year, children develop the ability for social imitation, cooperative problem solving, and role reversal during play (Brownell, 1986; Eckerman, Davis, & Didow, 1989; Eckerman & Stein, 1982; Goldman & Ross, 1978; Howes, 1988; Howes & Matheson, 1992; Howes, Unger, & Matheson, 1992; Howes, Unger, & Seidner, 1989; Ross, 1982). When roles are reversed in play children recognize one other as full social partners who can complement one another's actions.

This recognition of self/other reversability and the social sensitivity needed for cooperative problem solving are fundamental aspects of friendship. Children who are friends perceive each other as social partners who can engage in coordinated social games or play. Indeed, friendships are difficult to imagine without evidence of these behaviors. Accordingly, if two children are to be considered friends, they must be observed in complementary and reciprocal interaction. Complementary/reciprocal interaction can be defined as action role reversals, for instance, run-and-chase games (Howes & Matheson, 1992). Defining complementary and reciprocal interaction in this way makes it possible to infer the existence of a relationship from particular social interactions, a necessity owing to the children's preverbal nature.

Engagement in reciprocal and complementary interaction can be regarded as a second criterion (in addition to proximity) to be used in identifying friendship dyads (Howes, 1983; Howes & Phillipsen, 1992). This criterion, used alone, is actually somewhat more effective in identifying friendships than using proximity measures is. When comparing two methods of identifying friendships, preference and complementary/reciprocal interaction, there was less overidentification of friendships using the complementary/reciprocal criterion than there was using the preference criterion.

Complementary and reciprocal interaction is a less discriminating criterion for identifying friendships among preschoolers than among toddlers. Three- and four-year-old children can use their emerging capacities for symbolic communication to engage not only in more complex and skillful interactions (Howes et al., 1989), but also to gain access to a wide range of playmates who may or may not be friends (Howes, 1983, 1988). Preschool children can engage in sophisticated and complex play, such as complementary and reciprocal interaction, with new acquaintances as well as old friends who share common and well-rehearsed scripts for interaction (Howes, 1983, 1988).

*Similar social interactive skills as a basis for friendships*

Similarity in social interactive skills may serve as a basis for friendships in young children. In a recent analysis we investigated the basis for friendships in a longitudinal study of children enrolled in child care (Howes & Phillipsen, 1992). Three bases for friendship were examined: similarities in activity level, in social interaction style, and in social skills. There were no significant similarities among members of friendship dyads in activity level. Cross-gender, but not same-gender friends were similar in social interaction style, that is, sociability or use of aggressive behaviors. Toddler-age friends were more similar in social skill than were preschool-aged friends or nonfriend dyads, suggesting that similarities of this kind may undergird a social attraction among children whose skills are rudimentary but not among children whose social skills are more mature.

These findings support the argument, outlined earlier, that engagement in complementary and reciprocal interaction is intrinsic in friendship relations among very young children. Social interactions among these children are dependent on well-established and somewhat routinized games such as peek-a-boo instead of shared symbolic communication. For example, older children might use the same game structure but say, "I'll be the rabbit and you be the fox, and when I run you try to catch me." Children of any age will repeat experiences in which satisfaction is achieved in constructing play. With each repetition the interaction becomes easier because of common referents and scripts. Through this process friendships provide the children with opportunities to have fun and play together, that is, to be *companions*.

*The development of more skillful interaction within a friendship dyad*

Children who are friends are more compatible than children who do not share a friendship (Hartup, 1989). This is not surprising, considering that friendships are voluntary relationships and that one of the functions of friendship is to provide a partner for having fun. However, because infant- and toddler-age children are in a period of rapid development and, more specifically, because toddler-age friends may form friendships on the basis of their similar developmental status, friendships may be particularly important contexts for the acquisition of social skills.

Across the second, third, and fourth years, individual differences in some interactive behaviors, such as elaborated exchanges (Howes, 1983), successful group entry (Howes, 1988), and hostile aggression (Howes, Phillipsen, & Hamilton, 1993), remain fairly stable. In contrast, the complexity of both social play and social pretend play increases during these years (Howes, 1983, 1988; Howes & Matheson, 1992; Howes et al., 1989, 1993). These results have been obtained in both longitudinal (Howes, 1988; Howes & Matheson, 1992; Howes et al., 1993) and cross-sectional studies (Howes, 1983; Howes et al., 1989).

Consistent with these findings, we have examined play development within friends' relationships. In several instances, differences in the complexity of play were found between toddler-age friends and nonfriends (Howes, 1983; Phillipsen, 1990; Werebe & Baudonniere, 1991), suggesting that friendships supply young children the space and time needed to develop complex sequences in social interaction. We know from ethnographic studies (Corsaro, 1981) that young children have trouble both in initiating and maintaining play without being disrupted by other children. Because friends are more likely to respond to play initiations from the partner than nonfriends are (Howes, 1983), these relationships seem, then, to create a ''space'' in which play can develop. Furthermore, the time spent by children who are not friends negotiating whether play will occur can be used instead by friends to develop more complex sequences (Hartup, 1989).

As already discussed, preverbal and presymbolic children are limited play partners; the actions forming the basis for their play are idiosyncratic and based on meanings developed through repetitive play rather than common symbols. One difficult transition for these children extends from social play, which is based on literal actions (e.g., as running and chasing or playing peek-a-boo), to social pretend play, which is based on symbolic, nonliteral meanings (e.g., feeding one and other pretend food). Friendship appears to facilitate this transition. In one longitudinal study, complex forms of play emerged first in social pretend play with friends rather than with acquaintances (Howes & Unger, 1989). In fact, the first instance of complex play recorded for all children occurred with a friend.

Successful social pretend play depends on a number of factors including the players' willingness to use newly acquired symbolic behavior, their agreement that nonliteral symbols can be shared, and their willingness to interpret the private meanings of their companions. Children whose friendships predate the emergence of social pretend play actually have an experiential basis for believing that play can be constructed between inexperienced and inept partners. Such experiences permit them to experiment with the use of nonliteral symbols in communication.

This reasoning leads us to the working hypothesis that early friendships create a social context characterized by trust between the partners. In this case, trust means that partners are willing to work to interpret behavioral meanings during social communication. If this hypothesis is correct, then friendships among very young children are social contexts that resemble harmonious mother–child dyads. Successful early mother–child social pretend play is characterized by maternal interpretations of the child's early and imperfect symbolic actions (Howes, Unger, & Matheson, 1992). This joint pretend play is more harmonious and complex when the mother–child attachment is secure (Slade, 1987), suggesting that, when the child trusts the mother to interpret his or her attempts to construct nonliteral meanings, the child is better able to construct complex social pretend play.

## Summary

In summary, companionship has been operationalized in some studies as the time two children spend in proximity and, in others, as complementary and reciprocal social interaction. Studies are most successful in parsimoniously identifying friendship among young children when both proximity preferences and complementary and reciprocal interaction are used as friendship criteria. Skillful interaction may be a particularly interesting reflection of friendship among toddlers because these children lack the skills necessary to engage in complex peer interaction and are rapidly developing these skills. Furthermore, friendships serve as the context in which skillful interaction develops. Paradoxically, social skills are both a basis for friendship selection and a necessary component of friendship interaction.

## Affection and intimacy

Affection and intimacy are two other friendship criteria. According to most researchers the friendships of older children and adults are characterized by mutual liking or affection and by intimacy (Buhrmester & Furman, 1986; Parker & Gottman, 1989). Researchers interested in the earliest friendships have operationalized these functions of friendships in three different ways: defining friendships with reference to behavioral manifestations of mutual affection; examining friendships for evidence of emotional support; and examining the social pretend play of friends for evidence of intimacy.

### Defining friendships by mutual affection

Mutual enjoyment or shared positive affect has actually been used as a criterion in defining friendships through behavioral observation (Howes, 1983; 1988; Howes & Phillipsen, 1992). Shared affect is operationally defined as both partners smiling or laughing while looking at the other and engaged in an ongoing activity.

The construct and operational definition of shared affect originated in research describing the social interaction of mothers and children with varying attachment classifications. It was intended as a code to capture an affectionate social exchange and is believed to differentiate the harmonious and positive interaction of mother–toddler dyads earlier judged to have a secure attachment relationship from that of mother–child dyads judged earlier to be insecure (Matas, Arend, & Sroufe, 1978).

When three behavior criteria for identifying friendships were used, only the shared positive affect criterion as opposed to the preference and skillful play criteria did not overidentify friendships (Howes, 1983). That is, dyads were more likely to exhibit preference and skillful play than they were to engage in shared affect. This suggests that early friendships are not merely relationships created by children who are skillful at initiating and sustaining social interaction but are instead affective relationships based on children's mutual affection.

Considering friendships as affective relationships should not be confused with expecting friends to show affection. Our behavioral observations in child care find little evidence of hugs or other examples of physical affection between peers. Preschoolers may use the language of friendship to order their social relationships (see Corsaro, 1981), but are rarely observed to make verbal affirmations of liking or affection. Instead we must assume that shared positive affect is behavior from which we infer an internal representation of an affectionate relationship.

### Friendships and emotional support

If friendships between very young children are affective relationships, then they should provide children with emotional support. Because many of these friendships are observed in social contexts without the children's parents (child care arrangements), a compelling notion is that these relationships provide some measure of emotional support that compensates for the absence of parents. Some support for the notion of compensatory emotional support is found in Ispa's (1981) and Schwartz's (1972) studies in which children provided comfort for peers in a Strange Situation-like paradigm. And, in my own work when children moved between child care centers accompanied by well-acquainted peers, they fared better than did those who moved alone (Howes, 1988).

As research on infants and toddlers in child care has become more sophisticated, however, it becomes clear that although friendships may constitute affective resources for children, a stable adult caregiver who provides emotional support is also necessary for the development of social competence with peers (Howes, Phillips, & Whitebook, 1992). Without sensitive adults to provide emotional support and supervision, peer play and affectionate friendships fail to develop (Howes & Matheson, 1992).

Even if the emotional support received from friends cannot, in most cases, substitute for that received from caregivers in child care, infants and toddlers may still benefit from this function of friendships – at least in the short term. Evidence for these benefits comes from maternal reports and from studies of peer responses to distress. For example, most mothers in one study (Unger, 1991) of 2-year-olds reported that their children had emotional attachments to particular peers and would miss these relationship if they ended.

Observing the distress of peers is a frequent experience for children enrolled in child care programs (Howes & Farver, 1987). Given the limited perspective-taking ability of infants and toddlers, crying is most often ignored by peers, even by those within 3 feet of the child. Children who are friends, however, are three times more likely to respond to distress either with comfort or by alerting the teacher than are children who are not friends (Howes & Farver, 1987). Some measure of emotional support and comfort thus appears to be provided by toddler-age friends.

In summary, although the intimacy and affection criteria for friendships are used less often in early friendship research than the criterion of companionship, there is some evidence for defining earliest friendships as affective relationships. This is important because if they were not then it would be difficult to distinguish conceptually between friends and playmates in this literature.

*Intimacy and social pretend play*

Intimacy is the most difficult of the friendships criteria to infer from observations of children's behaviors. When researchers of friendships in adolescence use the construct of intimacy, they define it as self-disclosure, closeness, and the sharing of feelings (Laursen, 1993). With the exception of self-disclosure these characteristics are more easily described than observed. Thus it is not surprising that only self-disclosure has been used in friendship research with preschool and younger children. Parker and Gottman (1989) have coded self-disclosure from audio tapes of the conversations of preschool-age friends. Park and Waters (1984) q-set for rating friendship quality from the social interactions of friends includes self-disclosure items.

Theoretically, pretend play may serve as a form of self-disclosure for children too young to sustain intimate conversations. This idea was introduced by Parker and Gottman (1989), who argued that there is evidence within the themes of children's social pretend play for self-disclosure and thus intimacy. Howes et al. (1992) extend this argument to suggest that an important function of social pretend play, once children have become expert players, is the exploration of trust and intimacy. Both of these arguments rest on the premise that within pretend play children use fantasy to communicate information about themselves that they do not yet have the cognitive and linguistic sophistication to communicate within conversation. According to this premise children who, for example, are playing "afraid of the dark – pretend we were sleeping and a monster came" are self-disclosing their fears to their partner.

This premise of self-disclosure through pretend play is largely untested. There is, of course, a rich and controversial literature on the extent to which pretend play is a ''window'' into the emotional concerns of the child (see, e.g., Erickson, 1940; Piaget, 1962). However, if we accept the premise that self-disclosure can occur through social pretend play, there are a number of interesting research directions to pursue. For example, children may explore some fears within social pretend play, but reserve other fears for solitary pretend play. Self-disclosure during pretend play could strengthen a friendship if, perhaps, the children shared the same emotional concerns. Alternatively, the exploration of some themes within social pretend play may end other friendships. For example, Pauley (1988) reports that a preschool friendship was disrupted when one partner became a big brother in real life and refused to play any other role except that of baby in social pretend play.

Using social pretend play to explore issues of intimacy usually does not appear until children are near the end of early childhood (Howes, Unger, & Matheson, 1992), almost beyond the period in which the earliest friendships emerge. Nevertheless, some support exists to show that early friendships have a role in this process. Children who are friends at the time they attempt to master the sharing of nonliteral meanings are more likely to construct social pretend play than children who are not (Howes & Unger, 1989). Children who are friends are more likely to successfully negotiate conflicts over content, form, and script of the social pretend play than children who are not (Hartup, 1989). Finally, preschool-aged children whose friendships dated back to toddlerhood engaged in more intimate social pretend play than either contemporary friends or nonfriends (Howes, Matheson, & Wu, 1992). Intimacy in this last instance was operationalized as the incidence of self-disclosure in social pretend play.

The literature reviewed in this section of the chapter is more speculative than that in the section on the companionship criterion of friendship. One explanation for the relative paucity of research in this area is the tradition exemplified by Sullivan (1953) and Selman (1980), which assumes that a developmental progression occurs in friendship functioning so that children cannot achieve intimacy in peer relationships until preadolescence. An alternative explanation is that peer researchers have been reluctant to make inferences on the nature of relationships from observational data. Proximity and play complexity are more easily observed than emotional support or intimacy and thus are used more easily to define early friendships.

## Conclusions

Two rich literatures exist that explore the companionship, affection, and intimacy of friends across the first two decades of life – toddlerhood to adolescence.

Although each research literature is distinctive, each informs the other. The earliest friendship literature is extremely descriptive in nature. On the other hand, the literature on older children has focused on friendship functions, for example, reliable alliance, children's perceptions of their friendships and their satisfaction with them, without much emphasis on observing and understanding the behaviors of children within these social relationships.

By exploring the "goodness of fit" between the constructs of companionship, affection, and intimacy as used first in work on older children and now in research on earliest friendships, we attempt to bridge two literatures. Further research will be necessary to further develop this integration exploring, for example, such questions as whether the relationship aspects that permit the construction of shared social pretend play in 2-year-olds are similar or different from those that permit preadolescents to engage in intimate discourse. Does the toddler who uses a friend as a secure base when her mother leaves her for the day in child care experience a similar or different relationship than the sixth grader who uses her friend as a secure base during the transition from elementary school to middle school?

If we accept the hypothesis that toddler-age children form internal representations of their friendship relationships and that these friendships function to provide companionship, affection, and intimacy there is much interesting research to be pursued. For instance, much of our research on friendship quality in childhood is based on a theoretical model that suggests that the quality of the relationships children form with their caregiving adults provides the internal working model of relationships for the construction of relationships with peers (see Park, this volume). The assumptions that toddlers form internal representations of friendship relationships and that their friendship relationships are characterized by companionships, affection, and intimacy suggest an alternative model. That is, children may draw on their internal representations of friendship relationships by constructing subsequent friendships much as they draw on their internal models of adult attachment relationships as they construct future relationships.

This hypothesis concerning the construction of peer relationships takes on added significance as more and more infants and toddlers have the opportunity for multiple, recursive interactions with a stable and small group of peers through out-of-home child care arrangements. Based on the hypotheses elaborated in this chapter these children construct internal models of relationships with both caregiving adults and with friends. Middle childhood developmental issues and group membership and adolescence issues of establishing close relationships, then, are met with similar or perhaps complementary working models of relationships, drawn from relationships with adults and with friends in early childhood. Although we know that subsequent experiences modify working models of relationships, we also know that the emotional security of care-giver–child relationships continues to influence children's relationships into later years (Bretherton, 1985). Representations of friendship relationships could continue to influence future friendship relationships so that the toddler who used a friend as a source of emotional comfort in child care becomes the child who is able to use friendships as a source of emotional support in the transition from elementary to middle school. Future research examining these ideas is badly needed because little or nothing is known about the long-term developmental consequences of close and intimate friendships beginning in early childhood.

### Note

1. Friendship scans are time-sampled scans of the entire peer group used to identify the occurrence of friendship behaviors between children.

### References

Ainsworth, M. S., Blehar, M. C., Waters, E., & Wall, S. (1978). *Patterns of attachment.* Hillsdale, NJ: Erlbaum.

Berndt, T. J. (1982). The features and effects of friendships in early adolescence. *Child Development, 53,* 1447–1460.

Berndt, T. J. (1989). Obtaining support from friends during childhood and adolescence. In D. Belle (Ed.), *Children's social networks and social support.* New York: Wiley.

Berndt, T. J., & Perry, T. B. (1986). Children's perceptions of friendships as supportive relationships. *Developmental Psychology, 22,* 640–648.

Bigelow, B. J. (1977). Children's friendship expectations: A cognitive-developmental study. *Child Development, 48,* 246–253.

Bigelow, B.J., & LaGaipa, J. J. (1975). Children's written description of friendship: A multidimensional analysis. *Developmental Psychology, 11,* 857–858.

Bowlby, J. (1969). *Attachment and loss: Vol 1. Attachment.* London: Hogarth.

Bretherton, I. (1985). Attachment theory: Retrospective and prospective. In I. Bretherton & E. Waters (Eds.), Growing points of attachment theory and research. *Monographs of the Society for Research in Child Development, 50,* 1–2, Serial No. 209.

Brownell, C. A. (1986). Convergent developments: Cognitive-developmental correlates of growth in infant/toddler peer skills. *Child Development, 57,* 275–286.

Bruner, J. (1983). *Child's talk.* New York: Norton.

Buhrmester, D. (1990). Intimacy of friendship, interpersonal competence and adjustment during preadolescence and adolescence. *Child Development, 61,* 1101–1111.

Buhrmester, D., & Furman, W. (1986). The changing functions of friends in childhood: A neo-Sullivinian Perspective. In V. J. Derlega & B. A. Winstead (Eds.), *Friendship and social interaction* (pp. 42–62). New York: Springer Verlag.

Corsaro, W. A. (1981). Friendship in the nursery school: Social organization in a peer environment. In R. Asher & J. M. Gottman (Eds.), *The development of children's friendships* (pp. 207–241). New York: Cambridge University Press.

Dunn, J. (1983). Sibling relationships in early childhood. *Child Development, 54,* 787–811.

Dunn, J. (1993). *Young children close relationships: Beyond attachment.* London: Sage.

Eckerman, C. O., Davis, C. C., & Didow, S. M. (1989). Toddlers' emerging ways of achieving social coordination with a peer. *Child Development, 60*, 440–453.

Eckerman, C. O., & Stein, M. R. (1982). The toddler's emerging interactive skills. In K. Rubin & H. Ross (Eds.), *Peer relations and social skills in childhood* (pp. 41–72). New York: Springer.

Emde, R. N. (1989). The infant's relationship experience: Developmental and affective aspects. In A. J. Sameroff & R. N. Emde (Eds.), *Relationship disturbances in early childhood*. New York: Basic.

Erickson, E. H. (1940). Studies in the interpretation of play. *Genetic Psychology Monographs, 22*, 557–671.

Freud, A., & Dann, S. (1951). An experiment in group upbringing. In R. Eisler (Ed.), *The psychoanalytic study of the child (Vol. 6)*. New York: International Universities Press.

Furman, W., & Buhrmester, D. (1985). Children's perceptions of the personal relationships in their social networks. *Developmental Psychology, 21*, 1016–1024.

George, S. W., & Krantz, M. (1981). The effects of preferred play partnership on communication accuracy. *Journal of Psychology, 109*, 245–253.

Gershman, E. S., & Hayes, D. S. (1983). Differential stability of reciprocated friendships and unilateral friendships among preschool children. *Merrill Palmer Quarterly, 29*, 169–177.

Goldman, B. D., & Ross, H. S. (1978). Social skills in action: An analysis of early peer games in J. Glick & K. A. Clarke-Stewart (Eds.), *The development of social understanding* (pp. 37–53). New York: Gardner Press.

Gottman, J., & Parker, J. (1986). *Conversations of friends: Speculations on affective development*. Cambridge: Cambridge University Press.

Hartup, W. W. (1983). Peer relations. In E. M. Hetherington & P. H. Mussen (Series Eds.), *Handbook of Child Psychology, Vol. 4: Socialization, personality and social development* (pp. 103–196). New York: Wiley.

Hartup, W. W. (1989). Behavioral manifestations of children's friendships. In T. J. Berndt & G. W. Ladd (Eds.), *Peer relationships in child development* (pp. 46–70). New York: Wiley.

Hay, D. (1985). Learning to form relationships in infancy: Parallel attainments with parents and peers. *Developmental Review, 5*, 122–161.

Hinde, R. A. (1979). *Towards understanding relationships*. New York: Academic Press.

Hinde, R. A., Titmus, G., Easton, D., & Tamplin, A. (1985). Incidence of "friendship" and behavior with strong associates versus nonassociates in preschoolers. *Child Development, 56*, 234–245.

Howes, C. (1983). Patterns of friendship. *Child Development, 54*, 1041–1053.

Howes, C. (1987). Social competence with peers in young children: Developmental sequences. *Developmental Review, 7*, 252–272.

Howes, C. (1988). Peer interaction of young children. *Monographs of the Society for Research in Young Children, 53* (Serial 217).

Howes, C., & Farver, J. (1987). Toddlers' responses to the distress of their peers. *Journal of Applied Developmental Psychology, 8*, 441–452.

Howes, C., & Matheson, C. C. (1992). Sequences in the development of competent play with peers: Social and social pretend play. *Developmental Psychology, 28*, 961–974.

Howes, C., Matheson, C. C., & Wu, F. (1992). Friendship and social pretend play. In C. Howes, O. Unger, & C. C. Matheson (Eds.), *The collaborative construction of pretend: Social pretend play functions*. Albany, NY: State University of New York Press.

Howes, C., Phillips, D. A., & Whitebook, M. (1992). Thresholds of quality in child care centers and children's social and emotional development. *Child Development, 63*, 449–460.

Howes, C., & Phillipsen, L. C. (1992). Gender and friendship: Relationships within peer groups of young children. *Social Development, 1*, 231–242.

Howes, C., Phillipsen, L. C., & Hamilton, C. E. (1993). Constructing social communication with peers: Domains and sequences. In J. Nadel & E. L. Camaionoi (Eds.), *New perspectives in early communicative development*. London: Routledge.

Howes, C., & Unger, O. A. (1989). Play with peers in child care settings. In M. Bloch & A. Pelligrini (Eds.), *The ecological contexts of children's play* (pp. 104–119). Norwood, NJ: Ablex.

Howes, C., Unger, O., & Matheson, C. C. (1992). *The collaborative construction of pretend: Social pretend play functions.* Albany, NY: State University of New York Press.

Howes, C., Unger, O., & Seidner, L. B. (1989). Social pretend play in toddlers: Parallels with social play and solitary pretend. *Child Development, 60,* 77–84.

Ipsa, J. (1981). Peer support among Soviet daycare toddlers. *International Journal of Behavior Development 4,* 255–269.

Ladd, G. W., & Golter, B. S. (1988). Parents' management of preschooler's peer relations: Is it related to children's social competence? *Developmental Psychology, 24,* 109–117.

Ladd, G. W., Hart, C. H., Wadsworth, E. M., & Golter, B. S. (1988). Preschoolers' peer networks in nonschool settings: Relationships to family characteristics and school adjustment. In S. Salzinger, J. Antrobus, & M. Hammer (Eds.), *Social networks of children, adolescents, and college students* (pp. 23–54). Hillsdale, NJ: Erlbaum.

Laursen, B. (1993). Close friendships in adolescence. *New direction for child development, 60.* San Francisco: Jossey-Bass.

Lee, L. C. (1973). *Social encounters of infants: The beginnings of popularity.* Paper presented at the biennial meeting of the Society for the Study of Behavioral Development, Ann Arbor, MI.

Matas, L., Arend, R. A., & Sroufe, L. A. (1978). Continuity of adaptation in the second year: The relationship between quality of attachment and later competence. *Child Development, 49,* 547–556.

Moller, L. (1991). *Toddler preferences.* Unpublished doctoral dissertation, Concordia University, Montreal.

Park, D. A., Lay, K., & Ramsay, L. (1990, March). Stability and change in preschoolers' friendship. Presented at the Conference of Human Development, Richmond, VA.

Park, K. A., & Waters, E. (1984). Security of attachment and preschool friendships. *Child Development, 60,* 1076–1081.

Parker, J. G., & Gottman, J. M. (1989). Social and emotional development in a relational context: Friendship interaction from early childhood to adolescence. In T. J. Berndt & G. W. Ladd (Eds.), *Peer relationships in child development* (pp. 95–132). New York: Wiley.

Pauley, V. G. (1988). *Bad guys don't have birthdays.* Chicago: University of Chicago Press.

Phillipsen, L. C. (1990). *Early friendships and social skills: Is there a relation?* Paper presented at the biennial meeting of the International Conference on Infant Studies, Montreal.

Piaget, J. (1962). *Play, dreams, and imitation in childhood.* New York: Norton.

Rubenstein, J., & Howes, C. (1976). The effects of peers on toddlers' interaction with mothers and toys. *Child Development, 47,* 597–600.

Rubin, Z., & Sloman, J. (1984). How parents influence their children's friendships. In M. Lewis (Ed.), *Beyond the dyad.* New York: Plenum.

Ross, H. S. (1982). Establishment of social games among toddlers. *Developmental Psychology, 18,* 509–518.

Ross, M., & Lollis, S. (1989). A social relations analysis of toddler peer relations. *Child Development, 60,* 1082–1091.

Schaffer, H. R., & Emerson, P. E. (1964). The development of social attachments in infancy. *Monographs of the Society for Research in Child Development, 29,* no. 94.

Schwartz, J. (1972). Effects of peer familiarity on the behaviors of preschoolers in a novel situation. *Journal of Personality and Social Psychology, 24,* 276–284.

Selman, R. L. (1980). *The growth of interpersonal understanding: Developmental and clinical analysis.* New York: Academic Press.

Slade, A. (1987). Quality of attachment and early symbolic play. *Developmental Psychology, 23,* 78–85.

Sullivan, H. S. (1953). *The interpersonal theory of psychiatry.* New York: Norton.

Unger, O. A. (1991). *Mothers as managers of their young children's social lives: Relationship to maternal beliefs, maternal strategies and social competence with peers.* Unpublished dissertation, University of California, Los Angeles.

Vandell, D., & Mueller, E. (1980). Peer play and friendship during the first two years. In H. C. Foot, A. J. Chapman, & J. R. Smith (Eds.), *Friendship and social relations in Childhood.* New York: Wiley.

Werebe, M. J., & Baudonniere, P. (1991). Social pretend play among friends and familiar peers. *International Journal of Behavioral Development, 14,* 411–428.

Weiss, R. S. (1974). The provisions of social relationships. In Z. Rubin (Ed.), *Doing unto others.* Englewood, NJ: Prentice Hall.

# 5     Determinants of friendship selection and quality: Developmental perspectives

*Frances E. Aboud and Morton J. Mendelson*

Children and adolescents are influenced by their friends (Deutsch & Mackesy, 1985; Nelson & Aboud, 1985), so it is important for both theoretical and practical reasons to understand why they make the friends they do. In the following discussion we consider children's characteristics that promote the development of close friendships. Specifically, we explore the personal and social attributes of youngsters who are likely to be selected as friends and who are apt to participate in high-quality friendships.

There is a long tradition of social psychological research on friendship under the topic of interpersonal attraction. The research concerns characteristics that individuals look for in prospective friends and it focuses largely on how similar friends are to one another. Yet studies of friendship in childhood and adolescence highlight two limitations of the social psychological research. First, it largely ignores the evolution of friendship, which is a lengthy process, especially for youngsters who have not fully mastered relevant social skills (Gottman, 1983). Thus, specific characteristics of friends may increase or decrease in importance from the time would-be friends are initially attracted to one another to later phases of friendship. Second, the social psychological research does not consider possible implications of developmental changes. Similarity and attraction may not be the same among younger and older children. As social and cognitive skills mature, behavioral and egocentric criteria for selecting and maintaining friends may become less central when the sharing of social and emotional experiences gains importance (Brown, 1981).

Here we examine studies with children and adolescents that address these limitations and focus on the criteria that youngsters use initially to select their friends and subsequently to maintain their friendships. The first section concerns characteristics of a peer – namely, similarity and personal attributes – that lead to attraction. Among youngsters, interpersonal attraction is highly influenced by

Preparation of this chapter was supported by a grant to the first author from the Social Sciences and Humanities Research Council of Canada.

similarities in sex, race, age, and activity preference, somewhat less so by similarities in attitudes, values, self-esteem, and social perception, and perhaps not at all by similarity in personality. Although a number of personal characteristics – including physical attractiveness, cognitive ability, sociability, aggression, and withdrawal – influence youngsters' popularity with their peers, there has been less research on the characteristics that influence friendships. The second and third sections deal with changes – associated with phases of friendship and age – in the characteristics that influence selection of a peer as a friend or maintenance of a friendship. Similarity is more important early in a relationship than later on, when other criteria related to the provision of social and emotional resources become significant. Similarity may also be more important in early childhood than in later childhood and adolescence, when personal attributes seem to become more influential. The final section identifies unresolved issues and directions for future research.

**Characteristics that lead to attraction**

Two general hypotheses guide most research on the characteristics that people look for in a friend. The first hypothesis is that people select friends who are similar to themselves. There are a number of ways to assess if *established* friends are similar to one another. Some researchers administer personality and attitude measures to two reciprocal friends and determine the degree of correlation between their scores. Other studies extend this by comparing correlations between friends' scores with correlations between nonfriends' scores. More stringent tests examine if the quality of, or individuals' satisfaction with, a friendship is associated with how similar the friends are. Few investigations with children or young adolescents have used this last design (e.g., Clark & Drewry, 1985; Parker & Asher, 1989b). We include research with undergraduates to evaluate the similarity-attraction hypothesis, because these studies often use the best designs. Moreover, such studies provide a reasonable endpoint – that is, late adolescence or early adulthood – for considering friendships in childhood and adolescence.

The second hypothesis concerning attraction is that people select friends who have desirable attributes – for example, particular social skills, ideal personality traits, and specific temperaments – or who simply like them in return. In some cases, researchers have used the similarity-attraction design to compare the relative importance of a friend's attributes with the degree of similarity between the friend's and the subject's attributes. In other instances, the person's attributes are examined in relation to the quality of the friendship.

Measures of attraction vary widely. Social psychologists studying interpersonal relations among older adolescents use rating scales to assess liking for another and desire to work with the other, which are thought to reflect attraction.

More recently, psychologists go beyond initial attraction to assess the strength and closeness of friendship with ratings of, for example, companionship, intimacy, satisfaction, and relationship stability. Child psychologists frequently examine attraction in terms of popularity. Instead of analyzing one child's attraction for another, researchers aggregate friendship nominations or liking ratings received by a child and compare children who receive many nominations or high ratings with those who do not. This strategy particularly specifies the personal attributes that distinguish popular children – to whom many peers are attracted – from average or rejected children. Yet, as in the adult literature, there is now increasing interest in deeper social and psychological qualities of friendship, especially because popularity and friendship are different aspects of children's peer relations (Bukowski & Hoza, 1989). Whereas popularity is general acceptance by agemates, friendship is a mutual dyadic relationship that may be influenced by attributes quite different from those that influence popularity (Mendelson, Aboud, & Lanthier, 1994).

*Similarity*

The dominant theory guiding social psychological research on adolescent friendship has been the similarity-attraction hypothesis, which states that liking is associated with similarity in one or more characteristics (Byrne & Griffitt, 1973). Similarity is presumed to be rewarding in at least two ways: The first involves consensual validation of one's attitudes and beliefs, which is provided by others who hold similar views. The second involves participating in enjoyable activities with others who have similar interests. Consistent with this hypothesis, adults' choices of friends are based on similarity in several demographic characteristics or social attributes (Verbrugge, 1979). Children are also similar to their friends in a number of ways (see Hartup, 1983, 1993), but some of the similarities derive from demographic factors that bring together similar individuals in a given neighborhood or school; that is, similarity and proximity are confounded with each other, which makes it difficult to draw conclusions about the similarity-attraction hypothesis solely from correlations of attributes between established friends.

Byrne and colleagues (see Byrne & Griffitt, 1966) introduced one procedure that avoids the confound between similarity and proximity in studying how similarity of attitudes and personality influences friend selection. Participants are given information about a fictitious stranger whose attitudes are either similar or dissimilar to their own; attraction to the stranger is then assessed by having participants rate how much they like, and want to work with, the stranger. The procedure has been used extensively with adults to assess the impact of various attributes, particularly attitudes, on attraction. Generally, level of attraction is directly related to the proportion of similar attitudes shared by two individuals (Byrne & Griffitt, 1973). Children in grades 4 to 12 are likewise influenced by the proportion of similar attitudes held by a fictitious stranger (Byrne & Griffitt, 1966). However, it is important to distinguish an experimental situation in which children are given information about how similar a stranger is to them from real situations in which children have to seek relevant information about a stranger and determine whether the stranger is similar or different. Moreover, initial attraction to a stranger who is similar in a limited number of ways is not necessarily related to long-term attraction and does not necessarily predict the quality of the friendship that might emerge over time – issues that will be addressed in the section on phases of friendship.

*Demographic variables.* Similarities in demographic features such as sex, age, race, occupation, employment status, education, marital status, and length of residence in the same area are important features of adult friendships (Verbrugge, 1979). Among these, similarities in sex, age, and race appear consistently in children's and adolescents' friendships (see Hartup, 1983, 1993).

*Sex.* Although other-sex friendships begin to develop during adolescence, children associate with those of the same sex – be they familiar or unfamiliar peers – from an early age (Maccoby, 1988, 1990). Maccoby discusses a number of possible explanations that rest on gender-based differences in styles of play, dominance, and influence, but she argues that the differences are not sufficiently categorical to account for the degree of gender self-segregation observed in childhood. Gender segregation appears to be a group phenomenon based on the binary distinction between male and female. According to Maccoby, this distinction organizes social functioning by clearly defining an in-group and an out-group and thereby promoting not only attraction to, and preferential treatment of, in-group members, but also stereotypic thinking about out-group members. Regardless of the explanation, there clearly are criteria in addition to gender that determine children's choice of friends and that account for variability in friendship quality.

*Age.* It is not surprising that children are typically friends with age-mates in countries that provide universal age-segregated education. Indeed, similarity in age between school friends – which is probably better called similarity in grade or class – is one of the clearest instances in which similarity and proximity are confounded. Further research would be necessary to determine the degree to which similarity in age between school friends is attributable to, for example, common abilities or interests rather than proximity. However, we know that children in mixed-age preschool groups form friendships based on age; that is, they self-select according to this criterion. Guralnick and Groom (1988) studied friendship patterns in mixed-age groups of normal 3-year-olds and normal and developmentally delayed 4-year-olds. Although only two developmentally delayed children formed reciprocal friendships, normal 4-year-olds formed reciprocal friendships predominantly with other normal 4-year-olds, and 3-year-olds predominantly with other normal 3-year-olds.

In neighborhoods, children spend a fair amount of time associating with peers who are more than 1 year older or younger (Ellis, Rogoff, & Cromer, 1981), so there is certainly the opportunity to form cross-age friends in this context. However, children in school-based societies may still categorize themselves and other children in terms of grade even when they are away from school. If they do, age-segregation may be explainable in terms similar to those that Maccoby (1988) used to account for gender segregation. Alternatively, even if children are attracted to children older than themselves, the older children may not reciprocate because they do not share interests or abilities or because they feel socially pressured not to befriend someone younger.

*Race.* Racial similarity is important in friendships throughout the school years. Children from preschool on tend to like, and play with, classmates of their own race to a greater extent than those of another race (e.g., Aboud, 1988; Finkelstein & Haskins, 1983; McCandless & Hoyt, 1961; Singleton & Asher, 1979). Yet, compared to white children, black and other minority children show greater attraction and friendship toward other-race peers (e.g., Finkelstein & Haskins, 1983; Hallinan & Teixeira, 1987a, 1987b; Howes & Wu, 1990), especially when whites are the majority (Hallinan, 1982). Race and sex also interact in affecting other-race preferences, with black girls having the most other-race friends, and white girls the fewest (e.g., Hallinan & Teixeira, 1987b; Schofield, 1982). As children approach adolescence, they seem to become more selective (Hallinan & Teixeira, 1987a) or – at least in Britain – show no change (Davey & Mullin, 1982; Denscombe, 1983) in their choice of same-race friends. Increasing selectivity based on race may be due less to the child's own racial prejudice than to social pressures from parents and peers. Adolescents' preferences for other-race peers are strongly affected by the disapproval they expect from parents and friends outside school for close cross-race friendships (Moe, Nacoste, & Insko, 1981). Inside school, the tendency to self-segregate by race during recreational group activities (Schofield, 1982) imposes a group-based categorization that, like gender, organizes social functioning.

Increasing racial similarity between friends, however, cannot be attributed to increasing prejudice, because with age, children actually become more positive in their attitudes toward other-race members (reviewed extensively in Aboud, 1988). Contact within the classroom and between individuals of different races is high (Schofield, 1982). Despite the preference for same-race peers, many children have reciprocal other-race friendships (Dubois & Hirsch, 1990), and these relationships are as stable and close as same-race friendships (Hallinan & Williams, 1987). Thus, even if racial similarity increases children's attraction to peers, race cannot explain variability in quality among same-race friendships or among cross-race friendships.

*Socioeconomic and school factors.* Although similarities in socioeconomic and school status appear to be important in late adolescence and in the college years (Griffin & Sparks, 1990), they may not be criteria for mutual friend choice in childhood. Many children choose friends who differ in ability and grades; nonetheless, differences along these dimensions – which necessarily mean an imbalance in status – may eventually lead to dissolution of a friendship (Epstein, 1983). For example, high-status youngsters who associate with low-status friends may experience or anticipate scorn from peers and consequently end their friendships, or they may simply end up in different high school classes from their friends and consequently lose contact with them.

*Activities.* Similarities in activity preferences seem to be important in friendship at all ages. Conversations aimed at establishing a common ground activity – but not at establishing other similarities and differences – are related to the quality of young children's interactions with a partner and predict whether pairs of children who meet for the first time will hit it off (Gottman, 1983). Additionally, friends are likely to engage in similar peer activities – like marijuana use – in adolescence (Kandel, 1978a) and to have similar activity preferences in college (Werner & Parmelee, 1979). Yet there is an interesting individual difference. Some people choose friends who are competent in an activity they prefer, whereas others choose friends who have a similar profile of preferences and attitudes (Snyder, Gangestad, & Simpson, 1983). The latter choose friends more consistently across activities because their selection criteria are not activity-specific.

*Attitudes and values.* The findings for similarities among friends in attitudes and values are mixed. Byrne and Griffitt (1973) argued that liking consistently increases as a function of the proportion of similar attitudes. Similarity in political preference is reportedly one of several features of adult friendships (Verbrugge, 1979); thus, scores on a scale of conservative versus liberal attitudes correlate moderately for friends, but not at all for pairs of nonfriends (Rushton, 1989). However, others have found that the attitudes of friends are as dissimilar as those of nonfriends (Aboud, 1993; Werner & Parmelee, 1979), that liking is unrelated to similarity of values early in a friendship (Duck & Craig, 1978; Hill

& Stull, 1981), and that liking is related only to similarity of values accepted by the friends but not to similarity of rejected values (Lea & Duck, 1982). Moreover, as discussed below, similarity between friends may be less important at older ages than early on; thus, unlike 7- to 8-year-old boys, 9- to 10-year-old boys are not more similar in attitudes to friends than to nonfriends (Erwin, 1985). However, more consistent results might be obtained for similarities between friends if researchers focused on attitudes and values that reflect central concerns for the samples in question.

*Personality.* Findings concerning the effects of similarity in personality on friend selection are also mixed for adults, and again there is very little research on the topic with children. Only one study with adults found supporting data. Similarities on interpersonal adequacy and character – dimensions of the California Personality Inventory – predict satisfaction with a roommate (Carli, Ganley, & Pierce-Otay, 1991); but similarities in achievement potential, intelligence, and interests do not. Other research indicates that adult friends are not more likely than nonfriends to be similar in intelligence, locus of control, or introversion-extroversion (Bailey, DiGiacomo, & Zinser, 1976; Blag, 1983; Duck & Craig, 1978; Feinberg, Miller, & Ross, 1981; Rushton, 1989). Among kindergarten children, pairs of friends are not similar on the subscales of Baumrind's (1968) Preschool Behavior Q-Sort – achievement orientation, alienation, approach orientation, autonomy, confidence, destructiveness, rebelliousness, and stress tolerance (Mendelson et al., 1994). Beginning in Grade 4, children form social networks with others who have similar levels of aggression (Cairns, Cairns, Neckerman, Gest, & Garieppy, 1988), but aggressive children may be forced together because they are rejected by nonaggressive peers, so similarity in aggression may be confounded with availability.

*Self- and social concepts.* Similarity in self-esteem is related to friendship; children who are mutual friends have more similar self-esteem scores than unilateral "friends" or nonfriend pairs (Clark & Drewry, 1985; Kurdek & Krile, 1982). Moreover, youngsters and adults appear to choose friends who validate their self-concepts. For example, Bailey and colleagues (1976) asked undergraduates to rate their own, and a friend's, intelligence. The correlation that indicated self-validation (i.e., between subject's and friend's estimates of subject's intelligence) was very high. Indeed, it was higher than the correlation that indicated actual similarity (i.e., between subject's and friend's intelligence scores) or the one that indicated perceived similarity (i.e., between subject's estimates of both subject's and friend's intelligence scores).

Friends are also more similar than nonfriends in terms of the generalized dimensions that they use for perceiving their own roles and those of significant others (Duck, 1973; Duck & Craig, 1978). Although role constructs change during adolescence from those that are mainly demographic to those that are physical, social, and psychological, the degree of similarity between friends is striking (Duck, 1975). Even if similarities in social perceptions are as much a consequence as a cause of friendship (Deutsch & Mackesy, 1985), the degree to which friends agree with, and adopt, each other's social perceptions may determine whether the friendship is maintained.

*Challenges to the similarity-attraction hypothesis.* So far, we have addressed how attraction may be influenced by actual similarities in demographic and psychological attributes. But perceiving similarity, being liked, and being different may be more potent selection criteria than actually being similar. Moreover, similarity between friends may just as much result from, as lead to, friendships.

*Perceived similarity.* Friends' perceptions of each other confirm the similarity-attraction hypothesis. People rate their friends as similar to themselves in activity preferences, attitudes, extroversion-introversion, locus of control, and competence (e.g., Bailey et al., 1976; Blag, 1983; Feinberg, Miller, & Ross, 1981; Tesser, Campbell, & Smith, 1984; Werner & Parmelee, 1979). Yet similarity may largely be in the eyes of the beholder as suggested by the "false-consensus" effect – the tendency to assume that most other people are similar to oneself. This may be especially true for individuals in close relationships, in which there are social incentives to perceive similarities. The differential effects of perceived and actual similarity point to a critical limitation of the fictitious-stranger paradigm. Participants in a fictitious-stranger study probably accurately perceive the stranger's clearly described characteristics, so the stranger's actual characteristics affect the participants' liking ratings. In real life, however, individuals commonly misperceive each other, which limits the impact of actual characteristics on liking.

*Being liked.* Reciprocal liking is one of the defining features of a close friendship, and assumptions about being liked by others may help explain the link between similarity and attraction (Aronson & Worchel, 1966). Early in a relationship, people infer that they are liked by others who are similar to them, and such an inference – valid or not – leads to attraction, perhaps even more than does similarity (Condon & Crano, 1988). Further research is necessary, however, to determine the extent to which children can accurately estimate how much would-be friends like them and whether they select friends based on their estimates.

*Ideal personality.* Wetzel and Insko (1982) undermined the hypothesis that similarity in personality leads to attraction. They discovered that liking a fictitious stranger is unrelated to similarity on several personality dimensions. Rather, the important criterion is the similarity between the stranger's personality and the subject's profile of an *ideal* personality. Perhaps fictitious strangers with ideal personalities are attractive because of an assumption that their socially desirable characteristics will reflect well on their friends and associates. Alternatively, ideal personality characteristics may be important when selecting friends because individuals strive to learn from, or emulate, a friend rather than simply have their own personalities validated.

*Complementarities.* Some complementary differences may be as important in a friendship as are similarities (Ashton, 1980), although complementarity has not been studied among children. Alternatively, differences may be important in the initial phases of friend selection, and attraction to similar peers may result from rejection of different ones. Thus, adults are more negatively affected by the difference between their attitudes and those of another person than they are positively affected by similarity in attitudes (Rosenbaum, 1986). People assume that others are similar to them in attitudes and values, so the impact of similarities on attraction is relatively weak compared to similarities on other dimensions or to other factors, such as personality. In contrast, differences, which are unexpected, are potent both affectively and motivationally. This implies a two-stage model of friendship selection in which the first stage involves weeding out those who are very dissimilar, and the second stage involves selecting, from among those who are more or less similar, friends who fit other criteria (Smeaton, Byrne, & Murnen, 1989).

*Selection criteria versus socialization effects.* The final challenge to the similarity-attraction hypothesis – or at least to empirical demonstrations of it – is that similarity may be just as much a consequence of friendship or companionship as it is a cause of attraction. Indeed, similarities in activities, attitudes, values, and social perceptions between friends increase over time (Deutsch & Mackesy, 1985; Hill & Stull, 1981; Kandel, 1978a; Lea & Duck, 1982; McCarthy & Duck, 1976). Therefore, similarities between long-standing friends cannot be interpreted as unequivocal support for the similarity-attraction hypothesis.

Increasing similarity between friends, at least in social perceptions, apparently results from conversations friends have about themselves and their acquaintances (Deutsch & Mackesy, 1985) during which they share, and perhaps even co-construct, their perceptions. Convergences between childhood friends may also be achieved through conversations: To maintain dramatic play episodes, pairs of young children achieve agreement by discussing context, character, and plot, and such agreement presumably enhances similarity not only in social perception but also in negotiation skills (Doyle & Connolly, 1989). In later childhood, friends who initially disagree on a solution to a social dilemma converge on the better of the two solutions, to a greater extent than nonfriends, by explaining their own positions to each other and criticizing the other's opinion (Nelson & Aboud, 1985). Several countervailing forces appear to be operating here. Children expect agreement from their friends (Aboud, 1993), and seek more information from an agreeing than from a disagreeing friend (Nelson & Aboud, 1985). However, when confronted with a disagreement, they evaluate the friend's judgment more positively and devalue their own (Aboud, 1989). Thus, socialization by friends may be strong because children respect their friends' judgments and feel secure enough to admit their own error and to change.

*Summary.* Friends in childhood and adolescence are characterized by similarities in sex, race, age, and activity preferences. Although similarities in attitudes and values seem to lead to interpersonal attraction, these similarities may be less important than others in friendship formation. There is also no evidence that similarity in personality affects youngsters' friendships. Nonetheless, childhood friends are similar in self-esteem. Friends also appear similar in social perception, but this may result from, rather than cause, the friendship, a direction of influence that calls into question many demonstrations of the similarity-attraction hypothesis – if not the hypothesis itself. Other potential threats to the hypothesis include findings that perception of similarity may be more important than actual similarity, that similarity may be confounded with an assumption about being liked, and that complementary differences may also be important. Although similarity clearly does not solely account for interpersonal attraction, more research is required to determine the extent to which it may be one of several relevant factors. Studies must investigate similarity along a number of different dimensions and, as suggested by research below, more work is needed on the role of similarity at different phases of a friendship and at different ages.

*Personal attributes.* Child psychologists have long been interested in the personal attributes of children that result in their being liked or disliked by their classmates (Hartup, 1983). But few studies have examined personal attributes that are sought by children in a friend or that foster good quality friendships. The personal attributes most often examined in relation to sociometric status are sociability (e.g., companionship and intimacy) and control of aggression, although a few studies have included measures of temperament and personality. The best designs involve different informants for assessing peer or friend attributes and for assessing popularity or friendship quality. For example, peer or friend attributes can be measured through teachers, self-reports, or observations, popularity through peer nominations, and friendship quality through child reports or independent observations.

Broadly, children's sociometric status is predicted by physical attractiveness, cognitive ability, sociability, aggression, and withdrawal (Furman & Buhrmester, 1985; Newcomb, Bukowski, & Pattee, 1993). Popular children tend to be attractive, cognitively and scholastically able, and sociable; in contrast, rejected children tend to be unattractive, to lack cognitive and social skills, and to be relatively aggressive and/or withdrawn. Although friendship and popularity differ conceptually, they overlap empirically in some ways: Popular school children have more friends, and may have better quality friendships, than do unpopular children (Parker & Asher, 1993); also, classmates favorably describe both friends and popular children (Bukowski & Hoza, 1989). Thus, the attributes of popular children might overlap with the attributes that are sought in a friend, but this is not known for certain. Alternatively, some attributes may make a child attractive to a peer initially, whereas other attributes are relevant to success in establishing and maintaining friendships (Bukowski & Hoza, 1989; Buhrmester, 1990; Mendelson et al., 1994; Stocker & Mantz-Simmons, 1993). And, as we will suggest, different attributes may be important in friendship at different stages of development.

Research related to the personal characteristics associated with friendship has been limited, and the findings are somewhat disjointed. The number of reciprocal friends is related to higher masculinity in both girls and boys and to higher femininity only in boys (Townsend, McCracken, & Wilton, 1988). Compared to youngsters who do not have close reciprocal friends, youngsters who have them are more independent and emotionally supportive (Cauce, 1986), more altruistic and sensitive to feelings (McGuire & Weisz, 1982), more excitable and less dominant, controlled, or tense (Clark & Ayers, 1988), and have higher self-esteem (Townsend et al., 1988). Children who stay friends throughout a school year are more prosocial and less aggressive than children who do not stay friends (Berndt & Das, 1987); closeness with, and low hostility to, a best friend is predicted by high sociability and low emotionality (Stocker & Dunn, 1990); cooperative play with a friend is also related to high sociability and to low problematic peer behavior and activity (Stocker & Mantz-Simmons, 1993). Among older children, ratings of companionship, intimacy, and satisfaction with a friend are associated with the friend's self-ratings of high interpersonal competence, sociability, and esteem and low anxiety/depression (Buhrmester; 1990). Among late adolescents, satisfaction with a friend is correlated with perception of the friend's competence in self-disclosure, initiation of encounters, conflict management, and, especially, emotional support (Buhrmester, Furman, Wittenberg, & Reis, 1988).

*Summary.* It is difficult to generalize from the literature about personal characteristics associated with friendship because the youngsters' ages and the measures of personal attributes and friendship have varied across the small number of relevant studies. Nonetheless, the literature provides some hints. Interpersonal competence (e.g., high sociability), self-control (e.g., low aggression), "friendship" skills (e.g., conflict management), emotional adjustment (e.g., low anxiety/ depression), and self-esteem seem to be associated with the experience of friendship. However, with few exceptions (e.g., Berndt & Das, 1987), the studies have provided correlational data that cannot indicate the direction of influence. Thus, certain personal characteristics may make youngsters more attractive as friends, may result from having close friends, or both, so further research is needed to disentangle these possibilities (see Newcomb, this volume). Moreover, as suggested by the following sections, it may be fruitful to consider how personal characteristics associated with friendship vary across phases of friendship and across stages of development.

## Phases of friendship

The similarity-attraction hypothesis concerns initial phases of attraction and not necessarily later phases of friendship. Demographic characteristics, which are extremely salient, may be used as preliminary criteria for seeking or rejecting partners. Children play overwhelmingly with peers who are similar in sex, age, and race, even if circumstances allow otherwise. This means not only that they choose to associate with others who are demographically similar, but also that they avoid associating with others who are different (Finkelstein & Haskins, 1983). Children may also avoid associating with peers who are physically unattractive and aggressive (Cairns et al., 1988). Yet, after what amounts to a broad screening, individuals subsequently choose friends from the resulting group of similar peers. And they base their choices on information – garnered from social interactions – that is relevant to a number of narrow criteria, such as personality, social constructs, being liked, and similarities in activity preferences and attitudes. This phase may involve selecting friends from a predefined group (e.g., all the boys in the class) and/or ending relationships with individuals who prove to be unsuitable (e.g., peers who are untrustworthy). In the following sections, we examine criteria that are important in consolidating and maintaining friendships beyond the initial phase of attraction. One set of criteria, which can be used to define friendship quality, relates to social resources exchanged in the relationship; other criteria relate to the characteristics of the exchange itself.

*Social resources*

A true test of friendship is that it lasts over time and develops certain qualities. Although friendship quality can be measured simply in terms of the satisfaction each partner derives from the relationship, more detailed conceptions of quality focus on the functions of friendship – that is, on the social, emotional, and instrumental resources sought in the relationship by one friend and provided by the other (Asher & Parker, 1989). The functional approach is particularly relevant here because it highlights criteria that individuals use in selecting friends. Measures of friendship quality generally assess six resources – stimulating companionship, help, intimacy, reliability, emotional security, and self-validation – that are provided more by friends than by nonfriends and that are related to satisfaction with the relationship (Bukowski, Hoza, Boivin, 1994; Furman & Buhrmester, 1985; Parker & Asher, 1989a; Sharabany, Gershoni, & Hofman, 1981; Wright, 1991).

Friendship quality is also related to its duration (Mendelson et al., 1994), which implies that ongoing interactions enhance a friendship and possibly provide information for deciding if a peer adequately fulfills friendship functions. Because most research involves current friends, not much is known about the process whereby friendships are terminated. In one study, 31% of fourth and eighth graders did not keep at least one best friend for 6 months (Berndt, Hawkins, & Hoyle, 1986); in another study, 67% of fifth to twelfth graders did not remain friends with their top three nominations for 12 months (Epstein, 1983). Even if these figures represent high estimates, a process of selection continues after the initial phases of attraction, and certain friendships are ended, whereas others are enhanced. The criteria for ending or continuing friendships are presumably more stringent – in the sense that they are likely based on multiple or more important dimensions – than are the criteria for selecting potential friends. Similarity and reciprocal liking may remain relevant, but additional criteria – such as the exchange of the six resources associated with friendship – become significant.

By analyzing the conversations of children in existing and emerging friendships, Gottman (1983) identified six elements in the process of friendship formation and maintenance: connected communication, information exchange, establishing common ground, self-disclosure of feelings, extending and elaborating each other's activities, and conflict resolution. Thus, similarity, connectedness, and agreement are part of the process; but so are self-expression, validating and extending the partner's viewpoint, and negotiating disagreements. To engage in this process, children and adolescents must have the requisite skills as well as the motivation, which comes from rewarding experiences of being liked, validated, and agreed with. But there is more to friendship than seeking and finding similarity and agreement.

Kandel (1978b) compared similarity of behaviors and attitudes in adolescent pairs who remained friends, who stopped being friends, or who became friends during a school year. Pairs who remained or became friends were more similar at the beginning of the year than pairs who stopped being friends. This is evidence of a process during which children seek and interpret information about similar attributes both from peers whom they selected at the beginning of the year and from those whom they rejected. Moreover, pairs who remained friends were more similar at the end of the year than at the beginning, which is evidence that friends socialize each other. However, the results were stronger for marijuana use than for the other dimensions measured – namely, educational aspirations, political orientation, and minor delinquency – so the conclusions cannot be generalized without caution.

Berndt and colleagues (1986) examined the development of children's and adolescents' friendships in the fall and spring of the academic year. Although perceived similarity was higher in reciprocated than in unilateral friends, it was not higher in the fall for the 69% of youngsters who remained friends than for the 31% who did not; that is, somewhat inconsistent with Kandel's (1978b) findings, perceived similarity did not predict friendship maintenance. However, some qualities of friendship – mutual liking, the frequency of interaction, and perceived intimacy – did predict which friendships would last and which would end. Children in stable friendships evaluated their friends equally positively in the fall and spring, so it appeared that they had already reached a plateau in their relationships, and the study did not provide information about the enhancement of friendship. However, children in unstable friendships evaluated their friends more negatively in the spring, so the study does provide information about criteria for ending relationships. It is necessary to assess at least the duration, if not the current phase, of friendships, to draw firm conclusions about how friendship quality may change as friendships develop.

Hays (1985) examined friendship development among newly acquainted undergraduates, 63% of whom became close friends by the end of the school term. Selection criteria were based on the social and emotional resources provided by the friend, particularly in the domains of communication and companionship. Pairs who were to become close friends steadily increased the intensity of their friendship at both casual and deeper levels of communication, companionship, consideration, and affection. Pairs whose ties weakened over the term never reached deep levels of the four dimensions of friendship and even experienced declines in casual levels of communication and companionship.

Other studies have examined developing friendships among undergraduates who were assigned as roommates. Although perceived similarity influences initial liking for the roommate, actual similarities in personality, values, religion, and father's education did not predict liking either initially or several months later (Duck & Craig, 1978; Hill & Stull, 1981). Indeed, demographic and academic similarities were negatively related to liking. The best predictors of later liking were initial liking, closeness, and similarity of social constructs (Duck & Craig, 1978; Hill & Stull, 1981).

## Exchange

Regardless of the resources involved, the basis of exchange between friends is another dimension that may change over the course of friendship. In early phases of friendship, fair exchange is maintained; but in later phases, a communal orientation prevails – that is, the friend's needs and desires determine what resources are offered, because each partner is concerned about the other's welfare (Clark, 1984; Clark & Mills, 1979). Thus, strangers attend more to what a partner contributes to an interaction, whereas friends attend more to their partners' expressed needs (Clark, Mills, & Corcoran, 1989). Similarly, friends and would-be friends are more likely than nonfriends to acquiesce in a friend's request and to reciprocate a favor (Lydon, Jamieson, & Holmes, 1993). However, unlike friends, would-be friends view their own and their friends' behavior in terms of a fair exchange that is necessary to foster the friendship. Friends do not believe that reciprocation has any implications for the relationship, so they do not see the need to reciprocate quickly; they assume the friend's behavior reflects personal attributes rather than attempts to maintain the friendship. In addition, individuals seem more satisfied with a relationship if a friend adopts a communal, rather than an exchange, orientation (Jones, 1991).

Good friendships have a long time frame, so it is difficult to study exchanges between close friends in short experimental sessions. Therefore, Hays (1989) asked close and casual friends to rate 15 interactions over a week in terms of the benefits received, the benefits offered, and the costs. The benefits received closely resemble five of the six resources that might be used to measure friendship quality: fun, task assistance, emotional support, intellectual stimulation, and information or advice. Benefits received are higher for close than for casual friends, but benefits offered and costs do not differ. For close friends, the amount of benefit received – especially fun, but also emotional support and information or advice – is the strongest predictor of satisfaction with the interaction; emotional support offered also predicts satisfaction. For casual friends, costs – especially feeling irritated and bored – are the strongest predictor of dissatisfaction with the interaction.

## Summary

Similarity appears relatively more important during initial phases of friendship, when individuals choose potential friends, than in later phases, when they establish long-lasting relationships. Nonetheless, similarity between friends may increase as relationships unfold and may help maintain them. But similarity becomes less important relative to other criteria. In particular, friends seek the social and emotional resources – companionship, emotional support, help, self-validation, and so on – that psychologists have identified as important qualities in a friend. Friends are less concerned about the costs of interactions than about the benefits, perhaps because costs are considered transitory in a long-term relationship, but benefits are important to maintaining it. To verify these notions we need more research on personal attributes that enable youngsters to provide social and emotional resources and on how such resources change in importance across different phases of friendship.

### Age-related changes

Developmental aspects of friendship have generally been studied in terms of age-related changes in children's ideas about friendship (e.g., Selman, 1980) or in other social-cognitive manifestations (e.g., Brown, 1981; Epstein, 1983; Tesch, 1983). During the preschool years, friends primarily serve a child's self-interest. Yet self-interest becomes relatively less important with age as sharing, for example, increases (Berndt et al., 1986; Birch & Billman, 1986; Jones, 1985). In middle childhood, friends are seen as cooperative partners in activities, but conflict is not easily tolerated. Thus, fourth graders focus on their friends' similarity and on prosocial behaviors (Berndt et al., 1986). Disagreements become less disruptive from childhood through adolescence (Enright & Lapsley, 1981), so friendships become more stable (e.g., Ladd, 1988). In preadolescence, stimulating companionship remains important in friendship, but exchanging intimacies gains significance (Berndt et al., 1986). However, it is not until adolescence that emotional support and autonomy are seen as essential in friendship. Thus, adolescents appear to be more attentive to what their friends need than to what they offer (Clark et al., 1989).

Children's conceptions of friendship imply criteria for selecting friends and maintaining friendships. To a certain extent, these implicit criteria overlap with the criteria already mentioned – for example, similar activities, cooperativeness, and attributes related to intimacy. But a cognitive developmental analysis of friendship necessarily highlights age-related changes, so it focuses on parallel changes in implicit friendship criteria. In contrast, a social-rewards analysis of friendship focuses on continuity (or stability) across age in the criteria for selecting friends and maintaining friendships. The criteria of similarity, personal attributes, and social resources discussed in previous sections are probably more consistent with a framework based on social reward than with one based on cognitive development.

*Similarity*

Despite age-related differences in children's conceptions of friendship and in the ''surface'' criteria implicit in them, similar ''basic'' or ''deep'' criteria seem to contribute to satisfaction with friendship throughout childhood and adolescence. Perceived similarity is important at all ages, as are actual similarities in demographic attributes and activities. With age, children attribute less importance to similarity and become more aware of how they differ from their friends (Ladd & Emerson, 1984), but, as we have indicated, perceived similarity remains important. Although the relative importance of common activities declines with age (Furman & Bierman, 1983, 1984), the importance of exciting companionship does not (e.g., Buhrmester & Furman, 1987; Jones & Dembo, 1989). The occurrence of intimacy increases with age (Berndt et al., 1986), but it is present even among preschoolers where it correlates with other measures of friendship quality (Mendelson et al., 1994). Thus, it is important to identify both changes and continuities across age in children's selection criteria and to examine whether cognitive and environmental changes associated with age affect the use of these criteria.

*Personal attributes*

The attributes of a friend that are associated with a good quality friendship may not be the same among children of all ages. But there is little research directly on this topic, and comparisons must be made across studies to ferret out possible developmental changes. Among preschoolers, security of attachment to the mother is an important determinant of children's enjoyment and cooperation with their friends (Park & Waters, 1989). Interactions of securely attached children paired with a securely attached friend are more harmonious, responsive, and happy and less controlling than interactions of other pairs of friends. Thus, the ability to develop, or the experience of, a trusting emotional bond is an important attribute for enhancing friendship. Research is needed to specify the advantages that secure attachments afford peer relations and to determine whether such advantages last beyond early childhood (see Park, this volume).

As mentioned earlier, interpersonal competence and self-control seem to be important attributes in childhood friends. Thus, a study with kindergarteners (Mendelson et al., 1994) yielded somewhat surprising findings. Children's ratings of companionship, similarity, and intimacy with their friends and observations of their partners' friendliness were predicted by the partners' destructiveness as rated by teachers. Children who were somewhat unconstrained by the rules of kindergarten and who were characterized by physical assertiveness, attention-seeking, and dominance with classmates were apparently most attractive as friends. Contrasted with findings from studies of older children, these results suggest that some of the attributes (e.g., assertiveness) associated with good quality friendships may change with age. Certainly, in middle childhood, friendships are related positively to sociability and negatively to emotionality (Stocker & Dunn, 1990). And in later childhood and adolescence, having close reciprocal friends is associated positively with, among other attributes, sociability, altruism, prosocial behavior, emotional supportiveness, sensitivity to feelings, competence in self-disclosures, independence, and self-esteem and negatively with, among other attributes, anxiety/depression, dominance, and aggression (Buhrmester; 1990; Buhrmester et al., 1988). One possibility is that such changes parallel changes in children's conceptions of friendship (e.g., Selman, 1980), but no study has related how attributes and judgments of quality might be related to conceptions.

## Changes influencing selection criteria

Two striking differences are apparent in the way children and adolescents select and maintain friends. First, with age, youngsters become more particular about who their friends are (Epstein, 1983). The number of nominated friends does not increase with age, but the number of reciprocated nominations does (e.g., Berndt & Hoyle, 1985), which means that children increasingly restrict their nominations to peers who like them in return. And, even though children's racial attitudes become more tolerant (Aboud, 1988), the number of other-race friends declines with age (Hallinan & Teixeira, 1987a), which suggests that children either use increasingly more criteria in choosing friends or that they apply certain criteria more stringently. With age, children also form increasingly stable friendships (e.g., Ladd, 1988) and gain fewer new friends throughout the year (Berndt & Hoyle, 1985), which suggests that older children's criteria for choosing friends are relevant for later phases of friendship; that is, older children use criteria that predict later satisfaction and, hence, durability.

Age-related increases in selectivity may be due partly to weakening environmental and parental constraints on youngsters' social contacts. Older children attend relatively large schools, have the freedom to participate in many extracurricular activities, and are allowed to travel independently to spend time with friends who live outside their own neighborhoods. Having access to many potential friends, they can afford to be choosy. Increased selectivity may also result from social-cognitive changes that enable older children to base their choices on more criteria. Older children more easily gather and evaluate information about both external and internal attributes of one another. They also have more elaborated self-schemas, so they can look for friends whose attributes overlap with, or complement, their own (Snyder et al., 1983).

The second way adolescents differ from children in selecting and maintaining friends concerns the time frame they adopt with respect to their relationships. As children grow older, they gain a longer perspective on friendships, a gain associated with social-cognitive skills that enable inferences about personality. Older children can evaluate what each partner gives and receives, aggregating this information over many interactions. Spontaneous inferences about traits and other internal attributes become increasingly common; and adolescents use such inferences to predict future behavior in different situations (Rholes & Ruble, 1984). Thus, a friend's good deeds are taken as an expression of the friend's personality and do not require immediate reciprocation; each partner trusts the other's long-term commitment to the relationship (Lydon et al., 1993).

Older children interpret a friend's behavior less in terms of immediate impact on themselves and more in terms of the partner's personality and how it affects long-term satisfaction with the relationship (e.g., Berndt et al., 1986; Birch & Billman, 1986; Clark et al., 1989). They also require less approval from peers (Barenboim, 1981) and become able both to consider simultaneously and to reconcile their own positive and negative emotions and experiences (Harter & Buddin, 1987). Thus, older children's disagreements with a friend do not necessarily lead to negative evaluations of the self or the other (Enright & Lapsley, 1981). Rather, older children overcome temporary conflicts and irritations in a relationship by reconciling them with their experiences and expectations. Disagreements become less disruptive (Enright & Lapsley, 1981; Ladd & Emerson, 1984) and can be resolved equitably (Hartup, 1992) or by agreeing to disagree (Aboud, 1989).

*Summary*

Similarities in sex, race, age, and activity preferences seem to be important in friendship at all ages. Similarities in socioeconomic and school status appear important beyond childhood, as do similarities in attitudes, values, and social perception. And, relative to other criteria, similarity appears to be more important for young children than for older children and adolescents.

Similarities and differences, however, may be selection criteria in two sequential phases of friendship. Children and adolescents initially exclude others of different race and gender from their group of associates, which effectively weeds out potential friends who are dissimilar in obvious demographic characteristics. Gradually, children discover other information about classmates and select friends based on finer-grained criteria, such as similarity, positive attributes, and mutual liking. Regardless, by 10 years of age, children are aware of differences between themselves and their friends in personality and temperament; and they may even consider certain complementary differences to be as important in a friendship as are similarities.

The personal attributes of physical attractiveness, cognitive ability, sociability, aggression, and withdrawal predict children's attraction to peers, although other attributes might be relevant to friendship. Yet there is little research on the attributes that are sought by children in a friend or that foster high quality friendships – and certainly not enough research to support generalizations across development – so this is one area that should prove fruitful in future research. Unlike the case for similarity, personal attributes may become relatively more important for older, than for younger, children. With age, youngsters become more selective about friends, have fewer environmental and parental constraints on their social contacts, and have a longer perspective on their friendships.

### Conclusions

We have reviewed the literature to discern criteria that youngsters may use to choose friends and maintain friendships. We examined how similarity and personal attributes of a peer might lead to attraction and then explored how the importance of such criteria might change with the phases of a friendship and with age. The review makes one thing apparent: More developmental research is needed on virtually every topic that we have addressed. In this section, we highlight important distinctions that must be considered in future studies and summarize areas ripe for investigation.

### *Friendship versus interpersonal attraction*

We echo others (e.g., Bukowski & Hoza, 1989) who stress the necessity of distinguishing between attraction (i.e., liking) and friendship. Friendship should not be equated with interpersonal attraction as measured hypothetically by the fictitious-stranger paradigm or even by sociometry. Rather, friendship and popularity appear to be distinct constructs, even in kindergarten, where the two facets of peer relations might be expected to be as similar as they ever are (Mendelson et al., 1994). Therefore, explanations of interpersonal attraction or popularity should not be generalized to friendship. At best, research on interpersonal attraction can be used to generate hypotheses about friendship, but these hypotheses must be tested directly with studies of friends or friendship.

### *Phases of friendship*

Our analysis highlights the importance of considering friendship as changing and dynamic. Interpersonal attraction may or may not be the first phase of friendship; this varies from relationship to relationship. Regardless, theoretical and empirical work is needed to identify how friendships unfold. Levinger and Levinger (1986) offered one framework for identifying causal conditions of friendship that incorporated the idea of phases of a relationship. Whether or not the five phases they specified – acquaintanceship, buildup, continuation and consolidation, deterioration, and ending – prove useful, questions remain concerning what factors are important to the relationship as it evolves.

## Quality of friendship

Merely identifying the presence or absence of a friendship does not seem sufficient. The issue of quality of friendship must be addressed. Quality might be related to phases of friendship. Thus, a consolidated friendship is presumably better than a simple acquaintanceship, but this begs the question about which dimensions of friendship characterize different phases. Moreover, friendships that are in the same phase – for example, long-standing consolidated relationships – can vary in quality.

It is useful to consider friendship quality in terms of the social, emotional, and instrumental resources sought in the relationship by one friend and provided by the other. Doing so transforms questions about precursors of friendship into questions about predictors of friendship quality. Moreover, a differentiated view of quality, like the one suggested here, means that different factors – say similarity on certain dimensions, particular personal attributes, or specific contexts – may predict different facets of friendship quality. For example, similarity of activity preferences may be associated with companionship, but a friend's empathy may be associated with intimacy.

## Developmental considerations

The issues addressed in this section so far are relevant to friendships at any age. Yet a number of other concerns especially relevant to developmental psychologists are raised. It is widely accepted that children's ideas about friendship change with age. This may not be due to the development of social cognition – that is, to changes in children's *understanding* about relationships that themselves do not differ with age. More likely, however, changes in children's ideas reflect real age-related changes in these relationships. Consequently, developmental research is needed on all the issues raised in this chapter, although the following questions strike us as particularly interesting: Does the influence of similarity on friendship change with age? Do friendship qualities change with age? And do different factors influence quality at different ages? These and other questions await further attention.

## References

Aboud, F. E. (1988). *Children and prejudice*. New York: Basil Blackwell.

Aboud, F. E. (1989). Disagreement between friends. *International Journal of Behavioral Development, 12*, 495–508.

Aboud, F. E. (1993). The developmental psychology of racial prejudice. *Transcultural Psychiatric Research Review, 30*, 229–242.

Aronson, E., & Worchel, S. (1966). Similarity versus liking as determinants of interpersonal attractiveness. *Psychonomic Science 5*, 157–158.

Asher, S. T., & Parker, J. G. (1989). Significance of peer relationship problems in childhood. In B. H. Schneider, G. Attili, J. Nadel, & R. P. Weissberg (Eds.), *Social competence in developmental perspective*. Dordrecht, Netherlands: Kluwer.

Ashton, N. L. (1980). Exploratory investigation of perceptions of influences on best friend relationships. *Perceptual and Motor Skills, 50*, 379–386.

Bailey, R. C., DiGiacomo, R. J., & Zinser, O. (1976). Length of male and female friendship and perceived intelligence in self and friend. *Journal of Personality Assessment, 40*, 635–640.

Barenboim, C. (1981). The development of person perception in childhood and adolescence: From behavioral comparisons to psychological constructs to psychological comparisons. *Child Development, 52*, 129–144.

Baumrind, D. (1968). *Manual for the Preschool Behavior Q Sort*. Berkeley: University of California Press.

Berndt, T. J., & Das, R. (1987). Effects of popularity and friendship on perceptions of the personality and social behavior of peers. *Journal of Early Adolescence, 7*, 429–439.

Berndt, T. J., Hawkins, J. A., & Hoyle, S. G. (1986). Changes in friendship during a school year: Effects on children's and adolescents' impressions of friendship and sharing with friends. *Child Development, 57*, 1284–1297.

Berndt, T. J., & Hoyle, S. G. (1985). Stability and change in childhood and adolescent friendships. *Developmental Psychology, 21*, 1007–1015.

Birch, L. L., & Billman, J. (1986). Preschool children's food sharing with friends and acquaintances. *Child Development, 57*, 387–395.

Blag, M. (1983). Perceived extraversion in a best friend. *Perceptual and Motor Skills, 57*, 891–894.

Brown, B. B. (1981). A life-span approach to friendship: Age-related dimensions of an ageless relationship. *Research in the Interweave of Social Rules, 2*, 23–50.

Buhrmester, D. (1990). Intimacy of friendship, interpersonal competence, and adjustment during preadolescence and adolescence. *Child Development, 61*, 1101–1111.

Buhrmester, D., & Furman, W. (1987). The development of companionship and intimacy. *Child Development, 58*, 1101–1113.

Buhrmester, D., Furman, W., Wittenberg, M. T., & Reis, H. T. (1988). Five domains of interpersonal competence in peer relationships. *Journal of Personality and Social Psychology, 55*, 991–1008.

Bukowski, W. M., & Hoza, B. (1989). Popularity and friendship: Issues in theory, measurement, and outcome. In T. J. Berndt & G. Ladd (Eds.), *Peer relationships in child development*. New York: Wiley.

Bukowski, W. M., Hoza, B., & Boivin, M. (1994). Measuring friendship quality during pre- and early adolescence: The development and psychometric properties of the friendship qualities scale. *Journal of Social and Personal Relationships, 11*, 471–484.

Byrne, D., & Griffitt, W. (1966). A developmental investigation of the law of attraction. *Journal of Personality and Social Psychology, 4*, 699–702.

Byrne, D., & Griffitt, W. (1973). Interpersonal attraction. *Annual Review of Psychology, 24*, 317–336.

Cairns, R. B., Cairns, B. D., Neckerman, H. J., Gest, S. D., & Garieppy, J. L. (1988). Social networks and aggressive behavior: Peer support or peer rejection? *Journal of Personality and Social Psychology, 24,* 815–823.

Carli, L. L., Ganley, R., & Pierce-Otay, A. (1991). Similarity and satisfaction in roommate relationships. *Personality and Social Psychology Bulletin, 17,* 419–426.

Cauce, A. M. (1986). Social networks and social competence: Exploring the effects of early adolescent friendships. *American Journal of Community Psychology, 14,* 607–628.

Clark, M. L., & Ayers, M. (1988). The role of reciprocity and proximity in junior high school friendships. *Journal of Youth and Adolescence, 17,* 403–411.

Clark, M. L., & Drewry, D. L. (1985). Similarity and reciprocity in the friendships of elementary schoolchildren. *Child Study Journal, 15,* 251–264.

Clark, M. S. (1984). Record keeping in two types of relationships. *Journal of Personality and Social Psychology, 47,* 549–557.

Clark, M. S., & Mills, J. (1979). Interpersonal attraction in exchange and communal relationships. *Journal of Personality and Social Psychology, 37,* 12–24.

Clark, M. S., Mills, J. R., & Corcoran, D. M. (1989). Keeping track of needs and inputs of friends and strangers. *Personality and Social Psychology Bulletin, 15,* 533–542.

Condon, J. W., & Crano, W. D. (1988). Inferred evaluation and the relation between attitude similarity and interpersonal attraction. *Journal of Personality and Social Psychology, 54,* 789–797.

Davey, A. G., & Mullin, P. N. (1982). Inter-ethnic friendship in British primary schools. *Educational Research, 24,* 83–92.

Denscombe, M. (1983). Ethnic group and friendship choice in the primary school. *Educational Research, 25,* 184–190.

Deutsch, F. M., & Mackesy, M. E. (1985). Friendship and the development of self-schemas: The effects of talking about others. *Personality and Social Psychology Bulletin, 11,* 399–408.

Doyle, A. B., & Connolly, J. A. (1989). Negotiation and enactment in social pretend play: Relations to social acceptance and social cognition. *Early Childhood Research Quarterly, 4,* 289–302.

Dubois, D. L., & Hirsch, B. J. (1990). School and neighborhood friendship patterns of Blacks and Whites in early adolescence. *Child Development, 61,* 524–536.

Duck, S. W. (1973). Personality similarity and friendship choice: Similarity of what, when? *Journal of Personality, 41,* 543–558.

Duck, S. W. (1975). Personality similarity and friendship choices by adolescents. *European Journal of Social Psychology, 5,* 351–365.

Duck, S. W., & Craig, G. (1978). Personality similarity and the development of friendship: A longitudinal study. *British Journal of Social and Clinical Psychology, 17,* 237–242.

Ellis, S., Rogoff, B., & Cromer, C. C. (1981). Age segregation in children's social interactions. *Developmental Psychology, 17,* 399–407.

Enright, R. D., & Lapsley, D. K. (1981). Judging others who hold opposite beliefs: The development of belief-discrepancy reasoning. *Child Development, 52,* 1053–1063.

Epstein, J. L. (1983). Examining theories of adolescent friendships. In J. L. Epstein & N. Karweit (Eds.), *Friends in school: Patterns of selection and influence in secondary schools.* New York: Academic Press.

Erwin, P. G. (1985). Similarity of attitudes and constructs in children's friendships. *Journal of Experimental Child Psychology, 40,* 470–485.

Feinberg, R. A., Miller, F. G., & Ross, G. A. (1981). Perceived and actual locus of control similarity among friends. *Personality and Social Psychology Bulletin, 7,* 85–89.

Finkelstein, N. W., & Haskins, R. (1983). Kindergarten children prefer same-color peers. *Child Development, 54,* 502–508.

Furman, W., & Bierman, K. L. (1983). Developmental changes in young children's conceptions of friendship. *Child Development, 54,* 549–556.

Furman, W., & Bierman, K. L. (1984). Children's conceptions of friendship: A multimethod study of developmental changes. *Developmental Psychology, 20,* 925–931.

Furman, W., & Buhrmester, D. (1985). Children's perceptions of the personal relationships in their social networks. *Developmental Psychology, 21*, 1016–1024.

Gottman, J. M. (1983). How children become friends. *Monographs of the Society for Research in Child Development, 48* (3, Serial No. 201).

Griffin, E., & Sparks, G. G. (1990). Friends forever: A longitudinal exploration of intimacy in same-sex friends and platonic pairs. *Journal of Social and Personal Relationships, 7*, 29–46.

Guralnick, M. J., & Groom, J. H. (1988). Friendships of preschool children in mainstreamed playgroups. *Developmental Psychology, 24*, 595–604.

Hallinan, M. T. (1982). Classroom racial composition and children's friendships. *Social Forces, 61*, 56–72.

Hallinan, M. T., & Teixeira, R. A. (1987a). Opportunities and constraints: Black–white differences in the formation of interracial friendships. *Child Development, 58*, 1358–1371.

Hallinan, M. T., & Teixeira, R. A. (1987b). Students' interracial friendships: Individual characteristics, structural effects, and racial differences. *American Journal of Education, 95*, 563–583.

Hallinan, M. T., & Williams, R. A. (1987). The stability of students' interracial friendships. *American Sociological Review, 52*, 653–664.

Harter, S., & Buddin, B. J. (1987). Children's understanding of the simultaneity of two emotions: A five-stage developmental acquisition sequence. *Developmental Psychology, 23*, 388–399.

Hartup, W. W. (1983). Peer relations. In P. H. Mussen (Series Ed.) and E. M. Hetherington (Vol. Ed.), *Handbook of child psychology, Vol. 4: Socialization, personality, and social development.* New York: Wiley.

Hartup, W. W. (1992). Conflict and friendship relations. In C. U. Shantz & W. W. Hartup (Eds.), *Conflict in child and adolescent development.* New York: Cambridge University Press.

Hartup, W. W. (1993). Adolescents and their friends. In B. Laursen (Ed.), *Close friendships in adolescence.* San Francisco, CA: Jossey-Bass.

Hays, R. B. (1985). A longitudinal study of friendship development. *Journal of Personality and Social Psychology, 48*, 909–924.

Hays, R. B. (1989). The day-to-day functioning of close vs. casual friendships. *Journal of Social and Personal Relationships, 6*, 21–37.

Hill, C., & Stull, D. E. (1981). Sex differences in effects of social and value similarity in same-sex friendship. *Journal of Personality and Social Psychology, 41*, 488–502.

Howes, C., & Wu, F. (1990). Peer interactions and friendships in an ethnically diverse school setting. *Child Development, 61*, 537–541.

Jones, D. C. (1985). Persuasive appeals and responses to appeals among friends and acquaintances. *Child Development, 56*, 757–763.

Jones, D. C. (1991). Friendship satisfaction and gender: An examination of sex differences in contributors to friendship satisfaction. *Journal of Social and Personal Relationships, 8*, 167–185.

Jones, G. P., & Dembo, M. H. (1989). Age and sex role differences in intimate friendships during childhood and adolescence. *Merrill-Palmer Quarterly, 35*, 445–462.

Kandel, D. B. (1978a). Similarity in real-life adolescent friendship pairs. *Journal of Personality and Social Psychology, 36*, 306–312.

Kandel, D. B. (1978b). Homophily, selection, and socialization in adolescent friendships. *American Journal of Sociology, 84*, 427–436.

Kurdek, L. A., & Krile, D. (1982). A developmental analysis of the relation between peer acceptance and both interpersonal understanding and perceived social competence. *Child Development, 53*, 1485–1491.

Ladd, G. W. (1988). Friendship patterns and peer status during early and middle childhood. *Journal of Developmental and Behavioral Pediatrics, 9*, 229–238.

Ladd, G. W., & Emerson, E. S. (1984). Shared knowledge in children's friendships. *Developmental Psychology, 20*, 932–940.

Lea, M., & Duck, S. (1982). A model for the role of similarity of values in friendship development. *British Journal of Social Psychology, 21*, 301–310.

Levinger, G., & Levinger, A. C. (1986). The temporal course of close relationships: Some thoughts about the development of children's ties. In W. W. Hartup & Z. Rubin (Eds.), *Relationships and development*. Hillsdale, NJ: Erlbaum.

Lydon, J. E., Jamieson, D. W., & Holmes, J. G. (1993). *The meaning of social exchange in the transition from acquaintanceship to friendship*. Manuscript submitted for publication.

McCandless, B. R., & Hoyt, J. M. (1961). Sex, ethnicity and play preferences of preschool children. *Journal of Abnormal and Social Psychology, 62*, 683–685.

McCarthy, B., & Duck, S. W. (1976). Friendship duration and responses to attitudinal agreement-disagreement. *British Journal of Social and Clinical Psychology, 15*, 377–386.

Maccoby, E. E. (1988). Gender as a social category. *Developmental Psychology, 24*, 755–765.

Maccoby, E. E. (1990). Gender and relationships: A developmental account. *American Psychologist, 45*, 513–520.

McGuire, K. D., & Weisz, J. R. (1982). Social cognition and behavior correlates of preadolescent chumship. *Child Development, 53*, 1478–1484.

Mendelson, M. J., Aboud, F. E., & Lanthier, R. P. (1994). Personality predictors of friendship and popularity in kindergarten. *Journal of Applied Developmental Psychology, 15*, 113–135.

Moe, J. L., Nacoste, R. W., & Insko, C. A. (1981). Belief versus race as determinants of discrimination: A study of southern adolescents in 1966 and 1979. *Journal of Personality and Social Psychology, 41*, 1031–1050.

Nelson, J., Aboud, F. E. (1985). The resolution of social conflict between friends. *Child Development, 56*, 1009–1017.

Newcomb, A. F., Bukowski, W. M., & Pattee, L. (1993). Children's peer relations: A meta-analytic review of popular, rejected, neglected, controversial, and average sociometric status. *Psychological Bulletin, 113*, 99–128.

Park, K. A., & Waters, E. (1989). Security of attachment and preschool friendship. *Child Development, 60*, 1076–1081.

Parker, J. G., & Asher, S. R. (1989a). Friendship Quality Questionnaire–Revised: Instrument and administration manual. University of Michigan.

Parker, J. G., & Asher, S. R. (1989b). Peer relations and social adjustment: Are friends and group acceptance distinct domains? University of Michigan.

Parker, J. G., & Asher, S. R. (1993). Friendship and friendship quality in middle childhood: Links with peer group acceptance and feelings of loneliness and social dissatisfaction. *Developmental Psychology, 29*, 611–621.

Rholes, W. S., & Ruble D. N. (1984). Children's understanding of dispositional characteristics of others. *Child Development, 55*, 550–560.

Rosenbaum, M. E. (1986). The repulsion hypothesis: On the nondevelopment of relationships. *Journal of Personality and Social Psychology, 51*, 1156–1166.

Rushton, J. P. (1989). Genetic similarity in male friendships. *Ethology and Sociobiology, 10*, 361–373.

Schofield, J. W. (1982). *Black and white in school: Trust, tension or tolerance?* New York: Praeger.

Selman, R. L. (1980). *The growth of interpersonal understanding: Developmental and clinical analyses*. New York: Academic Press.

Sharabany, R., Gershoni, R., & Hofman, J. E. (1981). Girlfriend, boyfriend: Age and sex differences in intimate friendship. *Developmental Psychology, 17*, 800–808.

Singleton, L. C., & Asher, S. R. (1979). Racial integration and children's peer preferences: An investigation of developmental and cohort differences. *Child Development, 50*, 936–941.

Smeaton, G., Byrne, D., & Murnen, S. K. (1989). The repulsion hypothesis revisited: Similarity irrelevance or dissimilarity bias? *Journal of Personality and Social Psychology, 56,* 54–59.

Snyder, M., Gangestad, S., & Simpson, J. A. (1983). Choosing friends as activity partners: The role of self-monitoring. *Journal of Personality and Social Psychology, 45,* 1061–1072.

Stocker, C. M., & Dunn, J. (1990). Sibling relationships in childhood: Links with friendships and peer relationships. *British Journal of Developmental Psychology, 8,* 227–244.

Stocker, C. M., & Mantz-Simmons, L. A. (1993). *Children's friendships and peer status: Links with sibling relationships, temperament and social skills.* Manuscript submitted for publication.

Tesch, S. A. (1983). Review of friendship development across the life span. *Human Development, 26,* 266–276.

Tesser, A., Campbell, J., & Smith, M. (1984). Friendship choice and performance: Self-evaluation maintenance in children. *Journal of Personality and Social Psychology, 46,* 561–574.

Townsend, M. A. R., McCracken, H. E., & Wilton, K. M. (1988). Popularity and intimacy as determinants of psychological well-being in adolescent friendships. *Journal of Early Adolescence, 8,* 421–436.

Verbrugge, L. M. (1979). The structure of adult friendship choices. *Social Forces, 56,* 576–597.

Werner, C., & Parmelee, P. (1979). Similarity of activity preferences among friends: Those who play together stay together. *Social Psychology Quarterly, 42,* 62–66.

Wetzel, C. G., & Insko, C. A. (1982). The similarity–attraction relationship: Is there an ideal one? *Journal of Experimental Social Psychology, 18,* 253–276.

Wright, P. H. (1991). *The Acquaintance Description form: What it is and how to use it.* Unpublished manuscript, University of North Dakota.

*Part II*

# Interdependence of relationship systems

# 6  Parents' interpersonal relationships and children's friendships

*Anna Beth Doyle and Dorothy Markiewicz*

Several recent reviews have summarized the extant research and theory on the role of the family in children's peer relations (e.g., Dunn, 1988; Parke, Mac-Donald, Beitel, & Bhavnagri, 1988; Putallaz & Heflin, 1990; Cohn, Patterson, & Christopoulos, 1991; Parke & Ladd, 1992). Although a broad range of relationships has been highlighted as being of importance within the family (Hinde & Stevenson-Hinde, 1988), until recently little attention has been paid to the multiple types and ways in which family relationships can affect children's friendships. There is a significant need also to examine how these potential influences may operate differentially across the child's various developmental periods. Some of these relationships operate within the family system (e.g., the spousal relationship) and some in the family's wider social context (e.g., the parents' relationships with adult friends). The parent–child relationship, including the quality of parent–child attachment (e.g., Sroufe, 1983; Park & Waters, 1989) and general parenting style (e.g., Baumrind, 1975; Putallaz & Heflin, 1990), have been viewed as of primary importance, to the neglect of other relationships. In this chapter we examine the role of family relationships and the mechanisms through which these may affect child friendships.

Friendship is a unique peer relation, distinguished from others primarily by its intense, mutually positive, dyadic nature (Bukowski & Hoza, 1989). Because family relationships are often similarly close and dyadic, there is considerable reason to expect family relationships to contribute to children's friendships. Moreover, relationships have qualities, features, and functions that emerge from the interactions of the members and are not individual characteristics per se. Thus, similarities may be more apparent between two relationships than between a relationship and the characteristics and behavior of individuals (Sroufe & Fleeson, 1986, 1988).

In this chapter two major questions are addressed: (a) How do family rela-

This chapter was prepared with the support of a grant from the Quebec Fonds FCAR.

tionships contribute to the likelihood of a child's having friends? (b) How do family relationships contribute to the quality of the child's friendships? Each of these questions will be dealt with in turn, and then relevant data from our own research will be presented. Focus is on the prevalence and quality of children's friendships, in part because of evidence that participation in and quality of friendship predict social adjustment and perceptions of well-being over and above predictions from general peer acceptance (Bukowski, Hoza, & Boivin, 1993; Parker & Asher, 1993; Berndt, this volume). For example, participation in a friendship and the quality of that relationship have been found to ameliorate loneliness at all levels of popularity (Parker & Asher, 1993). Though considerable overlap exists between the set of factors and processes affecting friendship participation and quality, selected qualities of friendship may be affected exclusively or differentially by particular family factors, and these effects may vary with the developmental level of the child. Thus, participation in and quality of friendship will be examined separately.

Two influential theoretical frameworks, attachment theory (Ainsworth, Blehar, Waters, & Wall, 1978; Bowlby, 1969/1982, 1973, 1980, 1988) and social learning theory (Bandura & Walters, 1963; Bandura, 1971, 1977; Mischel, 1976), suggest specific mechanisms through which family relationships may influence children's friendships. Family systems theory (Minuchin, 1974) also adds an important perspective. Differential predictions from each of these theoretical approaches are highlighted in addressing the questions we have posed.

**Family factors and the prevalence of child friendships**

The majority of children participate in friendships by middle childhood, but between 11% and 40% do not (Putallaz and Gottman, 1981; Berndt, Hawkins, & Hoyle, 1986; Parker & Asher, 1993). Research has highlighted particular factors associated with friendship participation for children in preschool, early- and middle-childhood, and adolescence. Individual differences in friendship participation may be attributable to affective/motivational factors, cognitive/behavioral skills, or a combination of these. Less is known about the affective/motivational bases of friendship participation. We do know, however, that children vary in their desire or need to form friendships, which may facilitate their acquiring and keeping friends or, in the extreme, interfere with friendship acquisition (Selman & Schultz, 1990).

With respect to cognitive/behavioral skills that contribute to friendship participation, at the preschool and early elementary-school level, children who communicate clearly and relevantly with a peer, exchange information, resolve conflict, and establish a common ground of activity are more likely to make friends (Gottman, 1983; Putallaz, 1983; Putallaz & Wasserman, 1990). By middle childhood, initiating interaction, being nice and respectful of others and self, exhibiting prosocial behaviors, providing social support, managing conflict, and not engaging in psychological aggression, negative self-presentation, or antisocial acts, such as fighting, lying, and the like, are identified as contributing to making friends (Ladd & Mize, 1982; Wentzel & Erdley, 1993). Also, by this age children who engage in negative gossip while maintaining common ground are more likely to become friends, whereas in adolescence, self-disclosure, the exploration of similarities and differences, and problem solving take on importance (Gottman & Mettetal, 1986). Each of these motivations, cognitions, and/ or skills may have roots in the context of family relationships.

*Parent–child relationships*

Earlier work on parent–child relationships and peer relations focused on two dimensions of parenting: warmth/rejection and control/permissiveness (e.g., Schaefer, 1959; Baumrind, 1971; Maccoby & Martin, 1983). Warmth, which includes affection, approval, encouragement, and physical and psychological availability, is associated with friendly, prosocial behavior with peers (Hinde & Tamplin, 1983; Attili, 1989); absence of parental warmth has been associated with social maladjustment and delinquency (Lytton, Watts, & Dunn, 1986; Siegelman, 1966).

Maternal warmth and availability are closely related to maternal responsiveness, which attachment theory highlights as being central to the establishment of a secure child–parent bond (e.g., Bowlby, 1969/1982, 1988). Securely attached children show greater social competence with peers at all ages. That is, securely attached preschool children have been found to engage in more reciprocal and less hostile or negative interaction with peers (Pastor, 1981) and to receive more positive interaction bids from peers (Jacobson & Wille, 1986). Secure preschool children are also more competent and affectively positive with classmates (Waters, Wippman, & Sroufe, 1979). With respect to friendships specifically, at age 10–11 secure children are more likely to make friends, to select securely attached children as friends, and to spend extensive time with these friends at day camp. These secure children are also more popular (Elicker, Englund, & Sroufe, 1992). However, Lewis and Feiring (1989) found that securely attached 9-year-old boys, but not girls, were more likely to have friends compared with insecurely attached children.

It is interesting to note that the findings linking attachment status to participation in mutual friendships are reported no earlier than middle childhood. The specific influences of family relationships on children's friendship participation may not appear earlier because in middle childhood issues of intimacy and loyalty central to attachment relations are beginning to take on importance

(Buhrmester & Furman, 1987; Buhrmester, 1990), distinguishing mutual friendships from peer relations in general.

Attachment theory identifies the major mechanism hypothesized to account
for these outcomes as the working model of attachment (Bowlby, 1969/82). In
the parent this cognitive model leads to responsive parenting and the development of a similar working model in the child (Main, Kaplan, & Cassidy, 1985).
Through memory, attributions, and expectations, the secure child's working
model of self as lovable and other as responsive is postulated to have increasing
autonomous influence over actual experience during his or her development.
This working model may affect friendship participation in a number of ways.
It may act as an acquired trait such as ego-resiliency (Block & Block, 1980),
self-esteem (Park, 1989), or felt security (Bowlby, 1969/82), or as a motiva-
tional/attributional system triggered by specific social situations that the child
then brings to later peer interactions (Sroufe & Fleeson, 1986, 1988). If the
working model of attachment functions as a trait, its expression would be expected to be consistent across situations and targets, including the early stage
of friendship formation and other peer relations. Support for the trait interpretation comes from the findings cited earlier of associations between attachment
security and a broad spectrum of peer relations (e.g., Waters et al., 1979), not
just with friendships. On the other hand, if the working model operates as a
motivational system, it would be expected to function only when the peer relation is experienced as a close relationship (Bowlby, 1969/82; Main et al.,
1985). That is, children's motivation to participate in a friendship may be quite
distinct from their motivation to participate with peers in general. The child's
definition of the relationship as ''close'' may elicit emotions, cognitions, and
behavior that are different from those elicited by the peer group in general.
More research distinguishing attachment associations with friendship from those
with general peer acceptance are needed.

It must also be noted that working models of insecurely attached children and
adults are heterogeneous, such that some avoid attachment figures whereas others cling to them. Some insecurely attached children are expected to avoid peer
friendships, whereas others, as noted earlier, may seek friends but display un-
reasonable expectations and, thus, be less likely to keep close friends (e.g.,
Selman & Schultz, 1990).

Though the mechanism by which the attachment system might affect later
social relationships is not yet clear, it is evident that attachment theory places
more emphasis on the motivational and attributional consequences rather than
the direct behavioral consequences of the parent–child relationship. In contrast,
social learning theorists focus on specific parent behaviors that may be learned
by children in the context of family relationships. For example, through observing maternal behaviors modeled in mother–child interaction, children may ac-

quire some of the social behavioral repertoire they utilize with peers (Putallaz, 1987). In playful interactions with parents, children may also learn to modulate affect (Parke, Cassidy, Burks, Carlson, & Boyum, 1992). That is, parents' tendency to elicit positive affect during play with their preschool child has been found to be associated with the child's social competence with peers, whereas parental overstimulation was associated with peer rejection (MacDonald & Parke, 1984; MacDonald, 1987). Other research also highlights the predictive power of parental expressed emotion for older children's social acceptance (Cassidy, Parke, Butkovsky, & Braungart, 1992). These authors observed that parents' emotional expressiveness was related to their kindergarten and first-grade children's popularity. With respect to friendships, children who express feelings inappropriately may alienate others and thus have difficulty making friends.

In a developmental extension of social learning theory, MacDonald (1992) postulates that parental warmth contributes to the development of a motivational system specifically relevant to friendship, characterized by attraction to the rewards of intimacy and affection, and by a tendency to seek out and enjoy intimate, affectionate relationships. Warmth may also contribute to the learning of specific social skills relevant to the formation of friendships, which should be optimally acquired because the warm parent's approval would be a powerful social reinforcer, warm mothers would serve as models of warm behaviors, and their teaching strategies would be more effective (Putallaz & Heflin, 1990).

## Spousal relationships

In addition to the parent–child relationship, marital adjustment has been identified as significant for children's peer relations (Grych & Fincham, 1990). Divorce and/or marital conflict have been found to be associated with children's lack of social competence with peers (Hetherington, Cox, & Cox, 1979; Johnson & O'Leary, 1987; Long, Forehand, Fauber, & Brody, 1987; Gottman & Katz, 1989). We expect that children in families with poor marital relationships will be less likely to have friends.

With respect to the mechanisms accounting for these associations, an attachment framework focuses on the tendency of adults to seek romantic relationships that are consistent with their working models of self and other, and actively, though perhaps unconsciously, to shape such relationships to conform to the model (Sroufe & Fleeson, 1986, 1988). For securely attached adults, the working model for the marital relationship is apt to lead to more harmonious and satisfying relationships. Considerable research on adult close relationships, including the romantic, spousal, and friendship relationships (Hazan & Shaver, 1987; Bartholomew, 1990; Collins & Read, 1990; Simpson, 1990; Kobak & Hazan, 1991), supports this interpretation. Adults securely attached in their families of origin may also marry spouses of similar orientation (Cohn, Silver, Cowan, Cowan, & Pearson, 1991). Such adults are also likely to have securely attached children (Main et al., 1985; Howes & Markman, 1989; Fonagy, Steele, & Steele, 1991). Therefore, an association between marital adjustment and the child's participation in friendship is expected, based on similar working models of attachment held by the child and the parents. However, in an attachment framework, associations between marital adjustment and child friendship are primarily indirect and not necessarily causal, the parent–child relationship is of principal importance, and greater predictability from the parent–child relationship to child friendships than from the marital relationship to child friendships is expected at all ages.

Similar predictions concerning an association between marital adjustment and children's participation in friendship would be made on the basis of social learning theory. The postulated mechanism, however, is parental modeling of specific social behaviors that are conducive to the formation and maintenance of a friendship. In particular, reciprocity of positive social exchanges and conflict resolution skills of disengagement and compromise (Kelley, Berscheid, Christensen, Harvey, Huston, Levinger, McClintock, Peplau, & Peterson, 1983; Laursen, 1993) may be fostered by parents who model such behavior in their marital relationship. Conversely, parents in discordant marriages may model negative behavior. Interadult anger has been shown to have negative effects on children, leading to distress in younger girls and anger in younger boys (Cummings, Vogel, Cummings, & El-Sheikh, 1989) and the reverse in older children (Cummings, Ballard, & El-Sheikh, 1991). Children from maritally discordant homes showed more preoccupation and upset in response to interparental anger than did other children (Cummings, Pellegrini, Notarius, & Cummings, 1989). We might speculate that such children would also experience more distress in their own conflicts with close friends, and, because they witness poor conflict resolution at home, would be less able to successfully regulate conflict in their own friendships. These reactions are likely to affect their ability to form and maintain friendships. Such children would also be less likely to observe and learn behaviors conducive to making friends. Thus, social learning theory implies a direct, causal relation between parental discord and friendship participation. To the extent that modeling is greater if the model is perceived as similar, interactions with friends by older adolescents might be expected to be influenced more by their parents' marital relationship than those of younger children.

In both attachment theory and social learning theory, focus is on one family dyad at a time (e.g., mother–child, spouses), and its effect on the child's friendships (Sroufe & Fleeson, 1986, 1988). In systems theory (e.g., Minuchin, 1974), an analysis of parent influences on children's friendships is expanded beyond the dyadic context to the family system as a whole. Other relationships in the family context are recognized as potentially influencing the child's development. Although the attachment and learning theory approaches suggest that children's friendships will be positive if the parent–child relationship is positive, a systems analysis includes the valence of other family relationships, as well as the strength of ties among family members, the permeability of boundaries between subsystems, and the hierarchical position of members. According to Minuchin, a healthy family system is characterized by a good marital relationship and by a clear parental subsystem, with a permeable boundary between that subsystem and the child subsystem. The parental subsystem functions as the executive, with the collaboration of both parents in providing guidance and support to the children. The children would be able to perform the appropriate roles of exploration and involvement inside and outside the family system, and therefore would be expected to form good interpersonal relationships, including friendships.

In Minuchin's view, when the spousal relationship is not adequate, one or both parents might form an unhealthy, overinvolved bond with a child or the other spouse ("enmeshed"), or move to a peripheral, distant position from the family ("disengaged"). Any of these configurations would be expected to affect the child's ability to function adequately. Children in "enmeshed" parent–child relationships might be constrained from engaging in intimate peer relations, whereas those in "disengaged" positions might form compensatory close friendships or be afraid to form them.

The bulk of the evidence suggests an association between a supportive marital relationship and positive mother–child interaction (Brody, Pellegrini, & Sigel, 1986; Easterbrooks & Emde, 1988; Engfer, 1988; Quinton & Rutter, 1987) and security of attachment (Belsky, 1984; Goldberg & Easterbrooks, 1984; Howes & Markman, 1989). Thus, the spousal relationship may affect child friendships through the mother–child relationship. Such connections would be predicted by attachment theory or social learning theory as outlined earlier. However, systems theory suggests that "enmeshed" children, who might appear to have warm, positive relationships with one or both parents, might have difficulty forming friendships.

### Adult friendships

A third set of parental relationships that may be of significance to children is the parents' friendships with adult peers. Parents' recollections of their own peer relations in childhood have been found to be associated with differential social status of their children and with differential attempts by mothers to influence their children's peer relations (Putallaz, Costanzo, & Smith, 1991). Mothers who had predominantly anxious and lonely recollections of their childhood peer experiences had children who were rated more competent by peers than were the children of mothers who had positive or negative recollections, perhaps because the anxious recollection mothers invested more effort in optimizing their children's peer experiences. In another study, parents' current possession of regularly seen, dependable friends and affiliation with formal organizations were associated positively with children's adjustment, including participation in a friendship network (Homel, Burns, & Goodnow, 1987). These authors interpreted their findings as due to parents' modeling of friendship patterns and provision of child access to community resources. From an attachment viewpoint, the findings could also be interpreted as reflecting secure working models of attachment for both parents and children that extended to their friendships.

Despite their emphases on different mechanisms, all the previous theoretical approaches suggest that children experiencing family disequilibrium would have a lower probability of having friends. That is, children from families in which parents have insecure attachment styles, discordant marital relations, enmeshed parent–child relations, and/or no adult friendships are less likely to participate in friendships.

### Family factors and the quality of the child's friendships

Though most children participate in friendships, these may vary considerably in quality (Bukowski et al., 1993; Parker & Asher, 1993). Quality is higher in closer and more stable friendships (Bukowski, Hoza, & Boivin, 1994; Hardy, Doyle, Markiewicz, & Spector, 1993).

An extensive body of developmental research on the quality of children's friendships indicates that the preschooler's focus on companionship and shared activities shifts by adolescence to a greater importance on loyalty and intimacy characterized by self-disclosure (Bigelow & LaGaipa, 1975; Berndt & Perry, 1986; Gottman & Mettetal, 1986; Buhrmester & Furman, 1987; Buhrmester, 1990). It is possible that conceptions/perceptions of friendship become more differentiated with age. Wright (1985) enumerates more adult friendship qualities than do researchers of child friendship qualities (Buhrmester & Furman, 1986; Bukowski et al., 1994; Parker & Asher, 1993). On the basis of these developmental studies of the features and complexity of children's friendships, we may also anticipate age differences in associations between parent and child relationships. That is, though links may exist between family relationships and young children's friendships, these links may be difficult to discern because of qualitative differences in the form and complexity of the child and family relationships in question. Especially when complex adult relationships (e.g., the spousal relationship and adult friendships) are examined, links may be most apparent with older children's friendships, whose friendships may be similar in structure to those of adults. Emotional and instrumental support, intimacy, security or loyalty, ability to resolve conflict, and companionship are common qualities of friendship from middle childhood through adulthood (Aboud & Mendelson, this volume).

Differential associations of qualitiative features of friendship with family relationships may help clarify the essential features of children's friendships. That is, though there is considerable consensus about the qualitative features of children's friendships, the extent to which these features are empirically independent of each other is not yet well established (Bukowski et al., 1994; Furman, this volume). In addition, though the family factors that predict friendship participation are also expected to influence the quality of the friendship, it is possible that selected qualities of friendship may be affected differentially. Such differential associations may aid in distinguishing among the various theories implicated in explanations for family relationship–child friendship associations.

### Parent–child relationships

A few studies conducted within an attachment framework provide data on associations between parent–child relationships and the quality of children's friendships. Park and Waters (1989) assessed attachment security in 4-year-olds with the mother version of the Attachment Q-set (Waters & Deane, 1985) and observed the quality of the child's play with a best friend. Secure–secure pairs played more harmoniously, and were less controlling, more responsive, and happier than secure–insecure pairs. Youngblade and Belsky (1992) related parent–child attachment in infancy and quality of parent–child interaction at age 3 years to child–friend interaction at 5 years. Security of attachment to the mother, and mother– and father–child interaction, predicted connectedness, synchrony, and cognitive level of play with friends as expected. Though relations of father–child attachment (as measured in the Strange Situation) to child play were counterintuitive, Q-sort father–child attachment security at 12 months of age predicted the affective tone of 5-year-old-child interaction with a friend as expected (Youngblade, Park, & Belsky, in press). These findings provide support for attachment theory in accounting for mother–child relationship influences on children's friendships, but raise questions about the measurement of attachment to father and its significance for peer relations. In addition, a lack of associations between attachment security and parent–child play suggests the possibility of multiple independent parental contributions to children's friendship quality.

With reference to older children, modest but positive correlations between the specific qualities of adolescents' relationships with parents and with friends are reported, with higher correlations for dimensions of insecurity than security (Furman & Wehner, 1994; Furman, this volume). Continuity between the quality of adolescents' relationships with their parents and their friends is also reported by Haynie and McLellan (1992). One limitation of these studies, however, is that all measures are derived from adolescent self-report. Findings should be substantiated utilizing procedures that minimize shared method variance.

In social construction theory (Sullivan, 1953; Youniss, 1980), differences in structure and function between parent–child and child–peer relationships are highlighted, with the former characterized by unilateral adult authority and child constraints to adult norms and the latter by reciprocal cooperation and mutual engagement. Relations with adults are considered of little importance or potentially interfering with the development of mutuality, standards of worth, respect for equality, interpersonal sensitivity, and the primacy of the need for relation. Accordingly, social construction theory would predict few correlations between the quality of parent–child relationships and peer friendships.

Nevertheless, parent–child relationships vary in reciprocity and egalitarianism individually and with age. More reciprocal parent–child relationships characterize securely attached preschool-aged children and their mothers, who engage in a "goal-corrected partnership" (Bowlby, 1969/1982; Greenberg & Speltz, 1988). Social learning theory, in contrast to social construction theory, predicts that such children should behave in more reciprocal, egalitarian ways with their peers, and therefore should be more likely to have friendships that are characterized by mutual helpfulness, and closeness. Moreover, from a social learning viewpoint, all aspects of relationships seen and reinforced are candidates for learning, including conflict-management, frequency of interaction, and emotional support. In particular, MacDonald's (1992) analysis of parental warmth implies that similarity between parent relations and child friendships may be mediated through motivation to seek close, affectionate social relationships. Thus, greatest similarity in parent and child relationships might be evidenced in closeness and affection, particularly for children with warm parents. Skills learned in parent–child relationships should affect both close friendships and relations with peers in general, namely, popularity.

Within an attachment framework, the qualities of friendship most relevant – maximizing felt security, seeking protection from anticipated dangers, and minimizing the negative emotions of fear and anxiety – are expected to be most influenced by family relationships. In particular, children who are securely attached to at least one parent should report more security in their friendships than insecurely attached children, because they are more likely to be friends with other securely attached children (Elicker et al., 1992) and because of their working models of close relationships. The concept of responsiveness central to secure attachment also leads to the prediction that a securely attached child might be more sociable and helpful with friends, though not necessarily higher in self-disclosure and intimacy than an insecurely attached child. Less significant or smaller differences would be expected on other dimensions of friendship quality, such as companionship. The empirical findings to date highlight effects of attachment security on the reciprocity, positive affect, and responsiveness of young children's friendships (Park & Waters, 1989; Youngblade & Belsky, 1992) and on companionship in older children (Park, 1993). It is possible that attachment may impact first on certain friendship qualities (e.g., security and helpfulness) and later on others (e.g., companionship). More research is needed in which a range of friendship qualities is examined across the different phases of friendship.

As noted earlier, attachment theory also implies that manifestations of working models of attachment with friends could be quite distinct from behavior and relationship quality exhibited in less close relationships with the general peer group (MacDonald, 1992). Thus, if attachment beyond infancy is relationship-specific rather than a personality trait, little consistency is predicted between the quality of children's friendships and the quality of their less close peer relations. It is also possible that close and less close relationships might diverge in quality only after middle childhood, when, as already noted, issues of trust and loyalty become particularly salient in friendship (Buhrmester & Furman, 1986, 1987; Buhrmester, 1990). Again, further research is necessary to test these predictions.

Support for these predictions derived from attachment theory would be most probable in a setting that aroused attachment motivation. Thus, observations of friends interacting together in an enjoyable environment might not reveal differences in the security of their relationships as a function of attachment history, whereas questions or observations tapping security in stressful situations might elicit these differences. Observational studies of adults who differ in attachment styles support the view that these are associated with different patterns of responding in stressful or emotionally laden situations (Kobak & Hazan, 1991; Simpson, Rholes, & Nelligan, 1992). On the other hand, differences in quality of friendship and interaction between securely and insecurely attached young children in dyadic free play (Park & Waters, 1989; Youngblade & Belsky, 1992) suggest that attachment status may affect friendship in a variety of situations.

*Spousal relationships and adult friendships*

Because attachment theory predicts similarity between parent and child internal working models of attachment, positive correlations between the quality of the spousal, parent–child, child–friend, and parent–peer relationships are expected. Findings noted earlier support this view. That is, adult attachment orientations predict adult friendship patterns as well as romantic relationships (Bartholomew, 1990; Bartholomew & Horowitz, 1991) and child attachment security predicts quality of children's interactions with friends (Park & Waters, 1989; Youngblade

& Belsky, 1992). Nevertheless, as noted in the discussion of friendship participation, the primacy of the parent–child attachment relationship would suggest
that the quality of the parents' relations with each other and with their own
friends would not directly or significantly affect the quality of the child's friendships.

From a social learning framework, it is likely that parents who are warm to
their children would place high value on interpersonal issues and prosocial behavior, and thus model and reward this behavior both with their children and
with their spouses and friends. Such parents would be more likely to have marriages characterized by affection and satisfaction. They would also be more
likely to have close adult friendships characterized as being rewarding and supportive both emotionally and instrumentally. Thus we would expect children
from these families to have friendships characterized by these qualities. Concerning the relative influence of different sources of parental modeling/condi-
tioning, it is reasonable to postulate that children witness more parental
interaction and are more affected emotionally by parental interaction than by
parent–friend interaction (e.g., Cummings & Ballard, 1991). Thus, a modeling
framework would predict stronger associations between child friendship qualities
and the qualities of the parental marital relationship than with parental friendships. In addition, the salient features of these relationships for the child would
be expected to change with child age due to social and cognitive development.
For example, younger children might attend to the gross emotional tone of
relating, the frequency of interacting, or the types of activities, whereas older
children might focus on more subtle qualities such as loyalty, affirmation of self,
or reciprocity (Buhrmester and Furman, 1987; Buhrmester, 1990). Adolescents
with their newly developed cognitive skills (Youniss & Smollar, 1985) may be
more attuned to parental modeling of mutuality and reciprocity with spouse and
adult friends.

### Maternal interpersonal relationships and child friendships

Our own research deals with the importance of a broad range of family relationships, including mother's friendships, marital harmony, the mother–child
relationship, and marital status, in children's friendship participation and quality
(Doyle, Markiewicz, & Hardy, 1994). In this exploratory study, we were primarily interested in the extent to which the qualities of the mother's relationships
were associated with the presence and quality of children's friendships, and child
popularity.

A sample of 154 mothers provided data on maternal friendship quality, marital
status and quality, and the mother–child relationship. One of their children, aged
8 to 12 years, provided information about their participation in friendships and

the quality of their best friendship. Thus, independent sources provided data on family relationships and child peer relations.

Children were identified as having a stable, mutual best friend (49%); only a stable, mutual good friend (22%), or no stable friend (29%) on the basis of classroom sociometrics. All rated the qualities of their best friendship in terms of companionship, help, closeness, security, and conflict on the *Friendship Quality Scale* (Bukowski et al., 1994).

Mothers rated the quality of their closest, same-sex friendship on nine subscales of the *Acquaintance Description Form* (Wright, 1985), including: stimulation value, self-affirmation value, ego support value, security value, utility value, maintenance difficulty, global favorability, voluntary interdependence, and person-qua-person. The first four subscales were categorized by Wright as self-referent rewards, referring to their contribution to the person's positive sense of self. Mothers also evaluated the quality of their marriage on the *Dyadic Adjustment Scale* (Spanier, 1976) and were interviewed about acceptance of their child as an index of the mother–child relationship (Rothbaum, 1986, 1988). Thus, though attachment was not directly assessed in order to preserve independence of family and child friendship data sources, the role of maternal acceptance and responsiveness to the child was examined as a potential mediating variable.

### Family factors and child friendship participation

Friendship participation was predicted by only one of the family relationship variables, the quality of the mother's closest friendship. When popularity was held constant, children were more likely to have a best friend if their mothers perceived their own best friends as providing more stimulating ideas and activities, but also felt somewhat less secure in that friendship. This finding parallels the association between mothers' anxious recollections of their own peer relations in childhood with greater child social acceptance found by Putallaz et al. (1991). Marital status, marital harmony, and mother–child relationship quality did not predict friendship status.

### Family factors and child friendship quality

Among children who had a stable friendship, mothers whose friendships were higher in stimulation value of the friend's ideas and activities had children who perceived their own best friend to be more helpful and supportive. Moreover, mothers who felt their friends were supportive of their achievements tended to have children who experienced more closeness/intimacy with their own friend. This association is noteworthy in that the closeness/intimacy of the child's best friendship is the dimension that most exemplifies MacDonald's (1992) postu-lated motivational system determining the seeking of close, affectionate rela-tionships. The mother's view of her friend as ego-supportive can also be conceived of as an index of positive affection in that friendship. Thus, maternal friendship quality was linked to child friendship quality; specifically, the pres-ence, closeness, and helpfulness of children's friendships were associated with self-referent aspects of the mother's best friendship. In contrast to predictions from social learning theory, the quality of the spousal relationship was not as strongly related to child friendship quality as was the quality of the mother's friendship. Only one child friendship quality – security – was associated with marital quality. In two-parent families, mothers who were positive about their marriage were more likely to have children who felt secure in their best friend-ship. It is noteworthy that marital quality predicted the child's sense of security with friends. These associations suggest that both measures tap relationship se-curity that may be associated with the attachment system.

Finally, the marital status of the family (divorced/separated *versus* two parent) was strongly related to the child's perception of the qualities of their best friend-ship, with children from two-parent families reporting more companionship, help and support, closeness, and security in their best friendship. For child compan-ionship and closeness, marital status of the parents was a significant predictor only for boys. These findings suggest the powerful influence of the family sys-tem on child relationships, especially on those of boys, perhaps in the form of residual effects of conflict and discord. It is noteworthy that marital status was a strong predictor of friendship quality, but unrelated to friendship participation.

Our measure of the mother–child relationship, maternal acceptance of the child, did not predict either child friendship quality or status. The failure to establish a link between the mother–child relationship, at least as measured in this study, and child friendship quality fails to support the view that family influences on children's friendships are mediated primarily through the mother–child attachment relationship.

*Family factors and child popularity*

Child popularity was predicted differently from family variables than was child friendship participation. The difficulty a mother experienced in maintaining a relationship with her best friend significantly predicted child popularity but not friendship status. Moreover, child popularity and friendship status were related in opposite fashion to mothers' perceptions of their friends as sources of inter-esting ideas and activities, the relation being negative for child popularity and positive for child friendship status. Finally, popularity was not related to moth-ers' friendship quality among children who had a friend. Other family relationships did not predict child popularity. Thus, these findings are consistent with other research indicating that popularity and friendship are two conceptually distinct aspects of children's peer relations, with related but nonidentical antecedents and functions in children's social development (Bukowski et al., 1993; Parker & Asher, 1993; Vandell & Hembree, 1994).

*Summary*

In summary, this study provides evidence of associations between family relationships and children's friendships. In particular, we observed links between the degree to which the mother's best friendship was personally rewarding and her child's participation in friendship and the quality of that relationship. The quality of the mother's best friendship was also the only significant predictor of child popularity, though the pattern of relationships differed. Marital quality was a less frequent predictor of child friendship quality. Evidence from this study did not support the view that these findings were mediated through attachment security, though other operationalizations of the mother–child relationship merit further study. On the other hand, the relative lack of prediction from the quality of the marital relationship did not support predictions from social learning theory. The findings thus lead us to conclude that there are underlying similarities between adult friendships and child friendships and/or that modeling effects are specific to particular categories of relationships. Because the observed associations between the family and child variables in our research are between methodologically independent measures of parent relationships and child friendships, they are particularly interesting and worthy of further study.

**Conclusions**

This review illustrates that children's friendships reflect and are likely to be influenced by qualities of their parents' interpersonal relationships. There is extensive evidence that positive parent–child relationships, for example, those characterized by warmth and responsiveness, are associated with good peer relations, including participation in close, supportive, and secure friendships. Moreover, the literature and our own preliminary results justify investigation of the impact on children's friendships of an expanded set of family relationships, including both spousal and adult friendships. In addition, the influence of fathers' relationships singly and in combination with mothers needs to be studied fully. There is some suggestion that fathers may be more important influences than mothers on children's peer relations, especially for boys (Parke et al., 1992). Sex differences in these family influences must also be examined.

Further research needs to clarify the causal mechanisms underlying the associations observed between parent relationship variables and child friendship participation and quality. This review provides support both for and against predictions derived from attachment theory and/or from social learning theory. These theories overlap considerably, including an emphasis on similar mechanisms, for instance, on working models, schemas, and expectations (Bandura, 1971, 1977; Bowlby, 1988; Crittenden, Partridge & Clausen, 1991). One point of difference, however, is in the importance accorded to the parent–child relationship, with attachment theory identifying it as primary, and social learning theory allowing for considerable observational learning from modeling by spouses and adult friends. The relative and joint contributions of these two theoretical viewpoints to understanding the associations between parental social relationships and child friendships could be clarified further by examining evidence for mediating variables, such as self-esteem, motivation for closeness, motivation for stimulation and enjoyment, and parent and child working models of attachment. More specific operationalizations of children's working model of self in relation to others, and more study of the generality of that model across the relationships experienced by a child at different ages, are needed in order to test the hypothesized mechanisms of attachment theory. For example, study of the degree to which secure attachment affects interactions with close friends in comparison to interactions with other peers at preschool, middle childhood, and adolescence would provide evidence relevant to attachment theory explanations of intergenerational similarity in relationships. More extensive study of children's awareness of their parents' values and behavior with friends and spouse would provide more specific data relevant to the importance of modeling.

Because the aim of this chapter was to highlight family influences on children's friendships, in discussions of attachment theory emphasis has been placed almost exclusively on a unidirectional model of such influence. However, attachment theory also points out that working models not only assimilate new relationships but also accommodate to changing relationship circumstances and experiences (Bowlby, 1973, 1980; Kobak & Hazan, 1991). That is, working models are revised according to whether an individual's experiences confirm or negate the accuracy of the attachment schema, and individuals also differ in the extent to which they are open to revising their models. Thus, changes in the spousal relationship and adult friendships can alter parents' working models. More important, children's friendships may alter the working model of the child, especially with increasing age, contributing to potential divergence from the parental model.

Future research into associations between relationships across generations would be facilitated by measures that are parallel in structure and valid for both children and adults. Furman's *Network of Relationships Inventory* and *Behavioral Systems Questionnaire* (Furman, this volume) make a considerable contribution in this regard. Measures of attachment typology that are parallel and that are suitable for infants, children, and adults have contributed greatly to the advancement of research in that field (George, Kaplan, & Main, 1985; Waters & Deane, 1985).

Finally, careful study of friendships over time is needed to determine the effects of family factors on different stages of friendship development, for example, valuing friendship, initiating friendship, conflict resolution during friendships, and long-term friendships. Studies of family determinants at different phases of friendship offer the possibility of distinguishing primary from secondary influences.

## References

Ainsworth, M., Blehar, M., Waters, E., & Wall, S. (1978). *Patterns of attachment.* Hillsdale, NJ: Erlbaum.

Attili, G. (1989). Social competence versus emotional security: The link between home relationships and behavior problems at school. In B. H. Schneider, G. Attili, J. Nadel, & R. P. Weissberg (Eds.), *Social competence in developmental perspective* (pp. 293–311) London: Kluwer.

Bandura, A. (1971). *Social learning theory.* New York: General Learning Press.

Bandura, A. (1977). Self-efficacy: Toward a unifying theory of behavioral change. *Psychological Review, 84,* 191–215.

Bandura, A., & Walters, R. H. (1963). *Social learning and personality development.* New York: Holt, Rinehart, and Winston, Inc..

Bartholomew, K. (1990). Avoidance of intimacy: An attachment perspective. *Journal of Social and Personal Relationships, 7,* 147–178.

Bartholomew, K., & Horowitz, L. M. (1991). Attachment styles among young adults: A test of a four-category model. *Journal of Personality and Social Psychology, 61,* 226–244.

Baumrind, D. (1971). Current patterns of parental authority. *Developmental Psychology, 4,* 103–112.

Baumrind, D. (1975). The contribution of the family to the development of competence in children. *Schizophrenia Bulletin, 14,* 12–37.

Belsky, J. (1984). The determinants of parenting: A process model. *Child Development, 55,* 83–96.

Berndt, T. J., Hawkins, J. A., & Hoyle, S. G. (1986). Changes in friendship during a school year: Effects on children's and adolescents' impression of friendship and sharing with friends. *Child Development, 57,* 1284–1297.

Berndt, T. J., & Perry, T. (1986). Children's perceptions of friendships as supportive relationships. *Developmental Psychology, 22,* 640–648.

Bigelow, B., & LaGaipa, J. (1975). Children's written descriptions of friendship: A multidimensional analysis. *Developmental Psychology, 11,* 857–858.

Block, J. H., & Block, J. (1980). *The California child Q-set.* Palo Alto, CA: Consulting Psychologists Press.

Bowlby, J. (1973). *Attachment and loss: Vol. 2. Separation.* New York: Basic.

Bowlby, J. (1980). *Attachment and loss: Vol. 3. Loss, sadness and depression.* New York: Basic Books.

Bowlby, J. (1982). *Attachment and loss: Vol. 1. Attachment.* New York: Basic Books. (Original work published 1969.)

Bowlby, J. (1988). *A secure base: Parent–child attachment and healthy human development.* New York: Basic Books.

Brody, G. H., Pellegrini, A. D., & Sigel, I. E. (1986). Marital quality and mother–child and father–child interactions with school-aged children. *Developmental Psychology, 22,* 291–296.

Buhrmester, D. (1990). Intimacy of friendship, interpersonal competence, and adjustment during preadolescence and adolescence. *Child Development, 61*, 1101–1111.

Buhrmester, D., & Furman, W. (1986). The changing functions of friends in childhood: A neo-Sullivanian perspective. In V. J. Derlaga & B. A. Winstead (Eds.), *Friendship and social interaction*. New York: Springer-Verlag.

Buhrmester, D., & Furman, W. (1987). The development of companionship and intimacy. *Child Development, 58*, 1101–1113.

Bukowski, W. M., & Hoza, B. (1989). Popularity and friendship: Issues in theory, measurement and outcome. In T. J. Berndt & G. W. Ladd (Eds.), *Peer relationships in child development*. New York: Wiley.

Bukowski, W. M., Hoza, B., & Boivin, M. (1993). Popularity, friendship and emotional adjustment during early adolescence. In B. Laursen (Ed.), *New directions for child development: Close friendships in adolescence*. San Francisco: Jossey-Bass.

Bukowski, W. M., Hoza, B., & Boivin, M. (1994). The friendship qualities scale: Development and psychometric properties (Version 3.4). *Journal of Social and Personal Relationships, 11*, 471–485.

Cassidy, J., Parke, R. D., Butkovsky, L., & Braungart, J. M. (1992). Family–peer connections: The roles of emotional expressiveness within the family and children's understanding of emotions. *Child Development, 63*, 603–618.

Cohn, D. A., Patterson, C. J., & Christopoulos, C. (1991a). The family and children's peer relations. *Journal of Social and Personal Relationships, 8*, 315–346.

Cohn, D. A., Silver, D. H., Cowan, P. A., Cowan, C. P., & Pearson, J. L. (1991b, April). *Working models of childhood attachment and marital relationships. Paper presented at meetings of the Society for Research in Child Development, Seattle.*

Collins, N. L., & Read, S. J. (1990). Adult attachment, working models, and relationship quality in dating couples. *Journal of Personality and Social Psychology, 58*, 644–663.

Crittenden, P. M., Partridge, M. F., & Claussen, A. H. (1991). Family patterns of relationship in normative and dysfunctional families. *Development & Psychopathology, 3*, 491–512.

Cummings, E. M., & Ballard, M. (1991). Responses of children and adolescents to interadult anger as a function of gender, age and mode of expression. *Merrill-Palmer Quarterly, 37*, 543–560.

Cummings, E. M., Ballard, M., & El-Sheikh, M. (1991). Responses of children and adolescents to interadult anger as a function of gender, age, and mode of expression. *Merrill Palmer Quarterly, 37*, 543–560.

Cummings, J. S., Pellegrini, D. S., Notarius, C. I., & Cummings, E. M. (1989). Children's responses to angry adult behavior as a function of marital distress and history of interparent hostility. *Child Development, 60*, 1035–1043.

Cummings, E. M., Vogel, D., Cummings, J. S., & El-Sheikh, M. (1989). Children's responses to different forms of expression of anger between adults. *Child Development, 60*, 1392–1404.

Doyle, A. B., Markiewicz, D., & Hardy, C. (1994). Mothers' and children's friendships: Intergenerational associations. *Journal of Social and Personal Relationships*.

Dunn, J. (1988). Relations among relationships. In W. Duck (Ed.), *Handbook of personal relationships* (pp. 193–209). Wiley.

Easterbrooks, M. A., & Emde, R. N. (1988). Marital and parent–child relationships: The role of affect in the family system. In R. Hinde & J. Stevenson-Hinde (Eds.), *Relationships within families*. Oxford: Clarendon Press.

Elicker, J., Englund, M., & Sroufe, L. A. (1992). Predicting peer competence and peer relationships in childhood from early parent–child relationships. In R. D. Parke & G. W. Ladd (Eds.), *Family–peer relationships: Modes of linkage* (pp. 77–106). Hillsdale, NJ: Erlbaum.

Engfer, A. (1988). The interrelatedness of marriage and the mother–child relationship. In R. A. Hinde & J. Stevenson-Hinde (Eds.), *Relationships within families: Mutual influences*. Oxford: Clarendon Press.

Fonagy, P., Steele, H., & Steele, M. (1991). Maternal representations of attachment during pregnancy predict the organization of infant–mother attachment at one year of age. *Child Development, 62,* 891–905.

Furman, W., & Wehner, E. A. (1994). Romantic views: Toward a theory of adolescent romantic relationships. In R. Montmayor (Ed.), *Advances in adolescent development, Vol. 6: Relationships in adolescence.* Newbury Park, CA: Sage.

George, C., Kaplan, N., & Main, M. (1985). *Attachment interview for adults.* Unpublished manuscript, University of California, Berkeley.

Goldberg, W. A., & Easterbrooks, M. A. (1984). The role of marital quality in toddler development. *Developmental Psychology, 20,* 504–514.

Gottman, J. M. (1983). How children become friends. *Monographs of the Society for Research in Child Development, 48, (Serial No. 201).*

Gottman, J. M., & Katz, L. F. (1989). Effects of marital discord on young children's peer interaction and health. *Developmental Psychology, 25,* 373–381.

Gottman, J. M., & Mettetal, G. (1986). Speculations about social and affective development: Friendship and acquaintanceship through adolescence. In J. M. Gottman & J. G. Parker (Eds.), *Conversations of friends: Speculations on affective development* (pp. 192–240). New York: Cambridge University Press.

Greenberg, M. T., & Speltz, M. L. (1988). Contributions of attachment theory to the understanding of conduct problems during the preschool years. In J. Belsky & T. Nezworski (Eds.), *Clinical implications of attachment.* Hillsdale, NJ: Erlbaum.

Grych, J. A., & Fincham, F. (1990). Marital conflict and children's adjustment: A cognitive-contextual framework. *Psychological Bulletin, 108,* 267–290.

Hardy, C., Doyle, A. B., Markiewicz, D., & Spector, E. (1993). *Friendship and sociometric status: Associations with self-concept in middle-childhood. Unpublished manuscript, Concordia University.*

Haynie, D., & McLellan, J. (1992). *Continuity in parent and peer relationships.* Presented at the fourth biennial meeting of the Society for Research on Adolescence, Washington.

Hazan, C., & Shaver, P. (1987). Romantic love conceptualized as an attachment process. *Journal of Personality and Social Psychology, 52,* 511–524.

Hetherington, E. M., Cox, M., & Cox, R. (1979). Play and social interaction in children following divorce. *Journal of Social Issues, 35,* 26–49.

Hinde, R., & Stevenson-Hinde, J. (1988). *Relationships within families.* Oxford: Clarendon Press.

Hinde, R., & Tamplin, A. (1983). Relations between mother–child interaction and behavior in preschool. *British Journal of Developmental Psychology, 1,* 231–257.

Homel, R., Burns, A., & Goodnow, J. (1987). Parental social networks and child development. *Journal of Social and Personal Relationships, 4,* 159–177.

Howes, P., & Markman, H. J. (1989). Marital quality and child functioning: A longitudinal investigation. *Child Development, 60,* 1044–1051.

Jacobson, J. L., & Wille, D. E. (1986). The influence of attachment pattern on developmental changes in peer interaction from the toddler to the preschool period. *Child Development, 57,* 388–347.

Johnson, P. L., & O' Leary, K. D. (1987). Parental behavior patterns and conduct disorders in girls. *Journal of Abnormal Child Psychology, 15,* 573–581.

Kelley, H. H., Berscheid, E., Christensen, A., Harvey, J. H., Huston, T. L., Levinger, G., McClintock, E., Peplau, L. A., & Peterson, D. R. (1983). *Close relationships.* New York: Freeman.

Kobak, R. R., & Hazan, C. (1991). Attachment in marriage: Effects of security and accuracy of working models. *Journal of Personality and Social Psychology, 60,* 861–869.

Ladd, G. W., & Mize, J. (1982). A social-cognitive learning model of social-skill training. *Psychological Review, 90,* 127–157.

Laursen, B. (1993). Conflict management among close friends. In B. Laursen (Ed.), *Close friend-*

*ships in adolescence: New directions for child development* (pp. 39–54). San Francisco: Jossey-Bass.

Lewis, M., & Feiring, C. (1989). Early predictors of childhood friendship. In T. J. Berndt & G. W. Ladd (Eds.), *Peer relationships in child development* (pp. 246–273). New York: Wiley.

Long, N., Forehand, R., Fauber, R., & Brody, G. (1987). Self-perceived and independently observed competence of young adolescents as a function of parental marital conflict and recent divorce. *Journal of Abnormal Child Psychology, 15*, 15–27.

Lytton, H., Watts, D., & Dunn, B. E. (1986). Stability and predictability of cognitive and social characteristics from age 2 to age 9. *Genetic, Social & General Psychology Monographs, 112*, 363–398.

Maccoby, E., & Martin, J. (1983). Socialization in the context of the family. In E. M. Hetherington (Ed.), *Handbook of child psychology: Vol. 4. Socialization, personality, and social development* (pp. 1–102). New York: Wiley.

MacDonald, K. (1987). Parent–child physical play with rejected, neglected, and popular boys. *Developmental Psychology, 23*, 705–771.

MacDonald, K. (1992). Warmth as a developmental construct: An evolutionary analysis. *Child Development, 63*, 753–773.

MacDonald, K., & Parke, R. D. (1984). Bridging the gap: Parent–child play interaction and peer interactive competence. *Child Development, 55*, 1265–1277.

Main, M., Kaplan, N., & Cassidy, J. (1985). Security in infancy, childhood and adulthood: A move to the level of representation. In I. Bretherton and E. Waters (Eds.), *Growing points in attachment theory and research. Monographs of the Society for Research in Child Development, 50*, 66–106.

Minuchin, S. (1974). *Families and family therapy.* Cambridge, MA: Harvard University Press.

Mischel, W. (1976). *Introduction to personality.* New York: Holt, Rinehart, & Winston.

Park, K., & Waters, E. (1989). Security of attachment and preschool friendships. *Child Development, 60*, 1076–1081.

Park, K. A. (1989). *Self-esteem: One mediator of the relation between security of attachment and behavioral conduct.* Paper presented at the biennial meeting of the Society for Research in Child Development, Kansas City, MO.

Park, K. A. (1993, March). *A longitudinal examination of links between mother–child attachment and children's friendships in early childhood.* Paper presented at the biennial meeting of the Society for Research in Child Development, New Orleans.

Parke, R., MacDonald, K., Beitel, A., & Bhavnagri, N. (1988). The role of the family in the development of peer relationships. In R. Peters & R. McMahon (Eds.), *Social learning systems approaches to marriage and the family.* New York: Brunner Mazel.

Parke, R. D., Cassidy, J., Burks, V. M., Carson, J. L., & Boyum, L. (1992). Familial contribution to peer competence among young children: The role of interactive and affective processes. In R. D. Parke & G. W. Ladd (Eds.), *Family–peer relationships: Modes of linkage* (pp. 107–134). Hillsdale, NJ: Erlbaum.

Parke, R. D., & Ladd, G. W. (1992). *Family–peer relationships: Modes of linkage.* Hillsdale, NJ: Erlbaum.

Parker, J., & Asher, S. (1993). Friendship and friendship quality in middle childhood: Links with peer group acceptance and feelings of loneliness and social dissatisfaction. *Developmental Psychology, 29*, 611–621.

Pastor, D. (1981). The quality of mother–infant attachment and its relationship to toddlers' initial sociability with peers. *Developmental Psychology, 17*, 326–335.

Putallaz, M. (1983). Predicting children's sociometric status from their behavior. *Child Development, 54*, 1417–1426.

Putallaz, M. (1987). Maternal behavior and children's sociometric status. *Child Development, 58*, 324–340.

Putallaz, M., Costanzo, P. R., & Smith, R. B. (1991). Maternal recollections of childhood peer relationships: Implications for their children's social competence. *Journal of Social and Personal Relationships, 8,* 403–422.

Putallaz, M., & Gottman, J. (1981). Social skills and group acceptance. In S. Asher & J. Gottman (Eds.), *The development of children's friendships.* New York: Cambridge University Press.

Putallaz, M., & Heflin, A. H. (1990). Parent–child interaction. In S. R. Asher & J. Coie (Eds.), *Peer rejection in childhood.* New York: Cambridge University Press.

Putallaz, M., & Wasserman, A. (1990). Children's entry behavior. In S. R. Asher & J. Coie (Eds.), *Peer rejection in childhood* (pp. 60–89). New York: Cambridge University Press.

Quinton, D., & Rutter, M. (1987). *Parenting breakdown: The making and breaking of intergenerational links.* Aldershot: Gower.

Rothbaum, F. (1986). Patterns of parental acceptance. *Genetic, Social and General Psychology Monographs, 112,* 435–458.

Rothbaum F. (1988). Maternal acceptance and child functioning. *Merrill-Palmer Quarterly, 34,* 163–184.

Schaefer, E. S. (1959). A circumplex model for maternal behavior. *Journal of Abnormal and Social Psychology, 59,* 226–235.

Selman, R., & Schultz, L. H. (1990). *Making a friend in youth.* Chicago: University of Chicago Press.

Siegelman, M. (1966). Loving and punishing parental behavior and introversion tendencies in sons. *Child Development, 37,* 985–992.

Simpson, J. A. (1990). Influence of attachment styles on romantic relationships. *Journal of Personality and Social Psychology, 59,* 971–980.

Simpson, J. A., Rholes, W. S., & Nelligan, J. S. (1992). Support seeking and support giving within couples in an anxiety-provoking situation: The role of attachment styles. *Journal of Personality and Social Psychology, 62,* 434–446.

Spanier, G. B. (1976). Measuring dyadic adjustment: New scales for assessing the quality of marriage and similar dyads. *Journal of Marriage and the Family, 38,* 15–28.

Sroufe, L. A. (1983). Infant–caregiver attachment and patterns of adaptation in preschool: The roots of maladaptation and competence. In M. Perlmutter (Ed.), *Minnesota symposium in child psychology. Vol. 16* (pp. 41–81). Hillsdale, NJ: Erlbaum.

Sroufe, L. A., & Fleeson, J. (1986). Attachment and the construction of relationships. In W. W. Hartup & R. Rubin (Eds.), *Relationships and development* (pp. 57–71). Hillsdale, NJ: Erlbaum.

Sroufe, L. A., & Fleeson, J. (1988). The coherence of family relationships. In R. A. Hinde & J. Stevenson-Hinde (Eds.), *Relationships within families: Mutual influences* (pp. 28–47). Oxford: Clarendon Press.

Sullivan, H. S. (1953). *The interpersonal theory of psychiatry.* New York: Norton.

Vandell, D., & Hembree, S. (1994). Peer social status and friendship: Predictors of children's social and academic adjustment. *Merrill-Palmer Quarterly, 40,* 461–477.

Waters, E., & Deane, K. E. (1985). Defining and assessing individual differences in attachment relationships: Q-methodology and the organization of behavior in infancy and early childhood. In I. Bretherton and E. Waters (Eds.), Growing points of attachment theory and research. *Monographs of the Society for Research in Child Development, 50,* 41–65.

Waters, E., Wippman, J., & Sroufe, A. (1979). Attachment, positive affect and competence in the peer group: Two studies in construct validation. *Child Development, 50,* 821–829.

Wentzel, K. R., & Erdley, C. A. (1993). Strategies for making friends: Relations to social behavior and peer acceptance in early adolescence. *Developmental Psychology, 29,* 819–826.

Wright, P. H. (1985). The acquaintance description form. In S. Duck & D. Perlman (Eds.), *Understanding personal relationships: An interdisciplinary approach.* London: Sage Publications.

Youngblade, L. M., & Belsky, J. (1992). Parent–child antecedents of 5-year-olds' close friendships: A longitudinal analysis. *Developmental Psychology, 28,* 700–713.

Youngblade, L. M., Park, K. A., & Belsky, J. (in press). Measurement of young children's close friendship: A comparison of 2 independent assessment systems and their associations with attachment security. *International Journal of Behavioural Development.*

Youniss, J. (1980). *Parents and peers in social development: A Sullivan-Piaget perspective.* Chicago: University of Chicago Press.

Youniss, J., & Smollar, J. (1985). *Adolescent relations with mothers, fathers, and friends.* Chicago: University of Chicago Press.

Youniss, J., & Smollar, J. (1989). Adolescents' interpersonal relationships in social context. In T. J. Berndt & G. W. Ladd (Eds.), *Peer relationships in child development* (pp. 330–318).

# 7 Individual differences in friendship quality: Links to child–mother attachment

*Kathryn A. Kerns*

The purpose of this chapter is to discuss how children's friendships differ from one another and to speculate on the source of individual differences in friendship. By friendship I mean a close, affective tie between two peers. The focus will be on qualitative differences in friendship. I argue that: (a) It may be important to apply an individual differences approach to the study of children's friendships; (b) a consideration of friendship theories may aid in identifying the most salient features of friendship at a particular age; and (c) one source of individual differences in friendship may be a child's relationships with caregivers.

### Taking an individual differences perspective on friendship

Most of the research and theory on children's friendships is devoted to identifying normative changes in friendship. For example, Gottman (Gottman, 1983; Gottman & Mettetal, 1986; Parker & Gottman, 1989) has proposed a model of peer relationships in which different issues (e.g., coordinated play) are proposed to be salient in peer relationships during different developmental periods. By contrast, individual differences in friendship generally have been treated as error variance rather than as interesting phenomena in their own right. As a consequence, there have been few attempts to describe variations in children's friendships.

It is important to recognize that the study of normative changes in friendship and the study of individual differences in friendship are complementary perspectives. There can, of course, be stable individual differences in friendship even during periods of normative changes. For example, Park, Lay, and Ramsay

I wish to thank the following students, all of whom made significant contributions to the studies reported in this chapter: AmyKay Cole, Victoria Harlett, Lisa Klepac, and Amy Stevens. The studies reported in this chapter were funded by grants from the Kent State University Research Council and a Biomedical Research Support Grant, awarded to the author. This chapter was completed while the author was supported by a grant from NIMH (MH48787).

(1993) observed preschool friend pairs once at age 4 and once at age 5. These investigators found that friend pairs were more positively oriented and displayed more coordinated play at age 5. At the same time, there was evidence of individual differences in children's friendships being maintained over time: Scores on positive orientation, cohesiveness, and control from the two time points were moderately correlated. These findings illustrate that evidence of normative change does not preclude finding meaningful individual differences in friendship; rather, the normative change and individual differences perspectives answer different questions about friendship.

In addition, research and theory on normative changes in friendship can inform the study of individual differences. It may be most fruitful for investigators to look for variation in aspects of friendship identified as those most salient at a given age. For example, Sullivan's (1953) theory of friendship suggests that companionship is the key feature of friendship in middle childhood whereas intimacy is the key feature of friendship in adolescence. This suggests that there may be changes with age in which features of friendship have the greatest impact on a child's adjustment. Consistent with this hypothesis, Buhrmester (1990) found that intimacy in friendship was more strongly related to adjustment for adolescents than for preadolescents. Thus, variation on the developmentally relevant friendship dimension may prove to be the best indicator of friendship quality at a given age.

For a number of reasons it may be important to study individual differences in friendship. First, although children may share similar ideas about what constitutes an ideal friendship, it is not the case that all friendships achieve the ideal. For example, although friendships are thought of as egalitarian relationships, not all preschool friendships are egalitarian (Park et al., 1993). The substantial variation in children's friendships suggests that different friendships may have different impacts on children. Second, it is now recognized that peer acceptance and friendship are two distinct aspects of peer relationships that may contribute differentially to social development (Bukowski & Hoza, 1989). Thus, any account of how peers contribute to development will be incomplete if it does not include a role for experiences in friendship. Given that almost all children have at least one friend, studying individual differences in friendship may enhance our understanding of how friendships contribute to development.

### Individual differences in friendship quality: Mapping the domain

As a first step to studying individual differences in children's friendships, it is necessary to map the domain. In what ways will children's friendships differ from one another? To what degree is it necessary to study different features of friendship at different ages?

Bukowski and Hoza (1989) proposed a hierarchical, three-level model of friendship that is useful for defining how friendships may differ from one another. First, one can determine whether a child is involved in a reciprocated friendship. Thus, the first level deals with the presence of a friendship. At the second level, the number of reciprocated friendships in which a child is involved can be assessed. The third assessment level focuses on describing the quality of a child's friendships. Assessments at the three levels are thought to provide somewhat distinct information about children's friendships. There has been some work conducted on the presence and stability of friendship (e.g., Berndt & Hoyle, 1985), but investigators have typically ignored qualitative differences in friendship. This chapter focuses on the third level, friendship quality.

Friendship quality refers to the essential character or nature of friendship. Two attributes that seem particularly useful for describing friendships, especially if friends are observed, are the content of the interactions and the qualities of the interactions (Hinde, 1979; Hartup & Sancilio, 1986). Content refers to what two people do together; qualities refer to how individuals engage in activities and behaviors (Hinde, 1979). Information about both content and qualities of interaction is often necessary for characterizing the nature of a relationship. For example, two sets of friends may both be fighting, but we would probably draw different inferences about the friendships if one pair was fighting in a playful way and the other in a hateful way. To take another example, we are likely to describe a friendship as intimate if the friends: (a) self-disclose personal and potentially embarrassing information to one another (i.e., intimate content), and (b) the friends appear attentive and interested when listening to the disclosures of their partner (i.e., engaged). By contrast, in the absence of these conditions we may infer that a friendship is low in intimacy.

There are many other ways to distinguish pair-to-pair variations in children's friendships aside from examining the content and qualities of friendship. For example, one could study friendship stability, patterning of interactions between friends, or similarity of individuals who are close friends. (For a more complete presentation of how children's friendships might differ, see Hartup and Sancillo, 1986, and Hinde, 1979). For the purposes of this chapter, I will focus on global dimensions that capture both the content and qualities of friendship.

Even if one defines friendship quality in terms of global dimensions that describe the relationship, it is still necessary to define more precisely how children's friendships will differ. The study of individual differences in friendship quality may be informed by examining the literatures on other types of close relationships. Responsiveness and control are identified as two core features of parent–child relationships (Maccoby & Martin, 1983), and they may be manifested in friendships as well. The data bear this out in that both responsiveness and control are evident in pre-shoolers' friendships. Children are more responsive to friends than to peer acquaintances or strangers (Foot, Chapman, & Smith, 1977; Gottman, 1983; Howes, 1983). In addition, the dimensions of responsiveness and control have been useful in distinguishing individual differences in children's friendships (Park et al., 1993; Park & Waters, 1989). Given that these features are present in young children's friendships, and that they capture meaningful variation in friends' interactions, they also may be useful for describing variations in friendship across childhood.

Owing to normative changes in the nature of friendship, some dimensions of friendship may be most salient in a particular developmental period. I propose there are substantial individual differences in the degree to which friendships achieve the norm. For example, although coordinated play may be the hallmark of friendship in early childhood (Gottman, 1983; Gottman & Mettetal, 1986) there are likely to be individual differences in the degree to which any preschool friend pair is able to establish and maintain coordinated play. When studying individual differences in friendship, it may be most fruitful to study those aspects of friendship that are most salient in the age period studied. For example, when studying preschool friendships it may be more important to examine variations in coordinated play than to examine variations in intimacy; the opposite is likely to be true when studying adolescent friendships.

When identifying friendship issues that may be most salient at a particular age, it is useful to divide childhood into three periods: early childhood (ages 3–7), middle childhood (ages 8–12), and adolescence (13–19). Two themes emerge from observational studies of peer interaction in early childhood. First, the ability to establish coordinated play with another is a hallmark of friendship (Gottman, 1983; Howes, 1983). Consistent with this hypothesis, young children define a friend as someone with whom you play (e.g., Selman, 1980). In addition, children display more coordinated and advanced play with friends than with acquaintances (Howes, 1988; Vespo, 1991). Maintaining a climate of agreement and regulating conflict is a second feature of young children's friendships (Hartup, 1989; Gottman, 1983). Children who are friends, relative to children who are not friends, use disagreement more frequently in conflict resolution (Hartup, Laursen, Stewart, & Eastenson, 1988) and maintain a climate of agreement more consistently during play (Gottman, 1983). These two themes were also identified in two observational studies of individual differences in preschoolers' interactions with friends (Park & Waters, 1989; Youngblade, Park, & Belsky, 1993). In both studies, a broad-band assessment was performed to describe the interactions of friend pairs, and two dimensions that emerged from principal components analyses of the data were positive interaction and coordinated interaction. Thus, maintaining harmony and staying engaged in play are two distinct features of friendship in early childhood, with meaningful individual differences along these two dimensions.

In middle childhood, children are concerned with finding companions and avoiding isolation from the peer group (Gottman & Mettetal, 1986; Sullivan, 1953). Children work to develop a sense of solidarity with peers in order to be accepted by the larger peer group (Gottman & Mettetal, 1986). In addition, children can stay connected with peers and avert loneliness by forming an alliance with another child. Sullivan (1953) suggested that preadolescents are motivated to form a close, one-on-one relationship with a particular peer, what Sullivan termed a *chumship*. The development of a chumship is thought to prevent a child from experiencing loneliness, provide validation of one's self-worth, and foster the development of interpersonal sensitivity (Sullivan, 1953). There is some empirical support for Sullivan's hypotheses in that preadolescents with a close friend have been found to be less lonely, have higher self-esteem, and behave more altruistically than do children who do not have a close friend (Mannarino, 1980; McGuire & Weisz, 1982; Parker & Asher, 1993). In studying individual differences in friendship in middle childhood, it may be important to tap companionship and solidarity in friendship.

The major change in friendship from preadolescence to adolescence is an increase in intimacy (Berndt, 1982; Buhrmester, 1990; Gottman & Mettetal, 1986). A close, intimate relationship with a peer is thought to provide an adolescent with a safe environment in which to explore and define the self (Gottman & Mettetal, 1986). Although Sullivan (1953) suggested that friendships may provide intimacy as early as preadolescence, self-report studies have found that intimacy in friendship increases from preadolescence to adolescence (Buhrmester & Furman, 1987; Furman & Buhrmester, 1992; Sharabany, Gershoni, & Hofman, 1981). Girls tend to report more intimacy in friendship than do boys, suggesting that intimacy is particularly important for adolescent girls. The empirical evidence supports the hypothesis that intimacy may become particularly salient in adolescence. Thus, investigators interested in individual differences in adolescents' friendships may find it most useful to examine intimacy in friendship (see Buhrmester, 1990).

The dimensions discussed do not represent an exhaustive cataloguing of individual differences in friendship; instead, this section is intended to illustrate some of the ways in which friendships differ. The particular dimensions of friendship studied may depend in part on the investigator's methodological strategies. Self-report techniques may provide valid measurement of dimensions, such as intimacy, which are based on private and subjective evaluations of the friendship. Other dimensions, such as responsiveness, may be more reliably assessed by an outside observer. Therefore, a variety of methodological approaches will be needed to provide a complete description of variations in the quality of children's friendships.

In addition, the choice of which dimensions of friendship to study may depend on the children's ages. Some dimensions, such as responsiveness, may be applicable to the friendships of both younger and older children. Other dimensions, such as coordinated play or intimacy, may be most salient at a given age and therefore may provide the most sensitive index of individual differences in friendship in particular age periods. In short, investigators may wish to apply a developmental analysis to the study of individual differences in friendship.

## The roots of individual differences in friendship: Family influences

In these two relations lies the root of a mother's importance, unique, without parallel, established unalterably for a whole lifetime as the first and strongest love-object and as the prototype of all later love-relations – for both sexes. (Freud, 1949, p. 45)

Although there has been some work on the correlates of friendship, little attention has been paid to what might produce individual differences in friendship quality. There are no doubt many factors that influence the quality of children's friendships. The mother–child relationship is one possible influence. Parke et al. (1989) suggest that the influence of parents on peer relationships may be both direct and indirect. Direct influences include actions or activities in which parents engage for the specific purpose of fostering their children's peer relationships (e.g., starting a play group or instructing a child on how to make friends). Indirect parental influences on peer relationships include actions or activities by parents that influence peer relationships even though they are not engaged in specifically for this purpose. For example, an indirect effect of a mother establishing a harmonious interaction style with her child may be that her child will generalize this interaction style to the peer setting and subsequently have less difficulty interacting with peers. (See Putallaz & Heflin, 1990, for an alternative way of defining direct and indirect influences and a discussion of how these effects are mediated.)

This chapter is devoted to one indirect influence on peer relationships – the quality of a child's tie to his or her mother. Quality of parent–child relationships can be measured in many ways. This discussion explores how security in child–parent attachments is related to peer relationships. I am testing the hypothesis that the mother–child bond serves as a prototype or template for later close relationships, including friendships (Sroufe & Fleeson, 1986). Note that this hypothesis is somewhat broader than Freud's (1949) and Bowlby's (1982) claim that the mother–child bond has implications for later love relations. Although the research is correlational, and therefore direction of influence is difficult to determine, I am working on the assumption that children learn within the mother–child relationship ways of thinking, feeling, and behaving that subsequently generalize to their own friendships.

In my research I have used attachment theory (Ainsworth, Blehar, Waters, & Wall, 1978; Bowlby, 1973, 1982; Bretherton, 1985; Main, Kaplan, & Cassidy, 1985; Sroufe & Fleeson, 1986; Waters, Kondo-lkemura, Posada, & Richters, 1991) as the theoretical framework for conceptualizing individual differences in child–parent relationships. According to the theory, all children form attachments, typically with individuals who are stronger and wiser than themselves and who provide care, comfort, and security (Bowlby, 1982). In this chapter, the term *attachment* has this specific meaning and should not be taken to be synonymous with other descriptors of relationships, such as close. Thus, children's relationships with parents and other caregivers are attachments but, except in unusual circumstances (Freud & Dann, 1976), relationships with friends would not be termed attachments. A corollary of this view is that there are qualitative differences between parent–child relationships and friendships.

Attachment bonds vary in the degree to which they provide the child with a sense of security. By definition, a child who has formed a secure attachment to a particular caregiver is one who has developed confidence in the responsiveness and availability of that caregiver. This confidence in the caregiver allows the child to use the attachment figure as a secure base from which to explore and a haven of safety in times of distress. By contrast, an insecurely attached child is one who has not developed confidence in the caregiver's responsiveness and/ or availability. Consequently, the insecurely attached child has difficulty using the caregiver as a secure base; the child may be unwilling to tolerate separation from the attachment figure or may try to emotionally distance the self from the caregiver.

Although children form attachments to more than one person, Bowlby (1982) believed that children are biased to direct attachment behavior toward one principal attachment figure. Thus, although children may form attachments with multiple caregivers, including fathers as well as mothers, Bowlby's (1982) notion of a central attachment figure suggests that attachment relationships may be arranged in a hierarchy of importance, with the principal attachment relationship likely to have the greatest impact on a child's social development. In most Western societies, the mother serves as a child's primary caregiver and therefore the mother–child relationship is predicted to be the most important attachment relationship.

Whether this is so, or whether mother–child and father–child attachments might have a different set of external correlates, is an empirical question. Resolving this question requires conducting studies in which children's attachments to both mother and father are assessed. Studies of mother–child and father–child attachment may address the question of whether a secure attachment relationship can compensate for an insecure one, and whether it matters whether the secure relationship is formed with mother or father. Main's work on the correlates of parental attachments (Main & Weston, 1981; Main et al., 1985) suggests that : (a) mother–child attachment is more strongly related to social development outcomes than is father–child attachment; (b) the number of secure parental attachments (0, 1, or 2) is positively related to indices of social functioning; and (c) in cases where children have formed one secure and one insecure parental attachment, children who form the secure attachment to the mother have been rated more socially competent. Other research has not explicitly examined the question of compensatory effects, but instead separately examined mother–child and father–child attachments. Father–child attachment has been linked to preschoolers' interactions with peers (Easterbrooks & Goldberg, 1990; Suess, Grossman, & Sroufe, 1992; Youngblade et al., 1993), suggesting the need to articulate and examine the role of child–father attachment in social development.

Although it is recognized that both fathers and mothers can serve as attachment figures, relatively few studies have examined both child–mother and child–father attachments. Thus, one direction for future research will be to understand the importance of children's attachments to fathers. The focus on the child–mother relationship in this chapter should not be interpreted as indicating that child–father attachments play no role in social development. This chapter focuses on the mother–child relationship because examining children's primary attachments provides the strongest test of attachment theory.

One tenet of attachment theory is that the security of the mother–child relationship has implications for the quality of a child's other attachments (Bowlby, 1982) or close relationships (Sroufe & Fleeson, 1986). An important question is *why* the development of a secure attachment would facilitate relationships with peers. First, a secure attachment to a caregiver may support exploration of the environment (Ainsworth et al., 1978), including interactions with peers (Sroufe & Waters, 1977). That is, a child who is confident in the responsiveness and availability of a caregiver may be more willing to initiate relationships with peers. In addition, children may develop a particular behavioral style through interactions with caregivers that is carried over into other relationships (Youngblade & Belsky, 1992). For example, children whose caregivers have been responsive to their social bids may subsequently adopt a responsive interaction style in other close relationships. Thus, learned behavior patterns may generalize from the mother–child relationship to other close relationships.

Another way in which attachments may influence friendships is through their impact on an individual's beliefs about the self or others, what Bowlby (1973) termed *working models*. Working models are described as schemes or scripts (Bretherton, 1985) or rules (Main et al., 1985) that summarize an individual's experiences in and expectations about relationships. According to Bowlby, children develop working models of the self and others, based on interactions with attachment figures, which are thought to be mutually confirming. That is, children who view the self as loveable tend also to hold positive views of others. Sroufe and Fleeson (1986) suggest that children also develop an understanding of both sides of the attachment relationship. For example, a child who has had a sensitive attachment figure expects others to be sensitive and will treat others with sensitivity. Sroufe and Fleeson (1986) suggest that a child's understanding of the whole attachment relationship is carried forward into later close relationships.

Working models may be one mechanism linking experiences in attachment relationships with peer relationships. For example, a child with a positive view of self may have greater social confidence and may better handle the rebuffs that all children face (Sroufe, 1990). In addition, a child who has found caregivers to be trustworthy and responsive may initiate relationships with peers because he or she believes peers will respond in a positive way to his or her social overtures. This same child may also be responsive to peers' overtures. Finally, beliefs about others and relationships may influence how others' actions are perceived. For example, children who have experienced rejection from a caregiver may subsequently be more likely to make hostile attributions about a peer's ambiguous actions (Suess et al., 1992).

Bowlby (1979) suggested that working models are built up across infancy, childhood, and adolescence. Thus, at any age working models are a product of an individual's attachment history. Not all attachment experiences may carry equal weight, however, in shaping a person's expectations about relationships. Early experiences may have special importance because they provide the framework in which later events are interpreted and experienced. As with other schemas or beliefs, it is predicted that individuals will seek confirmation of the basic tenets of their working model and interpret ambiguous information in ways that are consistent with their beliefs. As a consequence, the ways in which current relationships are experienced are in part shaped by earlier attachments.

Of course, this does not lead to the conclusion that early experiences override all subsequent life experiences. Expectations about relationships may be modified, particularly in the context of other attachment relationships (Main et al., 1985). In addition, links between attachment at one point in childhood and subsequent socialization outcomes may be mediated by other variables such as parental child-rearing practices (Waters et al., 1991). It is therefore easiest to interpret links between child–mother attachment and peer relationships when the two are assessed concurrently.

In summary, the development of a secure attachment to the primary caregiver is predicted to support exploration of the social environment, to provide a context for the development of a behavioral style, and to shape children's beliefs and expectations of self, others, and relationships. As a consequence, securely attached children are expected to: (a) show an interest in establishing relationships with peers, and (b) work to establish the type of close, responsive relationships with friends that they developed with their caregivers.

*Evidence of links between child–mother attachment and*
*peer relationships*

Many studies have investigated how child–mother attachment predicts or is concurrently related to children's competent interactions with peers in early childhood. Children securely attached to their mothers have been found to be more responsive, outgoing, empathic, and less aggressive toward strangers and acquaintances than are children insecurely attached to their mothers (Kestenbaum, Farber, & Sroufe, 1989; LaFreniere & Sroufe, 1985; Lieberman, 1977; Pastor, 1981; Sroufe, 1983; Troy & Sroufe, 1987; Waters, Wippman, & Sroufe, 1979; but see Jacobson & Wille, 1986, for an exception; consistent effects for boys only, Cohn, 1990; Turner, 1991). Attachment at age 1 also has been found to predict peer competence in a camp setting at age 10 (Elicker, Englund, & Sroufe, 1992). For the most part, the data suggest that securely attached children display a more socially competent interaction style with peers than do insecurely attached children.

Although these findings attest to the developmental significance of mother–child attachment, they do not provide a test of the hypothesis that attachment influences close peer relationships because: (a) children were not observed with friends, and (b) peer assessments focused on the competencies of the child rather than on the quality of relationships. Four studies have investigated whether attachment is related to the incidence of friendship. A secure attachment to mother in infancy predicts the number of friendships preschoolers form with classmates (Sroufe, 1983) and preadolescents form at a day camp (Elicker et al., 1992) or in their peer network (Grossman & Grossman, 1991), with securely attached children forming more friendships. A fourth study (Lewis & Feiring, 1989) did not find an association between infant attachment and number of friends at age 9 for girls; for boys, infant attachment was related only to the number of male friends (boys secure as infants had more male friends). Attachment may be more highly related to the quality than to the quantity of children's friendships. A better test of the hypothesis that mother–child attachment serves as a prototype or template for other close relationships would be provided by examining links between attachment and the quality of children's friendships.

There has been some speculation about how the friendships of securely and insecurely attached children might differ (Hartup, 1986; Kerns, 1994; Sroufe & Fleeson, 1986). Some friendship variables may be related to attachment across childhood because they are linked with interaction styles that develop early and are maintained. For example, securely attached children may develop a responsive interaction style with caregivers that carries over into friendships, with attachment linked to responsiveness in friendship across childhood. Other differences in the friendships of securely and insecurely attached children may be most pronounced during particular developmental periods. Two examples illustrate this point. Hartup (1986) suggests that securely attached children's friendships may function more smoothly than insecurely attached children's friendships. This difference may emerge in early childhood given that maintaining a climate of agreement (Gottman & Mettetal, 1986) is a salient feature in preschoolers' friendships. Hartup (1986) also suggests that securely attached children are more likely than insecurely attached children to form stable friendships, a difference that may emerge in preadolescence when the establishment of a chumship becomes important (Sullivan, 1953) and children have more choice of friends.

## Associations between attachment and friendship in early childhood

Two studies have examined associations between attachment and friendship quality in preschoolers. Youngblade et al. (1993) examined how mother–child and father–child attachment, assessed at ages 1 and 3, predicted a child's interactions with a friend at age 5. Mother–child attachment, assessed with both the Strange Situation and the Attachment Q-set, did not predict friends' interactions. Unexpectedly, children classified as securely attached to their fathers in Strange Situation assessments at age 1, compared to those classified as insecure, were in friendships rated as less positive and coordinated. However, father–child attachment security, assessed with the Attachment Q-set, was related to positive interactions in the friend dyad. Interpretation of the findings is complicated by the fact that attachment data were available only for one member of the friend dyad. Park and Waters (1989) also examined relations between mother–child attachment and the behavior of friend dyads. In the Park and Waters study, attachment and friendship quality were assessed concurrently and attachment data were collected for both children in the friend dyad. Friend dyads in which both children were securely attached were compared to dyads in which one child was securely attached and the other insecurely attached to his or her mother. Mother–child attachment was predictive of friends' interactions: The secure–secure friend pairs were rated higher on measures of positive interaction (e.g., harmony, responsiveness) than were the secure–insecure friend pairs. These findings are consistent with the suggestion that securely attached preschoolers may have less difficulty maintaining a climate of agreement in friendship.

## Associations between attachment and friendship in middle childhood

No published studies have examined links between attachment and friendship quality beyond early childhood. The lack of research is not due to a decline in the need for attachment figures. As Bowlby (1979, p. 103) stated, "The require-ment of an attachment figure, a secure personal base, is by no means confined to children though, because of its urgency during the early years, it is during those years that it is most evident and has been most studied." In older children the maintenance of physical proximity becomes less important, and availability of the attachment figure becomes the set goal of the attachment system (Bowlby, 1973, p. 204; Bowlby, 1987, cited in Ainsworth, 1990). Availability of the attachment figure is determined by a child's belief that the attachment figure is open to communication, physically accessible, and responsive if called upon for help (Bowlby, 1987, cited in Ainsworth, 1990). Although Bowlby (1982) sug-gested that the mother–child relationship becomes a goal-directed partnership in the preschool years, with children becoming aware of and able to take into account their mothers' goals, plans, and motives, Waters et al. (1991) suggest that the mother–child relationship does not become a true negotiated partnership until the middle childhood years. According to Waters et al. (1991), the goal of the attachment system is to maintain a degree of supervision and contact when the child is away from the parent, with the responsibility for maintaining contact shared more equally between parent and child in middle childhood than at younger ages.

Based on these ideas, it seems reasonable to propose the following about attachment in middle childhood. Children are still in need of a secure base. Parents may fulfill the role of a secure base by being accessible, available, responsive, and willing to communicate openly with their children. In middle childhood, children take more responsibility for maintaining contact with the parent than they did at an earlier age. Children's feelings of security in the child–mother relationship serve either to inhibit or facilitate children's explo-ration when the attachment figure is not physically accessible.

Several well-validated measures of child–mother attachment are available for assessing attachment in early childhood: the Strange Situation (Ainsworth et al., 1978), the Attachment Q-set (Vaughn & Waters, 1990; Waters & Deane, 1985), and the separation–reunion procedure (Main & Cassidy, 1988; Main et al., 1985). By contrast, there are no widely accepted, well-validated techniques for assessing child–mother attachment in middle childhood. The assessments of at-tachment in early childhood all rely on using observations of children's secure base behavior to assess attachment security. The frequency and intensity of attachment behavior declines across childhood (Bowlby, 1982, 1979), suggesting that at older ages it may be more fruitful to assess attachment by tapping chil-dren's representations of the attachment relationship (Main & Cassidy, 1988).

I have recently begun to explore associations between child–mother attach-ment and friendship in preadolescence (ages 9–12). In this work, I have used a self-report measure (Park & Hazan, 1990) to assess children's feelings of security in the mother–child relationship. The Security Scale is a 15-item measure of the degree to which a child feels that a particular caregiver is trustworthy, responsive, and physically and emotionally available (i.e., willing and able to serve as a secure base). Each item is rated on a 4-point scale with items presented in the "Some kids . . . Other kids . . ." format developed by Harter (1982). The scale has now been used in a series of studies and has demonstrated evidence of internal consistency. Efforts to validate the scale have focused on relating children's security scores to other self-reports obtained from the child, to ratings of peer acceptance obtained from classmates, and to reports of maternal acceptance obtained from mothers. Children's reports of security in the mother–child relationship are significantly correlated with maternal reports of acceptance of the child. In addition, children more securely attached to their mothers have been found to have higher self-esteem. More secure children also report higher levels of peer acceptance and receive higher liking ratings from peers. Some evidence of discriminant validity has been obtained in that security scores are not significantly correlated with school grade-point average or self-perceptions of athletic competence. Collectively, the data suggest that the security scale may provide one reliable and valid method of assessing security of child–mother attachment in preadolescence.

One way of examining links between attachment and friendship would be to relate self-reports of attachment and friendship quality. In a developmental perspective, I expected attachment to be related to the most salient features of friendship in preadolescence, companionship and validation (Sullivan, 1953; Buhrmester & Furman, 1986). In addition, I expected that securely attached children would feel less lonely (Kerns, 1994). In a study of fourth and fifth graders, we obtained reports of child–mother attachment using the Security Scale. In addition, children completed five scales from the Parker and Asher (1993) Friendship Inventory: companionship and recreation, validation and caring, intimate disclosure, conflict and betrayal, and conflict resolution. Children also completed a shortened version of the loneliness scale (Asher, Hymel, & Renshaw, 1984). Consistent with predictions, children's security scores were significantly related to reports of companionship and validation in their best friendship. Security scores were not related to reports of intimacy in the friendship. The fact that attachment was not correlated with intimacy suggests that the findings cannot be parsimoniously subsumed by a response bias or halo explanation. Security scores were also inversely related to the amount of conflict and betrayal in the friendship, suggesting that securely attached children were better at averting conflicts with friends. Securely attached children also reported feeling less lonely. In summary, securely attached children reported more positively about their friendships, particularly with respect to the key features of friendship in preadolescence.

It is important to note a major limitation of this approach to testing links between attachment and friendship. Friendships are inherently dyadic, involving two people, each of whom has established a relationship with his or her primary attachment figure. It is therefore problematic to talk about the friendships of securely attached children or insecurely attached children unless some consideration is given to the security of the *partner*, because a securely attached child may develop qualitatively different friendships with a securely attached and an insecurely attached friend. Thus, if one has attachment data on only one member of a friend dyad, any lack of association between the child's attachment security and the quality of the friendship is difficult to interpret. For example, Park (1992) examined how preschoolers react when a friendship ends because the friend moves away. More securely attached preschoolers were reported by mothers to talk more about their best friends prior to the move but did not show more sadness after their best friend moved away. From this pattern of findings, it is difficult to conclude whether more securely attached children form more significant friendships. One complication in interpeting the study findings is that information about the friend's security of attachment was not available. It is most informative if one knows the composition of the friendship dyad when studying links between attachment and friendship. Thus, one strategy to investigate links between attachment and friendship would be to compare friend dyads in which both children are securely attached to mother to friend dyads in which one child is securely attached and the other insecurely attached to mother. This approach takes into consideration each child's attachment to his or her mother.

Although this approach may clarify links between attachment and friendship, it introduces a complication in the assessment of friendship because the friend dyad, rather than the individual child, becomes the unit of study. This seems appropriate given that friendship is conceived of as a dyadic relationship. One could, of course, separately code the behavior of each dyad member (e.g., Gottman, 1983). However, given that the behavior of two people interacting is not independent, this is a viable solution only if one is interested in studying sequential patterns of behavior between dyad members. One could not, for instance, code the behavior of both members of a secure–insecure friend pair and treat the observations as independent. An alternative approach would be to code the behavior of the friend dyad. In my work, I have addressed this problem by developing behavioral coding schemes in which the friend dyad is used as the unit of description. Thus, an observer is asked to rate the degree to which a behavioral characteristic (e.g., responsiveness) is descriptive of a particular dyad. One advantage of this approach is that dyadic properties of interaction that cannot be described with reference to one individual, such as cohesiveness or balance of power, can be rated. In addition, this approach takes into consideration the behavior of each dyad member and thereby avoids the problem of describing a dyadic relationship with reference to one person's behavior.

A dyadic approach was used in a second study examining links between child–mother attachment security and friendship quality among 10–12 year-old best friend pairs. The Security Scale was used to measure security of mother–child attachment. Scale scores were used to classify children as securely or insecurely attached. Associations between attachment and friendship were examined by comparing secure–secure and secure–insecure friend pairs. Self-report and observational techniques were used to assess friendship quality. Children completed three subscales from the Network of Relationships Inventory (Buhrmester & Furman, 1987; Furman & Buhrmester, 1985; Furman & Buhrmester, 1992), which assessed companionship, intimacy, and affection. Reports of the children were averaged to obtain dyad scores for these variables. Children were also videotaped talking about two topics: their mothers and kids they both know. Observers later rated the tapes for intimacy, responsiveness, and criticism.

The secure–secure friend pairs reported higher levels of companionship in their friendship than did the secure–insecure pairs. The groups did not differ on reports of intimacy or affection in the friendship. Thus, as with the other study discussed earlier, there was evidence that attachment security is related to perceptions of companionship in friendship.

The associations between attachment and qualitative ratings of behavior during the conversations depended on the conversation topic. When talking about their mothers, secure–secure pairs were less critical than secure–insecure pairs. For ratings of intimacy, there was an interaction between attachment and gender. An examination of the group means indicated that the conversations of secure–insecure girls were the most intimate and the conversations of secure–insecure boys were the least intimate. The secure–insecure boy and girl pairs displayed moderate levels of intimacy. The finding that secure–insecure boys engaged in less intimate conversations about their mothers is consistent with the suggestion that securely attached children are more open and at ease when communicating about intimate topics (Bretherton, 1987). The high levels of intimacy for secure–insecure girls appeared to be due to their choice of topics: These pairs tended to discuss intimate information in the context of criticizing their mothers. For example, some secure–insecure girls discussed times they felt rejected by their mothers. This interpretation is supported by the fact that scores on criticism and intimacy were correlated for girls but not for boys.

Although there were no group differences on responsiveness ratings when children talked about their mothers, secure–secure friend pairs were more responsive than secure–insecure pairs were when discussing kids they both knew. Observers noted that the children seemed more at ease and relaxed when discussing the "kids" topic and this may have contributed to finding a difference for the responsiveness category. The attachment groups did not differ on ratings of intimacy or criticism when discussing other children.

In summary, the study of friend dyads suggests that child–mother attachment has implications for both children's perceptions of and interactions in friendship. The findings also point to one of the complications in using behavioral assessments of friendship: The context may influence the nature of the interaction and therefore the individual differences that are most salient. Is attachment related to intimacy in friendship in preadolescence? The observational results suggest the answer depends in part on what topic children discuss. Similarly, evidence of a link between mother–child attachment and responsiveness was found only when children were asked to discuss kids they knew. Additional use of multiple assessments of friendship, with observations of friends in different contexts, will be needed to clarify the exact nature of the links between attachment and friendship quality in middle childhood.

## Conclusions

A review of the literature suggests a number of conclusions about child–mother attachment and friendship. Earlier work had documented that attachment security in the child–mother relationship is positively associated with peer competence when children are observed interacting with strangers or acquaintances. More recent work (Park & Waters, 1989; Troy & Sroufe, 1987) demonstrates that attachment security predicts the quality of particular relationships formed by peers. Associations between attachment and peer relationship quality have been found most consistently when investigators have varied the security combination of friendship dyads. For example, interactions of secure–secure friend dyads are more positive than the interactions of secure–insecure friend dyads (Park & Waters, 1989).

Given the ample evidence of links between attachment and peer relationships in young children, it seems timely to move the field forward by studying links between child–mother attachment and the peer system in middle childhood. Children are in need of an attachment figure across childhood, even though the frequency and intensity of attachment behaviors decline and physical proximity becomes less important (Bowlby, 1979, 1982; Main & Cassidy, 1988). As physical availability becomes less important, children's expectations about an attachment figure's accessibility and responsiveness become more important (Bowlby, 1982). The studies reported in this chapter suggest that children's reports of the attachment relationship in middle childhood have a meaningful set of correlates. In particular, attachment security was associated with the quality of peer relationships. For example, children reporting a more secure attachment to their mothers were more responsive when interacting with friends and reported more companionship in friendship. Thus, it appears that there are links between child–mother attachment and the peer system in middle childhood.

A number of questions were raised that cannot presently be answered. This chapter focused on the developmental significance of child–mother attachment and ignored how other relationships within the family may influence friendship. For example, given the similarities between peer and sibling interaction, it could be that children learn from siblings how to relate to peers. Consistent with this hypothesis, Gruys, Park, and Kelleher (1992) found that the warmth and closeness of a preschooler's closest sibling relationship predicted the quality of that child's friendships at preschool. A more comprehensive understanding of how family relationships influence children's friendships requires a consideration of different types of family relationships.

Second, the findings suggest that a variety of methodological approaches are needed to map the links between child–mother attachment and friendship. In part, this requires using different data collection techniques. Use of observational as well as self-report techniques to assess both child–mother attachment and friendship would provide different perspectives on how attachment and friendship are linked. Different techniques are needed in part because some techniques are more suited for measuring particular relationship qualities. In addition, the two techniques provide descriptions at a different level of analysis: Self-report techniques typically provide for more global assessments whereas observational techniques are more sensitive to the influence of context.

At a more conceptual level, it will be necessary to develop assessment tools that can capture the dyadic nature of friendship. For the most part, tools to assess friendship tap an individual's perspective on friendship. If friendships are conceptualized as dyadic, then dyadic assessments would provide a closer match between theory and measurement.

Third, the research documenting age-related changes in friendship serves as a reminder that friendship has a different meaning to children in early childhood, middle childhood, and adolescence. These changes may have some effect on the nature of the links between attachment and friendship. Testing the hypothesis that links between attachment and friendship may change with age will require studying multiple- rather than single-age groups.

Finally, the links between child–mother attachment and friendship described in this chapter are not an explanation but represent associations to be explained (Waters et al., 1991). That is, finding that child–mother attachment predicts friendship quality does not explain development; there is still a need to search for mechanisms and to examine plausible third variables that may account for associations between attachment and friendship. It may be easier to identify mechanisms once there is further documentation of how a child's tie to mother is related to the quality of a child's friendships.

## References

Ainsworth, M. D. S. (1990). Epilogue: Some considerations regarding theory and assessment relevant to attachments beyond infancy. In M. T. Greenberg, D. Cicchetti, & E. M. Cummings (Eds.), *Attachment in the preschool years* (pp. 463–488). Chicago: University of Chicago Press.

Ainsworth, M. D. S., Blehar, M.C., Waters, E., & Wall, S. (1978). *Patterns of attachment: A psychological study of the Strange Situation.* Hillsdale, NJ: Erlbaum.

Asher, S. R., Hymel, S., & Renshaw, P. R. (1984). Loneliness in children. *Child Development, 55,* 1456–1464.

Berndt, T. J. (1982). The features and effects of friendship in early adolescence. *Child Development, 53,* 1447–1460.

Berndt, T. J., & Hoyle, S. G. (1985). Stability and change in childhood and adolescent friendships. *Developmental Psychology, 21,* 1007–1015.

Bowlby, J. (1973). *Attachment and loss: Vol. 2. Separation: Anxiety and Anger.* New York: Basic Books.

Bowlby, J. (1979). *The making and breaking of affectional bonds.* New York: Tavistock.

Bowlby, J. (1982). *Attachment and loss: Vol. 1. Attachment.* New York: Basic Books.

Bretherton, I. (1985). Attachment theory: Retrospect and prospect. In I. Bretherton & E. Waters (Eds.), *Monographs of the SRCD, 50* (Serial No. 209).

Bretherton, I. (1987). New perspectives on attachment relations: Security, communication, and internal working models. In J. D. Osofsky (Ed.), *Handbook of infant development* (2nd ed.) (pp. 1061–1100). New York: Wiley.

Buhrmester, D. (1990). Intimacy of friendship, interpersonal competence, and adjustment during preadolescence and adolescence. *Child Development, 61,* 1101–1111.

Buhrmester, D., & Furman, W. (1986). The changing functions of friends in childhood: A neo-Sullivanian perspective. In V. J. Derlaga & B. A. Winstead (Eds.), *Friendship in social interaction* (pp. 41–62). New York: Springer-Verlag.

Buhrmester, D., & Furman, W. (1987). The development of companionship and intimacy. *Child Development, 58,* 1101–1113.

Bukowski, W. M., & Hoza, B. (1989). Popularity and friendship: Issues in theory, measurement, and outcome. In T. J. Berndt & G. W. Ladd (Eds.), *Peer relationships in child development* (pp. 15–45). New York: Wiley.

Cohn, D. A. (1990). Child–mother attachment of six-year-olds and social competence at school. *Child Development, 61,* 152–162.

Easterbrooks, M. A., & Goldberg, W. A. (1990). Security of toddler–parent attachment: Relation to children's sociopersonality functioning during kindergarten. In M. T. Greenberg, D. Cicchetti, & E. M. Cummings (Eds.), *Attachment in the preschool years* (pp. 221–244). Chicago: University of Chicago Press.

Elicker, J., Englund, M., & Sroufe, L. A. (1992). Predicting peer competence and peer relationships in childhood from early parent–child relationships. In R. Parke & G. Ladd (Eds.), *Family–peer relationships: Modes of linkage* (pp. 77–106). Hillsdale, NJ: Erlbaum.

Foot, H. C., Chapman, A. J., & Smith, J. R. (1977). Friendship and social responsiveness in boys and girls. *Journal of Personality and Social Psychology, 35,* 401–411.

Freud, S. (1949). *An outline of psycho-analysis.* New York: Norton.

Freud, A., & Dann, S. (1976). An experiment in group upbringing. In A. Skolnick (Ed.), *Rethinking childhood* (pp. 287–317). Boston, MA: Little, Brown, and Company.

Furman, W., & Buhrmester, D. (1985). Children's perceptions of the personal relationships in their social networks. *Developmental Psychology, 21*, 1016–1024.

Furman, W., & Buhrmester, D. (1992). Age and sex differences in perceptions of networks of personal relationships. *Child Development, 63*, 103–115.

Gottman, J. M. (1983). How children become friends. *Monographs of the SRCD, 48* (Serial No. 201).

Gottman, J., & Mettetal, G. (1986). Speculations about social and affective development: Friendship and acquaintanceship through adolescence. In J. M. Gottman & J. G. Parker (Eds.), *Conversations of friends* (pp. 192–237). New York: Cambridge University Press.

Grossman, K. E., & Grossman, K. (1991). Attachment quality as an organizer of emotional and behavioral responses in a longitudinal perspective. In C. M. Parkes, J. Stevenson-Hinde, & P. Marris (Eds.), *Attachment across the life cycle* (pp. 93–114). London: Routledge.

Gruys, A. K., Park, K. A., & Kelleher, T. A. (1992). Links between qualities of sibling and peer relationships in preschoolers. Paper presented at the American Psychological Association Annual Conference, Washington, D.C.

Harter, S. (1982). The perceived competence scale for children. *Child Development, 53*, 87–97.

Hartup, W. W. (1986). On relationships and development. In W. W. Hartup & Z. Rubin (Eds.), *Relationships and development* (pp. 1–26). Hillsdale, NJ: Erlbaum.

Hartup, W. W. (1989). Behavioral manifestations of children's friendships. In T. J. Berndt & G. W. Ladd (Eds.), *Peer relationships in child development* (pp. 46–70). New York: Wiley.

Hartup, W. W., Laursen, B., Stewart, M. I., & Eastenson, A. (1988). Conflict and friendship relations of young children. *Child Development, 59*, 1590–1600.

Hartup, W. W., & Sancilio, M. F. (1986). Children's friendships. In E. Schopler & G. B. Mesibor (Eds.), *Social behavior in autism* (pp. 61–79). New York: Plenum.

Hinde, R. A. (1979). *Towards understanding relationships*. New York: Academic Press.

Howes, C. (1983). Patterns of friendship. *Child Development, 54*, 1041–1053.

Howes, C. (1988). Peer interaction of young children. *Monographs of the SRCD, 53* (Serial No. 217).

Jacobson, J. L., & Wille, D. E. (1986). The influence of attachment pattern on developmental changes in peer interaction from the toddler to the preschool period. *Child Development, 57*, 338–347.

Kerns, K.A. (1994). A developmental model of the relations between mother–child attachment and friendship. In R. Erber & R. Gilmour (Eds.), *Theoretical frameworks for personal relationships* (pp. 129–156). Hillsdale, NJ: Erlbaum.

Kestenbaum, R., Farber, E. A., & Sroufe, L. A. (1989). Individual differences in empathy among preschoolers: Relation to attachment history. In N. Eisenberg (Ed.), *New directions for child development, 44*, 51–64.

LaFreniere, P., & Sroufe, L. A. (1985). Profiles of peer competence in the preschool: Interrelations between measures, influence of social ecology, and relation to attachment history. *Developmental Psychology, 21*, 56–68.

Lieberman, A. F. (1977). Preschoolers' competence with a peer: Relations with attachment and peer experience. *Child Development, 48*, 1277–1287.

Lewis, M., & Feiring, C. (1989). Early predictors of childhood friendship. In T. J. Berndt & G. W. Ladd (Eds.), *Peer relationships in child development* (pp. 246–273). New York: Wiley.

Maccoby, E. E., & Martin, J. A. (1983). Socialization in the context of the family: parent–child interaction. In P. H. Mussen (Ed.), *Handbook of child psychology* (4th edition), pp. 1–101. New York: Wiley.

McGuire, K. D., & Weisz, J. R. (1982). Social cognition and behavior correlates of preadolescent chumship. *Child Development, 53*, 1478–1484.

Main, M., & Cassidy, J. (1988). Categories of response to reunion with the parent at age 6: Predictable from infant attachment classifications and stable over a 1-month period. *Developmental Psychology, 24,* 415–426.

Main, M., Kaplan, N., & Cassidy, J. (1985). Security in infancy, childhood, and adulthood: A move to the level of representation. In I. Bretherton & E. Waters (Eds.), *Monographs of the SRCD, 50* (Serial No. 209).

Main, M., & Weston, D. R. (1981). The quality of the toddler's relationship to mother and to father: Related to conflict behavior and the readiness to establish new relationships. *Child Development, 52,* 932–940.

Mannarino, A. P. (1980). The development of children's friendships. In H. C. Foot, A. J. Chapaman, & J. R. Smith (Eds.), *Friendship and social relations in children* (pp. 45–63). Chichester, England: Wiley.

Park, K. A. (1992). Preschoolers' reactions to loss of a best friend: Developmental trends and individual differences. *Child Study Journal, 22,* 233–252.

Park, K. A., & Hazan, C. (1990). Correlates of attachment security and self-worth in middle childhood. Paper presented at the International Conference on Personal Relationships, Oxford, England.

Park, K. A., Lay, K. L., & Ramsay, L. (1993). Individual differences and developmental changes in preschoolers' friendships. *Developmental Psychology, 29,* 264–270.

Park, K. A., & Waters, E. (1989). Security of attachment and preschool friendships. *Child Development, 60,* 1076–1081.

Parke, R. D., MacDonald, K. B., Burks, V. M., Carson, J., Bhavnagri, N., Barth, J., Beitel, A. (1989). Family and peer systems: In search of the linkages. In K. Kreppner & M. Lerner (Eds.), *Family systems of life-span development* (pp. 65–92). Hillsdale, NJ: Erlbaum.

Parker, J., & Asher, S. (1993). Friendship and friendship quality in middle childhood: Links with peer group acceptance and feelings of loneliness and social dissatisfaction. *Developmental Psychology, 29,* 611–621.

Parker, J., & Gottman, J. M. (1989). Social and emotional development in a relational context. In T. J. Berndt & G. W. Ladd (Eds.), *Peer relationships in child development* (pp. 95–131). New York: Wiley.

Pastor, D. L. (1981). The quality of mother–infant attachment and its relationship to toddler initial sociability with peers. *Developmental Psychology, 17,* 323–335.

Putallaz, M., & Heflin, A. H. (1990). Parent–child interaction. In S. R. Asher & J. D. Coie (Eds.), *Peer rejection in childhood* (pp. 189–216). New York: Cambridge University Press.

Selman, R. L. (1980). The child as friendship philosopher. In S. R. Asher & J. M. Gottman (Eds.), *The development of children's friendships* (pp. 242–272). New York: Cambridge University Press.

Sharabany, R., Gershoni, R., & Hofman, J. E. (1981). Girlfriend, boyfriend: Age and sex differences in intimate friendship. *Developmental Psychology, 17,* 800–808.

Sroufe, L. A. (1983). Infant–caregiver attachment and patterns of adaptation in preschool: The roots of maladaptation and competence. In M. Perlmutter (Ed.), *Minnesota symposium in child psychology* (Vol. 16, pp. 41–81). Hillsdale, NJ: Erlbaum.

Sroufe, L. A. (1990). An organizational perspective on the self. In D. Cicchetti & M. Beeghly (Eds.), *The self in transition: Infancy to childhood* (pp. 281–307). Chicago: University of Chicago Press.

Sroufe, L. A., & Fleeson, J. (1986). Attachment and the construction of relationships. In W. W. Hartup & Z. Rubin (Eds.), *Relationships and development* (pp. 57–71). Hillsdale, NJ: Erlbaum.

Sroufe, L. A., & Waters, E. (1977). Attachment as an organizational construct. *Child Development, 48,* 1184–1199.

Suess, G. J., Grossman, K. E., & Sroufe, L. A. (1992). Effects of infant attachment to mother and father on quality of adaptation in preschool: From dyadic to individual organization of self. *International Journal of Behavioral Development, 15,* 43–65.

Sullivan, H. S. (1953). *The interpersonal theory of psychiatry.* New York: Norton.

Troy, M., & Sroufe, L. A. (1987). Victimization among preschoolers: Role of attachment history. *American Academy of Child and Adolescent Psychiatry, 26,* 166–172.

Turner, P. J. (1991). Relations between attachment, gender, and behavior with peers in preschool. *Child Development, 62,* 1475–1488.

Vaughn, B. E., & Waters, E. (1990). Attachment behavior at home and in the laboratory: Q-sort observations and Strange Situation classifications of one-year-olds. *Child Development, 61,* 1965–1973.

Vespo, J. E. (1991). Features of preschoolers' relationships. *Early Child Development and Care, 68,* 19–26.

Waters, E., & Deane, K. E. (1985). Defining and assessing individual differences in attachment relationships: Q-methodology and the organization of behavior in infancy and early childhood. In I. Bretherton & E. Waters (Eds.), *SRCD Monographs, 50* (Serial No. 209).

Waters, E., Kondo-Ikemura, K., Posada, G., & Richters, J. E. (1991). Learning to love: Milestones and mechanisms in attachment, identity, and identification. In M. Gunnar (Ed.), *Minnesota symposium on child psychology* (Vol. 24, pp. 217–255). Hillsdale, NJ: Erlbaum.

Waters, E., Wippman, J., & Sroufe, L. A. (1979). Attachment, positive affect, and competence in the peer group: Two studies in construct validation. *Child Development, 50,* 821–829.

Youngblade, L. M., & Belsky, J. (1992). Parent–child antecedents of 5-year-olds' close friendships: A longitudinal analysis. *Developmental Psychology, 28,* 700–713.

Youngblade, L. M., Park, K. A., & Belsky, J. (1993). Measurement of young children's close friendship: A comparison of 2 independent assessment systems and their associations with attachment security. *International Journal of Behavioral Development, 16,* 563–587.

# 8 Need fulfillment, interpersonal competence, and the developmental contexts of early adolescent friendship

*Duane Buhrmester*

Children's and adolescents' friendships are played out within nested sets of contexts. Although the notion of "contexts" commonly refers to situational settings, social strata, or cultures, in this chapter I explore three somewhat different types of contexts. The first, and most pervasive, is the developmental context in which friendship takes place. Children face a series of developmental tasks or issues, each of which serves as a context for friendship. Here I consider some of the developmental issues that children of different ages face and I explore how friendships feed into, and grow out of, these developmental issues. The second context is a child's network of interpersonal relationships. Children are involved in networks of personal relationships with parents, siblings, teachers, friends, and peer groups. I examine where close friendships fit within the overall organization of social relationships and consider the unique contributions friendships make to development. The third context is that of gender. The important differences in the social developmental pathways of girls and boys appear to be especially pronounced in friendship. In this chapter I consider the ways that the social worlds of girls' and boys' friendships differ and speculate about the roles these differences might play in the development of gender-linked characteristics of children that extend beyond friendship.

It would be difficult to fully address this broad set of issues in one book chapter. My goal, therefore, is to address these broader issues as they come to bear on two more focused questions. First, what role do friendships play in fulfilling social needs? The focus here is on understanding the *immediate ongoing impact* that friendships have on children's daily socioemotional lives. Second, what role do friendships play in the development of the social competencies called for in mature close relationships? The focus here is on the longer-term *formative impact* that friendships have on the developing child (Hartup, in press).

The formative and immediate impacts of friendships are closely intertwined

158

with one another. Accordingly, it is important to consider them in the same chapter. On the one hand, the levels of social competence that children bring to peer relationships affect their likelihood of succeeding at forging friendships that satisfy, rather than frustrate, personal needs. That is, the formative influences of past relationships with friends (as well as with family members) have shaped the competencies that determine ongoing outcomes of friendship and their immediate impact on socioemotional adjustment. On the other hand, ongoing experiences with friends cumulatively constitute their formative influence. Responses by friends that satisfy personal needs serve to reinforce competent behavior patterns, whereas responses by friends that frustrate needs prompt the development of alternative patterns of behaving and coping. In short, need fulfillment and interpersonal competence reciprocally affect one another over both the short and long run.

Questions concerning need fulfillment and interpersonal competence have been the focus of my program of research over the past several years. The conceptual impetus for this work finds its roots in the work of H. S. Sullivan (1953). Because I have rather freely modified Sullivan's ideas and wed them with those of other theorists, my conceptual orientation is better viewed as "neo-Sullivanian," and is not strictly limited to Sullivan's original formulations.

This chapter is organized into two major sections, the first dealing with the need-fulfilling role of friendship, and the second focusing on the role friendship plays in the development of interpersonal competence. Each section considers, in turn, the developmental, network, and gender contexts of friendships.

## Friendship and need fulfillment

Many of the important theories of psychology argue that human behavior is organized around striving to fulfill a number of basic needs. Several theorists have emphasized the importance of *social needs* (e.g., Adler, 1927; Maslow, 1971; Murray, 1938). H. S. Sullivan (1953), in particular, argued that social needs for tenderness, companionship, acceptance, and intimacy organize interpersonal relationships and individuals' personalities. The core assumption of this formulation is that people need certain forms of social input or social interaction to remain happy and psychologically healthy. Positive regard, loving affection, entertaining interaction, and assistance in coping with stress are all examples of social inputs that are experienced as rewarding and needed for well-being. Robert Weiss (1974) describes these inputs as "social provisions" that are "exchanged" either directly through specific aspects of social discourse and less directly through the attitudes and meanings that are conveyed through interactions.

An additional assumption of the social needs formulation is that when social life fails to supply these provisions, people experience different forms of personal distress and maladjustment. The form of distress depends on the particular need in question. For example, lack of positive regard from significant others leaves a person with a low sense of self-esteem and a sense of worthlessness (Rogers, 1951). Similarly, absence of a personal audience with whom to disclose intimate aspects of oneself gives rise to a sense of social isolation and loneliness (Weiss, 1974). Sullivan assumed that people's personalities and forms of psychopathology are outgrowths of the ways they develop either to satisfy their social needs, or to defend themselves against the pain and anxiety caused by failing to address those needs.

Social needs, however, are only part of the picture. Indeed, many theorists believe that there are two broad categories of human needs (see McAdams, 1988, for a more complete review). Theorists such as Freud (1933), Angyal (1941), Bakan (1966), and McAdams (1985) argue that one cluster of needs or motives is directed toward gaining *agency, power, and excitement*, whereas the other cluster is directed toward gaining *communion, intimacy, and love*. The former needs are individualistic in nature (referred to in this chapter as "agentic" needs) and the latter needs are social or interpersonal in nature (referred to here as "communal" needs; Bakan, 1966). This dualism has variously been described in terms of death (aggressive) and life (erotic) instincts (Freud, 1933), needs for autonomy and surrender (Angyal, 1941), striving for superiority and social interest (Adler, 1927), and the ethics of individuation and interdependence (Gilligan, 1982).

In a recent series of studies of adults, Karen Prager and I investigated the empirical validity of these two broad categories of needs (Prager & Buhrmester, 1992). We identified 20 personal needs that major personality, social-psychological, and developmental theorists have described as common human needs. Factor analysis of need satisfaction ratings, as well as cluster analysis of similarity judgments, revealed three superordinant clusters or dimensions of personal needs. Table 8.1 presents the results of a factor analysis of 20 multi-item rating scales assessing need satisfaction. In general, the observed factor structure supports the dualistic perspective. The first factor represents agentic needs, such as needs for achievement, power/authority, recognition/status, approval/acceptance, autonomy, identity, and self-esteem. The second factor represents communal needs, such as needs for affection/love, intimacy, support, companionship, nurturance, fun/enjoyment, and sexual fulfillment. Whereas the first factor captures the concerns discussed by Erikson (1968) and Veroff and Veroff (1980), the second factor includes the social needs and provisions described by Sullivan (1953) and Weiss (1974). In this analysis a third factor represents needs that are less psychological than those in the first two factors. This factor seems to capture basic physical or "survival" needs, including needs for physical

Table 8.1. *Rotated factor coefficients for adults' ratings of satisfaction with 20 personal needs*

| | Factors | | |
|---|---|---|---|
| Need scales | Agentic needs | Communal needs | Survival needs |
| Self-esteem | .94 | — | — |
| Identity | .93 | — | — |
| Self-actualization | .92 | — | — |
| Meaning/purpose | .92 | — | — |
| Power/authority | .86 | — | — |
| Structure/control | .81 | — | — |
| Achievement | .77 | — | — |
| Recognition/status | .71 | — | — |
| Approval/acceptance | .65 | — | — |
| Money | .53 | — | — |
| Autonomy | .51 | — | — |
| Sexual fulfillment | — | .95 | — |
| Affection/love | — | .87 | — |
| Intimacy | — | .75 | — |
| Receive support | — | .70 | — |
| Provide nurturance | .37 | .55 | — |
| Companionship | .36 | .50 | — |
| Fun/enjoyment | .35 | .48 | — |
| Physical safety | — | — | .93 |
| Health/shelter/food | — | — | .72 |

*Note*: Each need scale score was based on 5 to 6 Likert-type items. Coefficients are factor pattern weights from an obliquely rotated principal axis factor analysis. Coefficients less than .30 are deleted for clarity. Factor intercorrelations: Agentic-Communal, $r = .59$; Agentic-Survival, $r = .50$; and Communal-Survival, $r = .37$.

safety, food, health, and shelter. Maslow (1971) suggests that needs falling in the communal and agentic clusters become prominent only after physical well-being needs have been addressed.

Social life seems to involve a dynamic interplay between the pursuit of agentic and communal forms of satisfaction (Cantor & Malley, 1991; Carson, 1979; Shaver & Buhrmester, 1983). In some instances, agentic and communal needs may be in direct competition with one another, such as when beating a friend in a game brings individual glory at the expense of hard feelings in the friendship. In other instances, agentic and communal aims are in concert with one another, such as when a team victory simultaneously engenders an agentic sense of achievement for each individual team member, along with a communal sense of close comradeship among teammates. Moreover, successful living, within this framework, involves behaving in ways that balance the satisfaction of both agentic and communal needs (Bakan, 1966; Carson, 1979).

## The developmental context of need fulfillment

When viewed from a developmental perspective, it appears that there are changes over the life course in the salience of different needs, especially during childhood and adolescence (Veroff & Veroff, 1980). Sullivan (1953) provided a speculative developmental timetable of when different social needs "emerge" or initially make themselves evident during childhood (see Buhrmester & Furman, 1986). Briefly, he contended that: (a) infants have a strong need for tender contact from caregivers (i.e., security); (b) toddlers and preschoolers develop a need to have other people co-participate with them in playful and entertaining activities; (c) children in the early elementary-school years develop a need to be accepted by, and have status within, the peer group; (d) preadolescents acquire an increased desire for interpersonal intimacy; and (e) adolescents experience a heightened desire for sexual involvement.

Other theorists have speculated about the developmental emergence of agentic needs (e.g., Erikson, 1968; Veroff & Veroff, 1980). For example, Erikson (1968) argued that concerns about autonomy intensify in the second year of life, followed, in succession, by unfolding concerns about initiative, industry (achievement), and identity. He characterized development within each period as being organized around these preoccupying issues or "crises," the resolution of which bear on the child's evolving sense of individuality (Franz & White, 1985). Although Erikson did not refer to these as needs per se, it is clear from his description that each preoccupying issue motivates children to seek out particular outcomes or forms of feedback that bear on the issue at hand. As will be made clear in a moment, this is precisely the sense in which I wish to employ the concept of "need."

Although assertions about developmental sequences of emerging needs are intuitively appealing, few studies have investigated developmental changes in needs empirically (Buhrmester & Furman, 1987). One factor impeding research has been the conceptual ambiguities surrounding the construct of "need." For example, Sullivan did not clearly define the construct of need, and said little about whether the developmental emergence of needs was controlled by endogenous or exogenous factors. Whereas the long history of motivational concepts like needs and motives in psychological theorizing attests to their intuitive appeal (Cofer & Appely, 1964; Hall & Lindzey, 1970), this long history also means that the constructs carry several meanings that can confuse our contemporary usage.

There are at least two general ways the construct of need has been employed.

First, the concept has been used to connote an internal "drive" that explains behavior. For example, Henry Murray (1938) conceptualized needs and motives as "internal forces" that causally energize and direct thought and behavior; in this usage, needs and motives are used to "explain" individual differences in behavior and personality. Second, the concept of need has been used more descriptively. Abraham Maslow (1971) used this concept to describe how people seemingly "need" to resolve certain categories of issues and concerns (e.g., basic concerns about food, shelter, and safety) before they become preoccupied with other categories of issues and concerns (e.g., social belongingness, self-esteem, etc.). Maslow did not use the concept of need to denote hypothetical internal forces or drives, but rather uses the concept as a heuristic means of describing categories of concerns and outcomes to which people attend.

Maslow's descriptive usage of needs as "preoccupying concerns" seems to be compatible with contemporary psychological models, whereas the explanatory usage of needs as "internal energizing forces" is based on the outdated drive theory of motivation (Cantor & Malley, 1991). Indeed, the conceptualization of needs as preoccupying concerns is consistent with cognitively oriented theories of social learning and personality (Bandura, 1986; Mischel, 1980), with social-cognitive concepts of plans, goals, and strategies (Cantor & Malley, 1991; Fiske & Taylor, 1991), and with attachment theory's concept that level of preoccupation about "felt security" is a central feature of "internal working models" of relationships (Sroufe & Fleeson, 1986). In my own work, and throughout this chapter, I view needs in this descriptive sense as sets of preoccupying concerns rather than as the internal drive states.

What does it mean, then, to say that needs "emerge" over the course of development? In general terms, children acquire new needs in the sense that they become preoccupied with new issues and concerns. That is, to the extent that emergent issues or concerns prompt youngsters to seek out new classes of communal or agentic inputs to address those concerns, a "need" for a new form of social input can be said to have emerged. In Sullivan's developmental scheme, for example, the infant's preoccupation about issues of security embodies a need to be treated tenderly by parents; similarly, the juvenile's preoccupation with social involvement and status comprises a need to be accepted by the peer group. In each case, children come to need a new type of social input or social provision that directly speaks to an emergent set of concerns.

What, then, controls the substance and developmental timing of emerging concerns and needs? Figure 8.1 depicts some of the possible factors involved. It is very unlikely that one single factor, such as "maturation" or "experience," is solely responsible. Rather, a complex interplay of multiple factors including biological maturation, cognitive development, cultural expectations, and individuals' histories of experiences probably converge to influence the issues and

Figure 8.1. Developmental emergence of concerns, needs, and relationship features.

concerns that youngsters are consciously and unconsciously preoccupied with at any point in development. For example, what Sullivan described as the emergence of the need for intimacy during preadolescence seems, in reality, to be a coalescence of several issues that achieve prominence at this time, including concerns about social self-definition and social validation that are dealt with through private and self-revealing conversations (Buhrmester & Prager, 1995). The timing of the emergence of the need for intimate confidants seems linked to a number of factors, including pubertal maturation, the growth of formal-operational cognitive abilities to reflect on oneself more abstractly, and cultural values that encourage individual identity exploration through conversation with others. In this sense, then, the substance of children's needs and the timing of their emergence are controlled by the full array of factors that influence children's concerns.

Given this conceptual framework, one task for developmental researchers is to identify normative developmental changes in the issues that are of preoccupying concern to youngsters. To date, little research has been designed to directly gain such information. In one pioneering study, Gottman and his colleagues analyzed the thematic content of children's naturalistic conversations with friends and identified developmental changes in the themes and concerns that dominated children's conversations (Gottman & Mettetal, 1986; Parker & Gottman, 1989). They found that in early childhood, maximizing excitement and entertainment through coordinated play was the focal concern. During middle childhood, the focal concerns of inclusion by peers, avoidance of rejection, and self-presentation become central themes in evaluative gossip between friends. In early adolescence, emergent concerns about self-exploration and self-definition lead to considerable self-disclosure and supportive problem solving among friends. It is interesting that these findings closely parallel, in many respects, Sullivan's account of emerging social needs. The progression from play modulation, to inclusion by peers, to self-exploration is very similar to Sullivan's description of the emerging needs for co-participation in play, peer-group acceptance, and intimate exchange, respectively.

More research is needed to document developmental changes in the concerns and needed types of social input that organize youths' social lives. A variety of research methodologies could be employed toward this end. Projective techniques like the Thematic Apperception Test (TAT) may be useful for identifying the issues and concerns that preoccupy children's conscious and unconscious thoughts (McAdams, 1984). In addition, thought and activity sampling techniques, like the Experience Sampling Method developed by Csikszentmihalyi and Larson (1984), may also prove useful.

In what ways, then, do developmental changes in social needs act as a context for changes in friendships? The general answer is rather straightforward: Developing concerns and needs dictate, to a sizable degree, the social provisions and relationship features that are sought in friendship. That is, the nature of friendship changes as youngsters seek different types of social input to address their changing concerns and needs. Gottman and his colleagues' study nicely illustrates the links between friendship and developing concerns and needs. During each stage of development, the central features and interactional qualities of friendship change in tandem with the issues and concerns that are at the forefront of individual development. Since children who are friends are typically preoccupied with similar developmental issues, their friendships provide them with a unique opportunity to wrestle with the issues of most central concern to them both.

At this juncture, it is worth noting that all of my own empirical work (as well as the bulk of the work in the field) has been done with American children, teenagers, and adults, who are mainly of lower-middle-class to upper-middle-class economic backgrounds. Although the samples in my studies have been somewhat heterogeneous in terms of the ethnic/racial backgrounds of participants (i.e., 15% to 35% combined African-American, Hispanic, and Asian participants), the small samples of specific subpopulations have made it impossible to make meaningful comparisons among different ethnic/racial and socioeconomic subgroups. As such, the conclusions derived from the reported data throughout this chapter cannot reasonably be generalized beyond the types of populations studied. At a conceptual level, I do not assume that friendship phenomena are universal across cultures or subcultures. Rather, as suggested in Figure 8.1, I expect that the issues and concerns out of which the needs for friends grow vary from one culture or subculture to another.

## The changing role of friendship in the social network

I now turn to discuss the nature of changes that occur in friendship within the broader context of youths' networks of social relationships. Robert Weiss (1974) emphasized that people are embedded in a network of social relationships, and that any one social need can be addressed through relationships with any of a number of different network members, but that different types of relationships are specialized in how effectively they supply particular social provisions. For example, he thought friends especially depend on each other for entertaining companionship and intimacy, whereas parents and children depend upon each other to address needs for attachment and nurturance, respectively. Moreover, the role that any particular type of relationship plays in socioemotional life can be understood according to the profile of need-fulfilling provisions that are sought from it.

What role, then, do friends play in fulfilling needs? Perhaps the single most important and unchanging function of friends across the entire life course is the fulfillment of needs for enjoyable companionship (Savin-Williams & Berndt, 1990). Even infants and toddlers turn to peers for stimulation and excitement (Howes, 1987). During childhood, adolescence, and adulthood, "playing together," "hanging out," and "doing things together" are consistently reported as among the most important features of friendships (Savin-Williams & Berndt, 1990). It is interesting to note that because this is such an obvious and developmentally constant function of friendship, the provision of companionship has probably not received as much attention by researchers as it deserves, particularly compared to the role of friendship in supplying intimacy.

Most developmentalists have focused their attention on those aspects of friendship that undergo notable change during childhood and adolescence. Sullivan was among the first to describe developmental changes in the need-fulfilling roles of friendships. Some of these changes are brought on by the emergence of new concerns and needs, whereas other changes involve reorganizations in terms of which network members are most depended upon to address established needs. In particular, Sullivan argued that as children enter early adolescence, there is increased impetus to depend on intimate friendships to address social needs.

Within the conceptual framework depicted in Figure 8.1, these changes are viewed as resulting from a number of cognitive, pubertal, and sociocultural changes that take place during early adolescence and that give rise to heightened concerns about social validation, self-clarification, and obtaining coping assistance (Buhrmester & Prager, 1995). These concerns, in turn, lead to changes in the types of interactions and relationship features that teenagers seek in friendship. Young teens come to desire or need intimate confidants with whom they can share and explore their opinions about others and their concerns about themselves (Parker & Gottman, 1989; Harter, 1990). Through conversation and action, friends can consensually validate one another's opinions about peers and about themselves. Because such self-revealing disclosures are potentially risky, children come to value "loyal" or "true" friends who will not breech confidences or "talk behind your back," and who will sensitively understand personal admissions (Rawlins, 1992). In short, these emergent concerns increase the need to establish the type of intimate friendships that will address these concerns.

Although Sullivan gave little consideration to family relationships during adolescence, other theorists contend that changes in friendship occur against the backdrop of important changes in family relationships (Blos, 1979; Grotevant & Cooper, 1986; Hill & Holmbeck, 1986; Youniss & Smollar, 1985). Especially during early adolescence, a certain degree of distancing from parents is thought to occur as adolescents become preoccupied with concerns about autonomy and self-governance (Hill & Holmbeck, 1986; Steinberg, 1988). These emergent concerns set in motion a transformation of the dependency structure of parent–child relationships (Youniss & Smollar, 1985). Thus, in theory, dependence on friends to address needs for intimacy and support seems to be increasing at the same time that dependence on parents to address certain needs is decreasing.

Wyndol Furman and I have conducted a number of studies documenting developmental changes in the contributions that friends compared to those mothers, fathers, siblings, and romantic partners make to the fulfillment of communal needs (Buhrmester & Furman, 1987; Furman & Buhrmester, 1985, 1992). Our samples have ranged from second graders up through college freshmen. Recently, as part of her dissertation, Julie Carbery (1993) extended this work by studying three groups of young adults: (a) single adults who were not romantically involved, (b) married adults with no children, and (c) married adults with young children. In each of these studies, participants completed the Network of Relationships Inventory (Furman & Buhrmester, 1985), which includes self-report rating scales assessing each of the seven social provisions described by Robert Weiss (1974).

Figure 8.2 aggregates data from several studies for ratings of intimate self-disclosure to different confidants. The findings for other provisions are somewhat different, but generally follow the same pattern. As can be seen, there is a substantial increase during early and middle adolescence in the *relative* importance of friends as confidants. Reported dependence on friends rises during this period while dependence on parents falls. It is interesting to note that the pattern changes again in young adulthood. Friends' importance relative to spouses as intimate confidants decreases during the married-without-children phase as couples report depending on each other more exclusively to address their needs for intimate disclosure. When offspring enter the picture in the married-with-children phase, there is yet another reshuffling of patterns of dependencies, with friends and parents showing a modest resurgence in importance. Overall, these data suggest that friendships reach their peak of relative importance as intimate confidants during adolescence.

These findings alert us to the systemic nature of developmental changes in

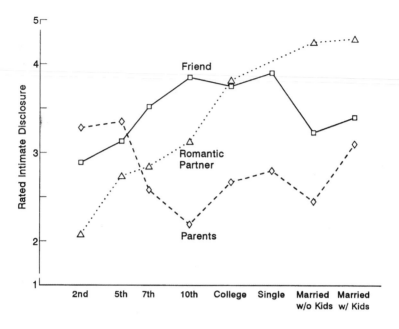

Figure 8.2. Age trends in reported self-disclosure to parents and peers.

social needs and in the network members that are sought to fulfill needs. It is difficult, if not impossible, to fully understand developmental changes in the roles played by friends without simultaneously considering changes in the roles played by other important network members.

*The gender context of friendship*

Not shown in Figure 8.2 are several noteworthy gender differences in the role that friends play in addressing youths' social needs (which will be described shortly). In recent years, an increasing number of theorists have noted the different "cultures" that are manifest in boys' and girls' peer relationships (Brown & Gilligan, 1992; Tannen, 1990). Maccoby (1990) notes that female–female interactions place priority on the building of interpersonal connections, whereas male–male interactions are more directed toward the enhancement of individual status. Maccoby then argues that gender differences in peer relationships represent a powerful socializing influence that shapes the development of these gender-related interaction styles. In addition, she suggests that the socializing influences of peer relationships rivals, and in some respects surpasses, the socializing influence of parents. Because boys and girls segregate themselves by gender starting at an early age, they each experience notably different "peer gender cultures" that actively reinforce and punish gender-norm appropriate and inappropriate patterns of relating, respectively.

It is worth noting that there is nothing in Maccoby's reasoning to suggest that the content of gender norms is in any way innately determined. To the contrary, the assumption is that children naturally seek to discover gender-linked norms present in the broader culture and then actively try to shape their own and their peers' behavior to conform to those norms. In this sense, children socialize one another to conform to what they infer to be the cultural ideal. Because peer and family relationships can represent fairly independent spheres of functioning, it is not surprising that the gender-socializing influence of peers can run counter to the efforts of parents to instill either traditional or nontraditional gender norms.

If Maccoby's contentions are accurate, then the gender of a child and his or her friends would seem to provide a decidedly different context for the development of personal needs: Boys' friendships more extensively focus on agentic concerns and needs, whereas girls' friendships focus more on communal concerns and needs. The gender context of friendship, therefore, is hypothesized to affect personal needs in at least two ways. First, boys' and girls' friendships provide differential opportunities for the fulfillment of needs, with communal needs being more readily met in girls' friendships and agentic needs being more readily met in boys' friendships. Second, boys' and girls' friendships may differentially socialize children's levels of concerns about, and appetites for, agentic and communal outcomes; boys' friendships are likely to foster an increased desire for agentic rewards, whereas girls' friendships are likely to nurture a heightened desire for communal rewards.

Existing empirical findings support the first of these two hypotheses. There is extensive documentation that, beginning in early adolescence, girls report more frequent interactions of an intimate and supportive nature with female friends than boys do with male friends (see Buhrmester & Prager, 1995, for review). Data from our recent study of 200 12- to 15-year-old adolescents illustrate this difference (Buhrmester & Carbery, 1992). Young teenagers were interviewed by telephone each evening over a 5-day period and asked to recount the social events of the preceding 24-hour period. For each interaction lasting 10 minutes or longer, the interviewer recorded the types of partners present (i.e., same-sex friends, parents, siblings, etc.) and then asked subjects to rate the extent of self-disclosure and emotional support that took place using a 7-point scale.

The findings were clearly consistent with the contention that female friendships provide more opportunity than male friendships for the fulfillment of communal needs (see Table 8.2). Females reported somewhat more frequent interactions with friends than males did, and they reported substantially higher

Table 8.2. *Gender differences in adolescents' daily interactions with same-sex friends*

| Daily interaction variables | Males | Females | t | p |
|---|---|---|---|---|
| Number of interactions with all same-sex friends | 5.51 | 7.76 | 2.81 | .001 |
| Number of interactions with best friend | 1.30 | 1.92 | 1.98 | .05 |
| Rated self-disclosure when interacting with best friend | 2.74 | 3.91 | 6.57 | .001 |
| Rated emotional support when interacting with best friend | 3.04 | 4.26 | 5.45 | .001 |

levels of self-disclosure and emotional support than males did in daily interactions. These findings are consistent with those of a good number of other studies.

Although the data are more sparse, there is suggestive evidence supporting the contention that male friendships provide more frequent opportunities for the fulfillment of agentic needs. In contrast to female friendships' "face-to-face" emphasis on talking, Paul Wright (1982) characterizes male friendships as a "side-by-side" orientation focused on doing things together. These shared activities often involve agentic pursuits, chiefly sports and competitive games (Lever, 1976, 1978). When male friends do talk, their discussions often focus on agentically oriented issues, such as the accomplishments of sports figures or the evaluation of peers' prowess in sports and school. Thus, the activity basis and norms of boys' friendships seem more often to put males in situations that directly bear on agentic needs for achievement, recognition, and power.

There is scattered evidence bearing on the second hypothesis that boys' and girls' friendships contribute to the socialization of gender differences in the strength of the appetite for agentic and communal rewards. Two questions are relevant to this hypothesis. First, are there gender differences in the strength of personal needs? Restated in terms of the framework presented in Figure 8.1, do girls evidence greater preoccupation with certain issues and concerns that lead them to have a stronger desire for certain social provisions than boys do (and vice versa)? Second, do gender differences in the socialization experiences that occur in friendships play a causal role in amplifying or attenuating the strength of levels of concern about agentic and communal outcomes?

The layperson's perception is that girls and women have a stronger need to "talk" and seek emotional support than do boys and men (Rosenkrantz, Vogel, Bee, Broverman, & Broverman, 1968). Although there is substantial evidence that women and girls do, in fact, engage in more intimate self-disclosure than men do (at least in interactions with same-sex peers), there is less evidence bearing directly on whether females have a stronger need for intimacy than do males (McAdams, 1984). Girls are more likely than boys to spontaneously mention wanting emotional support and the opportunity for intimate disclosure when they describe an ideal friend (e.g., Bigelow & La Gaipa, 1980). In addition, although few global sex differences have been found in the strength of adults' intimacy motives as measured by TAT stories (McAdams et al., 1984), McAdams and Constantian (1983) found that females reported nearly twice as high a mean percentage of interpersonal thoughts as did men when they were paged at various times of the day and asked to record their thoughts.

At the same time, the layperson's perception is that boys and men have a stronger need to display their agentic prowess in social interaction than do girls and women (Maccoby, 1990). The large disparity between the number of males and the number females participating in organized youth and adult sports reinforces the perception that overt competition is a more pressing concern for males than for females. Again, there is little organized evidence documenting that males are more preoccupied with, or have a stronger need for, establishing their personal efficacy in social relationships than do females. Studies utilizing projective TAT stories find few global gender differences in power motives (McAdams, 1984). However, McAdams and his colleagues did find that males expressed more agentic striving in stories about friendship episodes than did females. More research is clearly needed to determine if, and when, gender differences in the strength of communal and agentic needs manifest themselves during childhood and adolescence.

Assuming for the moment that there are gender differences in the strength of communal and agentic needs, how might friendship play a role in the socialization of these needs? Following Maccoby's reasoning, it seems likely that same-sex friendships play a major role in actively shaping children's appetites for communal and agentic rewards. At least two processes may be involved. First, increased exposure to one type of reward may contribute to a stronger "acquired taste" for that type of outcome. By simple analogy, just as adults acquire a strong "need" for coffee through repeated consumption, so too may the need for agentic or communal outcomes be heightened by repeated exposure. The more frequent exposure to communal rewards afforded by girls' friendships thus may foster a stronger need for communal exchanges, whereas the more frequent exposure to agentic rewards provided through males' friendships may foster stronger agentic concerns and needs.

Second, the norms and expectations that govern boys' and girls' friendships may lead friends to overtly discourage the pursuit of some needs and encourage the pursuit of other needs. Several authors (Brown & Gilligan, 1992; Maccoby, 1990; Tannen, 1990) note that the norms for girls' friendships seem to actively reward intimate self-disclosure and the provision of emotional support, but actively discourage open competition and attempts to draw attention to status differences. In contrast, Maccoby (1990) points out that the agentic style fostered by boys' friendships often runs counter to the building of intimate connections. There is evidence that male–male friendships actively discourage the expression of communal needs through norms prohibiting ''mushy'' sentimentality and the open expression of ''love'' for a male friend (Parker & Gottman, 1989).

At the same time, the norms of male–male friendship may contribute in important ways to the socialization of agentic needs. In general, our culture seems to prize males (and to a lesser extent females) who are motivated toward agentic ends. The pursuit of fulfillment of needs for individual achievement, a clear sense of identity and purpose, and interpersonal influence are valued and rewarded in most Western societies. The greater competitiveness, status-related bantering, and focus on ''doing things together'' (i.e., co-accomplish) of boys' friendships may play an important role in the socialization of agentic motivation. As Lever (1978) pointed out, boys' friendships provide more opportunities than girls' friendships to learn to thrive on playing games with complex rules where winning and losing are at stake. For boys, spending so much time interacting in activities that heavily emphasize agentic issues must, most certainly, contribute to shaping their concerns about, and need for, agentic outcomes. To date, friendship researchers have given only limited attention to the role that friendships play in the socialization of needs and motives. Indeed, even Maccoby (1990) in her discussion of the socializing influence of peers focused mainly on the negative socializing effects of male–male interactions, suggesting that they result in a ''constricting'' and ''derailing'' interaction style. The arguments considered here suggest that researchers should also investigate how boys' friendships contribute to the positive aspects of an agentic orientation.

### Friendship and interpersonal competence

As noted at the outset, the fulfillment of personal needs requires the exercise of competent instrumental action. No matter whether children are trying to address needs for individual achievement, or needs for interpersonal closeness, they must possess certain knowledge, skills, and behaviors in order to gain desired outcomes. Although this chapter is primarily concerned with social rather than agentic forms of competence, social competence cannot be equated simply with the fulfillment of communal needs. Children come to social interactions with several needs and agendas. Some of the agenda items involve seeking to fulfill social needs by building communal relationships, whereas other items are more agentic in nature, such as seeking tangible gain or wanting to demonstrate superiority; these latter goals, by their very nature, can create interpersonal distance and conflict. The challenge is to exercise the social knowledge, interpersonal skills, and self-regulatory capabilities that enable a balanced fulfillment of both communal and agentic needs in the context of social relationships (Bakan, 1966).

In the peer relations literature, the meaning of the term "social competence" varies from being narrowly equated with a child's sociometric standing to being so broadly defined as to include any and all factors that affect adjustment. My own work has explicitly focused on the competencies called for in *close relationships*, such as relationships with parents, close friends, and spouses (Buhrmester et al., 1988). I have adopted the term *interpersonal competence* – in contrast to the broader term *social competence* – to denote the competencies called for in close interpersonal relationships. Thus, for my purposes here, interpersonal competence refers to the tendency to establish and maintain close personal relationships that fulfill communal needs and facilitate the fulfillment of agentic needs.

Two sorts of questions can be asked about the development of interpersonal competence. First, what is the normative developmental sequence involved in the growth of adultlike ways of relating in close relationships? In this chapter, I am primarily interested in the development of competencies called for in friendships. Second, what factors are responsible for the development of individual differences in interpersonal competence? Again, my interest here is in the role that friendship experiences play in shaping individual differences in competence.

## The developmental course of interpersonal competence

Developmental changes in both communal and agentic needs motivate children, at least in part, to enter into new types of relationships, and to restructure existing relationships. Different qualities of close relationships, in turn, demand different competencies. For example, Sullivan (1953) noted that the emergence of the desire to engage in play with others motivates preschool children to establish playmate relationships with peers. These new playmate relationships are based on principles of symmetrical reciprocity that require children master new arenas of social competence that were not called for in previous parent–child relationships (Piaget, 1932; Youniss, 1980). Later during the early elementary-school years when children begin to develop social-comparative criteria for classifying peers into the "acceptable" in-group or the "unacceptable" out-group, they then must master the interpersonal demands created by social-status structures. Here, the desire to individually excel must be balanced against the desire to be liked and accepted by members of the group.

Much of my research has focused on the new demands that close friendships make upon early adolescents (e.g., Buhrmester, 1990). Several important changes seem to occur in friendships that require adolescents to master new interpersonal competencies; four changes are especially important. First, friendships become more "talk focused" than "play focused" (Parker & Gottman, 1989; Smollar & Youniss, 1982), requiring that teenagers become more skilled at initiating and sustaining interesting conversation. Second, friendships move outside the confines of the classroom and school playground, necessitating that teenagers acquire greater individual initiative in striking up conversations, calling new friends on the phone, and making plans to spend time together. Third, friendships become an important forum for self-exploration and a source of emotional support (Harter, 1990), requiring that teenagers learn to appropriately self-disclose personal thoughts and be able to empathically provide emotional support to friends. Fourth, as teenagers become more dependent upon friends to meet their needs, they more frequently find themselves in situations where they must work through conflicts of interest and disagreements with friends, thus requiring teenagers to be able to manage conflicts in ways that effectively reduce tension and maintain the intimacy of the relationship.

In light of the changes in the demands of friendship during early adolescence, it follows that teenagers who lack these interpersonal competencies are more likely to have difficulty establishing need-fulfilling friendships. They are likely to have fewer friendships, and the friendships they succeed in forming are more likely to be superficial or conflicted in nature. In short, during early adolescence levels of close relationship competence should play an increasingly important role in causally determining the quality of friendship experiences, and consequently, the fulfillment of needs.

The goal of a recent study was to determine whether, in fact, these competencies became more essential to success in friendship during early adolescence (Buhrmester, 1990). Although a large number of studies had demonstrated that social skills play an important role in determining younger children's sociometric status in the peer group (e.g., Dodge et al., 1986), few studies had investigated the competencies that correlate with the qualities of adolescents' dyadic friendships. A questionnaire that my colleagues and I recently developed, the Interpersonal Competence Questionnaire (ICQ; Buhrmester et al., 1988), was used to assess five domains of interpersonal competence relevant to adolescence and adult close relationships: (a) initiating interactions and relationships, (b) appropriately disclosing personal information, (c) providing emotional support to partners, (d) asserting displeasure with partners, and (e) managing interpersonal conflicts. Self- and friend-ratings of both interpersonal competence and friendship quality were gathered from samples of preadolescents (10–13-year-olds) and early adolescents (13–16-year-olds). The results revealed that the quality of friendship was more strongly correlated with these interpersonal competencies for the early adolescent sample than for the preadolescent sample. In particular, competence in initiating interactions, self-disclosure, and the provision of support most strongly predicted intimacy in adolescents' friendships. Moreover, the overall pattern of findings was consistent with the view that the competencies called for in close friendships emerge as important correlates of interpersonal success and personal well-being during early adolescence.

## The contributions of friends and other network members to the development of competence

The links between interpersonal competence and the quality of relationships can be viewed from two different directions. So far I have talked as if interpersonal competence plays a causal role in determining the quality of adolescents' friendships. This linkage can also be viewed from the reverse direction: Friendship experiences may play a causal role in shaping the development of interpersonal competence (Hartup & Sancilio, 1986).

Friendship experiences might contribute to the development of competence in two general ways. First, adolescents may at a minimum need to be involved in a close friendship in order to be exposed to the interpersonal demands that prompt them to acquire more mature competencies. For example, an adolescent without close friends may seldom or never be called upon to provide emotional support or discuss personal thoughts and feelings, and thus will not have the opportunity to try out and refine these interpersonal skills. In this sense, friendships provide the *opportunities* needed to master competencies. Second, variation in the *feedback* received through *interactions* with friends may play an important role in shaping individual differences in interpersonal competence. When adolescents' efforts to exercise new competencies are met by a positive reception from friends, this feedback serves to reinforce skillfulness. Conversely, when efforts bring forth negative or punitive responses from friends, this feedback undermines the use of these skills in the future. For example, if an adolescent's initial attempts at disclosure of personal anxieties are met with support and confidentiality by friends, then these experiences should foster the continued use and refinement of self-disclosing behaviors. However, if disclosure is met with indifference, ridicule, or a breach of confidentiality, this may inhibit future disclosure and, in addition, may foster the development of coping responses, such as an avoidance of opening up to others or an exaggerated neediness for intimate validation.

Relationships with friends are not the only ones that contribute to the development of close relationship competence. Obviously, experiences with parents, siblings, and other social network members provide opportunities to learn competencies and shape individual differences. Indeed, investigators within the parent–child attachment tradition have contended that most important elements of social competence are laid down in early attachment relationships and that the competencies and behavioral styles manifest in later relationships with friends and romantic partners are in part recapitulations of early attachment experiences (Sroufe & Fleeson, 1986; also see chapters by Parke and by Price in this volume). This attachment perspective emphasizes the *primacy of early parent–child relationships* and *continuity of functioning across different types of relationships*.

Sullivan's and Piaget's perspectives on relationship experiences and their contributions to the growth of competence contrast with the attachment view. Sullivan and Piaget emphasized the *discontinuities in functioning across family and peer relationships* and the *unique incremental contributions* that relationships with parents and peers make to the growth of competence. In their view, because relationships with parents and peers are structured differently, each realm of relationships requires children to master different types of skills. Although children may learn to deal with the demands of parent–child relationships chronologically first, early parent–child relationships do not call forth all the competencies that are needed for success in all forms of later relationships. Over the course of development, children encounter new and evermore complex relationships with peers (and parents), each of which requires that children add new competencies to their repertoires of interpersonal skills. Rather than emphasizing early experience and continuity (i.e., lack of change) as stressed by the attachment tradition, this "incremental growth" perspective focuses on developmental change and on the unique contributions that all relationships and periods of development make to the growth of social maturity.

Although limited, the extant research provides mixed support for both the continuity and incremental growth perspectives. In my own work, my colleagues and I regularly find moderate correlations between ratings of intimacy in relationships with best friends and relationships with mothers and fathers, $r = .20$ to .40. Other researchers have reported similar levels of continuity across relationships with parents and friends during adolescence (Bartholomew, 1993; Furman, 1989). These findings indicate, at least in terms of self-, friend-, and mother-reported relationship intimacy, that there is at best moderate continuity across relationships with parents and friends. When viewed from the other perspective, however, these same findings indicate that there is also considerable discontinuity across these relationships: The intimacy of relationships with friends is far from perfectly predicted by relationships with parents (i.e., 80% to 90% of the variance is not shared across relationships). Moreover, the data suggest that friendships represent a realm of relationships that is fairly orthogonal to parent–child relationships.

The incremental growth perspective suggests that relationships with parents and friends each make important and unique contributions to the growth of interpersonal competence. In particular, friendship theorists have argued that it is in friendship that children learn many of the interpersonal competencies that are important in adult close relationships, especially romantic relationships (Hartup & Sancilio, 1986; Savin-Williams & Berndt, 1990; Sullivan, 1953). This is because friendships are structurally more similar to romantic relationships than are asymmetrically structured parent–child relationships. This view stands in contrast to the continuity of early experience perspective, which, at its extreme, argues that social competence is shaped more by experiences in parent–child relationships than in friendships (Hazan & Shaver, 1987).

The findings from our recent study of 200 13- to 16-year-old adolescents shed at least preliminary light on this issue. We reasoned that the extent to which relationships are involved in the development of close relationship competencies should be reflected in the strength of the correlation between the quality of those relationships and individual variation in interpersonal competence. That is, if the quality of experiences in friendships plays a formative role in shaping adolescents' levels of interpersonal competence, then friendship quality and interpersonal competence should be significantly correlated. In addition, if both friendships and parent–child relationships make unique contributions to the growth of interpersonal competence, then the quality of each type of relationship should account for unique proportions of the variance in interpersonal competence.

Composite interpersonal competence scores were created by averaging total Interpersonal Competency Questionnaire scores across self-, friend-, and mother-report ratings of subjects' competence. Friendship intimacy scores were created by averaging self- and friend-report intimacy ratings, whereas composite mother–adolescent relationship intimacy scores were created by averaging self- and mother-report ratings. Correlational analyses revealed that although friendship intimacy and mother–adolescent intimacy scores were modestly correlated with each other, $r = .19$, scores for both relationships were moderately correlated with interpersonal competence scores, $r = .46$ and $r = .39$, respectively. When interpersonal competence scores were regressed on the two relationship intimacy scores, the latter two scores jointly accounted for 33% of the variance in competence, with friendship intimacy accounting uniquely for roughly 16% of the variance and mother–adolescent intimacy accounting uniquely for 9% of the variance. These findings are consistent with the incremental growth perspective's hypothesis that experiences in adolescent friendship have a sizable impact on the socialization of close relationship competence that is independent from the impact of the mother–adolescent relationship. Although there are obviously other possible interpretations of these correlational findings, the results are strong enough to warrant further study of the unique role friends play in the development of close relationship competence. Longitudinal and experimental studies are needed to fully evaluate the causal role that friendship plays in shaping the competencies that carry forward to adult intimate relationships.

*Gender and interpersonal competence*

As noted earlier, Maccoby (1990) has argued that same-sex peer relations are an important socializing context that shape the development of gender differences in social-interaction styles. Female–female friendships are thought to foster a communal-oriented style of relating, whereas male–male friendships are thought to foster an agentic-oriented style of relating. Although Maccoby's assertions are not entirely new, her theoretical framing of the issues opens new lines of inquiry for friendship researchers (Buhrmester, 1993).

The evidence reviewed previously suggests that early adolescence is a period in which youth develop an increased interest in, and capacity for, forming adultlike intimate relationships with friends. It seems to follow, then, that friendship experiences during this period may be especially influential in shaping gender differences in a number of intimacy-related social-style traits, including "communal" close relationship competencies such as intimate self-disclosure and the provision of emotional support.

Given this working hypothesis, three general questions present themselves. First, do boys and girls differ in their levels of communal-promoting interpersonal competencies? Table 8.3 presents gender differences in adolescents' interpersonal competency as rated by self, friend, and mother. Whereas adolescent girls are rated higher than boys for nearly all five domains of competence, the magnitude of the gender differences is greatest for the disclosure and support competence domains, averaging well over one-half standard deviation. The fact that ratings by mothers and friends also evidence this same pattern of gender differences bolsters confidence that these findings do not merely reflect a self-report bias, but rather represent a perceived reality shared among significant others who are well acquainted with adolescents.

Second, are there differences in the qualities of male and female adolescents' interactions with friends, and are these differences likely to foster greater communally oriented skills among females? Table 8.4 presents self- and friend-ratings of *mean levels* of companionship, conflict, self-disclosure, emotional support, and satisfaction in adolescents' friendships. Although there were negligible gender differences in reported companionship, conflict, and satisfaction, there were sizable gender differences in reported self-disclosure and emotional support. On average, girls reported roughly one standard deviation more disclosure and support in their friendships than did boys. Thus, the greater disclosure

Table 8.3. *Gender differences in adolescents' interpersonal competence*

| Interpersonal competence scales | Males | Females | t | p |
|---|---|---|---|---|
| *Self-reported* | | | | |
| Negative assertion | 3.42 | 3.52 | 1.04 | .30 |
| Relationship initiation | 3.33 | 3.64 | 2.63 | .01 |
| Conflict management | 3.24 | 3.55 | 2.63 | .01 |
| Self-disclosure | 3.14 | 3.77 | 5.37 | .001 |
| Emotional support | 3.56 | 4.14 | 5.36 | .001 |
| *Friend-reported* | | | | |
| Negative assertion | 3.53 | 3.73 | 1.66 | .10 |
| Relationship initiation | 3.52 | 3.82 | 2.25 | .03 |
| Conflict management | 3.39 | 3.67 | 2.13 | .04 |
| Self-disclosure | 3.34 | 3.81 | 3.71 | .001 |
| Emotional support | 3.51 | 4.13 | 5.27 | .001 |
| *Mother-reported* | | | | |
| Negative assertion | 3.39 | 3.51 | 1.35 | .18 |
| Relationship initiation | 3.35 | 3.56 | 1.67 | .10 |
| Conflict management | 3.19 | 3.41 | 2.08 | .04 |
| Self-disclosure | 2.99 | 3.41 | 3.49 | .001 |
| Emotional support | 3.47 | 3.98 | 4.92 | .001 |

and support reported in girls' friendships may, indeed, provide girls with more opportunities to exercise and refine disclosure and support competencies.

Third, are differences in friendships related to variations in interpersonal competency in a fashion that supports the assertion that friendship experiences play an important role in shaping competence? Table 8.5 presents findings suggesting that experiences in males' and females' same-sex friendships may contribute to gender differences in interpersonal competence. The two relationship questionnaire subscales that evidenced the largest gender differences – levels of self-disclosure and emotional support – were combined to create a composite intimacy score. Correlational analyses revealed that levels of intimacy in friendship were significantly predictive of competence at self-disclosure and the provision of emotional competence. It is interesting that the patterns of correlations for males and females were similar, suggesting that the basic processes that link intimacy to disclosure and support competence are the same for both sexes; that is, the more intimacy achieved in friendship, the more competent adolescents tend to be. What is different between the sexes, however, is that girls' friendships provide more of the intimacy experiences (as shown by the higher mean scores in Table 8.4) that presumedly foster girls' greater skill in self-disclosure and the provisions of emotional support.

Table 8.4. *Gender differences in self- and friend-reported features of adolescents' same-sex friendships*

| Relationship questionnaire scales | Males | Females | t | p |
|---|---|---|---|---|
| *Self-reported* | | | | |
| Companionship | 4.34 | 4.47 | 1.39 | .16 |
| Conflict | 1.97 | 1.73 | −1.80 | .07 |
| Self-disclosure | 3.44 | 4.52 | 7.56 | .001 |
| Emotional support | 3.18 | 4.46 | 8.81 | .001 |
| Satisfaction | 4.50 | 4.63 | 2.11 | .04 |
| *Friend-reported* | | | | |
| Companionship | 4.23 | 4.10 | − .92 | .36 |
| Conflict | 2.02 | 1.93 | − .50 | .62 |
| Self-disclosure | 3.52 | 4.16 | 3.82 | .001 |
| Emotional support | 3.30 | 4.12 | 5.07 | .001 |
| Satisfaction | 4.50 | 4.39 | −1.28 | .19 |

Obviously, the direction of cause could run in the opposite direction: Girls' greater skill at self-disclosure and provision of support may enable them to have more intimate friendships. In either case, the evidence clearly suggests that experiences in same-sex friendships are integrally tied to gender differences in interpersonal competence. The entire issue of the role played by friendship in the socialization of gender differences represents a promising arena of investigation that should be pursued in further research. Especially needed are studies that examine the role that boys' friendships play in the socialization of agentic forms of competence.

## Summary and conclusions

The first half of this chapter explored the idea that children's and adolescents' social behavior is directed toward addressing personal needs that grow out of the issues and concerns that preoccupy their attention. It is useful to conceive of two general classes of needs, those dealing with communion, or interpersonal connectedness, and those focusing on agency, or individual accomplishment. These two classes of needs evolve and change over the course of development, resulting in developmental changes in the types of outcomes children and adolescents seek through their social relationships.

Within this general conceptual framework, developmental changes in the nature and qualities of friendship are viewed as an outgrowth of changes in the concerns and needs that friendships address. This point was illustrated by discussing how the observed increase in self-disclosure to friends that occurs during

Table 8.5. *Correlations between adolescents' intimacy with same-sex friend
and interpersonal competence*

| Friendship intimacy | Male | Female |
|---|---|---|
| *Interpersonal competence* | | |
| Negative assertion | .18 | .06 |
| Relationship initiation | .38[b] | .17 |
| Conflict management | .23[a] | .12 |
| Self-disclosure | .48[b] | .44[b] |
| Emotional support | .53[b] | .36[b] |

*Note*: Friendship intimacy scores averaged across self- and friend-report ratings. Interpersonal Competence scores were a composite of the five subscales of Buhrmester's (1990) Adolescent Interpersonal Competence Questionnaire averaged across self-, friend-, and mother-report ratings.
[a]$p < .05$; [b]$p < .01$.

early adolescence may be linked to broader changes in teenagers' concerns and needs for social validation, self-clarification, and self-expression. Further research is needed to more carefully document developmental changes in basic concerns and needs, and to investigate how changes in the features of friendship grow out of, and feed back in to, broader developmental changes in concerns and needs.

Gender differences in concerns and needs may be the result of, as well as the cause of, gender differences in the features of friendships. It was argued that higher levels of concern by females for communal outcomes may, on the one hand, account for the more frequent disclosing and supportive interactions that are reported in girls' friendships. At the same time, the more frequent disclosing and supportive interactions of girls' friendships may be an important socializing influence in the development of a stronger appetite by females for communal outcomes. In the case of males' friendships, a greater concern about agentic outcomes may account for the more frequent competitive and status-oriented interactions that occur in boys' friendships, whereas these types of interactions may, in turn, play an important role in fostering males' appetite for agentic outcomes. These possible links between gender differences in friendships and agentic and communal needs are at this time largely speculative, but represent interesting directions for future friendship research.

Overall, a personal needs perspective appears to hold promise as a way of understanding friendship development within the broader context of individual development. The constructs of concerns and needs provide a conceptual means of linking changes in the nature of friendship to more basic developmental considerations. Moreover, friendship appears to provide a window into the "leading edge" issues and concerns of individual development (Buhrmester & Prager, 1995). The second half of the chapter considered how developmental changes in interpersonal competence are linked to changes in friendship. Interpersonal competence is viewed as the ability to forge relationships that facilitate the fulfillment of both communal and agentic needs. The basic contention put forth was that developmental changes in concerns and needs bring about changes in the nature and demands of friendship, and that these changes challenge children to learn new and more mature forms of interpersonal competence.

The qualities of children's friendships are thought to be partially determined by individual differences in competence, and contribute to shaping individual differences in competence. Two different theoretical perspectives on the relative contributions of parents and friends to the growth of interpersonal competence were considered: the attachment view and the incremental growth view. Findings presented from a study of young adolescents were most consistent with the incremental growth view's expectations of only moderate continuity in functioning across relationships with parents and friends. In addition, the quality of relationships with parents and friends uniquely accounted for individual variation in interpersonal competence, with friendship quality accounting for the greatest amount of variance. Although these findings are by no means definitive, they do suggest that further study of the processes through which interactions with friends may shape interpersonal competence is warranted.

Finally, the role of friendship in the development of gender differences in interpersonal competencies was explored. It was suggested that gender differences in the qualities of interactions with same-sex friends play an important role in the socialization of communal and agentic forms of competence. Findings were reviewed that were consistent with the view that the greater intimacy observed in adolescent girls' friendships contributes to girls' greater competence in self-disclosure and the provision of emotional support. Further research is needed to explore the possible ways in which boys' friendships contribute to the development of agentic forms of competence. Moreover, the broader issue of the potentially important role that same-sex friendships play in the socialization of gender roles appears to represent a relatively unexplored frontier for friendship research.

## References

Adler, A. (1927). *Practice and theory of individual psychology.* New York: Harcourt, Brace, & World.
Angyal, A. (1941). *Foundation for a science of personality.* New York: Commonwealth.

Bakan, D. (1966). *The duality of human existence.* Boston: Beacon Press.

Bandura, A. (1986). *Social foundations of thought and action: A social cognitive theory.* Englewood Cliffs, NJ: Prentice-Hall.

Bartholomew, K. (1993). From childhood to adult relationships: Attachment theory and research. In S. Duck (Ed.), *Learning about relationships* (pp. 30–62). London: Sage Publications.

Bigelow, B. J., & LaGaipa, J. J. (1980). The development of friendship and values and choice. In H. C. Foot, A. J. Chapman, & J. R. Smith (Eds.), *Friendship and social relations in children.* New York: Wiley.

Blos, P. (1979). *The adolescent passage.* New York: International Universities Press.

Brown, L. M., & Gilligan, C. (1992). *Meeting at the crossroads: Women's psychology and girls' development.* Cambridge, MA: Harvard University Press.

Buhrmester, D. (1990). Intimacy of friendship, interpersonal competence, and adjustment during preadolescence and adolescence. *Child Development, 61,* 1101–1111.

Buhrmester, D. (1993, April) *Adolescent friendship and the socialization of gender differences in social-interaction style.* Paper presented at the biennial meeting of the Society for Research on Child Development, New Orleans.

Buhrmester, D., & Carbery, J. (1992, March). *Daily patterns of self-disclosure and adolescent adjustment.* Paper presented at the biennial meeting of the Society for Research on Adolescence, Washington D. C.

Buhrmester, D., & Furman, W. (1986). The changing functions of friendship in childhood: A neo-Sullivanian perspective. In V. J. Derlega & B. A. Winstead (Eds.), *Friendship and social interaction* (pp. 43–62). New York: Springer-Verlag.

Buhrmester, D., & Furman, W. (1987). The development of companionship and intimacy. *Child Development, 58,* 1101–1113.

Buhrmester, D., Furman, W., Wittenberg, M., & Reis, H. (1988). Five domains of interpersonal competence in peer relationships. *Journal of Personality and Social Psychology, 55,* 991–1008.

Buhrmester, D., & Prager, K. (1995). Patterns and functions of self-disclosure during childhood and adolescence. In K. J. Rotenberg (Ed.), *Disclosure processes in children and adolescents.* New York: Cambridge University Press.

Cantor, N., & Malley, J. (1991). Life tasks, personal needs, and close relationships. In G. J. O. Fletcher & F. D. Fincham (Eds.), *Cognition in close relationships.*

Carbery, J. (1993). *The changing significance of friendship across three young adult phases.* Unpublished doctoral dissertation, University of Texas at Dallas.

Carson, R. C. (1979). Personality and exchange in developing relationships. In R. L. Burgess & T. L. Houston (Eds.), *Social exchange in development relationships* (pp. 247–269). New York: Academic Press.

Cofer, C. N., & Appely, M. H. (1964). *Motivation: Theory and research.* New York: Wiley.

Csikszentmihalyi, M., & Larson, R. (1984). *Being adolescent.* NY: Basic Books.

Dodge, K. A., Pettit, G. S., McClaskey, C. L., & Brown, M. A. (1986). Social competence in children. *Monographs of the Society for Research in Child Development, 51* (2, Serial No. 213).

Erikson, E. (1968). *Identity: Youth and crisis.* New York: Norton.

Fiske, S. T, & Taylor, S. E. (1991). *Social cognition.* New York: McGraw-Hill.

Franz, C., & White, K. M. (1985). Individuation and attachment in personality development: Extending Erickson's theory. *Journal of Personality, 53,* 224–256.

Freud, S. (1993). *Beyond the pleasure principle.* New York: International Psychoanalytic Press.

Furman, W. (1989). The development of children's social networks. In D. Belle (Ed.), *Children's social networks and social supports.* New York: John Wiley & Sons.

Furman, W., & Buhrmester, D. (1985). Children's perceptions of the personal relationships in their social networks. *Developmental Psychology, 21,* 1016–1024.

Furman, W., & Buhrmester, D. (1992). Age and sex differences in perceptions of networks of personal relationships. *Child Development, 63*, 103–115.

Gilligan, C. (1982). *In a different voice: Psychological theory and women's development.* Cambridge, MA: Harvard University Press.

Gottman, J. M., & Mettetal, G. (1986). Speculations about social and affective development: Friendship and acquaintanceship through adolescence. In J. M. Gottman and J. G. Parker (Eds.), *Conversations of friends: Speculations on affective development* (pp. 192–240). New York: Cambridge University Press.

Grotevant, H., & Cooper, C. (1986). Individuation in family relationships: A perspective on individual differences in the development of identity and role-taking skill in adolescents. *Human Development, 29*, 82–100.

Hall, C. S., & Lindzey, G. (1970). *Theories of personality* (2nd ed.). New York: Wiley.

Harter, S. (1990). Self and identity development. In S. S. Feldman & G. R. Elliot (Eds.), *At the threshold: The developing adolescent* (pp. 352–387). Cambridge: Harvard University Press.

Hartup, W. W. (in press). Friendships and their developmental significance. In H. McGurk (Ed.), *Contemporary issues in childhood social development.* London: Routledge.

Hartup, W. W., & Sancilio, M. F. (1986). Children's friendships. In E. Schopler & G. B. Mesibov (Eds.), *Social behavior in autism* (pp. 61–80). New York: Plenum.

Hazan, K., & Shaver, P. (1987). Conceptualizing love as an attachment process. *Journal of Personality and Social Psychology, 52*, 511–524.

Hill, J. P., & Holmbeck, G. N. (1986). Attachment and autonomy during adolescence. *Annals of Child Development, 3*, 145–189.

Howes, C. (1987). Peer interaction in young children. *Monographs of the Society for Research in Child Development, 53* (Serial No. 217).

Lever, J. (1976). Sex differences in games children play. *Social Problems, 32*, 478–487.

Lever, J. (1978). Sex differences in the complexity of children's play and games. *American Sociological Review, 43*, 471–483.

McAdams, D. P. (1984). Human motives and personal relationships. In V. J. Derlega (Ed.), *Communication, intimacy, and close relationships* (pp. 41–70). New York: Academic Press.

McAdams, D. P. (1985). *Power, intimacy, and the life story: Personological inquiries into identity.* Homewood, IL: Dorsey Press.

McAdams, D. P. (1988). Personal needs and personal relationships. In S. W. Duck (Ed.), *Handbook of personal relationships* (pp. 7–22). New York: Wiley.

McAdams, D. P., & Constantian, C. A. (1983). Intimacy and affiliation motives in daily living: An experience sampling analysis. *Journal of Personality and Social Psychology, 45*, 851–861.

Maccoby, E. E. (1990). Gender and relationships: A developmental account. *American Psychologist, 45*, 513–520.

Maslow, A. (1971). *The farther reaches of human nature.* New York: Viking.

Mischel, W. (1980). Personality and cognition: Something borrowed, something new? In N. Cantor & J. Kihlstrom (Eds.), *Personality, cognition, and social interaction.* Hillsdale, NJ: Erlbaum.

Murray, H. A. (1938). *Explorations in personality.* New York: Oxford University Press.

Parker, J., & Gottman, J. M. (1989). Social and emotional development in relational context: Friendship interaction from early childhood to adolescence. In T. J. Berndt and G. W. Ladd (Eds.), *Peer relationships in child development* (pp. 95–131). New York: John Wiley and Sons.

Piaget, J. (1932). *The moral judgment of the child.* New York: Harcourt.

Prager, K. J., & Buhrmester, D. (1992, August). *Assessing agentic and communal need fulfillment and life satisfaction.* Paper presented at the annual meeting, American Psychological Association, Washington, D.C.

Rawlins, W. K. (1992). *Friendship matters: Communication, dialectics and the life course.* New York: De Gruyter.

Rogers, C. (1951). *Client-centered therapy: Its current practice implication and theory.* Boston: Houghton-Mifflin.

Rosenkrantz, P., Vogel, S., Bee, H., Broverman, I., & Broverman, D. M. (1968). Sex-role stereotypes and self-concept in college students. *Journal of Consulting and Clinical Psychology, 32*, 287–295.

Savin-Williams, R. C., & Berndt, T. J. (1990). Friendship and peer relations. In S. S. Feldman, & G. R. Elliot, (Eds.), *At the threshold: The developing adolescent.* Cambridge: Harvard University Press.

Shaver, P., & Buhrmester, D. (1983). Loneliness, sex-role orientation, and group life: A social needs perspective. In P. B. Paulus (Ed.), *Basic group processes* (pp. 259–288). New York: Springer-Verlag.

Smollar, J., & Youniss, J. (1982). Social development through friendship. In K. H. Rubin & H. S. Ross (Eds.), *Peer relations and social skills in childhood.* NY: Springer-Verlag.

Sroufe, L. A., & Fleeson, J. (1986). Attachment and the construction of relationships. In W. W. Hartup & Z. Rubin (Eds.), *Relationships and development.* Hillsdale: Erlbaum.

Sullivan, H. S. (1953). *The interpersonal theory of psychiatry.* NY: Norton.

Steinberg, L. D. (1988). Reciprocal relation between parent–child distance and pubertal maturation. *Developmental Psychology, 24*, 122–128.

Tannen, D. (1990). Gender differences in topical coherence: Creating involvement in best friends' talk. *Discourse Processes, 13*, 73–90.

Veroff, J., & Veroff, J. B. (1980). *Social incentives: A life-span developmental approach.* New York: Academic.

Weiss, R. S. (1974). The provisions of social relationships. In Z. Rubin (Ed.)., *Doing unto others* (pp. 17–26). Englewood Cliffs, NJ: Prentice-Hall.

Wright, P. H. (1982). Mens' friendships, women's friendships and the alleged inferiority of the latter. *Sex Roles, 8*, 1–20.

Youniss, J. (1980). *Parents and peers in social development: A Sullivan-Piaget Perspective.* Chicago: The University of Chicago Press.

Youniss, J., & Smollar, J. (1985). *Adolescent relationships with mothers, fathers, and friends.* Chicago: The University of Chicago Press.

# 9 Closeness and conflict in adolescent peer relationships: Interdependence with friends and romantic partners

*Brett Laursen*

Close relationships with peers play an increasingly important role in socialization across adolescence. As the social worlds of parents and peers grow distinct, adolescents devote greater time and energy to relationships with agemates (Csikszentmihalyi & Larson, 1984). These changes coincide with a shift from parents to peers as a primary source of companionship and intimacy (Furman & Buhrmester, 1992). Still, parents and peers tend to be complementary, not competitive, forces. Even though adolescents look for support from agemates who share these new experiences, parents continue to provide a stable base from which to explore unfamiliar settings.

Given the widespread recognition of social changes during the adolescent years, the paucity of knowledge concerning friendships and romantic relationships is somewhat surprising. We know much more about adolescent relationships with parents than with peers; paradoxically, most extensive studies of friendship extend only through middle childhood, when parents are arguably more important socialization influences. One possible reason for this lack of research is the dearth of theory concerning adolescent close peer relationships. The usual practice is to invoke the seminal works of Sullivan (1953) or Youniss (1980) in introductory remarks, and then "proceed with empirical business as usual" (Furman, 1993, p. 90). The unintended effect of this theoretical neglect is a field littered with disparate findings that are difficult to integrate thematically.

The purpose of this chapter is twofold. The first is to elaborate a comprehensive model of adolescent close peer relationships. The second is to summarize recent research supporting this theoretical view. A social relational model of

The thoughtful comments of my colleagues David G. Perry and Deborah R. Richardson are gratefully acknowledged. As always, Bill Hartup proved to be a gentle and inspirational editor. Research described in this chapter was supported, in part, by the Johann Jacobs Foundation Young Investigator Grants Program.

adolescent development, incorporating principles of interdependence in peer relationships, will be advanced. New research derived from this perspective illustrates distinctive features of adolescent relationships with friends and romantic partners. A trio of questions are central to understanding the significance of close peer relationships (i.e., friendships and romantic relationships) during adolescence. What processes distinguish friends and romantic partners, from each other and from other relationships? How does the nature of close peer relationships change across adolescence? What role do relationships with friends and romantic partners play in social development? Although studies strongly support the notion that peers provide a critical context for development during adolescence, the nature of these processes and the unique contributions of friendships and romantic relationships remain to be elaborated (Collins & Repinski, 1994; Furman & Wehner, 1995).

The chapter is divided into six sections. The first reviews exchange theory and recent developmental revisions encompassed within a social relational model. Interdependence, a central concept of exchange theory, may be conceptualized in terms of closeness and conflict; this balance of rewards and costs offers insight into the form and function of adolescent peer relationships. The second section summarizes literature on closeness and conflict with friends and romantic partners. In the third and fourth sections, the dynamics of adolescent peer relationships are described. Consistent with interdependence models, closeness and conflict distinguish close peer relationships from other relationships; rewards and costs also discriminate between friendships and romantic relationships. In the fifth section, social relational models are modified according to distinctions between close peer relationships. It is proposed that developmental changes in interconnections with friends and romantic partners alter patterns of adolescent relationship interdependence. The final section identifies research directions designed to fulfill the developmental potential inherent in social relational models of close peer relationships.

## Exchange theory, interdependence, and adolescent close relationships

During the 1960s and 1970s a general theory of social behavior, *exchange theory*, was advanced by social psychologists and applied to a variety of interpersonal phenomena (Kelley & Thibaut, 1959; Thibaut & Kelley, 1978; Walster, Berscheid, & Walster, 1973). In the 1980s, exchange theory spurred research advances into the establishment, maintenance, and dissolution of close relationships (see Clark & Reis, 1988, for review). With few exceptions (e.g., Berscheid, 1986), however, developmental aspects of the theory were largely overlooked. Following a decade of research on infant attachment, which underscored the developmental significance of close relationships, social relational models evolved in the 1990s applying interdependence to children's relationships with parents and friends.

*Exchange theory: Origins and overview*

Not unlike other social psychological perspectives, exchange theory begins with the assumption that humans are selfish: "Individuals will try to maximize their outcomes (where outcomes equal rewards minus costs)" (Walster et al., 1973, p. 151). Cultures maximize collective rewards by institutionalizing systems that reward individuals who treat others fairly in social interactions. Based on these simple postulates, exchange theory proved to be a powerful predictor of interpersonal attraction (Berscheid & Walster, 1969). Simply put, interactions between two individuals can be understood in terms of the rewards and costs each provides the other. If an initial interaction is mutually rewarding, participants seek each other out for future interactions (and rewards). Interpersonal attraction describes not just a preference for a particular partner, but also a desire for the rewards provided by interactions with that partner.

*Interdependence* develops as interactions continue to be mutually rewarding and parties increasingly depend on one another for rewards (Kelley et al., 1983). In an interdependent relationship the thoughts, behaviors, and emotions of two parties are causally interconnected. Interdependent affiliations that endure over an extended period of time with strong, recurring, diverse interconnections are considered close relationships. *Equity* is essential for most forms of interdependence; the rewards and costs associated with a relationship must be equitable (equally shared by participants) for interdependence to develop. Difficulties arise as a result of inequity, the perception that interactions are more rewarding for one individual than the other. Inequity may also arise if costs are not divided between relationship participants.

Conceptualizations of rewards and costs in interdependent relationships have been refined. Originally, rewards encompassed propinquity, similarity, and cooperation, whereas costs included competition and aggression (Berscheid & Walster, 1969). Recent advances provide greater specificity: Rewards are now equated with closeness, costs with conflict (Kelley et al., 1983). Closeness describes rewards that occur frequently and in a variety of settings, exerting a strong influence on participants. Conflict, defined in terms of behavioral opposition or interference, represents the main cost associated with interdependence (Peterson, 1983). Conflict often implies inequity, positive and/or negative features of affiliation that are unevenly distributed.

As an interdependent relationship develops, many rewards and costs become restricted to the relationship. Thus, interdependence implies mutual reliance. Differences between interdependent relationships emerge as a function of how dependencies are manifest and which features of equity are emphasized (Clark, Mills, & Powell, 1986; Mills & Clark, 1982). Two distinct types of relationship interdependence, communal and exchange, emerge from a consideration of equity.

In a *communal* relationship, participants emphasize equity in meeting one another's needs, rather than equity in the contributions made by each party. Individuals in communal relationships strive to meet their partner's needs, assuming that over the course of the relationship their relative contributions will be roughly equivalent. For instance, rather than keep track of exactly how much each partner contributes to maintaining the household, spouses focus more on the extent to which the other responds to special needs for support. The emphasis is on equity of need fulfillment: Is he (or she) there when you need him (or her)? During adolescence, communal relationships include those with family members, romantic partners, and friends (Collins & Repinski, 1994).

An *exchange* relationship, in contrast, consists of interdependent individuals who feel no special responsibilities for one another. Participants track equity in terms of the contributions of each individual to the relationship; attaining a balance of need satisfaction is less of a consideration than is parity in the overall value of rewards attained and costs incurred. For instance, relationships between neighbors tend to be driven more by a timely return of favors proffered than by sensitivity and responsiveness to personal needs. The emphasis is on equity of outcomes received: What has he (or she) done for you lately? During adolescence, exchange relationships encompass associations with neighbors, work associates, teachers, and classmates.

In sum, equity directs the dynamics of interpersonal relationships; interdependence is the key to understanding behavior within this framework. When rewards in a relationship are evenly distributed and consistently exceed costs, interdependence develops. As a result, the behaviors, emotions, and thoughts of participants become causally interconnected. Differing facets of equity distinguish between interdependent relationships. Participants in communal relationships are motivated to maintain rewards and avoid costs that could disrupt interconnections. As a consequence, interactions are driven by need fulfillment. Participants in exchange relationships, although also motivated to maintain interdependence, have less invested in long-term relationship stability. Thus, interactions are grounded in balancing contributions to the relationship.

*Applying exchange theory to adolescent relationships*

Unique influences differentiate the close relationships of adolescents from those of children and adults. This section describes developmental considerations prompting revisions to interdependence models. Because factors that determine interdependence vary with development, adult close relationships, which served as the model for exchange theory applications, imperfectly reflect relationships during childhood and adolescence. Early adolescent peer relationships differ substantially from those of adults, because the accoutrements of friendships and romantic relationships are acquired slowly. Accordingly, a social relational model of development holds that interdependence in close peer relationships emerges gradually with individual maturation and social experience (Collins & Repinski, 1994; Hartup & Laursen, 1991; Laursen & Collins, 1994).

Relationships grow and change over time, and so do their participants. When one or both parties in a relationship is an adolescent, change may be experienced in multiple arenas. At the most basic level, individual development alters on-going reward exchanges, as when an adolescent in a romantic relationship attains sexual maturity. Furthermore, interdependencies change as the relationship matures. For instance, adolescent romantic relationships often begin platonically and progress through various stages of sexual involvement. Finally, general expectations about interactions within a relationship change with maturation. Young children who are "going steady" have different conceptions about interconnections between romantic partners than do older adolescents.

Development also influences the degree of external influences placed on individuals in a relationship. Interpersonal attraction between adults is predicated on the assumption that participants are free to establish and dissolve relationships as they choose. Adolescents, in contrast, do not have total control over their close relationships. For instance, parents can (and often do) place roadblocks in the way of romantic relationships and friendships. They further discourage (even prohibit) certain interconnections. With age, the constraints that adults place on interactions with close peers are gradually removed, permitting exploration of the full range of rewards (and costs) offered by friends and romantic partners.

The hierarchy and composition of communal relationships also change with development. Although young adults give much of their attention to romantic relationships, this is not necessarily the case for adolescents. Because romantic relationships emerge later than other close relationships do, most children and many adolescents maintain communal relationships exclusively with same-sex friends, siblings, and parents. Interdependencies within relationships change with development; new and different close relationships are established during adolescence. A developmental consideration of close relationships, therefore, must necessarily encompass a wide and shifting array of potential affiliations.

Finally, the nature and significance of close relationships are altered with development. During adolescence, communal relationships comprise two distinct groups in which the principles of interdependence are applied differently (Collins & Laursen, 1992). *Involuntary relationships* include associations with family members, wherein kinship, customs, and laws dictate behavior. Power tends to be unevenly divided between participants in these relationships. Still, regardless of inequities resulting from this imbalance of power, family relationships are inherently stable and unlikely to be severed. As a consequence, family members may be more tolerant of inequitable interactions than unrelated individuals. The stability of the relationship does not, however, ensure interdependence. Conflict may increase and closeness may disappear even as the relationship continues. *Voluntary relationships* consist of associations with friends and romantic partners. These relationships are somewhat tenuous and unstable, since peers compete with one another for rewards. Friendships and romantic relationships are also egalitarian in that participants hold roughly equal power. Interactions are based on trust and commitment, not on familial bonds. Aside from investment in the rewards associated with the relationship, there is nothing to hold parties together should inequity arise. Close peers, therefore, are more sensitive to variations in interdependence than family members.

As children mature cognitively and gain social experience, distinctions between involuntary and voluntary communal relationships become more apparent. Since a full appreciation of what is required to maintain positive outcomes in voluntary relationships does not emerge until adolescence, awareness of equity requirements in relationships with friends and romantic partners is not evident until this age. Behaviors considered appropriate with close peers and family members reflect the interaction of developmental status and relationship type (Hartup, 1992; Selman, 1981). For example, the incidence of conflict in voluntary communal relationships may increase with age, as adolescents become more sensitive to the need for maintaining interdependence and resolving interpersonal difficulties; young children, only vaguely aware that inequity is harmful, may simply avoid conflict to avert any potential disruption of rewards. Interactions in involuntary communal relationships, by virtue of their stability, probably evince less variability across ages.

In sum, social relational revisions to interdependence models take into account developmental status and relationship characteristics. Close peers, unlike family members, have relationships that are susceptible to disruption; interactions in voluntary communal relationships are particularly influenced by developmental change. Friends and romantic partners become aware that to maintain voluntary relationships, costs and inequity must be avoided. Adolescent close peer affiliations reflect the transition from child to adult relationships, as the application and appreciation of equity and interdependence transform interactions with friends and romantic partners.

**Interdependence in adolescent close peer relationships**

Developmental extensions of exchange theory fill a void in our understanding of adolescent peer relationships, in addition to providing a coherent framework for organizing empirical efforts. Alternative accounts of adolescent development primarily focus on changes in parent–child relationships: psychoanalytic (e.g., Blos, 1979), cognitive-developmental (e.g., Smetana, 1988), and sociobiological (e.g., Steinberg, 1989) perspectives all emphasize disjunctive alterations with adolescent maturation. Parent–child relationships are purportedly disrupted at mid-adolescence, forcing concomitant revisions in friendships and romantic relationships. In contrast, social relational models of adolescent development (e.g., Collins & Repinski, 1994; Laursen & Collins, 1994) depict close relationships as a stable context for development. From this perspective, gradual transformation best characterizes changes in adolescent close relationships.

This section presents evidence consistent with social relational models of development, focusing on characteristics of close peer relationships across the adolescent years. Interdependencies among friends and romantic partners are discussed in light of research on closeness and conflict. A common theme concerns the steady ascendance of peers, relative to other close relationships, as central figures in the lives of adolescents. With development, closeness between friends and romantic partners eclipses family members; similarly, conflict with close peers is increasingly managed to minimize the disruptive potential of the dispute.

*An overview of closeness in adolescent peer relationships*

Recent literature reviews, although not grounded in exchange theory, reiterate themes of interdependence in adolescent friendships. According to Savin-Williams and Berndt (1990), intimacy and loyalty are the primary characteristics that distinguish adolescent friendships from other relationships. Intimacy entails openness that reveals thoughts and feelings, whereas loyalty implies an interpersonal commitment to share attitudes, values, and activities. Three similar foci were identified by Hartup (1993): reciprocity, commitment, and equality. Reciprocity includes expectations of intimacy, as well as common interests and activities. Commitment entails loyalty and trust. Equality describes shared power. These attributes are consistent with a relationship model that depicts interdependence as interconnections exerting strong and frequent influence over the behaviors, thoughts, and feelings of participants (Kelley et al., 1983). Several investigations illustrate the emerging developmental significance of closeness in adolescent peer relationships.

The first, a short-term longitudinal study of children in grades 2 through 8, compared attributes of friends with classmates who were neither liked nor disliked (Berndt & Perry, 1986). In a composite rating of positive relationship features (including association, intimacy, attachment, and loyalty), friends were viewed as more supportive than nonfriends. Friendship intimacy increased across grades. Social interaction was an important marker of friendship: Frequent interactions were indicative of children who remained friends for the duration of the school year; declining rates predicted the eventual demise of the friendship (Berndt, Hawkins, & Hoyle, 1986).

A second study examined reports by children in grades 5 through 11 of intimacy with same-sex friends and opposite-sex friends (including romantic partners) (Sharabany, Gershoni, & Hofman, 1981). A composite rating of intimacy (comprised of eight dimensions including sensitivity, common activities, trust, and exclusivity) remained constant across grades for same-sex friends, while increasing dramatically in opposite-sex relationships. Greater intimacy with same-sex relative to opposite-sex friends diminished with age until there were no differences between the relationships of the oldest subjects.

Several provisions of close peer relationships were examined with the Network of Relationships Inventory (NRI: Furman & Buhrmester, 1985). Across grades 2 through 8, intimacy and companionship increased with friends and romantic partners, but decreased with family members, classmates, and adults (Buhrmester & Furman, 1987). Across grades 4 through 10, a composite index of support (including intimacy, companionship, affection, and reliable alliance) increased among friends and romantic partners, whereas it decreased with parents, siblings, and teachers (Furman & Buhrmester, 1992). Neither investigation revealed differences between friendships and romantic relationships during adolescence, although younger children reported that friends provided greater intimacy, companionship, and support than romantic partners. Finally, subjects ranging from 11 to 19 years old reported that on most NRI scales support from friends declined between early and mid-adolescence; admiration, companionship, reliable alliance, and satisfaction diminished further between mid- and late adolescence (Clark-Lempers, Lempers, & Ho, 1991). Friendship intimacy was the exception, which remained constant across adolescence. Reports of relationships with parents indicated that support declined linearly across the adolescent years.

Adolescent friendships and romantic relationships share many similar characteristics. Intimacy, companionship, and commitment are but three manifestations of interdependence in both adolescent relationships. These characteristics provide a unique source of rewards to participants, thus setting close peer relationships apart from all other relationships. Developmental differences between close peer relationships, however, also emerge. Closeness with same-sex friends increases across childhood, peaking during early to mid-adolescence – the "chumship" stage (Sullivan, 1953) – and then declining across late adolescence. Intimacy with opposite-sex friends and romantic partners, in contrast, increases steadily throughout adolescence.

*An overview of conflict in adolescent peer relationships*

Although conflict is consistently invoked as an important mechanism in peer interactions, the nature and purpose of disputes in close relationships are poorly understood (Rizzo, 1992; Shantz, 1987). Most accounts incorporate some features of interdependence to describe the special role of conflict in friendships and romantic relationships. It is often assumed that because the potential costs of disagreement threaten voluntary relationships, friends and romantic partners should go to great lengths to minimize negative conflict outcomes (Laursen, Hartup, & Koplas, in press). Representations of the costs of conflict have been described in terms of the overall rate of disagreement and the product of specific behaviors within the dispute. Sensitivity to conflict costs increases with age, as adolescents appreciate that the threat to close peer relationships depends not just on the presence of a disagreement, but also on how participants comport themselves during the disagreement.

When costs are equated with conflict frequency, voluntary communal relationships appear to fare better than involuntary communal relationships: Adolescents quarrel less with close peers than with family members. In two studies, adolescents of various ages reported that conflict (i.e., quarreling, arguing, getting mad) with friends and romantic partners occurred at a rate between parents and siblings on the one hand, and teachers and grandparents on the other hand (Clark-Lempers et al., 1991; Furman & Buhrmester, 1992). Close peer relationships are not devoid of conflicts; interviews suggest that adolescent friends "fight" and "argue" as much as nonfriends (Berndt & Perry, 1986).

Family members remain the greatest source of conflict across adolescence: The primacy of conflict with mothers and siblings remains predictably constant. Relative rates of disagreement in peer relationships, however, change with age. Literature reviews find that conflict with same-sex friends declines during adolescence, whereas that with romantic partners increases (Collins & Laursen, 1992; Laursen & Collins, 1994). Thus, across the adolescent years, greater costs – more frequent conflicts – are associated with involuntary than with voluntary communal relationships.

Similar results emerge when relationship costs are equated with conflict behaviors, especially the management and outcome of a disagreement: Friends and romantic partners handle conflict in ways that minimize the potential for relationship disruption. Reports of hypothetical and actual conflicts indicate that adolescents compromise and negotiate more with close peers than with adults (Selman et al.; 1986; Youniss & Smollar, 1985). A recent meta-analysis of peer conflict describes the influence of age and relationship on resolutions (Laursen, 1993a). Overall, close peer relationships contain fewer negative interactions than do relationships with other peers and siblings. Conflict is resolved by mitigation more often with friends and romantic partners than either with nonfriends or siblings, a trend that accelerates with age. Negotiation is the most common method of resolving conflict between close peers, especially romantic partners; coercion occurs infrequently. Coercion dominates conflict with nonfriends and siblings, whereas negotiation in these relationships is rare. Across peer relationships, coercion declines and negotiation increases with age. Differences between reports of hypothetical and actual disagreements reveal a growing cognitive awareness of the costs associated with peer conflict. Although young children overwhelmingly endorse negotiation in hypothetical disputes, they nearly always practice coercion inactual disputes; the discrepancy between perception and reality narrows during adolescence and by early adulthood reports of negotiation in hypothetical peer conflict were similar to levels of negotiation actually displayed.

Additional evidence affirms that friends and romantic partners are aware of the dangers posed by conflict. Across adolescence, poorly managed disagreements are increasingly regarded as forces that threaten close peer relationships (Selman, 1981). Females are particularly sensitive to the potential costs of conflict with friends: Relative to males, females more often emphasize the importance of resolving disagreements through compromise (see Collins & Laursen, 1992, for review). This distinction grows with age, leading Youniss and Smollar (1985) to suggest that a sizable minority of adolescent males has yet to develop a mature appreciation of the potential costs of conflict and the behaviors required to preserve friendships and romantic relationships.

To summarize, research indicates that conflict is an important concomitant of close relationships. Adolescents are increasingly cognizant of the costs associated with conflict and, although disagreements cannot be avoided altogether (to some extent conflict is necessary to raise concerns about inequity), they can be managed so as to minimize negative outcomes and reestablish interdependence. Regardless of how costs are calculated, there are fewer of them in relationships with friends and romantic partners than in relationships with parents and siblings. Overall, less conflict occurs with close peers than with family members; similarly, disputes with close peers are more likely to involve compromise, thus avoiding damage to the relationship. Because development brings greater awareness of the dangers to close peer relationships inherent in poorly managed disputes, mitigation increases with age.

*Limitations in the literature on closeness and conflict*

Attaining a balance between closeness and conflict appears essential to inter-dependence in relationships with friends and romantic partners. Research findings are consistent with claims that, in voluntary communal relationships, the rewards of affiliation are carefully weighed against the costs. But the data are suggestive only. Interpretations are strictly post-hoc assessments, because few studies operationalize variables in terms of interdependence. The considerable overlap across reports of rewards in friendships and romantic relationships does not obviate the need for an explicit test of closeness. The same is true of the extant conflict literature: Although global depictions suggest that conflict and its management are critical to the maintenance of close peer relationships, a detailed account of the costs associated with these interactions is lacking.

What emerges from the literature is the need for a framework that integrates accounts of friendships and romantic relationships. Distinctive and shared features of these relationships remain to be explicated. Similarly, mechanisms responsible for interaction processes must be considered. Rewards describe but one side of the coin; costs must be reckoned as well. A social relational model of interdependence offers promising insight into these dynamics, detailing the balance of closeness and conflict with friends and romantic partners, and accounting for gradual transformations in these relationships across the adolescent years.

**Advances in the study of closeness**

What is the nature of closeness with close peers? What distinguishes the rewards of friendships and romantic relationships from those of other relationships? To address these questions, new research describes interdependence and closeness within the framework of a social relational model of development. In several recent studies, the Relationship Closeness Inventory (Berscheid, Snyder, & Omoto, 1989) was completed by adolescents to ascertain three central features of interdependence: (1) the *frequency* of social interactions; (2) the *diversity* of social interactions; and (3) the *influence* or strength of these interactions. Frequency is the amount of daily interaction that occurs between participants. Diversity is the number of different activities participants engage in during a week. The strength of the relationship's impact (measured with a 34-item scale) describes the partner's influence on the subject's thoughts, feelings, and behaviors (e.g., happiness, basic values), as well as future plans and goals (e.g., vacations, finances). An overall relationship closeness score is obtained by standardizing and summing these three domains.

The inventory, initially designed for young adults, offers a glimpse into relationship interdependence. In a sample of college students, 47% selected romantic partners as their closest relationship (Berscheid et al., 1989); friends were the second most frequently nominated relationship (36%), followed by family members (14%). Across these relationships, overall levels of closeness were highest with romantic partners. There were no differences in closeness with friends and family members.

Two recent studies administered a modified version of the Relationship Closeness Inventory to adolescents and neither found age-related differences in closeness with same-sex friends. Fifth through eighth graders indicated that overall closeness with parents declines with age (Repinski, 1992). Seventh through eleventh graders also reported that closeness with parents steadily diminishes (Repinski, 1993). Parents, however, failed to verify this trend: Their perceptions of closeness with children did not decline. Both parents and children indicated that, regardless of age, adolescents were closer to their mothers than to their fathers and their friends.

### Closeness in adolescent relationships

New research is under way in our laboratory to elaborate patterns of closeness within different adolescent relationships. Participants included a total of 121 rural New England (U.S.A.) high school students ($M = 17.1$ years). Five versions of the Relationship Closeness Inventory were administered to adolescents, one each for best friend, romantic partner, mother, father, and sibling. Not all adolescents participated in each relationship: Thus, 94% reported on best friends, 78% on romantic partners, 100% on mothers, 94% on fathers, and 88% on siblings.

Overall relationship closeness was highest with romantic partners and lowest with siblings. In between, friends and mothers had similar levels of closeness, followed by fathers. Relationships also differed on the attributes that comprised closeness (i.e., interaction frequency, interaction diversity, strength of influence). Romantic partners ranked highest in all three domains; in addition to wielding the most influence, boyfriends and girlfriends reported an average of 50 minutes more daily social interaction ($M = 120$ minutes) and three to four additional weekly activities ($M = 11$ activities) compared to the next closest relationship. After romantic partners, similar levels of daily social interaction and weekly activities were reported with mothers and friends ($M = 70$ minutes and 7 to 8 activities), followed by siblings ($M = 55$ minutes and 6 activities), and then fathers ($M = 40$ minutes and 4 activities). Patterns of relationship strength differed somewhat from interaction frequency and diversity: After romantic partners, mothers and fathers had the most influence over adolescents, followed by friends, and then siblings. Another study from our laboratory, which includes 500 rural New England (U.S.A.) subjects ranging from early adolescence through young adulthood, extends and replicates these findings. Closeness with parents and siblings declined with age. Closeness with best friends peaked at mid-adolescence and then decreased. Closeness with romantic partners increased steadily with age, surpassing siblings during mid-adolescence, and parents and friends during late adolescence. Social interaction and activities in all family relationships declined precipitously with age; the frequency and diversity of interactions with friends peaked during mid-adolescence, whereas both steadily increased with romantic partners across the adolescent years. Parental influence remained strong at all ages, in contrast to that of siblings and friends, which was relatively weak. The influence of romantic partners, already greater than that of siblings and friends at early adolescence, increased with age, surpassing that of parents during late adolescence.

These results indicate that manifestations of relationship closeness are not uniform. During late adolescence and young adulthood, romantic partners emerge as the closest relationship in all three domains of interdependence. Despite frequent social interactions in diverse activities, however, adolescents perceive friends to be relatively uninfluential. The curvilinear trend for closeness with friends (peaking at mid-adolescence) and the linear trend for closeness with romantic partners (increasing across adolescence) appears to be the result of an escalation in the number and type of interactions in close peer relationships, with a switch in emphasis from same-sex to opposite-sex peers following pubertal maturation. Across ages, mothers rank fairly high in all closeness domains, whereas fathers retain influence disproportionate to the frequency and diversity of their social interactions. Indeed, parental influence scarcely wanes throughout adolescence, even while engagement plummets. Finally, siblings tend not to be very close during early adolescence and they become less so with age.

Some close peer relationships are more equal than others. Friends enjoy fewer rewards than do romantic partners. Closeness in romantic relationships cuts across rewards, yet among friends closeness is restricted to companionship and affiliation. Although friends undoubtedly attain influence in specific domains, the relative strength of their overall influence does not compare to that of romantic partners (or parents). These age-related trends suggest that friendships pave the way for romantic relationships, providing the necessary forum for critical social experiences and an avenue for partial disengagement from families. The emerging picture of gradually shifting rewards is consistent with the social relational model of stability and transformation in close peer relationships across the adolescent years.

## Advances in the study of conflict

What is the nature of conflict with close peers? What distinguishes the costs of friendships and romantic relationships from those of other relationships? To address these questions, recent research combines contemporary views of interpersonal conflict with models of adolescent interdependence. A central feature of these studies is Shantz's (1987) definition of conflict as behavioral opposition (an individual objects to or resists the actions of another), which distinguishes conflict from negative affect and aggression. Accordingly, conflicts are disagreements, dyadic exchanges comprised of discrete temporal components, including onset, affective intensity, resolution, and outcome.

The costs associated with a conflict include the potential to harm a relationship. Anger and coercive conflict resolutions tend to produce inequitable outcomes, discontinued social interaction, and worsened relationships (Gottman, 1979; Laursen & Hartup, 1989). Disagreements do not automatically result in negative outcomes; some conflicts carry great relationship costs, whereas others have neutral or beneficial results. Although costs may be envisioned as either a product of disagreement per se, or the result of specific behaviors within a disagreement, conflict management strategies may be better indices than conflict rates for determining the impact of disagreement on a relationship because they associate costs with coercion (Perry, Perry, & Kennedy, 1992).

Because amicable resolutions tend not to disrupt rewards, participants in voluntary communal relationships should be careful to manage disputes so as to maintain interdependence. Indeed, preschool friends, relative to nonfriends, avoid angry and coercive tactics during free play, settling conflicts with equitable outcomes and thereby continuing social interactions (Hartup, Laursen, Stewart, & Eastenson, 1988). Grade-school friends also manage conflict so as to avoid disrupting the relationship, often disengaging or "agreeing to disagree" rather than forcing a potentially divisive issue (Rizzo, 1992). Adolescents are even more sensitive than children about the costs of disagreement to close peer relationships, but the dynamics of adolescent conflict with friends and romantic partners have yet to be demonstrated. To this end, several studies are under way to determine the costs associated with daily conflict in adolescent close relationships.

## Conflict in adolescent relationships

In questionnaires that explored interpersonal conflict within a social relational model of adolescent development, costs were equated with three features of conflict (Laursen, 1993c, 1995): negative affect, continued social interaction, and perceived relationship impact. Conflict rates, another potential metric of costs, were also ascertained. A total of 685 suburban midwestern (U.S.A.) tenth and eleventh graders ($M = 16.7$ years) provided information about daily conflict in interdependent communal relationships – voluntary (friends, romantic partners) and involuntary (parents, siblings) – as well as in interdependent exchange relationships (classmates, teachers, work associates, employers). Conflict was defined in terms of disagreement and behavioral opposition. Subjects were instructed that disagreements range from "differences of opinion" to "quarrels and arguments." Adolescents reviewed a list of 34 conflict issues (adapted from Prinz, Foster, Kent, & O'Leary, 1979; Robin & Foster, 1984); for each issue, subjects indicated whether a conflict had arisen the previous day and, if so, who it involved.

Conflict rate represented the mean number of daily disagreements in a relationship, adjusted for frequency of social interaction. Affective intensity, during and after the conflict, was rated on a 5-point scale ranging from very friendly to very angry. Post-conflict social interaction assessed whether a disagreement disrupted ongoing social interaction. Adolescents selected one of three postconflict alternatives: remained together, continued talking; remained together, stopped talking; and not together. Relationship impact described the perceived consequence of a conflict for the relationship. One of three outcomes was possible: made the relationship better; no impact; and made the relationship worse.

Adolescents reported an average of seven to eight disagreements per day (Laursen, 1995). Mother–adolescent conflict was most frequent, with two to three daily disagreements. Friends, romantic partners, siblings, and fathers followed, with approximately one disagreement each. Conflict rates were lowest with peers, teachers, and employers, averaging less than one disagreement a day. Thus, conflict appears to vary as a function of interdependence, with disagreements more frequent in communal than in exchange relationships.

Close peers avoided negative affect and minimized the disruptive potential of conflict (Laursen, 1993c). Despite feeling somewhat angry during their disagreement, positive affect returned to participants in voluntary communal relationships afterward, whereas negative or neutral affect characterized involuntary communal as well as exchange relationships. Four out of five conflicts between close peers were followed by continued social interaction, compared to only half (or less) in other relationships. Adolescents also perceived that conflicts with close peers had the fewest negative and the most positive relationship outcomes. Disagreements that improved the relationship usually involved close peers. Among romantic partners, conflicts made the relationship better as often as they had no impact (41% of disagreements fell into each category). Disagreements between friends made the relationship better less often (23%), tending instead to have no impact (63%). Few conflicts with close peers worsened relationships (10%–14%). Conflicts with parents and siblings were about as likely to improve

(9%–14%) as harm (15%–18%) the relationship; most (68%–75%) had no long-term impact. Conflict with teachers, employers, and other peers more often made relationships worse (27%–34%) than better (5%–18%), with no impact (48%–64%) on the prevalent outcome. Thus, in terms of relationship consequences, close peers reported an optimal balance of conflict rewards to costs: Positive outcomes for friends exceeded negative ones, and rewards for romantic partners were twice as high as costs.

Telephone interviews with approximately 200 suburban midwestern (U.S.A.) high school students confirmed the role of conflict management in relationship costs. Responding to a list of conflict issues read aloud by the interviewer, adolescents identified all conflicts from the previous day, as well as their participants, affective intensity, resolutions, and immediate outcomes. Across relationships, negative affect and resolution strategy strongly predicted conflict outcomes: Coercion produced unequal outcomes and negative affect, whereas compromise was associated with the greatest levels of equal outcomes and positive affect (Laursen & Koplas, in press). Ongoing analyses indicate that friends and romantic partners avoided expressions of anger and minimized winner/loser outcomes by eschewing coercive strategies of conflict management. In contrast, angry, coercive disagreements with inequitable outcomes were the rule in all other relationships.

In sum, conflict costs vary across adolescent relationships. More conflicts are reported in communal relationships than in exchange relationships. Conflict with friends and romantic partners, although less frequent than with mothers, occurs at a rate similar to that with siblings and fathers. Nevertheless, relative to disagreements with family members, close peers report less anger during conflict and fewer unequal outcomes, as well as more positive affect and continued social interaction afterward. Despite (or because of) the potential for detrimental consequences, conflict with close peers contains fewer costs and more rewards than those in other relationships. Conflict management may be the key to understanding these relationship differences. Meta-analytic results indicate that with friends and romantic partners, adolescents tend to avoid coercion, preferring softer modes of conflict resolution (disengagement and negotiation) instead (Laursen, 1993b). In contrast, coercion is the most common resolution of disputes with parents, and other peers and adults; negotiation in these relationships is quite rare. Thus, close peers defuse the costs of conflict by avoiding anger and heavy-handed tactics.

Conflict costs also illustrate distinctions between close peer relationships. Compared to friends, romantic partners evince fewer coercive conflict management tactics and, as a result, disagreements are more likely to improve the relationship. When conflict arises, friends are apparently content to close off the dispute and leave well enough alone. Romantic relationships, however, engender special efforts to turn an episode fraught with costs into one that is ultimately rewarding.

## Toward a revised theory of interdependence

Rewards and costs, manifest in closeness and conflict, reflect relationship interdependence. In this section, evidence for the social relational model of adolescent development will be reviewed. Two important revisions to the model are suggested. First, interdependence with friends differs from that with romantic partners, suggesting critical distinctions between relationships in the extent to which rewards and costs govern interactions. Second, the form and function of interdependence in relationships with friends and romantic partners changes with age and maturation. Clearly, adolescence represents a transitional period in manifestations of close relationships, with principles of exchange emerging as increasingly important features differentiating friendships from romantic relationships.

### Accounting for differences between close relationships

Questionnaire reports of rewards and costs in adult relationships underscore the special properties of voluntary communal relationships with friends, romantic partners, and spouses, when compared to involuntary communal relationships with family members and exchange relationships with neighbors and work associates (Argyle & Furnham, 1983). Subjects ranging from 18 to 51 years old evaluated relationships in terms of rewards or satisfaction (e.g., emotional support, shared interests) and costs or conflict (e.g., emotional conflict, criticism). Spouses and romantic partners described both the most satisfaction and the most conflict. Friends ranked next in both categories. Family members reported levels of conflict that rivaled friends, but levels of satisfaction that were somewhat less than those with friends. Exchange relationships scored significantly lower on satisfaction and slightly lower on conflict than communal relationships. Relationship outcomes, represented by the ratio of conflict to satisfaction, encapsulate patterns of interdependence. Communal relationships were marked by more positive outcomes (greater satisfaction relative to conflict) than were exchange relationships. Thus, interactions with friends, romantic partners, spouses, and family members contained relatively fewer costs and relatively more rewards than those with neighbors and work associates. Voluntary communal relationships, especially those with friends, differed from involuntary communal relationships with family members in that the former contained more positive outcomes than the latter.

Similar comparisons of rewards and costs illustrate interdependence in adolescent relationships, depicting differences between close peers and family members, as well as highlighting distinctions between friends and romantic partners. Research described in this chapter indicates that rewards (overall closeness) are greatest with romantic partners, followed by mothers and friends, then fathers and siblings. Costs (coercive conflict behaviors and negative conflict outcomes) are higher with family members than with either friends or romantic partners (Laursen, 1993b, 1993c). In sum, more positive outcomes (greater rewards and fewer costs) are associated with friends and romantic partners than with parents and siblings.

Comparisons of relative rewards and costs also suggest distinctions between friends and romantic partners. The evidence indicates that extant models of interdependence better characterize interactions between romantic partners than between friends. Overall closeness is greater with romantic partners than with friends, and so too is the likelihood of conflict improving the relationship. During mid- and late adolescence, friends enjoy fewer social interactions and less influence than romantic partners, while at the same time friends appear less concerned than romantic partners about the possibility that conflict may terminate rewarding interconnections.

What are the sources of differences between adolescent friendships and romantic relationships? Sex-role socialization, relationship stability, and societal expectations undoubtedly combine to make friends more tolerant of inequity than romantic partners. First, gender differences in close relationships are evident; females are more intimate with friends than males, who instead emphasize companionship and affiliation (Youniss & Smollar, 1985). Opposite-sex relationships may be closer than same-sex friendships, because girlfriends prompt boyfriends to be intimate. Second, the greater inherent stability of the relationship provides friends with more resilience than romantic partners in the face of inequity (Berscheid et al., 1989). As it does with family members, the relative permanence of friendship protects against relationship disruption. Third, Western culture endorses a relationship hierarchy that accords more status to romance than to friendship. Adolescents adopt these expectations, remarking in interviews on the frequency with which a boyfriend or a girlfriend will usurp a best friend as their closest relationship (Shulman, 1993).

Finally, we must not overlook the possibility that with pubertal maturation a genetic propensity, designed to maximize reproductive potential, emerges favoring romantic partners over friends. Over the course of human evolutionary history opposite-sex relationships were required for reproduction. A close relationship between participants may have increased the involvement of fathers in child rearing and improved chances of the offspring's survival. To encourage reproduction and investment in parenting, physical rewards, absent from platonic same-sex friendships, are inherent in romantic relationships (Kenrick & Trost,

1989). Application of these preferential rewards need not be exclusively heterosexual; regardless of their evolutionary origins in reproductive activities, a similar reward structure may be extended to romantic homosexual relationships. The point is simply that sexuality provides an arena for additional interdependence between romantic partners.

Keeping in mind distinctions between voluntary communal relationships with peers and involuntary communal relationships with family members, differentiation between friends and romantic partners may also be the result of stability and relationship function. Friends provide adolescents with companionship and shared activities; the relationships are primarily affiliative. Loyalty and expectations of stability support the continuation of rewards. Romantic partners offer something more than affiliation, including the rewards and status associated with sexual activity and reproduction. In this sense, greater interdependence develops between romantic partners than between friends, because the rewards associated with interactions specific to romantic relationships go beyond those included in most friendships.

*Anticipating developmental changes in close relationships*

Although complete data are not yet available on the distribution of relationship rewards and costs across childhood and adolescence, it is reasonable to conclude that age-related shifts occur in interdependencies. Such an assumption is an integral part of many social developmental theories. Sullivan (1953), for instance, believed that changes occurred in the primacy of relationships, shifting from mothers during infancy, to family members during early childhood, to chums and friends during middle childhood and early adolescence, and finally to romantic partners during late adolescence.

What accounts for developmental shifts in relationship interdependence? Certainly, biological maturation alters interpersonal experiences. Sociobiological accounts stress that greater conflict and diminished closeness are the result of physical maturation; thus, adolescents are pushed out of the home and into the waiting arms of peers (Steinberg, 1989). Alternatively, cognitive advances provide a more sophisticated understanding of close relationships that, in turn, alter social interactions (Selman, 1981; Youniss & Smollar, 1985). Adolescent cognitive maturity prompts reformulation of relationship conceptions, revising patterns of closeness and conflict in interactions (Smetana, 1988).

Finally, the relationship itself provides an important context for development. Two social relational themes capture mechanisms of adolescent development. First, social skills improve with experience, enabling abilities acquired in one set of relationships to be applied to others (Hartup & Laursen, 1991). This bootstrapping strategy describes the adaptation of successful patterns of interaction from previous relationships and age-periods. Second, developmental shifts in interdependence result from systematic reductions in environmental constraints (Collins & Repinski, 1994; Laursen & Collins, 1994). The behavior of children is influenced by settings and authority figures that demand specific interaction outcomes (e.g., getting along), effectively restricting unfettered distribution of rewards and costs in a relationship. Across adolescence, there is less adult supervision of peer relationships and less interference with the selection of interaction partners. Consequently, principles of interdependence assume greater importance in determining features of peer relationships as adolescents grow older.

Consistent with these social relational tenets, it is proposed that the full implications of interdependence are not realized until adolescents make the transition from a social world dominated by parents to one comprised of peers. Thus, interdependence should increasingly influence voluntary communal relationships with friends and romantic partners. Family relationships, although communal, are more circumscribed relative to those with peers; the behavior of children toward their parents and siblings remains bound by kinship, regardless of age. No similar glue binds friends and romantic partners. As supervisory dictates are lifted, adolescents must discover rules of conduct appropriate for close peer relationships. Principles of interdependence, growing in importance as the stature of the relationship increases, help to fill this void (Laursen et al., in press). Cognitive advances promote new conceptualizations of friendships and romantic relationships, deepening the appreciation of the need to maintain interdependence even as greater autonomy and improved social skills expand abilities to act on this awareness. Thus, interdependence in close peer relationships gradually develops during adolescence, prompted by the removal of external constraints on interactions.

## Fulfilling the developmental potential of interdependence models

Social relational models of close peer relationships offer considerable promise as an explanatory framework. Research suggests that adolescents carefully balance rewards and costs in voluntary communal relationships with friends and romantic partners, so as to maintain interdependence and ensure continuation of positive outcomes. Such behavior is not apparent in involuntary communal relationships with family members and in exchange relationships with work and school associates; consequently, these relationships are marked by less closeness and more disruptive conflicts.

Although more similar than dissimilar, important differences between friends and romantic partners have been identified. Romantic relationships, for instance, contain more positive outcomes (rewards relative to costs) than friendships. To accommodate these findings, social relational models of adolescent relationships must account for differences between interdependent peers whose rewards are strictly affiliative and those whose rewards offer potential sexual activity. Developmental considerations should also be incorporated into models of interdependence, in light of evidence that manifestations of closeness and conflict in communal relationships vary with age. Since behavior during childhood is subject to multiple external constraints, a developmental perspective suggests that adolescence may be the earliest age in which the full impact of interdependence is appreciated in close peer relationships.

Empirical research on friendships and romantic relationships during adolescence lags behind that of other developmental periods (Furman, 1993). A growing number of scholars, however, are turning their attention to adolescent peer relationships and tremendous advances are anticipated in the near future. Social relational models, as an alternative to traditional perspectives on adolescent development, offer new avenues of study for investigators interested in close relationships as a central developmental construct. Among the many areas of adolescent close peer relationships that await further explication, three directions for future study stand out as being particularly amenable to research within a social relational framework: (1) elaborating distinctions between interdependent relationships; (2) delineating linkages between rewards and closeness, costs and conflict; and (3) determining contextual influences on interdependence.

Social relational models of development emphasize continuity and gradual transformation. Yet, as currently envisioned, relationships are qualitatively distinct: interdependent or not interdependent, communal or exchange, voluntary or involuntary. These categories oversimplify the complex reality of social relationships. Quite probably, all relationships display varying amounts of these attributes, and their characteristics change over time as interconnections within the relationship are altered. This raises several questions about nuances in relationship interdependence that the current framework is neither conceptually nor methodologically capable of addressing. Are communal and exchange relationships mutually exclusive? Do voluntary and involuntary attributes represent two poles of a single dimension of interdependence or are they orthogonal variables that operate independently? These empirical questions require immediate attention; the distinct possibility that associations between interdependence variables vary as a function of development make it unwise to generalize about properties of close relationships from one age-period to another.

There is little evidence that closeness and conflict represent the full spectrum of the rewards and costs in a relationship, although this is conceptually appealing. In other words, closeness and conflict may not capture important properties of interdependence present in other types of interactions. For instance, new insight into interdependence may emerge if costs are conceptualized in terms of missed interaction opportunities. So too might depictions of closeness expand if rewards are defined as interpersonal problems avoided. In a similar vein, the relative importance of the various constructs representing closeness and conflict are not yet known. What are the unique contributions of intimacy and affiliation to closeness? Do coercive conflict management and negative affect represent equivalent relationship costs? The answers to these questions are also likely to differ with age, again underscoring the need for developmentally sophisticated research.

Finally, little is known about how culture and context influences interdependence. Because most investigations of adolescent relationships, especially friendships and romantic relationships, have considered only middle-class North American subjects, the universality of interdependence and its developmental applications remain to be demonstrated. Do representations of closeness and conflict in relationships with friends and romantic partners differ across cultures? Can the influence of a setting nullify principles of interdependence in close peer relationships? In light of evidence that setting shapes interactions in interdependent relationships (see Hartup & Laursen, 1993; Laursen & Collins, 1994, for review), it should not be surprising if additional contextual factors emerge as prominent determinants of behavior with friends and romantic partners. Because a developmental appreciation of relationship processes remains incomplete without a full accounting of contextual diversity, research on cultural and ecological variations in close peer relationships is imperative.

The study of adolescent close peer relationships, like most areas of adolescent development, offers a rich and ambitious research agenda. Even as scholars provide a better description of the form of friendships and romantic relationships, theoretical frameworks explicating transformations in close peer relationships are lacking (Furman, 1993). An interdependence model of close relationships offers a first step toward a more detailed account of adolescent development, bridging the gap between theory and empirical business as usual.

## References

Argyle, M., & Furnham, A. (1983). Sources of satisfaction and conflict in long-term relationships. *Journal of Marriage and the Family, 45*, 481–493.

Berndt, T. J., Hawkins, J. A., & Hoyle, S. G. (1986). Changes in friendship during a school year: Effects on children's and adolescents' impressions of friendship and sharing with friends. *Child Development, 57*, 1284–1297.

Berndt, T. J., & Perry, T. B. (1986). Children's perceptions of friendships as supportive relationships. *Developmental Psychology, 22*, 640–648.

Berscheid, E. (1986). Emotional experience in close relationships: Some implications for child development. In W. W. Hartup & Z. Rubin (Eds.), *Relationships and development*. Hillsdale, NJ: Erlbaum.

Berscheid, E., Snyder, M., & Omoto, A. M. (1989). The Relationship Closeness Inventory: Assessing the closeness of interpersonal relationships. *Journal of Personality and Social Psychology, 57*, 792–807.

Berscheid, E., & Walster, E. H. (1969). *Interpersonal attraction*. Reading, MA: Addison-Wesley.

Blos, P. (1979). *The adolescent passage*. New York: International Universities Press.

Buhrmester, D., & Furman, W. (1987). The development of companionship and intimacy. *Child Development, 58*, 1101–1113.

Clark, M. S., Mills, J., & Powell, M. C. (1986). Keeping track of needs in communal and exchange relationships. *Journal of Personality and Social Psychology, 51*, 333–338.

Clark, M. S., & Reis, H. T. (1988). Interpersonal processes in close relationships. *Annual Review of Psychology, 39*, 609–672.

Clark-Lempers, D. S., Lempers, J. D., & Ho, C. (1991). Early, middle, and late adolescents' perceptions of their relationships with significant others. *Journal of Adolescent Research, 6*, 296–315.

Collins, W.A., & Laursen, B. (1992). Conflict and relationships during adolescence. In C. U. Shantz & W. W. Hartup (Eds.), *Conflict in child and adolescent development*. New York: Cambridge University Press.

Collins, W. A., & Repinski, D. J. (1994). Relationships during adolescence: Continuity and change in interpersonal perspective. In R. Montemayor, G. Adams, & T. Gullotta (Eds.), *Personal relationships during adolescence*. Beverly Hills, CA: Sage.

Csikszentmihalyi, M., & Larson, R. (1984). *Being adolescent*. New York: Basic Books.

Furman, W. (1993). Theory is not a four-letter word: Needed directions in the study of adolescent friendships. In B. Laursen (Ed.), *Close friendships in adolescence: New directions for child development*. San Francisco: Jossey-Bass.

Furman, W., & Buhrmester, D. (1985). Children's perceptions of the personal relationships in their social networks. *Developmental Psychology, 21*, 1016–1024.

Furman, W., & Buhrmester, D. (1992). Age and sex differences in perceptions of networks of personal relationships. *Child Development, 63*, 103–115.

Furman, W., & Wehner, E. A. (1995). Romantic views: Toward a theory of adolescent romantic relationships. In R. Montemayor, G. Adams, & T. Gullotta (Eds.), *Personal relationships during adolescence*. Beverly Hills, CA: Sage.

Gottman, J. M. (1979). *Marital interaction: Experimental investigations*. New York: Academic Press.

Hartup, W. W. (1992). Conflict and friendship relations. In C. U. Shantz & W. W. Hartup (Eds.), *Conflict in child and adolescent development* (pp. 186–215). New York: Cambridge University Press.

Hartup, W. W. (1993). Adolescents and their friends. In B. Laursen (Ed.), *Close friendships in adolescence: New directions for child development*. San Francisco: Jossey-Bass.

Hartup, W. W., & Laursen, B. (1991). Relationships as developmental contexts. In R. Cohen & A. W. Siegel (Eds.), *Context and development*. Hillsdale, NJ: Erlbaum.

Hartup, W. W., & Laursen, B. (1993). Conflict and context in peer relations. In C. Hart (Ed.), *Children on playgrounds: Research perspectives and applications*. Albany, NY: State University of New York Press.

Hartup, W. W., Laursen, B., Stewart, M. I., & Eastenson, A. (1988). Conflict and the friendship relations of young children. *Child Development, 59*, 1590–1600.

Kelley, H. H., Berscheid, E., Christensen, A., Harvey, J. H., Huston, T. L., Levinger, G., McClintock, E., Peplau, L. A., & Peterson, D. R. (1983). *Close relationships*. New York: Freeman.

Kelley, H. H., & Thibaut, J. W. (1978). *Interpersonal relations: A theory of interdependence*. New York: Wiley.

Kenrick, D. T., & Trost, M. R. (1989). A reproductive exchange model of heterosexual relationships:

Putting proximate economics in ultimate perspective. In C. Hendrick (Ed.), *Review of personality and social psychology*, Vol. 10. Newbury Park, CA: Sage.

Laursen, B. (1993a, March). Age-related changes in the management of peer conflict. In B. Laursen (Chair), *The role of conflict in relationships with close peers and siblings: Getting along with agemates.* Paper presented at the meetings of the Society for Research in Child Development, New Orleans, LA.

Laursen, B. (1993b). Conflict management among close peers. In B. Laursen (Ed.), *Close friendships in adolescence: New directions for child development.* San Francisco: Jossey-Bass.

Laursen, B. (1993c). The perceived impact of conflict on adolescent relationships. *Merrill-Palmer Quarterly, 39*, 535–550.

Laursen, B. (1995). Conflict and social interaction in adolescent relationships. *Journal of Research on Adolescence, 5*, 55–70.

Laursen, B., & Collins, W. A. (1994). Interpersonal conflict during adolescence. *Psychological Bulletin, 115*, 197–209.

Laursen, B., & Hartup, W. W. (1989). The dynamics of preschool children's conflicts. *Merrill-Palmer Quarterly, 35*, 281–297.

Laursen, B., Hartup, W. W., & Koplas, A. L. (in press). Towards understanding peer conflict. *Merrill-Palmer Quarterly.*

Laursen, B., Koplas, A. L. (in press). What's important about important conflicts: Adolescents' perceptions of daily disagreements. *Merrill-Palmer Quarterly.*

Mills, J., & Clark, M. S. (1982). Exchange and communal relationships. In L. Wheeler (Ed.), *Review of personality and social psychology*, Vol 3. Beverly Hills, CA: Sage.

Perry, D. G., Perry, L. C., & Kennedy, E. (1992). Conflict and the development of antisocial behavior. In C. U. Shantz & W. W. Hartup (Eds.), *Conflict in child and adolescent development.* New York: Cambridge University Press.

Peterson, D. R. (1983). Conflict. In H. H. Kelley, E. Berscheid, A. Christensen, J. H. Harvey, T. L. Huston, G. Levinger, E. McClintock, L. A. Peplau, & D. R. Peterson (Eds.), *Close relationships.* New York: Freeman.

Prinz, R. J., Foster, S. L., Kent, R. N., & O'Leary, K. D. (1979). Multivariate assessment of conflict in distressed and non-distressed mother–adolescent dyads. *Journal of Applied Behavior Analysis, 12*, 691–700.

Repinski, D. J. (1992). *Closeness in parent–adolescent relationships: Contrasting interdependence, emotional tone, and a subjective rating.* Unpublished manuscript, State University of New York, Geneseo.

Repinski, D. J. (1993). *Adolescents' close relationships with parents and friends.* Unpublished Ph.D. thesis, University of Minnesota.

Rizzo, T. A. (1992). The role of conflict in children's friendship development. *Interpretive approaches to children's socialization: New directions for child development.* San Francisco: Jossey-Bass.

Robin, A. L., & Foster, S. L. (1984). Problem-solving communication training: A behavioral family systems approach to parent–adolescent conflict. In P. Karoly & J. J. Steffen (Eds.), *Adolescent behavior disorders: Foundations and contemporary concerns.* Lexington, MA: Heath.

Savin-Williams, R. C., & Berndt, T. J. (1990). Friendship and peer relations. In S. S. Feldman & G. R. Elliott (Eds.), *At the threshold: The developing adolescent.* Cambridge: Harvard University Press.

Selman, R. L. (1981). The development of interpersonal competence: The role of understanding in conduct. *Developmental Review, 1*, 401–422.

Selman, R. L., Beardslee, W., Schultz, L. H., Krupa, M., & Podorefsky, D. (1986). Assessing adolescent interpersonal negotiation strategies: Toward the integration of structural and functional models. *Developmental Psychology, 22*, 450–459.

Shantz, C. U. (1987). Conflict between children. *Child Development, 58*, 283–305.

Sharabany, R., Gershoni, R., & Hofman, J. E. (1981). Girlfriend, boyfriend: Age and sex differences in intimate friendship. *Developmental Psychology, 17*, 800–808.

Shulman, S. (1993). Close friendships in early and middle adolescence: Typology and friendship reasoning. In B. Laursen (Ed.), *Close friendships in adolescence: New directions for child development*. San Francisco: Jossey-Bass.

Smetana, J. G. (1988). Concepts of self and social convention: Adolescents' and parents' reasoning about hypothetical and actual family conflicts. In M. R. Gunnar & W. A. Collins (Eds.), *Minnesota symposia on child psychology*, Vol 21. Hillsdale, NJ: Erlbaum.

Steinberg, L. (1989). Pubertal maturation and parent–adolescent distance: An evolutionary perspective. In G. Adams, R. Montemayor, & T. Gullotta (Eds.), *Biology of adolescent behavior and development*. Newbury Park, CA: Sage.

Sullivan, H. S. (1953). *The interpersonal theory of psychiatry*. New York: Norton.

Thibaut, J. W., & Kelley, H. H. (1959). *The psychology of groups*. New York: Wiley.

Walster, E., Berscheid, E., & Walster, G. W. (1973). New directions in equity research. *Journal of Personality and Social Psychology, 25*, 151–176.

Youniss, J. (1980). *Parents and peers in social development: A Piaget-Sullivan perspective*. Chicago: University of Chicago Press.

Youniss, J., & Smollar, J. (1985). *Adolescent relations with mothers, fathers, and friends*. Chicago: University of Chicago Press.

*Part III*

**Friendship and its associations with other aspects of development**

# 10 Cooperation, close relationships, and cognitive development

*Willard W. Hartup*

Relatively little is known about children's friendships as contexts for cognitive development. Peer interaction sometimes contributes to problem-solving efficacy although outcome studies are not entirely consistent (Azmitia & Perlmutter, 1989; Tudge & Rogoff, 1989). Even so, few investigators have asked what friends might contribute to cognitive development, that is, whether experience with friends accounts for significant variance in cognitive functioning beyond that which child–child interaction generally accounts for.

Close relationships and their variations are mostly ignored in theories of cognitive development. Although social interaction has long been recognized as a determinant of cognitive growth (Vygotsky, 1986/1934; Mead, 1934), the emotional and instrumental interdependencies that constitute "closeness" in relationships between the social agent and the child are rarely taken into account. Social agents are usually thought to influence cognitive development through what they know rather than through the quality of their relationships with the child. Mothers, for example, are regarded as significant contributors to cognitive development more often for reasons having to do with their knowledge about the world than for reasons relating to the attachments existing between themselves and their children. Similarly, friends are regarded as significant cognitive resources (if at all) because of the time they spend together rather than because of the unique qualities of these relationships.

New interest is evident in close relationships and what they may contribute to cognitive development. For example, secure attachments between mothers and infants are now known to promote utilization of social resources in problem-solving better than insecure ones (Matas, Arend, & Sroufe, 1978); mothers are especially able to articulate new information with what the child already knows

The author wishes to thank Margarita Azmitia, Ellen Berscheid, Andrew Collins, Rochel Gelman, Barbara Rogoff, Jonathan Tudge, and Kees van Lieshout for their careful reading of the first version of this manuscript, and for their many comments and suggestions. Support from the Rodney S. Wallace Endowment, University of Minnesota, is also gratefully acknowledged.

213

(Rogoff, 1990). Bits of evidence are also accumulating to suggest that friends contribute something unique to cognitive functioning, but this literature is scattered and thin.

Since cooperation (collaboration) between the child and the social agent is believed to have special significance in cognitive development (Rogoff, 1990; Schaffer, 1992), this chapter begins with a consideration of cooperation as a social imperative. Cooperation and collaboration are used synonymously here to refer to conditions in which individuals work together toward common goals or shared rewards.

Cooperation and its role in cognitive development is then discussed. The term *cognitive development* refers here to normative changes in problem solving, communication, and creative activity. In the contemporary literature, the word *cognition* encompasses almost every known perceptual or intellectual function. Close relationships, however, are not likely to affect the development of basic processing functions or their organization, but are likely to affect task-mastery and creativity, especially in social contexts (Hartup, 1985). As yet, no taxonomy exists with which to specify exactly which "problem" solutions might be sensitive to social experience and which may not be. Social agents are nevertheless known to affect performance in situations in which questions are raised for inquiry, consideration, or solution; communication with other persons established and maintained; and materials and language manipulated creatively (play, creative writing, or dramatics). Although no one knows exactly which cognitive domains are linked to the social context, sufficient research has been conducted to suggest that these three are (Schaffer, 1992).

Whether friends differ from nonfriends during collaboration on cognitive tasks is discussed next, with special attention being given to why collaboration should differ between children and their friends as compared to children and their acquaintances. Friendships are close relationships whose normative essentials consist of reciprocity and commitment, and which occur between individuals who see themselves more or less as equals. Some writers consider friendships to be "affiliative" relationships rather than "attachments" (Weiss, 1986) but children make considerable investment in these relationships, go to considerable lengths to maintain them, and separate themselves from their friends with reluctance. Various studies now show that friends cooperate readily with one another (conflict also occurs), thus engaging in the social exchanges thought to be relevant to cognitive development.

Other questions addressed in the chapter include the following: Are some friends better suited to collaboration (and to cognitive advancement) than others? Are children who have friends better collaborators and more cognitively mature than children who do not have friends? From several different perspectives, then, this discussion ties together three constructs: cooperation, close relationships (between children and their friends), and cognitive development.

## Cooperation as a social imperative

Although the evolutionary basis for cooperation has not been specified to everyone's satisfaction, coordinated activity between human beings is ubiquitous. Social collaborations among children are evident in every culture, appearing early in development; differences among children in cooperation are salient in person perception and social attribution; and these differences are moderately stable across time. Scattered evidence supports these conclusions and, taken together, suggests that cooperation is a necessity in human development and adaptation. Whether these necessities include contributions to cognitive development is not certain, although this is widely believed.

### Cooperation in evolutionary perspective

The extent to which cooperation, in contrast to competition, is fundamental in natural selection has been debated since evolutionary theory was first promulgated. Some writers (e.g., Charlesworth, 1991) argue that cooperation is always competitively motivated, and thus is not an evolutionary imperative in its own right. Others argue that natural selection favors cooperation and altruism (as well as competition) among both related and nonrelated individuals. According to these arguments: (a) Cooperation may be selected among related individuals when a greater number of one's genes survive through one's relatives than through one's own offspring (Hamilton, 1964). (b) Among nonrelatives, cooperation can arise through mutualism (in which cooperation mutually benefits the two parties), induced altruism (in which one individual coerces altruism from another), or reciprocal altruism (between individuals who reciprocate); see Axelrod and Hamilton (1981). Everyone recognizes that cooperative and competitive motives can be intermingled, so that two individuals may compete with one another while, at the same time, they cooperate. Similarly, two individuals may cooperate while simultaneously competing with outsiders. But sociobiological thought has swung increasingly to the view that natural selection favors cooperation as well as competition in supporting the reproduction of the individual's genetic material.

Some investigators (LaFreniere, 1991) argue that friendship relations serve some of the same adaptive functions as kin relations and that, consequently, the interaction between friends should be marked by greater cooperation than interaction between nonfriends. The argument assumes that friendship selection rests on similarities in age, sex, race, social class, and neighborhood. These similarities enhance social attraction and establish reciprocity as the normative basis for social interaction (Berscheid & Walster, 1969). Reciprocity norms, in turn, determine that friends will cooperate more extensively than nonfriends. The similarity/attraction hypothesis thus provides a basis for reciprocal altruism between friends even though friends do not share genes.

*Cultural universals*

Some aspects of cooperative interaction among children are invariant across cultures. Cooperation appears universally in child and family relations in both hunter-gatherer and subsistence societies. Certain features occur again and again. When scarce resources are involved (an opportunity, for example, to view a cartoon through a narrow aperture in an experimental apparatus), children in cooperating groups simultaneously compete with one another in many different cultures (Charlesworth, 1991).

At the same time, the world's cultures vary in the extent to which cooperation versus competition is emphasized in child rearing, and children behave accordingly. Hunter-gatherer societies (as well as industrialized ones) favor competition whereas agricultural societies favor cooperation (Whiting, 1981). Rural Mexican children thus cooperate more readily than Mexican-American or Anglo-American children (Kagan & Madsen, 1971; Knight & Kagan, 1977).

*Cooperation emerges early in development*

Cooperation emerges early in both adult–child and child–child relations. Babies' actions are coordinated with their caregivers' actions (both actively and passively) from birth onward, suggesting a genetic bias that favors coordinated action systems. Coordinated interaction between children emerges more slowly: Certain coordinated elements – visual regard, touching and reaching, pushing and pulling – are evident early in child–child interaction but with rudimentary social results (Walker, Messinger, Fogel, & Karns, 1992).

Changes occur, however, toward the end of the second year: "skills for initiating and maintaining interactions [emerge] as well as more general abilities to coordinate interaction around a theme, goal, or plan, to behave reciprocally, and to communicate effectively" (Brownell & Brown, 1992, p. 196). Cooperative problem solving in a wide variety of tasks advances according to this timetable. One example: coordinating one's actions with those of another child in order to obtain an otherwise unobtainable reward occurs rarely among 12-month-olds, intermittently among 18-month-olds, but quickly and easily among most 24-month-olds (Brownell & Carriger, 1990).

Social coordinations are thus evident from birth onward in the child's commerce with the environment. In the beginning, the child's actions must occur in interaction with an adult to effect an appropriate adaptation. Social coordinations with other children are evident within a short time and, by the end of the second year, cooperative interaction is common.

### Stability of cooperation

As a personality dimension, cooperativeness is relatively stable in early childhood. For example, the occurrence of responsivity and reciprocity in mother–child interaction (i.e., sensitivity) disposes toward cooperation between mother and child in problem solving later on (Matas et al., 1978); being temperamentally easy or difficult (agreeable) is moderately stable (Thomas, Chess, & Birch, 1969).

Other evidence showing cooperative stability is based on observations and teacher ratings of children's activities in nursery school and extend over 1- and 2-year intervals between 12 and 24 months, 24 and 36 months, and 36 and 60 months (Howes, 1988). One-year stability coefficients among nursery school children for engaging in cooperative play are about .50. Stability estimates using measures aggregated across different settings and extending over longer time intervals have been obtained with ratings based on four play sessions (each with different unacquainted partners) at 12, 24, and 42 months as well as three play sessions (each with two different acquainted partners) at 60 months (de Roos & Riksen-Walraven, 1992). Aggregated cooperation scores were moderately stable from 12 to 42 months ($r = .33$ and .45, respectively) but not extending on to 60 months. The 60-month results may mean that dyadic cooperation (the situation used with the younger children) simply does not predict triadic cooperation (the situation used with the older children). Other data (Cillessen, van Lieshout, & Haselager, 1992) show that aggregated cooperation scores based on observations in triads and teacher ratings are stable across 1- and 2-year intervals in middle childhood.

### Salience in person perception

Cooperation is well differentiated in person perception among both children and adults. Children employ "cooperative schemas" in organizing and remembering information about one another. In one investigation (Bukowski, Kramer, & Watson, 1992), evidence of schematic organization among nursery school children was derived from a task measuring the extent to which the children used information about a child from one hypothetical situation to make inferences about that child in other situations. Consistency in these generalizations was greater than chance when other children were described as "having someone to play with," "liking to be nice," and "being very helpful to others," suggesting the existence of an "agreeableness" or "cooperativeness" schema among these children. Concordance has also been demonstrated between kindergarten children's expectations about one another's prosocial behavior and their subsequent actions (Cillessen, 1991).

Adults organize their social thinking using a limited number of constructs, among which is "agreeableness" (Graziano & Eisenberg, in press). This construct is grounded in altruism and friendliness as well as in cooperativeness, and the cluster is always evident in the language that adults use to describe people. Adults in most countries use this construct cluster to encode and utilize information about children as well as to organize information about adults, suggesting that it is broadly salient in natural language (Halverson, Kohnstamm, & Martin, 1994). Whether children utilize agreeableness as consistently as adults evince the construct and the extent to which children employ the construct cluster in their relations with other children are not entirely clear. Agreeableness, however, is salient by early adolescence when youngsters describe one another in a manner that is congruent with adult descriptions. Self-descriptions in early adolescence also reveal an agreeableness factor that is substantially congruent with adult language (van Lieshout & Haselager, in 1994).

*Summary*

Cooperation is most likely a social imperative. Behavioral coordinations and working together toward common goals are evident from early childhood in both social behavior and social cognition. Cooperation emerges in interactions with other children toward the end of the second year; early differences among individuals are moderately stable across time; adults organize their information about children in terms of these differences; children and adolescents do too. Although developmental data are lacking, one can guess that cooperative behavior may be the substrate from which the cooperative lexicon emerges. Our attention now turns to the dialectics that link cooperation and cognitive activity.

**Cooperation and cognitive development**

Three ancestries can be identified among theories dealing with the significance of cooperative/collaborative experience and cognitive development: *equilibration theory* (Piaget, 1932, 1985/1975), *sociohistorical theory* (Vygotsky, 1986/1934), and *symbolic interactionism* (Mead, 1934, 1938). Great significance is attached in these formulations to the necessity for the child to interact with cultural representatives in order to bring about cognitive growth. Recent formulations ascribe an especially important role to the child, who actively selects and creates learning opportunities (Rogoff, 1990; Lave & Wenger, 1991). At the same time, little attention is given in this literature to close relationships and their implications. The "social agent" remains an abstraction in these formulations (a person, an adult, a peer) rather than a "warm body" with emotional and interactive attachments to the child.

## Piaget and equilibration

Piaget (1926) assumed that cognitive development derives from coordinating ideas and overcoming contradictions through a complex process known as *equilibration*. In his early writings, conflicts between children and their companions (within a cooperative context) were believed to be a major impetus for "disequilibrium" and, hence, cognitive growth. Piaget is usually interpreted as arguing that conflicts between one's own and others' views precipitate cognitive conflicts within the individual, thereby instantiating disequilibrium. Children's encounters with views different from their own are thus critical events in cognitive development, even though the process does not involve consensus building. Actually, the relevance of conflict *content* to cognitive change is not well specified in this literature and, most commonly, these notions are understood as suggesting that "for Piaget, the meeting of minds involved two separate individuals, each operating on the other's ideas, using the back-and-forth of discussion for each to advance his or her own development" (Rogoff, 1990, p. 149).

Peer interaction is believed to contribute to cognitive development because interaction between social and cognitive equals generates the confrontations necessary for schematic coordination. Conflicts with adults, according to these notions, are resolved via conformity rather than cooperation because adults always have greater power and knowledge about the world than the child does. Peer interaction is uniquely relevant to cognitive development because it forces the child to coordinate his or her views with those of the companion (i.e., to restructure his or her own views) rather than to conform to them.

Children working with other children have been shown many times to solve more difficult problems than children working on their own, with effects that generalize to other, similar problems (Doise & Mugny, 1984; Perret-Clermont & Brossard, 1985). Such effects do not necessarily depend on interacting with a more knowledgeable partner (sometimes a *less* able partner will do) nor does observational learning mediate changes in the subject's performance. Rather, cooperating children seem to structure new strategies in problem solving that are better than those either child can generate alone. In some instances, investigators have not been able to show facilitating effects of social conflict and cooperation on cognitive development (Bearison, Magzamen, & Filarde, 1986).

In others, though, contributions to cognitive development clearly derive from social conflict and the cooperative experience.

And yet, neither earlier nor more recent notions about equilibration suggest that the qualitative dimensions of children's relationships may moderate these effects. Most experiments demonstrating that conflict and cooperation affect cognitive development are based on observations of acquainted children (at best) or strangers. Frequently, friends are excluded from the experimental design in order to maintain comparability across experimental conditions. Friends and acquaintances, however, are not equivalent companions (Hartup, 1983), so it is risky to assume that they are equivalent cognitive agents.

*Vygotsky and internalization*

"Social relations or relations among people [onto]genetically underlie all higher functions and their relationships" (Vygotsky, 1981, p. 163). The importance of social interaction in cognitive development is thus assumed. The dialectics between society and the individual that undergird selective attention, concept formation, memory development, and motivation were thought by Vygotsky to consist of "interpsychological processes" involving small groups (including dyads) engaged in social interaction and explainable in terms of group dynamics. Some social exchange or event was believed always to be antecedent to mental function, that is, "everything internal was once external." These transmutations are thus known collectively as "internalization."

Speech and dialogue were identified as the most important mediators of internalization. Dialogues resulting in developmental change involve finely tuned coordinations between the child and the social agent and must occur within a "zone of proximal development," defined as the difference between the child's current functioning (measured by his or her independent problem solving) and the child's competence (measured by problem solving with adult guidance or in collaboration with more capable peers). The social agent tunes the problem-solving attempt to a level just beyond the actual development of the child, who is not a passive actor in these exchanges but engages in active transformation of his or her social skills. The social agent mediates the decontextualization of the skill, usually through indirect or inductive suggestions. Gradually, abstractions (internal) are elaborated by the child that are not situation-specific and that do not need to be supported by concrete social interactions. Wertsch and his colleagues (1980, 1985) documented this scenario in mother–child interaction, showing that the dialogic sequence is similar from child to child although participation and control of the dialogue may vary greatly (e.g., between learning disabled and normally achieving children).

The most effective partners in these dialogues are not equal in cognitive skill (the mother and child represent the prototype in most studies). Among children, the best partners differ from one another in expertise. Not surprisingly, then, the evidence shows that conversations among toddlers are more mature when they interact with children 2 years older than themselves than when they interact with agemates (Lougee, Grueneich, & Hartup, 1977; Howes & Farver, 1987). Depending on the task, however, two novices can contribute to problem solving (Azmitia, 1988; Daiute & Dalton, 1991) and, in some respects, novice–novice and expert–novice dialogues are structured similarly. Agemates, for example, use generative strategies as well as reflective ones during collaborative writing (including disagreeing about story content) and also take turns in "master/apprentice" roles (Daiute & Dalton, 1991).

Beyond demonstrating that collaboration among children contributes generally to cognitive development, researchers are now identifying the skills most likely to benefit and the qualities in peer interaction most likely to be responsible (Azmitia & Perlmutter, 1989; Tudge & Rogoff, 1989) for this development. Conversation or modeling is necessary in order for internalization to occur (Light & Glachan, 1985); especially effective are dialogues dealing with task-related issues and strategies (Ellis & Rogoff, 1986) as well as "transactive" dialogues (conversations in which the children discuss one another's strategies and reasoning; see Kruger, 1992; Tudge & Winterhoff, 1993).

Once again, very little is known about friends as compared with nonfriends in collaborative problem solving. Children's conversations with friends during problem solving are only beginning to be compared with children's conversations with nonfriends in the same tasks (see the next section). Sociohistorical theory generally ignores closeness in relationships as a determinant of cognitive development although the theory implies that collaborators must know one another well in order for a zone of proximal development to be created. Although consensus that close relationships have considerable developmental significance is emerging elsewhere (Hartup, 1989), one cannot draw from sociohistorical theory the prediction that cognitive dialogues between friends are better than those between nonfriends.

*Mead and symbolic interaction*

The idea that certain cognitive attributes originate in social interaction was shared by George Herbert Mead (1934, 1938). Best known for his theory concerning the social origins of the self, Mead worked out a comprehensive theory of action in which interactive exchanges are assumed to be the basis of cognitive development. Symbolically transmitted interactions between persons (conversations with gestures) were assumed to be the basis for the construction of symbolic thought; linguistic and other symbols occurring in interaction are internalized, not mere imitations. "The probable beginning of human communication was in cooperation, not in imitation, where the conduct differed and yet where the act of the one answered to and called out the act of the other" (Mead, 1909, p. 406). Communication and cooperation are events during which individuals adjust to one another, exchanging meaningful gestures realized linguistically and symbolically. Actions become significant symbols when, in social interaction, they implicitly arouse in one individual the same responses they explicitly arouse (or are supposed to arouse) in others. Social interaction thus furnishes the basis for symbolic thought, even before the child can make self-other distinctions and before self-consciousness emerges. More like Vygotsky, then, than Piaget, Mead argued that mind and self are constituted through the interiorization of symbols and linguistic behavior that originate in social interaction.

Mead's theory of action has never been as widely appreciated as his ideas about socialization, especially his notions about the "generalized other" and the social origins of self (see Higgins, 1991, for a notable exception). The manner in which culture becomes internalized is widely known, probably because Mead was first read by sociologists (fragmentary versions of his works began to appear in sociological writings during the 1920s and 1930s; (see Vari-Szilagyi, 1991). This theory of action, however, has broad implications as a theory of mental development, and rests on the assumption that cooperation between individuals (most commonly between individuals who know one another well) contains the symbolic interaction most relevant to cognitive growth. Social interaction within close relationships may contain a gestural and symbolic language that differs from interaction when close relationships do not exist (i.e., with social agents abstractly conceived) but this assumption was never made explicit.

*Summary*

Quoting Perret-Clermont and Brossard (1985):

For Piaget, social factors are necessary for the completion of the structures of intelligence, *but they are not at the source of these structures* [authors' italics]. To assimilate the contributions of social experience, the child must already be endowed with mental structures which make this assimilation possible. . . . For Mead, thought appears as the interiorization of the conversation of gestures . . . especially when verbal behaviors are mixed with the conversation of gestures. . . . For Vygotsky, this transformation of an interpersonal process into an intrapersonal one can be generalized to all higher functions . . . and to the cognitive ones in particular. (pp. 310–312)

Cooperation, collaboration, intersubjectivities, and interdependencies in social interaction are thus stressed in each of these theories – even though implications for cognitive development differ. Relatively little recognition has been given, however, to the possibility that cooperative interaction and collaborative dialogues might differ according to the affective relationships existing between children and their social agents.

## Cooperation among friends and nonfriends: The evidence

Cooperation and friendship are linked in both children's thinking and their behavior. Children behave cooperatively in order to become friends, but also to remain friends (Bigelow, 1977; Furman & Bierman, 1984). The extent to which children and their friends cooperate with one another as cognitive resources, however, is difficult to determine. Various assessments tell us that friends want to work under cooperative conditions more than nonfriends (Philp, 1940); cooperative experiences increase children's attraction to one another (Johnson, Johnson, & Scott, 1978); and cooperation occurs more frequently in socializing among friends than among nonfriends (Masters & Furman, 1981). Nevertheless, friends are frequently not allowed to work together on classroom tasks because teachers believe they won't maintain task-orientation and will disrupt others. Elementary school teachers allow girls greater freedom in this regard than boys (Azmitia, personal communication) but an "anti-friends" bias among classroom teachers is pervasive. Which bias is correct?

In this section, friends and nonfriends are compared in terms of their interaction during problem solving. Most of the evidence comes from the laboratory rather than from naturalistic settings. A sufficient number of studies has been completed, however, to determine: (a) whether friends cooperate more readily during problem solving than nonfriends; and (b) the specific ways in which social interaction during problem solving differs between friends and nonfriends.

*Seeking scarce resources*

Various situations have been used to compare cooperation between friends and between nonfriends when access to scarce resources is limited. One experiment (Newcomb, Brady, & Hartup, 1979) demonstrated that school-aged children's success in a block-building task was not related to friendship status although social interaction was: Friends interacted more frequently, smiled and laughed with each other more, gave greater attention to equity rules, and turned their conversations toward mutual ends rather than individualized ones. Similar differences were obtained when school children were asked to explore a many-faceted "creativity box" with either a friend or a nonfriend (Newcomb & Brady, 1982). More extensive exploration occurred among children with their friends; conversation was more extensive and mutually oriented; the emotional tenor of the exchanges was more positive. Most important, when tested subsequently, the children who explored the box with a friend remembered more about it afterward. Other studies using a simplified version of the prisoners' dilemma (Matsumoto, Haan, Yabrove, Theodorou, & Carney, 1986) show attraction between children to be correlated with mutual orientation to the task as well as with equalization in task negotiations.

Observations of school-aged children playing a board game under closed-field conditions revealed that disagreements occurred more frequently between friends (thereby setting the stage for cognitive conflict) than between nonfriends and lasted longer (Hartup, French, Laursen, Johnston, & Ogawa, 1993). Conflict talk varied according to friendship and sex: With friends, boys used assertions *without rationales* more frequently than girls but girls used assertions *with rationales* more frequently than boys. Sex differences were not evident during conflicts between nonfriends. Girls' greater concerns about relationships and well-being as well as boys' concerns about mastery and status – usually assumed to reflect general sex differences (cf. Maccoby, 1990) – thus appear to be manifestations of relationships rather than manifestations of individuals. No cognitive outcomes were assessed in this instance.

Larger groups of friends also interact differently from nonfriends when seeking access to a scarce resource. Friends working in tetrads with a movie viewer obtain the resources more efficiently than do nonfriends, turn-taking is more common, social interaction is more harmonious, and average viewing time is greater (Charlesworth & LaFreniere, 1983).

*Problem solving*

More traditional problem-solving tasks have not been used very often to compare friends and nonfriends. One investigator (Philp, 1940) employed a marble-dropping task, reporting that the children were more interactive with "preferred partners," dropped more marbles, and were more helpful to one another. In another instance (Lebediker & Thompson, 1992), small groups of adolescent friends were differentiated according to their cohesiveness and stability over a 5-month interval and then asked to complete several combinatorial reasoning tasks. The most stable and cohesive groups talked more during their sessions, used more interactive (as opposed to noninteractive) utterances, and directed more utterances toward specific companions (as opposed to nondirected talk). Data were not obtained concerning the relation between the talk measures and problem-solving outcome, but the talk measures that differentiated the groups have been shown elsewhere to be optimal for cognitive development. Still other investigators (Shaw & Shaw, 1962) showed that friends are more democratic, friendly, and cooperative during spelling lessons, although in subsequent encounters friends felt freer than nonfriends to stop studying.

One elegant experiment dealing with friendship and problem solving centers on dialogues between fifth graders who were solving "isolation of variables" problems either with friends or acquaintances (Azmitia & Montgomery, 1993). These problems require deductive reasoning to determine which of several variables causes a specified outcome (e.g., which pizza ingredients cause malaise among certain characters described in a story). Problem solving was studied across four sessions: pretest (individual problem solving), two collaborations (during which conversations were also recorded), and posttest (individual). Results showed, first, that friends spontaneously justified their own proposals more readily than acquaintances, elaborated on their partners' proposals, engaged in a greater percentage of conflicts during their conversational transactions, and more often checked their results. Second, the children who collaborated with friends outperformed the children who collaborated with acquaintances on the posttest, but only on the most difficult versions of the task. Thus, "a friend in need is a friend indeed," that is, children must sense that they really need assistance before the advantages of interaction with a friend are evident. Finally, the data show that the main link between the children's dialogues and improved problem solving on the posttest was their engagement in transactive conflicts. Cognitive change was thus facilitated to a greater extent between friends than between nonfriends through free airing of the children's differences within a cooperative, task-oriented dialogue.

*Written narratives*

Creative writing is a complex problem-solving situation in which narrative content must be generated, narrative structure developed, and linguistic mechanics utilized. Collaborative writing is used in schools to replicate and extend, through the conversations that occur during collaboration, the inner dialogues required in mature writing. Daiute and her colleagues (Daiute & Dalton, 1991) have shown that children's collaboratively written stories are more advanced than individually written ones and, furthermore, that the benefits of collaborative writing carry over into independent composition. As mentioned earlier, collaborative conversations between children encompass generative as well as reflective talk (including criticisms and disagreements) as well as alternations in taking "expert" and "novice" roles. Conversations among collaborating writers also include more repetition and more co-construction than occur in conversations between actual experts and novices.

With computer-literate 10-year-olds from an inner-city school, we examined conversations between friends and between nonfriends while the children wrote collaboratively (Hartup, Daiute, Zajac & Sholl, 1995; Sholl, 1992; Zajac, 1992). Children were divided into three groups: (a) youngsters who wrote stories on four occasions, always alone; (b) youngsters who wrote one story alone, two stories with a best friend, and one more alone; and (c) children who wrote first alone, then twice with an acquaintance (nonfriend), and once again alone. Children were assigned to groups on the basis of a classroom questionnaire designed to determine whether they participated in a reciprocal friendship; within this constraint, group assignments were random except that sociometric status was counterbalanced. The stories themselves were written in response to standard prompts, each asking the children to write about an adventure in the rain forest. (All children in the experiment completed a 6-week project on rain forest ecology approximately 2 months before the testing began.)

Results show, first, that friends did not talk more during their collaborative conversations than nonfriends. Nevertheless, friends engaged in more mutually oriented and less individualistic utterances than nonfriends; they repeated their own and their partners' assertions proportionally more often, posed alternatives, and provided elaborations more frequently; they agreed with one another proportionally more often (but did not disagree more readily); and they spent about twice as much time as nonfriends talking about the content and vocabulary being used in their writing as well as writing mechanics (conversely, nonfriends expended proportionally more utterances on "off task" matters).

The stories themselves show that, overall, the collaboratively written ones were rated as having better quality than the individually written ones. Additionally, texts written by collaborators (both friends and acquaintances), as compared to texts written by individuals, contained: (a) more solutions, (b) more solutions to story problems, (c) more frequent reference to motivating conditions, and (d) fewer syntax and word-use errors. Stories written collaboratively by friends, as compared with stories by nonfriends, contained more personal pronouns, but fewer affect words and fewer references to present events. These results are consistent with the conversational differences that occurred as the texts were being produced. Although talk and text variables do not match one on one, the tendency for friends to take a mutual orientation to their task is consistent with the greater interpersonal orientation shown in the stories written by friends as compared with nonfriends. The tendency for friends to be more task-oriented and more generative in their interactions than the nonfriends did not, however, appear to transfer into greater use of any specific story elements.

Connections between the talk and text variables, as well as changes in the texts written by friends, nonfriends, and individuals are still being studied. Stories written by children who collaborated (both friends and nonfriends) stand out as containing more problems and story conflicts than stories written by children individually. Greater interpersonal emphasis marked the final, individually written texts of children who collaborated with friends than texts written by children who collaborated with nonfriends or wrote individually through the experiment: Authors' names, first-person pronouns, affect words, and interpersonal relations occurred more frequently in friends' stories than in stories written by the others. Additional analyses will include regressing story qualities on the conversational measures separately for friends and nonfriends so that friendship interaction may be connected to task outcome.

Certain dimensions in children's writing, then, vary with the opportunity to collaborate (consistent with earlier collaborative writing studies), whereas others vary with the relationship that exists between the collaborators. Stated differently: When children write, the affordances of collaboration differ from the affordances of solitude and, during collaboration, the affordances of "being friends" differ from the affordances of "being acquaintances."

*Normative discussion*

Five studies, comparing children's discussions about normative issues between friends and nonfriends, have been conducted. Results are not consistent and the reasons for the inconsistencies are not evident. First, one early study showed that, when conformity to a social norm is involved (resisting temptation), friends were more efficacious as models than nonfriends are (Grosser, Polansky, & Lippitt, 1951). Second, when discussing a series of social issues, friends exchanged explanations and criticism more frequently than nonfriends as well as took more mature stances on the issues being discussed (Nelson & Aboud, 1985); in one other instance, friends and nonfriends did not differ (Feltham, 1990). Third, "close friends" smiled more than "lukewarm friends" during discussion of a sociomoral problem (and only among girls; von Salisch, 1991). Fourth, friends and nonfriends did not differ in the frequency of either agreements or disagreements observed during academic conversations (Berndt, Perry, & Miller, 1988).

*Summary and comment*

Scattered evidence thus suggests that friends provide one another with problem-solving contexts different from those of nonfriends. By collating the results from the studies already described, six behavioral constellations that differentiate friends from nonfriends in collaborative problem solving can be identified: talk, mutuality and affirmativeness, equity, conflict management, task orientation, and affect. These constellations are evident in at least three studies each and, except

for conflict occurrence (as opposed to conflict management), directional differences are concordant.

Specifically, friends engage in more extensive discourse with one another than
nonfriends do during problem solving, offer suggestions more readily to one
another, and are more supportive as well as more critical in these interactions.
Mutuality is more evident and, affectively, the interaction between friends is
more positive and equally balanced. Task orientation is greater and, depending
on the task, equity concerns, overt cooperation, and altruism are more evident.
Thus, social interaction between friends, more than between nonfriends, matches
the social experiences that theoretically facilitate cognitive development.

## Why should cooperation between friends and nonfriends have different cognitive affordances?

Why should social interaction between friends be especially well suited to cognitive development? What attributions and motives underlie the better collaborations that seem to occur between friends than occur between nonfriends?
Definitive answers to these questions are difficult to come by, but the current
literature suggests four possibilities: (a) Friends know one another better than
nonfriends; (b) friends and nonfriends have different expectations of one another; (c) friends provide one another with affective contexts that facilitate
problem solving; and (d) friends are more motivated than nonfriends to maintain
contact with one another and to behave in ways that continue their interaction.

### Knowledge of one another

Companions cannot contribute to cognitive development unless their collaboration occurs within the zone of proximal development or unless cognitive conflicts can be reconciled. Accordingly, one can argue that effective cooperation
between children requires mutual understanding of one another's needs and capacities. Relationships require that "one know the other's needs and goals and
how the individual impinges on those, know the responses the other is likely to
exhibit in reaction to the individual's own behavior, and, then, possess the ca-
pability of performing the responses necessary to bring about the desired effect"
(Berscheid, 1985, p. 71). And, indeed, recent studies show that mutual friends
know one another better than do nonfriends, and that they are more accurate
than "unilateral associates" in assessing the characteristics they have in common as well as their differences (Ladd & Emerson, 1984). Assuming the necessary expertise, then, friends ought to be better teachers and collaborators than
strangers or acquaintances. Just as mothers may be more knowledgeable about
their children than fathers may be and thus better "bridges" in language de-

velopment (Tomasello & Farrar, 1986), friends may be better cognitive bridges than nonfriends because they know one another better.

## Expectations

Specific expectations supporting friendships among children and adolescents consist mainly of reciprocity, commitment, and equality. *Reciprocity* undergirds these relationships throughout childhood even though younger children expect relations with their friends to involve concrete exchanges and older ones expect self-disclosure and empathy. Sharing and self-disclosure are behavioral manifestations of reciprocity; cooperation is its essence. Almost by definition, then, the reciprocity necessary for friendship formation and maintenance maximizes the coordinations in social interaction that favor cognitive development.

*Commitment* and *trust* are manifest in friendship relations even before children can articulate these expectations. School-aged children expect loyalty from their friends (Bigelow, 1977) and also a commitment to spending time with one another. These expectations would seem to originate in the early interactions between children; trust emerges when two individuals discover through cooperation that they can depend and rely on one another according to consensual norms (Rotenberg & Pilipenko, 1983–1984). Trust, in turn, elicits among children attributions of sincerity, truthfulness, and constancy, which attract individuals to one another and strengthen their commitment (Collins & Repinski, 1994). Trust may constitute a cognitive affordance in several ways: (a) Companions who trust one another are freer to disagree and criticize one another without jeopardizing their continued interaction; (b) information provided by a trustworthy companion may be believed more readily than information provided by an untrustworthy associate; (c) communication between individuals who trust one another may be more effective than communication between those who do not (Armsden & Greenberg, 1987).

Friendship relations are also understood to be *egalitarian* and to involve a more equal power base than adult–child relationships (Furman, 1989). Power relations have important behavioral implications. Both communication patterns and strategies for conflict resolution are related directly to them (Cowan, Drinkard, & MacGavin, 1984). Once again, the expectations and attributions typifying friendship relations would seem to support the cooperative and "balanced" interactions that, theoretically, are believed to facilitate cognitive development.

## Affective substrates

Relatively little is known about the manner in which friendship emotions support cognitive development. Schwartz (1972) discovered that preschool-aged children were more active in exploring a strange situation with a friend than with a nonfriend and were less anxious – conditions that should promote knowledge acquisition and problem solving similar to the manner in which attachments between children and their adult caregivers bring about these outcomes. Affective exchanges between friends may also support selective attention and otherwise influence problem solving, for example, by increasing the child's motivation to persist with difficult problems. Existing studies provide relatively little evidence, however, concerning these speculations (but see Ladd, this volume).

*Contact maintenance*

Friends are motivated to spend time together, so much so that spending time together is a defining feature of these relationships (Hinde, Titmus, Easton, & Tamplin, 1985). Children who have friends necessarily engage in reciprocities and egalitarian exchanges in order to maintain these relationships. As a consequence, children who have friends have more ready access to the egalitarian social interaction that supports cognitive development than children who do not. Spending time with one another thus may mediate exposure to the social interaction required for cognitive development rather than affect cognition directly.

*Summary and comment*

Friendship relations may affect cognitive development through the special knowledge that friends possess about one another, their expectations of one another, the affective substrate, and the time they spend together. Better understanding of these conditions is badly needed in order to better understand the manner in which close relationships serve as contexts for cognitive development.

Motives and attributions concerning friends, however, change with age. Among preschool children, friendship expectations center on common pursuits and concrete reciprocities; among preadolescents, friends expect one another to display mutual understanding, loyalty, and trust (Bigelow, 1977). Whether these differences represent elaborations of the child's understanding of social reciprocity (Youniss, 1980), structural transformations in the child's understanding of social relations (Selman, 1980), or the cumulative assimilation of basically unrelated expectations (Berndt, 1981) has not been determined. Most important, these age differences have not been linked to collaboration between friends and the manner in which such collaboration differs from collaboration between nonfriends. Although developmental considerations thus need to be taken into account generally when speculating about friendship affordances, these are difficult to specify.

## Collaborative outcomes among friends and nonfriends

Unfortunately, cognitive outcomes were assessed superficially in most of the studies cited, so that we know more about the social exchanges occurring between friends than their cognitive consequences. Actually the various studies tell us that friends as compared with nonfriends: (a) explored a creativity box more extensively and remembered more about it (Newcomb & Brady, 1982); (b) obtained more time with a scarce resource (Charlesworth & LaFrienere, 1983); (c) more easily solved difficult, but not easy, deductive reasoning problems (Azmitia & Montgomery, 1993); (d) wrote more complex and creative stories (Zajac, 1992); and (e) exhibited greater changes in social reasoning in one instance (Nelson & Aboud, 1985). About the only evidence suggesting that friends actually internalize their social interaction more extensively than nonfriends comes from our own studies: Friends, more than nonfriends, included relational content, names, and affirmative interaction in their stories about adventures in the rain forest.

Elsewhere (Hartup, 1985), I argue that the cognitive functions deriving from close relationships ought to be the "executive regulators": The planning, monitoring, and outcome-checking skills involved in problem solving and creative activity (e.g., predicting one's capactity limitations, being aware of one's repertoire for problem solving, identifying the problem, generating ideas and planning strategy, monitoring the routines one uses, evaluating outcomes, and using them to make adjustments in one's activities). Most commonly, collaborative conversations deal with how to assemble various actions in some kind of order, how to make sense of a task, and how to monitor one's behavior. To the extent that conversations between friends are more mutually oriented, more task-oriented, and more sensitively regulated than conversations between nonfriends, friendship experience can be hypothesized to contribute to cognitive regulation rather than to other cognitive capacities. Whether the social interactions occurring between friends are more effective in memory, logical operations, and other basic cognitive functions is much more uncertain.

Certain results suggest that friends may affect cognitive outcomes on some tasks but not others. For example, friends appear to contribute most to cognitive efficacy when tasks are difficult or the situation is extremely uncertain (Azmitia & Montgomery, 1993). Moreover, self-reliance may be the rule when one's own self-evaluation is at stake whereas reliance on one's friends occurs when the task reflects the friend's ego-involvements (Tesser, 1984).

*Summary*

The cognitive outcomes associated with cooperation between friends have not been well studied. Arguments can be advanced to the effect that these outcomes should consist mainly of regulative functions. Nevertheless, friends and non-friends are likely to affect outcomes differently according to the task and the situation.

**Other issues**

Several other issues related to friendship and cognitive development can be singled out: (a) Are some friendships better suited to collaboration than others? (b) Are children who have friends better collaborators than those who do not? (c) Are children who have friends more cognitively mature than children who do not? (d) Are friendships significant factors in school learning and adaptation? Unfortunately, answers to these questions are not available. Cause and effect, in any event, are difficult to disentangle.

Scattered studies show that children who have reciprocated friendships evidence more mature perspective taking (Jones & Bowling, 1988); engage in more cooperative play (Howes, 1988); have fewer school-related problems (Kurdek & Sinclair, 1988); and are more involved in school and have higher achievement test scores (Berndt & Hawkins, 1991). But these findings are difficult to interpret. Generally, research relating to these issues requires longitudinal analysis; friendship-to-friendship variations must be examined.

Friendships are not all alike. Berndt and Keefe (1992), for example, differentiated ''positive'' from ''negative'' friendships in terms of emotional support, on the one hand, and conflicts and rivalry, on the other, in order to understand implications of these relationships for school adjustment. Regression analyses showed that adolescents whose friendships were intimate and supportive at the beginning of the year became more involved in school over time whereas those whose friendships were marked by conflict and rivalry became more disruptive and less involved. School grades were *not* related to these relationship variations, however, creating some uncertainty about cognitive implications. Once again, one suspects that relationships affect cognitive development indirectly as well as directly.

**Conclusion**

The evidence suggests that cooperation between friends differs from cooperation between nonfriends. Empirical studies are not numerous but friends, as compared with nonfriends, are more talkative, mutually oriented, task-oriented, affectively expressive (positively), affirmative as well as argumentative, and equitable in managing conflicts. Not every data set supports these assertions but the weight of the evidence is consistent with these claims.

Because friendships subsume these coordinations and because these coordinations, in turn, are believed to support cognitive development, friendships may be relevant to individual cognition. But the cognitive outcomes deriving from friendship experience are not well documented. Certain evidence suggests that these outcomes consist mainly of cognitive regulation, especially as utilized in problem solving, communication, and creative activity in everyday life. The evidence also supports the broad conclusion that close relationships are important cognitive resources owing to the mutually oriented coordinations they encompass.

## References

Armsden, G. C., & Greenberg, M. T. (1987). The inventory of parent and peer attachment: Individual differences and their relationship to psychological well-being in adolescence. *Journal of Youth and Adolescence, 16,* 427–454.

Axelrod, R., & Hamilton, W. D. (1981). The evolution of cooperation. *Science, 211,* 1390–1396.

Azmitia, M. (1988). Peer interaction and problem solving: When are two heads better than one? *Child Development, 59,* 87–96.

Azmitia, M., & Montgomery, R. (1993). Friendship, transactive dialogues, and the development of scientific reasoning. *Social Development, 2,* 202–221.

Azmitia, M., & Perlmutter, M. (1989). Social influences on children's cognition: State of the art and future directions. In H. W. Reese (Ed.), *Advances in child development and behavior* (Vol. 22). New York: Academic Press.

Bearison, D. J., Magzamen, S., & Filarde, E. K. (1986). Socio-cognitive conflict and cognitive growth in young children. *Merrill-Palmer Quarterly, 32,* 51–72.

Berndt, T. J. (1981). Relations between social cognition, nonsocial cognition, and social behavior: The case of friendship. In J. H. Flavell & L. Ross (Eds.), *Social cognitive development.* Cambridge: Cambridge University Press.

Berndt, T. J., & Hawkins, J. A. (1991). *Effects of friendship on adolescents' adjustment to junior high school.* Unpublished manuscript, Purdue University.

Berndt, T. J., & Keefe, K. (1992). Friends' influence on adolescents' perceptions of themselves in school. In D. H. Schunk & J. L. Meece (Eds.), *Student perceptions in the classroom.* Hillsdale, NJ: Erlbaum.

Berndt, T. J., Perry, T. B., & Miller, K. E. (1988). Friends' and classmates' interactions on academic tasks. *Journal of Educational Psychology, 80,* 506–513.

Berscheid, E. (1985). Interpersonal modes of knowing. In E. W. Eisner (Ed.). *Learning the ways of knowing. The 85th yearbook of the national society for the study of education.* Chicago: University of Chicago Press.

Berscheid, E., & Walster, E. (1969). *Interpersonal attraction.* Reading, MA: Addison-Wesley.

Bigelow, B. J. (1977). Children's friendship expectations: A cognitive developmental study. *Child Development, 48,* 246–253.

Brownell, C. A., & Brown, E. (1992). Peers and play in infants and toddlers. In V. B. Van Hasselt & M. Hersen (Eds.), *Handbook of social development*. New York: Plenum.

Brownell, C. A., & Carriger, M. S. (1990). Changes in cooperation and self–other differentiation during the second year. *Child Development, 61*, 1164–1174.

Bukowski, W. M., Kramer, T. L., & Watson, J. (1992). *Preschool children's use of schemas for information about prosociability, aggression, and social withdrawal in peers*. Unpublished manuscript, Concordia University.

Charlesworth, W. R. (1991, July). *Cooperation as competition: Contributions to a developmental and evolutionary model*. Paper presented at the XIth Biennial Meetings of the International Society for the Study of Behavioral Development, Minneapolis.

Charlesworth, W. R., & LaFreniere, P. (1983). Dominance, friendship, and resource utilization in preschool children's groups. *Ethology and Sociobiology, 4*, 175–186.

Cillessen, A. H. N. (1991). *The self-perpetuating nature of children's peer relationships*. Ph.D. dissertation, University of Nijmegen.

Cillessen, A. H. N., van Lieshout, C. F. M., & Haselager, G. J. T. (1992, September). *Effects of early consistent rejection by peers on children's social and emotional adjustment in late elementary school years*. Paper presented at the 5th European Conference on Developmental Psychology, Seville.

Collins, W. A., & Repinski, D. J. (1994). Relationships during adolescence: Continuity and change in interpersonal perspective. In R. Montemayor, G. Adams, & T. Gullotta (Eds.), *Advances in adolescent development, Vol. 5, Personal relationships during adolescence*. Beverly Hills, CA: Sage.

Cowan, G., Drinkard, J., & MacGavin, L. (1984). The effects of target age, and gender on use of power strategies. *Journal of Personality and Social Psychology, 47*, 1391–1398.

Daiute, C., & Dalton, B. (1991). *Collaboration between children learning to write: Can novices be masters?* Unpublished manuscript, Harvard University.

de Roos, S. A., & Riksen-Walraven, M. (1992, September). *Stability of peer interactions in the first five years of life*. Paper presented at the 5th European Conference on Developmental Psychology, Seville.

Doise, W., & Mugny, G. (1984). *The social development of the intellect*. Oxford: Pergamon Press.

Ellis, S., & Rogoff, B. (1986). Problem solving in children's management of instruction. In E. C. Mueller & C. R. Cooper (Eds.), *Process and outcome in peer relationships*. Orlando, FL: Academic Press.

Feltham, R. (1990). *Social determinants of social-cognitive growth in children: The effects of racial group and friendship*. Unpublished Ph.D. dissertation, Concordia University (Montreal).

Furman, W. (1989). The development of children's social networks. In D. Belle (Ed.), *Children's social networks and social supports*. New York: Wiley.

Furman, W., & Bierman, K. L. (1984). Children's conceptions of friendship: A multi-dimensional study of developmental changes. *Developmental Psychology, 20*, 925–931.

Graziano, W. G., & Eisenberg, N. H. (in press). Agreeableness: A dimension of personality. In S. Briggs, R. Hogan, & W. Jones (Eds.), *Handbook of personality psychology*. San Diego: Academic Press.

Grosser, D., Polansky, N., & Lippitt, R. (1951). A laboratory study of behavioral contagion. *Human Relations, 4*, 115–142.

Halverson, C. F., Kohnstamm, G. A., & Martin, R. P. (1994). *The developing structure of temperament and personality from infancy to adulthood*. Hillsdale, NJ: Erlbaum.

Hamilton, W. D. (1964). The genetical evolution of social behaviour: I, II. *Journal of Theoretical Biology, 7*, 1–52.

Hartup, W. W. (1983). Peer relations. In E. M. Hetherington (Ed.), & P. H. Mussen (Series Ed.), *Handbook of child psychology, Vol. 4, Socialization, social development, and personality*. New York: Wiley.

Hartup, W. W. (1985). Relationships and their significance in cognitive development. In R. A. Hinde, A.-N. Perret-Clermont, & J. Stevenson-Hinde (Eds.), *Social relationships and cognitive development*. Oxford, UK: Clarendon Press.

Hartup, W. W. (1989). Behavioral manifestations of children's friendships. In T. J. Berndt & G. W. Ladd (Eds.), *Peer relationships in child development*. New York: Wiley.

Hartup, W. W., Daiute, C., Zajac, R., & Sholl, W. (1995). *Collaboration in creative writing by friends and nonfriends*. Unpublished manuscript, University of Minnesota.

Hartup, W. W., French, D. C., Laursen, B., Johnston, M. K., & Ogawa, J. R. (1993). Conflict and friendship relations in middle childhood: Behavior in a closed-field situation. *Child Development, 64*, 445–454.

Higgins, E. T. (1991). Development of self-regulatory and self-evaluative processes: Costs, benefits, and tradeoffs. In M. Gunnar & L. A. Sroufe (Eds.), *Minnesota symposia on child psychology, Vol. 23: Self processes and development*. Hillsdale, NJ: Erlbaum.

Hinde, R. A., Titmus, G., Easton, D., & Tamplin, A. (1985). Incidence of "friendship" and behavior with strong associates versus non-associates in preschoolers. *Child Development, 56*, 234–245.

Howes, C. (1988). Peer interaction of young children. *Monographs of the Society for Research in Child Development, 53* (1, Serial No. 217).

Howes, C., & Farver, J. (1987). Social pretend play in 2-year-olds: Effects of age of partner. *Early Childhood Research Quarterly, 2*, 305–314.

Johnson, D. W., Johnson, R. T., & Scott, L. (1978). The effects of cooperative versus individualized instruction on student attitudes and achievement. *Journal of Social Psychology, 104*, 207–216.

Jones, D. C., & Bowling, B. (1988, March). *Preschool friends and affective knowledge: A comparison of mutual and unilateral friends*. Paper presented at the Conference on Human Development, Charleston, SC.

Kagan, S., & Madsen, M. C. (1971). Cooperation and competition of Mexican, Mexican-American, and Anglo-American children of two ages under four instructional sets. *Developmental Psychology, 5*, 32–39.

Knight, G. P., & Kagan, S. (1977). Acculturation of prosocial and competitive behaviors among second- and third-generation Mexican-American children. *Journal of Cross-Cultural Psychology, 1977, 8*, 273–284.

Kruger, A. C. (1992). The effect of peer and adult–child transactive discussions on moral reasoning. *Merrill-Palmer Quarterly, 38*, 191–211.

Kurdek, L. A., & Sinclair, R. J. (1988). Adjustment of young adolescents in two-parent nuclear, stepfather, and mother-custody families. *Journal of Consulting and Clinical Psychology, 56*, 91–96.

Ladd, G. W., & Emerson, E. S. (1984). Shared knowledge in children's friendships. *Developmental Psychology, 20*, 932–940.

LaFreniere, P. J. (1991, July). *Cooperation as a conditional strategy among peers: The role of frustration tolerance and affective synchrony*. Paper presented at the XIth Biennial Meetings of the International Society for the Study of Behavioral Development, Minneapolis.

Lave, J., & Wenger, E. (1991). *Situated learning: Legitimate peripheral participation*. Cambridge: Cambridge University Press.

Lebediker, J., & Thompson, C. (1992, May). *Collaborative problem solving in adolescent peer groups*. Paper presented at the 22nd annual Symposium of the Piaget Society, Montreal.

Light, P., & Glachan, M. (1985). Facilitation of individual problem solving through peer interaction. *Educational Psychology, 5*, 217–225.

Lougee, M. D., Grueneich, R., & Hartup, W. W. (1977). Social interaction in same-and mixed-age dyads of preschool children. *Child Development, 48*, 1353–1361.

Maccoby, E. E. (1990). Gender and relationships: A developmental account. *American Psychologist, 45*, 513–520.

Masters, J. C., & Furman, W. (1981). Popularity, individual friendship selections, and specific peer interaction among children. *Developmental Psychology, 17*, 344–350.

Matas, L., Arend, R., & Sroufe, L. A. (1978). Continuity of adaptation in the second year of life: The relationship between quality of attachment and later competence. *Child Development, 49*, 547–556.

Matsumoto, D., Haan, N., Yabrove, G., Theodorou, P., & Carney, C. C. (1986). Preschoolers' moral actions and emotions in prisoner's dilemma. *Developmental Psychology, 22*, 663–670.

Mead, G. H. (1909). Social psychology as a counterpart to physiological psychology. *Psychological Bulletin, 6*, 401–408.

Mead, G. H. (1934). *Mind, self and society*. Chicago: University of Chicago Press.

Mead, G. H. (1938) *The philosophy of the act*. Chicago: University of Chicago Press.

Nelson, J., & Aboud, F. E. (1985). The resolution of social conflict between friends. *Child Development, 56*, 1009–1017.

Newcomb, A. F., & Brady, J. E. (1982). Mutuality in boys' friendship relations. *Child Development, 53*, 392–395.

Newcomb, A. F., Brady, J. E., & Hartup, W. W. (1979). Friendship and incentive condition as determinants of children's task-oriented social behavior. *Child Development, 50*, 878–881.

Perret-Clermont, A.-N., & Brossard, A. (1985). On the interdigitation of social and cognitive processes. In R. A. Hinde, A,-N. Perret-Clermont, & J. Stevenson-Hinde (Eds.), *Social relationships and cognitive development*. Oxford: Clarendon Press.

Philp, A. J. (1940). Strangers and friends as competitors and operators. *Journal of Genetic Psychology, 57*, 249–258.

Piaget, J. (1926). *The language and thought of the child*. New York: Harcourt Brace.

Piaget, J. (1932). *The moral judgment of the child*. Glencoe, IL: Free Press.

Piaget, J. (1985). *The equilibration of cognitive structures*. Chicago: University of Chicago Press. (Original work published in 1975.)

Rogoff, B. (1990). *Apprenticeship in thinking*. New York: Oxford University Press.

Rotenberg, K. J., & Pilipenko, T. A. (1983–1984). Mutuality, temporal consistency, and helpfulness in children's trust in peers. *Social Cognition, 2*, 235–255.

Schaffer, H. R. (1992). Joint involvement episodes as context for development. In H. McGurk (Ed.), *Childhood social development: Contemporary perspectives*. Hove, UK: Erlbaum.

Schwartz, J. C. (1972). Effects of peer familiarity on the behavior of preschoolers in a novel situation. *Journal of Personality and Social Psychology, 24*, 276–284.

Selman, R. L. (1980). *The growth of interpersonal understanding*. New York: Academic Press.

Shaw, M. E., & Shaw, L. M. (1962). Some effects of sociometric grouping upon learning in a second grade classroom. *Journal of Social Psychology, 57*, 453–458.

Sholl, W. C. (1992). *Children's conversations during creative writing: Friends compared to nonfriends*. Unpublished B. A. honors thesis, University of Minnesota.

Tesser, A. (1984). Self-evaluation maintenance processes: Implications for relationships and for development. In J. C. Masters & K. Yarkin-Levin (Eds.), *Boundary areas in social and developmental psychology*. New York: Academic Press.

Thomas, A., Chess, S., & Birch, H. (1969). *Temperament and behavior disorders*. New York: New York University Press.

Tomasello, M., & Farrar, M. J. (1986). Joint attention and early language. *Child Development, 57*, 1454–1463.

Tudge, J. R. H., & Rogoff, B. (1989). Peer influences on cognitive development: Piagetian and Vygotskian perspectives. In M. Bornstein & J. Bruner (Eds.), *Interaction and human development*. Hillsdale, NJ: Erlbaum.

Tudge, J. R. H., & Winterhoff, P. (1993). *Can young children benefit from collaborative problem solving? Tracing the effects of partner competence and feedback*. Unpublished manuscript, University of North Carolina, Greensboro.

van Lieshout, C. F. M., & Haselager, G. J. T. (1994). The big five personality factors in Q-sort descriptions of children and adolescents. In C. F. Halverson, G. A. Kohnstamm, & R. P. Martin (Eds.), *The developing structure of temperament and personality from infancy to adulthood.* Hillsdale, NJ: Erlbaum.

Vari-Szilagyi, I. (1991). G. H. Mead and L. S. Vygotsky on action. *Studies on Soviet thought, 42,* 93–121.

von Salisch, M. (1991, April). *Conflicts between friends: Gender differences in expression and regulation of emotion.* Paper presented at the biennial meetings of the Society for Research in Child Development, Seattle.

Vygotsky, L. S. (1981). The genesis of higher mental functions. In J. V. Wertsch (Ed.), *The concept of activity in Soviet psychology.* Armonk, NY: M. E. Sharpe.

Vygotsky, L. S. (1986). *Thought and language* (rev. ed.). Cambridge, MA: MIT Press. (Original work published in 1934.)

Walker, H., Messinger, D., Fogel, A., & Karnes, J. (1992). Social and communicative development in infancy. In V. B. Van Hasselt & M. Hersen (Eds.), *Handbook of social development.* New York: Plenum.

Weiss, R. S. (1986). Continuities and transformations in social relationships from childhood to adulthood. In W. W. Hartup & Z. Rubin (Eds.), *Relationships and development.* Hillsdale, NJ: Erlbaum.

Wertsch, J. V., McNamee, G. D., McLane, J. B., & Budwid, N. A. (1980). The adult–child dyad as a problem-solving system. *Child Development, 51,* 1215–1221.

Wertsch, J. V., & Sammarco, J. G. (1985). Social precursors to individual cognitive functioning: The problem of units of analysis. In R. A. Hinde, A.-N. Perret-Clermont, & J. Stevenson-Hinde (Eds.), *Social relationships and cognitive development.* Oxford, UK: Clarendon Press.

Whiting, J. W. M. (1981). Environmental constraints on infant care practices. In R. H. Munroe, R. L. Munroe, & B. B. Whiting (Eds.), *Handbook of cross-cultural human development,* New York: Garland.

Youniss, J. (1980). *Parents and peers in social development: A Piaget-Sullivan perspective.* Chicago: University of Chicago Press.

Zajac, R. J. (1992). *Friends and nonfriends: Collaboration on a written text.* Unpublished B. A. honors thesis, University of Minnesota.

# 11 Friendship and morality: (How) are they related?

*William M. Bukowski and Lorrie K. Sippola*

## Introduction

In developmental psychology, research on friendship and research on morality have been undertaken relatively independent of each other. Indeed, some authors have gone so far as to suggest that they are two separate domains of development, each with its own set of issues and processes (Turiel, 1983). This divergence between friendship and morality is reasonable given psychology's usual treatment of morality as an *intra*personal phenomenon and friendship as an *inter*personal phenomenon. Whereas friendship has been treated as a relational construct and is frequently studied according to patterns of interactions between friends, research on morality has typically been focused on the individual's use of abstract principles in the resolution of moral dilemmas. More recently, however, questions have been raised about the definition of morality generally used by developmental psychologists (Gilligan, 1982). The central point of much of this recent discussion is that there is a relational or interpersonal component to morality. In this same vein of thought, concerns have been expressed about the tendency in child psychology to emphasize cognitive features of moral development to the detriment of other features such as moral emotions and moral character (Haste, 1990).

In this chapter, we argue that friendship and morality are interrelated. Specifically, we propose that friendship is defined and constrained by moral parameters and that it serves as a context in which morality is learned and achieved. At the same time, we argue that morality is largely an interpersonal construct in the sense that moral issues frequently arise in our relations with

Work on this chapter was supported by a W. T. Grant Foundation Faculty Scholars Award to the first author and an award from the Fonds pour la formation des chercheurs et pour l'aide a recherche (gouvernement du Québec) to the second author. The authors are grateful to Bill Hartup, Nina Howe, Andy Newcomb, and Deborah Vineberg for their comments on previous versions of this chapter. They are grateful also to several fellow "eudomainiacs" for their advice and encouragement, including Tom Berndt, Thomas Paul Bukowski, Bill Damon, Sue Dwyer, Sheila Mullett, Charlotte Patterson, and James Youniss.

friends and that a significant portion of our experiences with others consists of moral struggles, involving issues of loyalty, trust, commitment, and honesty. Because these issues are among the most basic features of the friendship relation, we believe that friendship can be regarded as a fundamentally moral phenomenon.

Our goal is to consider how the integration of theory from the literature on friendship and the literature on morality can enrich our understanding of both constructs. Two arguments, both from outside of the traditional literature on child psychology, serve as points of departure for our discussion. The first argument is found in MacIntyre's (1981) work on the role of virtue in social theory. MacIntyre proposed that philosophers and social scientists would be wise to recognize the centrality of morality in persons' thoughts about others and in the regulation of their social behavior. He believed that by considering morality, social scientists would acquire a powerful means for understanding why people behave as they do. MacIntyre's proposal suggests that by understanding the processes underlying morality, psychologists may better understand the processes in the development and maintenance of friendship.

The second argument comes from the American psychologist William Bevan (1991) who asked why contemporary psychology has become so narrow and fragmented. Part of his answer is that psychologists no longer care about the basic philosophical issues that contributed to the beginnings of psychology over a century ago. With respect to the current topic, it is clear that persons who study friendship usually do so from within the confines of specific theories, such as those from psychology or sociology. As a group, friendship researchers have not paid much attention to ideas and concerns expressed in philosophy. It is in this spirit that we embarked on our consideration of how ideas about morality can inform our understanding of friendship during childhood and adolescence.

In this chapter we consider three broad issues. We first examine how friendship has been discussed in the philosophical literature on morality. Using Aristotle's model of friendship and morality as our main point of discussion, our goal in this section is to consider the relevance of philosophical themes regarding friendship and morality for the psychological study of friendship. Second, we consider whether the processes of friendship affect morality and moral development. This discussion focuses on the psychological literature on moral development. And finally, we ask if friendship can be antagonistic to morality. For each of these questions we discuss theory and empirical studies (when available) to illuminate the links between these constructs. Although our primary concern is with the friendships of children and adolescents, we will refer to and borrow from theory and research with adults.

### Friendship and morality: The philosophical perspective

For at least 22 centuries, the idea that friendship and morality are interconnected has been evident in Western thought. In particular, among the many philosophical writings of Aristotle from the fourth century B.C., one can identify a well-articulated and relatively coherent model of friendship and morality. Our present discussion is largely centered on Aristotle because more than other writers he has embedded the processes of friendship within his conceptualization of the morally "good" person. Moreover, Aristotelian thought has exerted a strong influence over the study of morality and friendship in philosophy. However, in psychology, Aristotle's views of morality and friendship have largely been overshadowed by the emphasis on other thinkers, such as Kant (c.f. Blum, 1980). Accordingly, the aim of our discussion of the philosophical perspective is to demonstrate the relevance of Aristotle's views, and those of moral philosophy in general, for contemporary psychological theory about friendship and moral development.

*Aristotle: Father of friendship?*

In order to understand Aristotle's model of friendship and morality, we must first consider his conceptualization of "goodness." For Aristotle, goodness is a transcendent phenomenon and as such it cannot be defined in terms of its contents (e.g., as a list of traits). Instead, he regarded goodness as an end point or a state toward which one wishes to move (i.e., a state of well-being). In this regard, as Nussbaum (1986) has shown, Aristotle saw goodness not as a "thing" but as a form of activity. That is, goodness is not merely an end point but is also the activity by which one would reach a particular end point. She notes that Cooper (1980) has translated Aristotle's term for goodness, *eudaimonia*, as "human flourishing." According to MacIntyre (1981), Aristotle believed goodness was a property of all our actions that are directed toward this particular aim. Goodness is not simply one's sense of immediate pleasure, but is instead a long-lasting sense of vital well-being, happiness, and satisfaction in which one experiences the fullness of one's potential, particularly with respect to one's rational or intellectual capacities. From these different descriptions, it is clear that the concept of goodness is a complex and multidimensional phenomenon involving both process (i.e., activity) and a goal (i.e., eudaimonia).

A second aspect of Aristotle's model is the notion of virtue. Virtues are the qualities that allow a person to achieve goodness. Virtues are not only necessary for goodness, but they are also a manifestation of it. In this respect, virtue and goodness are not the same and yet one cannot separate one from the other either.

One can identify five interrelated themes in Aristotle's model of friendship and morality: (a) that goodness is characteristic of the highest form of friendship; (b) that goodness is required if a person is to appreciate friendship; (c) that the goal of the highest form of friendship is rooted in goodness; (d) that friendship is a relationship between equals; and (e) that friendship requires both justice and benevolence. In the following sections we discuss each of these points.

## Types of friendship

Aristotle distinguished among three types of friendships. One type, referred to as *utility friendships*, is centered on the benefits that a person would enjoy as a result of being someone's friend. Persons would enter such a friendship because it offered certain beneficial opportunities. A second type, *pleasure friendship*, is predicated on one's satisfaction in interacting with the other. Thus, a person engages in this form of friendship because it is enjoyable. Participation in either of these two forms of friendship is intended to bring the individuals involved either pleasure or particular benefits.

The first two forms of friendship described by Aristotle are essentially self-centered. In contrast, the third form of friendship requires a greater appreciation or understanding of the "other" in that it is based on the recognition of goodness in the other person. Furthermore, rather than being based on either advantage or pleasure, friendships based on goodness are characterized by virtue (e.g., kindness, benevolence, justice). This is not to say that *goodness friendships* would not provide pleasure or benefits, but that these features would be incidental to considerations of goodness.

For Aristotle, goodness is the central feature of the highest form of friendship. He argued in particular that goodness is essential for the longevity and maintenance of satisfaction in friendship. He noted that, in friendship, pleasure and utility do not contribute to the consistency of the relationship in the sense that if either of these two motivations were to disappear, so would the friendship. Moreover, he argued that pleasure and benefits are, by their very nature, more transitory because they are dependent on particular circumstances or events. On the other hand, he believed that virtue and goodness are unlikely to be linked to specific contexts. Consequently, he believed that an appreciation of goodness would maximize the depth and longevity of friendship as it facilitates the consistency of the friendship across time and circumstances.

## Friendship requires goodness

A second important feature of Aristotle's model is that the highest form of friendship requires goodness. That is, without goodness, a person would be incapable of participating in these friendships for two reasons. First, one would not be able to recognize the virtues in another person, and also would not have these characteristics that could be appreciated by others. Second, one must have a concern for goodness in one's friend. Cooper (1980) argues that Aristotle was not saying that friendship is possible only among "moral heroes," but that instead friendship is facilitated by a concern or appreciation for constructs related to goodness, such as generosity, honesty, kindness, loyalty, and authenticity. In other words, what matters is a concern for and interest in goodness rather than perfection.

*Goal of friendship is goodness*

Following from these first two points, Aristotle believed that a goal of friendship is to do good for one's friend. That is, in an extension of his view that goodness is the basis of friendship he also saw goodness as the goal of friendship. As Cooper (1980) has pointed out, the argument that the goal of friendship is to "do well by someone for his own sake . . . not out of concern for oneself" (p. 302) is a central feature of Aristotle's model of ethics. Cooper proposed that Aristotle went so far as to indicate that one should not regard justice as the only important moral goal, but that friendship and the goodness inherent in friendship should also be important moral goals. In other words, friendship is so intimately linked to virtue and goodness that it is a moral goal in itself.

*Equality necessary for the highest form of friendship*

A further point of Aristotle's model is that friendships between "unequals" would be very difficult. Aristotle referred to two manners in which individuals could be unequal. First, persons could be unequal in status, such as in the relationship between masters and slaves in antiquity. Second, individuals could be unequal in their virtue. Goodness friendships between persons who differ significantly in their virtue are problematic because this lack of similarity impedes the development of mutual respect and an appreciation for each other's moral character. Aristotle did not suggest that absolute equality was necessary between friends. Indeed, Aristotle described several types of friendship that could occur between people of unequal status (e.g., husbands and wives, in Aristotle's era). However, the essential point of this perspective is the necessity for a reciprocal or mutual process within friendship. In this respect, Aristotle does not see goodness as a simple feature of friendship, but he instead sees it as a powerful force that holds the friendship together. That is, the dynamic mutual processes between equals are necessary for the longevity of the friendship and the continued sense of appreciation between friends. Insofar as this equality persists, the friendship is also likely to persist; if an imbalance should occur, the continuity of the friendship would be jeopardized. Aristotle believed that for these reasons friendship between unequals would be unlikely because mutual processes would not emerge (see Laursen, this volume).

This aspect of Aristotle's model has implications for our understanding of both the development and dissolution of friendship relations. According to Aristotle's perspective, peers who become friends will share similar values and goals for friendship. Moreover, the model suggests that identification with the virtues and goals of the other is a fundamental process underlying the development and maintenance of friendship. Finally, Aristotle's theory implies that the disintegration of friendships may be traced to emerging differences in the values held by the individuals involved in the relationship.

### Justice, benevolence, and friendship

A final important theme in Aristotle's writing is his concern for the role of the virtues in friendship. On this topic, Aristotle implies that both the virtue of "justice" and the virtue of "love" or benevolence are essential to lasting friendships. However, how these virtues interact in friendship is not clear from Aristotle's writing. On the one hand, Aristotle implies that justice is incidental to the phenomenon of friendship when he states that "while men [*sic*] are friends they have no need of justice, while when they are just they need friendship as well, and the truest form of justice is thought to be a friendly quality" (p. 471, "Nicomachean Ethics"). Rather, he attributes the lasting feature of goodness friendships to the virtue of "love" of the other for the other's own sake and not for the sake of pleasure or usefulness of the friend. However, in a later section, Aristotle proposed that friendships based on goodness place particular demands on the persons involved to act in a just manner:

> Friendship and justice seem ... to be concerned with the same objects and exhibited between the same persons. For in every community there is thought to be some form of justice, and friendship. ... And the demands of justice also seem to increase with the intensity of the friendship ... (pp. 484–485, "Nicomachean Ethics")

Implicit in Aristotle's writing are the ideas that as a consequence of the love between friends, friendship instills certain obligations (rights) on the part of the friends to treat the other in a just and benevolent manner. Badhwar (1985) provides some insight into this idea. She suggests that the recognition of a friendship implies a recognition of how friends *ought* to act, especially in terms of making judgments about the other. For example, friends expect to be treated in a just manner when they commit a transgression in the friendship. "If she was really my friend she would understand and forgive me" would be a commonly heard statement in these types of situations. Thus, Badhwar (1985) suggests that the closer the relationship, the more attention is required to understanding the facts and issues involved in the situation when rendering a moral judgment and deciding upon an action in the situation. Consequently, Badhwar suggests that supererogation is not only a natural feature of friendship but, at times, it also becomes a moral standard that aids in the maintenance of the friendship relation. That is, for example, in friendship it could be considered morally wrong not to forgive and thereby threaten the continuation of the relationship.

## Contemporary philosophical perspectives

Although the work of several philosophers is apparent in the theoretical framework of many psychologists interested in moral development (e.g., the influence of Kant and Rawls in Kohlberg's work), Aristotle's views have generally been neglected (see Blasi, 1991). In contrast to the situation in developmental psychology, however, Aristotle's views are echoed in the writings of some modern philosophers (Blum, 1980; Friedman, 1989; Noddings, 1984; Raymond, 1986). In general, these modern views resemble Aristotle's in that they identify concern for the other person for his or her own sake as an important feature of friendship. Although these contemporary philosophers do not describe a hierarchy of friendship similar to Aristotle's, they do appreciate the moral virtues inherent in close, reciprocated friendships. Furthermore, they expand upon Aristotle's ideas by providing a more detailed description of the qualities of friendship that reflect these virtues. There are, however, important differences between the ideas of Aristotle and the ideas of many of these moderns. These differences suggest a revision of Aristotle's theoretical framework that may have important implications for developmental psychology.

One means by which modern philosophers have expanded upon Aristotle's view of friendship is by describing in greater detail the features that Aristotle used to distinguish friendships based on goodness from his other two friendship types. In describing their impression of what constitutes "morally superior friendships," modern philosophers have emphasized qualities such as concern, caring, sympathy, sensitivity to the friend's needs or wants, identification with the other, and a willingness to give of one's self to the friend for his or her own sake. They are careful to distinguish self-giving within a friendship from self-giving per se in that a friend's response to the other is based on the knowledge acquired of this friend's particular needs. Noddings (1984), for example, argued that giving, which does not address the specific needs of the receiver, indicates a lack of sensitivity to others and therefore is not a true form of benevolence or caring. Further, she distinguished between philanthropy and friendship in that she viewed giving in friendship as often involving greater self-sacrifice to meet the specific needs of an individual. Philanthropy or charity, she argued, typically involves little self-sacrifice and is not necessarily based on meeting the specific needs of an individual for his or her own sake.

One important difference between these contemporary authors and Aristotle concerns the issues perceived to be at the center of friendship relations. Whereas Aristotle emphasized the importance of the moral character of the individuals involved, contemporary writers identify the depth of the concern for the other person as being the most important property of friendship. Indeed, Blum (1980) has argued that this quality of friendship is the distinguishing feature of what he calls "morally excellent" friendships. Blum suggested that Aristotle's description of morally superior friendships reflects an "overmoralized view of friendship" (p. 82) that contradicts a fundamental concept of virtue. He argued that (a) caring for a friend because of his or her moral worthiness is not caring for his or her own sake, and (b) that our friends do not need to be virtuous to receive our care. Rather, friends tend to seek out and emphasize whatever morally virtuous qualities are inherent within each other. Blum's perspective highlights other features of friendship such as liking and care that are overshadowed by Aristotle's emphasis on moral character.

Finally, for these contemporary philosophers the concept of "commitment" to both the relationship and the friend is fundamental. Aristotle implied that loyalty, which could be conceived as a form of commitment, was only one of several virtues of friendships. In contrast, current philosophers view it as the primary feature of friendship with important implications for morality. Friedman (1989), for example, suggested that friendship provides a balance between commitment to abstract ideals and commitment to particular persons. Indeed, she argued that commitment to friendship reminds one of the purpose of morality in the first place.

In summary, Aristotle's views on the link between friendship and morality continue to be represented in the views of some modern philosophers. However, these authors have made important conceptual contributions to Aristotle's views that are relevant to developmental psychology. First, they point to the importance of understanding how friendships are developed and maintained. Second, they have proposed that particular qualities are essential for "morally excellent" friendships. These qualities include: (a) a deep concern for the other for his or her own sake; (b) intimate knowledge of the emotional and moral world of the other based on mutual self-disclosure; (c) high levels of trust and commitment to the relationship; and (d) conflict resolution styles that contribute to the emotional well-being of the individuals involved. Whether these qualities are essential and whether other qualities should be examined are both philosophical and empirical questions (T. Berndt, personal communication, December, 1994).

**Empirical findings relevant to the link between friendship and morality**

A systematic program of psychological research that examines the links between friendship and morality found in philosophy is currently lacking. Some evidence to support this model is scattered throughout the psychological literature. In this section we bring together evidence that is relevant to the issues raised by philosophers, especially Aristotle, regarding the associations between these domains.

*Types of friendship*

Is there evidence from empirical studies to support the three-factor model of friendship proposed by Aristotle? Research conducted with adult subjects has shown that this three-factor model can be applied successfully to friendship during early adulthood (Bukowski, Nappi, & Hoza, 1987; Murstein & Spitz, 1974), but there has been no direct test of the proposal that adult friendships based on goodness are of longer duration than are friendships based on pleasure or utility. In the child and adolescent literature, one study has specifically examined the Aristotelian model. Reisman and Shorr (1978) showed that children's, adolescents', and adults' descriptions of their friendships could be coded according to the three factors of Aristotle's model. Moreover, the importance of pleasure was highest among the youngest subjects (e.g., grades 2 and 3) and declined with age, whereas the emphasis on utility was infrequent among the youngest subjects and then increased with age. Contrary to their expectation that virtue or goodness would be most pronounced among their adolescent and adult subjects, there was no age trend associated with this feature of friendship, perhaps because it was mentioned infrequently at any age level.

Evidence from the literature on friendship conceptions provides some indirect evidence in support of Aristotle's three-factor model of friendship (e.g., Bigelow, 1977; Damon, 1977). This literature suggests that at nearly all ages children refer to pleasurable companionship as a feature of friendship and that older children emphasize the importance of virtue-related constructs such as loyalty and genuineness (Bigelow, 1977). Damon's (1977) three-level developmental model of children's understanding of friendship is especially pertinent to this issue. At the first level in Damon's framework, children's friendships are pleasure-based. At this level children describe friends as people with whom they like to play. At the second level children use psychological characteristics (e.g., helpfulness, trustworthiness) to distinguish friends from other peers. The psychological characteristics preferred by children at this stage tend to emphasize concrete or material interchanges such as physical helpfulness or kindness. Thus, these characteristics are parallel to Aristotle's notion of utility friendship. Damon's third level of friendship understanding reflects many of the qualities of friendship inherent in Aristotle's notion of "goodness." Children at this stage begin to describe friendships in terms of an understanding of the other person for his or her own sake. Damon describes this as a sense of "mutual ease, that one can be 'oneself' with a friend" (p. 164). It should be pointed out that children's descriptions of friendship at this level also imply a certain amount of moral "courage" (MacIntyre, 1981) in that friends take psychological risks with each other in the process of developing and maintaining the relationship. Finally, according to Damon's description of the third level, children begin to understand the long-standing nature of friendships and that effort is required to maintain and develop these types of friendships.

In summary, there is both direct and indirect evidence to support Aristotle's three-factor model of friendship. Taken together, both social scientists and children appear to agree that Aristotle's conceptualization of friendship is of value to the current understanding of this relationship. In the next section we consider whether "goodness" promotes friendship.

### Friendship requires goodness

The argument that the highest level of friendship is more likely among persons who appreciate goodness has not been directly studied. However, research from three different aspects of children's friendships provides some support for this argument. These three aspects are: (a) peer conflicts, (b) behavioral characteristics of friended and friendless children, and (c) friendship continuity.

Research on peer conflicts indicates that although there are no differences in the frequency of conflict between friends and nonfriends, friendship formation and maintenance are related to the means by which children try to resolve their conflicts (Hartup, Laursen, Stewart, & Eastenson, 1988; Kramer, 1991). Kramer, for example, found that children who use selfish strategies (e.g., winner-take-all) to resolve conflicts were less likely to form friendships than were children who used strategies based on equity.

As a further assessment of Aristotle's view that friendship is more likely among persons who are "good" than among others, we compared characteristics of children with friends to those of children without friends on dimensions that are reflections of "goodness" (Bukowski, Sippola, & Hoza, 1994). We compared friended and friendless children from a sample of 236 pre- and early adolescent boys and girls on the following two items taken from Masten, Morison, and Pellegrini's (1985) *Revised Class Play*: "someone you can trust" and "helps other people when they need it." Differences were found on each of these dimensions, with the friended children receiving higher scores than the friendless children. The differences observed between these two groups of children on these items were larger than those observed on items referring to other aspects of sociability or social skill (e.g., "someone who plays fair") or to either aggression or withdrawal. These findings are, of course, correlational, and one cannot derive from them any evidence of causality. Nevertheless, they show that friendship is more strongly linked to these "goodness" items than to other aspects of sociability.

Finally, there is also evidence that the continuity of children's friendships is related to the moral dimensions suggested by Aristotle. In Berndt, Hawkins, and Hoyle's (1986) study of fourth and eighth graders, friendship quality scores on the dimension of loyalty/faithfulness were twice as high for stable friendship pairs than for nonstable pairs.

In summary, evidence from three sources supports the Aristotelian argument that goodness enhances and promotes friendship. Friendship pairs that resolve conflicts via techniques that reflect goodness and that emphasize constructs such as loyalty and faithfulness are more likely to continue in a friendship relation than are other friendship pairs. Moreover, children who possess characteristics that are related to "goodness" are more likely to engage in friendship relations.

*Goal of friendship is goodness*

Evidence to support Aristotle's argument that a central goal of friendship is goodness can be taken from the literature on friendship conceptions. This evidence is particularly apparent in the research of Damon (1977) and Smollar and Youniss (1982). From approximately preadolescence onward, children's construction of the friendship relation relies on notions of moral obligation such as the importance of cooperation and mutual respect. Indeed, the importance of doing good for one's friend is explicit in the comments of their adolescent subjects. Smollar and Youniss reported that adolescents in general, and girls in particular, believed that it is important to be supportive of one's friends because this support would contribute to the friend's well-being. And as we pointed out earlier, children at the third stage of Damon's developmental model describe friendships in terms of doing "good" for their friend for the friend's own sake.

*Equality and friendship*

Direct evidence regarding the role of equality in friendship is somewhat sparse. Certainly, as Furman (this volume) and Laursen (this volume) have argued, concepts such as balance and equity have been identified by psychological theorists as central processes in friendship. And there are at least two sources of indirect evidence to support this view. First, research with adults has generally shown that interpersonal similarity facilitates friendship (see Berscheid & Walster, 1978). Research with children has also supported this view but there have been relatively few studies. The best-known relevant study is Kandel's (1978) report that interpersonal similarity, especially in self-reported drug use, was not only a feature of friendship pairs, but that it also (a) existed prior to the formation of the friendship; (b) predicted the continuity of the friendship relation; and (c) increased as the friendship continued.

A second form of evidence showing that equality and friendship are linked is the repeated observation that reciprocity is a central feature of friendship. This observation can be gleaned from observational studies (e.g., Newcomb & Brady, 1982) and from studies of friendship conceptions (e.g., Youniss & Volpe, 1978). Together, these studies have shown the centrality of reciprocity and mutuality in children's friendships. Insofar as reciprocity is a form of equality, these studies support the notion that equality is necessary for friendship. Nevertheless, the meaning of equality and its place in children's friendship has not been systematically explored. It is conceivable that many forms of inequality may be tolerated within friendship.

*Justice, benevolence and friendship*

Again, direct evidence is unavailable, but some literatures provide indirect support for the role of justice and benevolence in friendship. Certainly, children's comments about their relationships with friends reveal a concern with fairness. This has been shown by Damon (1977, 1980), Smollar and Youniss (1982), and Youniss and Volpe (1978). La Gaipa (1979) observed that the issue of justice and benevolence was particularly salient in the dissolution of girls' friendships. One of the most important factors observed to be involved in the dissolution of girls' friendships was the issue of disloyalty as indicated by a failure to maintain confidentiality of shared disclosures. Moreover, La Gaipa's (1979) summary demonstrates that loyalty is perceived by adolescents as a more important dimension of best friendships than of ''good'' friendships or relationships with an acquaintance.

Clearly, more research is required to understand the interaction between different aspects of morality in the development and maintenance of friendships. It remains unclear, for example, how differential concerns with ''care'' and ''justice'' (Gilligan, 1982) may affect friendship and whether these concerns vary for boys and girls.

*Summary*

Some empirical evidence can be found to support the basic positions taken by Aristotle and other philosophers. Although much of this evidence is indirect, it nevertheless provides an opportunity to evaluate the positions taken by Aristotle and others regarding friendship and morality. Overall, these findings show that the model of friendship and morality that was originally proposed by Aristotle and recapitulated, with some revisions, in the work of modern philosophers is remarkably consistent with research on friendship. This evidence from the empirical study of friendship by psychologists alludes to the power of the ideas of Aristotle and other philosophers for the psychological study of friendship and morality. Because many of the studies we reviewed were not designed as direct tests of philosophical positions, they cannot be used to examine subtle or particular points from philosophical positions. Such inquiries, however, may be useful. At the least, the application of philosophical ideas may give psychologists a new interpretive scheme by which data from old and new studies can be understood.

## Friendship and moral development

In the previous sections we have considered how friendship and morality may be associated. The goal of the present section is to consider how friendship relates specifically to moral development. We begin by examining the question of the goal of moral development. We argue that an examination of the links between friendship and morality reveals a narrow view of moral development inherent in psychological research.

### What is the goal of moral development?

In some areas of human development the end point or goal is clearly defined and readily observable. The end point of language development, for example, may be the ability to communicate thoughts or ideas with other speakers. In our opinion, however, the end point of moral development is less clear. The influence of a particular philosophical perspective can be observed in the dominant theory of moral development articulated by Lawrence Kohlberg.

Based on the Kantian definition of morality, the ultimate goal of moral development in the cognitive-developmental tradition is the acquisition of prescriptive, universally applicable principles of justice (Kohlberg, 1984). At the final stage of development one does what is right because, as a rational being, one grasps the validity of these principles and is committed to following them. Thus, the end point of moral development is viewed as the ability to rationally resolve moral conflicts by using these principles regardless of the nature of the social context of the conflict. It should be noted that, more recently, proponents of this view have attempted to integrate the concept of benevolence by suggesting that moral "maturity" involves the integration of judgments of "justice'' with judgments of benevolence (Kohlberg, Boyd, & Levine, 1990). However, moral development continues to be viewed primarily as a cognitive process and the moral position from which resolutions to moral conflicts are achieved are presumed to be oblivious to the particular nature of the social relationships involved.

In describing the influences on moral development, Kohlberg focused most of his attention on the context of the parent–child relationship. According to Kohlberg (Kohlberg & Diessner, 1991), two different processes are involved in the development of moral reasoning. The first process forms the basic conditions for moral development that are involved in any sociomoral interaction regardless of the special nature of the relationship. This process includes exposure to internal cognitive moral conflict, exposure to disagreements between persons, and role-taking opportunities. The second process, identified by Kohlberg as ''moral attachment,'' involves the processes of basic imitation and perceived likeness to persons with whom the child has formed a close relationship. In Kohlberg's theory, this refers specifically to one's parents. Through these secondary processes, children develop a sense of a ''shared self'' with others. This experience of profound sharing with another person sensitizes them to social reinforcement contingencies and creates a feeling of obligation or responsibility to the other's welfare, their expectations, and to the maintenance of the relationship itself.

As Pence (1991) has suggested, an emphasis on the cognitive aspects of moral development underestimates the fundamentally social (i.e., interpersonal) aspects involved in morality. According to Pence, the cognitive-developmental view suggests that moral concepts develop outside of the individual's interpersonal history and diminish the importance of specific types of relational experiences for moral development. However, Piaget's theory, which forms the foundation for much of Kohlberg's work, implies that moral maturity also involves the development of a sensitivity toward others and an understanding of others that occurs within the context of particular relationships.

As Youniss and Damon (1992) have noted, Piaget proposed that the child develops two different types of moral values as a result of qualitatively different types of interactions with parents and peers. In order to make sense of a world in which there is an imbalance of power between adult and child, the child must learn respect for authority and social tradition. Piaget called this ''unilateral respect'' (1932, p. 44). However, peers provide the child with an opportunity to develop ''mutual respect'' that, in turn, contributes to a transformation in understanding of the origins of morality. According to Piaget, it is through cooperation with others of an equal status that morality ceases to be external to the individual. It is through relations with one's peers that the child ''will not only discover the boundaries that separate his self from the other person, but will learn to understand the other person and be understood by him. . . . In this way, autonomy succeeds heteronomy'' (Piaget, 1932, p. 90).

For Piaget, moral development occurs as a function of cooperative construction between equals. The kind of cooperation and mutual sensitivity that Piaget describes as fundamental to the process of moral development has been observed to occur between friends (e.g., Newcomb & Brady, 1982). Moreover, whereas Kohlberg placed a heavy emphasis on the importance of cognitive processes underlying moral development, Piaget saw the importance of the affective ties between persons. By suggesting that affective ties and mutual respect lead to processes of collaboration and cooperation, Piaget implied a unique role for friendship in moral development.

*What are the processes underlying moral development?*

Sullivan (1953) argued that a sense of collaboration emerges between friends during preadolescence corresponding with an increased need for interpersonal intimacy, particularly with a same-sex friend. According to Sullivan, it is through collaboration with friends that early adolescents develop an increasing sensitivity to others' needs. In other words, it is in friendship that an early adolescent develops a sense of ''what I should do to contribute to the happiness or to support the prestige and feeling of worth-whileness of my chum'' (Sullivan, 1953, p. 245). Clearly, Sullivan sees the affective ties of friendship as a source of motivation for friendship and as a precondition for the acquisition of particular moral sensitivities.

In parallel to the Sullivan's views, some modern philosophers (e.g., Blum, 1980; Friedman, 1989), have pointed out that friendships based on mutual trust provide opportunities to share, vicariously, the moral conflicts of our friends. Friendships thus allow the individuals involved access to a greater range of moral experiences against which to evaluate their own moral standards. These writers have also proposed that sharing moral experiences with close and trusted friends provides an important context in which to evaluate and, if necessary, modify one's moral standards or principles. In other words, friendship is viewed as an opportunity in which persons can evaluate their moral standards. Friedman (1989) suggested that, through friendships, persons gain insight into their own moral life and are also moved beyond the self to see the moral world from the perspective of others. Thus, she argued, friendships serve not only to validate our own moral experiences (i.e., through sharing of past experiences and conflicts), but may also inspire the individual to consider new values and principles.

Friedman (1989) has also suggested that friendships provide the opportunity for the development of fundamentally moral characteristics. She argues, for example, that morally excellent friendships develop with time and require a substantial amount of effort on the part of the individuals involved. She suggests that maintaining these relationships through conflict and disagreement is a process in which trust can develop because it provides the opportunity to express a commitment between persons and to the relationship in spite of their differences. Working through disagreements within a caring relationship leaves both individuals relatively "intact" emotionally and creates a context in which persons can acquire greater insight into both the self and the other. Friedman referred to close friends as providing a "reliable moral witness" into our moral values. This context provides a unique opportunity for the moral growth of the individuals involved, thus expanding upon the moral knowledge developed first within the context of the family.

An even more explicit proposal regarding the link between friendship and morality can be found in the writing of Nussbaum (1990). She pointed out that Aristotle stated clearly that the bonds of friendship are important for the development of interpersonal understanding. In describing Aristotle's model, Nussbaum states:

trusting the guidance of a friend and allowing one's feelings to be engaged with that other person's life and choices, one learns to see aspects of the world that one had previously missed. One's desire to share . . . with the friend motivates this process. (1990, p. 44)

An essential point of this perspective is that it is the *affective* features of friendship that facilitate or motivate the *cognitive* processes that Kohlberg emphasized. Consistent with this view, Damon (1988) argued that the moral significance of friendship is primarily motivational in the sense that friendship leads children to recognize the importance of moral standards such as honesty, justice, and kindness.

*Summary*

An examination of the role of friendship in moral development ultimately leads to the question of *what* should be studied in moral development. The construct of morality is clearly a multidimensional construct consisting of moral reasoning, the motivation to act upon one's moral judgments, the courage to commit one's self to a moral position, and moral character (Colby & Damon, 1992; Rest, 1983) The development of these various features of morality may be influenced by different relational experiences. Thus, one may consider, in an Aristotlean tradition, that the development of friendship relationships may, in itself, be considered as one important feature of moral development. That is, the development of the processes of responsiveness, reciprocity, and commitment to others that occur within the context of particular relationships such as friendship may be fundamental markers of moral maturity. Certainly, one would expect that the processes that Blum, Friedman, and others have discussed will be more important as children grow older. Indeed, as Keller and Eidelstein (1991) have already suggested, changes in the child's understanding of friendship are accompanied by changes in the moral issues raised within the context of these relationships. Moreover, individual differences are consistently observed in the quality of children's friendships. That is, some friendships have qualities that others lack. Accordingly, children who lack friendships that contain certain features may have more difficulty in developing particular moral sensibilities than children whose friendships possess these qualities. Clearly, what these features are and how they develop are empirical questions.

Finally, one might ask if these processes will be equally salient for boys and girls. It has been suggested that boys and girls have different forms of experience with their peers, with boys' friendships being extensive, that is, oriented toward a group of peers, and girls' friendships being intensive, that is, oriented toward processes experienced at the level of the dyad (Waldrop & Halverson, 1975). Therefore, it is conceivable that peer experiences may lead to different moral concerns for boys and girls (Gilligan, 1982). Because boys engage in group-oriented peer settings, they may be more likely than girls to have experiences that promote the development of a morality that can be used to regulate the behavior of an individual within a group. That is, the concern that would derive from group experiences is a concern with developing rules related to the functioning of the group. In contrast, girls' friendship experiences at the dyadic level may lead to an emphasis on issues concerned with the maintenance of relationships and the protection of trust and intimacy. If this is the case, then friendship relations may lead to the development of different moral constructs for girls and boys.

### Are friendship and morality antithetical?

Ironically, the very properties that make friendship a context for moral development may also present particular challenges for moral development. The powerful affect and sense of interpersonal commitment and differentiation that are central features of friendship may lead persons to treat friends and nonfriends in very different ways. Moreover, from a sociological perspective, friendship has been regarded as "asocial" in the sense that it is occurs on the level of personal experience and is outside the regulation of informal and formal social institutions (Paine, 1969). Accordingly, friendship may not be subject to the same moral prescriptions as other forms of interaction. In this section, we consider whether friendship and morality can be antithetical forces for children. The concern we raise is an old one, namely, whether the inherent partiality of friendship poses particular problems for morality (see Baron, 1991). How can a child engage in a relationship that is based on partiality and yet at the same time show equal consideration to all others? How do children resolve the tension between their affection for their friends and concerns about being impartial to others? To address these issues, we examine three questions: (a) why would we expect friendship to pose a challenge to morality during childhood? (b) is there any evidence that children reach different moral conclusions for friends and nonfriends? and (c) how do philosophers and children deal with these problems?

### Why would friendship pose a challenge to morality?

There are at least two reasons to think that friendship may present particular problems for morality. The first derives from the differences in one's sense of fairness and one's desire to be responsible for one's friends. Insofar as the features of friendship include constructs such as loyalty and commitment, it is to be expected that children may feel a stronger sense of responsibility to their friends than to others. Moreover, because children may have a more positive affective orientation toward friends than toward nonfriends, they may have different motivations for helping friends and nonfriends. For example, because of a sense of commitment and loyalty, children might feel a greater sense of responsibility to help a friend than a nonfriend. As a result of one's differential affect for friends and nonfriends, children may feel a greater sense of empathy and concern for their friends and, as a consequence, will be more likely to help them.

Second, the affective biases of friendship are also likely to influence how children interpret the behavior of friends and nonfriends. Based on Heider's (1958) notion of evaluative consistency, Hymel (1986) proposed that children's impressions of a target child's behavior as good or bad would depend on how much they liked the child. Consistent with this view, Hymel's findings indicate that children were more likely to blame a child for a negative behavior when the child was a disliked peer rather than a liked peer. These results suggest that the differences in children's affect toward friends and nonfriends will influence their moral evaluations or interpretations of the behavior of their peers.

### Evidence of differences in moral decisions for friends and nonfriends

Is there evidence that children make different moral decisions for friends and nonfriends? To our knowledge there is only limited empirical research on this issue. One available study is Slomkowski and Killen's (1992) assessment of preschool children's evaluations and interpretations of transgressions committed by friends and nonfriends. Several findings from their study are of interest.

First, some acts, such as having one's toys taken away, were regarded as "ok" if the transgressor was a friend rather than a nonfriend. These findings show that children's impressions of the "morality" of an act were affected by the friendship status of the persons involved. Second, and more important, in children's explanations of transgressions they were more likely to appeal to psychological interpretations for acts that involved a friend rather than a nonfriend, whereas they were more likely to interpret a transgression as a violation of a moral rule when the transgressor was a nonfriend rather than a friend. These findings show that friendship status affects children's moral interpretations. Nevertheless, different results might be obtained if older children were studied. As Damon (1977) has pointed out, the association between the concepts of friendship and justice may be more strongly fused for preschool children than for older boys and girls for whom these concepts have become progressively differentiated.

A second pertinent study examined the effects of friendship on prosocial behavior and intentions (Berndt, 1981). In this study, children from kindergarten and grades 2 and 4 were paired with a friend or an acquaintance for a sharing task. Before the task, each child was asked how they intended to behave toward the friend or acquaintance. The children's behavior on a sharing task was observed and results indicated sex differences in both their intentions and their behavior. Girls stated that they would treat the friend better than they would treat the acquaintance. Boys, on the other hand, stated that they would treat friends and acquaintances equally. However, on the behavioral measures, girls ultimately treated friends and acquaintances equally during the sharing task whereas boys treated acquaintances better than they treated their friends.

A third type of evidence comes from studies of gang behavior. In Sherif, Harvey, White, Hood, and Sherif's (1961) widely known Robbers Cave study, an experimental manipulation (a) increased levels of intragroup loyalty and (b) resulted in differences in the interactions between boys and their in-group colleagues and members of the "other" group. This study can be interpreted as indicating that a consequence of loyalty to one's closest companions can be a reduction in one's concerns for others. Again, we see that attitudes or experiences with particular others can compromise one's attitudes toward others.

Each of these studies demonstrates that friendship, or experiences with particular others, affects the moral interpretation of events (Slomkowski & Killen, 1992), sharing (for boys) with peers (Berndt, 1981), and treatment of "outgroup" members (Sherif et al., 1961). It may be that children have separate moral codes or different moral motivations with respect to friends and nonfriends. Considering the importance of this issue for moral development, understanding how children construct and resolve moral issues with respect to friends and nonfriends should be an important research question.

*Resolutions of the tension between friendship and morality*

Can this potentially antithetical association between friendship and morality be resolved? And more important for psychologists, how do individuals resolve these tensions in their daily lives? With regard to this first question, some philosophers (e.g., Kant) have argued that this problem cannot be solved – friendship poses a threat to morality and therefore it is our responsibility to be certain that our moral decisions are not swayed by our particular feelings toward others. Other philosophers (e.g., Baron, 1991) have taken alternative positions, usually affirming that impartiality is an important feature of any moral system but that friendship and other personal relationships (e.g., being a parent) give persons unique responsibilities to particular others. LaFollette (1991) noted that according to this view there is an impartial requirement that persons be "partial." That is, there is a general moral rule that requires persons treat persons with whom they are intimate differently than they treat others. This view can also be seen in the writing of Williams (1981), who claims that allegiance to one's friends and intimates is part of the generally accepted moral code of Western society. He claims that partiality is acceptable, just so long as it does not lead to unfairness: One's decision to treat one's friends differently from others would be moral only if no one would, as a consequence, be treated unfairly.

MacIntyre (1981) proposes a more complex solution to this problem. He draws a distinction between two types of moral considerations: justice and courage. Whereas justice refers to principles of fairness and equality, courage refers to reliability at times of need. MacIntyre states that the relevance of these moral considerations will vary considerably for our interactions and experiences with friends and nonfriends. According to his perspective, justice, by its very definition, should be uniform and impersonal. That is, he believes that we owe justice to everyone. One's decisions about fairness should not be affected by matters of friendship. On the other hand, he points out that courage – that is, being unconditionally reliable – is both a virtue and a property of friendship. In this regard, courage is to be expected in friendship relations more than in other relationships because of its connections with properties of friendship such as care and concern. Therefore, some moral considerations should be impartial, whereas others may be influenced by partiality.

To our knowledge there have been no empirical studies relevant to the question of how individuals deal with questions of impartiality. There have been some studies (Berndt, 1993) of how persons resolve tensions that fall along a self/other dimension (e.g., whether to study for a test so as to improve one's own grade or to help a classmate who is having trouble). Expanding on this approach to include a consideration of different types of others – friends, acquaintances, strangers – is essential to our understanding of how relationship properties affect moral decisions. Knowing when and why persons make "partial" decisions about moral issues regarding friends and nonfriends would contribute significantly to our understanding of the links between friendship and morality.

## Summary and conclusion

One of the fundamental challenges facing researchers of moral development concerns the definition of morality. This question is basic in that it has important implications for the (a) our conceptualizations of the goals of moral development, (b) the processes involved in this development, and, finally (c) the empirical tools or approaches used to assess development (Sippola & Bukowski, 1994). Considering the strong influence that particular philosophical views of morality have held in the empirical literature, it is understandable how friendships could have been overlooked as a factor involved in moral development or even viewed as antithetical to morality. However, beginning with the writings of Aristotle and continuing into the contemporary period several philosophers have pointed to the inextricable links between friendship and morality. Although this view is not always seen in psychological theory, research demonstrates that friendship is constructed upon particular moral principles. Indeed, it may be that morality plays a significant role in the processes that regulate the formation and direction of friendship. Moreover, it is possible that morality contributes to the meaning and benefits that persons derive from their experiences with friends. Theory also proposes that friendship is an important context for the development and emergence of morality. In their relationships with friends, children have opportunities to learn about others' needs and feelings and to experience the desire or motivation to be responsive to these needs. Such experiences are likely to form the basis of children's acquisition of concepts such as justice and courage or care.

The many avenues by which friendship and morality are interrelated show that morality should be of interest to persons who study friendship and that friendship should be of interest to persons who study morality. Several challenging questions could form the center of a research program for the study of these two constructs. How do children extract moral principles from their friendship relations? How does morality influence the maintenance and continuity of relationships? How do children deal with potential conflicts between one's affection and "partiality" toward a friend and one's desire to adhere to an impartial morality? The answers to these questions and others will contribute greatly to the understanding of friendship and to the understanding of morality and its development.

# References

Aristotle (1973). Nicomachean Ethics. In Richard McKeon (Ed.), *Introduction to Aristotle* (2nd ed.). Chicago: University of Chicago Press.

Badhwar, N. K. (1985). Friendship, justice, and supererogation. *American Philosophical Quarterly, 22*, 123–131.

Baron, M. (1991). Impartiality and friendship. *Ethics, 101*, 836–857.

Berscheid, E., & Walster, E. H. (1978). *Interpersonal attraction (Second edition)*. Reading, MA: Addison Wesley.

Berndt, T. (1981). Effects of friendship on prosocial intentions and behavior. *Child Development, 52*, 636–643.

Berndt, T. (March, 1993). *The morality of friendship*. Presented at the biennial meetings of the Society for Research in Child Development, New Orleans, Louisiana.

Berndt, T., Hawkins, J., & Hoyle, S. (1986). Stability and change in childhood and adolescent friendships. *Developmental Psychology, 21*, 1007–1297.

Bevan, W. (1991). A tour inside the onion. *American Psychologist, 46*, 475–483.

Bigelow, B. J. (1977). Children's friendship expectations: A cognitive-developmental study. *Child Development, 48*, 246–253.

Blasi, A. (1991). How should psychologists define morality? In T. Wren (Ed.)., *The moral domain* (pp. 38–70). Cambridge, MA: MIT.

Blum, L. (1980). *Friendship, altruism, and morality*. London: Routledge and Kegan Paul.

Bukowski, W. M., Nappi, B. J., & Hoza, B. (1987). A test of Aristotle's model of friendship for young adults' same-sex and opposite-sex relationships. *Journal of Social Psychology, 127*, 595–603.

Bukowski, W. M., Sippola, L. K., & Hoza, B. (1994). *Comparisons of children with and without friends on indices of social behavior*. Unpublished manuscript, Concordia University, Montréal, Québec.

Colby, A., & Damon, W. (1992). *Some do care: Contemporary lives of moral commitment*. New York: Free Press.

Colby, A., & Kohlberg, L. (1987). *The measurement of moral judgment*. New York: Cambridge University Press.

Cooper, J. M. (1980). Aristotle on friendship. In A. Rorty (Ed.), *Essays on Aristotle's ethics* (pp. 301–340). Berkeley: University of California Press.

Damon, W. (1977). *The social world of the child*. San Francisco: Jossey-Bass.

Damon, W. (1980). Patterns of change in children's social reasoning. *Child Development, 51*, 1010–1017.

Damon, W. (1988). *The moral child*. New York: Free Press.

Friedman, M. (1989). Friendship and moral growth. *The Journal of Value Inquiry, 23*, 3–13.

Gilligan, C. (1982). *In a different voice*. Cambridge, MA: Harvard University Press.

Hartup, W. W., Laursen, B., Stewart, M. I., & Eastenson, A. (1988). Conflict and the friendship relations of young children. *Child Development, 59*, 1590–1600.

Haste, H. (1990). Moral responsibility and moral commitment: The integration of affect and cognition. In T. Wren (Ed.)., *The moral domain*. Cambridge, MA: MIT.

Heider, F. (1958). *The psychology of interpersonal relations*. New York: Wiley.

Hymel, S. (1986). Interpretations of peer behavior: Affective biases in childhood and adolescence. *Child Development, 57*, 431–455.

Kandel, D. (1978). Similarity in real-life adolescent friendship pairs. *Journal of Personality and Social Psychology, 36*, 306–312.

Keller, M., & Eidelstein, W. (1990). The emergence of morality in personal relationships. In T. Wren (Ed.)., *The moral domain* (pp. 255–281). Cambridge, MA: MIT.

Kohlberg, L. (1984). *Essays on moral development. Vol. 2: The psychology of moral development.* San Francisco: Harper & Row.

Kohlberg, L., Boyd, D. R., & Levine, C. (1990). The return of stage 6: Its principle and moral point of view. In T. E. Wren (Ed.), *The moral domain: Essays in the ongoing discussion between philosophy and the social sciences.* Cambridge: MIT Press.

Kohlberg, L., & Diessner, R. (1991). A cognitive-developmental approach to moral attachment. In J. L. Gewirtz & W. M. Kurtines (Eds.), *Intersections with attachment.* Hillsdale, NJ: Erlbaum.

Kramer, T. (1991). *The relation between conflict management and liking during the initial interactions of preschool children.* Unpublished dissertation, Department of Psychology, University of Maine, Orono, Maine.

LaFollette, K. (1991). Personal relationships. In P. Singer (Ed.), *A companion to ethics.* Oxford: Blackwell.

La Gaipa, J. J. (1979). A developmental study of the meaning of friendship in adolescence. *Journal of Adolescence, 2,* 201–213.

MacIntyre, A. (1981). *After virtue.* Notre Dame: University of Notre Dame.

Masten, A. S., Morison, P., & Pellegrini, D. (1985). A revised class play method of peer assessment. *Developmental Psychology, 21,* 523–533.

Murstein, B., & Spitz, L. (1974). Aristotle and friendship: A factor analytic study. *Interpersonal Development, 4,* 21–34.

Newcomb, A., & Brady, J. (1982). Mutuality in boys' friendship relations. *Child Development, 53,* 392–395.

Noddings, N. (1984). *Caring: A feminine approach to ethics and moral education.* Berkeley: University of California.

Nussbaum, M. C. (1986). *The fragility of goodness.* New York: Cambridge University Press.

Nussbaum, M. C. (1990). *Love's knowledge.* New York: Oxford.

Paine, R. (1969). In search of friendship: An exploratory analysis in "middle-class" culture. *Man, 4,* 505–524.

Pence, G. (1991). Virtue theory. In P. Singer (Ed.), *A companion to ethics* (pp. 249–257). Cambridge, MA: Basil Blackwell.

Piaget, J. (1932). *The moral judgement of the child.* London: Routledge & Kegan Paul.

Raymond, J. (1986). *A passion for friends.* Boston: Beacon.

Reisman, J. M., & Shorr, S. E. (1978). Friendship claims and expectations among children and adults. *Child Development, 49,* 913–916.

Rest, J. (1983). Morality. In Mussen, P. H. (Series Ed.), *Handbook of Child Psychology* (Vol. 4), E.M. Hetherington (Ed.), *Socialization, personality, and social development* (pp. 556–629). New York: Wiley.

Sherif, M. Harvey, O. J., White, B. J., Hood, W. R., & Sherif, C. (1961). *Intergroup conflict and cooperation: The Robbers Cave experiment.* Norman, OK: University Book Exchange.

Sippola, L. K., & Bukowski, W. M. (November, 1994). *A dangerous liaison: Unresolved issues in the association between philosophy and the psychology of moral development.* Paper presented at the 20th Annual Conference of the Association for Moral Education. Banff, Alta.

Slomkowski, C., & Killen, M. (1992). Young children's conceptions of transgressions with friends and nonfriends. *International Journal of Behavioral Development, 15,* 247–258.

Smollar, J., & Youniss, J. (1982). Social development through friendship. In K. Rubin & H. Ross (Eds.), *Peer relations and social skills in childhood* (pp. 279–298). New York: Springer-Verlag.

Sullivan, H. S. (1953). *The interpersonal theory of psychiatry.* New York: Norton.

Turiel, E. (1983). *The development of social knowledge: Morality and convention.* New York: Cambridge University Press.

Waldrop, M. F., & Halverson, C. F. (1975). Intensive and extensive peer behavior: Longitudinal and cross-sectional analyses. *Child Development, 46,* 19–26.

Williams, B. (1981). Persons, character, and morality. In B. Williams (Ed.), *Moral luck*. Cambridge: Cambridge University Press.

Youniss, J., & Damon, W. (1992). Social construction in Piaget's theory. In H. Beilin & P. B. Pufall (Eds.), *Piaget's theory: Prospects and possibilities* (The Jean Piaget Symposium series), Pp. 267–286. Hillsdale, NJ: Erlbaum.

Youniss, J., & Volpe, J. (1978). A relationship analysis of children's friendship. In W. Damon (Ed.), *Social cognition*, (New Directions for Child Development, #1). San Francisco: Jossey-Bass.

## 12 Friendships of maltreated children and adolescents: Contexts for expressing and modifying relationship history

*Joseph M. Price*

Embedded in the research and theory on children's friendships are two widely accepted premises. The first is that there is a link between children's early family experiences and their abilities to form and maintain friendship relationships with peers. Through their interactions and experiences with family members children develop their initial understanding of themselves, others, and relationships, and learn specific social behavioral orientations. These representations and behavioral patterns, in turn, serve to guide the nature and course of their friendships. This premise is supported by a growing empirical literature (Park, this volume; Ladd, 1991; Parke & Ladd, 1992). Complementing this first premise is the proposal that child and adolescent friendships make unique contributions to social and emotional growth and development. From their experiences with friends, children learn various social competencies, extend their knowledge of themselves, and derive emotional support. This premise has also gained empirical and theoretical support (e.g., Buhrmester & Furman, 1986; Sullivan, 1953).

Recently, Cicchetti (1989) has argued that research and theoretical models of normal development can be greatly enhanced by the study of children who are at high risk for developmental deviation and psychopathology. Through the study of children who have experienced divergent socialization experiences, theories of normal development can be affirmed and challenged. Following this line of reasoning, the study of the friendships of children who have experienced maladaptive family relationships should contribute to our understanding of the links between family relationships and friendships and the unique functions of children's friendships.

One group of children likely to have experienced maladaptive family relationships, and therefore be at risk for psychopathology, is made up of children who have been maltreated (Mueller & Silverman, 1989). The family environ-

This chapter was written with the support of the W. T. Grant Foundation Faculty Scholars Program.

ments of these children are often characterized by poor parent–child interactions, familial stress and disorganization (Garbarino & Gilliam, 1980), social isolation and family discord (Gil, 1970), and persistent poverty (Pelton, 1978). Given these characteristics, Bronfenbrenner (1979) suggests that maltreatment provides an "experiment in nature." If indeed there is a link between children's early family experiences and friendship relationships, then children who have experienced some form of maltreatment should evidence difficulties in forming and maintaining friendships. Also, if friendships do provide unique functions, such as social support, then maltreated children who can form friendships should be at less risk for later pathology than maltreated children who are unable to form friendships. Therefore, the friendships of maltreated children and adolescents are hypothesized as serving as a context for both the expression and modification of their early family experiences. Empirical support for this hypothesis would complement the friendship research with "normal" children and will, therefore, either affirm and/or challenge our present understanding of children's friendships.

The primary objective of this chapter is to present and discuss the theoretical and empirical work supporting the hypothesis that the friendships of maltreated children and adolescents can both express and modify their early relationship histories. Another objective is to propose directions for future research that will provide a more comprehensive examination of this hypothesis. Before discussing these issues, however, the literature on the friendships of maltreated children will be reviewed.

## Friendships of maltreated children and adolescents

Although few investigations have focused exclusively on the peer relationships of maltreated children, several consistent findings have emerged from the research (see Conaway & Hansen, 1989; Mueller & Silverman, 1989; also Cicchetti, Lynch, Shonk, & Manly, 1992, for reviews of this literature). To begin, maltreated children, especially those who have been physically abused, appear on average to be more aggressive toward their peers than nonmaltreated "normal" children (Alessandri, 1991; Hoffman-Plotkin & Twentyman, 1984; Kaufman & Cicchetti, 1989; Reidy, 1977). Second, maltreated children are less competent and prosocial in social interactions than nonmaltreated children (Alessandri, 1991; Hoffman-Plotkin & Twentyman, 1984; Howes & Espinosa, 1985; Lewis & Schaeffer, 1981). Finally, some maltreated children are also withdrawn and avoidant of interaction with peers, although this pattern of withdrawal may be more prevalent in neglected children than in physically abused children (e.g., Hoffman-Plotkin & Twentyman, 1984). Even when peers make friendly overtures, maltreated children respond inappropriately (e.g., with aggression) (Howes

& Espinosa, 1985; Main & George, 1985). Given that the behavioral orientations of maltreated children are more aggressive, less competent, and that some maltreated children actively withdraw from social interaction, it is not surprising that these children are less well liked by their peers than nonmaltreated children (Haskett & Kistner, 1991; Salzinger, Feldman, Hammer, & Rosario, 1993).

Given their behavioral patterns, it seems reasonable to suggest that maltreated children would also experience difficulties in both forming and maintaining friendships. Unfortunately, there is little data addressing the quality of maltreated children's friendships. The data that do exist suggest that compared with nonmaltreated children, maltreated children experience difficulties in forming friendships with their peers, and that their interactions with their friends may differ subtly from those of nonmaltreated children and their friends. We recently examined the emergence of friendships among unfamiliar children in small play groups (Price & Van Slyke, 1991). Eight play groups were formed, each consisting of one maltreated child and three nonmaltreated matched comparisons. Each play group met for a half-hour, twice a week for 4 weeks. Following each play session, interviews were conducted to determine how well each child liked the other members of the play group. Friendship was operationalized as reciprocal liking nominations between two children during three of the last four play sessions. Based on this definition, only one maltreated child formed a reciprocal friendship, whereas nine of the nonmaltreated children formed friendships during this period. However, given the relationship histories of maltreated children, brief encounters with a limited number of unfamiliar peers over 4 weeks may not have been conducive to forming friendships. Howes (1984) found that the maltreated children in her study who attended full-time therapeutic day care eventually established friendships, although only with other maltreated children. Given enough time with consistent play partners, maltreated children may be able to form friendships.

Additional evidence for maltreated children's difficulties in establishing friendships comes from an investigation conducted by Salzinger et al. (1993) with physically abused elementary-aged children, ages 8 to 12. These authors found that in comparison to nonabused children, the abused children received significantly fewer reciprocal best-friend nominations from their classmates at school. Furthermore, the abused children were also more likely to receive disliking nominations from the peers they nominated as friends. Although it is too early to draw firm conclusions about the extent to which maltreated children exhibit difficulties informing friendships, it does appear that at least some maltreated children may be less successful in establishing friendships with their agemates than children who have not experienced some form of maltreatment.

In spite of the apparent difficulties some maltreated children experience in establishing a friendship, at least some maltreated children can eventually form friendships (e.g., Howes, 1984; Lynch & Cicchetti, 1991; Parker, Levendosky, & Okun, 1993). However, their interactions with their friends appear to differ from the interactions of nonmaltreated children and their friends. Recently, Parker et al. (1993) examined the cooperative and competitive behavior of abused and nonabused elementary-school aged children with their best friends. The friendships of abused girls involved less mutual cooperative activity and were more likely to continue competitive and unproductive stalemates than those of other girls. Abused girls were also more likely to be exploited by their friends than were other girls. The authors suggest that this might be because the abused girls are very trusting. In contrast, the friendships of abused boys were more cooperative and less competitive than those of nonabused boys. In fact, dyads with an abused boy were the least competitive of all dyads. The authors concluded that the friendships of abused boys may be conflict avoiding. This may have been because abused boys reacted negatively to dyadic conflict. Furthermore, the friends of abused boys avoided using betrayal during the competitive activity, perhaps, as the authors suggest, to avoid provoking their abused friend.

Consistent with the findings on the friendships of maltreated children are data suggesting that maltreated exhibit certain social cognitive orientations that may undermine their efforts to form and maintain friendships. To begin, maltreated children's representations of their relationships appear to be different from those of nonmaltreated children. Lynch and Cicchetti (1991) examined children's reports of relatedness to multiple relationship figures (i.e., their parents, their teachers, and their best friends). The dimensions of relatedness examined included emotional quality (i.e., the valence of emotions that children have when they are with a specific partner) and psychological proximity-seeking (i.e., the degree to which children wish they were psychologically closer to their partner). Among maltreated children there was virtually no relation between the two dimensions of relatedness across all three relationship types. That is, the feelings maltreated children reported experiencing when with a particular partner were unrelated to their desire to be psychologically closer to that partner. Although a maltreated child may feel extremely positive about a particular relationship, he or she may still desire to be closer to that person. Maltreated children were unsatisfied with how close they were to both their mothers and their best friends. In contrast, among nonmaltreated children there was a significant negative relation between emotional quality and proximity-seeking. For these children the more positive their reported feelings were when they were with a particular partner, the less they felt the need to be psychologically closer, presumably because the child already felt close to that partner.

Maltreated children also appear to exhibit difficulties in interpersonal trust. Recently, Bernath, Feshbach, and Gralinski (1993) examined abused children's feelings and reasoning about trust. In response to hypothetical scenarios involving keeping promises and secrets, abused children responded with an all-or-nothing pattern of trust. In comparison to nonabused children, physically abused children responded more frequently to hypothetical peers with either no trust or a whole lot of trust. Either extreme in trust could be an obstacle to establishing and maintaining friendships.

Besides exhibiting these extremes in trust, Barahal, Waterman, and Martin (1981) found that in comparison to nonabused children, abused children were less sensitive and were less able to identify appropriate feelings in others. Not only were the abused children less accurate in labeling the emotions of others, but they were also less articulate in describing the social and interpersonal causes of the specific emotions. In contrast, nonabused children were better in perspective-taking skills, manifesting views that were not as egocentric as the views of the abused children. Complementing these findings are data based on behavioral observations that suggest that physically abused children are less likely to display concern or empathy toward a distressed peer than nonabused children (George & Main, 1979; Howes & Espinosa, 1985) and are more likely to respond negatively (e.g., fear, aggression) (George & Main, 1979; Howes & Espinosa, 1985; Klimes-Dougan & Kistner, 1990). Taken together, these data suggest that maltreated children have difficulties both in understanding others' feelings and in expressing concern or empathy toward their peers. These types of deficits would hinder the formation and maintenance of friendships.

Maltreated children's conceptualizations of peer relationships may pose yet another barrier to friendship. In their investigation of maltreated children's conceptions of parental and peer relationships, Dean, Malik, Richards, and Stringer (1986) found that when responding to hypothetical situations, maltreated children were less likely to describe peer interactions as reciprocal in nature than nonmaltreated children. That is, in comparison to nonmaltreated children, maltreated children were less likely to expect kind acts to be reciprocated by peers. These expectations could hinder establishing behavioral reciprocity between peers and, consequently, serve as an obstacle to friendship (Price & Ladd, 1986).

Finally, besides their representations of others, maltreated children's representations of themselves could undermine their ability to form friendships with peers. The evidence suggests that maltreated children and adolescents manifest impairments in self-system processes (Cicchetti, Beeghly, Carlson, & Toth, 1990), and that these children exhibit deficits in self-esteem (Egeland, Sroufe, & Erickson, 1983; Kazdin, Moser, Colbus, & Bell, 1985). More specifically, maltreated children express more negative feelings about themselves (Schneider-Rosen & Cicchetti, 1984) and talk less about themselves than comparison children (Cicchetti & Beeghly, 1987). Negative evaluations of themselves and their inability to talk about their feelings could be a hindrance to the formation and maintenance of friendship, especially during adolescence when intimate self-disclosure becomes important to friendship (Parker & Gottman, 1989).

Taken as a whole, the existent research suggests that maltreated children may indeed experience difficulties in forming and maintaining friendships. This is not surprising, given that the social-cognitive and behavioral orientations of maltreated children are not conducive to establishing or keeping friends. However, what are the explanations for why the experiences associated with maltreatment lead to the development of representations and behavioral patterns that would hinder the development of friendship? This question will be addressed in the following section.

## Theoretical perspectives on the impact of maltreatment

Fortunately, there are several theoretical perspectives that address the reasons maltreated children would experience difficulties in forming and maintaining friendships. Those perspectives include attachment theory, Sullivan and neo-Sullivan theories of personality development, cognitive-social learning theories, and social-network theory. Although there is often overlap between perspectives, each theory offers a unique perspective to the reasons underlying the friendship difficulties of maltreated children.

### Attachment theory

Perhaps the most widely used theoretical perspective guiding the research on maltreated children is attachment theory (Crittenden, 1990; Lynch & Cicchetti, 1991). According to attachment theory, children's attachment relationships with their parent(s) provide the initial context in which children learn about themselves, others, and relationships. In turn, these representations shape and influence children's relationships with peers. This proposition is supported by empirical data that demonstrate a link between the quality of children's attachments to their parents and their social competence and acceptance among peers (Sroufe, 1983). Children who have been classified as securely attached to their caregivers during infancy or toddlerhood are more socially competent and better liked by their peers than children who have been classified as insecure (Lafreniere & Sroufe, 1985). There is also evidence of a specific link between the quality of parent–child attachments and children's friendship (see Park, this volume).

Several mechanisms have been hypothesized to link early attachment with children's peer relationships. First, through caregiver sensitivity and responsiveness, children are provided with a "secure base" from which to explore their physical and social environments. This social exploration, in turn, leads to varied experiences and greater competency in dealing with others. Second, through their interactions with their parents, children are provided with initial models of reciprocity and sharing, as well as a context for learning how to take the perspective of another. Therefore, the quality of the parent–child attachment plays an instrumental role in the development of conceptions of reciprocity and sharing, and in the growth of perspective-taking and interpersonal understanding (Mueller & Silverman, 1989). Finally, through interactions with his or her caregiver the child develops a set of representations about the specific caregiver, a complementary set of representations about the self, and a set of representations about the relationship between self and others (Bowlby, 1969, 1973, 1980). These specific models, in turn, contribute to the development of more generalized models of relationships that are applied to subsequent relationships (Crittenden, 1990).

Maltreated children are more likely to have insecure attachments with their primary caregivers than are nonmaltreated children (Crittenden, 1988; Egeland & Sroufe, 1981). More specifically, for most maltreated children their attachments could be classified as "disorganized/disoriented" (Lyons-Ruth, Connel, Zoll, & Stahl, 1987; Carlson, Cicchetti, Barnett, & Braunwald, 1989). This attachment style is characterized by approach and avoidant behavioral patterns toward the parent, "undirected" expression of fear or distress, and freezing and stilling movements. Main and Hesse (1990) suggest that this pattern of disorganization is a consequence of the inconsistent care by their caregivers and the frightening behavior displayed by their abusing parents. The consequences of a "disorganized" attachment are that the maltreated child develops a sense of self as unworthy of love and affection, as well as early representational models of others as untrustworthy and threatening.

According to the attachment perspective, there are several explanations for why maltreated children could experience difficulties in forming and maintaining friendships. First, maltreated children lack a secure emotional base from which to explore their social environment and develop new relationships. Second, because of the disorganized interaction patterns between parent and child, maltreated children miss the first opportunities to develop skills for engaging in reciprocal and cooperative exchanges with others and for perspective-taking. Finally, maltreated children would be expected to develop distorted representational models of self, others, and relationships that would lead to ambivalence about forming friendships, and perhaps even uncertainty about the value of friendships.

*Sullivan and neo-Sullivan perspectives*

Similar to attachment theory, Sullivan (1953) and neo-Sullivan (Buhrmester & Furman, 1986) theories of social-personality development emphasize the importance of early parent–child interactions. However, unlike attachment theory, these perspectives acknowledge that other types of relationships are important for development as well. Sullivan believed that throughout the lifespan, an individual's personality is shaped by one's "key" relationships, primarily those with parents, siblings, teachers, and peers. Depending on the developmental stage, these key relationships function to fulfill the basic social needs that emerge during development (e.g., tenderness, acceptance by others, and interpersonal intimacy). Key relationships also serve as contexts in which interpersonal competencies are formed. Because the types of interactions within each key relationship may vary, the specific competencies required in each relationship will also vary (Buhrmester & Furman, 1986). Thus, each key relationship offers new interpersonal challenges and opportunities for developing different social skills.

Given the importance of key relationships in development, failure to form the key relationships of a particular period, or difficulties in those relationships can have negative consequences for the individual. To begin, a developmental arrest could result. Usually, "an arrest involves the child adopting a maladaptive coping pattern in order to deal with an anxiety-provoking interpersonal situation" (Buhrmester & Furman, 1986, p. 45). Another consequence of a maladaptive key relationship is that one or more of the basic social needs may remain unfulfilled. Finally, a child or adolescent who was unable to establish the functional key relationship for their developmental period would miss opportunities to learn important social competencies. Since the acquisition of social competencies follows a hierarchical path, failure to develop certain competencies at one period of development would hinder the acquisition of competencies at the next period.

Parent–child relationships are viewed as "key" from infancy through preadolescence. This relationship meets many basic needs and provides a context for learning many social competencies. Therefore, a child who is unable to develop an adaptive relationship with his or her parents would continue to have unmet needs, would miss opportunities to learn important competencies, and could develop a "malevolent transformation," which involves the child developing the belief that his or her parents are enemies. Thus, according to the Sullivan and neo-Sullivan perspectives, the experiences associated with maltreatment (e.g., abuse from one's parents, neglect, negative interaction patterns with parents) would likely lead to maladaptive relationships with parents early in development. Consequently, these children carry forward with them in development maladaptive representations of relationships and unsatisfied needs that would undermine future key relationships with peers. Furthermore, these children may also lack the social competencies necessary to form future key relationships, which include friendships during preadolescence and adolescence.

## Cognitive-social learning theory

Recently, several theoretical models of the links between family and peer relationships have emerged from the cognitive-social learning perspective (e.g., Parke, MacDonald, Beitel, Bhavnagri, 1988; Pettit & Mize, 1993; Putallaz & Heflin, 1990). These models share two common characteristics. First, a distinction is made between direct and indirect influences on children's social development. Direct influences often refer to parents' attempts to teach about and manage children's peer relationships. Direct influences also refer to coaching or teaching of specific social skills, providing advice when social dilemmas arise, and managing and supervising play activities. Indirect influences refer to the manner in which parents interact with their children, which, in turn, influences how children relate to their peers. These influences include parental disciplinary styles, quality of parent–child interactions, and the degree of emotional warmth and support displayed by parents toward their children. Another indirect influence is parental modeling of social behaviors.

Another feature of these models is that children's social cognitions (e.g., relational schema, social information processing patterns) and their abilities to recognize and express emotion are viewed as mechanisms mediating the relation between family and peer relationships (Pettit & Mize, 1993). Because of both direct and indirect parental influences, children develop mental representations (''schemas'') of self, others, and relationships. These schemas influence the processing of social information (e.g., encoding of social and emotional cues, interpretations of others' intentions, and selection and evaluation of response options). In turn, social cognitive processes guide children's social behavior and interactions with peers. The notion that cognitive and affective mechanisms mediate the relation between early family experiences and children's peer relations is similar to the position advanced by the attachment perspective.

From a cognitive-social learning perspective, the family environments of maltreated children would not be conducive to the development of the mental representations and processing patterns and behavioral orientations necessary for forming and maintaining friendships. In comparison to the parents of nonmaltreated children, maltreating parents are, in general, more aversive and display less positive behavior toward their children (Bousha & Twentyman, 1984). They also spend less time interacting with their children, are less engaged (Lewis & Schaeffer, 1981), are less sensitive to the children's distress cues, and lower in socioemotional growth-fostering behavior (Bee, Disbrow, Johnson-Crowley, &

Barnard, 1981). Furthermore, besides inadequacies in their caregiving behavior, maltreating parents have also been found to display many other deficits that would make them less adequate role models, including poor impulse control, social skill deficits, and poor stress-coping ability (see Azar & Twentyman, 1986, a review).

Supporting the predictions derived from cognitive-social learning models, maltreated children have been found to display social cognitive patterns previously linked to incompetent and aggressive behavioral orientations (Dodge, Bates, & Pettit, 1990; Rieder & Cicchetti, 1989). Price and Van Slyke (1991) examined the social-information processing skills of maltreated children. In response to hypothetical social situations, maltreated children were less accurate in encoding social cues and generated a higher proportion of aggressive solutions than did the comparisons.

*Social network theory*

In contrast to the other theoretical perspectives, the social-network model proposes relative independence between parent–child and child–friend relationships. As articulated by Lewis and Feiring (1989), the development of relationships is not necessarily sequential. Within each type of relationship a child forms, the child learns the skills and competencies necessary for that type of relationship. Although the quality of the parent–child relationship can have an effect on children's friendships, it is not through a direct causal relation. There are two pathways by which a parent–child relationship can have an effect on children's friendships. First, parents play a pivotal role in determining the amount of peer contact a child receives. Parents can, through either design or neglect, fail to provide their child with adequate peer experiences. The absence of experience or contact will prevent the child from learning how to interact with peers. Thus the cause of difficulties in forming friendships is the lack of peer experience per se, and not the quality of the parent–child relationship. The second pathway is through generalized fear of others. Because of inappropriate parental behaviors, the child develops a fear of others. This fear might have the effect of inhibiting contact with others.

According to this perspective, maltreated children would likely experience difficulties forming friends. Because maltreating parents are not well integrated into an established support system and tend to be socially isolated from their communities (Garbarino & Gilliam, 1980), their children would be afforded few opportunities to develop interaction skills and warm and trusting relationships with others outside the family. The effects of social isolation would likely be greatest during early childhood when parents possess the greatest amount of control over their children's peer experiences.

*Summary*

Based on theoretical perspectives reviewed and empirical evidence supporting these perspectives, the experiences associated with maltreatment are expected to influence the ability of a child or adolescent to form and maintain friendships. The pathways through which these influences are predicted to travel include: (a) the quality of the parent–child attachment; (b) more general parent–child interactions; and (c) the provision of opportunities for peer interaction. The relevant child processes hypothesized to be affected by maltreatment experiences include: conceptualizations, evaluations, and expectations of self, others, and relationships, and social cognitive and behavioral skills. Yet several important issues remain unresolved. As is becoming evident within the maltreatment literature, the effects of maltreatment on children's psychosocial development may vary as a function of the type and severity of the maltreatment (e.g., abuse or neglect) and the age of the child at the time of the maltreatment and at the time of the assessments (Bukowski, 1992; Crittenden, 1990). Thus, although maltreated children may have difficulties forming and maintaining friendships, the individual explanations for their difficulties may vary, depending upon these factors.

**Functions of friendships**

As previously mentioned, in spite of their family histories, some maltreated children and adolescents do manage to form friendships (Howes, 1984; Lynch & Cicchetti, 1993). Given this, it is hypothesized that for those maltreated children and adolescents who can form a friendship, their relationships may act as a buffer or protective factor, and by that serve as a context for modifying their relationship histories. As pointed out in several chapters in this volume, as well as in previous theoretical and empirical work, friendships appear to serve a variety of functions for children. For example, in Parker and Gottman's (1989) model, friendships are viewed as an important context for social and emotional growth. Theoretical and empirical work from Furman and his colleagues (Furman & Buhrmester, 1985; Furman & Robbins, 1985) suggest that, among other things, friendships function to provide opportunities for intimacy and affection, provide support and companionship, and enhance self-esteem. Similarly, Hartup and Sancilio (1986) and Bukowski and Hoza (1989) suggest that friendships serve as a context for growth in social competence, provide emotional security and support, and serve as precursors of later relationships. Furthermore, Sullivan (1953) argues that friendships, particularly as they emerge in preadolescence, even have the potential to help adolescents overcome negative experiences of childhood. Similarly, proponents of the social-network perspective suggest that peer experiences can help children overcome poor parental interaction and its negative effects on children's social behavior (Lewis & Schaeffer, 1981).

In this section, the potential functions of friendships for maltreated children and adolescents will be discussed. Although each function theorized to be provided by friendships is important, given the family histories of maltreated children, it is hypothesized that those functions that may be particularly important include: (a) providing a context for learning specific relationship competencies and developing alternative representional models of relationships; (b) enhancing the formation of self-concept and self-esteem; and (c) providing emotional support and security.

### Context for learning relationship competencies

There is theoretical and empirical work suggesting that friendships provide children and adolescents with unique interactional experiences that facilitate the growth of various social competencies (e.g., Sullivan, 1953; Buhrmester & Furman, 1986). Howes and her colleagues have found that friendships contribute to the development of social skills among young children. In one study (Howes, 1983), the greatest increase in complexity of social interaction (e.g., number of successful initiations, the number of elaborated exchanges, time spent in complementary and reciprocal peer play, and time spent in positive affective exchanges) were observed within stable friendship pairs. In another study (Howes & Unger, 1989), friendships assisted young children in negotiating the transition from social play that is based on literal actions (e.g., playing chase) to social pretend play based on symbolic, nonliteral meanings (using a table as a house).

According to Sullivan (1953) and neo-Sullivan theories (Buhrmester & Furman, 1986) friendships are particularly important to the growth of social skills during preadolescence and adolescence. During this period, children begin to develop a greater need for intimacy and these feelings are often expressed within peer relationships. Presumably, intimate interactions that occur in friendships not only validate the self but also increase the individual's sensitivity to the needs of the friend. Sensitivity acquired in this manner is thought to generalize to subsequent peer relationships. Youniss (1980) integrates elements of Piaget's and Sullivan's theories and suggests that children's awareness of the unique interactions that occur with friends is an impetus for the elaboration of such concepts as cooperation, mutual respect, and interpersonal sensitivity. Once learned, these concepts generalize to other peer interactions.

Given that social interactive patterns within the families of maltreated children tend to be aversive and lacking in opportunities for engaging in positive reciprocal exchanges, friendships may provide maltreated children with a "remedial" socialization context in which to learn and rehearse certain social skills. If, as the theoretical and empirical literatures suggest, friendships during childhood and adolescence contribute to the development of a variety of social competencies, then maltreated children who form relationships may be afforded opportunities to learn social skills they never learned from their parents. These competencies could, in turn, be conducive to the formation and maintenance of future relationships. Furthermore, through positive and reciprocal exchanges with friends, maltreated children may extract an understanding of friend relationships that is in opposition to the more general representations of relationships they initially developed through interactions with their parents. This specific representational model of friendship may, in turn, lead to the modification of the child's more general relational knowledge structures.

### Development of self-concept

Another function friendships may serve for maltreated children is in operating as a context in which the maltreated child's negative and distorted sense of self can be modified. As previously mentioned, because of acts of abuse and insecure attachment relationships, maltreated children exhibit deficits in self-esteem. However, Sullivan (1953) argues that interactions with parents are not the only interpersonal forces that shape children's self-esteem. According to Sullivan, peer relations make important contributions to children's self-concepts, especially during the school-age and early adolescent years. As children enter preadolescence they begin to develop close friendships with same-sex peers. Within this context of interactions between co-equals, preadolescents receive important validation of self-worth. In support of Sullivan's assertions, Bukowski, Hoza, and Newcomb (1991) found that over a 1-year interval, having friends enhanced the self-esteem of a group of fourth and fifth graders.

Maltreated children who form relationships during preadolescence and adolescence may be afforded opportunities to modify negative views of themselves and to develop a more adequate sense of self. However, simply having friends may not be enough to modify or change a maltreated child's distorted sense of self. More important may be the quality of the child's friendships, and whether these relationships are characterized by mutual trust and acceptance.

### Emotional support

Finally, the friendships of maltreated children may serve as a resource for emotional support and security. It appears that friendships can be a source of emotional support for both children (e.g., Howes & Farver, 1987; Ispa, 1981; Ladd & Price, 1987; Schwarz, 1972) and adolescents (Furman & Buhrmester, 1985).

However, as the results from a recent investigation by Howes and Matheson (1992) suggest, for young children, the presence of a stable, affectionate caregiver may be essential to the development of supportive friendships.

Given the disrupted relationships maltreated children experience with their parents and the lack of provisions of emotional support within the family, friendships may be a very important source of emotional security for maltreated children and adolescents. This support may be particularly important during times of stress, such as during periods of heightened family conflict, or family instability, or during major life transitions (e.g., beginning junior high school). Having friends with whom a child can either play or confide may be critical in determining how a maltreated child or adolescent will cope with a particular stressor. A stable friend may be one of the few interpersonal resources available to a maltreated child or adolescent.

*Summary*

As the theoretical and empirical evidence suggests, friendships appear to provide a variety of functions for children and adolescents. Unfortunately, there is no direct evidence that supports the hypothesis that the friendships of maltreated children and adolescents provide these functions. Clearly, empirical work in this area is required. As this work begins, it is important that researchers attend to Hartup's (1993) admonishment that attention be given to the characteristics of the "company they keep."

Hartup (1993) has argued that when addressing the significance of friendships, it is important to distinguish between three dimensions of friendship: (a) having friends; (b) the identity of one's friends; and (c) the quality of one's friends. Furthermore, these three dimensions must be regarded as different variables with different implications. Simply having a friend or group of friends may serve a specific function. For example, Ladd (1990) recently found that having friends at entrance into elementary school was predictive of favorable school perceptions in the early months. As another example, Bukowski, Hoza, and Newcomb (1991) found that for fourth and fifth graders friendship was causally related to self-reports about social competence. Yet besides having a friend, Hartup (1993) points out that the characteristics of the individuals with whom children and adolescents form their friendships may also be significant, particularly among adolescents. Friendships can contribute either positively or negatively to an individual's socialization. If a particular friend behaves in a normative manner, then the contribution is likely to be positive. Alternatively, if the friend's behavioral orientation is aggressive or disruptive, then the influence may in fact be negative (Hartup, 1993).

Finally, not all friendships are alike. Although some may be characterized by cooperation, intimacy, and mutual support, others are characterized by conflict, and lacking in both intimacy and support. Thus, for some functions, such as the provision of emotional support, the qualities of an individual's friendships may be more important than whether the individual simply has a friend.

## Future directions

The primary goal of this chapter has been to examine the possibility that the friendships of maltreated children and adolescents serve as a context for both the expression and modification of their family relationship histories. Although the existent theoretical and empirical evidence supports this hypothesis, additional research is necessary before making firm conclusions. In this section four directions for future empirical research are proposed.

### Friendship patterns

The first step to understanding the friendships of maltreated children is to collect descriptive information on their friendship patterns. The information that needs to be collected includes: (a) the proportion of maltreated children who actually form friendships; (b) the average size of their friendship networks; (c) the characteristics of the children with whom maltreated children form friendships; and (d) the relative stability of their friendships. This information is critical for addressing both aspects of the central hypothesis of this chapter. First, if the experiences associated with maltreatment do in fact have an effect on children's abilities to form and maintain friendships, then it would be expected that maltreated children would exhibit different friendship patterns from those of nonmaltreated children. If as the theoretical perspectives reviewed in this chapter suggest and the experiences associated with maltreatment have deleterious effects on children's abilities to form and maintain friendships, then it would be expected that in comparison to nonmaltreated children, maltreated children would be less likely to have a friend, would have a smaller friendship network, and would have less stable friendships. It might also be expected that the characteristics of the children with whom maltreated children formed friendships would be different from those of nonmaltreated children's friends. Support for this speculation comes from an investigation by Ladd (1983) on the peer networks of popular, average, and rejected children. In comparison to popular and average children, most of rejected children's interactions occurred in small groups and were distributed among younger or unpopular companions. Presumably, if a rejected child formed a friendship it would be with these network partners. In fact, the rejected children in this study mentioned having friends who were significantly younger than those reported by children in the other two status groups. Given that maltreated children are not well liked by their peers, the peer networks of maltreated children might resemble those of rejected children.

Information on maltreated children's friendship patterns is also important for evaluating the second aspect of the hypothesis of this chapter – that friendships provide important functions for maltreated children and by that provide a context in which their relationship histories can be modified. Whether maltreated children have friends, the stability of their friends, the size of their friendship networks, and the characteristics of their friends are crucial to determining the functions of their friendships. Obviously, understanding the functions of friendships for maltreated children is limited to those children who actually have a friend. Beyond this, previous research has shown that the stability of a child's friendships is an important factor in determining the functions of friendships (Howes, 1983). Additionally, as pointed out earlier, Hartup (1993) has argued that the identity (characteristics) of one's friends is also important when addressing the functions of children's friendships.

There are several approaches investigators could use to assess the friendship patterns of maltreated children. The most common are nomination measures, by which friendships are identified by reciprocal friendship nominations. Unfortunately, nomination procedures may not always be feasible for use with maltreated samples. For a variety of reasons, it may not be possible to have access to the peers of maltreated children or adolescents. Parents and/or social service agencies may want to protect the confidentiality of the child and therefore not want to risk the possibility of having the child singled out in any fashion. Second, in most studies of maltreated children, subjects are spread across several classrooms or schools. The time and expense of obtaining parental permission from each child in each classroom, and of conducting the assessment procedures, may make this approach impractical. There are, however, some alternatives.

For preschool-age and school-age children, behavioral assessments for friendship, such as those developed by Howes (1983) and Ladd and Price (1987), may be alternatives. As another alternative, verbal reports from a knowledgeable informant could be used. This approach typically requires that mothers or teachers identify ''friends'' from among neighborhood or school playmates. The most obvious advantage of this assessment procedure is relative ease of administration. In addition, most parents and teachers are willing to provide information on children's friendships. Furthermore, a great deal of information about children's friendship patterns can be obtained, including the number of friends, the frequency of contact between the child and each friend, and the duration of the relationship. Although this measure of friendship is a less direct assessment of reciprocal friendships than either nomination or behavioral procedures, both parent and teacher reports of children's friendships are considered reliable and accurate (Howes, 1983; Ladd, 1990; Ladd & Emerson, 1984; Ladd & Golter, 1988; Ladd & Price, 1987).

In our longitudinal investigation of the social adjustment of maltreated children in early grade school, children's friendship patterns are being assessed via parent and teacher reports of friendship. Using a modified version of a questionnaire developed by Ladd and Price (1987) to assess children's peer experiences and networks, both parents and teachers are asked to provide information on children's peer networks. Each informant lists the target child's most frequent play partners, designates the type of relationship the child has with the partner, provides information about each partner (e.g., age, gender), and the relationship the child has with each partner (e.g., frequency of contact, duration of the relationship, frequency of conflict). Thus, the extensivity of children's school and neighborhood friendships, as well as some dimensions of the qualities of those friendships, are being assessed.

*Behavioral interactions*

Although there is some data on the behavioral interactions of maltreated children and their peers, we know very little about how maltreated children behave with their peers when they are in the process of forming friendships or how they interact with their friends once the relationships are established. Research in this area will further our understanding of the effects of maltreatment on an individual's ability to form and maintain close relationships outside the family, and aid in understanding the functions friendships serve for maltreated children. As Hartup (1993) argues, a clear description of friendship interaction is a prerequisite to understanding the functions of friendship.

Since cooperation and conflict management are important to both the formation and maintenance of friendships (Hartup, 1983), observations of maltreated children and their friends in situations requiring cooperation could prove most insightful. Although observations of naturally occurring cooperative and competitive situations as they arise in the classroom or on the playground would be revealing, contrived situations may allow for more systematic assessment of these behaviors. Recently, Parker et al. (1993) utilized a mixed-motive game based on the Prisoner's Dilemma task for adults to examine cooperation and competition between physically abused children and their friends. As noted earlier, the results of this investigation revealed subtle differences between the interactions of physically abused children with their friends and the interactions of comparison children with their friends.

As part of our longitudinal investigation of the social adjustment of maltreated children, we are examining the process by which maltreated children become acquainted and begin to form friendships with unfamiliar peers. To examine this process, the contrived play group design developed by Coie and Dodge and their colleagues (e.g., Coie & Kupersmidt, 1983; Dodge, 1983) is being used. Each play group is composed of maltreated and nonmaltreated children, matched on gender and age. Groups meet for 45 minutes a day for 5 consecutive days, and each play session is videotaped. Following each session, each child is interviewed privately and asked a series of questions designed to solicit his or her feelings and perceptions of each of the other group members. Both the observation and interview data will be used to track the day-to-day progression of dyadic relationships. Plans include examining the interactions of maltreated children with their established friends.

*Children's cognitions about relationships*

The third proposed direction for research is to assess children's conceptions and expectations of their relationships. Both attachment and cognitive-social learning models theorize that the relation between maltreatment experiences and children's social behavior is mediated by a set of cognitive and affective mechanisms. Within an attachment perspective, these mechanisms are referred to as "internal working models" or "representational models." Social cognitive theorists term these mental constructs "knowledge structures," or "schema" and suggest that these structures, in turn, guide the child's processing of information in future situations. Thus, common to both theoretical perspectives is the proposition that understanding the working models or relationship schema of maltreated children and the development of these mental structures is important to understanding how maltreatment history is translated into relationship problems.

It is hypothesized that measures of children's conceptions and expectations of friendships, perceptions of qualities of their friendships, and their social goals tap into dimensions of children's understanding of friendship relationships. Assessing these constructs could, therefore, provide valuable insights into the knowledge structures of maltreated children. The findings of Lynch and Cicchetti (1991) and Dean et al. (1986) suggest that when assessing children's cognitions of friendships, investigators should also assess children's cognitions of their relationships with their parents. The value of this simultaneous assessment of relationship constructs is that it is then possible to examine the relation between the knowledge structures that develop within the maltreating family environment and those that develop later within the context of peer interactions (e.g., conceptions of friendships). The stronger the similarity between these different relationship knowledge structures, the stronger the evidence for the linkages between these structures. The next step in this line of research would be to determine whether relationship cognitions are related to children's interactions with their friends, and whether these mental structures do indeed mediate the relation between maltreatment and behavior with friends. Even greater detail could be obtained if parent–child interactions were assessed in maltreating families rather than by using the global descriptions of "abuse" and "neglect."

One of the components of our program of research involves developing methods of assessing maltreated children's representations of their relationships, including friendships. The goal of this work is to begin to delineate some of the cognitive and affective processes underlying maltreated children's social behavior. Toward this end we have constructed and piloted measures of children's attributions of their parents, peers, and friends and measures of social goals. We are also assessing children's conceptions and expectations of friendships. Finally, we are assessing maltreated children's social information processing patterns to determine whether processing patterns serve as cognitive mediators in the relation between maltreatment and social behavior.

## Functions of friendships

Given the current literature, one can only speculate about the possible functions friendships serve for maltreated children and adolescents. As stated earlier, friendships are hypothesized to serve three important functions for maltreated children and adolescents. First, friendships may provide a context for maltreated children and adolescents to learn relationship skills and to modify their representations and conceptualizations about relationships. Second, based on Sullivan's assertions (1953), it is expected that friendships have the potential to aid children, and especially adolescents, in reformulating their perceptions of self. Finally, friendships are expected to serve as a resource for emotional security and support. Clearly, longitudinal studies such as those conducted by Howes (e.g., 1983) and Ladd (1990) are necessary so that we can begin to tease apart the causal direction between friendships and individual competence and adjustment.

When examining the potential functions of friendships for maltreated children, an alternative strategy to group designs, in which maltreated children are compared with nonmaltreated children, is a within-group approach in which multiple regression techniques are used. Friendship variables can be added into a multiple regression equation as a predictor of individual competence or adjustment. Thus the effects of friendship can be assessed after taking into account other predictors, such as the severity and chronicity of abuse and measures of family dysfunction. This approach has been used by Ladd and his colleagues (Ladd, 1990; Ladd & Price, 1987) to assess the role of friendships in children's social and school adjustment. In our current research, the role of children's friendships in moderating the relation between maltreatment and personal and school adjustment is being examined.

## Conclusions

The hypothesis explored in this chapter has been that the friendships of mal-treated children and adolescents serve as a context for both the expression and modification of their relationship histories. Theoretical and empirical research relevant to both aspects of this hypothesis was reviewed. Regarding the first component of this hypothesis, there is clear theoretical support from several perspectives that children who have experienced some form of maltreatment would experience difficulties forming and maintaining friendships. A growing accumulation of empirical research supports this claim. There is also some the-oretical support for the proposal that friendships may provide maltreated children with a context for modifying their relationship histories. Unfortunately, the em-pirical support for this aspect of the hypothesis is derived from research with children who have not experienced maltreatment. The potential benefits of friendships for maltreated children have not yet been examined directly. As the chapters in this volume show, there have been significant advances in the study of children's friendships. Similarly, great strides have also been made in the study of maltreated children (Cicchetti, 1989). Therefore, both conceptual and methodological tools are available for investigating the friendships of maltreated children.

Obviously, research in these areas has the potential to further our understand-ing of (a) the extent of the impact of the experiences associated with maltreat-ment on the psychosocial development of maltreated children and adolescents; (b) of the pathways and processes by which maltreatment has an impact; and (c) the potential benefits of friendships for maltreated children. In addition, an empirical examination of the central hypothesis of this chapter has the potential to contribute to our general understanding of the links between family and peer relationships and the possible variations and functions of friendships. Further-more, by accepting Bronfenbrenner's (1979) assertion that maltreatment is an "experiment in nature," the results from the study of the friendships of mal-treated children and adolescents can be used to affirm and challenge current knowledge and theories about the friendships of children and adolescents.

## References

Alessandri, S. M. (1991). Play and social behavior in maltreated preschoolers. *Development and Psychopathology, 3*, 191–205.

Azar, S. T., & Twentyman, C. T. (1986). Cognitive-behavioral perspectives on the assessment and treatment of child abuse. *Advances in cognitive-behavioral research and therapy, Vol. 5* (pp. 237–267). New York: Academic Press.

Barahal, R., Waterman, J., and Martin, A. P. (1981). The social-cognitive development of abused children. *Journal of Consulting and Clinical Psychology, 49*, 508–516.

Bee, H. L., Disbrow, M. A., Johnson-Crowley, N., & Barnard, K. (1981, April). *Parent–child interactions during teaching in abusing and nonabusing families.* Paper presented at the biannual meetings of the Society for Research in Child Development, Boston.

Bernath, M. S., Feshbach, N. D., & Gralinski, H. J. (1993, March). Physical maltreatment and trust in peers: Feelings, reasons, and behavioral intentions. Paper presented at the biennial meetings of the Society for Research in Child Development, New Orleans.

Bousha, D., & Twentyman, C. T. (1984). Abusing, neglectful and comparison mother–child interactional style: Naturalistic observation in the home setting. *Journal of Abnormal Psychology, 93,* 106–114.

Bowlby, J. (1969/1982). *Attachment and loss, Vol. I: Attachment.* New York: Basic Books.

Bowlby, J. (1973). *Attachment and loss, Vol. II: Separation.* New York: Basic Books.

Bowlby, J. (1980). *Attachment and loss, Vol III: Loss.* New York: Basic Books.

Bronfenbrenner, U. (1979). *The ecology of human development: Experiments by nature and design.* Cambridge, MA: Harvard University Press.

Buhrmester, D., & Furman, W. (1986). The changing functions of friends in childhood: A neo-Sullivanian perspective. In V. J. Derlega & B. A. Winstead (Eds.), *Friendship and social interaction* (pp. 41–62). New York: Springer-Verlag.

Bukowski, W. M. (1992). Sexual abuse and maladjustment considered from the perspective of normal developmental processes. In W. O'Donohue & J. Geer (Eds.), *The sexual abuse of children:Theory and research Volume I* (pp. 261–282). Hillsdale, NJ: Lawrence Erlbaum.

Bukowski, W. M., & Hoza, B. (1989). Popularity and friendship: Issues in theory, measurement, and outcome. In T. J. Berndt & G. W. Ladd (Eds.), *Peer relationships in child development* (pp. 95–132). New York: Wiley.

Bukowski, W. M., Hoza, B, & Newcomb, A. F. (1991). Friendship, popularity, and the self during early adolescence. Unpublished manuscript Concordia University.

Carlson, V., Cicchetti, D., Barnett, D., & Braunwald, K. (1989). Disorganized/disoriented attachment relationships in maltreated infants. *Developmental Psychology, 25,* 525–531.

Cicchetti, D. (1989). How research on child maltreatment has informed the study of child development: Perspective from developmental psychopathology. In D. Cicchetti & V. Carlson. *Child maltreatment: Theory and research on the causes and consequences of child abuse and neglect* (pp. 377–431). New York: Cambridge University Press.

Cicchetti, D., & Beeghly, M. (1987). Symbolic development in maltreated youngsters: An organizational perspective. *New Directions for Child Development, 36,* 5–29.

Cicchetti, D., Beeghly, M., Carlson, V., & Toth, S. (1990). The emergence of the self in atypical populations. In D. Cicchetti & M. Beeghly (Eds.), *The self in transition: Infancy to childhood* (pp. 309–344). Chicago: The University of Chicago Press.

Cicchetti, D., Lynch, M., Shonk, S., & Manly, J. T. (1992). An organizational perspective on peer relations in maltreated children. In R. D. Parke & G. W. Ladd (Eds.), *Family-peer relationships* (pp. 345–384). Hillsdale, NJ: Erlbaum.

Coie, J. D., & Kupersmidt, J. (1983). A behavioral analysis of emerging social status in boys' groups. *Child Development, 54,* 1400–1416.

Conaway, L. P., & Hansen, D. J. (1989). Social behavior of physically abused and neglected children: A critical review. *Clinical Psychology Review, 9,* 627–652.

Crittenden, P. M. (1988). Disordered patterns of relationship in maltreating families: The role of internal representational models. *Journal of Reproductive and Infant Psychology, 6,* 183–199.

Crittenden, P. M. (1990). Internal representational models of attachment relationships. *Infant Mental Health Journal, 11,* 259–277.

Dean, A. L., Malik, M. M., Richards, W., & Stringer, S. A. (1986). Effects of parental maltreatment on children's conceptions of interpersonal relationships. *Developmental Psychology, 22,* 617–626.

Dodge, K. A. (1983). Behavioral antecedents of peer social status. *Child Development, 54,* 1386–1399.

Dodge, K. A., Bates, J. E. & Pettit, G. S. (1990). Mechanisms in the cycle of violence. *Science, 250,* 1678–1683.

Egeland, B., & Sroufe, L. A. (1981). Developmental sequelae of maltreatment in infancy. *New Directions for Child Development, 11,* 77–92.

Egeland, B., Sroufe, L. A., & Erickson, M. (1983). The developmental consequences of different patterns of maltreatment. *Child Abuse and Neglect, 7,* 459–470.

Furman, W., & Buhrmester, D. (1985). Children's perceptions of the personal relationships in their social networks. *Developmental Psychology, 21,* 1016–1024.

Furman, W., & Robbins, P. (1985). What's the point: Selection of treatment objectives. In B. Schneider, K. H. Rubin, & J. E. Ledingham (Eds.), *Children's peer relations: Issues in assessment and intervention* (pp. 41–54). New York: Springer-Verlag.

Garbarino, J., & Gilliam, G. (1980). *Understanding abusive families.* Lexington, MA: Lexington Press.

George, C., & Main, M. (1979). Social interactions of young abused children: Approach, avoidance, and aggression. *Child Development, 50,* 306–318.

Gil, D. B. (1970). *Violence against children: Physical child abuse in the United States.* Cambridge, MA: Harvard University Press.

Hartup, W. W. (1983). Peer relations. In P. Mussen (Ed.), *Handbook of child psychology* (Vol. 4) (pp. 103–196). New York: Wiley.

Hartup, W. W. (1993). Adolescents and their friends. In B. Laursen (Ed.), *New directions for child development: Close friendships in adolescence* (pp. 3–22). San Francisco: Jossey-Bass.

Hartup, W. W., & Sancilio, M. F. (1986). Children's friendships. In E. Schopler & G. B. Mesibov (Eds.), *Social behavior in autism* (pp. 61–80). New York: Plenum.

Haskett, M., & Kistner, J. A. (1991). Social interactions and peer perceptions of young physically abused children. *Child Development, 62,* 979–990.

Hoffman-Plotkin, D., & Twentyman, C. (1984). A multimodal assessment of behavioral and cognitive deficits in abused and neglected preschoolers. *Child Development, 55,* 794–802.

Howes, C. (1983). Patterns of friendship. *Child Development, 54,* 1041–1053.

Howes, C. (1984). Social interactions and patterns of friendships in normal and emotionally disturbed children. In T. Field, J. Roopnarine, & M. Segal (Eds.), *Friendships in normal and handicapped children.* Norwood, NJ: Ablex.

Howes, C., & Espinosa, M. P. (1985). The consequences of child abuse for the formation of relationships with peers. *Child Abuse and Neglect, 9,* 397–404.

Howes, C., & Farver, J. (1987). Toddlers' responses to the distress of their peers. *Journal of Applied Developmental Psychology, 8,* 441–452.

Howes, C., Matheson, C. C. (1992). Sequences in the development of competent play with peers: Social and social pretend play. *Developmental Psychology, 28,* 961–974.

Howes, C., & Unger, O. A. (1989). Play with peers in child care settings. In M. Bloch & A. Pelligrini (Eds.), *The ecological contexts of children's play* (pp. 104–119). Norwood, NJ: Ablex.

Ispa, J. (1981). Peer support among Soviet day care toddlers. *International Journal of Behavioral Development, 4,* 255–269.

Kaufman, J., & Cicchetti, D. (1989). Effects of maltreatment on school-age children's socioemotional development: Assessments in a day-camp setting. *Developmental Psychology, 25,* 516–524.

Kazdin, A. E., Moser, J., Colbus, D., & Bell, R. (1985). Depressive symptoms among physically abused and psychiatrically disturbed children. *Journal of Abnormal Psychology, 94,* 298–307.

Klimes-Dougan, B., & Kistner, J. (1990). Physically abused preschoolers' responses to peers' distress. *Developmental Psychology, 26,* 599–602.

Ladd, G. W. (1983). Social networks of popular, average, and rejected children in school settings. *Merrill-Palmer Quarterly, 29,* 283–307.

Ladd, G. W. (1990). Having friends, keeping friends, making friends, and being liked by peers in the classroom: Predictors of children's early school adjustment. *Child Development, 61,* 1081–1100.

Ladd, G. W. (1991). Family–peer relations during childhood: Pathways to competence and pathology? *Journal of Social and Personal Relationships, 8,* 307–314.

Ladd, G. W., & Emerson, E. S. (1984). Shared knowledge in children's friendships. *Developmental Psychology, 20,* 932–940.

Ladd, G. W., & Golter, B. S. (1988). Parents' initiation and monitoring of children's peer contacts: Predictive of children's peer relations in non-school and school setting? *Developmental Psychology, 24,* 109–117.

Ladd, G. W., & Price, J. M. (1987). Predicting children's social and school adjustment following the transition from preschool to kindergarten. *Child Development, 59,* 986–992.

LaFreniere, P. J., & Sroufe, L. A. (1985). Profiles of peer competence in the preschool: Interrelations between measures, influence of social ecology, and relation to attachment history. *Developmental Psychology, 21(1),* 56–69.

Lewis, M., & Feiring, C. (1989). Early predictors of childhood friendship. In T. J. Berndt & G. W. Ladd (Eds.), *Peer relationships in child development* (pp. 246–273). New York: Wiley.

Lewis, M., & Schaeffer, S. (1981). Peer behavior and mother–infant interaction in maltreated children. In M. Lewis & L. A. Rosenblum (Eds.), *The uncommon child: The genesis of behavior* (pp. 193–223). New York: Plenum Press.

Lynch, M., & Cicchetti, D. (1991). Patterns of relatedness in maltreated and nonmaltreated children: Connections among multiple representational models. *Development and Psychopathology, 3,* 207–226.

Lyons-Ruth, K., Connel, D., Zoll, D., & Stahl, J. (1987). Infants at social risk: Relations among infant maltreatment, maternal behavior, and infant attachment behavior. *Developmental Psychology, 23,* 223–232.

Main, M., & George, C. (1985). Responses of abused and disadvantaged toddlers to distress in agemates: A study in the day care setting. *Developmental Psychology, 21,* 407–412.

Main, M., & Hesse, E. (1990). Parents' unresolved traumatic experiences are related to infant disorganized attachment status: Is freighted and/or frightening parental behavior the linking mechanism? In M. Greenberg, D. Cicchetti, & M. Cummings (Eds.), *Attachment during preschool years* (pp. 161–182). Chicago: University of Chicago Press.

Mueller, N., & Silverman, N. (1989). Peer relations in maltreated children. In D. Cicchetti & V. Carlson (Eds.), *Child maltreatment: Theory and research on the causes and consequences of child abuse and neglect* (pp. 529–578). New York: Cambridge University Press.

Parke, R. D., & Ladd, G. W. (1992). *Family–peer relationships: Modes of linkage.* Hillsdale, NJ: Erlbaum.

Parke, R. D., McDonald, K. B., Beitel, A., & Bhavnagri, N. (1988). The role of the family in the development of peer relationships. In R. De V. Peters & R. J. McMahan (Eds.), *Marriages and families: Behavioral treatments and processes,* (pp. 17–44). New York: Brunner Mazel.

Parker, J. G., & Gottman, J. M. (1989). Social and emotional development in a relational context: Friendship interaction from early childhood to adolescence. In T. J. Berndt & G. W. Ladd (Eds.), *Peer relationships in child development* (pp. 95–132). New York: Wiley.

Parker, J. G., Levendosky, A., & Okun, A. (1993, March). Cooperative and competitive behavior among abused children and their close friends. Poster presented at the biennial meetings of the Society for Research in Child Development, New Orleans.

Pelton, L. (1978). Child abuse and neglect: The myth of classlessness. *American Journal of Orthopsychiatry, 48,* 608–617.

Pettit, G. S., & Mize, J. (1995). Substance and style: Understanding the ways in which parents teach children about social relationships. In S. Duck (Ed.), *Understanding relationship processes, Vol. 2: Learning about relationships* (pp. 118–151). Newbury Park, CA: Sage.

Price, J. M., & Ladd, G. W. (1986). Assessment of children's friendships: Implications for social competence and social adjustment. In R. Prinz (Ed.), *Advances in behavioral assessment of children and families, Volume II* (pp. 121–149). Greenwich, CT: JAI Press Inc.

Price, J. M., & Van Slyke, D. (1991, April). Social information processing patterns of maltreated children. Poster presented at the biennial meetings of the Society for Research in Child Development, Seattle.

Putallaz, M., & Heflin, A. H. (1990). Parent–child interaction. In S. R. Asher & J. C. Coie (Eds.), *Children's status in the peer group* (pp. 189–216). New York: Cambridge University Press.

Reidy, T. J. (1977). The aggressive characteristics of abused and neglected children. *Journal of Clinical Psychology, 33*, 1140–1145.

Rieder, C., & Cicchetti, D. (1989). Organizational perspective on cognitive control functioning and cognitive-affective balance in maltreated children. *Developmental Psychology, 25*, 382–393.

Salzinger, S., Feldman, R. S., Hammer, M., & Rosario, M. (1993). The effects of physical abuse on children's social relationships. *Child Development, 64*, 169–187.

Schneider-Rosen, K., & Cicchetti, D. (1984). The relationship between affect and cognition in maltreated infants: Quality of attachment and the development of visual self-recognition. *Child Development, 55*, 648–658.

Schwarz, J. C. (1972). Effects of peer familiarity on the behavior of preschoolers in a novel situation. *Journal of Personality and Social Psychology, 24*, 276–284.

Sroufe, L. A. (1983). Infant–caregiver attachment and patterns of adaptation in preschool. The roots of maladaptation and competence. In M. Perlmutter (Ed.), *Minnesota symposium on child psychology* (Vol. 16) (pp. 41–81). Minneapolis: University of Minnesota.

Sullivan, H. S. (1953). *The interpersonal theory of psychiatry*. New York: Norton.

Youniss, J. (1980). *Parents and peers in social development*. Chicago: University of Chicago Press.

*Part IV*

**Friendship and adaptation**

# 13 The developmental significance of children's friendship relations

*Andrew F. Newcomb and Catherine L. Bagwell*

The linkages between peer relations and developmental outcome are of considerable interest to developmental and child clinical psychologists. In fact, the introductions to most articles on childhood peer relations include an obligatory paragraph affirming this connection. As the adage suggests: Say it loud enough, and often enough, and words become truth. This chapter asks whether investigators interested in peer and friendship relations are listening to their data or to the echoes of their introductions. Specifically, we are interested in examining two questions: What is the developmental significance of children's friendship relations, and where should future research efforts be directed to clarify the contributions of these relationships?

In addressing these questions, we focus on the benefits of having friends and on the implications of not having friends. We begin by tracing the philosophical and psychological origins of current conceptualizations about the developmental significance of friendship. At the heart of this chapter, we use two lines of investigation to inform our understanding of friendship's contribution to developmental outcome. First, we report findings from a quantitative review of the empirical literature on friendship in childhood and adolescence. These meta-analytic findings, based on studies comparing reciprocal friends and acquaintances, are used to clarify the unique nature of friendship relations and to identify the socialization opportunities potentially afforded by friendship. We continue the discussion of these findings with a consideration of the implications and limitations of this work, and we draw special attention to the need for longitudinal studies and the need for investigation of moderator influences created by the age of the child, the identity of the child's friends, and the quality of the relationship. Second, we examine the literature that has considered differences

The completion of this chapter was supported by a University of Richmond Faculty Research Grant to the first author and by a University of Richmond Summer Undergraduate Research Fellowship to the second author.

between children who have and who do not have friends. Potential methodological problems associated with this literature are discussed, and we present findings from a longitudinal investigation of adults who did or did not have a stable, mutual best friend in preadolescence. In our conclusion, we summarize the current state of knowledge in these areas and suggest key issues that will determine our success in furthering this body of evidence.

## Philosophical and psychological viewpoints on the contribution of friendship relations

The recent surge of interest in empirically studying the significance of children's peer and friendship relations hardly represents a new discovery; instead, contemporary psychologists are resurrecting questions and hypotheses that have intrigued philosophers and writers from all corners of the earth across all periods in history. Gabirol, a Hebrew poet writing in the eleventh century, captures three frequently cited notions about friendship: "There are three types of friends: those like food, without which you can't live; those like medicine, which you need occasionally; and those like an illness, which you never want." Indeed, although researchers today do not hold these three positions as mutually exclusive, different aspects of friendship have been thought to be developmental necessities, developmental advantages, or even developmental hindrances.

### The role of friendship in developmental outcome

Viewed as developmental necessities, friendships are believed to be vital to the acquisition of skills and competencies essential to a child's social, cognitive, and emotional development. Thus, friendship provides a unique context for development, for what is gained in a friendship relation cannot be as effectively achieved in any other relationship. Philosophers have elucidated the indispensable nature of friendship for many centuries. Erasmus, for example, portrayed friendship as "the most desirable of all things; more necessary than either air, fire, or water," and William Blake contended that friendship is as essential to human beings as a nest to a bird or a web to a spider.

These ideas are mirrored in the views of some developmental theorists and researchers. Sullivan's (1953) interpersonal theory of development incorporates a "necessity view" as he argues that friendships emerge in the preadolescent period when the need for acceptance, fulfilled by participation in general peer group interactions in the juvenile era, shifts to the need for interpersonal intimacy. Experience with friends is believed to afford a unique context for satisfying the need for interpersonal intimacy, and in this process, certain social skills and competencies evolve in the interactions between friends. Friendships are collaborative relationships in which individuals are driven by a concern for one another's satisfaction and success, and validation of personal worth is an essential derivative of the collaborative relationship.

Sullivan proposes that without the experience of a mutual, collaborative friendship, opportunities to acquire a repertoire of effective social behaviors are lost. Accordingly, the affective, cognitive, and social experiences afforded in friendship relations may be as requisite in development as experiences in family relations (Hartup, 1983). In addition to the importance of friendships in the acquisition of skills and competencies, friendship relations also provide a context for improving aspects of a child's well-being that have gone awry in previous developmental stages. In this way, friendships are valuable therapeutically, and without the experience of a collaborative friendship relation in early adolescence, a child's developmental success is restricted (Sullivan, 1953).

The developmental necessity viewpoint casts friendship relations in the strongest light, yet given the plasticity of development and the complementarity of other socialization agents, it would be surprising to find that friendships are completely indispensable. Alternatively, the benefits that might accrue in friendship can be viewed as developmental advantages. In this way, the collaborative relationship between friends is assumed to be advantageous but not essential for positive developmental outcome. C. S. Lewis describes the beneficial nature of friendship in vivid terms, proposing that "friendship is unnecessary, like philosophy, like art. . . . It has no survival value; rather it is one of those things that give value to survival." In this vein, friendship is viewed as a positive contribution to a child's developmental success. Nevertheless, it is not an essential context for the acquisition of social skills and competencies or for securing an adaptive developmental pathway.

Mark Twain presented friendship as an advantage in his portrayal of the relationship between Huck Finn and Jim in *The Adventures of Huckleberry Finn*. As their relationship strengthens, Huck and Jim experience shared loyalty, mutual trust, and intimate disclosure. Similarly, within developmental psychology, Smollar and Youniss (1982) propose that friendship affords a context for the development of cooperation, mutual respect, and interpersonal sensitivity that may then be projected onto other social relationships. The friendship between Huck and Jim is a valuable source for the development of these components of social effectiveness. Friendship, however, is not the unique domain for the evolution and enhancement of any of these social behaviors (Hartup & Sancilio, 1986; Price & Ladd, 1986). Instead, friendship provides only a developmental advantage that facilitates the acquisition of these social provisions.

Although the developmental advantage hypothesis tempers the developmental necessity argument, the potential negative consequences of friendship also require consideration. One possibility is that friendship relations are generally advantageous, yet particular features of the relationship or consequences of interactions between friends may sometimes lead to negative outcomes. Alternatively, some friendships may simply be of poor quality and thus of little developmental advantage or may even be detrimental to the participants. The hypothesis that friendships represent developmental hindrances has seldom been advanced, per se, in the developmental literature. Developmental psychologists, however, may be ignoring evidence of the negative features of friendship (Berndt, 1992). In particular, in interviews about conceptions of friendship, there are frequent reports of conflict, but far greater attention is given in the literature to the positive aspects of these relationships. As a developmental hindrance, experience in friendship relations would be expected to push a child toward a maladaptive developmental pathway by promoting deviance.

Possible avenues for exploring the developmental hindrance argument include investigation of the negative features of friendship, the characteristics of a child's friends, and the quality of friendships. Berndt (this volume) contends that friendship quality is determined by both positive and negative features of the interactions between friends. These features are two separate dimensions of friendship quality and investigators may often need to ask children about both positive and negative aspects of their relationship. He names conflict and inequality as negative friendship features whereas intimacy, loyalty, and prosocial behavior are examples of positive features of friendship quality. Friendships that contribute to poor adjustment are expected to be high in negative features. Berndt further reports that early adolescents whose friendships are characterized by more negative features had lower self-esteem and were less involved in school than students whose friendships were high in positive features.

The characteristics or identity of the child's friends may also help explain how friendship can be viewed as a developmental hindrance. Friends are important socializing agents, and children and adolescents who engage in delinquent or antisocial behavior are likely to be attracted to other individuals like themselves (Snyder, Dishion, & Patterson, 1986). Furthermore, as the resulting cliques and crowds increase in salience, friendship networks may have an increasingly maladaptive influence. Adolescents who are initially attracted to one another by their mutual interest in antisocial behavior may subsequently engage in more antisocial activities as the friendship network promotes deviance through further opportunities for socialization in deviant behavior.

Mark Twain presents a literary example of the way in which friendships may represent developmental hindrances in *The Adventures of Tom Sawyer*. Tom and his two friends, Huck and Joe, run away to Jackson's Island to be pirates. When Joe wants to return home and ease the worries of his family, his friends encourage and coerce him into staying with them. As the boys remain on the island, they begin to plot their return home. Their desire to impress their friends and their collaboration lead them to devise a plan much more deviant and elaborate than either of the boys would have considered on his own. The intricate bond of friendship between Tom, Huck, and Joe illustrates how the negative features both in the friendship and in the individuals who make up the relationship can lead to deviance or other negative outcomes.

Friendships thus can vary both among individuals and within specific dyads or groups. At times, friendship may serve a nearly indispensable role in socialization or at least be developmentally advantageous. Yet poor- and high-quality friendships have the potential to lead to both positive and negative consequences. In particular, negative features within high-quality friendships may sometimes lead to negative consequences. Similarly, the negative features in poor-quality friendships would be expected to result in unfavorable adaptation. At the same time, friendships of both high and low quality may promote particular positive outcomes.

*Models to explain the role of friendship in development*

An important question is whether these varied contributions of friendship can be combined into a comprehensive model. Previously, most writing in this area has relied on theoretical models focused on the developmental functions of peer relations in a general sense, and two principal models have undergirded these writings (see Parker & Asher, 1987, for a comprehensive review). In the first model, poor peer relations are thought to have a direct causal role in the development of maladjustment. That is, children who present problematic aggressive and/or withdrawn behavior do not occupy a central place in the peer group and are severely disadvantaged by this absence of socialization opportunity; the lack of experience with peers leads directly to poor developmental outcome. Positive peer relations are thus seen as developmental necessities, for peers serve unique functions in the socialization process.

The second model does not assume a direct link between peer relations and developmental outcome. Instead, individual differences in the propensity for maladjustment first result in aberrant social behavior. Behavioral deviance then leads to poor developmental outcome and only incidentally to peer rejection. Thus, poor peer relations do not determine maladjustment in this model; rejection by peers merely marks the underlying disorder. Kupersmidt, Coie, and Dodge (1990) provide an interesting variant to this model, proposing that positive peer relations can attenuate the influence of preexisting potential for maladjustment, thereby resulting in a more positive developmental outcome.

In trying to understand the contribution of friendship to developmental outcome, an obvious starting point is to build upon what we know about the role of general peer relations in social development. Well-controlled prospective studies are not numerous, but findings are generally concordant. Parker and Asher's (1987) review of these studies provides support for a link between childhood peer rejection and later criminality, psychopathology, and premature school withdrawal; the link between poor peer relations and adult psychopathology, however, is not as strong as the other connections. Potentially, only a small leap of faith is required to extend these results to the conclusion that friendship relations are also valuable. Logically, if peer relations are significant to developmental outcome, then the more intense affective ties afforded by friendships could only be that much more potent.

As attractive as this extrapolation may be, there needs to be a concurrent realization that although friendship relations and peer relations are related, they may represent different socialization experiences. Bukowski and Hoza (1989) discuss this distinction; they propose that popularity is a group-oriented, unilateral concept marking the opinions of the group about the individual, whereas friendship indexes a mutual, dyadic relationship occurring between two individuals. Unfortunately, prior study of the connection between poor peer relations and developmental outcome has given limited consideration to this distinction between general peer relations and closer social relationships and to the effect of these relationship differences on causal and incidental processes.

Consequently, we are faced with a series of challenging questions. For example, assuming that peer and friendship relations have unique social definitions, can the causal models describing the mechanisms of peer influence be directly extended to explain the contribution of friendship relations? Do peer and friendship relations serve complementary functions, or are their respective contributions redundant, making either relation superfluous? Are friendship relations always beneficial, or might these relations, like peer relations, contribute to developmental deviance?

## A quantitative assessment of friend versus acquaintance differences

In answering these and other questions, we argue that identifying the ways in which friendship and acquaintanceship differ is critical. In our current work, we use meta-analysis to establish a quantitative basis for the differences between these relations (Newcomb & Bagwell, 1995). A primary strategy in this research literature has been to compare dyads of friends with dyads of nonfriends on a variety of behavioral and affective dimensions. Clearly, this empirical approach does not afford a direct test of the relation between friendship experience and developmental outcome. Instead, the friend–nonfriend literature sheds light on the potential context that friendship affords for children to experience and exercise particular behaviors. As a result, developmental significance must be inferred and the mechanisms whereby friendship relations contribute to different developmental pathways must be deduced indirectly. In the present context, however, our expectation is that an assessment of where we have been as investigators of children's friendship relations will serve an integral role in guiding future research on the developmental significance of children's friendship.

Our use of meta-analysis to address this question differs from narrative reviews that have addressed either the specific question of the developmental significance of children's friendships (e.g., Hartup, 1992a; Hartup & Moore, 1990) or have completed global considerations of friendship relations (e.g., Berndt, 1988; Buhrmester & Furman, 1986; Hartup, 1992b). Although these narrative reviews have been beneficial for both identifying trends in the friendship relations literature and generating hypotheses for future research, even the best narrative review is subject to criticism as being subjective, unsystematic, and nonquantitative (Cooper & Rosenthal, 1980). Alternatively, establishing the quantitative magnitude of a friendship relations effect through a systematic and comprehensive evaluation affords the opportunity to specify more clearly the potential role of friendship relations in developmental outcome.

Consequently, we used meta-analysis to quantify the extent to which friendships differ from nonfriend relations. Computerized searches of *Psychological Abstracts*, ERIC, and *Dissertation Abstracts* were used to identify published and unpublished articles that met the following inclusion criteria: (1) The age of the participants ranged between preschool years and early adolescence and (2) the design of the study included either an observational comparison of friends versus nonfriends or a nonobservational assessment of friend versus nonfriend differences, that is, interviews or questionnaires, hypothetical situations, or similarity evaluations. In all, we located 82 published and unpublished studies that satisfied our inclusion criteria. Our organization and coding of the study variables within the friendship relations literature was based primarily on a descriptive approach. In particular, we identified four clusters or broad-band categories that describe variables important in all aspects of close social relationships: Positive engagement, Conflict management, Task activity, and Relationship properties. Each of these codes was further broken down into a series of narrow-band categories.

Our quantitative strategy was based on Hedges's (1982) approach of fitting categorical models to effect sizes. In the initial step, we computed the effect size $g$, which is defined as the mean of the friendship group minus the mean of the comparison group divided by the pooled standard deviation of both groups; $g$ represents the standardized difference between the experimental and control group means for each variable. Consistent with the distinction between $g$ and $d$ offered by Hedges and Olkin (1985), the estimator $g$ was corrected for bias, and the unbiased effect size estimator was the basis for our calculations. Positive values of $d$ represented higher levels of a behavior for the friendship group than for the nonfriend comparison group.

The meta-analytic findings discussed in the present chapter draw from a limited subset of a larger meta-analysis. Here, we focus on those studies that included comparisons between reciprocal friends – each member of the dyad chooses the other as a best friend – and acquaintances – children do not select one another either as friends or as disliked peers. This specific contrast was selected to insure the most stringent comparison of the friendship relation to neutral peer relationships. This approach excludes comparisons of reciprocal friends with unilateral friends, strangers, or disliked peers. In all, 38 studies included assessments of reciprocal friends and acquaintances. Exercising the restriction that any given study could contribute only one effect size per narrow band category per each age level and methodology, the initial data set was reduced by approximately 45%, and 161 effect sizes remained for the current analysis.

*Disaggregation of broad-band categories*

Our first goal was to determine whether a common effect size could describe behavioral differences between reciprocal friends and acquaintances. After outliers were removed, a weighted integration of study outcomes resulted in a mean effect size labeled $d+$, which served as an overall estimate of differences between friends and acquaintances. Hedges's method for disaggregating $d$ by categorical models was used to further analyze $d+$. This approach determines whether the overall heterogeneous effect size may be broken down by variable characteristics to obtain homogeneous effect size estimates. Our analytic process began with the disaggregation of the overall effect size into the four broad-band categories. The broad-band categories were next conceptualized as individual overall effect sizes, and these clusters were further broken down into their respective narrow-band codes.

To those investigators interested in friendship relations, the meta-analytic findings from our broad-band categories are reassuring as these results verify the predominant assumptions and theories associated with friendship relations. First, these findings quantitatively demonstrate significant differences in the interactions of children with their friends as compared to interactions with their acquaintances, and the friend-versus-acquaintance differences represent a moderate order of magnitude (Glass, McGaw, & Smith, 1981). Second, the findings provide quantitative support for the argument that friendship relations are marked by more intense affective and affiliative features than are relations among acquaintances.

Table 13.1. *Magnitude of reciprocal friend versus acquaintance differences on broad- and narrow-band categories*

| Categories | | | | Effect sizes excluding outliers | | |
|---|---|---|---|---|---|---|
| | | | | | 95% confidence | |
| Broad band | Narrow band | $n$ | $d+$ | interval for $d+$ | | $Q$ |
| Overall | | 150 | .322[c] | .280 / | .365 | 332.61[c] |
| Positive | | | | | | |
| engagement | | 65 | .396[c] | .328 / | .463 | 118.27[c] |
| | Social contact | 17 | .419[c] | .280 / | .559 | 22.78 |
| | Talking | 15 | .360[c] | .220 / | .499 | 32.97[b] |
| | Cooperation | 19 | .385[c] | .258 / | .512 | 28.28 |
| | Positive affect | 13 | .365[c] | .223 / | .508 | 23.98[a] |
| Conflict | | | | | | |
| management | | 19 | .118[a] | .005 / | .231 | 43.30[c] |
| | Instigation | 13 | .077 | −.058 / | .211 | 24.42[a] |
| | Resolution | 6 | .478[c] | .256 / | .700 | 3.48 |
| Task | | 11 | .214[b] | .063 / | .365 | 13.03 |
| activity | | | | | | |
| | Communication | 6 | .129 | −.059 / | .318 | 9.28 |
| | Performance | 5 | .369[b] | .115 / | .622 | 1.55 |
| Relationship | | | | | | |
| properties | | 52 | .363[c] | .294 / | .432 | 120.47[c] |
| | Similarity | 8 | .316[c] | .168 / | .465 | 42.82[c] |
| | Equality | 10 | .304[c] | .143 / | .466 | 14.03 |
| | Dominance | 15 | −.171[b] | −.302 / | −.039 | 5.65 |
| | Mutual liking | 5 | .743[c] | .504 / | .982 | 7.45 |
| | Closeness | 8 | .676[c] | .489 / | .862 | 10.73 |
| | Loyalty | 5 | .703[c] | .422 / | .984 | 3.93 |

*Note*: Significance of $d+$ is assessed by the normal $z$ distribution, and nonsignificant $Q$ reflects homogeneity within category. Significance levels: [a]$p < .05$, [b]$p < .01$, and [c]$p < .001$. The Dominance narrow-band code was inverse-scored throughout the disaggregation process so that the absolute difference between friends and acquaintances would not be masked by one narrow-band code. However, the true direction of $d+$ for the Dominance category is shown above.

The disaggregation of the overall effect size into broad-band categories resulted in greater homogeneity than in the overall comparison. As shown in Table 13.1, reciprocal friends evidenced significantly more Positive engagement, Conflict management, Task activity, and Relationship properties in their interactions than did acquaintances. In a comparison of effect sizes across the broad-band categories, the magnitude of difference between friends and acquaintances in Positive engagement and Relationship properties was greater than the friend–acquaintance difference in Conflict management.

*Disaggregation of narrow-band categories*

The disaggregation of the broad-band categories into their narrow-band components delineates the potential sources of interpersonal competency that might be promoted by friendship relations (see Table 13.1). Furthermore, these narrow-band findings allow us to gain a comprehensive assessment of what a friendship relation is like and how it differs from more general peer relations. In discussing the narrow-band results, we have organized our commentary around the four broad-band categories. We first present findings for the specific narrow-band categories and then discuss the implications of these results for friendship as a context for social, emotional, and cognitive development. As these findings identify interpersonal skills and competencies that may be more effectively achieved in relationships with friends as opposed to relationships with acquaintances, the meta-analysis serves as an important step in furthering our understanding of the developmental significance of friendship relations in childhood.

*Positive engagement.* Positive engagement incorporates behaviors that establish and maintain a common base for future interactions and thus preserve and perpetuate the relationship. This category is operationally defined to include four narrow band codes that describe positive interactions between individuals – Social contact, Talking, Cooperation, and Positive affect. These study variables index children engaging in frequent interaction; participating in verbal communication exchanges; sharing and cooperating; or smiling, looking, laughing, and touching one another.

Although all of these positive engagement behaviors may be found in the interactions of acquaintances, the meta-analysis reveals that each is more extensive in friends' interactions. In comparison to acquaintances, friends spend more time in one another's company and engage in play behaviors and activities that promote proximity and mutual involvement. In addition, friends talk more with one another and are more likely to share and cooperate with one another than are acquaintances. The affiliative bond between friends is further reflected in greater affective expression than that displayed between acquaintances.

Children's positive engagement with their friends suggests venues in which friendship may serve as a context for social, emotional, and cognitive development. Within friendship relations, children develop competencies associated with effective interpersonal interaction. Learning to sustain social contact and gaining experience in cooperating and helping others appear to be achieved more readily in relationships with friends as compared to acquaintances. The developmental significance of these friendship features may rest in the opportunity they afford children to experience and to practice these critical components of effective interpersonal relations.

The affective ties associated with friendship provide children with an ongoing opportunity to develop intense relations outside the family, and these extrafamilial relations may serve as valuable precursors to future social relationships. Experience with the strong bond of friendship also fosters emotional development. Friendship offers an important context in which to acquire skills in regulating emotional expression through the opportunity to practice displays of positive affect. Furthermore, helping and cooperating are behavioral manifestations of emotion that are more prevalent in interactions between friends than between acquaintances, and, as discussed below, this cooperation and collaboration may also promote cognitive development.

*Conflict management.* Conflict management represents a salient feature of children's interactions with one another (Hartup, French, Laursen, Johnston, & Ogawa, 1992). This broad-band cluster, made up of the Conflict instigation and Conflict resolution narrow-band codes, allows us to distinguish between behaviors that precipitate conflict and those that rectify the disagreement. Our meta-analytic findings indicate that friends and acquaintances do not differ in their instigation of conflict. In contrast, however, the commitment that friends have to their relationship is evinced in their greater likelihood to settle their disagreements. In other words, friends are just as likely as acquaintances to argue and disagree with one another, yet friends are more likely to engage in strategies of conflict resolution. There is more at stake in friendship relations, and children do not want to place their friendships in jeopardy by failing to work through their conflicts. Furthermore, by promoting the development of the interpersonal skill of conflict resolution, friendship provides an important base of experience upon which other social relationships can build.

*Task activity.* In this category, we include the narrow-band codes of Task communication and Task performance, and we require that variables in these narrow-band categories be drawn only from studies that were directly concerned with children's interactions during the completion of a specified task. Within this context, both verbal and nonverbal interactions related to the accomplishment of a goal are incorporated in Task communication while the Task performance category indexes the performance or outcome of task-related activities. Although relatively few studies have examined differences in the task activity of friends and acquaintances, our disaggregation of the Task activity broad-band category into the Communication and Performance clusters enables us to better understand the significance of children's goal-oriented behaviors with their peers.

Previously, researchers have tended to use performance in task activity as an indicator of cognitive growth, and the meta-analytic results reveal that friends are more successful in task outcomes and engage in more task-related behaviors with one another than do acquaintances. In contrast, verbal and nonverbal task-related communication between pairs of friends and pairs of acquaintances does not differ. In sum, although the Task activity findings must be interpreted with caution due to the small number of effect sizes available for consideration, the present findings indicate that something other than specific task-related communication contributes to friends' greater success in task activities than acquaintances'.

Several explanations have been offered to clarify processes, other than task-related communication, that may result in friends' more successful task activity. Azmitia and Montgomery (1993) propose that three mechanisms combining communicative and performance-related factors are potentially responsible for promoting greater cognitive growth in friends' interactions. First, friends are more likely than nominal peers to exchange ideas in their conversations and to share and cooperate. Second, the balanced, mutual involvement and equality that is part of friendship facilitates more effective collaboration. Finally, the greater trust and loyalty among friends increases success in problem solving by encouraging the candid exchange of viewpoints and the testing of ideas.

Alternatively, Hartup (this volume) presents a series of related processes to explain how friendship affords a better context for cognitive growth than does the relationship between acquaintances. Whereas Azmitia and Montgomery (1993) focus on more specific features of the relationship between friends, Hartup discusses four contextual properties of friends' cooperation that may enhance cognitive development. Specifically, friends know one another better than acquaintances and thus better understand one another's needs and abilities. Second, friends and acquaintances have different expectations for one another. Reciprocity, commitment, trust, and equality are expectations of friendship that support the cooperation and mutuality suggested to promote cognitive growth. Third, the affective context of friendship is believed to support problem-solving endeavors, and fourth, children are highly motivated to maintain friendship relations and spend time together. Friendships thus expose children to the specific kinds of social interaction that are necessary for cognitive development.

*Relationship properties.* Whereas the first three broad-band categories index patterns of interactions between friends, Relationship properties, the fourth broad-band category, reflects more global properties of the friendship (cf. Hinde, 1979; Hinde & Stevenson-Hinde, 1987). This final broad-band cluster includes six narrow-band categories examining properties of children's social relationships. The Similarity, Equality, and Dominance codes reflect demographic and behavioral concordances between children, maintenance of balance in the relationship, and assertion of control over the relationship by one individual. The final three narrow-band clusters incorporate more intimate components of a close relationship between two children. In particular, the Mutual liking code assesses the affective and affiliative bonds between the children; the Closeness category incorporates demonstrations of emotional support and understanding; and the Loyalty narrow-band code indexes reflections of faithfulness between the two children.

The meta-analysis reveals that the more global properties that character-ize children's relationships with their peers differ between friends and acquain-tances. Similarity and equality, often considered hallmarks of children's peer relations, are indeed greater between friends than between acquaintances (see also Aboud & Mendelsohn, this volume). Furthermore, friends are less likely to exert dominance in their relationships than are acquaintances. These findings for Equality and Dominance indicate that when compared to acquaintances, the relationship between friends is more balanced.

With respect to developmental significance, these findings, combined with the evidence that friends share, cooperate, and help more than acquaintances do, suggest that friendship may maintain a relational homeostasis that affords an advantaged context for social development. Within the give-and-take that typi-fies interpersonal relationships, friends are buffered by their goal of sustaining the relationship. Consequently, although friends and acquaintances engage in similar levels of conflict, friends maintain a greater commitment to conflict res-olution. Similarly, as friends strive for greater equality and exert less dominance, their relationship affords a balanced middle ground for emotional exchange. Furthermore, as we have already suggested, the opportunity for collaboration characterized by balanced, mutual involvement encourages cognitive develop-ment (Azmitia & Montgomery, 1993).

The remaining three Relationship properties – the narrow-band categories of Mutual liking, Closeness, and Loyalty – represent more intimate and intense properties of children's relationships. Again, relationships between reciprocal friends include higher levels of these properties than relationships between ac-quaintances. It is also important to note that the effect-size estimates for Mutual liking, Closeness, and Loyalty are the largest effect sizes for any of the narrow-band categories considered. Thus, the most extensive difference between friends and acquaintances appears to be in their expressions of amity, manifestations of closeness, and demonstrations of faithfulness with one another.

Amongst friendship features, the three relationship properties of Mutual lik-ing, Closeness, and Loyalty may best reveal how friendships contribute to social, emotional, and cognitive development. In particular, closeness and loyalty are competencies that provide a base for the development of future sustained social relationships. Gaining fundamental experience with these skills in childhood friendships allows for greater success in the more complex intricacies of adult relationships. As the emotional demands of interpersonal relationships increase with age, the earlier intense emotional experience of friendship, characterized by strong mutual liking and closeness, better prepares an individual for the emotional interplay in adolescent and adult relationships. A corollary benefit of the loyalty and closeness in friendships may be to encourage free and candid exchange of ideas, each of which is critical to rewarding same- and opposite-sex relations later in life.

## Implications and limitations of friend versus acquaintance investigations

Although the results of the meta-analysis provide an important backdrop for understanding the developmental significance of children's friendships, it is also necessary to acknowledge that there are a variety of critical issues that the meta-analytic findings do not cover. First, this analysis reveals that friends, as compared to acquaintances, engage in more extensive and intensive interactions, yet the role of friendship in the origin, maintenance, and refinement of these patterns of interaction is unknown. There is an urgent need for longitudinal research to begin to address these questions of causality. Second, although friendship has been studied at all ages, friendship has not been studied developmentally. Identification of when, or if, friendship is more or less important over the course of development is critical to our understanding of the developmental significance of friendship relations. Third, the meta-analysis is constrained inasmuch as the friendship literature has not as yet extensively addressed issues of individual differences in friendship relations. The meta-analytic findings reveal what it is like to have a friend at the normative level, but the particular type of company a child keeps, that is, the identity of one's friends, and the differences in the quality of individual friendships, is not examined. Each of these individual difference variables is likely to be an important moderator of the contribution that friendship makes to developmental outcome.

### Longitudinal designs

Although the argument that friendship relations constitute a context for social, emotional, and cognitive development is compelling, the reader must remember that these speculations are not based on causal data. At best, the meta-analysis encourages us to pursue the fundamental longitudinal research that is needed to answer the question of causality. In this quest, arguments for the developmental significance of friendship relations have drawn on causal models linking peer relations and developmental outcome. A cadre of longitudinal studies of peer relations is usually cited (Cowen, Pederson, Babigian, Izzo, & Trost, 1973; Parker & Asher, 1987; Roff, 1961; Roff, Sells, & Golden, 1972) and may unjustifiably reinforce the impression that friendship difficulties are also predictive risk factors for later maladjustment. Although the predictive function of peer-acceptance and rejection has received some empirical consideration, the longitudinal examination of friendship relations has unfortunately been extremely limited.

One notable exception is Ladd's (1990) longitudinal study of preschoolers' transition into kindergarten. Friendship experience was found to contribute to both school and social adjustment. Noteworthy amongst his findings are data suggesting that the type of friendship, in addition to merely having friends, influences different aspects of adjustment. For example, existing friendships may facilitate adaptation to new situations, and new friendships provide bases of support and promote learning, whereas stable friendships may improve coping as school demands increase over time (see Ladd, this volume). In this instance, a naturally occurring event – the transition to kindergarten – is used to study the value of friendship relations. Such studies offer possibilities for examining elements in friendship experience not readily accessible by one-time or cross-sectional designs, and as such, these prospective designs enhance understanding of the long-term significance of friendship.

Although longitudinal research can clarify the contribution of friendship to development, follow-up designs also have an important role vis-à-vis intervention studies designed to assist children in making and keeping friends (see Asher, Parker, & Walker, this volume). From this perspective, intervention research has applied implications and is also important for identifying the possible developmental contributions of friendship relations. In their application, intervention programs can help children and adolescents develop important social skills and competencies. In addition, if an intervention designed to help children establish friendships also demonstrates stable improvement in the quality of other aspects of these children's social and emotional development, friendships can be considered to have a casual role in this enhanced developmental outcome.

## Developmental changes

The use of longitudinal designs also has direct implications on our understanding of developmental changes in friendship. As part of our larger meta-analytic investigation (see Newcomb & Bagwell, 1995), we examined the cross-sectional literature on age differences. First, the meta-analysis revealed age-related differences between childhood and preschool friends and between early adolescent and childhood friends. In contrast, nonfriend relations did not differ across these same three age levels. These findings are consistent with age-related differences in children's conceptions of friendship (e.g., Bigelow, 1977) and theoretical writings (Sullivan, 1953). Second, subsequent analyses revealed that the magnitude of the friend–nonfriend difference at each age level significantly differed only in the Relationship properties category. Specifically, the magnitude of the preschool friend–nonfriend difference in Relationship properties was significantly smaller than the difference between early adolescent friends and nonfriends.

How then do these quantitative findings compare to the conclusions drawn by prior narrative reviewers? In the preschool period, friendships are typically thought to include shared activities and opportunities for play. Although these relationships are considered to be precursors of later development, the relationships themselves are far less stable than those found in later childhood (Furman, 1982). Parker and Gottman (1989) suggested that, during the school-age period, friends provide knowledge of behavioral norms and facilitate the acquisition of skills in the self-regulation of emotion. Friendships during this period are generally based on reciprocity, equality, and cooperation. Although these features remain salient foundations of friendship at all stages, intimacy is thought to emerge as the essential hallmark of friendship in early adolescence (Sullivan, 1953).

The strongest support for these conclusions is evident in our findings for the Relationship properties category. The intimacy, trust, and commitment reflected in this category are more prevalent in friendships among early adolescents than among children, and the degree to which friends and nonfriends differ on these relationship properties is significantly greater in early adolescence than during the preschool years. The findings regarding early adolescent friendships support Sullivan's assumption that intimacy is at its height of importance at this later developmental period. Despite these meta-analytic results, age differences in other categories were not as prevalent as might be expected for two possible reasons: (a) the small number of studies in which age-related differences were reported, and (b) the focus of these studies on the quantity of particular behaviors displayed between friends and nonfriends rather than on differences in the function of those behaviors at various age levels.

Just as behavior may serve different functions at different age levels, the character and importance of relationships may also vary developmentally. For example, friendship relations may operate primarily at the level of the dyad in early childhood, but by early adolescence, become embedded in broader social networks, that is, friendship cliques or groups (Cairns, Cairns, Neckerman, Gest, & Garieppy, 1988). Similarly, whether examining children in dyads or in larger networks, researchers need to assess friendship relations across a wide range of environments. Moving out of the school classroom to the lunchroom, the playground, and the neighborhood would provide a more thorough examination of the significance of friendship relations and might help identify how features of friendship differentially influence social and emotional development in various social ecologies among children of different ages.

*Identity of one's friends*

In examining the effect of the identity of a child's friends on adjustment and developmental outcome, researchers acknowledge that not all friendships are the same. Although friends have considerable influence on one another, this influence appears to come in different forms. As such, the characteristics of the individual friend may determine whether the friendship facilitates positive social development or whether the relationship contributes to poor adjustment. Critical to any consideration of the nature of this moderator effect is an understanding of the processes through which friends influence one another.

The influence friends have on one another is manifested in their similarity, and Kandel (1978) specified two processes that precipitate similarity in friendship relations. First, individuals are attracted to others like themselves; consequently, friendship selection is fostered by similarity. Even more salient for understanding friends' mutual influence is the process whereby friends become more similar over time. These socialization effects have been documented for smoking and drinking, delinquency, and educational achievement and motivation (Hartup, 1993). Among educational aspirations, political orientation, marijuana use, and delinquency, the strongest socialization effect was reported for marijuana use (Kandel, 1978). Fueling the popular belief that peer pressure is negative, this finding suggests that children and adolescents whose friends are involved in antisocial, delinquent, or other negative behaviors are influenced to behave in similar delinquent ways.

Friends' influences, however, are not unidirectional, and the identity of one's friend is an important determinant of the direction of this influence. For example, although an individual's grades may fall if his or her friends do not do well in school, school motivation may increase if one's friends care about academic success (Berndt, 1992). Friends' influence on one another's affective and academic behavior shows these effects. Middle and high school students who initially scored either high or low on measures such as college plans, English and math standardized achievement, and self-reliance and who had high-scoring friends received higher scores one year later than students with low-scoring friends (Epstein, 1983). Regardless of the students' own initial scores, the socialization effect of high-scoring friends facilitated the students' high scores the following year.

A final illustrative study of the effects of friends' characteristics addresses the interaction between biological and social influences on delinquency. In this instance, early maturing girls reported significantly more delinquent acts than girls who were either on-time or late maturers (Magnusson, Stattin, & Allen, 1985). Most important, the interaction between maturation and friendship mediated participation in delinquency: Early maturers with older friends were involved in significantly more delinquent behavior than were early maturers without older friends. In fact, this latter group did not differ from on-time or late maturers. Thus, even seemingly neutral demographic characteristics such as the age of one's friends may be important identity factors in determining the influence that friends have on one another.

*Friendship quality*

Not only do characteristics of the child's friends influence development, but the quality of the dyadic relationship itself has an impact on developmental outcome. Correlational and predictive investigations have led investigators to recognize that the developmental significance of friendship may rest both in having friends and in having friendships of high quality (e.g., Bukowski, Hoza, & Boivin, 1993; Cauce, 1986). Thus, the quality of the relationship needs to be examined as a critical moderator of the potential role friendship plays in developmental outcome.

Fundamental to exploring friendship quality is the development of scales to measure specific domains of relationship quality. Nevertheless, investigators differ in their ideas about what qualities and how many qualities to assess. For example, the *Friendship Qualities Scale* (FQS) indexes five dimensions of friendship quality – companionship, conflict, help, security, and closeness – with relatively low intercorrelations amongst these domains (Bukowski, Hoza, & Boivin, 1994). Alternatively, the FQS has been augmented and reorganized to include six features – companionship and recreation, help and guidance, validation and caring, intimate exchange, conflict and betrayal, and conflict resolution (Parker & Asher, 1993). Even so, the quality of a friendship may depend on still more domains. For example, security, diversity, balance of power, and commitment may be additional markers of relationships of differing quality (Hartup, 1993)

In another approach to the measurement of friendship quality, features of friendship are placed under the broad umbrellas of positive or negative features that in turn determine the quality of the relationship (Berndt & Perry, 1986; Berndt & Keefe, 1992; Berndt, this volume). This assessment of friendship quality is accomplished through a three-step process (Berndt, this volume). In particular, researchers must first define friendship quality and calculate composite scores for positive and negative friendship features. Correlational designs that examine relationships between quality and various aspects of social development are then used to determine areas of functioning that appear most related to friendship quality. Finally, longitudinal investigations that include both observational and experimental studies are needed for testing hypotheses about friendship quality and development.

Regardless of how quality is measured, empirical studies show that friendship quality affects developmental outcome and psychological well-being. In particular, path analyses have linked popularity, mutual friendship, and friendship quality with feelings of belongingness and loneliness (Bukowski, Hoza, & Boivin, 1993). Mutual friendship and the quality of that relationship in early adolescence are directly related to loneliness, and mutual friendship is also indirectly related to loneliness via friendship quality. Thus, nonmutual friendships do not seem to provide the high quality experiences that ward off loneliness. Friendship quality, as measured by relationship closeness, is similarly related to psychological adjustment in early adolescence. Specifically, experiencing greater closeness with a best friend is a prophylactic against a decline in children's perceptions of their social acceptance after rejection by their peers (Vernberg, 1990).

## Investigations of children with and without friends

Although comparisons of friends and acquaintances provide one means to examine the developmental implications of having friends, an alternative approach has been to compare children who have friends and children who do not have friends. As seen in Table 13.2, we consider the very small literature in this area in two parts. First, we review the studies that have simply examined differences between friended and friendless children. These studies afford a static approach to investigating the importance of having versus not having a friend, and we pay particular attention to the methodological problems that constrain interpretation of these findings. The alternative dynamic approach, which includes longitudinal designs that follow-up on friendless children, has been given very little attention. In a second section, we consider two studies as examples of the dynamic approach. Studies such as these hold particular promise for untangling some of the questions that surround the developmental significance of children's friendships.

### A static approach to the study of friended and chumless children

A small body of research on children's friendships concerns the behavioral correlates of the friendship experience by comparing children who have a friend with children who are chumless. In these investigations, different criteria have been used to assign children either to the friended or the friendless group, and

Table 13.2. *Characteristics of studies comparing friended and chumless children*

| Authors | Aspects of friendship measured | | | | Inclusion criteria[c] | | Sociometric status | Dependent variables |
| | Mutuality[a] | Stability | Quality[b] | | Friended | Chumless | | |
|---|---|---|---|---|---|---|---|---|
| *Static approaches* | | | | | | | | |
| Bukowski & Newcomb (1987) | Yes | No | No | | All (1) | None | Controlled | Cognitive competence<br>Social competence<br>Physical competence<br>General self-worth |
| Buzzelli (1988) | Yes ($R_3$) | No | No | | All (1) | None | Yes | Trust |
| Clark & Drewry (1985) | Yes ($R_3$) | No | No | | All (1) | None | No | Self-concept<br>Personal characteristics |
| Eason (1985) | Yes ($R_3$) | No | No | | All (1) | None | No | Social skills<br>Friendship conceptions |
| Guralnick & Groom (1988) | Yes (33%) | No | No | | All (1) | None | No | Play interactions |
| Howes (1988) | Yes ($R_3$) | No | No | | All (1) | None | No | Entry behaviors<br>Play interactions<br>Affect |
| Howes, Matheson, & Wu (1992) | Yes ($R_3$)[d] | Yes | No | | All (2) | None | No | Play interactions |
| Hoza (1989) | Yes ($R_1$) | No | No | | All (1) | None | Yes | Self-concept<br>Externalizing behavior<br>Adaptive functioning |

| Study | | | | | | Controlled[e] | Measures |
|---|---|---|---|---|---|---|---|
| Kaye (1991) | Yes (R$_3$) | No | No | All (1) | None | Controlled | Self-perceptions<br>Peer perceptions<br>Teacher perceptions |
| Mannarino (1976) | No | Yes | Yes (2) | All (3) | Only 2 | Controlled | Altruism |
| Mannarino (1978a) | No | Yes | Yes (2) | All (3) | Only 2 | Controlled | Self-concept |
| Mannarino (1978b) | Yes (R$_2$) | Yes | Yes | All (3) | Only 1 | Controlled | Chumship features |
| Mannarino (1979) | Yes (R$_2$) | Yes | Yes (2) | All (4) | Only 1 | Controlled | Altruism |
| McGuire & Weisz (1982) | Yes (R$_2$) | Yes | Yes | All (3) | Only 1 | Yes | Altruism<br>Perspective taking |
| Roopnarine & Field (1984) | Yes (66%) | No | No | All (1) | < 25% | No | Play interactions |
| *Dynamic approaches* | | | | | | | |
| Bagwell, Newcomb, & Bukowski (1994) | Yes (R$_1$) | Yes | No | All (2) | None | Controlled | Social adjustment |
| Ladd (1990) | Yes (R$_u$)[f] | No | No | All (2) | None | Controlled | School adjustment |

[a] The value in parentheses reflects the degree of mutuality of the friendship choice or the percentage of observed interactions with a particular child, e.g., R$_3$ indicates that each child chose the other as any one of his or her three friend nominations.

[b] Indicates whether an assessment of friendship quality was a part of the inclusion criteria, and the number in parentheses reflects the number of quality measures included.

[c] The number of aspects of friendship measured that must be met to be included in the friended and chumless groups.

[d] A high liking score could replace one reciprocal nomination.

[e] The sample included only rejected and neglected children.

[f] The study allowed unlimited friendship choices and also included a teacher measure of friendship.

the potential effects of these methodological differences have important implications for our understanding of being chumless. In some instances, the measures of friendship were taken concomitantly with the measures of social skills and adjustment; this approach represents a static examination of the developmental significance of being friendless. Nevertheless, this research literature provides a base to develop a profile of the friendless child and to illuminate the potential negative consequences associated with not having the close, affective tie of friendship.

Classifying children as friended and friendless is based on two principal factors – mutuality and stability. Mutuality has been considered an important feature of dyadic friendship relations (Bukowski & Hoza, 1989) as studies that do not include a criterion of mutuality may actually assess liking or unilateral attraction (Mannarino, 1979). The primary methodology used to determine mutuality in friendship relations is a nomination procedure in which children name their best friends. As shown in Table 13.2, the degree of stringency in the use of this criterion varies. Approximately half of the studies require that the first or second named friend reciprocate an equivalent level of choice, whereas the others define friendship as any reciprocated choice. Rates of interaction have often been substituted for peer nomination procedures when examining friendship status in younger children (e.g., Guralnick & Groom, 1988; Roopnarine & Field, 1984). In these studies, children are observed during periods of interaction with their peers, and children are considered to be mutual friends if they direct a particular percentage of their interactions to specific companions.

When stability is added as a criterion for classification as friended, the nomination procedure is repeated after a designated interval. To be classified in the friended group, children must have the same reciprocated friendship at both assessments (Mannarino, 1978b; McGuire & Weisz, 1982). As seen in Table 13.2, reciprocity and stability are rarely used concurrently, and consequently, identification of the "truest" mutual friends is seldom achieved. As a practical matter, employing less stringent classification criteria would logically decrease the distinction between friended and friendless children and thus potentially attenuate group differences.

Methodological variations in the stringency of the criteria employed for defining membership in the friendless group are critical in the interpretation of findings. Some investigators have included children in the friendless group based solely on the criterion that their first friendship choices were not reciprocated (e.g., Hoza, 1989). In other studies, a child could be classified as friendless even if his or her first friendship choice was reciprocated as long as that choice was not stable and the child's behavioral involvement with the friend was not extensive (Mannarino, 1979; McGuire & Weisz, 1982). Clearly, some of these children are not truly friendless. As a result of these discrepancies, findings must be interpreted carefully; one cannot be sure whether methodological procedures for establishing comparison groups account for the results. Consequently, in our discussion of the friend versus friendless literature, we organize the existing studies around methodological approaches as opposed to dependent variables.

Methodological concerns render the earliest studies of friended and friendless children especially difficult to interpret. In two of them, friendship choices were not mutual; instead, three unilateral criteria defined friendship (Mannarino, 1976; 1978a). Friended children had only to nominate the same friend over a 2-week period, characterize that friendship as having extensive interpersonal contact, and prefer being with their friend over activities with a group of peers. Even more problematic than the lack of mutuality in the friended group was the decision to include children in the chumless group who met two of the three friendship criteria. As a result, the observed group differences on altruism and self-concept might be attributable to having versus not having a friend, but they might also be associated with the intensity of children's friendship relations as some children in the friendless group may actually have a friend.

The mutuality criterion has been handled in various ways. In two other early studies, mutuality was added as a requirement for inclusion in the friended group along with extensive contact and preference for activities with the friend. Although friendless children could meet only one of the three friendship criteria, as before, these ''friendless'' children could still have a mutual friend. Thus the findings that friendless girls displayed lower levels of altruism than girls who have friends (Mannarino, 1979) and that chumless males engaged in fewer social contact activities and less intimate disclosure than did friended boys (Mannarino, 1978b) are again suspect. The possibility that the friendless children actually had a friend suggests that these results may be due to differences in the strength of the relationships.

Amongst preschool-aged children, investigators have frequently used rate-of-interaction methodologies to index mutuality. For example, if children reciprocally directed 33% of their positive interactions at one another they were considered to be friended. In an analog playgroup setting, children with these friendships engaged in a greater frequency of positive interactions than preschool children without them (Guralnick & Groom, 1988). A similar, yet more stringent, methodology identified friended children as those who interacted with a particular peer more than 66% of the time, whereas chumless preschoolers did not interact with the same peer more than 25% of the time. Preschoolers without friends watched their peers' activities more often than did friended children. Moreover, chumless children were also less likely to verbalize to peers, direct peers' activities, as well as to make statements, commands, or requests (Roopnarine & Field, 1984).

Membership in the friended or chumless groups can also be determined by sociometric ratings. In one investigation of this kind, preschool children with mutual friends were more successful at entering groups and were less likely to be rebuffed upon group entry than were children without friends. Furthermore, friended children engaged in more reciprocal and cooperative play, and evinced more positive affect than chumless children (Howes, 1988). By combining the nomination methodology with behavioral observations of the stability of friendship relations, both mutuality and stability can be assessed. With this approach, friended preschoolers were found to engage in higher levels of self-disclosure, cohesion, and coordinated and harmonious social pretend play than friendless children were in a free play session (Howes, Matheson, & Wu, 1992).

Whether defined by rates of interactions or by peer nominations, each of these studies reveals that friendless preschoolers are less successful in peer interaction than are preschoolers with friends. In particular, friendless children's lack of experience in mutual, dyadic friendship relations is associated with difficulties in initiating play with peers and in achieving positive play interactions. Nevertheless, the causal nature of these difficulties has not been established. Although being friendless may indeed contribute to problematic peer interactions, it is also possible that failure to interact positively with peers causes a child to be friendless. Moreover, the absence of a friendship at this age is more likely a marker for general problems in peer relations than for specific difficulties in friendship. Investigation of the long-term consequences of being chumless in preschool will require longitudinal designs that can separate the relative contributions of peer and friendship relations, as well as the salient contributions of the family, to developmental outcome.

What happens to these children as they become older? Although the static approach allows only for an assessment of age differences and not age changes, the existing data suggest that school-aged children who do not have friends have considerable difficulties in social adaptation. These investigations also demonstrate that the methodological challenges in studying older children are no less complex than in studying preschoolers. In particular, investigators continue to differ on the criteria for membership in the friended and friendless groups.

When mutuality is the only criterion for friendship, school-age children with friends had higher developmental levels of friendship conceptions than those of friendless children. Furthermore, friendless children displayed less appropriate social skills than did children with friends (Eason, 1985). In a second study with mutuality as the only friendship criterion, peer ratings of children's characteristics revealed that children with reciprocated friendship choices were viewed as more popular, more physically attractive, more nicely dressed, more fun to be with, more likely to be successful, and neater than children whose choices were not reciprocated (Clark & Drewry, 1985).

Along with using mutuality as the primary criterion for friendship, studies of friendless children have also been significantly enhanced when the factor of social acceptance is added to the experimental design. The resulting 2 × 2 factorial design, which includes dichotomous measures of both high versus low popularity and friended versus friendless status, affords an assessment of the differential effects of popularity and friendship status. In one such study, only friendship status produced significant effects; friended children displayed higher levels of both altruism and affective perspective taking than did chumless children (McGuire & Weisz, 1982).

In contrast, the interaction of popularity and friendship is apparent in other studies. For example, low-accepted children with no friends received lower peer ratings of sociability-leadership and likability than rejected and neglected children with friends (Kaye, 1991). In addition, peers rated unpopular friendless children higher on sensitive-isolated and aggressive-disruptive behavior than did popular friendless children or either popular or unpopular friended children (Hoza, 1989). In the same comparison, teachers rated unpopular, friendless children higher on externalizing and lower on adaptive functioning than the children in the other three groups (Hoza, 1989). Rejected children who were friended have also been found to be more trusting of others than were rejected children who have no friends (Buzzelli, 1988).

Similarly, friendless children who are low in popularity evidence lower general self-worth and cognitive self-competence than friended children (Hoza, 1989). In studies controlling for social acceptance, friended as compared to chumless children scored higher on a measure of self-concept (Mannarino, 1978a) and higher on measures of cognitive, social, and physical perceived competence and general self-worth (Bukowski & Newcomb, 1987). In contrast, Clark and Drewry (1985) report no differences on total self-concept, personal self-concept, social self-concept, and intellectual self-concept in their comparison of children who have reciprocated friendships and those who do not. Clark and Drewry (1985) did not, however, make the distinction between friendless children of low and high popularity, and the effect of friendship status on self-concept in their study may have been confounded by the children's social acceptance.

Taken together, the research literature comparing school-aged children with and without friends reveals a distinct pattern of characteristics related to being friendless. Friendless children display less adaptive social competencies and social skills when interacting with peers. They are less likely to show altruism and trust toward peers, their play with peers is less coordinated and positive, and they have less mature conceptions of friendship relations. The social reputations of friendless children amongst their peers are further characterized by greater negativity including less sociability and greater isolation and disruption. Children without a mutual friend are less well adjusted and are more negatively perceived by themselves and others than are children who experience the affective bond of friendship. Furthermore, results from studies that have examined both friendship status and popularity indicate that children who are both low in popularity and without friends are at a definite disadvantage. At the same time, friendship may serve as a buffer against the negative effects associated with low peer acceptance or peer rejection.

## A dynamic approach to the study of friended and chumless children

Despite the evidence supporting the hypothesis that children without friends are at risk for social difficulties, the direction of the effect of friendship cannot be determined by these results. Specifically, although experience in friendship relations may be important for healthy development, well-adjusted children may simply be better able and more likely to participate in friendship relations. The studies we have reviewed here are all correlational in design, and therefore a causal relationship in which friendship experience contributes positively to adjustment cannot be inferred. Thus, future researchers who aim to identify the developmental significance of friendship relations will need to conduct prospective longitudinal studies that provide a dynamic approach to the study of the relation between adjustment and having friends.

As mentioned earlier, longitudinal studies are nearly absent from the friendship literature. Ladd's (1990) short-term prospective study is an exception, and results show that friendship relations contribute to positive social outcome. Children's friendship relations, sociometric status, and school adjustment were assessed at three times throughout their kindergarten year. Children who had more classroom friends when they entered school had more favorable school perceptions by the early school months than did those with few friends. Furthermore, those children who maintained their friendships continued to show more positive school perceptions throughout the year, and establishing new friendships was associated with increases in school performance. Rejection by peers, however, predicted more negative perceptions of school, greater school avoidance, and lower performance over the course of the school year. Most notably, the direction of these effects indicates that friendship relations predicted adjustment in school better than adjustment forecasted friendship experience.

When we turned our attention to adolescents, we investigated friendship experience as a predictor of success in the transition to young adulthood (Bagwell, Newcomb, & Bukowski, 1994). In particular, we examined both friendship status (having versus not having a mutual friend) and peer preference in early adolescence (the average standardized social preference score obtained in two fifth-grade assessments) as predictors of adult adjustment. Male and female fifth-grade students ($n = 334$, mean age = 10 years, 11 months) participated in two data collections separated by a 1-month interval. The students were asked to choose classmates for 14 roles in a hypothetical class play and to list their three best friends and their three least-liked peers. On the basis of the friendship nominations, two groups of participants were selected for a 12-year follow-up. Members of the friended group chose the same first best friend at both fifth-grade assessments, and this friendship choice was reciprocal, that is, the named first best friend nominated the participant as his or her first best friend at both time periods. The chumless group consisted of participants who did not receive a reciprocal nomination by any one of their three friendship choices at either fifth-grade assessment.

In the follow-up phase of the investigation, 30 friended and 30 chumless participants (15 males and 15 females in each group, mean age = 23 years, 2 months) completed a comprehensive assessment protocol. Of particular interest were the participants' responses to an adapted version of the Status Questionnaire (Morison & Masten, 1991), which assessed functioning in the nine domains of school, work, family status, aspiration level, social life, activities, trouble with the law, psychopathology, and overall adjustment from middle school to the present time. Coders independently rated each questionnaire on a 5-point scale (except for the 3-point psychopathology scale), and reliability estimates ranged from $r = .84$ to $r = .96$.

The analysis consisted of two components – group and predictive analyses. In the group analyses, one-way analyses of variance first assessed friended and chumless group differences. Children with friends scored significantly better than chumless children on the four composite fifth-grade measures of aggression, class competence, prominence, and withdrawal. Furthermore, friended children evidenced significantly better adjustment in young adulthood than did chumless children in the domains of school, family, trouble with the law, and overall adjustment. The second step of the group analyses used analyses of covariance to control for the subjects' fifth-grade peer preference. Once peer preference was controlled, the friended and chumless groups did not differ on the fifth-grade roles or on the nine domains of adult adjustment.

The second component of our analyses employed standard regression analyses to examine whether friendship status and peer preference could predict adult adjustment. In the first analysis, friendship status and peer preference were entered into the equation after the variance explained by the subjects' sex was removed. School success, aspiration level, social life, trouble with the law, and overall adjustment were predicted by friendship status and peer preference in combination. However, an examination of the unique contributions of each predictor variable indicated that only peer preference explained a unique proportion of the variance for the school success, aspiration level, and social life adjustment scales. In contrast, friendship status uniquely explained a marginally significant portion of the variance in family status. The second aspect of the predictive analyses controlled for the stability of each adjustment trait using fifth-grade role scores. After the effects of the role scores and sex were removed, friendship status and peer preference did not predict adjustment in any of the nine domains measured by the Status Questionnaire.

This longitudinal study is the first to examine the relationship of friendship status and peer preference in early adolescence to later adjustment. In interpreting the results, it is important to consider how findings vary at different levels of analysis. While group analyses reveal that friended and chumless children differ in their adjustment, controlling for peer preference erases these differences. Similarly, the findings for friendship and peer preference as predictors are eliminated when the stability of adjustment is controlled. As a result, we did not find strong support for the predictive function of having a friend or of being popular.

Instead, our findings point to the complexity of the relation between friendship and developmental outcome, suggesting that the link between them is indirect rather than direct. Although we have no data on the source of fifth-grade adjustment problems among the friendless children, differences in fifth-grade role scores indicate that those children evidenced more adjustment difficulties than friended children. Furthermore, these problems were stable over the 12-year study period, suggesting that individual differences in the propensity for maladjustment in fifth grade are maintained in young adulthood. Thus, the lack of friends in fifth grade appears to be a marker, as opposed to a source, of adjustment difficulties. A series of short-term longitudinal studies is needed to clarify the role of friendship leading up to the theoretically important period of preadolescence.

## Summary and conclusions

Historically, descriptive investigations have dominated the literature on children's peer and friendship relations. Less attention has been given to studying the processes that form and maintain these relationships and the processes through which these relationships leave their marks on the individual. As a result, we know something about what children's friendships look like but relatively little about the effects of friendships on children's lives. The intention of this chapter was to focus on the benefits of having a friend and on the implications of lacking a friend. In the process, we sought to specify the status of the quest for uncovering friendship's contribution to development and to outline directions for future research.

Our quantitative review of the literature comparing friends and acquaintances provided support for the notion that friendship relations are supportive contexts for development. Friendships are associated with enhanced opportunities to exercise behaviors related to social, emotional, and cognitive growth. In particular, friends' interactions are characterized by more intense social activity (including cooperation, talking, and sustained contact) and by greater concern with conflict resolution. Perhaps most consistent with theoretical reasoning about the benefits of friendship are the meta-analytic findings that children's relationships with their friends are marked by greater reciprocal and intimate properties of affiliation than are their relationships with acquaintances. Friends display greater closeness, loyalty, mutual liking, and equality than acquaintances do, and all of these experiences are important for the acquisition of interpersonal skills and competencies, for success in future relationships, and for emotional well-being.

Although the meta-analysis does not provide any direct evidence of developmental significance, it helps identify potential areas in which friendship experience contributes to social adaptation. In contrast, comparisons between children with and without friends provide a more direct assessment of the benefits of having a friend. Although the literature comparing friended and chumless children is complicated by methodological problems, these results provide a characterization of the friendless child and help ascertain specific competencies that are best developed within the context of friendship relations. The weight of the evidence suggests that friendless children display less adaptive social competencies and skills than friended children do; furthermore, the problems associated with being chumless are exacerbated among children with low sociometric standing.

Attention to five issues can significantly enhance comparisons between friends and acquaintances and between friended and chumless children. First, understanding friendship's developmental significance requires longitudinal designs that test causal models linking friendship and developmental outcome. Second, even though investigators have given some attention to studying friendship at different ages, we have hardly begun to explore developmental changes in friendship or how the importance of the friendship experience may vary with age. Third, investigators are increasingly sensitive to the fact that not all friendships are the same. As such, we must explore the vicissitudes of the friendship experience as a function of the identity of one's friend. Fourth, just as the identity of one's friend varies, the quality of individual relationships differs, and friendship quality also needs to be explored as a determinant of developmental outcome. Finally, the dynamic interplay between friendship relations and other social systems (e.g., the family and peers) undoubtedly has an impact on whatever contribution friendship makes to social adaptation. Although progress has been made in exploring these complex interrelationships, considerable work lies ahead.

What then is the developmental significance of children's friendship relations?

We can conclude only by saying that the jury remains out. So far, the data provide at least some support for Gabirol's ideas about friendship: "some are like food, some like medicine, and others like an illness." However, it is also evident that this holistic view of friendship is flawed as these relations are not singularly viewed as a necessity, an advantage, or a hindrance. Instead, high-quality friendships can at times have negative consequences and low-quality friendships may provide some positive outcomes. The task ahead is to carefully attend to design and conceptual issues as we go about our business of examining the contribution of friendship experience to child and adolescent development. We must commit ourselves to executing investigations that can provide causal explanations for the developmental significance of friendship. Until that time, we are left with little more than our conviction that the friendships of children and adolescents have a special place in development.

## References

Azmitia, M., & Montgomery, R. (1993). Friendship, transactive dialogues, and the development of scientific reasoning. *Social Development, 2*, 202–221.

Bagwell, C. L., Newcomb, A. F., & Bukowski, W. M. (1994). *Early adolescent friendship as a predictor of adult adjustment: A twelve-year follow-up investigation.* Unpublished manuscript, University of Richmond.

Berndt, T. J. (1988). The nature and significance of children's friendships. In R. Vasta (Ed.), *Annals of child development,* Vol. 5. Greenwich, CT: JAI Press.

Berndt, T. J. (1992). Friendship and friends' influence in adolescence. *Current Directions in Psychological Science, 1,* 156–159.

Berndt, T. J., & Keefe, K. (1992). Friends' influence on adolescents' perceptions of themselves at school. In D. G. Schunk & J. L. Meece (Eds.), *Student perceptions in the classroom.* Hillsdale, N.J.: Erlbaum.

Berndt, T. J., & Perry, T. B. (1986). Children's perceptions of friendships as supportive relationships. *Developmental Psychology, 22,* 640–648.

Bigelow, B. J. (1977). Children's friendship expectations: A cognitive developmental study. *Child Development, 48,* 246–253.

Buhrmester, D., & Furman, W. (1986). The changing functions of friends in childhood: A Neo-Sullivanian perspective. In V. J. Derlega & B. A. Winstead (Eds.), *Friendship and social interaction.* New York: Springer-Verlag.

Bukowski, W. M., & Hoza, B. (1989). Popularity and friendship: Issues in theory, measurement, and outcome. In T. Berndt & G. Ladd (Eds.), *Peer relationships in child development.* New York: Wiley.

Bukowski, W. M., Hoza, B., & Boivin, M. (1993). Popularity, friendship, and emotional adjustment during early adolescence. In B. Laursen (Ed.), *Close friendships in adolescence.* San Francisco: Jossey-Bass.

Bukowski, W. M., Hoza, B., & Boivin, M. (1994). Measuring friendship quality during pre- and early adolescence: The development and psychometric properties of the *Friendship Qualities Scale. Journal of Social and Personal Relationships, 11,* 471–484.

Bukowski, W. M., & Newcomb, A. F. (1987, April). *Friendship quality and the "self" during adolescence.* Paper presented at the biennial meeting of the Society for Research in Child Development, Baltimore, MD.

Buzzelli, C. A. (1988). The development of trust in children's relations with peers. *Child Study Journal, 18,* 33–46.

Cairns, R. B., Cairns, B. D., Neckerman, H. J., Gest, S., & Garieppy, J. L. (1988). Peer networks and social behavior: Peer support or peer rejection? *Developmental Psychology, 24,* 815–823.

Cauce, A. M. (1986). Social networks and social competence: Exploring the effects of early adolescent friendships. *American Journal of Community Psychology, 14,* 607–628.

Clark, M. L., & Drewry, D. L. (1985). Similarity and reciprocity in the friendships of elementary school children. *Child Study Journal, 15,* 251–264.

Cooper, H. M., & Rosenthal, R. (1980). Statistical versus traditional procedures for summarizing research findings. *Psychological Bulletin, 87,* 442–449.

Cowen, E. L., Pederson, A., Babigian, H., Izzo, L. D., & Trost, M. A. (1973). Long-term follow-up of early detected vulnerable children. *Journal of Consulting and Clinical Psychology, 41,* 438–446.

Eason, L. J. (1985). *An investigation of children's friendships: The relationship between cognitive social development and demonstration of prosocial behaviors.* Unpublished doctoral dissertation, University of Georgia.

Epstein, J. L. (1983). The influence of friends on achievement and affective outcomes. In J. L. Epstein & N. Karweit (Eds.), *Friends in school: Patterns of selection and influence in secondary schools.* New York: Academic Press.

Furman, W. (1982). Children's friendships. In T. Field, G. Finley, A. Huston, H. Quay, & L. Troll (Eds.), *Review of Human Development.* New York: John Wiley.

Glass, G. V., McGaw, B., & Smith, M. L. (1981). *Meta-analysis in social research.* Beverly Hills, CA: Sage.

Guralnick, M. J., & Groom, J. M. (1988). Friendships of preschool children in mainstreamed playgroups. *Developmental Psychology, 24,* 595–604.

Hartup, W. W. (1983). Peer relations. In E. M. Hetherington (Ed.), *Handbook of child psychology: Vol. 4. Socialization, personality, and social development.* New York: Wiley.

Hartup, W. W. (1992a). Friendships and their developmental significance. In H. McGurk (Ed.), *Contemporary issues in childhood social development.* London: Routledge.

Hartup, W. W. (1992b). Peer relations in early and middle childhood. In V. B. Van Hasselt & M. Hersen (Eds.), *Handbook of social development: A lifespan perspective.* New York: Plenum.

Hartup, W. W. (1993). Adolescents and their friends. In B. Laursen (Ed.), *Close friendships during adolescence: New directions for child development.* San Francisco: Jossey-Bass.

Hartup, W. W., French, D. C., Laursen, B., Johnston, M. K., & Ogawa, J. R. (1992). *Conflict and friendship relations in middle childhood: Behavior in a closed-field situation.* Unpublished manuscript, University of Minnesota, Minneapolis, MN.

Hartup, W. W., & Moore, S. G. (1990). Early peer relations: Developmental significance and prognostic implications. *Early Childhood Research Quarterly, 5,* 1–17.

Hartup, W. W., & Sancilio, M. F. (1986). Children's friendships. In E. Schopler & G. B. Mesibov (Eds.), *Social behavior in autism.* New York: Plenum Press.

Hedges, L. V. (1982). Fitting categorical models to effect sizes from a series of experiments. *Journal of Educational Statistics, 7,* 119–137.

Hedges, L. V., & Olkin, I. (1985). *Statistical methods for meta-analysis.* Orlando: Academic Press.

Hinde, R. A. (1979). *Toward understanding relationships.* London: Academic Press.

Hinde, R. A., & Stevenson-Hinde, J. (1987). Interpersonal relationships and child development. *Developmental Review, 7,* 1–21.

Howes, C. (1988). Peer interaction of young children. *Monographs of the Society for Research in Child Development.* Serial No. 217, Vol. 53.

Howes, C., Matheson, C., & Wu, F. (1992). Friendship and social pretend play: Illustrative study #6. In C. Howes, O. Unger, & C. C. Matheson (Eds.), *The collaborative construction of pretend*. State University of New York Press.

Hoza, B. (1989). *Development and validation of a method for classifying children's social status based on two types of measures: Popularity and chumship*. Unpublished doctoral dissertation, University of Maine.

Kandel, D. B. (1978). Homophily, selection, and socialization in adolescent friendships. *American Journal of Sociology, 84,* 427–436.

Kaye, C. D. (1991). *Do low-accepted children benefit from having friends? A study of self versus others' perspectives of socioemotional adjustment and quality of friendship*. Unpublished doctoral dissertation, The University of Texas at Dallas.

Kupersmidt, J. B., Coie, J. D., & Dodge, K. A. (1990). The role of poor peer relationships in the development of disorder. In S. R. Asher & J. D. Coie (Eds.), *Peer rejection in childhood*. New York: Cambridge University Press.

Ladd, G. W. (1990). Having friends, keeping friends, making friends, and being liked by peers in the classroom: Predictors of children's early school adjustment? *Child Development, 61,* 1081–1090.

McGuire, K. D., & Weisz, J. R. (1982). Social cognition and behavior correlates of preadolescent chumship. *Child Development, 53,* 1478–1484.

Magnusson, D., Stattin, H., & Allen, V. L. (1985). Biological maturation and social development: A longitudinal study of some adjustment processes from mid-adolescence to adulthood. *Journal of Youth and Adolescence, 14,* 267–283.

Mannarino, A. P. (1976). Friendship patterns and altruistic behavior in preadolescent males. *Developmental Psychology, 12,* 555–556.

Mannarino, A. P. (1978a). The interactional process in preadolescent friendships. *Psychiatry, 41,* 308–312.

Mannarino, A. P. (1978b). Friendship patterns and self-concept development in preadolescent males. *Journal of Genetic Psychology, 133,* 105–110.

Mannarino, A. P. (1979). The relationship between friendship and altruism in preadolescent girls. *Psychiatry, 42,* 280–284.

Morison, P., & Masten, A. S. (1991). Peer reputation in middle childhood as a predictor of adaptation in adolescence: A seven-year follow-up. *Child Development, 62,* 991–1007.

Newcomb, A. F., & Bagwell, C. L. (1995). Children's friendship relations: A meta-analytic review. *Psychological Bulletin, 117,* 306–347.

Parker, J. G., & Asher, S. R. (1987). Peer relations and later personal adjustment: Are low accepted children "at risk"? *Psychological Bulletin, 102,* 357–389.

Parker, J. G., & Asher, S. R. (1993). Friendship and friendship quality in middle childhood: Links with peer group acceptance and feelings of loneliness and social dissatisfaction. *Developmental Psychology, 29,* 611–621.

Parker, J. G., & Gottman, J. M. (1989). Social and emotional development in a relational context: Friendship interaction from early childhood to adolescence. In T. J. Berndt & G. W. Ladd (Eds.), *Peer relationships in child development*. New York: John Wiley & Sons.

Price, J. M., & Ladd, G. W. (1986). Assessment of children's friendships: Implications for social competence and social adjustment. In R. J. Prinz (Ed.), *Advances in behavioral assessment of children and families*, Vol. 2. Greenwich, CT: JAI Press Inc.

Roff, M. (1961). Childhood social interactions and young adult bad conduct. *Journal of Abnormal and Social Psychology, 63,* 333–337.

Roff, M., Sells, S. B., & Golden, M. M. (1972). *Social adjustment and personality development in children*. Minneapolis: University of Minnesota.

Roopnarine, J. L., & Field, T. M. (1984). Play interactions of friends and acquaintances in nursery school. In T. Field, J. L. Roopnarine, & M. Segal (Eds.), *Friendships in normal and handicapped children.* Norwood: Ablex Publishing Corporation.

Smollar, J., & Youniss, J. (1982). Social development through friendship. In K. H. Rubin & H. S. Ross (Eds.), *Peer relationships and social skills in childhood.* New York: Springer-Verlag.

Snyder, J., Dishion, T. J., & Patterson, G. R. (1986). Determinants and consequences of associating with deviant peers during preadolescence and adolescence. *Journal of Early Adolescence, 6,* 29–43.

Sullivan, H. S. (1953). *The interpersonal theory of psychiatry.* New York: Norton.

Vernberg, E. M. (1990). Psychological adjustment and experiences with peers during early adolescence: Reciprocal, incidental, or unidirectional relationships? *Journal of Abnormal Child Psychology, 18,* 187–198.

# 14 Linkages between friendship and adjustment during early school transitions

*Gary W. Ladd and Becky J. Kochenderfer*

Many researchers have argued that friends are important socializers who make substantial, and possibly unique contributions to children's social and cognitive development (see Berndt & Ladd, 1989). Hartup and Sancilio (1986), for example, contend that friendships provide children with: (1) contexts for skill learning and development, (2) emotional and cognitive resources, and (3) models for later relationships. In the pages that follow, we consider how functions such as these may affect children's adjustment during early ecological transitions.

More specifically, our aim in this chapter is to explore the potential contributions that children's peer relationships, especially friendships, make to children's adjustment during their transition to grade school. In recent years, our research agenda has broadened beyond asking questions about *how* children develop certain behavioral competencies, form relationships with peers, and acquire specific social reputations to include questions about the contributions of children's peer relationships – in particular, how children's existing peer relations, including the quality of them, affect their social adjustment and well-being. We have begun to pursue this research agenda by examining the linkage between children's peer relations and their adjustment during early school transitions.

To date, much of the research on the determinants of early school adjustment has been focused on personal characteristics of the child. Among the variables that have received the most empirical attention are organismic factors, such as children's gender and mental maturity, and children's behavioral styles. Investigators who have studied these dimensions find that girls, for example, are more likely to develop lower or inaccurate (underestimated) perceptions of their competence (Block, 1983; Dweck, 1986; Ladd & Price, 1986) and boys are at risk for conduct problems in the classroom (Garmezy, Masten, & Tellegen, 1984; Ladd & Price, 1987). Children's IQ and basic academic skills have been found to predict achievement in the early primary grades (Stevenson, Parker, Wilkinson, Hegion, & Fish, 1976) and their behavioral styles (e.g., prosocial vs. aggressive) forecast later peer rejection, classroom disruption, and school avoidance (see Ladd & Price, 1987; Parker & Asher, 1987).

Children's experiences and relationships in the family and neighborhood have also been studied, as have the extent and quality of their preschool experience. Findings from this research show that exposure to stressful life events in the family place children at risk for school maladjustment (see Cowen, Lotyczewski, & Weissberg, 1984; Garmezy et al., 1984; Sandler & Ramsay, 1980). Additionally, various socialization practices in the family, such as parents' management of children's peer relations, have a bearing on children's school adjustment (Ladd & Golter, 1988; Ladd & Hart, 1992; Ladd, Profilet, & Hart, 1992). Studies of prior preschool experience also suggest that children with considerable preschool experience may well have mastered tasks such as separating from parents, accepting teacher's authority, negotiating large group settings, and so forth and thus face fewer adjustment demands as they enter school (Ladd & Price, 1987).

Less well studied have been the potential contributions of children's peer relationships to children's adjustment during early school transitions. A few researchers have investigated whether the friendships children form prior to school entrance or in nonschool settings (e.g., neighborhoods) have any bearing on their later school adjustment (see Cowen et al., 1984; Ladd & Price, 1987). Ladd and Price (1987), for instance, have shown that children who choose to relate to younger companions in the neighborhood tend to have more difficulty adjusting to grade school classrooms. This finding suggests that because of the asymmetrical nature of such relationships, these children might lack the experience and social skills needed to establish ties with agemates in kindergarten, which, in turn, could lead to less interest and satisfaction with their new school environment.

However, until recently the potential contributions of children's *classroom* peer relationships (e.g., relationships in the school context) to their adjustment during early school transitions have been largely overlooked. Yet, as we illustrate in subsequent sections, there is growing evidence to suggest that the relationships that children form with peers *in classrooms* will affect their adjustment in this setting. Thus, another objective of this chapter is to distinguish between the types of relationships young children form with classroom peers, and the potential functions those relationships serve during early school transitions.

We begin this chapter by considering the nature of early school transitions and, more specifically, the features of this context that may provide investigators with opportunities to study the impact of children's peer relationships on their adjustment in this setting. Because our focus is on the linkages between children's peer relationships (e.g., friendships) and their adjustment in classrooms, we also provide a working definition of the construct of *school adjustment*, and identify key variables and indices that represent this dimension.

In subsequent sections, we consider recent theory and evidence that may shed light on the adaptive features of children's classroom peer relations (e.g., resources or provisions that children may derive from friendships with classmates), and the role that these provisions may play in the process of school adjustment. Three forms of classroom peer relations will be considered: friendships, acquaintanceships, and peer group acceptance.

### Early school transitions as a context for research on friendships

Changes in school environments represent one type of ecological transition that all children face, and this transition may take several forms including school entrance (e.g., the transition from home to preschool or day care; see Ladd, Hart, Wadsworth, & Golter, 1988), the progression from one level of schooling to another (e.g., the transition from preschool to kindergarten; see Ladd & Price, 1987; Ladd, 1990), and school transfers (e.g., moves that necessitate changes in classrooms or schools; Bogat, Jones, & Jason, 1980; Holland, Kaplan, & Davis, 1974). In most American communities, the first year of grade school (kindergarten) places substantial demands upon children, and therefore it is an important context for observing early social adaptation and adjustment. For example, as children move from preschool to kindergarten, they must cope with novel school environments and personnel, gain acceptance into new peer groups, confront more difficult academic tasks, and respond to higher performance standards (Ladd & Price, 1987). As we shall see, the relationships that children possess or form may provide important resources or "adaptational advantages" (Hartup & Sancilio, 1986) that may enhance their capacity to cope with these changing environmental and interpersonal demands.

### The concept of school adjustment

Although the concept of school adjustment has not been well defined in previous literature, we use it here to refer to young children's perceptions and feelings about the school environment, and the degree to which they embrace and succeed in this context. Specifically, school adjustment is defined as the degree to which children become interested, engaged, comfortable, and successful in the school environment (for further treatment of this concept, see Ladd, 1989). Therefore, as children enter grade school, adjustment is reflected by the degree to which they: (a) develop positive versus negative perceptions of school; (b) feel comfortable versus anxious in new classrooms; (c) become involved versus withdraw from or avoid school and school-related activities; and (d) progress versus fall behind at academic tasks (Bogat, et al., 1980; Ladd, 1990; Ladd & Price, 1987). Each of these adjustment dimensions is assumed to be an important precursor of children's subsequent educational progress. For example, we hypothesize that children who like school and become involved in classroom activities are more likely to learn and profit from their educational experiences. Conversely, children who develop negative attitudes toward school, or an inclination to avoid or withdraw from the school environment, are likely to have additional adjustment problems and disrupted progress.

## The role of peer relations in children's early school adjustment

As we mentioned earlier, although we view school adjustment outcomes as multiply determined, our aim is to provide a detailed examination of one dimension of our model. That is, in the remaining pages we examine the hypothesis that children's *classroom* peer relations affect their initial adjustment to grade school (kindergarten).

### *Types of classroom peer relations*

Within classrooms, it is possible to define and study children's peer relations at different levels of analysis. On the one hand, peer relations can be defined at the level of the dyad. Friendships, for example, can be thought of as ties that children form with individual peers. On the other hand, social relations can also be defined at the level of the peer group. At this level of analysis, the individual is seen as a member of a larger social unit, and the relation between the individual and the group is defined in terms of the individual's status within the group or in terms of the group member's regard for the individual.

In our efforts to understand the impact of classroom peers on children's early school adjustment, we have focused on three relationship constructs: friendship, acquaintanceship (familiar peers), and peer group acceptance. It is hypothesized that each of these three forms of relations have different features, and, as a result, differ in their contributions to school adjustment.

*Friendship.* The concept of a classroom friendship is defined at the level of the dyad and refers to a relationship that is both voluntary in nature (i.e., not imposed by one member) and mutually regulated (i.e., controlled and maintained by both partners). Friendship as a construct implies the presence of a reciprocated emotional or affiliative bond between the child and another classmate. In research with young children, the presence of the bond is usually inferred from one or more empirical indicators (see reviews by Ladd & Coleman, 1993; Price & Ladd, 1986), including evidence indicating that the dyad members: (a) mutually nominate each other as "best friends" (e.g., Ladd, 1990); (b) frequently interact or consistently seek out each other's company (e.g., Hinde, Titmus, Easton, & Tamplin, 1985); (c) display positive affect during interactions (see Howes, 1983, 1988); (d) mutually adjust their behaviors to "fit" their partners or achieve more sophisticated forms of interaction (Howes, 1983, 1988; Ross & Lollis, 1989).

*Acquaintanceship.* Acquaintanceship is also a dyadic construct, yet in comparison to friendships, it refers to "weak" interpersonal ties between children and individual classmates. We define classroom acquaintances as peers children "know," but with whom they have no close, reciprocated ties. For example, as children enter school, acquaintances are essentially no more than "familiar" classmates – that is, peers children have known before entering school, but with whom they have had no regular contact or close relationship.

It is important to note that many investigators have used the term *familiar peers* when referring to dyadic relationship pairs that may be more appropriately labeled *acquaintances*. However, because writers often do not define familiar peers or provide an explanation of the procedures used to operationalize this construct, it is not always possible to draw careful distinctions between these two concepts. Consequently, in reviewing the pertinent literature for this chapter, we have chosen to preserve investigators' terminology rather than infer concepts that were not originally intended or measured. Therefore, we use the terms familiar peers and acquaintances relatively interchangeably when a nonfriend dyadic relationship is implied. We feel, however, that it is important for researchers to address these concepts with greater conceptual precision in future investigations – that is, define more precisely what is meant by familiar peers (e.g., the extent of familiarity, not merely that they are nonfriends).

*Peer group acceptance.* The concept of peer group acceptance or popularity differs from that of friendship or acquaintanceship in that it refers to the quality of a child's peer relations within a group rather than the relationship a child has with an individual peer. Specifically, the concept of peer group acceptance or popularity is defined as the degree to which a specific child is liked by members of his or her peer group. Thus, relations between a child and the peer group may differ depending on the sentiments that group members develop toward the child, and the degree to which these sentiments are shared by group members or become consensual. For example, children who are liked by the majority of their peers can be thought of as well-accepted or popular members of the group. In contrast, those who are disliked by a majority of group members are defined as being low-accepted or rejected in their peer group.

Data from several studies show that the quality of children's relations with group members differs depending on their popularity or group acceptance (Ladd, 1983). Findings reported by Masters and Furman (1981) reveal that young children are more likely to interact in a nonpunitive manner with liked peers than with less-liked classmates. Similarly, in a study conducted on mixed-age school playgrounds, Ladd (1983) found that the interactions of popular and rejected children differed in quality (i.e., rejected children's interactions were more negative), and tended to be directed at peers of similar status (e.g., popular children tended to play with other popular children).

There is also evidence to suggest that once children are rejected by the peer group, they change the nature of their play and contact patterns with peers. Ladd, Price, and Hart (1990) found that, whereas popular children appeared to become more selective over time and focused their interactions upon a relatively small number of consistent play partners, rejected children appeared to maintain extensive play contacts, and often "bounced" from one playmate to another. Once children become disliked, they may be increasingly avoided by peers, and thus are forced to search out playmates among a broad range of peers.

Thus, as defined here, the construct of peer group acceptance differs from friendship in two important ways. First, these two constructs imply differing levels of social context or relational spheres. Group acceptance or popularity is a collective index of the quality of a child's relations with members of a peer group, and evidence of consensual liking or disliking is typically used to define a child's social standing in the group. Friendship, in contrast, refers to a dyadic relationship between the child and an individual peer. Second, popularity also differs from friendship in that classroom peer groups are seldom voluntary or mutually regulated; therefore children have little choice over their participation. For example, in schools, the peer composition of most classrooms is established by administrative decree, and changes in room assignments are seldom permitted. Once children enter a classroom, they become part of the "liking hierarchy" whether or not they choose to participate in it.

## Hypothesized functions of classroom peer relations

How might children's classroom peer relations affect their adjustment to school? This question poses an intriguing mystery – one for which there are important conceptual and empirical clues but, as of yet, no firm conclusions.

One assumption that has guided our recent work is that children's classroom peer relations function either as supports or stressors, depending on the extent to which they help children cope with the demands of school, and foster feelings of security, worth, belongingness, and competence. The basis for this premise lies in recent theory and research on the contributions of peer relations to children's development. In this section, we elaborate upon this premise by surveying recent theoretical perspectives on the functions of children's peer relationships.

*Functions of friendships.* The concept of friendship implies the presence of a relationship – specifically, a voluntary reciprocated emotional tie between child and peer. Recently, a number of investigators have argued that friendships, like other types of close relationships, provide certain psychological benefits (and costs) for children (see Berndt, 1989; Berndt & Perry, 1986; Buhrmester & Furman, 1987; Bukowski & Hoza, 1989; Furman & Buhrmester, 1985; Parker & Asher, 1989, 1993; Sharabany, Gershoni, & Hofman, 1981). These "social provisions," as Weiss (1974) referred to them, may be present to varying degrees in children's friendships, depending on the nature of the relationship (e.g., quality, stability) and the needs, interests, and characteristics that the partners bring to the relationship.

In recent years, a number of investigators have developed models of potential friendship features (see the dimensions listed in Table 14.1), and devised measures to assess individual and developmental differences in the quality of children's friendships. We propose that these features can be further broken down into two categories that would have implications for how investigators define and measure the features or qualities of children's friendships. More specifically, we are making a theoretical distinction between relationship *processes* and *provisions.* Some of the constructs investigators have used to distinguish friendship features refer to what we see as relationship "processes" – for example, observable forms of exchange or interaction between partners that may affect the development or quality of the relationship (e.g., self-disclosure, frankness and spontaneity, conflict, conflict resolution). Other proposed features refer to putative benefits that children derive from their participation in friendship. We are inclined to see as these as "provisions" (cf. Furman & Buhrmester, 1985). Examples of friendship provisions would include constructs such as "security," "intimacy," "trust," and so on.

Provisions may, as we conceive of them, be the product or outcome of specific friendship processes. For example, friends who self-disclose or gossip may enhance each other's feelings of intimacy or "closeness" (see also Parker & Gottman, 1989). Also, by offering each other companionship or help and guidance, friends may increase their partner's sense of security or repertoire of social skills. Of course, friendship processes may not always be balanced, or yield the same provisions for each partner. Partners may, for example, differ in their ability to self-disclose, keep secrets, resolve conflicts, offer instruction or guidance, and so forth. In such friendships, the provisions experienced by each partner might be quite different or imbalanced.

Table 14.1. *Features of children's friendships as defined by investigators*

| Investigator | Friendship features (categories) |
| --- | --- |
| Weiss (1974) | Attachment (affection, security, intimate disclosure)<br>Reliable alliance<br>Enhancement of worth<br>Social integration<br>Guidance<br>Opportunity for nurturance |
| Sharabany, Gershoni, & Hofman (1981) | Frankness and spontaneity<br>Sensitivity and knowing<br>Attachment<br>Exclusiveness<br>Giving and sharing<br>Imposing and taking<br>Common activities<br>Trust and loyalty |
| Furman & Burhmester (1985) | Provisions:<br>  Reliable alliance<br>  Enhancement of worth<br>  Instrumental help or guidance<br>  Companionship<br>  Affection<br>  Intimacy<br>Other features:<br>  Relative power<br>  Conflict<br>  Satisfaction<br>  Importance of relationship |
| Berndt & Perry (1986) | Play/association<br>Prosocial behavior<br>Intimacy<br>Loyalty<br>Attachment and self-esteem enhancement<br>Conflict |
| Bukowski, Boivin, & Hoza (1991) | Companionship<br>Security<br>  Reliable alliance<br>  Transcending problems<br>Conflict<br>Help<br>  Aid<br>  Protection from victimization<br>Closeness<br>  Affective bond<br>  Reflected appraisal |

Table 14.1. (cont.)

| Investigator | Friendship features (categories) |
| --- | --- |
| Parker & Asher (1993) | Validation and caring<br>Help and guidance<br>Companionship and recreation<br>Intimate exchange<br>Conflict and betrayal<br>Conflict resolution |

The processes that occur in young children's classroom friendships may yield a number of provisions that affect their school adjustment (see Figure 14.1). For the purposes of this chapter, we limit our analysis to provisions that: (a) are likely to be present in the friendships of young children, and (b) have some demonstrated empirical validity.

*1. Friendship as a context for skill development.* Among young children, skill development may be an important friendship provision. Investigators working with young children, such as Howes (1983), have argued that many of the skills required for complex social interactions develop in stable dyads, or early friendships. Friends, it is contended, are more receptive and responsive to their partners than they are to other peers and, therefore, initiate and maintain interactions more easily. Also, by increasing the success of each other's overtures, friends create an interactional context that is mutually facilitive of each other's skills – that is, they mutually collaborate (e.g., encourage each other to elaborate upon familiar interaction themes) and, in the process, devise increasingly sophisticated skills.

Howes's (1983) observations of young friends in child care settings provide preliminary support for this hypothesis. Toddlers and preschoolers were observed over the course of a school year, and changes in their social interactions and play behaviors were examined. Results indicated that gains in the complexity of play and social interaction were greatest for children who were members of stable friendship dyads.

*2. Friendship as a source of emotional support/security.* Emotional support or security can also be viewed as a key friendship provision (e.g., Bukowski, Boivin, & Hoza, 1991; Parker & Asher, 1989; Weiss, 1974). Young friends, particularly in child care or school settings, may function as important "attachment" figures for children in the absence of parents or their primary caretakers (Howes, 1983, 1988).

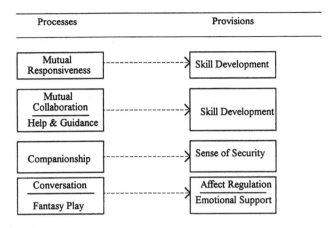

Figure 14.1. Hypothesized linkages between friendship processes and provisions.

Support for this rationale can be found in a study conducted by Schwarz (1972). Schwarz observed the behavior of 4-year-olds in an unfamiliar room containing both novel and familiar toys. Children were encouraged to explore the room under one of three conditions: with a close friend, with an unfamiliar peer, or alone. Schwarz found that children who were paired with a close friend explored the novel environment more freely and displayed higher levels of positive affect than did peers in the other two conditions, and concluded that friends had more of a distress-inhibiting effect on children than did unfamiliar peers.

Further evidence of the emotional significance of young children's friendships is borne out in research on conversational data (see Parker & Gottman, 1989). As these investigators have shown, young friends mutually create complex forms of conversation and fantasy play that allow them to express, share, and work through their own emotions.

With somewhat older samples (preadolescents), Bukowski and Hoza (1990) have shown that specific friendship features are predictive of affective outcomes such as loneliness. These investigators followed fifth and sixth graders over a 1-year interval and found that friends whose relationships were initially characterized by security and closeness were less likely to report feelings of loneliness at later points in time.

*3. Other friendship provisions.* Several other friendship features have been studied with school-age samples, and may be relevant to the study of young children's classroom friendships. Of these features, the following strike us as relationship "provisions" that may warrant further attention in studies of early school adjustment: trust and loyalty (Berndt & Perry, 1986; Sharabany, Gershoni, & Hofman, 1981); closeness, intimacy (Berndt & Perry, 1986; Bukowski, Boivin, & Hoza, 1991; Furman & Buhrmester, 1985; Parker & Asher, 1993); and enhancement of worth or self-esteem (Berndt & Perry, 1986; Furman & Buhrmester, 1985).

*Functions of acquaintances/familiar peers.* Unlike friendship, acquaintanceship implies the absence of a close, reciprocated emotional tie between child and peer. However, like friendship, several investigators have found evidence to suggest that acquaintanceship, or mere familiarity with one's peers, also affects children's social-emotional competence and adjustment. The perspectives offered by these investigators are similar in that peer acquaintanceship or familiarity is: (a) defined in terms of prior exposure or interaction (between child and peer) rather than as a form of "relationship" and, (b) viewed as having salutary effects upon children. However, investigators differ in their views of the mechanisms responsible for these effects.

   *1. Familiar peers as a facilitator of attraction, interaction, and skill development.* Prominent among these perspectives is the view that familiarity is an important determinant of both attraction and interaction. Scholtz and Ellis (1975) and Zajonc (1968) have argued that "mere exposure" may cause children to feel attracted to each other and, in turn, attraction raises the probability that they will seek each other's company or pursue interactions in the future.

   Another important function that familiarity may serve, according to Lewis, Young, Brooks, and Michaelson (1975), is that of facilitating the young child's social responsiveness. These writers point out that infants and young children often display more wariness and behavioral inhibition in the presence of strange or novel stimuli, including unfamiliar peers. Conditions that reduce strangeness or novelty, such as repeated exposures or interactions with the same peer, are hypothesized to have a disinhibiting effect. That is, familiarity between an infant and a peer reduces wariness and inhibition and promotes interpersonal engagement and social responsiveness (e.g., proximity seeking, physical, vocal, gestural contact).

   In a series of studies designed to explore this hypothesis, Lewis et al. (1975) found that infants engaged in behavior patterns that were more socially responsive and engaging when they were in the presence of familiar rather than unfamiliar peers. Compared to their unacquainted counterparts, familiar infants displayed higher levels of proximity seeking, physical contact, and imitation.

   Expanding on the Lewis et al. position, Doyle, Connolly, and Rivest (1980) contend that peer familiarity also affects children's behavioral development.

Their view is that repeated interactions with the same partner allow both members of the dyad to develop new skills and shared ways of relating (e.g., similar behavioral repertoires, complementary play styles). Over time, children begin to view peers with whom they have developed shared experiences and skills as attractive play partners, and they prefer them over unfamiliar peers as potential companions.

Data gathered by Doyle et al. (1980) and others provide preliminary support for this contention. To investigate the effects of peer familiarity, Doyle et al. observed 3-year-olds as they interacted with both familiar and unfamiliar peer partners during 50-minute laboratory play sessions. In the company of familiar peers, children engaged in more sociable forms of play (e.g., associative, cooperative play), and fewer nonsocial behaviors (e.g., onlooking, unoccupied). During interactions, familiar partners also tended to exhibit more sophisticated or mature forms of play, and succeeded more often at influencing their partner's behaviors. Other investigators have reported similar findings. For example, Mueller and Brenner (1977) found that male toddlers with repeated experience in the same play groups developed more sophisticated and coordinated forms of play than did boys with less play group exposure. Also, Howes (1988) found that toddlers who had been in child care with the same peers for an extended period of time (i.e., a year or more) tended to develop more skillful forms of interaction.

Studies conducted with much younger subjects reveal similar findings. Becker (1977) found that 9-month-olds who played with the same peer partner across many play sessions tended to develop more frequent and complex forms of social interaction than did infants who played with less familiar peers. However, the effects attributed to familiarity may be less robust under some conditions. Becker (1977), for example, compared the frequency of infants' interactions with acquainted peers both in their own homes and the homes of peers. Findings produced by this study showed that infants interacted less often when they played in the more novel of these two settings, that is, the homes of peers. In another study, Jacobson (1981) found that infants played less with familiar partners when toys were present in the play sessions. Thus, it would appear that situational constraints may mitigate the impact of partner familiarity. Nonetheless, as a whole, these findings would seem to imply that acquaintanceship, or experience with a particular partner, facilitates the young child's social competence.

*2. Familiar peers as a source of emotional support.* Social psychologists were among the first to propose that people's reactions to stressful and aversive situations are mitigated by the presence of a companion. However, after several decades of research on both animal and human subjects (adults), the evidence gathered to test this hypothesis has been mixed. In one of the last major reviews of this literature, Epley (1974) concluded that there was little evidence to suggest that the mere physical presence of a companion was responsible for such effects. Rather, it would appear that such effects are contingent upon the companions' characteristics and behaviors. In particular, adults who face threatening or aversive stimuli appear to benefit most from companions who model calm responses or invent distractions.

Developmental psychologists have begun only recently to speculate about the effects of peer companions on children's emotional states, so less is known about this phenomenon. Formal theories about how peer companions impact children's emotional states, and the psychological mechanisms that might be responsible for such effects, have yet to be articulated. However, investigators such as Ispa (1981) have asserted that the level of familiarity that exists between a child and peer is an important determinant of young children's affective reactions. Ispa's rationale for this hypothesis bears a strong resemblance to the tenets found in attachment theory. Specifically, Ispa proposes that children who are acquainted share weak emotional bonds (i.e., emotional ties that are not as strong as parent–child attachments) that, in turn, function as "havens for security" within stressful situations. In other words, familiarity with one's companions provides children with a sense of security, and the impact of this type of emotional support is most evident in stressful situations (e.g., strange, novel environments).

To explore this hypothesis, Ispa (1981) placed toddlers in a strange (unfamiliar) situation, and monitored their affective reactions under three conditions: accompanied by a familiar peer, accompanied by an unfamiliar peer, or alone (no peer companion). Note that Ispa's design was similar to Schwarz's (1972) earlier work, except that Schwarz had children enter the room with a close friend, rather than a familiar peer. As anticipated, children who were paired with a familiar peer displayed lower levels of distress than did those who were paired with unfamiliar peers. However, even an unfamiliar peer appeared to be more comforting than no peer at all. That is, children in the peer-absent condition were significantly more distressed than their counterparts in either the familiar or unfamiliar peer conditions.

*Functions of peer group acceptance.* Although there is no clear consensus among researchers as to the functions that are served by children's status in peer groups, a number of hypotheses can be culled from recent conceptual and empirical articles. Among the most widely cited hypotheses (see Ladd, 1988) are that low peer acceptance inhibits children's social learning (e.g., by excluding them from peer-mediated learning opportunities), forces them to occupy low-power or potentially abusive positions in groups (e.g., more exposure to ridicule, victimization), and reduces their sense of belongingness, competence, and self-esteem. A number of findings are consistent with these premises, including those indicating that compared to well-liked peers, rejected children are less likely to extricate themselves from marginal group roles (Coie & Dodge, 1983; Ladd, Price, & Hart, 1990) and are more likely to be victims of peer aggression (Perry, Kusel, & Perry, 1988), to feel lonely in school (Asher, Hymel, & Renshaw, 1984; Asher & Wheeler, 1985), have negative self-perceptions (Boivin & Begin, 1989), and show lower levels of self-confidence (Wheeler & Ladd, 1982).

There is also a sizable body of correlational evidence from prospective and retrospective studies to suggest that low-accepted children are at risk for a variety of adjustment problems at later points in the life span (see Kohlberg, LaCrosse, & Rickes, 1972; Kupersmidt, Coie, & Dodge, 1990; Parker & Asher, 1987). For example, a longitudinal study conducted by Kupersmidt (1983) revealed that children who were neglected by peers in fifth grade had higher levels of truancy in high school, and rejected fifth graders tended to develop higher levels of juvenile delinquency. Not surprisingly, several investigators who have recently analyzed the literature on early social risks (Kupersmidt, Coie, & Dodge, 1990; Parker & Asher, 1987) have concluded that low peer status in childhood is an important antecedent of adjustment problems in adolescence and adulthood.

*Linkages between classroom peer relations and school adjustment*

In this section, we examine the implications of the preceding perspectives on the functions of children's classroom peer relationships for research on early school adjustment. Conceptually, we explore the question of whether differing forms of relations, such as friendship, acquaintanceship, and peer group acceptance make important (and possibly differential) contributions to children's school adjustment. We also examine the relation between theory and data in this domain, and the heuristic value of specific hypotheses.

Our efforts to elucidate the functions of children's classroom peer relations are guided by the ecological (child-by-environment) model we are using to study early school adaptation (see Ladd, 1989). To resummarize, we think that the demands children face as they enter school and progress through their first year of kindergarten will determine the types of provisions they will most need and, in turn, benefit from in their relations with peers. In the paragraphs that follow, we consider some of the demands that children face as they enter school, and the role that classroom peer relations play in children's efforts to cope with these demands.

*Classroom friends and acquaintances.* For most young children, tasks such as separating from parents and entering new schools and classrooms are likely to trigger feelings of wariness and insecurity. One way that children may resolve these feelings is to seek out familiar classmates or form friendships with one or more peers in their classrooms. Seeking out the familiar, or establishing a "secure base," may allow children to feel more comfortable in school, and consequently, enable them to explore and learn more freely in the classroom. Moreover, such a hypothesis would seem to follow well from Schwarz's (1972) and Ispa's (1981) work showing that friends and familiar peers can function as supports for children in novel situations. Recall that studies by Schwarz and Ispa showed that young children displayed less distress and more exploratory behavior in novel surroundings when they were accompanied by a close friend (Schwarz, 1972) or a familiar peer (Ispa, 1981).

In fact, Ladd and Price (1987) found that the number of familiar peers present in children's kindergarten classrooms correlated positively with measures of their initial school adjustment. Data from this study indicated that children who entered kindergarten with familiar peers tended to develop positive attitudes toward school and exhibited lower levels of school avoidance (e.g., absences, requests to see the school nurse) at the beginning of the kindergarten year. Unfortunately, the familiar peers measure employed by Ladd and Price (1987) was a global one, and did not distinguish among the types of peer relations children had with their kindergarten classmates. Familiar peers, as they were defined by this study, consisted of all classmates a child had known prior to school entrance. Thus, it was not possible for the investigators to distinguish between the contributions of familiar peers versus friends.

However, in an extension of the Ladd and Price (1987) investigation, Ladd (1990) further explored the relation between children's peer relationships in new kindergarten classrooms and their school adjustment. Measures included both the number of acquaintances and the number of "prior" friends (i.e., peers who were "close" friends or "other" friends with the child prior to the start of school) who were enrolled in children's kindergarten classrooms at the beginning of the school year. This more differentiated look at the peer composition of children's classrooms showed that only the classroom friendship measures were associated with early school adjustment. Specifically, children's initial attitudes toward school tended to be more positive if they began school with a larger number of "prior" friends in their classrooms. No relation was found between the number of familiar peers or acquaintances in children's classrooms and their attitudes toward school (or any of the other measures of school adjustment). This finding suggests that prior friendships provide important affective benefits for children in the early weeks of the school year by reducing the strangeness of the environment, thus making it seem more familiar and accommodating, in turn, resulting in more positive perceptions of school.

Lack of familiarity with the school environment or separation issues may become of less concern for children once they have completed the initial weeks of kindergarten. Gradually, these "entry" tasks may be replaced by demands that might be characterized as "the everyday business of school." Essentially, as the school year progresses, children must learn to function both independently and collaboratively within a larger classroom "community." As members of this community, they are expected to embrace rather than resist or withdraw from many new learning tasks and activities, accept criticism and feedback and modify their performance accordingly, and conform to a variety of new rules, regulations, and routines.

We contend that friendships in the classroom, particularly *stable* classroom friendships, supply a number of provisions (e.g., emotional support, interpersonal skills, and validation) that may then facilitate the young child's ability to cope with the challenging demands of school. This logic is consistent with that articulated in recent theories about the nature and functions of early friendships. Howes (1988), for example, has argued that stable friendships function as peer "attachments" for young children, and as such, foster not only higher levels of security, but also competence. Parker and Gottman (1989) also emphasize the impact of early friendships on children's coping and adaptation. In their view, developments that emerge in stable friendships, such as complex fantasy play, allow children to explore their emotions (e.g., fears, doubts, anxieties), and defuse everyday frustrations. Further support for this view comes from a study by Newcomb and Brady (1982) in which they showed that affect is mutually regulated in friendships. Newcomb and Brady (1982) contend that this regulation of affect helps children manage their emotions (e.g., anxiety) which, in turn, may have been responsible for the finding that friends perform better than acquaintances on problem-solving tasks that require mutual effort. In addition, as Howes (1983) has argued, maintained friends may also be more receptive and responsive social partners for children. Because of this, children who establish lasting classroom friendships may have ready access to a network of rewarding exchanges, or natural communities of reinforcement. This resource may enable children with stable classroom friendships to view school as an engaging and rewarding environment.

Ladd (1990) found, consistent with this logic, that the potential benefits of prior classroom friendships may be fleeting, unless these relationships are maintained in the school setting. Although the number of prior classroom friendships predicted children's initial school attitudes (i.e., at the second month of kindergarten), they bore little relation to long-term changes in children's school perceptions (i.e., changes in attitudes across the school year). Rather, the results of this study showed that children who maintained their prior friendships over the school year tended to develop more favorable attitudes toward school.

Kindergarten is also a period during which children are subjected to ever-increasing scholastic demands. As preparation for first grade, most kindergarten children are expected to master a "readiness" curriculum that consists of many pre-reading and pre-mathematics skills (e.g., visual-spatial, auditory, language, and quantitative skills and concepts). Many of the lessons that are designed to teach these skills are conducted in small groups and activity centers where children are encouraged to collaborate with peers. In such contexts, children's friends may be the most influential and responsive collaborators in the classroom. Such a view is consistent with those of recent writers (e.g., Bukowski et al., 1991; Furman & Buhrmester, 1985; Howes, 1983, 1988; Parker & Asher, 1989, 1993) who have argued that friends who offer help and guidance, information, instrumental aid, and so forth enhance each other's learning and development.

It is interesting that Ladd (1990) found that children's tendencies to form *new* friendships in kindergarten were associated with gains in scholastic performance over the course of the school year. We reasoned that, by making friends with previously unfamiliar peers in the classroom, children may have formed a friendship with someone whom they shared similar academic interests and skills and, thus expanded the number of persons they could turn to for help-seeking and other forms of academic collaboration.

*Classroom peer acceptance.* As children enter school, they must also negotiate a large and, in most cases, relatively unfamiliar peer group. Children's success at this task, or the level of classroom peer acceptance or rejection they achieve, can be viewed as an indicator of the child's integration and participation in the school culture and classroom peer group (Ladd, 1983, 1988, 1989). Highly accepted children are likely to be more integrated into peer activities in the classroom and on the playground and, thus, feel a greater sense of belongingness, worth, effectance, and well-being. Low-accepted or rejected children tend to be excluded from peer activities and, therefore, are more likely to develop a sense of alienation, discomfort, and incompetence in school. Exclusion from peer activities may also prevent children from participating in a variety of collaborative learning situations with peers and possibly delay or retard the development of interpersonal and academic skills.

Findings from the Ladd (1990) investigation provide some support for these rationales. In addition to friendships, Ladd (1990) also explored linkages between children's classroom peer acceptance and their adjustment to kindergarten over the school year. Results indicated that rejection by one's classmates early in the school year forecasted less favorable school perceptions, higher levels of school avoidance, and lower levels of scholastic readiness by the end of the school year. Supplementary analyses designed to explore the opposite direction of effect (i.e., to determine whether early differences in school adjustment forecasted changes in children's peer acceptance) failed to produce significant findings.

**Future directions**

Thus far, our empirical work suggests that the friendships children possess or develop in classrooms may facilitate their adjustment in this setting. As children enter new or "strange" classrooms, the presence of prior friends may make them feel more secure and, therefore, interested in school. Moreover, by maintaining these friendships or forming new ones, children can continue to receive provisions such as emotional and instrumental support throughout the year as they cope with ever-increasing school demands. In contrast, low peer acceptance or rejection by classmates early in the year appears to function as a stressor in the new school context and may impair many aspects of children's school adjustment.

Although we are encouraged by these early findings, it is clear to us that a number of important issues remain to be addressed. For instance, how we conceptualize and investigate the "contributions" of children's classroom peer relations is one such issue that deserves further attention. Recent writers (e.g., Bukowski & Hoza, 1989) have encouraged investigators to think less about the quantity of children's friendships and more about the quality of these ties (specific relationship provisions). Thus far, we have focused on features such as children's access to friends (i.e., availability of prior friendships, formation of new friendships in the classroom) and the stability of children's classroom friendships. However, the effects of specific features or friendship processes and provisions have received less attention. In fact, very little effort has been devoted to defining the qualities of young children's friendships, especially in school settings, and constructing reliable measures of these functions.

In view of this need, we (Ladd, Kochenderfer, & Coleman, in press) developed a friendship features interview for preschool and kindergarten children. This measure consisted of 24 questions that were adapted from dimensions and items employed with older samples (Bukowski, Boivin, & Hoza, 1991; Parker & Asher, 1993), and was designed to provide information about several friendship *processes* (e.g., validation, aid, disclosure of negative affect, conflict, and exclusivity). Using this measure with a sample of kindergarten children, we found that all five of the friendship processes could be reliably assessed, and processes such as validation and conflict were predictive of children's satisfaction with their friendships, and the stability of these relationships. Furthermore, perceived conflict in friendships was associated with multiple forms of school maladjustment for boys, including higher levels of school loneliness and avoidance and lower levels of school liking and engagement. For both boys and girls, validation and aid forecasted gains in perceived support from classmates, and aid also predicted improvements in children's school attitudes. We hope to use this scale to learn more about the nature of young children's friendships, and to further probe linkages between specific friendship processes and children's school adjustment.

Another important, yet largely unaddressed question is whether the functions served by children's classroom friendships and peer group relations make unique versus overlapping contributions to their school adjustment (see Bukowski & Hoza, 1989; Ladd, 1988). On the one hand, classroom friendships and peer group status can be conceptualized as separate relational systems that make *unique* contributions to school adjustment. Such a model would lead us to expect differential (i.e., independent) "effects" for each type of relation – that is, we would expect friendship and peer status to predict different types of school adjustment outcomes.

On the other hand, friendship and peer status can be conceptualized as different relational systems that serve similar functions and, therefore, yield *overlapping* "effects." Models based on this premise would be supported by evidence indicating that both forms of relation contribute to the same adjustment outcomes. In such cases, the relative contributions of friendship versus peer status become of interest, and may be construed as: redundant (i.e., friendship and status make equal and identical contributions to the same outcome), additive (i.e., both friendship and status contribute to the same outcome, but one makes a larger contribution than the other, or both contribute uniquely), or contingent (i.e., the contribution of friendship depends on how well liked or rejected children are among classmates and vice versa).

Evidence gathered thus far offers some support for both models. That is, there are data to suggest that friendships and peer status make unique *and* overlapping contributions to children's adjustment. Bukowski and Hoza (1989), for example, have shown that friendship and peer status make differential (unique) contributions to adjustment outcomes. In their study of preadolescents, friendship qualities were found to be stronger predictors of affective outcomes such as loneliness than were indices of peer group status. Conversely, children's status in their peer group bore a stronger relation to measures of their self-perceived abilities. Coleman and Ladd (1993) also found that friendships and peer status make differential contributions to the prediction of changes in children's adjustment to kindergarten from one term to the next. Results of their study showed that the number of friends predicted changes in school attitudes (school liking) and anxiety, but peer status did not. Additionally, peer status but not friendship was associated with changes in social dissatisfaction (Coleman, 1993; Coleman & Ladd, 1993).

Other studies suggest that classroom friendships and peer status make overlapping contributions to children's school adjustment. Findings from our own research show that friendship and peer status make additive contributions to certain adjustment outcomes. Specifically, Ladd (1990) found that, in addition to classroom friendship measures, scores indexing children's classroom peer acceptance significantly enhanced the prediction of several types of adjustment criteria, including children's school perceptions, avoidance, and performance. Parker and Asher (1993) reported similar findings in a study that was designed to predict grade-school children's loneliness from measures of their classroom friendships and peer status. Results from Coleman's (1993; Coleman & Ladd, 1993) investigation show that the number of friendships children form makes an additive contribution to the prediction of loneliness. Conversely, peer status emerged as the better predictor of competence-related outcomes, such as children's academic progress and school readiness and teachers' perceptions of children's classroom behavior. Furthermore, Coleman (1993) found that peer status and friendships are redundant predictors of school absences – that is, they accounted for equal (overlapping) amounts of variance in this outcome.

A third issue concerns the validity of our inferences about the impact peer relations have on children's adjustment. Clearly, our interpretations rest upon causal assumptions that require further empirical investigation and support. Conceptually, our efforts to probe the linkage between children's classroom peer relations and their school adjustment has been guided by the hypothesis that relationships affect adjustment. Equally plausible, however, is the hypothesis that variations in children's early school adjustment influence the nature and quality of their classroom peer relations.

Although a number of such linkages might be proposed, several strike us as particularly important, and therefore, worthy of further empirical scrutiny. First, it is possible that children who feel uncomfortable in school, or develop avoidant reactions (e.g., frequent absences) may become emotionally or physically withdrawn from their classmates as potential play and learning partners. Such reactions may become a basis for peer ridicule or rejection, and may reduce children's opportunities to make new friends or maintain existing friendships in the classroom. Similar difficulties may be experienced by children who develop negative school attitudes, or who fail to keep up with peers academically.

Evidence of such relations, although small in magnitude, were obtained in data gathered by Ladd (1990). Specifically, in addition to forecasting changes in school adjustment from measures of classroom peer relations, we also attempted to predict changes in children's peer relations from early indices of school adjustment. These data revealed that children who disliked school, or who tended to avoid it during the early weeks of kindergarten, were less likely to maintain their classroom friendships over the course of the school year.

Clearly, we need to develop more precise and specific theories not only about the functions of children's peer relations, but also about the roles that different types of peer relations play in children's development and adjustment. Moreover, in order for this conceptual work to be fruitful, it seems likely that we must also consider factors such as the types of relationship functions that are available to children at different ages, the value of specific relationship provisions in different contexts or ecologies (e.g., school vs. neighborhood) and, conversely, the potential role that adjustment plays in determining children's access to peer relationships and the provisions they acquire within them.

## References

Asher, S. R., Hymel, S., & Renshaw, P. D. (1984). Loneliness in children. *Child Development, 55*, 1456–1464.

Asher, S. R., & Wheeler, V. A. (1985). Children's loneliness: A comparison of rejected and neglected peer status. *Journal of Consulting and Clinical Psychology, 53*, 500–505.

Becker, J. (1977). A learning analysis of the development of peer-oriented behavior in nine-month-old infants. *Developmental Psychology, 13*, 481–491.

Berndt, T. J. (1989). Contributions of peer relationships to children's development. In T. J. Berndt & G. W. Ladd (Eds.), *Peer relationships in child development.* New York: Wiley & Sons.

Berndt, T. J., & Ladd, G. W. (1989). *Peer relationships in child development.* New York: Wiley & Sons.

Berndt, T. J., & Perry, T. B. (1986). Children's perceptions of friendships as supportive relationships. *Developmental Psychology, 22*, 640–648.

Block, J. (1983). Differential premises arising from differential socialization of the sexes. *Child Development, 54*, 1335–1354.

Bogat, G. A., Jones, J. W., & Jason, L. A. (1980). School transitions: Preventive intervention following an elementary school closing. *Journal of Community Psychology, 8*, 343–352.

Boivin, M., & Begin, G. (1989). Peer status and self-perception among early elementary school children: The case of the rejected children. *Child Development, 60*, 591–596.

Bukowski, W., Boivin, M., & Hoza, B. (1991). The friendship qualities scale: Development and psychometric properties. Unpublished manuscript: Concordia University.

Bukowski, W., & Hoza, B. (1989). Popularity and friendship: Issues in theory, measurement, and outcome. In T. J. Berndt & G. W. Ladd (Eds.), *Peer relationships in child development.* New York: Wiley & Sons.

Bukowski, W., & Hoza, B. (1990, April). *Peer relations and loneliness during early adolescence.* Paper presented at the annual meetings of the Society for Research in Adolescence, Atlanta, GA.

Burhmester, W., & Furman, W. (1987). The development of companionship and intimacy. *Child Development, 58*, 1101–1113.

Coie, J. D., & Dodge, K. A. (1983). Continuities and changes in children's social status: A five-year longitudinal study. *Merrill-Palmer Quarterly, 29*, 261–282.

Coleman, C., & Ladd, G. W. (1993, April). How children who dislike school feel about their classroom peer relationships. Paper presented at the annual meetings of the American Educational Research Association, Atlanta, GA.

Coleman, C. (1993). *Relative contributions of classroom friendship and peer status to children's early school adjustment.* Unpublished master's thesis, University of Illinois at Urbana-Champaign, Champaign, IL.

Cowen, E. L., Lotyczewski, B. S., & Weissberg, R. P. (1984). Risk and resource indicators and their relationship to young children's school adjustment. *American Journal of Community Psychology, 12,* 353–367.

Doyle, A. B., Connolly, J., & Rivest, L. P. (1980). The effect of playmate familiarity on the social interactions of young children. *Child Development, 51,* 217–223.

Dweck, C. S. (1986). Motivational processes affecting learning. *American Psychologist, 41,* 1040–1048.

Epley, S. W. (1974). Reduction of the behavioral effects of aversive stimulation by the presence of companions. *Psychological Bulletin, 81,* 271–283.

Furman, W., & Buhrmester, D. (1985). Children's perceptions of the personal relationships in their social networks. *Developmental Psychology, 21,* 1016–1021.

Garmezy, N., Masten, A., & Tellegen, A. (1984). The study of stress and competence in children: A building block for developmental psychopathology. *Child Development, 55,* 97–111.

Hartup, W. W., & Sancilio, M. F. (1986). Children's friendships. In E. Schopler & G. B. Mesibov (Eds.), *Social behavior in autism.* New York: Plenum.

Hinde, R. A., Titmus, G., Easton, D., & Tamplin, A. (1985). Incidence of "friendship" and behavior toward strong associates versus nonassociates in preschoolers. *Child Development, 56,* 234–245.

Holland, J. V., Kaplan, D. M., & Davis, S. D. (1974). Interschool transfers: A mental health challenge. *Journal of School Health, 64,* 74–79.

Howes, C. (1983). Patterns of friendship. *Child Development, 54,* 1041–1053.

Howes, C. (1988). Peer interaction of young children. *Monographs of the Society for Research in Child Development, 53,* (1, Serial No. 217).

Ispa, J. (1981). Peer support among Soviet day care toddlers. *International Journal Of Behavioral Development, 4,* 255–269.

Jacobson, J. L. (1981). The role of inanimate objects in early peer interaction. *Child Development, 52,* 618–626.

Kohlberg, L., LaCrosse, J., & Rickes, D. (1972). The predictability of adult mental health from childhood. In B. Wolman (Ed.), *Manual of child psychopathology.* New York: McGraw-Hill.

Kupersmidt, J. B. (1983, April). *Predicting delinquency and academic problems from childhood peer status.* Presented at the biennial meeting of the Society for Research in Child Development, Detroit.

Kupersmidt, J. B., Coie, J. D., & Dodge, K. A. (1990). The role of poor peer relationships in the development of disorder. In S. R. Asher & J. D. Coie (Eds.), *Peer rejection in childhood.* New York: Cambridge University Press.

Ladd, G. W. (1983). Social networks of popular, average, and rejected children in school settings. *Merrill-Palmer Quarterly,* (Invitational Issue), 29, 283–307.

Ladd, G. W. (1988). Friendship patterns and peer status during early and middle childhood. *Journal of Developmental and Behavioral Pediatrics, 9,* 229–238.

Ladd, G. W. (1989). Children's social competence and social supports: Precursors of early school adjustment? In B. Schneider, G. Attili, J. Nadel, & R. Weissberg (Eds.), *Social competence in developmental perspective* (pp. 277–292). Amsterdam: Kluwer Academic Publishers.

Ladd, G. W. (1990). Having friends, keeping friends, making friends, and being liked by peers in the classroom: Predictors of children's early school adjustment? *Child Development, 61,* 1081–1100.

Ladd, G. W., & Coleman, C. (1993). Young children's peer relationships: Forms, features, and functions. In B. Spodek (Ed.), *Handbook of research on the education of young children* (pp. 57–76). New York, NY: Macmillan Publishing Co.

Ladd, G. W., & Golter, B. S. (1988). Parent's initiation and monitoring of children's peer contacts: Predictive of children's peer relations in nonschool and school settings? *Developmental Psychology, 24,* 109–117.

Ladd, G. W., & Hart, C. H. (1992). Creating informal play opportunities: Are parents and preschoolers' initiations related to children's competence with peers? *Developmental Psychology, 28*, 1179–1187.

Ladd, G. W., Hart, C. H., Wadsworth, E. M., & Golter, B. S. (1988). Preschoolers' peer networks in nonschool settings: Relationship to family characteristics and school adjustment. In S. Salzinger, J. Antrobus, & M. Hammer (Eds.), *Social networks of children, adolescents, and college students*. Hillsdale, NJ: Erlbaum.

Ladd, G. W., Kochenderfer, B. J., & Coleman, C. (in press). The friendship features interview for young children. *Child Development*.

Ladd, G. W., & Price, J. M. (1986). Promoting children's cognitive and social competence: The relation between parents' perceptions of task difficulty and children's perceived and actual competence. *Child Development, 57*, 446–460.

Ladd, G. W., & Price, J. M. (1987). Predicting children's social and school adjustment following the transition from preschool to kindergarten. *Child Development, 58*, 1168–1189.

Ladd, G. W., Price, J. M., & Hart, C. H. (1990). Preschoolers' behavioral orientations and patterns of peer contact: Predictive of social status? In S. R. Asher and J. D. Coie (Eds.), *Peer rejection in childhood*. New York: Cambridge University Press.

Ladd, G. W., Profilet, S., & Hart, C. H. (1992). Parents' management of children's peer relations: Facilitating and supervising children's activities in the peer culture. In R. D. Parke and G. W. Ladd (Eds.), *Family–peer relationships: Modes of linkage* (pp. 215–253). Hillsdale, NJ: Erlbaum.

Lewis, M., Young, G., Brooks, J., & Michaelson, L. (1975). The beginning of friendship. In M. Lewis & L. A. Rosenblum (Eds.), *Friendship and peer relations*. New York: Wiley & Sons.

Masters, J. C., & Furman, W. C. (1981). Popularity, individual friendship selections, and specific peer interaction among children. *Developmental Psychology, 17*, 344–350.

Mueller, E., & Brenner, J. (1977). The origins of social skills and interaction among playgroup toddlers. *Child Development, 48*, 854–861.

Newcomb, A. F., & Brady, J. E. (1982). Mutuality in boys' friendship selections. *Child Development, 53*, 392–395.

Parker, J. G., & Asher, S. R. (1987). Peer acceptance and later interpersonal adjustment: Are low-accepted children at risk? *Psychological Bulletin, 102*, 357–389.

Parker, J. G., & Asher, S. R. (1989). Significance of peer relationship problems in childhood. In B. Schneider, G. Attili, J. Nadel, & R. Weissberg (Eds.), *Social competence in developmental perspective* (pp. 5–24). Amsterdam: Kluwer Academic Publishers.

Parker, J. G., & Asher, S. R. (1993). Friendship and friendship quality in middle childhood: Links with peer group acceptance and feelings of loneliness and social dissatisfaction. *Developmental Psychology, 29*, 611–621.

Parker, J. G., & Gottman, J. M. (1989). Social and emotional development in a relational context: Friendship interaction from early childhood to adolescence. In T. J. Berndt & G. W. Ladd (Eds.), *Peer relationships in child development*. New York: Wiley & Sons.

Perry, D. G., Kusel, S. J., & Perry, L. C. (1988). Victims of peer aggression. *Developmental Psychology, 24*, 807–814.

Price, J. M., & Ladd, G. W. (1986). Assessment of children's friendships: Implications for social competence and social adjustment. In R. J. Prinz (Ed.), *Advances in behavioral assessment of children and families, Vol. 2*. Greenwich, CT: JAI Press.

Ross, H. S., & Lollis, S. P. (1989). A social relations analysis of toddler peer relationships. *Child Development, 60*, 1082–1091.

Sandler, I. N., & Ramsay, T. B. (1980). Dimensional analysis of children's stressful life events. *American Journal of Community Psychology, 8*, 285–302.

Scholtz, G. J., & Ellis, M. J. (1975). Repeated exposure to objects and peers in a play setting. *Journal of Experimental Child Psychology, 19*, 448–455.

Schwarz, J. C. (1972). Effects of peer familiarity on the behavior of preschoolers in a novel situation. *Journal of Personality and Social Psychology, 24*, 276–284.

Sharabany, R., Gershoni, R., Hofman, J. E. (1981). Girlfriend, boyfriend: Age and sex differences in intimate friendship. *Developmental Psychology, 17*, 800–808.

Stevenson, H. W., Parker, T., Wilkinson, A., Hegion, A., & Fish, E. (1976). Longitudinal study of individual differences in cognitive development and scholastic development. *Journal of Educational Psychology, 68*, 377–400.

Weiss, R. (1974). The provisions of social relationships. In Z. Rubin (Ed.), *Doing unto others* (pp. 17–26). Englewood Cliffs, NJ: Prentice-Hall.

Wheeler, V. A., & Ladd, G. W. (1982). Assessment of children's self-efficacy for social interactions with peers. *Developmental Psychology, 18*, 795–805.

Zajonc, R. B. (1986). Attitudinal effects of mere exposure. *Journal of Social and Personality Psychology Monograph Supplement, 9* (2, Part 2), 1–27.

# 15 Exploring the effects of friendship quality on social development

*Thomas J. Berndt*

Throughout human history, writers have extolled the benefits of friendships for individuals and society. Philosophers and essayists have asserted that close friendships not only provide individuals with companionship and support, but also contribute to the moral character of individuals and therefore promote stability and justice in the social order (see van Vlissingen, 1970). Yet until recently, all writers focused exclusively on the friendships of adults. None considered the friendships of children and adolescents.

Empirical research on children's friendships began around 1900, when child psychology emerged as a distinct discipline (e.g., Monroe, 1898). The earliest studies were largely atheoretical. Specific hypotheses about the effects of friendships were not presented until several decades later, and these hypotheses were virtually ignored by most researchers until the 1970s. Since then, both theories and research on children's friendships have blossomed. Even so, many questions about the features and effects of friendships have not been answered.

In this chapter, I explore the effects of friendship quality on the social development of children and adolescents. My goal is not to provide an exhaustive review of the literature, but to evaluate the strategies that researchers have used to investigate these effects. When examining the strategies, I will use three phrases repeatedly: friendship features, friendship quality, and the effects of friendship. These phrases are common in the literature, but not all writers define them equivalently. My definitions relate to the major themes of the chapter, so I will introduce those themes as I define the terms.

The features of a friendship are its attributes or characteristics. Some examples of friendship features are intimacy, companionship, and conflict. As the examples imply, every friendship has multiple features. The same friend may be an intimate confidant, a companion in activities, and an opponent in conflicts. The examples also imply that friendships have both positive and negative features. The term *feature* is useful partly because its connotation is neutral, so it can refer to both positive and negative attributes of a friendship.

346

Friendships vary in their features, and the variations in different features are not independent. Friends who have a more intimate relationship, for example, also tend to spend more time as companions in activities. The first theme of the chapter is that the variations in friendship features can be placed on two broad dimensions, one for positive and one for negative features.

Many researchers have used the term *qualities* to define what I have called features (see, e.g., the chapters in this volume by Aboud & Mendelson, by Furman, and by Park). Unlike *feature*, the term *quality* is not affectively neutral. One definition of quality is the degree of excellence of something. Thus people talk about the quality of American cars, of different brands of ice cream, and of other products. I will refer to the quality of a friendship in a similar way.

The second theme of the chapter is that the positive and negative dimensions of friendship features, taken together, define the quality of a friendship. Friendships are higher in quality when they have more positive features, such as greater intimacy. They are lower in quality when they have more negative features, such as more intense conflicts. The friendships highest in quality are like those perfect or ideal friendships described in the writings of Aristotle, Cicero, and other writers of antiquity.

My final phrase, *the effects of friendship*, refers more specifically to the effects of friendship quality. Both classical writers and modern researchers have assumed that friendships higher in quality have more beneficial effects on the persons involved. Yet what, exactly, does it mean to say that friendships affect people? A simple definition is that something affects something else when the first thing has an influence on, or causes a change in, the second.

The final theme of the chapter is that researchers have too often settled for indirect evidence of the effects of friendship. Typically, researchers have correlated some measure of friendship quality with measures of the friends' self-esteem, social behavior, or psychological adjustment (see Berndt & Savin-Williams, 1993; Hartup, 1993). Significant correlations are consistent with the hypothesis that friendship quality affects individuals' characteristics, but other interpretations of the correlations are possible. Longitudinal studies allow more direct tests of hypotheses about cause and effect. Later, I will describe a longitudinal study of the effects of friendship quality on adolescents' self-esteem and school adjustment.

The chapter begins with a summary of two theories that sparked the initial research on children's friendships. In the next section, I discuss steps researchers might follow when studying the effects of friendship quality. Those steps provide the framework for a review of recent research. Then I evaluate current strategies for exploring the effects of friendship quality and suggest some alternatives.

## Early theories of the effects of friendship

The work of two theorists provided the foundation for the growing interest in friendships during the 1970s. Jean Piaget presented several developmental theories during his long career. Most relevant to children's friendships is the theory of moral development in his early book, *The Moral Judgment of the Child* (Piaget, 1932/1965). Harry Stack Sullivan presented a neo-Freudian theory of psychiatry in several sets of lectures, most of which were published after his death. His best-known statements about friendship are contained in a single chapter of *The Interpersonal Theory of Psychiatry* (Sullivan, 1953).

During the 1980s, several writers modified and extended Sullivan's theory (e.g., Buhrmester, this volume; Buhrmester & Furman, 1986), or proposed an integration of Piaget's and Sullivan's theories (Youniss, 1980). The focus of this chapter is on the original theories, not on the newer variants. My goal is to highlight Piaget's and Sullivan's assumptions about the features of friendship, the relation of these features to friendship quality, and the effects of friendship quality on social development.

### Piaget on reciprocity norms and love

Piaget's theory of moral development was the first formal theory to deal with children's friendships, but he did not refer to friendship directly. Instead, he described how social relations with peers foster the development of an autonomous morality. Unlike most other scholars, Piaget viewed parents as a largely negative influence on children's moral development. According to Piaget, children respect their parents' power and authority, but this respect is irrational because children do not understand the reasons for their parents' rules. He believed that such irrational respect cannot foster a morality based on justice and benevolence toward others.

By contrast, Piaget described social relations in children's peer groups as inherently egalitarian. Children lack the power to compel their peers to obey them, so they must cooperate with peers if they want to reach their goals. Cooperation is impossible without mutual respect, so children must respect each other as equals. In Piaget's view, cooperation and mutual respect depend, in turn, on children's acceptance of reciprocity norms. That is, children believe that they can do to their peers what their peers do to them and vice versa.

In other words, Piaget identified three features of social relations among peers. Cooperation is the standard for interactions among peers. Mutual respect is the attitude that promotes cooperation. Reciprocity norms state the principles that children accept as legitimate for peer interactions. These three features, taken together, define the central quality of peer relations, which is that peers see themselves as equals. For Piaget, less egalitarian relationships, such as those between older and younger children, have the defining features of ideal peer relations less often and, therefore, are lower in quality.

Although the acceptance of reciprocity norms was only one feature of ideal peer relations, Piaget gave it special attention. He did so because developmental changes in reciprocity norms were central to his hypotheses about moral development. Piaget argued that young children see reciprocity norms as a requirement for a satisfactory social life. One 8-year-old said, for example, that children should not tell lies because "if everyone lied, no one would know where they were" (Piaget, 1932/1965, p. 171). In more abstract terms, unless people are honest with each other, a stable social order is impossible.

Nevertheless, Piaget argued that simple reciprocity norms are not an adequate basis for morality. First, reciprocity norms can increase children's aggressive behavior by encouraging them to retaliate against peers whom they think have injured them. Second, reciprocity norms can reduce children's prosocial behavior by discouraging them from helping or sharing with anyone who has not previously helped or shared with them. Piaget expressed these concerns when he wrote that a morality based on reciprocity "will not take one very far, since the best adult consciences ask for something more than the practice of mere reciprocity. Charity and the forgiving of injuries done to one are, in the eyes of many, far greater things than sheer equality [or reciprocity]" (1932/1965, p. 323).

Piaget then argued that a developmental change occurs in the content of reciprocity norms. He described the change by saying,

> the child begins by simply practicing reciprocity. . . . Once he has grown accustomed to this form of equilibrium in his actions, his behavior is altered from within, its form reacting, as it were, upon its content. What is regarded as just is no longer merely reciprocal action, but primarily behavior that admits of indefinitely sustained reciprocity. The motto "Do as you would be done by," thus comes to replace the conception of crude equality. (p. 323)

Piaget summarized the change by saying, "Without leaving the sphere of reciprocity, generosity . . . allies itself to justice pure and simple" (p. 324).

Piaget's hypotheses about reciprocity norms are intriguing, but later researchers have differed greatly in their reactions to them. A few researchers have taken the hypotheses as the basis for a general theory of social development (e.g., Youniss, 1980). Most researchers, however, have focused on other aspects of Piaget's theory of moral development (but see Berndt, 1977, 1979). Some, in particular, have reexamined Piaget's findings that young children focus on the consequences of an actor's behavior when evaluating the actor, whereas older children focus on the actor's intentions (Rest, 1983).

An analysis of the structure of Piaget's theory helps to explain why researchers have differed in their reactions. Although Piaget assumed that reciprocity norms govern peer interactions, he considered the equality in peer relationships to be more central to moral development. But he never showed through empirical research that peer relationships are based on equality. In addition, he never directly examined the connections between peer relations and moral development. His hypothesis about the process by which peer interactions affect the development of moral principles is provocative, but he did not propose a research strategy to test the hypothesis.

Piaget's theory is still valuable for its description of important features of peer relations, such as cooperation (see Hartup, this volume). Piaget also suggested the significance for friendship quality of friends' acceptance of one another as equals. Research cited later has confirmed that friendships are lower in quality when the friends refuse to recognize one another as equals.

## Sullivan on love and friendship

In *The Interpersonal Theory of Psychiatry*, Sullivan argued that friendships are essential at one period in development, the years just before and during adolescence. According to Sullivan, true love first appears in children's relationships with a friend or chum. His statement of this hypothesis is worth quoting in full:

> All of you who have children are sure that your children love you; when you say that, you are expressing a pleasant illusion. But if you will look very closely at one of your children when he finally finds a chum – somewhere between eight-and-a-half and ten – you will discover something very different in the relationship – namely, that your child begins to develop a real sensitivity to what matters to another person. . . . Thus the developmental epoch of preadolescence is marked by the coming of the integrative tendencies which, when they are completely developed, we call love, or, to say it another way, by the manifestation of the need for interpersonal intimacy. (Sullivan, 1953, pp. 245–246)

In this quotation, Sullivan asserts that intimacy is a defining feature of a true friendship. He defined intimacy as closeness, "without specifying that which is close other than the persons" (p. 246). He also said that a true friendship involves collaboration, interactions in which friends try to adjust their behavior to meet the other's needs. According to Sullivan, intimacy and collaboration between friends contribute to the enhancement of self-esteem.

Sullivan contrasted the intimacy of true friendships with the competition between peers that prevails during the early school years. He assumed that competition between peers is natural, but that it will negatively affect personality development if it becomes a consistent interactional style. He also suggested that the development of intimate friendships reduces the competitiveness of preadolescents. In sum, Sullivan viewed friendships as high in quality when they were high in intimacy and collaboration but low in competition.

Sullivan's hypotheses about the central features of peer relationships differ from those of Piaget. Sullivan and Piaget also differ in their hypotheses about the effects of these relationships, with Piaget focusing on moral development and Sullivan on personality development. Moreover, Sullivan believed that peer interactions could have negative effects on development, if children were highly competitive, whereas Piaget wrote only about the positive effects of peer relationships.

In one critical respect, however, Sullivan's and Piaget's theories are comparable. Sullivan was a practicing psychiatrist and a teacher rather than a researcher, so he did not study the friendships of children and adolescents directly. Like Piaget, he did not propose a strategy for testing his hypotheses about the effects of friendship quality. The absence of an empirical base for the theory probably delayed researchers' acceptance of Sullivan's ideas.

Sullivan's most important contribution was in identifying intimacy as a critical feature of friendship, especially as children move into adolescence. Another important contribution was his hypothesis that intimate friendships increase adolescents' self-esteem. This hypothesis has provided direction for many researchers. Yet as indicated later, confirming the hypothesis has not been easy.

## Questions for research on the effects of friendship quality

My purpose in looking backward at Piaget's and Sullivan's theories was to see more clearly how current research can move forward. The look backward suggests four steps that researchers should follow when exploring the effects of friendship quality on social development. These steps can be stated most simply as questions. Taken together, the questions define a strategy for research on friendship quality.

1. Which features of a friendship are most strongly related to its quality? At the first step in research, the primary question is how friendships should be described. Several years ago, Hinde (1979) argued that description is the first step in all science, but that researchers who study interpersonal relationships have often tried to bypass it. Writers like Piaget and Sullivan set the example by defining features of peer relationships without studying these relationships systematically. Yet without systematic research, judging the accuracy of these writers' descriptions is difficult.

Hinde (1979) offered a taxonomy of features of interpersonal relationships, but apparently no researcher studying children's friendships has used his taxonomy explicitly. One reason may be that researchers did not want to document all the features of friendships – they wanted to focus on features that are most strongly related to friendship quality. Some researchers have asked children and adolescents to describe their best friendships, and then treated the features mentioned most often as defining the quality of friendships (e.g., Berndt, 1986a). Others have defined features a priori, and then examined the relations of these features to children's satisfaction with the friendship (e.g., Aboud & Mendelson, this volume). Fortunately, the different methods have yielded similar results. The lists of features presented by various researchers overlap greatly (Furman, this volume).

Once researchers have generated an acceptable list of friendship features, they must decide how to measure the variations in these features. For example, Sullivan suggested that personality development is impaired when adolescents lack intimate friendships. To test this hypothesis, researchers must be able to judge which adolescents have more and less intimate friendships.

One option would be to observe friends' conversations and record the frequency of their intimate disclosures to one another (e.g., Gottman & Mettetal, 1986). Some important features of friendship are not directly observable, however. For example, trying to judge adolescents' trust in friends by observing the adolescents' behavior will not work. The only way to judge adolescents' trust in friends is to ask them about it directly (Hestenes, Berndt, & Gruen, 1993). In most previous studies, adolescents' responses to questions during interviews or on questionnaires were the basis for measures of friendship features (see Furman, this volume). Therefore, only measures obtained by this method are discussed in the chapter.

As indicated earlier, the measures of various features of friendship are likely to be correlated. Both Piaget and Sullivan assumed that the important features of friendships are interlocking. Both writers had an implicit construct of friendship quality that subsumed several features. Apparently, they also assumed that friendship quality was unidimensional. These assumptions must be empirically evaluated. Testing the assumptions and creating reliable measures of friendship quality would answer the first question and complete the first step in the proposed research strategy.

2. Is the quality of children's friendships related to their social development? If so, with what measures of social development are measures of friendship quality correlated? The second step in this research strategy is to see whether friendship quality is correlated with specific facets of social development. If friendship quality affects children's moral development and self-esteem, as Piaget and Sullivan assumed, then correlations among the measures of these constructs would be expected.

Correlational data are not sufficient for testing hypotheses about the effects of friendship quality. When significant correlations are found, the direction of causality could be opposite to that assumed. For example, children's self-esteem could affect their ability to form high-quality friendships rather than vice versa (Savin-Williams & Berndt, 1990). But if measures of friendship quality are not correlated with self-esteem, the hypothesis that high-quality friendships enhance self-esteem becomes less credible. Of course, drawing conclusions from the lack of significant findings violates the rule against affirming the null hypothesis. Nevertheless, repeated failures to find a significant correlation between two measures that, in theory, are causally related must certainly weaken a causal hypothesis. Also, direct tests of causal hypotheses are difficult, so evaluating whether the correlations between measures are consistent with the hypotheses is a useful step in a larger research strategy.

3. Is the quality of children's friendships related to changes in aspects of their social development? The third step in the proposed research strategy is to assess the effects of friendship quality with a longitudinal design. With longitudinal data, researchers can see if variations in friendship quality at one time predict the changes over time in children's social development. If so, hypotheses that friendship quality affects social development are strengthened.

4. Besides longitudinal designs, what other approaches can be used to assess the effects of friendship quality? This question is more open-ended than the previous ones. When testing causal hypotheses, developmental researchers have probably relied more heavily on longitudinal designs than on other approaches. But longitudinal designs have limitations that are especially important when exploring the effects of friendship quality. Later, I will describe these limitations and suggest some alternative approaches. If different approaches yield comparable findings regarding the effects of friendship quality, then researchers can draw conclusions with greater confidence.

My research program has progressed through the first three steps that I have outlined. As I discuss those steps in more detail, I will summarize my own and other researchers' findings. When I reach the final step, I will say less about what has been done than what could be done.

## How do friendship features relate to friendship quality?

During the 1970s and early 1980s, many researchers examined the features of friendships by asking children and adolescents to describe their conceptions of friendship (see Berndt, 1986a; Youniss, 1980). The findings from different studies were comparable, even when researchers began with different theoretical assumptions. This kind of research had three limitations, however.

First, investigators often described only the positive features of friendship. This bias probably resulted from the emphasis on positive features in both Piaget's and Sullivan's theories, and in classical writings on friendship. Also, some researchers have viewed children's friendships as analogous to supportive social relationships among adults (Cohen & Wills, 1985; Sarason & Sarason, 1985). These researchers naturally emphasized the positive or supportive features of friendships.

When researchers broadened their perspective and asked about problems in friendship, they found that children reported conflicts, unpleasant competition, and rivalry with friends (Berndt, 1986a; Youniss, 1980). When researchers who studied adults' relationships asked more balanced questions, they discovered that many supportive relationships are sources of significant problems for people (e.g., Rook, 1984). These data show that researchers portray friendships inaccurately when they "accentuate the positive and eliminate the negative." To describe friendships accurately, researchers must give equal attention to the positive and negative features of these relationships.

The second limitation of the early research was the neglect of important features of friendship. One of these features was equality. Piaget assumed that all peers think of each other as equals. By contrast, observations of friends' interactions have shown that equality is not a given in friendship: It must be achieved (Berndt, 1986b). Children and adolescents often compete with friends, and the outcomes of the competition show whether they can maintain a belief that they are equals. Competition is most common in sports, but friends also compete in academics and in other arenas. Of course, a competition with a friend may be enjoyable, but if one friend acts as if he or she is superior to the other, the friendship may be threatened.

Even when competition is not involved, interactions with friends are not always egalitarian. For example, one friend may try to dominate or boss the other around (Youniss, 1980). Thus preserving equality between friends can be a constant challenge. Tensions over equality must be viewed as another negative feature of friendships.

Third, researchers have often assumed that friendships have many distinct features. One investigator classified children's ideas about friendship into more than 20 categories (Bigelow, 1977). In my research, however, measures of various features of friendship have been strongly correlated. In one study (Berndt & Perry, 1986), students in the second, fourth, sixth, and eighth grades reported on six features of friendship: intimacy, loyalty, prosocial behavior, conflicts, play or association, and attachment/self-esteem support.

At the second, fourth, and sixth grades, factor analyses of the scores on the six features yielded only one strong factor. This result implies that the students viewed their friendships as varying on a single dimension of quality. At the eighth grade, the measure of conflicts with friends loaded on a factor separate from that for positive features. In later studies (e.g., Berndt & Keefe, 1993), both conflicts and inequality in friendships were assessed. Analyses of the data always revealed two factors, one for positive features and one for negative fea-

Table 15.1. *Mean scores for features of students' very best friendships reciprocated as very best, second, or third friendships*

| Friends' report of friendship closeness | | Positive features | | Negative features | |
|---|---|---|---|---|---|
| | | Students' reports | Friends' reports | Students' reports | Friends' reports |
| Very best | *M* | 3.25 | 3.25 | .69 | .69 |
| (*N* = 40) | *SD* | (.44) | (.44) | (.51) | (.51) |
| Second | *M* | 3.13 | 2.86 | .42 | .65 |
| (*N* = 10) | *SD* | (.71) | (.53) | (.53) | (.37) |
| Third | *M* | 3.09 | 2.18 | .65 | 1.59 |
| (*N* = 10) | *SD* | (.69) | (.75) | (.78) | (.96) |

tures. These analyses suggest that positive features of friendship define one dimension of quality, and negative features define a second dimension. The two dimensions are only weakly correlated.

I conclude that friendship quality is best measured by asking children or adolescents to describe the positive and the negative features of their friendships, and then creating composite scores for positive features and negative features. Some writers regard questions about the dimensions of friendship quality as still open (see Furman, this volume); others argue for more than two dimensions of quality (e.g., Parker & Asher, 1993). The correlations among measures of multiple dimensions are always high, however. These measures also have similar correlations with other measures. Thus evidence for the discriminant validity of these multiple dimensions is lacking.

My conclusion does not resolve all issues concerning the assessment of friendship quality. Two more issues must be discussed briefly. First, every friendship involves two persons, who may disagree about the quality of their relationship. Data from a recent study suggest that such discrepancies are greatest when two friends disagree about how the friendship between them compares with their other friendships. The study included seventh graders who named their very best friend, their second-closest friend, and their third-closest friend. Then they described the features of these friendships.

Some students named very best friends who reciprocated their nomination. Most of these friends said that the student who nominated them was also *their* very best friend, but some said that student was only their second- or third-closest friend. Table 15.1 shows how the students and the friends in the different groups described their friendship.

The students' reports of friendship quality were related to how close they viewed the friendship to be, not how their friends viewed it. Students rated the friendship with the peer they named as a very best friend as high in positive features and low in negative features, even when the peer had said that the friendship was only his or her third closest. By contrast, the friends' ratings were affected by how close they judged the friendship to be. The friends rated the friendship as having more positive and fewer negative features when they considered it as their very best friendship rather than their second or third closest.

Such asymmetries in friendships are a reality, and should not be surprising. Like other relationships, a friendship may be more significant to one person than to his or her partner. Friendships are supportive relationships (Berndt, 1989; Furman & Buhrmester, 1992), but the support that one person provides to another does not always equal the support that the person receives from the other. Researchers must accept these asymmetries when assessing friendship quality (Furman, 1984, this volume). That is, researchers should let the child who presumably is affected by a friendship be the judge of its quality.

The second issue of assessment concerns the number of best friends that adolescents have. Sullivan's (1953) writings on friendships have sometimes been misinterpreted as suggesting that an adolescent can have only one best friend. Yet as indicated earlier, most adolescents name several best friends (Hartup, 1993); the quality of all these friendships can be expected to affect their social development. Of course, assessing multiple friendships is more difficult than assessing only one. In my research (Berndt & Keefe, 1993; Berndt & Miller, 1993), measures of multiple friendships had stronger correlations with other measures than did measures of one friendship, even when that was an adolescent's very best friendship. Still, the results were similar for the two types of measures. Therefore, the choice between the two should not strongly influence the conclusions drawn from research.

## What are the correlates of variations in friendship quality?

The second step in the proposed research strategy is to examine the correlates of variations in friendship quality. Many researchers have found significant correlations between the quality of adolescents' friendships and their self-esteem and social behavior (see Berndt & Savin-Williams, 1993; Hartup, 1993; Newcomb & Bagwell, this volume). For example, Kristelle Miller and I (Berndt & Miller, 1993) individually interviewed 153 seventh graders and asked them about the features of up to three best friendships. Then we created composite scores for positive and negative features based on students' descriptions of all their friendships. We assessed various facets of students' self-esteem with Harter's (1985) Self-perception Profile for Children. We assessed their school adjustment from their reports about the value they attached to their schooling and

Table 15.2. *Correlations of friendship features with self-esteem and school adjustment*

|  | Positive features | Negative features |
|---|---|---|
| *Self-esteem* |  |  |
| Scholastic competence | .21** | −.18* |
| Social acceptance | .27*** | −.14 |
| Athletic competence | .10 | −.04 |
| Physical appearance | .14 | −.11 |
| Behavioral conduct | .21** | −.25** |
| Global self-worth | .25** | −.15 |
| *School adjustment* |  |  |
| School value (self-report) | .24** | −.21** |
| Involvement (self-report) | .14 | −.22** |
| Involvement (teacher rating) | .11 | −.08 |
| Disruption (teacher rating) | −.05 | .14 |

$*p < .05.; **p < .01.; ***p < .001.$

their positive involvement in classroom activities. In addition, two of the students' teachers reported on their involvement and their disruptive behavior at school.

Students' reports on their friendships were significantly correlated with their self-esteem and school adjustment (Table 15.2). Students whose friendships had more positive features had higher scores on four subscales for self-esteem and valued their schooling more. Students whose friendships had more negative features had lower scores on two subscales for self-esteem. According to their self-reports, they valued school less and were less involved in school.

Keunho Keefe and I (Berndt & Keefe, 1993) did a similar study with nearly 300 seventh and eighth graders. The new study had a short-term longitudinal design, with assessments in both the fall and the spring of a school year. We also assessed the quality of students' friendships with a questionnaire rather than an interview. Again, students described the positive and negative features of up to three close friendships. Table 15.3 shows the correlations of the scores based on multiple friendships with self-esteem and school adjustment.

As in the first study, students whose friendships had more positive features had higher self-esteem and were more involved in school. Students whose friendships had more negative features had lower self-esteem. They were especially likely to perceive their conduct as poor and their global self-worth as low. In addition, they reported less involvement and more disruption at school than did students whose friendships had fewer negative features.

Correlations like these strengthen hypotheses about the benefits of supportive

Table 15.3. *Correlations of friendship features with self-esteem and school adjustment at each time*

|  | Positive features | | Negative features | |
|---|---|---|---|---|
|  | Fall | Spring | Fall | Spring |
| *Self-esteem* | | | | |
| Scholastic competence | .14* | .12* | −.12* | −.07 |
| Social acceptance | .33*** | .28*** | −.10 | −.12* |
| Athletic competence | .02 | −.06 | .01 | −.04 |
| Physical appearance | .06 | .02 | −.17** | −.11 |
| Behavioral conduct | .17** | .16** | −.24*** | −.26*** |
| Global self-worth | .16** | .18** | −.27*** | −.20*** |
| *School adjustment* | | | | |
| Involvement (self-report) | .24*** | .24*** | −.11* | −.17** |
| Involvement (teacher rating) | .21*** | .20*** | −.11 | −.04 |
| Disruption (self-report) | −.06 | −.08 | .29*** | .28*** |
| Disruption (teacher rating) | −.01 | −.01 | .17** | .06 |

$*p < .05.; **p < .01.; ***p < .001.$

friendships and the costs of troubled friendships. Yet as I noted earlier, high self-esteem and a good adjustment to school could make it easier for students to form good friendships. In short, the direction of causality could be from psychological adjustment to friendship quality rather than the reverse. To choose between these alternatives, more direct tests of the effects of friendship are needed.

### Does friendship quality predict changes in self-esteem and behavior?

To examine the effect of one variable on another, some separation of the presumed cause from the presumed effect is needed. Longitudinal designs make this separation possible. They therefore constitute the third step in exploring the effects of friendship quality. Longitudinal data make it possible to see if variations in friendship quality predict the changes over time in any facet of social development (cf. Dubow et al., 1991). The short-term longitudinal design of Berndt and Keefe (1993) allowed us to do analyses of this kind.

The measures of self-esteem and school adjustment in the spring were the criteria in multiple regression analyses with the corresponding fall measures as the first predictors. Then measures of friendship quality were entered if they accounted for a significant amount of the remaining variance. Such analyses

Table 15.4. *Beta weights for predictors of students' self-esteem and school adjustment in the spring*

|  | Corresponding | Fall friendships | |
|  | Fall measure | Positive features | Negative features |
|---|---|---|---|
| *Self-esteem* |  |  |  |
| Scholastic competence | .70*** | .03 | −.01 |
| Social acceptance | .71*** | .04 | −.07 |
| Athletic competence | .81*** | −.11*** | −.03 |
| Physical appearance | .75*** | −.06 | .03 |
| Behavioral conduct | .75*** | .03 | −.08 |
| Global self-worth | .67*** | .00 | .03 |
| *School adjustment* |  |  |  |
| Involvement (self-report) | .62*** | .07 | −.06 |
| Involvement (teacher rating) | .82*** | .01 | .03 |
| Disruption (self-report) | .62*** | −.02 | .16** |
| Disruption (teacher rating) | .83*** | −.02 | −.03 |

$*p < .05.; **p < .01.; ***p < .001.$

show whether friendship quality predicts scores for self-esteem and school adjustment that are controlled for variations in fall scores.

Table 15.4 summarizes the results. Most obvious is the high continuity in self-esteem and school adjustment during the school year. The large beta weights for the fall measures indicate that students high in self-esteem and school adjustment in the fall were usually high on the same measures in the spring. Thus individual differences in self-esteem and school adjustment were quite stable during the year.

Friendship quality was a significant predictor of changes in only two measures of self-esteem and school adjustment. The strongest effect was that of negative friendship features on self-reported disruption. With fall scores controlled, students who had more negative interactions with friends in the fall reported that they were more disruptive in the spring. This result suggests that students who had trouble getting along with their best friends became more troublesome in class as the school year progressed.

The other significant effect was that of positive friendship features on perceived athletic competence. The negative beta weight implies that students with more positive friendships in the fall perceived their athletic competence to be lower in the spring, with fall scores for athletic competence controlled. That is, students with better friendships showed a decrease during the year in their perceived athletic competence.

Finally, having friendships with more positive features did not enhance adolescents' self-esteem or school adjustment. These results are not consistent with widely accepted hypotheses about the benefits of friendship, but other researchers have reported similar findings (e.g., Dubow et al., 1991; Hirsch & Dubois, 1991; Vernberg, 1990). The consistent failure of researchers to obtain support for plausible hypotheses about friendship quality requires an explanation. I believe the explanation lies in the limitations of longitudinal research.

## Are there better ways to evaluate the effects of friendship quality?

Current evidence suggests that the longitudinal approach to testing hypotheses about the effects of friendship quality should be reexamined. Table 15.4 suggests one reason why hypotheses about the predictors of changes in self-esteem and adjustment are difficult to confirm. These variables do not change greatly, even over periods of several months. Most of the reliable variance in these measures is captured by their continuity over time. The fall measures of friendship quality predict little of the remaining variance, but measures of other constructs might not do a better job of predicting such small changes.

How, then, should the two significant effects in Table 15.4 be interpreted? The effect of negative friendship features on self-reported disruption is readily interpretable and practically significant. The continuity in self-reported disruption was relatively low, suggesting that students' perceptions of their disruptive behavior changed appreciably during the year. In addition, the correlations between negative features and self-reported disruption were stronger and more consistent across times than any other correlations in Table 15.3. These correlations bolster the argument that having friendships with many negative features increased students' disruption at school.

The process by which negative interactions with friends could enhance disruptive behavior is easy to specify. Students whose friendships have many negative features practice a style of interaction with friends that affects their interactions with other people. These students learn to tease, argue, and insist on their own way in conflicts with another person. It is not surprising, then, that they become more disruptive toward their classmates and teachers.

The other significant effect relates friendships with highly positive features to decreases in perceived athletic competence. To explain this effect, some writers might speculate that students with supportive friendships do not want to damage their friendships by competing intensely with friends in sports (cf. Sullivan, 1953). Yet by refraining from intense competition, these students could reduce their athletic success and so begin to view their athletic competence as low.

In my view, however, the relation of positive friendship features to decreases in perceived athletic competence is spurious, or a Type I error. If having supportive friendships was incompatible with competition in sports, then the measures of positive features and perceived athletic competence should be negatively correlated. Yet in our data, the correlations between these measures were nonsignificant. Moreover, the continuity in perceived athletic competence was higher than for any other facet of self-esteem. An argument thus could be made that no reliable changes in perceived athletic competence occurred during the year. If that is true, the significant effect for the measure of positive features could be attributed to chance.

To avoid the problems of nonsignificant or spurious results, some writers might suggest increasing the duration of longitudinal studies. After all, if scores on constructs like self-esteem change a small amount over 6 months, they might change a greater amount over 1 or 2 years. For example, Dubow et al. (1991) tried to use measures of friends' support to predict changes in school-related behaviors over 2 years. This strategy may create other problems, however. Best friendships in childhood and adolescence often last for several months, but few last for 2 years or more (Savin-Williams & Berndt, 1990). Therefore, researchers who increase the period between assessments might actually be trying to measure the effects of friendships that ended months before. And even when students remain best friends for more than a year, the quality of their friendship could change greatly over time.

Instead of lengthening the duration of longitudinal studies, researchers could try to identify variables more responsive to short-term influence. For example, an adolescent's mood on a specific day might be affected by whether he or she had a positive conversation with a best friend on that day. Similarly, an adolescent's concern about an upcoming test might be affected by whether he or she talked about it with a best friend.

To test hypotheses of this kind, researchers would need not only to adopt new methods of longitudinal research; they would also need to generate more refined hypotheses about the effects of friendship quality. Recently, Buhrmester (this volume) argued that the immediate impact of friendships on children's socioemotional lives should be distinguished from their formative impact on children's social development. For example, having a good friend may meet children's immediate needs for a companion, and thus prevent them from feeling bored on a particular day. In the longer term, having a good friend may increase interpersonal competence. During interactions with a good friend, a child may learn the social skills needed for initiating interactions with peers, carrying on an intimate conversation, and resolving conflicts with others.

The distinction between the immediate impact and the formative impact of friendships is not absolute. Friendships that affect temporary emotional states may also affect stable patterns of psychological adjustment (Buhrmester, this volume). For example, conflict with friends may not only give a negative emotional tone to an adolescent's day. Frequent conflicts may, as indicated earlier, teach children a negative style of social interaction. One goal for future theories should be to specify these connections more precisely, and then use them to guide research on the effects of friendship quality.

Another strategy for research would be the systematic observation of friends' interactions in natural settings. Such observations could fill a major gap in research. Current theories refer mostly to abstract features of friendship, such as intimacy. The connections of these features to actual behavior are virtually unknown. Observational studies, even purely descriptive ones, could begin to fill this gap.

Several methods of observational research could be adapted for studying friendships. For example, the Rochester Interaction Record has been used to assess the characteristics of adults' interactions with other people (e.g., Reis, Lin, Bennett, & Nezlek, 1993). Similar methods could be used to study the relations of friendship quality to the characteristics of friends' interactions.

More technologically complex is the Experience Sampling Method (Larson, 1989). Children or adolescents carry standard paging devices for all their waking hours during one week. They are beeped at random intervals and asked to report briefly on their activities and social partners. With this method, researchers have obtained valuable data on the frequency of friends' interactions and the emotional tone of these interactions (e.g., Larson & Richards, 1991). By varying the content of adolescents' reports, researchers could test hypotheses about the immediate impact of differences in friendship quality.

A radically different approach to testing causal hypotheses is to conduct an experiment. Many researchers have paired children either with a friend or with another classmate and then compared friends' and nonfriends' behavior under controlled conditions (e.g., Hartup, French, Laursen, Johnston, & Ogawa, 1993). Although these experiments show the effects of friendship itself, they do not show how the quality of children's friendships affects their social development. To conduct experiments on friendship quality, a researcher must manipulate the quality of friends' interactions and then see how the manipulation affects the friends' behavior toward other people. For example, a researcher might ask pairs of friends to work on a task under conditions that elicit either harmonious interactions or conflicts. Then the researcher would see how the friends behave when working on another task with a peer who is not a close friend. An experiment of this kind would test the hypothesis that conflicts with friends promote the development of a negative interactional style.

The boldest approach for future research would be an experimental intervention to improve children's friendships. A researcher might identify children with low-quality friendships and train them in skills that could increase the quality of their friendships. Then the researcher would see whether the training affected the children's social adjustment. Such an intervention might seem risky without more evidence on the effects of friendship quality. However, both correlational data and common sense suggest that helping children improve the quality of their friendships would not do any harm, and probably would do some good. Moreover, Bronfenbrenner (1977) argued convincingly that the best way to understand a phenomenon is to try to change it. Understanding of friendship quality would increase if researchers found that improving children's friendships improves other attitudes and behaviors. Therefore, interventions should be one approach that researchers consider as they expand their repertoire of strategies for exploring the effects of friendship quality.

## Conclusions

The central hypothesis of this chapter was that the quality of children's friendships affects their social development. In the proposed research strategy, the first step in exploring these effects is to define friendship quality. Measures of various positive features of friendship are strongly correlated, as are measures of various negative features. The correlations between positive and negative features are much weaker. These data suggest that friendship quality has two dimensions that can be assessed with composite scores for the positive features and the negative features of a friendship.

The second step in the research strategy is to examine the correlates of friendship quality with measures of social development. Significant correlations do not prove that friendship quality affects social development, but they are consistent with that hypothesis. Moreover, correlational studies are an efficient means of seeing whether causal hypotheses are plausible.

The third step is the use of longitudinal designs to determine whether variations in friendship quality predict the changes over time in aspects of social development. Frequent conflicts with friends seem to contribute to disruptive behavior at school, but having high-quality friendships seems not to affect adolescents' self-esteem. The traditional longitudinal designs are not ideal, however, for testing hypotheses about the effects of friendship quality on self-esteem. Observational studies, experimental studies, and new forms of longitudinal research may provide a better test of those hypotheses. With the new approaches, researchers can learn more precisely how high-quality friendships enhance, and low-quality friendships hinder, the social development of children and adolescents.

## References

Berndt, T. J. (1977). The effect of reciprocity norms on moral judgment and causal attribution. *Child Development, 48,* 1322–1330.

Berndt, T. J. (1979). Lack of acceptance of reciprocity norms in preschool children. *Developmental Psychology, 15*, 662–663.

Berndt, T. J. (1986a). Children's comments about their friendships. In M. Perlmutter (Ed.), *Minnesota Symposium on Child Psychology* (Vol. 18). *Cognitive perspectives on children's social and behavioral development* (pp. 189–212). Hillsdale, NJ: Erlbaum.

Berndt, T. J. (1986b). Sharing between friends: Contexts and consequences. In E. C. Mueller and C. Cooper (Eds.), *Process and outcome in peer relationships* (pp. 129–160). New York: Academic.

Berndt, T. J. (1989). Obtaining support from friends in childhood and adolescence. In D. Belle (Ed.), *Children's social networks and social supports* (pp. 308–331). New York: Wiley.

Berndt, T. J., & Keefe, K. (in press). Friends' influence on adolescents' adjustment to school. *Child Development*.

Berndt, T. J., & Miller, K. A. (1993). *The assessment and correlates of adolescents' friendships*. Unpublished manuscript, Purdue University.

Berndt, T. J., & Perry, T. B. (1986). Children's perceptions of friendships as supportive relationships. *Developmental Psychology, 22*, 640–648.

Berndt, T. J., & Savin-Williams, R. C. (1993). Variations in friendships and peer-group relationships in adolescence. In P. Tolan & B. Cohler (Eds.), *Handbook of clinical research and practice with adolescents* (pp. 203–219). New York: Wiley.

Bigelow, B. J. (1977). Children's friendship expectations: A cognitive-developmental study. *Child Development, 48*, 246–253.

Bronfenbrenner, U. (1977). Toward an experimental ecology of human development. *American Psychologist, 32*, 513–531.

Buhrmester, D., & Furman, W. (1986). The changing functions of friends in childhood: A Neo-Sullivanian perspective. In V. J. Derlega & B. A. Winstead (Eds.), *Friendship and social interaction* (pp. 145–166). New York: Springer-Verlag.

Cohen, S., & Wills, T. A. (1985). Stress, social support, and the buffering hypothesis. *Psychological Bulletin, 98*, 310–357.

Dubow, E. F., Tisak, J., Causey, D., Hryshko, A., & Reid, G. (1991). A two-year longitudinal study of stressful life events, social support, and social problem-solving skills: Contributions to children's behavioral and academic adjustment. *Child Development, 62*, 583–599.

Furman, W. (1984). Some observations on the study of personal relationships. In J. C. Masters & K. Yarkin-Levin (Eds.), *Boundary areas in social and developmental psychology* (pp. 15–42). Orlando, FL: Academic Press.

Furman, W., & Buhrmester, D. (1992). Age and sex differences in perceptions of networks of personal relationships. *Child Development, 63*, 103–115.

Gottman, J. M., & Mettetal, G. (1986). Speculations about social and affective development: Friendship and acquaintanceship through adolescence. In J. M. Gottman and J. G. Parker (Eds.), *Conversations of friends* (pp. 192–237). Cambridge: Cambridge University Press.

Harter, S. (1985). *Manual for the self-perception profile for children*. Denver: University of Denver.

Hartup, W. W. (1993). Adolescents and their friends. In B. Laursen (Ed.), *New directions for child development: Close friendships in adolescence* (pp. 3–22). San Francisco: Jossey-Bass.

Hartup, W. W., French, D. C., Laursen, B., Johnston, M. K., & Ogawa, J. R. (1993). Conflict and friendship relations in middle childhood: Behavior in a close-field situation. *Child Development, 64*, 445–454.

Hestenes, S. L., Berndt, T. J., & Gruen, G. E. (1993). *The development of trust in adolescent friendships*. Unpublished manuscript, Purdue University.

Hinde, R. A. (1979). *Towards understanding relationships*. New York: Academic Press.

Hirsch, B. J., & DuBois, D. L. (1991). Self-esteem in early adolescence: The identification and prediction of contrasting longitudinal trajectories. *Journal of Youth and Adolescence, 20*, 53–72.

Larson, R. (1989). Beeping children and adolescents: A method for studying time use and daily experience. *Journal of Youth and Adolescence, 18*, 511–530.

Larson, R., & Richards, M. H. (1991). Daily companionship in late childhood and early adolescence: Changing developmental contexts. *Child Development, 62*, 284–300.

Monroe, W. S. (1898). Social consciousness in children. *Psychological Review, 5*, 68–70.

Parker, J. G., & Asher, S. R. (1993). Friendship and friendship quality in middle childhood: Links with peer group acceptance and feelings of loneliness and social dissatisfaction. *Developmental Psychology, 29*, 611–621.

Piaget, J. (1965). *The moral judgment of the child.* New York: Free Press. (Originally published in 1932)

Reis, H. T., Lin, Y.-C., Bennett, M. E., & Nezlek, J. B. (1993). Change and consistency in social participation during early adulthood. *Developmental Psychology, 29*, 633–645.

Rest, J. R. (1983). Morality. In P. H. Mussen (Series Ed.), J. H. Flavell, & E. M. Markman (Vol. Eds.), *Handbook of child psychology. Vol. 3. Cognitive development* (pp. 556–629). New York: Wiley.

Rook, K. S. (1984). The negative side of social interaction: Impact, on psychological well-being. *Journal of Personality and Social Psychology, 46*, 1097–1108.

Sarason, I. G., & Sarason, B. R. (Eds.) (1985). *Social support: Theory, research and applications.* The Hague: Martinus Nijhof.

Savin-Williams, R. C., & Berndt, T. J. (1990). Friendships and peer relations during adolescence. In S. S. Feldman & G. Elliott (Eds.), *At the threshold: The developing adolescent* (pp. 277–307). Cambridge, MA: Harvard University Press.

Sullivan, H. S. (1953). *The interpersonal theory of psychiatry.* New York: Norton.

van Vlissingen, J. F. (1970). Friendship in history. *Humanitas, 6*, 225–238.

Vernberg, E. M. (1990). Psychological adjustment and experiences with peers during early adolescence: Reciprocal, incidental, or unidirectional relationships? *Journal of Abnormal Child Psychology, 18*, 187–198.

Youniss, J. (1980). *Parents and peers in social development.* Chicago: University of Chicago Press.

# 16 Distinguishing friendship from acceptance: Implications for intervention and assessment

*Steven R. Asher, Jeffrey G. Parker, and Diane L. Walker*

Efforts to intervene with children who experience peer relationships problems have been designed principally to improve the extent to which other children accept or reject them. Much less attention has been devoted to ways of helping children who are having problems forming or maintaining specific friendships. The distinction between peer acceptance/rejection, on the one hand, and friendship involvement, on the other, is subtle and not always recognized. However, in recent years a growing consensus has emerged among peer relationships researchers that these two dimensions of peer adjustment can be meaningfully distinguished. In this chapter we begin by discussing the distinction between acceptance and friendship, suggesting how each construct can be assessed, and discussing several lines of inquiry that validate the distinction between peer group acceptance and friendship. In the second major section, we reflect on the existing social skill training literature in terms of this distinction. Here we argue that previous social skills training studies have been fairly successful in promoting peer acceptance but have not yet demonstrated effectiveness in promoting friendships. Our view is that distinctive aspects of friendship making and friendship keeping must be attended to if researchers are to successfully shift their emphasis from promoting acceptance to promoting friendship. Accordingly, in the final major section we offer specific hypotheses about the kinds of interpersonal tasks and skills that must be emphasized if the goal is to help children form and maintain friendships. Our hope is that our hypotheses will help stimulate intervention research that promotes both friendship and acceptance.

The authors wish to thank Tsai-Yen Chung and Alan Peshkin for their careful reading and helpful feedback on an earlier draft of the chapter. We also wish to thank Matt Asher for his reading of the manuscript and for suggesting the friendship task we discuss in the conclusion to this chapter.

## Acceptance versus friendship

The distinction between acceptance and friendship has a long history within the literature on children's adjustment with peers. Indeed, the distinction appears in early writings of Moreno (1934) and, in some form, in many subsequent reviews of the literature on children's peer relationships (e.g., Asher & Hymel, 1981; Ausubel & Sullivan, 1970; Berndt, 1984; Bukowski & Hoza, 1989; Campbell, 1964; Furman, 1982, 1984; Gronlund, 1959; Hartup, 1970, 1983; Parker & Asher, 1987; Thompson, 1960). Even so, until recently the distinction has not figured prominently in actual research on peer relationships. For this reason, attention to its roots, utility, and methodological implications is warranted.

### Conceptual distinction

The constructs of acceptance and friendship address the adjustment of individual children to their peers, but do so through very different conceptual lenses. Peer acceptance refers to the extent to which a child is liked or accepted by other members of a peer group. Well-accepted children are warmly and positively regarded by most of their fellow group members. Poorly accepted children, on the other hand, are viewed negatively and disliked by their peers. Because group acceptance describes the central tendency of a group of peers' liking for a specific child, only the degree of liking is of consequence and not the particular source (Child A vs. Child B) of the judgment. Note that how the focal child views others in the peer group is irrelevant to the concept of group acceptance; indeed a particular child's peer acceptance can be ascertained without any input from the child him- or herself. For this reason, acceptance has been described as a one-way or unilateral construct (Berndt, 1984; Bukowski & Hoza, 1989; Furman, 1982).

Friendship, by contrast, is an inherently dyadic rather than group-level construct; implicitly, friends perceive and respond to one another as unique and irreplaceable (Wright, 1985). Whereas a child's acceptance is relatively unaffected by a single group member, the secession of either party from a friendship destroys the whole. Thus, unlike acceptance, the source as well as the nature of the peer's judgment matters greatly in friendship. Most important, because friendship is inherently dyadic, it is not possible to appraise a child's friendship without evidence of reciprocity of affection; hence, input from the focal child him- or herself is critical.

The distinction between acceptance and friendship comports well with theoretical accounts of children's motivational tendencies and interpersonal needs. Specifically, several authors have drawn a broad distinction between children's needs for a close confidant and their need to identify with and experience a sense of belonging to a larger peer group (Ausubel & Sullivan, 1970; Furman & Robbins, 1985; Havighurst, 1953; Shaver & Buhrmester, 1983). Representative of this view, and often cited in this connection, is the theoretical framework of personality theorist and psychiatrist Harry Stack Sullivan (1953). According to Sullivan, group acceptance and successful friendship experiences are both essential to healthy adjustment and development, but they have different underlying motivational origins, different developmental timetables, and are based on different substrates of underlying interpersonal skills. In Sullivan's view, acceptance by a group of important peers is particularly consequential to the development of healthy attitudes toward competition, conformity, and achievement. Sullivan surmised that difficulties in this sphere could lead to excessive anxiety or defensive attitudes concerning ostracism and social isolation. By contrast, he speculated that friendship was irreplaceable as a context for the development of empathy and perspective-taking skills, and that friendship serves to validate children's interests, hopes, and positive self-perceptions. Interestingly, Sullivan predicted that, because children's needs for a friend develop later than their need for group inclusion, successful friendship experiences might offset to some degree the negative effects of earlier difficulties in peer acceptance.

*Assessing acceptance versus friendship*

Although the distinction between acceptance and friendship has a long history, investigators have tried only recently to develop separate operational procedures for measuring each construct. Several investigators have noted that specific assessment techniques can preserve or obscure the friendship–acceptance distinction (e.g., Asher & Hymel, 1981; Berndt, 1984; Bukowski & Hoza, 1989; Parker & Asher, 1993a). It can be argued that the field was misdirected by using the same measure – positive friendship nominations (e.g., "Name your three best friends") – to assess both friendships and a child's overall standing in the group. This inevitably confounds how friendship and acceptance are assessed.

Researchers have posed different types of solutions concerning how best to operationalize friendship versus acceptance. Asher and his colleagues (Asher & Hymel, 1981; Asher, Singleton, & Taylor, 1982; Oden & Asher, 1977; Singleton & Asher, 1977, 1979) advanced the view that acceptance could best be operationalized by calculating the average rating a child received from peers on a rating-scale measure that asked children not about friendship but about how much they liked to play with, work with, or be in activities with each other child in their class. These researchers also suggested that friendship could be measured by the number of nominations received by peers on a friendship-nomination measure. What led to these recommendations were data suggesting that different patterns of results emerged from rating-scale versus nomination measures. For example, evidence on cross-race relationships appeared to be more positive on rating-scale measures than on traditional friendship-nomination measures (Asher et al., 1982; Singleton & Asher, 1977; Schofield & Whitley, 1983), suggesting that children may accept peers of different races without necessarily choosing them as friends. Furthermore, there was evidence (to be discussed in more detail later) that social skills interventions produced greater changes on rating-scale measures of acceptance than on nomination measures of best friendship. Together, these lines of inquiry lent validity to the acceptance–friendship distinction and to the use of rating-scale versus nomination measures to assess each construct.

More recently, Parker and Asher (1993a, 1993b) have reexamined the issue of how best to assess acceptance and friendship. Their approach to measuring acceptance once again used a rating-scale measure in which children are asked not about friendship but about how much they like each other member of the group. But Parker and Asher (1993a, 1993b), in agreement with Bukowski and Hoza's (1989) arguments about the need for defining friendship in terms of reciprocal choice, identified children as having a friend when the child is nominated not only by another child as a best friend but also reciprocates that choice. Parker and Asher and Bukowski and Hoza appear to differ, however, with regard to the recommended wording of the friendship assessment measure. Parker and Asher hold that because the term *friendship* has a particular meaning to children, the nomination item must include explicit reference to friendship. Bukowski and Hoza strongly emphasize reciprocity of choice, but are more open to varying types of item content. They include as indicators of friendship reciprocity of choice on various types of items (e.g., ''like most'' nominations, ratings of liking, etc.). Research is needed on the validity of different item content. Research is also needed on the subtle but potentially important issue of how requesting limited versus unlimited friendship nominations affects the picture that emerges.

Recent research suggests the utility of distinguishing acceptance, based on the average ratings children receive, from friendship, based on reciprocal friendship choices. The evidence consistently suggests that acceptance and friendship are nonoverlapping, albeit not wholly independent, dimensions of individual differences. One source of evidence concerns the extent to which children of different levels of peer acceptance tend to participate in friendship. Although involvement in friendship generally increases as group acceptance increases, many low-accepted children have friends and not all high-accepted children have friends (Parker & Asher, 1989, 1993b; Parker & Seal, 1993).

Research also suggests that considering friendship and acceptance simultaneously is superior to relying on either index alone for predicting children's feelings about their social lives. In examinations of how group acceptance and having a friend relate to children's subjective experiences of loneliness and social dissatisfaction at school, researchers find that children without best friends are lonelier than children with best friends, regardless of how well-accepted they are (Parker & Asher, 1989, 1993b). In other words, friendship seems to offer low-accepted children the same kind of buffer against loneliness that it offers better-accepted children, but in the context of a greater degree of loneliness in general.

Although the research we have described is promising, even more direct evidence is needed concerning the discriminant validity of our recommended procedures for assessing acceptance versus friendship. The finding that both acceptance and friendship predict to loneliness could simply result from the fact that two sociometric measures will predict better than one. What is needed in future research are criterion variables that might be expected to relate differentially to acceptance and friendship. Later in this chapter we suggest various skills that may be related more highly to friendship than to acceptance.

To summarize, in this section we have argued that there is value in distinguishing children's overall acceptance by peers from children's participation in friendship. We have also recommended specific ways of operationalizing each construct. In the next section, we review research on social skills training with children who are selected for intervention based on sociometric measures. In our review we focus on the extent to which existing interventions promote not only increased acceptance by peers but also increased participation in friendship.

## Social skills training with children

### Sociometrically oriented social skills training research

Social skills training interventions to improve children's peer relationships have a long history within developmental psychology, including notable early efforts by Jack (1934), Page (1936), and Chittenden (1942). What all such efforts share is an assumption that children who have peer-relationship difficulties lack the skills necessary to initiate and maintain relationships (see Asher & Renshaw, 1981). Within this broad approach one particularly promising direction of a more recent nature has been the development of interventions that involve selecting children on the basis of evidence of low sociometric status and teaching them social skills that previous descriptive research has found to discriminate between popular and unpopular children. The idea behind this approach is to select intervention content not based on theory or intuition alone, but based on findings from previous research on the social skills correlates of sociometric status. This approach to selecting social skills has been termed a ''competence-correlates'' approach (Asher, 1985). The logic behind this approach is straightforward. If skills can be identified that discriminate between children who get along well with their peers versus those who do so poorly, why not teach those skills to unpopular children in an effort to improve their relations with others?

The feature of selecting children on the basis of sociometric criteria also sets this recent approach apart from other approaches, especially the early efforts. In the early studies children were selected on the basis of evidence of especially high or especially low rates of particular behaviors. For example, Chittenden (1942) targeted children who were highly "dominative" in their interaction with others; other researchers have targeted children on the basis of, for example, the frequency with which they approach others, make eye contact, behave aggressively, or act aggressively.

The impetus in recent work for selecting children based on sociometric criteria comes from several sources. First, there is the longstanding awareness that a large number of children lack friends or are poorly accepted by their peers. Although estimates vary across studies, even a conservative estimate would suggest that about 10% of school-age children have serious difficulties with peer relations.

Second, there is the general recognition that children's sociometric status predicts to long-term outcomes, especially children's tendency to drop out of school (Kupersmidt, Coie, & Dodge, 1990; Parker & Asher, 1987). Across studies, between two to eight times the number of unpopular to popular children withdraw from school; in percentage terms, about 25% of unpopular children drop out of school compared to about 8% of popular children (Asher & Parker, 1989).

Third, a long tradition of research points to the social skill deficits of children who have peer relationship problems (see Asher & Renshaw, 1981; Coie, Dodge, & Kupersmidt, 1990; Dodge & Feldman, 1990; and Hartup, 1983, for reviews). This evidence comes from observations of children in natural settings, analogue settings, and newly formed play groups. Evidence also comes from hypothetical situations interviews in which children are asked how they would handle various types of social situations.

More recently, two other sources of evidence have emerged that reinforce a sociometric approach to the selection of children for intervention. One is the growing body of research on loneliness in childhood. This research suggests that children have a basic understanding of the concept of loneliness (Cassidy & Asher, 1992; Hayden, Tarulli, & Hymel, 1988; Williams & Asher, 1992), that a substantial number of children feel lonely (Asher, Hymel, & Renshaw, 1984), that feelings of loneliness can be reliably measured at various age levels (Asher et al., 1984; Barth & Parke, 1993; Cassidy & Asher, 1992; Heinlein & Spinner, 1985; Marcoen & Brumagne, 1985; Parkhurst & Asher, 1992), that feelings of loneliness are rather stable even over a 1-year period (Hymel et al., 1983; Renshaw & Brown, 1993), and that low sociometric status in the peer group is associated with greater feelings of loneliness and social dissatisfaction in early adolescence (Parkhurst & Asher, 1992), in middle childhood (e.g., Asher & Wheeler, 1985; Crick & Ladd, 1993), and even among children as young as 5 and 6 years of age (Cassidy & Asher, 1992). These findings about loneliness are important because they suggest that children having peer relationship problems, as measured sociometrically, do feel badly about their situation and might possibly want help.

Support for the use of sociometric selection criteria also comes from studies in which children with varying levels of sociometric status indicate whether they would like help if someone were available to teach them how to relate more successfully to peers (Asher, Zelis, Parker, & Bruene, 1991). A consistent finding of this research is that poorly accepted children are significantly more interested in receiving help. For example, in one study, 46.7% of poorly accepted children said "yes," 37.8% said "maybe," and only 15.6% indicated "no." By contrast, only 8.5% of highly accepted children said "yes," 48.9% said "maybe," and as many as 42.6% said "no." These data on self-referral, like the research on loneliness, suggest that many children with peer relationship problems would welcome intervention efforts. The data also speak effectively to the ethical concern that researchers have no justification for intervening without evidence that children themselves are interested in changing.

To summarize, various types of evidence provide researchers with the rationale for selecting children based on sociometric criteria and attempting to develop social skills training strategies for helping children at risk. In the discussion that follows we describe the kinds of social skills training studies that have been implemented with children selected on sociometric criteria. In particular, we focus on the findings that relate to the acceptance-versus-friendship issue.

### Social skills training programs and sociometric outcomes

As described hereafter, progress has been made in fostering children's acceptance by peers, but relatively little attention has been given to whether social skills training helps children make and maintain friendships. Indeed, within sociometrically oriented social skills training research, investigators have rarely distinguished between promoting acceptance and promoting friendship. Our intention is to review the existing literature as a backdrop for speculating in the next section about the kinds of intervention content that might be needed to influence children's capacity for friendship.

*Features of sociometrically oriented skills training research.* Table 16.1 contains descriptions of sociometrically oriented social skills training studies. The

Table 16.1. *Sociometrically oriented social skills training studies*

| Author(s) | Subject characteristics | Procedures/skills taught (P: Procedures; ST: Skills taught) | Sociometric outcomes (I: Immediate; M: Maintenance) |
|---|---|---|---|
| Gottman, Gonso, & Schuler (1976) | Third graders who received a low number (mean = 2.5) of best friend nominations (unlimited measure). | P: 1. Treatment condition ($n = 2$) consisted of individual coaching using videotaped vignettes, role-play, and a word-pair game (3 sessions). 2. Control condition ($n = 2$) consisted of attention from the experimenter by playing board games and talking about topics unrelated to the treatment. ST: Initiating interaction, making friends (i.e., greeting, asking for information, giving information, offering inclusion, leave-taking), distributing positive interaction (e.g., showing interest in what someone else is saying, giving approval, giving affection), referential communication (i.e., taking another's perspective). | I: Not assessed. M: Treatment group increased significantly on "play with" and "work with" ratings at 9-week follow-up. |
| Oden & Asher (1977) | Third–fourth graders who had low mean ratings from same-sex classmates on "play with" and "work with" ratings. The three lowest rated children of one sex were selected from each class. | P: 1. Coaching condition ($n = 11$) consisted of individual instruction, play with a same-sex classmate, and review of the concepts taught (6 sessions). 2. Peer-pairing condition ($n = 11$) consisted of playing games with same-sex classmates. 3. Control condition ($n = 11$) consisted of playing solitary games. ST: Participation, cooperation, communication, validation-support. | I: Coaching condition increased significantly on "play with" ratings. This change was significantly greater than the changes made by the other two conditions combined. No significant differences were found for "work with" ratings or friendship nominations. M: Coaching conditions showed continued progress on "play with" ratings at 1-year follow-up. |

Table 16.1. (cont.)

| | | P | I/M |
|---|---|---|---|
| Gresham & Nagle (1980) | Third–fourth graders who were the four lowest rated children in their class on the average of their "play with" and "work with" ratings from same-sex classmates. | P: 1. Coaching condition ($n = 10$) consisted of instructions, rehearsal, role-play, and feedback to dyads or triads of subjects (6 sessions). 2. Modeling condition ($n = 10$) exposed dyads or triads to a narrated videotape of child models. 3. Mixed abbreviated modeling and coaching condition ($n = 10$) consisted of a shortened exposure to the modeling video, instructions, and a brief practice period. 4. Control condition ($n = 10$) consisted of viewing videotapes of *Wild Kingdom*.<br><br>ST: Participation, cooperation, communication, validation-support, friendship making (i.e., greeting, asking for and giving information, offering inclusion, leave-taking), initiating and receiving positive interaction (i.e., expressing affection and making reinforcing comments), avoiding the initiation and receipt of negative behaviors. | I: No significant differences were found on the "play with" ratings, "work with" ratings, best friend nominations, "like to play with" nominations, or "like to work with" nominations.<br><br>M: All three treatment groups increased significantly on "play with" ratings from the pretest to the 3-week follow-up; there were no significant differences among the treatment groups. The control group decreased significantly on the "play with" ratings from the pretest to the 3-week follow-up. No other significant differences emerged. |
| La Greca & Santogrossi (1980) | Third–fifth graders who had below average "play with" and "work with" ratings in their class. | P: 1. Skills training condition ($n = 10$) consisted of videotapes of peer models, discussion of the content of the videotapes, coaching, role-playing and receiving feedback from the trainer, and "homework" assignments to foster practice of the skills taught. 2. Attention-placebo condition ($n = 10$) consisted of videotapes of TV shows, games, and nonpeer oriented "homework" assignments. 3. Waiting-list control condition ($n = 10$) did not provide any form of treatment.<br><br>ST: Smiling and laughing, greeting, joining, extending invitations, conversational skills, sharing and cooperation, verbal complimenting, physical appearance/ | I: No significant differences were found in the "play with" or "work with" ratings.<br><br>M: Not assessed. |

374

| Ladd (1981) | Third graders who were in the lowest third of their class in average "play with" ratings and who exhibited low rates of targeted social skills when observed. Six children, three of each sex, were selected from each class. | P: 1. Skill training condition ($n = 12$) consisted of coaching dyads, rehearsal, play with two additional peers, and self-evaluations elicited by the experimenter (8 sessions). 2. Attention control ($n = 12$) condition consisted of dyadic interaction with a same-sex peer and attention from the experimenter. 3. Nontreatment condition ($n = 12$) did not provide any form of treatment (the children did not leave their classroom). ST: Asking questions, offering suggestions and directions, making supportive statements. | I: Skill training and attention-control conditions both increased significantly on the "play with" ratings. M: Skill training condition increased significantly on the "play with" ratings from posttest to the 4-week follow-up. The attention-control condition declined significantly on the "play with" ratings from posttest to the 4-week follow-up. |
| Berler, Gross, & Drabman (1982) | 8–10-year-olds who were the lowest rated children in their class on "play with" and "work with" ratings and were reported by their teacher as having poor peer relationships. | P: 1. Experimental condition ($n = 3$) consisted of coaching, modeling, rehearsal, feedback, and praise administered to dyads by two group leaders (11 sessions). After each session, classroom teachers were asked to provide the children with feedback regarding their interactions with peers. 2. The control condition ($n = 3$) consisted of feedback from classroom teachers on the children's peer interactions. ST: Eye contact, responding to unfair criticism, initiating interaction, giving compliments, requesting new behavior. | I: No significant differences on "play with" or "work with" ratings were found. M: No significant differences emerged. |

Table 16.1. (*cont.*)

| | | | |
|---|---|---|---|
| Csapo (1983) | Third graders who were in the lowest third of their class on "play with" and "work with" ratings, the three least socially skilled children of each sex in their class when observed, and classified as socially withdrawn according to teacher reports. | P: 1. Experimental condition (*n* = 10) consisted of coaching in dyads of same-sex subjects, play with an untrained classmate, instructor feedback and self-evaluation (training continued until children displayed the social skills at the same frequency of their average peers; 32 sessions were necessary, on average). 2. The attention control condition (*n* = 10) consisted of pairs of children playing games with two untrained peers and receiving attention from the experimenter. 3. Nontreatment control condition (*n* = 10) did not provide any form of training.<br><br>ST: Asking questions, offering suggestions and directions to peers, praising and encouraging peers. | I: The experimental condition increased significantly on ratings; the experimental condition received significantly higher ratings than did the attention control or nontreatment control conditions at posttest.<br><br>M: Experimental condition showed continued progress on the ratings at 4-week follow-up; this condition also continued to receive higher ratings than did the other two conditions. |
| Siperstein & Gale (1983) | Fourth–sixth graders who received few friendship nominations (same-sex unlimited "best friend," and "other friend"), many rejection nominations (same-sex unlimited "not a friend" nominations), and low "play with" and "work with" ratings. A child of each sex was selected from each class when possible. | P: 1. Social skill training condition (*n* = 9) consisted of viewing pictures of a problem-solving situation and proposing possible solutions to the problem, relating the hypothetical situations to previous personal experiences and role-playing those experiences, and practicing the skills as "homework" (10 sessions). 2. Adult attention condition (*n* = 8) consisted of individually telling stories about pictures in a magazine to an experimenter.<br><br>ST: Joining (i.e., entry into existing group, initiations), social reinforcement (i.e., making positive statements, taking turns, following rules). | I: Social skill training condition increased significantly on "play with" ratings, "work with" ratings, and unlimited "other friend" nominations and decreased significantly on the unlimited "not a friend" nominations. No significant differences were found for unlimited "best friend" nominations.<br><br>M: Not assessed. |

Bierman &
Furman
(1984)

Fifth–sixth graders who were in the lowest third in friendship ratings in their class and had low ratings of conversational skill performance when observed in peer group interactions.

P: 1. Individual coaching ($n = 14$) condition consisted of individual instruction, practice, and feedback while making a videotape (10 sessions). 2. Group experience condition ($n = 14$) consisted of one identified child making a video with two same-sex classmates. 3. The group experience with coaching condition ($n = 14$) consisted of instructions, rehearsal, and feedback administered to a triad of one identified child and two same-sex peers while making a video. 4. The no-treatment condition ($n = 14$) did not provide any form of treatment.

ST: Conversational skills (i.e., self-expressions, questions, leadership bids).

I: Group experience and group experience with coaching conditions received significantly higher friendship ratings from classmates than did the individual coachings or control conditions. The group experience with coaching condition received significantly higher friendship ratings from "treatment partners" than did the group experience without coaching condition.

M: No continuing effects were found on the friendship ratings from classmates at the 6-week follow-up. The group experience with coaching condition maintained significantly higher friendship ratings from "treatment partners" than did the group experience without coaching condition at the 6-week follow-up.

Table 16.1. (*cont.*)

| | | | |
|---|---|---|---|
| Coie & Krehbiel (1984) | Fourth graders who were classified as rejected (see Coie, Dodge, & Coppotelli, 1982), reported by their teacher as starting fights and being disruptive, and had reading or math scores below the 36th percentile on the California Achievement Test. | P: 1. Academic skills training conditions ($n = 10$) consisted of individual tutoring in reading, math or both (30–35 sessions). 2. Social skills training condition ($n = 10$) consisted of individual instruction, play with a peer, and a review of the concepts taught (6 sessions in the fall). The training also included videotaped group game playing followed by a review and discussion of the videotaped play (6 sessions in the spring). 3. Combined academic and social skills training condition ($n = 10$) consisted of all aspects of both the academic and social skills training conditions. 4. Control condition ($n = 10$) did not provide any form of treatment.<br><br>ST: Participation, cooperation, communication, validation support. | I: All three treatment conditions increased significantly on "play with" ratings; academic skills training condition received significantly higher "play with" ratings than the social skills training condition. The academic skills training and social skills training conditions increased significantly on like-most nominations. All treatment groups decreased significantly on like-least nominations.<br><br>M: Ratings, positive nominations, and negative nominations not reported for 1-year follow-up. Conditions 1 and 3 maintained the same level of social preference from posttest to 1-year follow-up. |
| Bierman (1986)* | Fifth–sixth graders who were in the lowest third in friendship ratings in their class and had low conversational skill ratings when observed in peer interactions. | P: 1. Social skills training condition ($n = 13$) exposed triads (a target child and two same-sex classmates) to coaching, practice, feedback, and praise while making a videotape (10 sessions). 2. Peer experience condition ($n = 14$) consisted of triads of children making a videotape.<br><br>ST: Conversational skills (i.e., self-expression, questioning, leadership bids). | I: In-treatment rate of conversational skills was significantly related to friendship ratings.<br><br>M: In-treatment rate of conversational skills continued to be significantly related to friendship ratings at 6-week follow-up. |

378

| | | | |
|---|---|---|---|
| Tiffen & Spence (1986) | 7–12-year-olds who were the five most rejected or neglected children (see Peery, 1979) in their class. At least two rejected and two neglected children were selected from each class. | P: Social skills training condition ($n = 17$) exposed groups of eight or nine subjects to instructions, modeling (peer models, either live or videotape), role-play, and feedback (12 sessions). 2. Attention placebo control condition ($n = 16$) consisted of groups of subjects playing games. 3. No-treatment control condition ($n = 17$) did not provide any form of treatment.<br><br>ST: Facial expression, posture, gesture, eye contact, smiling, grooming, physical appearance, touching, body distance, tone of voice, listening, initiating, appropriate speech content, questioning, answering, taking turns, continuing the conversation, sharing, helping, complimenting, politeness, sportsmanship, relaxation, the Turtle Technique, self-control, self-reward, ignoring teasing, ignoring rejection, ignoring bullying, expression of anger, expression of rights, expression of requests, discrimination of assertion and aggression and passivity, dealing with an accusation, dealing with group pressures, decision making, situational relaxation skills, positive assertion (i.e., giving and receiving compliments.) | I: All three groups increased significantly on positive "work with" and positive "play with" nominations received; the three conditions were not significantly different from each other. Within the social skill training condition, the neglected children increased significantly more than the rejected children. No significant differences were found for negative "work with" and negative "play with" nominations received.<br><br>M: All three groups maintained their levels of positive "work with" and positive "play with" nominations at the 3-month follow-up; no significant differences among the groups emerged. The neglected children in the social skills condition continued to receive more positive "play with" and positive "work with" nominations than did the rejected children at the 3-month follow-up. No significant differences in the negative "work with" and negative "play with" nominations emerged. |

Table 16.1. (cont.)

| Bierman, Miller, & Stabb (1987) | First–third graders who received the most negative ("like least") nominations (limited measure) in their class and exhibited high levels of negative peer interactions when observed. | P: 1. Instructions condition ($n = 8$) consisted of coaching social skills, play activities, and token rewards contingent on behavior that were administered to each focal child in a rotating group of one, two, or three classroom peers (10 sessions). 2. Prohibitions condition ($n = 8$) consisted of rules prohibiting certain behaviors (e.g., no fighting), play activities, random token awards, and temporary removal of the opportunity to gain tokens if a rule violation occurred (also administered to a group with rotating peer participants). 3. Combined instructions and prohibitions condition ($n = 8$) consisted of coaching social skills and establishment of prohibitive rules, play activities, token reinforcement for skilled behavior, and removal of reward opportunities for negative behavior (also administered in the rotating group format). 4. No-treatment condition ($n = 8$) did not provide any form of treatment.

ST: Questioning others, helping and cooperating in play, sharing. | I: No significant differences were found on "play with" ratings, positive nominations, or negative nominations from classmates. Combined condition decreased significantly in the number of negative nominations from treatment partners and received significantly fewer negative nominations from treatment partners than did the prohibitions alone condition.

M: No differences for "play with" ratings or nominations from classmates emerged at 6-week or 1-year follow-ups. Combined condition maintained a lower number of negative nominations from treatment partners and received significantly fewer negative nominations from treatment partners than did subjects in the prohibitions alone or the instructions alone conditions at 6-week follow-up. |

| Study | Sample | Procedure | Results |
|---|---|---|---|
| Mize & Ladd (1990) | 4–5-year-olds who were low-status (rejected or neglected by criteria adapted from Coie et al., 1982) and showed below average use of social skills and/or above average use of aversive behavior when observed. | P: 1. Skill training condition ($n = 18$) with dyads consisted of modeling, instructions, and role-play using hand puppets, play with untrained peers and individualized feedback (8 sessions). 2. Attention-control condition ($n = 15$) with dyads focused on how to play with certain toys.<br><br>ST: Leading, asking questions, making comments, and supporting. | I: No significant differences were found on rating-scale, positive nomination, and negative nomination measures.<br><br>M: Skill training condition increased significantly on positive nominations from pretest to 1-month follow-up. No significant effects were found for ratings or negative nominations at 1-month follow-up. |
| Vaughn & Lancelotta (1990) | Second–fourth graders who were below the 20th percentile in their class on ratings from same-sex classmates and reported by their teacher to have difficulties interacting with peers. | P: 1. Interpersonal social skills training with high-status peers present condition ($n = 11$) consisted of role-plays, coaching, rehearsal, and homework assignments administered to groups of approximately six children (18 sessions). 2. Interpersonal social skills training without high-status peers condition ($n = 11$) consists of the same training components, without high-status peers present. 3. Contact control group condition ($n = 13$) consisted of game playing activities with peers.<br><br>ST: Establishing rapport, identifying and using feelings, understanding solutions in the long run and short run, four steps to solving problems, making and maintaining friends, group integration. | I: Skill training with high-status peers present condition received significantly higher ratings than did the contact control condition at posttest.<br><br>M: Not assessed. |

Table 16.1. (cont.)

| | | | |
|---|---|---|---|
| Lochman, Coie, Underwood, & Terry (1993) | Third graders who were classified as rejected (see Coie et al., 1982) and either aggressive ($n = 18$) or nonaggressive ($n = 34$) based on peer nominations for starting fights (aggressive children were greater than 1 SD above the mean). | P: 1. Social relations training condition ($n = 26$) consisted of videotapes to introduce concepts, discussions in which children generated alternative solutions to social problems, behavioral rehearsal, feedback, social reinforcement for competent solutions, and self-monitoring by children watching videotapes of their own behavior (26 individual and 8 small group sessions). 2. Control condition did not receive any form of attention or training.<br><br>ST: Social problem solving, playing and maintaining relationships with a partner (i.e., nonverbal communication, negotiation, cooperation, acceptance of rejection), entering groups, coping with anger. (The sequence and duration of the skills trained differed for the aggressive-rejected and nonaggressive-rejected groups.) | I: Aggressive-rejected training condition received significantly higher ratings than did the aggressive-rejected control condition at posttest. A parallel nonsignificant trend was found for social preference (i.e., "like most" nominations minus "like least" nominations).<br><br>M: Aggressive-rejected and nonaggressive-rejected training conditions tended to have higher ratings than the control conditions at 1-year follow-up. No significant differences in social preference emerged. |

*This study is a secondary analysis of the Bierman and Furman (1984) data.

382

studies are presented in chronological order. We identified these studies by consulting reviews of the social skills training literature (e.g., Coie & Koeppl, 1990; Ladd & Asher, 1985; Ladd & Mize, 1983; Schneider, 1992), and by searching for additional studies through the PsycLIT database and the Social Citation Index. Our criteria for including studies in Table 16.1 were three-fold. First, children had to be selected for intervention based on sociometric measures. Second, the intervention method had to involve some form of instruction in social relationship skills. Third, the design had to include some form of control condition with random assignment to conditions. As Table 16.1 indicates, we found only 16 intervention studies that meet these criteria. The relatively small number of studies in this area needs to be considered within the context of the limited number of well-designed psychosocial intervention studies with children more generally (see Kazdin, 1993).

Although in each of the 16 studies in Table 16.1 children were selected for participation based on sociometric measures, there is considerable variability in the particular selection criteria employed. First, the studies can be distinguished from one another by having selection criteria based solely on either sociometric measures or on the combined use of sociometric measures along with behavioral and/or academic criteria. Furthermore, as a close examination of Table 16.1 indicates, the studies vary considerably in the specific cut-off scores used to select children for intervention. As a result, in some studies the children selected were probably experiencing relatively mild peer relationship problems compared to other studies in which children with more serious peer relationship problems were selected.

There is also variability in the specific instructional procedures and contexts employed. For example, Oden and Asher (1977) taught children social interaction concepts in a one-to-one session with an adult. Children were then asked to try out the ideas they were taught by playing a game with another child. Following the game playing, children met once again with the adult to reflect on the ideas in terms of the child's recent game-playing experience. Other studies have also used direct instruction, practice, and feedback or review, but have supplemented them with procedures such as modeling or role playing (e.g., Berler, Gross, & Drabman, 1982; Lochman, Coie, Underwood, & Terry, 1993; Tiffen & Spence, 1986; Vaughn & Lancelotta, 1990). Other studies have taught children in dyads or small groups rather than individually (e.g., Bierman & Furman, 1984; Gresham & Nagle, 1980; Ladd, 1981), and have had children do other kinds of activities instead of games, such as cooperative video production (Bierman & Furman, 1984) or cooperative art projects (Bierman, Miller, & Stabb, 1987). Still other studies have strikingly different formats. Consider, for example, an interesting study by Siperstein and Gale (1983). These investigators engaged children in a social problem-solving situation by showing them pictures while reading a hypothetical interpersonal dilemma. The children were asked to help the story character solve the problem as well as think about how the elements of the dilemma might be similar to a social situation they had faced in their personal lives. The children were then asked to role play responses either to the hypothetical dilemma or to one of their own life experiences. Then, each child received individualized instruction on specific social skills. Children were also instructed to practice the skills in their classrooms.

There is also considerable variability across studies in program content. For example, Oden and Asher (1977) taught children about four general concepts: cooperation (e.g., taking turns, sharing materials), participation (e.g., getting started, paying attention), communication (e.g., talking with the other person, listening), and validation-support (e.g., smiling, offering encouragement). These four concepts have been used in some of the other studies included in Table 16.1, either alone (Coie & Krehbiel, 1984) or in conjunction with some additional foci such as initiating and receiving positive interaction (Gresham & Nagle, 1980). Others studies have emphasized different concepts. For example, Ladd (1981) taught children three specific social skills: asking questions, leading (e.g., offering suggestions and directions), and offering supportive statements. Program content similar to Ladd's has been used by several other researchers (Bierman & Furman, 1984; Csapo, 1983; Mize & Ladd, 1990; Siperstein & Gale, 1983). Moving beyond these two clusters of program content, the variability in skills taught increases dramatically (for examples, see Table 16.1, for studies by Berler et al., 1982, La Greca & Santogrossi, 1980, and Tiffen & Spence, 1986). Furthermore, the studies vary in the specificity versus generality of the skills being taught. Some of the skills seem rather molecular, whereas others emphasize general concepts. This is an important distinction, as Malik and Furman (1993) have pointed out. Moreover, not all of the skills children are taught have demonstrated links to success in the peer group. Accordingly, the concept of teaching children "competence-correlates" is probably not being applied consistently.

Another point concerning program content concerns the relevance of the skills taught to acceptance versus friendship. An examination of Table 16.1 indicates relatively little reference to the types of friendship tasks or skills that we speculate about later in this chapter. By and large, existing studies appeared to focus on skills for getting along with others more than on skills for building close friendships. Still, there are exceptions (for examples, see the skills listed in Table 16.1 for Gottman, Gonso, & Schuler, 1976, and for Gresham & Nagle, 1980).

Finally, it should be noted that the 16 studies in Table 16.1 vary in terms of the sociometric outcomes assessed at posttest and follow-up, and vary with regard to how soon after completion of the intervention the outcomes were assessed. Some investigators use rating-scale measures, some use nomination measures, and some use both. More important, to date, no one has included reciprocal friendship nominations among the outcomes assessed at intervention posttest or follow-up. This omission reinforces the point that the friendship–acceptance distinction, although long appreciated, has had remarkably little impact on actual research.

In sum, although the studies in Table 16.1 share certain features and assumptions, they vary considerably in design. This makes it difficult to draw firm conclusions about the success or failure of particular approaches. Indeed, given more intervention studies, reviewers could distinguish among various types of studies to assess the effectiveness of certain instructional approaches or certain types of program content. Unfortunately, lacking this opportunity, we are forced to make sense out of a small number of fairly disparate studies. Nevertheless, we continue by highlighting the tentative conclusions that emerge from our examination of these studies.

*Sociometric outcomes of social skills training research.* There are 14 studies listed in Table 16.1 that used a rating-scale sociometric measure as an index of children's acceptance by peers. Of these studies, ten provide evidence that children who were taught social-relationship skills made significant gains in acceptance either at immediate posttest or long-term follow-up (Bierman & Furman, 1984; Coie & Krehbiel, 1984; Csapo, 1983; Gottman et al., 1976; Gresham & Nagle, 1980; Ladd, 1981; Lochman et al., 1993; Oden & Asher, 1977; Siperstein & Gale, 1983; Vaughn & Lancelotta, 1990). Furthermore, among these 14 studies, when significant changes in acceptance occurred at immediate posttest and when follow-up assessments were made, there is evidence of maintenance of change.

It should be stressed, however, that not all studies have resulted in significant improvements in children's peer acceptance, and even in studies with successful outcomes not all children change (Asher & Renshaw, 1981). Moreover, sociometric change is sometimes accompanied by ambiguous findings with regard to behavioral change (see Coie & Koeppl, 1990, for a detailed discussion of this issue). This reality should lead researchers to search for a better understanding of the conditions under which intervention succeeds and fails. Unfortunately we lack even the most rudimentary understanding of this problem. For example, only one study has examined whether intervention is differentially effective with different types of disliked children (Lochman et al., 1993). We are hopeful that this issue will be more fully addressed soon, given the recent widespread attention to subgroups of peer-rejected children (Boivin, Thomassin, & Alain, 1989; Cillessen, Van Ijzendoorn, Van Lieshout, & Hartup, 1992; French, 1988; Hymel, Bowker, & Woody, 1993; Parkhurst & Asher, 1992; Rubin, LeMare, & Lollis, 1990; Williams & Asher, 1987). Though rejected children can be subcategorized as aggressive or as submissive/withdrawn, we know very little about whether these or other possible subtypes are differentially affected by existing social skill training procedures. Coie and Koeppl (1990) speculate that the more withdrawn child benefits from intervention, and that the aggressive-rejected child probably changes relatively little. Although the arguments for this position are plausible, more relevant data are needed.

Finally, it is important to stress that the studies in Table 16.1 have not focused sufficiently on whether children who receive intervention make gains with regard to their participation in best friendship. As we already noted, none of the studies calculated mutual choices from friendship-nomination measures; thus we cannot determine from the existing literature whether children are changing in this regard. However, in three studies children were asked to nominate their best friends and the investigators calculated the number of unilateral friendship nominations children received pre- and post-intervention. Although making inferences about friendship from unilateral measures can be risky, these studies do provide some basis for speculating about the impact of intervention on the friendship dimension. Oden and Asher (1977) is one such study. In addition to collecting rating-scale sociometric data, they asked children at pretest and posttest (but not at 1-year follow-up), to indicate the names of their three best friends. Results indicated that children in the coaching condition made somewhat greater gains in the number of friendship nominations received but the difference across conditions was not significant. Gresham and Nagle (1980) found similar results; children showed significant improvement 3 weeks after the intervention on the rating-scale measure, but not on a best-friends, limited-nomination measure. Likewise, Siperstein and Gale (1983) found on an immediate posttest assessment that children made no gains on an unlimited friendship nomination measure even though they had gained on a rating-scale measure. However, children did make gains on an unlimited nomination measure in which they were asked to name their "other friends." This could indicate that children were beginning to establish friendships, although perhaps not very close ones.

A potentially comparable finding to that of Siperstein and Gale (1983) emerges from Bierman and Furman's (1984) study. Bierman and Furman used a rating-scale measure that was anchored by reference to friendship. They labeled their 5-point scale as follows: 1 = "not friends," 2 = "so so," 3 = "friends," 4 = "good friends," and 5 = "best friends." Results indicated that where children benefited from intervention, children were rated at posttest near the middle of the scale. Given the label associated with the middle rating, this could mean that intervention had some effect on friendship. Alternatively, children may have been more likely to use the midpoint rating after intervention because the two lower ratings implied more negativity than they now felt. In other words, the improvement on their rating-scale measure may be more a reflection of changes in acceptance (i.e., decreased rejection) than the development of close friendships.

In future research, then, there is a need to assess reciprocated-friendship choice. There is also the need to perform long-term assessments of change in friendship as well as acceptance. Children might show long-term gains because over time they might consolidate and refine their newly acquired skills. Time could work to children's benefit in another way. As children move from one grade level to the next, the membership of their class changes, often considerably. The result is a new mix of peers and the opportunity, perhaps, for children who have received social skills training to exercise their new-found skills in a more receptive peer group (see Hymel, Wagner, & Butler, 1990, for a related discussion of the role of reputational factors).

To summarize, existing sociometrically oriented social skills training studies have been fairly successful in affecting changes in acceptance, but little attention has been given to promoting friendship or assessing friendship outcomes. In the next section we speculate about the types of tasks children face and the types of social skills that children need with regard to initiating and maintaining friendships. We do not believe that the skills for peer group acceptance are entirely distinct from the skills involved in friendship, since it seems likely that many of the skills that children need to form good relationships with children in general are relevant to being able to form and maintain a close friendship. Nonetheless, we do believe that the skills traditionally taught for promoting group acceptance are not sufficient and that there are distinct relationship skills that children must acquire to succeed in forming and maintaining friendships. Our hope is that the hypotheses we offer in the next section will help inform the design of intervention research for friendship.

## Some speculations on the social skills basis of friendship formation and maintenance

The formation and maintenance of a satisfactory friendship is an interpersonal achievement built upon a foundation of interpersonal skills. Some of these skills also contribute to social success in the broader sense of peer acceptance; others are specific to the requirements of friendship. To be sure, the features and course of friendship reflect an intermingling of the expectations and interpersonal skills of two participants, not one. In addition, broader encompassing social circumstances – such as structural interaction opportunities, changing group membership, and local and cultural group norms – also influence whether friendships form, what shape they take, and what trajectories they follow. However, the fact that there are two parties to the relationship or that some important influences on friendships are uncontrollable does not diminish the importance of an individual child's repertoire of social skills to the overall success of the relationship.

The literature on children's friendships has not progressed to a point where we can confidently enumerate the specific social tasks involved in friendship or the interpersonal skills either necessary or sufficient for friendship success, particularly those that may be specific to friendship success versus peer acceptance. Rather there is a great need for additional research that examines the correlates of friendship involvement, formation, and loss, and controls for peer acceptance. In other words, what is needed is a body of research on the "competence-correlates" of friendship, where children's level of acceptance is independently assessed and taken into account. Although such literature does not yet exist, we are not without clues to the requirements of successful friendship participation. Certainly, the literature on children's friendship conceptions suggests what children expect of friends and how they regard violations of their expectations (see Berndt, 1986). Likewise, much conceptual and empirical progress has been made recently in thinking about the positive, as well as the negative, features of children's friendships (e.g., Adler & Furman, 1985; Asher & Parker, 1989; Berndt, 1989; Furman & Robbins, 1985; Hartup, 1992b, 1993; Laursen, 1993a, 1993b; Parker & Gottman, 1989).

Drawing upon these and other sources, this final section offers hypotheses about the requirements for successful friendship adjustment. In these hypotheses, we attempt to think separately about factors that contribute to initiating friendships and factors that contribute to making friendships more satisfying to the participants and thereby more enduring. We hasten to add, however, that we recognize that many relational skills serve both initiating and maintenance functions, and thus this distinction can be ephemeral. We also want to emphasize that friendship tasks do not necessarily apply equally to all friendships. For example, some friendships may place considerable emphasis on companionship and little emphasis on intimacy. We do not believe, therefore, that a satisfying friendship necessarily requires that children master each of the tasks in our list. Still, mastery of each task should benefit children. Indeed, there is evidence that a wide range of friendship qualities predicts to children's relationship satisfaction (Parker & Asher, 1993b).

*Hypothesis 1: Children must conceive of friendship as a relationship that transcends a specific context, and children must possess social skills for initiating contact outside the setting where the children typically interact.* Acquaintances signal their interest in deepening their relationship through initiatives and invitations for further interaction opportunities. Further, one of the hallmarks of existing friendship is the partners' demonstrated eagerness to commit their free time to one another in the absence of pressures or constraints that are external to the relationship. Wright (1985) refers to this quality of existing friendships as "voluntary interdependence," and considers it important to the process of friends developing a highly personalized interest and concern for one another. Because acquaintances who interact regularly are often constrained to do so (by being members of the same classroom or team, for example), it can be difficult for children to interact with one another on an individualized basis rather than as mere role occupants. Thus, although friendships can mature in the settings in which they bud, they are assisted by invitations and opportunities for interaction outside the usual or original setting. Contact across multiple settings probably also contributes to a richer shared history among friends, makes friendships more multifaceted, and enhances friends' investment in, interdependency with, and commitment toward one another (Berscheid, 1986; Hinde, 1979).

One problem that children face in forming friendships is that their interaction opportunities can be constrained by parental decisions and community and geographic factors (Bryant & DeMorris, 1992; Du Bois & Hirsch, 1993; Ladd, Profilet, & Hart, 1992; Rubin & Sloman, 1984; Parke et al., 1989; Pettit & Mize, 1993). In urban neighborhoods, parents may impose limits on after-school activities that make it hard for two particular children to get together outside of school (Bryant, 1985), and in rural areas children can be separated by substantial distances making it difficult to achieve contact outside of school. Nevertheless, despite these kinds of constraints, children's own skills do play an important role. As we already noted, children must conceive of friendship as a relationship that transcends any specific context, and they must recognize that opportunities for outside interaction are an avenue for deepening a relationship. Even in the presence of such awareness, important obstacles remain. For example, children must also possess the confidence necessary to initiate outside contact and the specific social skills for extending and accepting social invitations (Du Bois & Hirsch, 1993). Children paralyzed by fear of rejection may let important opportunities for friendship pass. Persistence and resourcefulness may be of importance as it seems likely that a host of external pragmatic considerations could interfere with the likelihood on a given day of any particular request being accepted. In this regard it is worth noting that there is evidence of reliable individual differences in children's persistence in the face of social failure (Goetz & Dweck, 1980). These differences appear to be the result of children's attributions about the causes of success and failure. Finally, children need to be selective in extending invitations to potential friends. Children who initiate friendships with others who are unavailable due to their existing commitments may find the outcome disappointing.

*Hypothesis 2: Children must possess the skills and dispositions necessary to be perceived as fun, resourceful, and enjoyable companions.* Companionship provides some of our most enduring images of childhood friendship, and friends of all ages emphasize the enjoyment they derive from one another and from the activities they undertake jointly (Berndt, 1986). However, the nature of companionship among friends changes developmentally, with collaborative play giving way to intimate conversations involving gossip, humor, disclosure, and problem solving about relationships (Parker & Gottman, 1989). Enjoyment of activities is also central to forming as well as being friends (Gottman, 1983; Parker, 1986), and for this reason the companionship skills involved are likely to contribute to both the formation of new friendships and the enhancement and stability of existing ones. Children who can generate ideas, possess a good sense of humor and an up-beat mood, and who are skilled at games and sports activities are likely to be appealing to other children. Knowledge of elements of the broader culture that are of interest to children (e.g., specific current events; fashion trends; the names of superheroes, or television, sports and rock stars) is also helpful. Successful and stimulating shared experiences contribute to a sense of shared history, joint fate, and a perception of investment in the relationship. Thus, shared experiences are the crucible for friendship formation and probably play a large role in cementing friendships. Part of the skill that undergirds the companionship aspects of friendship, then, includes the skill to recognize that friendships develop out of common experiences. To successfully maintain a friendship, children must expend the effort to imagine, develop, and sustain common activities. And they must closely monitor the shifting interests of their friend. More than that, children must be willing to get involved at times in the interests and activities of their friend even when those interests are not originally their own.

*Hypothesis 3: Children must recognize and respect the "spirit of equality" that is the heart of friendship.* Friendships can be said to be "leveling," in the sense that – though friendships develop between individuals of different abilities or status – friends "participate as equals in the sense that those things that one person is eligible to do the other person is eligible to do" (Davis & Todd, 1982, p. 83). Further, the formation and success of friendship depend on the development of a general climate of reciprocity and balance between partners. The child who is responsive to his or her friend's needs and interests has the right to expect responsiveness in return. This concept of reciprocity is a core component of the definition of friendship, and is recognized as such by adults and relatively young children alike (see Berndt, 1986). For this reason the requirement of reciprocity in friendship carries a particularly strong moral force (Rawlins, 1992; Youniss & Smoller, 1985); children who do not appreciate this are likely to encounter difficulty. At the same time, children (and adults) expect reciprocity in friendship to be maintained without complicated and overt "accounting" practices. Just as swiftly as the child who fails to reciprocate, the child who insists on strict and immediate reciprocity will encounter resentment and difficulty. An important challenge to participants in childhood friendship, therefore, is to fulfill the very binding responsibilities of helping and sharing in such a way that their obligatory aspects are not salient. Friends need to believe that prosocial acts are genuinely motivated by concern and caring, even when those acts are due or overdue.

*Hypothesis 4: Children must possess skills for self-disclosure.* Many authors regard intimacy as the defining feature of friendship and are reluctant to label a relationship as a friendship in the absence of evidence that the parties are intimate with one another. The expression of intimacy includes reciprocal self-disclosure, or the revealing of private personal experiences and strongly held thoughts and feelings. Research on intimacy in children's actual friendships has emphasized developmental and sex differences in self-disclosure among friends (e.g., Berndt & Perry, 1986; Buhrmester, 1990; Buhrmester & Furman, 1987; Sharabany, Gershoni, & Hofman, 1981; Reid, Landesman, Treder, & Jaccard, 1989). However, it should be stressed that children of both genders and every age value the opportunity to be open and frank with someone who is open and frank with them.

Self-disclosure exposes areas of personal vulnerability, and therefore requires an existing basis of trust. Somewhat paradoxically, however, children base their trust partly on successful experience with self-disclosure. Thus, trust is both the means to self-disclosure as well as its end product. Research on children's conceptions of the requirements of friendship shows that references to trust appear initially during early adolescence and increase steadily thereafter (see Berndt, 1986). Individual differences in children's willingness to trust and to engage in self-disclosure have also been documented, and have been found to be related to children's social success and adjustment with peers (Buzzelli, 1988; Rotenberg & Silz, 1988).

The child who is unable to trust or who does not conceptualize friendship as an appropriate arena for self-disclosure will face difficulties initiating and maintaining friendships. The skills of self-disclosure go beyond a willingness to self-disclosure and an appreciation of the opportunity. Responsive listening is also required. Responsive listening is evidenced by verbal and nonverbal responses to a friend's disclosure. This type of listening may be especially important in the beginning stages of friendship, when partners' limited experience with each other creates conditions for considerable misunderstanding of meaning and background information. Appropriate social skills for self-disclosure also include the ability to exercise restraint around sensitive issues. As Rawlins (1992, p. 22) observes:

Friends expect and want to trust in the honesty of each other's remarks. However, they also trust their friends not to hurt them by candid comments on personally vulnerable issues about which only a close friend is likely to know. Self might reveal a sensitive concern to the other, expecting a restrained reaction. A discreet response would reinforce self's trust in him or her. . . .

*Hypothesis 5: Children must be able to express caring, concern, admiration, and affection in appropriate ways.* Beyond the specific communicative requirements of self-disclosure per se, friendship relies on related skills for expressing mutual caring, concern, admiration, and affection for one's partner. These behaviors have been rightly identified as contributing to an atmosphere of personal validation within friendship, which, in turn, may contribute positively to children's developing sense of self-worth. To quote Rawlins's (1992) excellent essay again:

> Interaction with a friend is widely and duly celebrated for its potential to validate one's self-concept and enhance one's self-esteem (Sullivan, 1953). People are at ease with their friends because they feel liked and accepted by someone . . . familiar with both their strengths and their weakness, their charming and their irritating qualities.

A feeling of acceptance, then, contributes to personal validation and to satisfaction and stability in the relationship by permitting spontaneity versus the feeling that one is "required to play a role, wear a mask, or inhibit expressions of their personal characteristics" (Davis & Todd, 1982, p. 83). Children feel accepted to the extent that they believe that they are valued for who they are and not under coercion to become a new, different person.

Childhood friends ordinarily express their concern and affection for each other intermittently, not continuously. The occasions for such displays are varied and require different social skills. For example, when children succeed at difficult endeavors friends are expected to recognize these achievements with congratulations and express admiration as appropriate. Children who do not do so, who do so begrudgingly, or who harbor or express jealousy not only fail to validate their friends' experiences and successes but contribute to an undercurrent of rivalry and disappointment that can undermine friendship stability. By contrast, social failure and negative events occasion quite different but equally important opportunities for displays of acceptance, affection, caring, and concern.

The forms that affection may take vary by gender, ethnicity, context, and local custom. For example, some expressions of physical affection are appropriate to some children but not others (e.g., hand-holding and hugging are more appropriate for girl friends than boy friends in Western, middle-class cultures), or in some circumstances (e.g., a frightening movie) but not others (e.g., the classroom). Certain kinds of nicknames that are endearing between close friends may not be tolerated between children who are less close. These unwritten display rules pose formidable challenges to children's social knowledge and social skills.

*Hypothesis 6: Children must be able to help their friends when their friends are in need.* Children, like adults, experience negative events in daily living. Their stresses can include minor daily hassles, such as misplaced homework assignments or forgotten lunches; normative changes, such as impending school transitions; social setbacks, such as embarrassing gaffes and romantic breakups; and more emotionally devastating major life events, such as the experience of parental separation or the death of a parent. Like adults, when children experience problems and stress they often turn to their friends for help, advice, comfort, and emotional support. Under these circumstances, friends may be called upon to express affection and concern, and to minimize or find solutions to their friends' problems. To be effective in response to this social task, children must recognize that a problem exists, understand the seriousness of the problem, the problem details, and the specific emotions associated with the problem. And they must insure that their affection and advice is perceived and received as selflessly motivated and genuine. Frank criticism may be called for in some circumstances, and children recognize that criticism from their friends indicates personal concern. However, to be effective, criticism must be tendered tactfully; also, presumably children need to recognize those circumstances when criticism, though justified, should not be expressed at all.

A further complicating challenge is that, although children enjoy the privilege of calling on their friends in times of need or distress, they also plainly value the liberty to make decisions without undue intrusion or interference by their friends. Rawlins (1992) refers to this tension between these partly incompatible aspects of friendship assistance as "the dialectic of the freedom to be independent and the freedom to be dependent" and points out that when not managed correctly the assistance and advice of partners can undermine rather than enhance friendship.

In addition to comfort and advice-giving skills, comfort and advice-seeking skills are also important. Help seeking requires specific skills for making direct requests, skills for recognizing and articulating one's internal emotions, and, as we have already discussed, skills for self-disclosure. Responsiveness may also be required to encourage the helper to persist to a satisfactory answer. These skills are obviously of direct benefit to the user; and they can strengthen the friendship itself by leading the helper to feel needed, irreplaceable, and effectual.

*Hypothesis 7: Children must be reliable partners.* Friends rely on one another, and if children are to be successful in maintaining or forming friendships they must be perceived as reliable partners. Presumably, reliability is founded initially in consistency of availability. To be perceived as reliable, children must exhibit a consistent willingness to spend time with their partner. If children attend to their relationships in a sporadic manner, it is unlikely that they will be perceived as a reliable partner regardless of the quality of those scattered interactions.

The content of children's friendship interactions also has significance in establishing perceptions of reliability. Keeping confidences, sticking up for someone, and being honest with someone are all behaviors that encourage perceptions of reliability. Therefore, a child who violates confidences, who acts disloyally with a friend when others are around, or who engages in deception toward a friend is likely to be perceived as unreliable and to experience persistent friendship difficulties. Moreover, as children get older, they increasingly stress consistency between ''words and deeds'' as the basis of judgments of whether to trust somebody (Rotenberg, 1980). It may be especially important to social success, therefore, for children to follow through on promises.

*Hypothesis 8: Children must be able to manage disagreements and to resolve (and to the extent possible, prevent) more serious conflicts.* The ''close quarters'' of friendship present seemingly endless opportunities for disagreements and conflicts, which, if not managed and resolved well, can dissolve friendships (Hartup, 1992a; Hartup & Laursen, 1993; Laursen, 1993b). Further, children who disagree far more than they agree are unlikely to become friends in the first place (Gottman, 1983). For some children the source of many conflicts are unrealistic expectations of friends and friendships (see Selman & Schultz, 1990). That is, many children encounter unnecessary difficulties because they expect their friends never to disappoint them, to know everything about them, or to be their friend exclusively. As Smilansky (1991, p. 61) comments: ''Such inflexibility and high expectations inevitably lead to disillusionment with friends and an inability to enjoy a variety of friends, friendship of varying degrees of intensity and various forms of relationships.''

Children must recognize the insidious effects of serious conflicts on relationships and thus recognize the need for effective conflict resolution strategies. When conflict is resolved successfully through frank discussion and compromise, progress toward friendship can be made and existing friendships can be strengthened (Hartup, 1992a). Skills for managing disagreement and preventing and resolving conflict include skills for social perspective-taking, frustration tolerance, the ability to delay gratification, skills for self-disclosure, social problem-solving skills, skills for managing the internal experience of emotion (appropriate attributions, self-calming strategies), knowledge of emotional display rules (e.g., masking disappointment in appropriate circumstances), and knowledge of potentially helpful environmental resources (e.g., parents, teachers, and reference information). These skills are general skills that are likely to be applicable to various conflict situations. However, children's specific strategies for resolving conflict must be responsive to the context of the disagreement. For example, there is evidence that friends resolve conflicts differently in ''closed'' versus ''open'' settings (see Hartup, 1992a). Closed settings are situations in which two children are required to be together and cannot determine for themselves with whom and for how long to interact. Open settings are situations in which many alternative partners are available. In open settings children are free to select a different partner or to withdraw from interaction entirely. Conflicts between friends are more intense in closed versus open settings, but are also more likely to be resolved.

*Hypothesis 9: Children must be able to forgive.* Forgiveness is an aspect of conflict resolution, but its salience and significance to friendship merits it separate consideration. Because hurt feelings, disappointment, and transgressions are an inevitable part of close friendship, the child who is unwilling or unable to forgive others will have difficulty forming friendships and special difficulty keeping close friendships. Even if friendships are maintained, children's satisfaction with these relationships will be diminished.

Forgiveness depends, in part, on the child's assessment of the intentionality behind hurtful acts. That is, the child's willingness to heal a wounded relationship is affected by the extent to which the child perceives the act as an intentional attempt to cause harm or embarrassment. Clearly, forgiveness is facilitated by perceiving the hurtful act as unintentional. Therefore, a child who cannot separate the intentions from the consequences of a hurtful act will face difficulties forgiving his or her friend. Forgiveness is probably also facilitated to the extent that the relationship had a firm foundation of trust and is characterized by respect and understanding. If a hurt child feels otherwise respected and broadly understood, occasional acts of betrayal and disappointment are more likely to be seen in their isolated context, and more likely to be forgiven. When children routinely find their friend's behavior puzzling and unpredictable, forgiveness may not be forthcoming. After forgiveness, a reestablishment of trust is required, which may take considerable time. Presumably, however, the process of forgiveness and the reestablishment of trust can result in a subsequently stronger friendship bond.

*Hypothesis 10: Children must recognize that friendships are embedded within the broader social network of the peer group and classroom, and children must be prepared to address issues within and outside the relationship that result from this fact.* Friendships are part of a broader structure that includes cliques and larger crowds. As Hartup (1992b) recently observed, we do not have very good models of how such nested systems operate. It is a safe bet, however, that tensions are created within and between these nested systems. For example, third parties introduce the prospects of jealousy, envy, and rivalry between friends (Salovey & Rodin, 1989). *Jealousy* may result when children in a friendship have differing conceptions of the appropriate level of exclusivity of friendship, and one member perceives potential for loss of a highly valued source of affection and companionship (Selman & Schultz, 1990). *Rivalries* can develop when two children who are friends find themselves vying for the exclusive friendship of another, outside child. Finally, one member of a dyad may become *envious* of their partner's friendship with a third child. The actions of outside children who are feeling jealousy, rivalry, or envy can also make it difficult for a pair of friends to sustain their relationship. Special skills for communication and diplomacy may be required in these common circumstances.

Another type of tension is introduced when children find themselves divided by incompatible loyalties to different friends (whether to share a secret that has bearing on another friend) or between their public (e.g., team leader, group member, or committee chair) and their private (e.g., friend, confidant, loyal supporter) responsibilities.

In addition, friendships and potential friendships are probably also significantly affected by constraints introduced by children's group status and crowd membership. For example, the crowds in middle schools and high schools often include the "jocks," "brains," "loners," "druggies," "populars," and "nerds" (see Brown, 1990; Castlebury & Arnold, 1988). Crowds place important restrictions on children's social contacts and relationships with peers (Brown, 1989; Eder, 1985). For example, cliques are generally formed within (vs. across) crowds, and some crowd boundaries (e.g., jocks and populars) are more permeable than others (e.g., populars and nerds) (see Brown, 1990). Furthermore, crowds have different levels of prestige, which poses special challenges. Eder (1985), for example, has suggested that as preadolescent girls become increasingly popular, it becomes more difficult for these girls to reciprocate the friendship overtures of lower-status girls. High-status girls who do so risk social disapproval from other high-status girls. However, as a consequence, these girls earn a reputation for being "snobbish" outside their elite, high-status group, making them less desirable as friends in most children's eyes. Obviously, a child's repertoire of social skills may be severely taxed by the operation of these outside constraints on friendship, and a child unprepared to recognize or respond to these realities is at risk for social failure and disappointment.

Finally, a child's repertoire of social skills is likely to be challenged in a different way when events within friendships spill over to influence the broader peer group. A short passage from an essay of one of our undergraduate students expresses this dilemma: "When I was in the third grade I had an argument with my best friend, Katie. Katie was the unspoken leader of our group of friends and because of this I was basically ostracized unitl Katie and I made up months later. During that time I was miserable." Again, our current knowledge of how and when this type of circumstance occurs, and how children can respond effectively, is very limited. Our undergraduate, for example, may have been spared some pain had some of her specific social skills been stronger; for example, had she been more skilled at explaining the event that precipitated the breakup to other (no doubt, skeptical) children, had she been more skilled at forcefully protesting the unfair exclusion, or had she been more persuasive at lobbying other high-status peers to her "cause." Alternatively, perhaps such processes must run their course, and in the long run what matters is whether the afflicted children can feign indifference or respond to the rejection with poise and grace.

Clearly, children must be resourceful in managing the vexing moral and social dilemmas posed by the task of maintaining friendships in a larger social context. In some cases, children must be prepared to anticipate these tensions, and act to forestall them. In other, less predictable circumstances, some form of remedial action or reparation may be required to restore balance or harmony.

## Conclusion

In the last decade, the study of children's friendships has come into its own within the broader field of research on children's adjustment with peers. As part of this focus a number of authors have argued for the careful conceptual discrimination between children's participation in friendship versus children's acceptance by the peer group more generally. Our purpose in this chapter has been to review this distinction, to consider its utility, to examine the existing social skill training literature with regard to friendship as well as acceptance outcomes, and to speculate about the kinds of skill foci that may need to be addressed if social skills training is to have an impact on friendship as well as acceptance. Our call in this chapter is for a new generation of social skills training studies. In this spirit, we offered some hypotheses about potential foci for intervention efforts.

Our hypotheses do not address the complete list of critical areas but they are a start toward a comprehensive mapping of the critical social tasks and skills in the friendship domain. Certainly, children confront other friendship tasks and need to acquire other friendship skills. For example, a further hypothesis might be that children need to learn how to cope with change in a relationship, given that friendships take unpredictable twists and turns over time. Partners develop new interests, face special opportunities, and experience normative and nonnormative outside life events (e.g., a school transition, a family divorce). Such changes challenge the survival of friendships, particularly when they do not happen in tandem to the two partners. A child may find that his or her friend is no longer available on Saturday afternoons, has formed a new friendship with another child in another neighborhood, has quit band, has joined the cheerleading squad, must stay home more to tend to a sick parent, and so on. If children do not cope flexibly with such changes, the friendship will not continue. We are sure, then, that there are many challenges to friendship that go beyond the list that we have identified here.

Interventions designed to foster successful friendship involvement will require not only a good understanding of the skills to be taught, but also a good understanding of the best practices for conveying these skills to children. Previous successful social skills training studies contain several elements. First, the focal child receives guided instruction from a knowledgeable adult about general and specific concepts of social interaction. Second, the child is given an opportunity to practice these concepts while interacting with peers. Third, the child is asked to reflect on the concepts being taught in light of their own experience. Our hunch is that interventions to improve friendship will be more effective if they, too, incorporate the important components of instruction, rehearsal, and reflection.

However, there are several other service delivery parameters to be considered. One of these is the size of the instructional group. In past social skills training studies, children have received individualized instruction, instruction in pairs, and instruction in small groups (see Table 16.1). Each of these contexts may offer special opportunities. Another parameter of service delivery concerns the instructional technique(s) used to teach children new concepts of social interaction. Concepts can be taught by an adult or peer, presented in media such as books or films, or could be taught more inductively by having concepts emerge from guided discussion (see Selman & Schultz, 1990, for an example). Our assumption is that any procedure for teaching new concepts will be more effective when it is augmented by providing children with opportunities for practice and reflection. For example, it seems unlikely that having children read friendship-advice books or fiction involving friendship themes will be very effective without opportunities for children to try out new ideas or reflect on their own friendship experiences.

The entire matter of how best to intervene for friendship will benefit from a developmental perspective (see Furman, 1984). Both the content of intervention and the procedures used to teach friendship skills must vary as a function of the children's developmental level. For example, it seems plausible that older children would have a greater capacity to reflect on more distal friendship experiences, whereas for younger children it may be critical to provide interaction opportunities that provide an immediate context for discussing relationship principles.

In concluding this chapter we want to stress that a special focus on intervening for friendship will have implications for the kinds of outcome assessments that are made in social skills training research. In addition to learning whether children make gains in peer acceptance, it will be important to assess a variety of outcomes that have not been typically included in social skills training research. One basic point that we have emphasized is that it is important to learn whether children have friends, as demonstrated by reciprocated friendship choices. But beyond the issue of whether a child has a friend, two other dimensions require special attention. One of these is the temporal aspects of friendship (Berndt,

Hawkins, & Hoyle, 1986; Ladd, 1990; Parker & Seal, 1993). We need to know not only whether children make new friends but whether they are successful at keeping them. This can be addressed by analyzing whether a child maintains particular friendships from posttest to long-term follow-up. It will also be important to assess the related matter of the quality of children's friendships. We need to ask, for example, whether friendships are characterized by high levels of companionship and recreation, by affection and support, by shared intimacy, and by a willingness to offer help and guidance. We must also ask whether friendships have high levels of conflict and whether the friends have the ability to resolve their conflicts. Fortunately, considerable progress has been made in the area of measuring friendship quality (e.g., see Berndt & Perry, 1986; Buhrmester, 1990; Bukowski & Newcomb, 1987; Furman & Buhrmester, 1985, Parker & Asher, 1993b; Reid et al., 1989; Sharabany et al., 1981). We are hopeful that these kinds of innovations in assessment will figure in the evaluation of future intervention efforts.

# References

Adler, T. F., & Furman, W. (1985). A model for children's relationships and relationship dysfunction. In S. Duck (Ed.), *Handbook of personal relationships* (pp. 211–232). New York: Wiley.

Asher, S. R. (1985). An evolving paradigm in social skill training research with children. In B. H. Schneider, K. H. Rubin, & J. E. Ledingham (Eds.), *Children's peer relations: Issues in assessment and intervention* (pp. 157–171). New York: Springer-Verlag.

Asher, S. R. (1993, March). Inviting children to self-refer. In Celia Fisher (Chair), *Ethical issues in the reporting and referring of research participants*. Symposium conducted at the biennial meeting of the Society for Research in Child Development, New Orleans.

Asher, S. R., & Hymel, S. (1981). Children's social competence in peer relations: Sociometric and behavioral assessment. In J. D. Wine & M. D. Smye (Eds.), *Social competence* (pp. 122–157). New York: Guilford.

Asher, S. R., Hymel, S., & Renshaw, P. D. (1984). Loneliness in children. *Child Development, 55,* 1456–1464.

Asher, S. R., & Parker, J. G. (1989). The significance of peer relationship problems in childhood. In B. H. Schneider, G. Attili, J. Nadel, & R. P. Weissberg (Eds.), *Social competence in developmental perspective* (pp. 5–23). Dordrecht, The Netherlands: Kluwer Academic Publishing.

Asher, S. R., & Renshaw, P. D. (1981). Children without friends: Social knowledge and social skill training. In S. R. Asher & J. M. Gottman (Eds.), *The development of children's friendships* (pp. 273–296). New York: Cambridge University Press.

Asher, S. R., Singleton, L. C., & Taylor, A. R. (1982, March). Acceptance versus friendship: A longitudinal study of racial integration. In Gary W. Ladd (Chair), *Racial integration and mainstreaming: Methodological and substantive issues*. Symposium conducted at the annual meeting of the American Educational Research Association, New York.

Asher, S. R., & Wheeler, V. A. (1985). Children's loneliness: A comparison of rejected and neglected peer status. *Journal of Consulting and Clinical Psychology, 53,* 500–505.

Asher, S. R., Zelis, K. M., Parker, J. G., & Bruene, C. M. (1991, April). Self-referral for peer relationship problems among aggressive and withdrawn low-accepted children. In Jennifer T. Parkhurst and David L. Rabiner (Chairs), *The behavioral characteristics and the subjective experiences of aggressive and withdrawn/submissive rejected children.* Symposium conducted at the biennial meeting of the Society for Research in Child Development, Seattle.

Ausubel, D., & Sullivan, E. V. (1970). *Theory and problems of child development* (2nd Ed.). New York: Grune & Stratton.

Barth, J. M., & Parke, R. D. (1993). Parent–child relationship influences on children's transition to school. *Merrill-Palmer Quarterly, 39,* 173–195.

Berler, E. S., Gross, A. M., & Drabman, R. S. (1982). Social skills training with children: Proceed with caution. *Journal of Applied Behavior Analysis, 15,* 41–53.

Berndt, T. J. (1984). Sociometric, social-cognitive, and behavioral measures for the study of friendship and popularity. In T. Field, J. L. Roopnarine, & M. Segal (Eds.), *Friendships in normal and handicapped children* (pp. 31–52). Norwood, NJ: Ablex.

Berndt, T. J. (1986). Children's comments about their friendships. In M. Perlmutter (Ed.), *Cognitive perspectives on children's social and behavioral development: Minnesota symposia on child psychology* (Vol. 18, pp. 189–212). Hillsdale, NJ: Erlbaum.

Berndt, T. J. (1989). Obtaining support from friends during childhood and adolescence. In D. Belle (Ed.), *Children's social networks and social supports* (pp. 308–331). New York: Wiley.

Berndt, T. J., Hawkins, J. A., & Hoyle, S. G. (1986). Changes in friendship during a school year: Effects on children's and adolescents' impressions of friendship and sharing with friends. *Child Development, 57,* 1284–1297.

Berndt, T. J., & Perry, T. B. (1986). Children's perceptions of friendships as supportive relationships. *Developmental Psychology, 22,* 640–648.

Berscheid, E. (1986). Emotional experience in close relationships: Some implications for child development. In W. W. Hartup & Z. Rubin (Eds.), *Relationships and development* (pp. 135–166). Hillsdale, NJ: Erlbaum.

Bierman, K. L. (1986). Process of change during social skills training with preadolescents and its relation to treatment outcome. *Child Development, 57,* 230–240.

Bierman, K. L., & Furman, W. (1984). The effects of social skills training and peer involvement on the social adjustment of preadolescents. *Child Development, 55,* 151–162.

Bierman, K. L., Miller, C. M., & Stabb, S. (1987). Improving the social behavior and peer acceptance of rejected boys: Effects of social skill training with instruction and prohibitions. *Journal of Consulting and Clinical Psychology, 55,* 194–200.

Boivin, M., Thomassin, L., & Alain, M. (1989). Peer rejection and self-perceptions among early elementary school children: Aggressive-rejectees vs. withdrawn-rejectees. In B. H. Schneider, G. Attili, J. Nadel, & R. P. Weissberg (Eds.), *Social competence in developmental perspective* (pp. 392–394). Dordrecht, The Netherlands: Kluwer Academic Publishing.

Brown, B. B. (1989). The role of peer groups in adolescents' adjustment to secondary school. In T. J. Berndt & G. W. Ladd (Eds.), *Peer relationships in child development* (pp. 188–215). New York: Wiley.

Brown, B. B. (1990). Peer groups and peer cultures. In S. S. Feldman & G. R. Elliott (Eds.), *At the threshold: The developing adolescent* (pp. 171–196). Cambridge, MA: Harvard University Press.

Bryant, B. K. (1985). The neighborhood walk: Sources of support in middle childhood. *Monographs of the Society for Research in Child Development* (Serial No. 210, Vol. 50, No. 3).

Bryant, B. K., & DeMorris, K. A. (1992). Beyond parent–child relationships: Potential links between family environments and peer relations. In R. D. Parke & G. W. Ladd (Eds.), *Family–peer relationships: Modes of linkage* (pp. 159–189). Hillsdale, NJ: Erlbaum.

Buhrmester, D. (1990). Intimacy of friendship, interpersonal competence, and adjustment during preadolescence and adolescence. *Child Development, 61,* 1101–1111.

Buhrmester, D., & Furman, W. (1987). The development of companionship and intimacy. *Child Development, 58,* 1101–1113.

Bukowski, W. M., & Hoza, B. (1989). Popularity and friendship: Issues in theory, measurement, and outcome. In T. J. Berndt & G. W. Ladd (Eds.), *Peer relationships in child development* (pp. 15–45). New York: Wiley.

Bukowski, W. M., & Newcomb, A. F. (1987, April). *Friendship quality and the "self" during early adolescence.* Paper presented at the biennial meeting of the Society for Research in Child Development, Baltimore.

Buzzelli, C. A. (1988). The development of trust in children's relations with peers. *Child Study Journal, 18,* 33–46.

Campbell, J. D. (1964). Peer relations in childhood. In M. L. Hoffman & L. W. Hoffman (Eds.), *Review of child development research* (Vol. 1, pp. 289–322). Sage: New York.

Cassidy, J., & Asher, S. R. (1992). Loneliness and peer relations in young children. *Child Development, 63,* 350–365.

Castlebury, S., & Arnold, J. (1988). Early adolescent perceptions of informal groups in a middle school. *Journal of Early Adolescence, 8,* 97–107.

Chittenden, G. F. (1942). An experimental study in measuring and modifying assertive behavior in young children. *Monographs of the Society for Research in Child Development, 7,* (Serial No. 31).

Cillessen, A. H. N., Van IJzendoorn, H. W. Van Lieshout, C. F. M., & Hartup, W. W. (1992). Heterogeneity of peer-rejected boys. *Child Development, 63,* 893–905.

Coie, J. D., Dodge, K. A., & Coppotelli, H. (1982). Dimensions and types of social status: A cross-age perspective. *Developmental Psychology, 18,* 557–570.

Coie, J. D., Dodge, K. A., & Kupersmidt, J. (1990). Peer group behavior and social status. In S. R. Asher & J. D. Coie (Eds.), *Peer rejection in childhood* (pp. 17–39). New York: Cambridge University Press.

Coie, J. D., & Koeppl, A. K. (1990). Adapting intervention to the problems of aggressive and disruptive rejected children. In S. R. Asher & J. D. Coie (Eds.), *Peer rejection in childhood* (pp. 309–337). New York: Cambridge University Press.

Coie, J. D., & Krehbiel, G. (1984). Effects of academic tutoring on the social status of low-achieving socially rejected children. *Child Development, 55,* 1465–1478.

Crick, N. R., & Ladd, G. W. (1993). Children's perceptions of their peer experiences: Attributions, social anxiety, and social avoidance. *Developmental Psychology, 29,* 244–254.

Csapo, M. (1983). Effectiveness of coaching socially withdrawn/isolated children in specific social skills. *Educational Psychology, 3,* 31–42.

Davis, K. E., & Todd, M. J. (1982). Friendship and love relationships. In K. E. Davis & T. Mitchell (Eds.), *Advances in descriptive psychology* (Vol. 2, pp. 79–122). Greenwich, CT: JAI Press.

Dodge, K. A., & Feldman, E. (1990). Issues in social cognition and sociometric status. In S. R. Asher & J. D. Coie (Eds.), *Peer rejection in childhood,* (pp. 119–155). New York: Cambridge University Press.

Du Bois, D. L., & Hirsch, B. J. (1993). School/nonschool friendship patterns in early adolescence. *Journal of Early Adolescence, 13,* 102–122.

Eder, D. (1985). The cycle of popularity: Interpersonal relations among female adolescents. *Sociology of Education, 58,* 154–165.

French, D. C. (1988). Heterogeneity of peer rejected boys: Aggressive and nonaggressive subtypes. *Child Development, 59,* 976–985.

Furman, W. (1982). Children's friendships. In T. Field, G. Finley, A. Huston, H. Quay, & C. Troll (Eds.), *Review of Human Development* (pp. 18–30). New York: Wiley.

Furman, W. (1984). Issues in the assessment of social skills of normal and handicapped children. In T. Field, J. L. Roopnarine, & M. Segal (Eds.), *Friendships in normal and handicapped children* (pp. 3–30). New York: Ablex.

Furman, W., & Buhrmester, D. (1985). Children's perception of the personal relationships in their social networks. *Developmental Psychology, 21,* 1016–1024.

Furman, W., & Robbins, P. (1985). What's the point?: Selection of treatment objectives. In B.

Schneider, K. H. Rubin, & J. E. Ledingham (Eds.), *Children's peer relations: Issues in assessment and intervention* (pp. 41–54). New York: Springer-Verlag.

Goetz, T. F., & Dweck, C. S. (1980). Learned helplessness in social situations. *Journal of Personality and Social Psychology, 39,* 246–255.

Gottman, J. M. (1983). How children become friends. *Monographs of the Society for Research in Child Development, 78* (3, Serial No. 201).

Gottman, J. M., Gonso, J., & Schuler, P. (1976). Teaching social skills to isolated children. *Journal of Abnormal Child Psychology, 4,* 179–197.

Gresham, F. M., & Nagle, R. J. (1980). Social skills training with children: Responsiveness to modeling and coaching as a function of peer orientation. *Journal of Consulting and Clinical Psychology, 18,* 718–729.

Gronlund, N. E. (1959). *Sociometry in the classroom.* New York: Harper.

Hartup, W. W. (1970). Peer interaction and social organization. In P. H. Mussen (Ed.), *Carmichael's manual of child psychology* (Vol. 2, pp. 361–456). New York: Wiley.

Hartup, W. W. (1983). Peer relations. In P. H. Mussen (Ed.), *Handbook of child psychology,* (Vol. 4, 4th ed., pp. 103–196). New York: Wiley.

Hartup, W. W. (1992a). Conflict and friendship relations. In C. U. Shantz & W. W. Hartup (Eds.), *Conflict in child and adolescent development* (pp. 185–215). New York: Cambridge University Press.

Hartup, W. W. (1992b). Friendships and their developmental significance. In H. McGurk (Ed.), *Childhood social development: Contemporary perspectives* (pp. 175–205). Hillsdale, NJ: Erlbaum.

Hartup, W. W. (1993). Adolescents and their friends. In B. Laursen (Ed.), *Close friendships in adolescence* (pp. 3–22). San Francisco: Jossey-Bass.

Hartup, W. W., & Laursen, B. (1993). Conflict and context in peer relationships. In C. H. Hart (Ed.), *Children on playgrounds: Research perspectives and applications* (pp. 44–84). Albany, NY: SUNY Press.

Havighurst, R. (1953). *Human development and education.* New York: Longmans, Green, & Co.

Hayden, L., Tarulli, D., & Hymel, S. (1988, May). *Children talk about loneliness.* Paper presented at the biennial meeting of the University of Waterloo Conference on Child Development, Waterloo, Ontario.

Heinlein, L., & Spinner, B. (1985, April). *Measuring emotional loneliness in children.* Paper presented at the biennial meeting of the Society for Research in Child Development, Toronto, Ontario, Canada.

Hinde, R. A. (1979). *Towards understanding relationships.* London: Academic Press.

Hymel, S., Bowker, A., & Woody, E. (1993). Aggressive versus withdrawn unpopular children: Variations in peer and self-perceptions in multiple domains. *Child Development, 64,* 879–896.

Hymel, S., Freigang, R., Franke, S., Both, L., Bream, L., & Borys, S. (1983, June). *Children's attributions for social situations: Variations as a function of social status and self-perception variables.* Paper presented at the annual meeting of the Canadian Psychological Association, Winnipeg, Manitoba, Canada.

Hymel, S., Wagner, E., & Butler, L. J. (1990). Reputational bias: View from the peer group. In S. R. Asher & J. D. Coie (Eds.), *Peer rejection in childhood* (pp. 156–186). New York: Cambridge University Press.

Jack, L. M. (1934). An experimental study of ascendant behavior in preschool children. *University of Iowa Studies in Child Welfare, 9,* 9–65.

Kazdin, A. E. (1993). Psychotherapy for children and adolescents. *American Psychologist, 48,* 644–657.

Kupersmidt, J. B., Coie, J. D., & Dodge, K. A. (1990). The role of poor peer relationships in the development of disorder. In S. R. Asher & J. D. Coie (Eds.), *Peer rejection in childhood* (pp. 274–305). New York: Cambridge University Press.

Ladd, G. W. (1981). Effectiveness of a social learning method for enhancing children's social interaction and peer acceptance. *Child Development, 57,* 171–178.

Ladd, G. W. (1990). Having friends, keeping friends, making friends, and being liked by peers in the classroom: Predictors of children's early school adjustment? *Child Development, 61,* 1081–1100.

Ladd, G. W., & Asher, S. R. (1985). Social skill training and children's peer relations. In L. L'Abate & M. Milan (Eds.), *Handbook of social skills training* (pp. 219–244). New York: Wiley.

Ladd, G. W., & Mize, J. (1983). A cognitive-social learning model of social-skill training. *Psychological Review, 90,* 127–157.

Ladd, G. W., Profilet, S., & Hart, C. H. (1992). Parents' management of children's peer relations: Facilitating and supervising children's activities in the peer culture. In R. D. Parke & G. W. Ladd (Eds.), *Family–peer relationships: Modes of linkage* (pp. 215–254). Hillsdale, NJ: Erlbaum.

La Greca, A. M., & Santogrossi, D. A. (1980). Social skills training with elementary school students: A behavioral group approach. *Journal of Consulting and Clinical Psychology, 48,* 220–227.

Laursen, B. (Ed.). (1993a). *Close friendships in adolescence.* San Francisco: Jossey-Bass.

Laursen. B. (1993b). Conflict management among close peers. In B. Laursen (Ed.), *Close friendships in adolescence* (pp. 39–54). San Francisco: Jossey-Bass.

Lochman, J. E., Coie, J. D., Underwood, M. K., & Terry, R. (1993). Effectiveness of a social relations intervention program for aggressive and nonaggressive, rejected children. *Journal of Consulting and Clinical Psychology, 61,* 1053–1058.

Malik, N. M., & Furman, W. (1993). Problems in children's peer relations: What can the clinician do? *Journal of Child Psychology and Psychiatry, 34,* 1303–1326.

Marcoen, A., & Brumagne, M. (1985). Loneliness among children and young adolescents. *Developmental Psychology, 21,* 1025–1031.

Mize, J., & Ladd, G. W. (1990). A cognitive-social learning approach to social skill training with low-status preschool children. *Developmental Psychology, 26,* 388–397.

Moreno, J. L. (1934). *Who shall survive? A new approach to the problem of human interrelations.* Washington, DC: Nervous and Mental Disease Publishing.

Oden, S., & Asher, S. R. (1977). Coaching children in social skills for friendship making. *Child Development, 48,* 495–506.

Page, M. L. (1936). The modification of ascendant behavior in preschool children. *University of Iowa Studies in Child Welfare, 12,* 7–69.

Parke, R. D., MacDonald, K. B., Burks, V. M., Carson, J., Bhavnagri, N., Barth, J., & Beitel, A. (1989). Family and peer systems: In search of linkages. In K. Kreppner & R. M. Lerner (Eds.), *Family systems and life-span development* (pp. 65–92). Hillsdale, NJ: Erlbaum.

Parker, J. G. (1986). Becoming friends: Conversational skills for friendship formation in young children. In J. M. Gottman & J. G. Parker (Eds.), *Conversations of friends* (pp. 103–138). New York: Cambridge University Press.

Parker, J. G., & Asher, S. R. (1987). Peer relations and later personal adjustment: Are low-accepted children at risk? *Psychological Bulletin, 102,* 357–389.

Parker, J. G., & Asher, S. R. (1989, April). Peer relations and social adjustment: Are friendship and group acceptance distinct domains? In W. M. Bukowski (Chair), *Properties, processes, and effects of friendship relations during childhood and adolescence.* Symposium conducted at the biennial meeting of the Society for Research in Child Development, Kansas City, MO.

Parker, J. G., & Asher, S. R. (1993a). Beyond group acceptance: Friendship adjustment and friendship quality as distinct dimensions of children's peer adjustment. In D. Perlman & W. H. Jones (Eds.), *Advances in personal relationships* (Vol. 4, pp. 261–294). London: Kingsley.

Parker, J. G., & Asher, S. R. (1993b). Friends and friendship quality in middle childhood: Links with peer group acceptance and feelings of loneliness and social dissatisfaction. *Developmental Psychology, 29,* 611–621.

Parker, J. G., & Gottman, J. M. (1989). Social and emotional development in a relational context: Friendship interaction from early childhood to adolescence. In T. J. Berndt & G. W. Ladd (Eds.), *Peer relationships in child development* (pp. 95–131). New York: Wiley.

Parker, J. G., & Seal, J. (1993, March). Temporal patterning and behavioral and affective correlates of boys' and girls' friendship involvement in middle childhood. In D. C. Jones (Chair), *Friendship and gender.* Symposium conducted at the biennial meetings of the Society for Research in Child Development, New Orleans.

Parkhurst, J. T., & Asher, S. R. (1992). Peer rejection in middle school: Subgroup differences in behavior, loneliness, and interpersonal concerns. *Developmental Psychology, 28,* 231–241.

Peery, J. C. (1979). Popular, amiable, isolated, rejected: A reconceptualization of sociometric status in preschool children. *Child Development, 50,* 1231–1234.

Pettit, G. S., & Mize, J. (1993). Substance and style: Understanding the ways in which parents teach children about social relationships. In S. Duck (Ed.), *Learning about relationships* (pp. 118–151). Newbury Park, CA: Sage.

Rawlins, W. K. (1992). *Friendship matters: Communication, dialectics, and the life course.* New York: Aldine De Gruyter.

Reid, M., Landesman, S., Treder, R., & Jaccard, J. (1989). "My family and friends": Six- to twelve-year-old children's perceptions of social support. *Child Development, 60,* 896–910.

Renshaw, P. D., & Brown, P. J. (1993). Loneliness in middle childhood: Concurrent and longitudinal predictors. *Child Development, 64,* 1271–1284.

Rotenberg, K. J. (1980). "A promise kept, a promise broken": Developmental bases of trust. *Child Development, 51,* 614–617.

Rotenberg, K. J., & Silz, D. (1988). Children's restrictive disclosure to friends. *Merrill-Palmer Quarterly, 34,* 203–215.

Rubin, K. H., LeMare, L. J., & Lollis, S. (1990). Social withdrawal in childhood: Developmental pathways to peer rejection. In S. R. Asher & J. D. Coie (Eds.), *Peer rejection in childhood* (pp. 217–249). New York: Cambridge University Press.

Rubin, Z., & Sloman, J. (1984). How parents influence their children's friendships. In M. Lewis (Ed.), *Beyond the dyad* (pp. 223–250). New York: Plenum.

Salovey, P., & Rodin, J. (1989). Envy and jealousy in close relationships. In C. Hendrick (Ed.), *Review of personality and social psychology* (Vol. 10, pp. 221–246). Newbury Park: Sage.

Schneider, B. H. (1992). Didactic methods for enhancing children's peer relations: A quantitative review. *Clinical Psychology Review, 12,* 363–382.

Schofield, J. W., & Whitley, B. E. (1983). Peer nomination vs. rating scale measurement of children's peer preference. *Social Science Quarterly, 46,* 242–251.

Selman, R. L., & Schultz, L. H. (1990). *Making a friend in youth: Developmental theory and pair therapy.* Chicago: University of Chicago Press.

Sharabany, R., Gershoni, R., & Hofman, J. E. (1981). Girlfriend, boyfriend: Age and sex differences in intimate friendship. *Developmental Psychology, 17,* 800–808.

Shaver, P., & Buhrmester, D. (1983). Loneliness, sex role orientation, and group life: A social needs perspective. In P. B. Paulus (Ed.), *Basic group processes* (pp. 259–288). New York: Springer-Verlag.

Singleton, L. C., & Asher, S. R. (1977). Peer preferences and social interaction among third-grade children in an integrated school district. *Journal of Educational Psychology, 69,* 330–336.

Singleton, L. C., Asher, S. R. (1979). Racial integration and children's peer preferences: An investigation of developmental and cohort differences. *Child Development, 50,* 936–941.

Siperstein, G. N., & Gale, M. E. (1983, April). *Improving peer relationships of rejected children.* Paper presented at the biennial meeting of the Society for Research in Child Development, Detroit.

Smilansky, M. (1991). *Friendship and adolescence and young adulthood.* New York: Psychosocial and Educational Publications.

Sullivan, H. S. (1953). *The interpersonal theory of psychiatry.* New York: Norton.

Tiffen, K., & Spence, S. H. (1986). Responsiveness of isolated versus rejected children to social skills training. *Journal of Child Psychology and Psychiatry, 27,* 343–355.

Thompson, G. C. (1960). Children's groups. In P. H. Mussen (Ed.), *Handbook of research methods in child development* (pp. 821–844). New York: Wiley.

Vaughn, S., & Lancelotta, G. X. (1990). Teaching interpersonal social skills to poorly accepted students: Peer-pairing versus non-peer-pairing. *Journal of School Psychology, 28,* 181–188.

Williams, G. A., & Asher, S. R. (1987, April). *Peer and self-perceptions of peer rejected children: Issues in classification and subgrouping.* Paper presented at the biennial meeting of the Society for Research in Child Development, Baltimore.

Williams, G. A., & Asher, S. R. (1992). Assessment of loneliness at school among children with mild mental retardation. *American Journal of Mental Retardation, 96,* 373–385.

Wright, P. H. (1985). The acquaintance description form. In S. Duck & D. Perlman (Eds.), *Understanding personal relationships* (pp. 39–62). Beverly Hills, CA: Sage.

Youniss, J., & Smoller, J. (1985). *Adolescent relations with mothers, fathers, and friends.* Chicago: University of Chicago Press.

# Author index

# Subject index